THE OXFORD HISTORY OF THE BRITISH EMPIRE

COMPANION SERIES

Wm. Roger Louis, CBE, D. Litt., FBA
Kerr Professor of English History and Culture, University of Texas, Austin and Honorary Fellow of St Antony's College, Oxford
EDITOR-IN-CHIEF

Black Experience and the Empire

Philip D. Morgan
Professor of History, Johns Hopkins University
EDITOR

and

Sean Hawkins
Professor of History, University of Toronto
EDITOR

OXFORD
UNIVERSITY PRESS

OXFORD
UNIVERSITY PRESS

Great Clarendon Street, Oxford OX2 6DP

Oxford University Press is a department of the University of Oxford.
It furthers the University's objective of excellence in research, scholarship,
and education by publishing worldwide in

Oxford New York

Auckland Cape Town Dar es Salaam Hong Kong Karachi Kuala Lumpur
Madrid Melbourne Mexico City Nairobi New Delhi Shanghai Taipei Toronto

With offices in

Argentina Austria Brazil Chile Czech Republic France Greece
Guatemala Hungary Italy Japan South Korea Poland Portugal
Singapore Switzerland Thailand Turkey Ukraine Vietnam

Oxford is a registered trade mark of Oxford University Press
in the UK and in certain other countries

Published in the United States
by Oxford University Press Inc., New York

First published 2004
First published in paperback 2006

British Library Cataloguing in Publication Data

Data available

Library of Congress Cataloging in Publication Data

Data available

Typeset by SPI Publisher Services, Pondicherry, India
Printed in Great Britain
on acid-free paper by
Biddles Ltd., King's Lynn, Norfolk

ISBN 978-0-19-929067-3 (Pbk.)

FOREWORD

The purpose of the five volumes of the Oxford History of the British Empire was to provide a comprehensive survey of the Empire from its beginning to end, to explore the meaning of British imperialism for the ruled as well as the rulers, and to study the significance of the British Empire as a theme in world history. The volumes in the Companion Series carry forward this purpose. They pursue themes that could not be covered adequately in the main series while incorporating recent research and providing fresh interpretations of significant topics.

Wm. Roger Louis

PREFACE

Black Experience and the Empire explores how people of African descent (those born in sub-Saharan Africa and their descendants) shaped the imperial world, and how in turn empire affected their lives. The chapters of this volume build on the substantial foundations of the *Oxford History of the British Empire*; five of the thirteen first appeared in the volumes of the original series, although in some cases now significantly revised. The majority of the essays in this volume have been newly recruited to do full justice to the considerable contributions blacks made to the British Empire and their often painful experiences of it.

In shifting the lens from the history of Empire to the black experience of Empire, the essays in this volume highlight the dialectic of inclusion and exclusion that was at the heart of the British Empire. No matter how oppressive and disdainful the Empire seemed to blacks, nothing could disguise its dependence on them as workers, traders, soldiers, producers, agents, clerks, missionaries, teachers, policemen, and rulers. Blacks negotiated this fault line for over four hundred years. Their experiences reveal the obvious power and cruelty of empire as well as its inherent weaknesses and attractive promises. Accordingly, black attitudes toward Empire were often ambivalent and contradictory, making them resistant to binary simplifications.

Although *black* is an awkward and unwieldy noun, it is a convenient shorthand. Nevertheless, in linking the experiences of people of African descent under the rubric *black*, the dangers of essentialism and homogenization must be strenuously avoided. That people of African descent shared certain features in their experiences of Empire speaks more to what Empire did to them than to what they had in common. Just because the British Empire came to call people of African descent *black* did not necessarily make them so. This identification has meaning or validity because people of African descent themselves came to use it, albeit contextually, not because they accepted the ideology of racism, but because they recognized their common experiences of racism as well as of such salient influences as forced migration and exploitation of labour. Although the black experience varied greatly across space and over time, no other people were more uprooted and dislocated; or travelled more within the Empire; or created more of a trans-imperial culture. In the crucible of the British Empire, blacks invented cultural mixes that were precursors to our modern selves—hybrid, fluid, ambiguous, and constantly in motion.

The chapters in this volume range from West Africa in the sixteenth century, through the history of the slave trade and slavery, to nineteenth- and twentieth-century participation of blacks in the Empire as workers, soldiers, members of colonial élites, and intellectuals. The first five essays tell the story of African and British slave traders, the Middle Passage, enslaved Africans in the Caribbean and North America, the origins of abolition as an ideology, and the end of slavery and its effects. The next two essays return to Africa to tell the story of the growth of the British Empire, following the abolition of slavery in the Caribbean and the changing tone of the imperial conversation during the period of imperial conquest. Another three essays probe different aspects of the black experience in twentieth-century Africa: the marginalization of women, the participation of crucial intermediaries such as chiefs and clerks, and the exploitation of workers. The last three essays examine the complicated movement toward the dissolution of Empire: first in the Caribbean where a race and class hierarchy was well entrenched, then to Britain where black workers and intellectuals came together to mount critiques of Empire, and finally back to Africa where the legacies of Empire still resonate.

CONTENTS

LIST OF MAPS AND TABLES

LIST OF CONTRIBUTORS

KWAME ANTHONY APPIAH (Ph.D., Cambridge) is Laurance S. Rockefeller University Professor of Philosophy and a member of the University Center for Human Values at Princeton University. He is the author of *In My Father's House: Africa in the Philosophy of Culture* as well as several books on the philosophy of mind and language, and political philosophy, the most recent of which is *An Introduction to Contemporary Philosophy.*

VIVIAN BICKFORD-SMITH (Ph.D., Cambridge) is a Professor in the Historical Studies Department at the University of Cape Town. He is the author of *Ethnic Pride and Racial Prejudice in Victorian Cape Town: Group Identity and Social Practice, 1875–1902* as well as co-author of two other books, both about Cape Town in the twentieth century.

CHRISTOPHER L. BROWN (D.Phil., Oxford) is an Assistant Professor in the Department of History at Johns Hopkins University. He is working on a book to be published by the Institute of Early American History and Culture and the University of North Carolina Press on British anti-slavery.

FREDERICK COOPER (Ph.D., Yale) is a Professor in the Department of History at New York University. He is the leading historian both of African labour history and new approaches to the study of colonialism. His most recent books are *Decolonization and African Society: The Labor Question in French and British Africa* and *Africa since 1940: The Past of the Present.*

SEAN HAWKINS (Ph.D., Cambridge) is an Associate Professor in the Department of History and Director of the New College African Studies Program at the University of Toronto. He is the author of *Writing and Colonialism: The Encounter Between the LoDagaa and 'the World on Paper'.*

GAD HEUMAN (Ph.D., Yale) is a Professor in the Department of History and Director of the Centre for Caribbean Studies at the University of Warwick. His publications include *Between Black and White: Race, Politics, and the Free Coloreds in Jamaica, 1792–1865* and *'The Killing Time': The Morant Bay Rebellion in Jamaica.* He has edited books on slave resistance and on labour, and is co-editor of the journal *Slavery and Abolition.*

WINSTON JAMES (Ph.D., London) is an Associate Professor in the Department of History at Columbia University. He specializes in Caribbean, African-American, and African Diaspora history. His publications include *Inside Babylon: The Caribbean Diaspora in Britain* (co-authored with Clive Harris) and *Holding Aloft the Banner of Ethiopia: Caribbean Radicalism in Early Twentieth Century America.*

DIANA JEATER, (D.Phil., Oxford) is Head of the the History School at the University of the West of England, Bristol. She is the author of *Marriage, Perversion and Power: The Construction of Moral Discourse in Southern Rhodesia 1894–1930*, and review editor of the *Journal of Southern African Studies.*

HOWARD JOHNSON (D.Phil., Oxford) is Alumni Distinguished Professor of History and Director of the Black American Studies Program at the University of Delaware. He is the author of *The Bahamas in Slavery and Freedom; The Bahamas from Slavery to Servitude, 1783–1993*, and editor of *After the Crossing: Immigrants and Minorities in Caribbean Creole Society.*

T. C. MCCASKIE (Ph.D., Cambridge) is Professor of Asante History and Director of the Centre of West African Studies at the University of Birmingham. He has published extensively on the Asante and is the author of *State and Society in Precolonial Asante* and *Asante Identities: History and Modernity in an African Village, 1850–1950.*

PHILIP D. MORGAN (Ph.D., London), is the Harry C. Black Professor in History at Johns Hopkins University. He is the author of *Slave Counterpoint: Black Culture in the Upper and Lower Souths in the Eighteenth Century* and co-editor of *Strangers Within the Realm: Cultural Margins in the First British Empire.*

DAVID NORTHUP (Ph.D., University of California at Los Angeles) is a Professor in the Department of History at Boston College and President of the World History Association. He is the author of *Trade Without Rulers: Pre-Colonial Economic Development in South-Eastern-Nigeria, Indentured Labor in the Age of Imperialism,* 1834–1922, and, most recently, *Africa's Discovery of Europe, 1450–1850.*

TIMOTHY H. PARSONS (Ph.D., Johns Hopkins) is an Associate Professor in the Department of History at Washington University in St Louis. He is the author of *The African Rank-and-File: Social Implications of Colonial Military Service in the King's African Rifles, 1902–1964* as well as *The British Imperial Century, 1815–1914: A World History Perspective.*

David Richardson (M.A., Manchester) is Professor of Economic History at the University of Hull. He is the editor of *Bristol, Africa, and the Eighteenth Century Slave Trade to America*, co-editor of *The Trans-Atlantic Slave Trade: A Database on CD-ROM*, and is the author of numerous articles on the transatlantic slave trade and its impact on Africa as well as Britain.

1

Blacks and the British Empire: An Introduction

SEAN HAWKINS AND PHILIP D. MORGAN

The British Empire was a vast, shifting constellation of territories held together in no small measure by its maritime connections and maintained as much by the constant motion of ships as by the force of troops. No other people experienced these links more intensely or for a longer period than did blacks (that is, Sub-Saharan Africans and their descendants). No people were more uprooted and dislocated; or travelled more within the Empire, by both sea and land; or created more of a trans-imperial culture—one that synthesized not only a great number of different African elements, but also many British traits, into a dynamic cultural fusion. In the crucible of the British Empire, blacks invented cultural mixes that were very much precursors to our modern selves: hybrid, fluid, ambiguous, and constantly in motion. In many ways, the experiences of blacks best embody the nature of the British Empire.

At the same time that blacks experienced displacement, movement, and cultural mixing, many whites in the Empire devoted much effort to fixing blacks in place and denying them cultural resources. Enslavement and plantation life, the dominant experiences for most blacks within the Empire during the first two centuries, was the ultimate denial of human expression. Even after emancipation, apprenticeship, plantation labour, indenture, repatriation to home villages, influx control into colonial cities, and restrictions on emigration into Britain all hampered movement. Furthermore, lack of educational provisions, reinforcement of 'tribal' authority, and reification of customary law were just some of the many ways to restrict cultural access.

Olaudah Equiano or Gustavus Vassa neatly captures these features of the British Empire. He was extraordinarily well-travelled, a picaresque figure, a cosmopolitan man of the world, who criss-crossed the Atlantic, visiting almost every corner of the British Empire. He also endured the horrors and terrors of slavery and, even when free, never escaped the indignities of discrimination and racism. He is a chameoleon-like figure, bearing many identities. His autobiography is a bricolage of literary genres and registers—spiritual autobiography, captivity narrative, travel adventure, Methodist sermon, economic treatise, antislavery polemic. Equiano adopts many masks—from naïve boy to sophisticated gentleman, from chivalrous warrior to deferential slave, from humble sailor to the first black official representative of the British government. His occupations range from field hand to surgeon's mate, musician to barber, money-lender to author. He had at least four names. First, Olaudah, signifying 'vicissitude, or fortunate, also one favoured and having a loud voice and well spoken', appropriate for a man of eloquence; then Michael, the Lord's angel and messenger, while crossing the Atlantic; followed in Virginia by Jacob, his first slave name, the progenitor of a chosen people who became enslaved; and finally, Gustavus Vassa, the Swedish freedom fighter, again so apt for the future antislavery advocate who hoped to liberate his people. He is a hybrid, malleable, transnational cultural figure, who resists the fixity of categorical definitions or simplistic ascriptions. He is an enigma, especially now that it is known that he might well have been born in South Carolina and not Igboland, as he claimed in his autobiography.

Whether born in Africa or not, he wished to be known binomially, his joint names symbolically joining the two identities that mattered most to him—his African ancestry and his adopted Britishness. He claimed and straddled both identities; he was a man of at least two worlds, a bicultural figure, passionately tied to Africa, his actual or ancestral continent of origin, and to Britain, his acquired homeland. Within a few years of arriving in England, he reported that he was 'almost an Englishman', feeling himself 'quite easy with these new countrymen', relishing 'their society and manners', wanting to 'resemble them [and] to imbibe their spirit, and imitate their manners'. As his political consciousness developed, he also began to refer to himself as 'the African'. In private and public, he wanted to be known as Gustavus Vassa, his very definite European-sounding name, but he was also the first Anglophone writer of African descent to use the definite article to refer to himself. Long before he wrote his autobiography, he had been signing petitions and newspaper articles as Gustavus Vassa 'the African', 'the Ethiopian', the 'Son of Africa', 'the oppressed African'. Like many another black person in the Atlantic world, he discovered in his contacts with Europeans that he was an African—perhaps not literally so but a person indisputably of

African descent. In the final chapter of his autobiography, he referred to a generalized 'African complexion', was pleased that the Quakers freed many of his 'oppressed African brethren', and spoke of the planned colony at Sierra Leone as a philanthropic project 'to send the Africans' from London 'to their native quarter'. The whole of Africa had become his ancestral home. His 'countrymen' were Africans in the most general sense.[1]

Of course all identities are constructed and therefore highly variable over space and time, so much so that some scholars prefer to call them identifications rather than identities. In the history of the British Empire, the words 'African' (or 'black') and 'British' meant different things to different people at different times in different places. By calling them identities, there is a danger that they are assumed to be inherently true or authentic, rather than strategic and political. Yet looking at how these terms were used by individual subjects and by British imperial and metropolitan authorities is to see that they were never stable, certainly not static in their meanings, and not necessarily mutually exclusive. As several of the following chapters demonstrate, blacks in the Empire sometimes claimed to be British for instrumental purposes, even if they fervently believed the truth of their claims. In some situations, the British Empire actively encouraged black subjects to think of themselves as British, especially when it called on them to make military sacrifices. Yet in other situations imperial authorities often refused to reciprocate these forms of loyalty, attempting to disqualify non-white subjects by imposing essential categories on them, such as African, black, or 'native'; these, they believed, were permanent and immutable identities that would maintain the racial boundaries of what it meant to be British. The British Empire oscillated between asserting the universality and exclusiveness of British identity, producing what has been called a 'dialectical of imperial affirmation and disavowal'.[2]

Similarly, what it meant to be black or African was something that changed a great deal over time and depended on context. At any point in time the Pan-African movement contained within itself multiple meanings

[1] Vincent Carretta, ed., *The Interesting Narrative and Other Writings* (New York, 1995), pp. 41, 63–64, 77–78, 220, 224, 226; Vincent Carretta, 'Olaudah Equiano or Gustavus Vassa?: New Light on an Eighteenth-Century Question of Identity', *Slavery and Abolition*, XX (1999), pp. 96–105. For more on Equiano's life, see the Chaps. by David Northrup and David Richardson in this vol.

[2] Rogers Brubaker and Frederick Cooper, 'Beyond "Identity" ', *Theory and Society*, XXIX (2000), pp. 5–6, 14; Simon Gikandi, *Maps of Englishness: Writing Identity in the Culture of Colonialism* (New York, 1996), pp. 50–52.

of 'African' as well as a diversity of potentially competing forms of identity; indeed, the multiplicity of meanings and diversity of possible alternatives was an inherent weakness of the movement, preventing stronger forms of solidarity and political action. Furthermore, identities cannot be understood in isolation; since they are the products of encounters, always subject to negotiation, they were always unstable and fluid. Winston James shows clearly how mutually implicating the ideas of being 'black' and 'British' were in twentieth-century Britain. The same was true throughout the history of the Empire. In large part because blacks in Britain were not free to call themselves British, many came to see themselves as African. Unlike in the eighteenth century when Equiano could maintain two identities at the same time, blacks in twentieth-century Britain were intensely disillusioned by the disjunction of what James calls the logic of the Empire, which told them that they were British, and the logic of the metropole, which persistently and often violently told them they were not. For many blacks, their experience of racism at the heart of the Empire led them to identify themselves as Africans. This sense of being African was a cultural and political reaction against racist exclusion from full imperial citizenship. It was different than Equiano's sense of being African, which was a personal and social reaction to the erasure of history and memory wrought by the dislocations of enslavement. Yet, even as many distanced themselves from the Empire, many blacks never gave up on their right to be counted as British, and continued to challenge the boundaries that racial thinking wanted to erect. As a result, they have slowly changed what being British means in important ways, challenging 'the mythology of the island nation' while reinventing the 'the core terms of Englishness'.[3]

To do justice to Equiano's life and the black experience within the Empire more generally, this introduction outlines five themes. First, it sketches some of the salient spatial and temporal dimensions of the black experience to give a sense of geography and chronology. Next, it probes the nature of this Empire, particularly the relation between imperial centre and colony, and the opportunities it provided for blacks to turn the idea and rhetoric of the British Empire against the British even as those ideas ensnared them. Third, the contradictions between the inclusionary and exclusionary aspects of the British Empire, between the idea of empire as a community of loyal British subjects and the idea of empire as an arena for the oppression and suppres-

[3] Gikandi, *Maps of Englishness*, pp. vxiii, 49. See Chap. by Winston James in this vol.

sion of blacks, are examined. The fourth theme is how subjecthood changed for all blacks, looking specifically at the effects of emancipation in the Caribbean and Indirect Rule in Africa. This section highlights the centrality of labour to the black experience and the importance of labour struggles to black negotiations within the Empire. Finally, the British Empire was an important crucible in which blacks created dynamic and syncretic cultures, distinct for their high degree of hybridity and invention, fusing many different elements together, yet using common forms, such as the English language. The shared forms ultimately provided the basis for a Pan-African identity that challenged the idea of black loyalty to the British Empire. Across the linked territories, blacks produced modes of expression that resonated throughout the Empire.

Geography and Chronology of the Black Experience

Black people were always a prominent and inescapable presence in the British Empire. A few Africans have been identified in Britain from Roman times, but not till the late fifteenth century did their appearance—often as musicians in English and Scottish courts—become noteworthy. In the early sixteenth century, English merchants began trading along the African coast, and in 1555 perhaps the first group of black Africans—five men from the Gold Coast—arrived in England to learn the language and serve as mediators on their return home. In the following decade, the first English slave-trading expeditions to Africa began. By about the middle of the seventeenth century, the English became the major carrier of enslaved Africans across the Atlantic, and for roughly the next 150 years about three times as many Africans as Europeans left their native lands in British ships for the New World. During this time, slave-produced commodities dominated world trade, and the West Indies, with their majority black populations, were the jewels in the imperial crown. As the West Indies declined in imperial importance during the nineteenth century, and as British Africa grew in extent, so the centre of gravity of the black experience within the Empire gradually shifted from Caribbean islands to the African continent.

In the late eighteenth and early nineteenth centuries, the number of blacks in the British Empire was fairly stable (at about one million), but in the last decades of the nineteenth century the British Empire began to expand territorially in Africa faster than it ever had anywhere else. The suddenness with which the map of Africa was painted red—extending to an area of almost 3 million square miles by the early twentieth century—far outpaced knowledge of how many subjects had been acquired. British authorities were largely guessing when they estimated that their African subjects numbered 43 million in 1901. In comparison, the British Empire in the West Indies, including British Honduras (Belize) and British Guiana (Guyana), once the focus of the black experience, amounted to only 1.6 million subjects living on just twenty thousand square miles of islands and mainland coastal possessions. Although Africa had become much more important economically to the Empire than the Caribbean, the effect of the British Empire on the cultures of the Caribbean was much deeper and more intense than it was on the cultures of Africa. Economics and statistics, while influential, are not the only measure of experience.

In the twentieth century prior to decolonization, the boundaries of Empire in both Africa and the Caribbean remained fairly stable, but the numbers of blacks in the Empire increased dramatically. In 1900 Nigeria had less than half as many people as Great Britain, but by the end of the century it was twice as populous as its former colonial ruler. In the mid-1930s, the British estimated (with more accuracy than earlier) that there were about 50 million African (i.e., native as opposed to white, Asian, or Coloured) subjects in Africa and roughly another 2 million blacks in the West Indies. By 1946 the total population of the British Caribbean, including an important but small minority of Indo-Caribbeans, was just over 3 million; and by the early 1950s the number of black subjects in British Africa had increased to perhaps 74 million. By 1960, just as wholesale decolonization began, about 110 million blacks inhabited the British Empire, if one includes those living in Ghana, which had recently gained its independence, and South Africa, which was about to leave the Commonwealth. At the end of the twentieth century, almost three times as many blacks, or people of African descent, lived in the Commonwealth of the former British Empire than had lived in the Empire just forty years before.[4]

London, the centre of the British Empire, was an important crossroads for blacks from both the Caribbean and Africa, but it was not the centre of the

[4] Great Britain, *Census of the British Empire, 1901* (London, 1906), pp. 1, 4–6; Robert R. Kuczynski, *Colonial Population* (London, 1937), pp. 3–4 17–20; Kuczynski, *Demographic Survey of the British Colonial Empire*, 3 vols. (London, 1948; 1949; 1953); I, p. 2; II, pp. 23, 99, 641, 651; III, p.4; Lord Hailey, *An African Survey: A Study of Problems Arising in Africa South of the Sahara* (London, 1957), pp. 120, 126, 143–44.

black experience, certainly not as measured in numbers, or even in terms of influence. The sub-empire of the black experience within the British Empire had no centre, but rather was made up of a multitude of locales connected by the movement of labour, the spread of culture, language, and ideas, and the terms of participation. Size of population in any of these places—colonies, territories, and protectorates—was not necessarily an indicator of their importance. Because of timing as well as the circumstances of its creation, Sierra Leone had a profound effect throughout West Africa. While colonial Nigeria, the part of the British Empire with the most blacks, produced Chinua Achebe, the most read black writer in the English-speaking world, and Wole Soyinka, winner of the Nobel Prize for literature, Derek Walcott, another recipient of the Nobel Prize for literature, along with W. A. Lewis, the Nobel Prize winner for economics, come from the tiny island of St Lucia (233 square miles). Centres and margins of experience were not determined by geography but by the nature of blacks' relationship to the Empire. Some slaves had more direct experiences of Empire than did others, but much depended on what type of work they were forced to do rather than where they did it. Just as the nature of slavery depended heavily on the type of crops grown, and hence the work regime to be endured, the experience of Empire had everything to do with local contexts, and these kept changing. For much of the nineteenth century African Creoles, who lived predominantly near ports, such as Cape Town, Freetown, or Lagos, and who were therefore closer to the ships that connected the Empire, enjoyed positions of privilege. In the late nineteenth century, however, racism had begun to marginalize them, and the 'native' élites far to the interior preoccupied British attention by the beginning of the twentieth century. British culture travelled well beyond colonial capitals and provincial towns, all the way to the seemingly remotest villages. The networks of the slave trade, the patterns of military recruitment, and the routes of migrant labourers meant that there were few places where the effects of Empire were not felt as well as few places within the Empire where blacks did not travel.

In the beginning, of course, this diaspora of people of African descent was almost exclusively involuntary. During the era of the slave trade, blacks reached a multitude of places, eventually spreading well beyond the obvious destinations in the American colonies and the Caribbean, from Ascension Island to Australia, from Heligoland to Hong Kong, and from Nova Scotia to the New Herbides. Not to be forgotten also were those African communities already uprooted by the trans-Saharan, Red Sea, and Indian Ocean slave trades before their communities in India, Pakistan, Arabia, and Iraq found themselves part of the British Empire. From the end of the slave trade up until the Second World War, opportunities for large-scale travel within the Empire were relatively restricted. But black missionaries, traders, students, and intellectuals did move frequently to different parts of the Empire, often to and through Britain, as they pursued evangelical, educational, commercial, and political opportunities. During the Second World War black soldiers were deployed as far away as South East Asia, and after the war blacks spread throughout the English-speaking world—a linguistic boundary that echoed the older territorial boundaries of the British Empire, just as the Commonwealth replaced former colonial ties. Many blacks migrated to the former American colonies, where they integrated into small Caribbean communities that had been established much earlier, yet which still remained connected to the islands. There they encountered a much larger African–American culture founded on an experience of the British Empire too distant to be recalled, and whose contemporary dynamics were conditioned by a different experience of racism—that is, as an oppressed minority rather than majority. At this time sizeable black populations also developed for the first time in the white Commonwealth, particularly in Britain and Canada. Although smaller than the forced migrations of the slave trade in absolute terms, and even smaller in relative terms, African emigration from former British colonies after the Second World War was more extensive, with blacks travelling well beyond the immediate Atlantic world (both within Africa and beyond the English-speaking world). Ghanaians have been most captivated by the wanderlust of post-colonial travel, with roughly 12 per cent of the population of the country in the 1990s living abroad, and accounting for the largest population of sub-Saharan Africans living in Europe. As Emmanuel Akyeampong notes, 'The voluntary sojourn of Ghanaians overseas has a long history'.[5]

The British Empire did not have a distinct beginning, just as it did not have a clear end. Indeed, it had several possible starting points, and its many legacies suggest that in some senses it has not ended but merely changed, albeit irrevocably, as its cultural and social bequests continue to play out both in former colonies and in the former metropole. The emergence of the concept, 'British Empire', as a political community encompassing the

[5] Emmanuel Akyeampong, 'Africans in the Diaspora: The Diaspora and Africa', *African Affairs*, XCIX (2000), pp. 189–93, 204.

Three Kingdoms of Britain and Ireland and the related colonies, plantations, and territories of the Western hemisphere was long drawn out, stretching at least from the mid-sixteenth century to the mid-eighteenth, and not crystallizing till the late seventeenth century at the earliest. Similarly, the Empire's orbit only gradually encompassed blacks: Anglo–African trade did not begin until the mid-sixteenth century; as late as the 1620s Englishmen were still declaring that they did not deal in slaves; and not until the mid-seventeenth century was the slave trade and the presence of blacks in certain New World colonies on a solid footing. Turning to Empire's end, the shadow of the British Empire survived the lowering of the Union Jack across the globe in the second half of the twentieth century, long after the sun had set. In this ghostly Empire, echoes of the black experience have had a significant impact on the wider culture of the former Empire.

Despite the indistinct temporal boundaries, there are identifiable watersheds that define the black experience. The abolition of the British slave trade in 1807 was one significant milestone. With the collapse of French and Dutch participation in the transatlantic slave trade in the 1790s, Britain's share of the transatlantic slave trade was at its highest in the decade before 1807. The hundreds of thousands of Africans who were spared the Middle Passage as a result of British abolition had reason to savour the event. An even more momentous caesura was emancipation in 1834. No event mattered more to blacks, but not because it ended exploitation or ushered in an era of racial equality. In fact, in many respects, the conditions of life remained much the same, perhaps even worsened. By outlawing private property in persons, however, the metropolitan government inevitably curtailed the prerogatives of private employers. Freed men and women voted with their feet whenever possible; they fled the plantations and sought land. Women were in the vanguard of withdrawal from plantation labour. For peoples of African descent, emancipation provided more autonomy and more bargaining power than they had possessed as slaves. C. L. R. James described it as 'our Norman conquest'.[6]

Other turning points were also important. In 1847 the defeat and deliberate humiliation of the Xhosa by Sir Harry Smith, the new Governor of the Cape Colony, ushered in a new era in British–African relations. Checks on settler encroachments on Xhosa land were abandoned, marking the beginning of the conquest of southern Africa by British settlement. Eighteen years later,

[6] C. L. R. James, *Beyond a Boundary* (1963; Durham, NC, 1993), p. 255.

the Morant Bay Rebellion in Jamaica was important for the government's brutal response and the outcry it produced. Although Governor Edward John Eyre was never committed for trial for the deaths of 400 blacks killed during the month-long period of martial law he imposed, serious questions were raised about colonial rule and governmental accountability. Crown Colony government became the norm thereafter throughout the West Indies. In 1897 the sack and looting of Benin City by a 'punitive expedition' was a sign that the British were unwilling to respect African sovereignty and were willing to use any pretext to invade and annex African territory as part of newly formed administrative colonies. In the 1920s Indirect Rule was widely implemented through Africa as London formally abandoned imperial pretensions about change in favour of a policy of conservation that cost little. And in the 1930s strikes and labour disturbances in the Caribbean and Africa forced a fundamental reassessment of imperial policy. With the passage of the Colonial Development and Welfare Act in 1940, London saw Africans and West Indians as part of the same colonial people for the first time, and the social existence of workers in both areas was finally acknowledged. Education, housing, and nutrition were suddenly factors that the Colonial Office concluded were crucial to a modern labour market. The costs of the Act's provisions proved to be too great once they were implemented after the war, so much so that decolonization became more attractive than attempting to find another ideology with which to justify imperial rule.

Just as the British Empire resonated beyond any temporal limits, it also reached beyond any geographical boundaries. Well before the British removed black people to areas of imperial sovereignty, the ancestors of many of the people who were to come under its rule had experienced the Empire, even if they did not see it as such, through the sheer force of its economic power. That the reach of the British Empire went far beyond its formal territory would have been well known to many people in West Africa, who lost over 3.4 million of their kin between 1562 and 1807. Each of the ten thousand voyages of British slave traders to the coast of West Africa left its mark on societies of the interior as well as on those of the coast. This trade, which became significant only in the 1660s (6,700 slaves a year) and reached its height in the 1760s (42,000 slaves a year), linked London, Bristol, and Liverpool merchants with African markets, and in so doing, African traders and consumers came into contact with East Indian (especially cloth and cowries) and British goods (from firearms to gin). The trading patterns along the West African coast created relationships with coastal societies that had an important influence on later patterns of colonial conquest. Proportionately, British traders took more slaves from the Bight of Biafra, the Gold Coast, Sierra Leone, and Senegambia than any other of the European slave trading nations; or to put it another way, today's countries: Nigeria, Ghana, Sierra Leone, and Gambia were already part of the British Empire before they became formal colonies at the end of the nineteenth century. The British Empire, then, was always more than a series of formally annexed pieces of territory. It was a network that reached well beyond its formal territorial boundaries.[7]

Nature and Meaning of the British Empire

For most blacks, their experience of the British Empire was mediated by their experience of colonialism; the two are obviously connected, but were not the same. Colonies, whether settler or administrative, had varying degrees of autonomy and their interests often were quite distinct from metropolitan or imperial concerns. For much of the time there were few differences, but when they arose, blacks often sided with the imperial over the colonial party; indeed, in appealing to imperial authority in order to check or question colonial authority, whether exercised by settlers or administrators or both, blacks brought implicit differences within the world of white authority into the open.

Blacks often resorted to metropolitan authority in their struggles with slave-owners. In 1787, five years after the British had left Georgia, fugitive slaves claiming to be 'the King of England's soldiers' continued to attack plantations along the Savannah River. Slaves in Barbados in 1816, Demerara in 1823, and Jamaica in 1831–32 defended their rebellions as efforts to support the Crown in its struggle with planters to end slavery. Aware of shifts in metropolitan thinking that had created tensions between London and the slave owners in the Caribbean, slaves in the region rebelled and appealed to the British government for assistance in their struggle against the oppression of white planters. Similarly, in the immediate aftermath of emancipation in 1834, but before full freedom in 1838, apprentices in Trinidad were rightly aggrieved by this compromise to their freedom, but they did not blame it on the King, who they believed had freed them completely, but on the planters and the Governor.[8]

[7] See in particular Chaps. by Northrup and Richardson.

[8] See Chaps. by Christopher L. Brown and Gad Heuman.

The same instrumentality is evident in African contexts. In 1878 the leaders of a community of largely Muslim fisherman from Cape Town objected to government interference by noting that 'We were always under the impression that we were emancipated in the reign of our most Gracious Majesty Queen Victoria, and freed from tyranny, but it seems that we are mistaken'. Similarly, when William Wade Harris, the charismatic founder of an independent church in West Africa, wished to express his dissatisfaction with élite rule in Liberia during the first decade of the twentieth century, he hoisted the Union Jack and was promptly arrested and put in prison. He was not embracing imperialism, but he was expressing preference for British rule over that on offer in Liberia. For many blacks, the idea of empire could often be a foil to the realities of colonialism, but more than merely a critical tool, it was also at times a source of hope and nostalgia.[9]

When political organizations interested in issues of race, class, and nationalism emerged in the Caribbean in the last century between the two world wars, they criticized the form of colonial rule but did not question the imperial connection. In part because there was no memory of a pre-colonial experience of political independence among blacks in the twentieth-century Caribbean, anti-colonialism was never as strong a force as it became in Africa and nationalist sympathies were limited largely to a section of the middle classes. As Howard Johnson argues, 'the main focus of working-class loyalty remained the British monarchy which was first associated with slave emancipation'. Colonial education and public ceremonies reinforced this loyalty in the twentieth century. Jervis Anderson, the author and critic, who grew up in Jamaica in the early twentieth century writes movingly of his boyhood recollections of the importance of Empire Day, 24 May, which memorialized the birth and symbolic achievements of Queen Victoria.[10]

The idea of a benevolent monarchy was one British colonial administrators worked hard at inculcating among their subjects in late nineteenth- and twentieth-century Africa. Unable to build on an act as convincing or memorable as emancipation was in the West Indies, both missionaries and colonial administrators laboured to create an image of the British monarchy that was in essence religious. Ceremonial and ritual attention sought to

[9] See Chap. by Vivian Bickford-Smith; Gordon MacKay Haliburton, *The Prophet Harris: A Study of an African Prophet and his Mass-Movement in the Ivory Coast and Gold Coast 1913–1915* (London, 1971), p. 30.

[10] See Chap. by Howard Johnson; Jervis Anderson, 'England in Jamaica: Memories from a Colonial Boyhood', *American Scholar*, LXIX, 2 (Spring 2000), pp. 15–30.

demonstrate that the monarch was almost divine. In the absence of frequent royal visits, the authority of this royal cult had to be maintained by frequent festivals, officiated by all ranks from District Commissioner to Governor. Whether or not Africans ever believed in this cult as fervently as the British who created it for them, 'clearly the symbol of monarchy appealed to the imagination'. At times it created an ideological consensus between Europeans and their African supporters, providing a theoretical model through which political relations could be negotiated.[11]

What sustained this political model was the distinction between colony and metropole; in their day-to-day lives, Africans did not live in the Empire, but within colonies that were part of the Empire. This same distinction allowed many blacks in the Caribbean and Africa to believe in the goodness of imperial intentions at the same time as they suffered from the injustices of colonial rule. For most blacks the British Empire was a remote entity, often as much a product of their own imaginations and yearnings as it was the product of imperial hegemony. Such is evident in the celebrations of Queen Victoria's Golden and Diamond Jubilees in 1887 and 1897, during which the British enclaves along the West Coast and the Cape Colony were flooded with images of the Queen and accompanying imperial propaganda. The Creole élites of these areas seemed to respond enthusiastically to these opportunities to profess love for their monarch. But, 'Such displays or protestations of loyalty "should not be interpreted as the product of a simple, unmediated absorption of an imperial creed." Rather "own meanings" [to use local parlance], were imposed on patriotism.' So in Sierra Leone, Queen Victoria was referred to as 'We Mammy' reflecting local ideas of reciprocity and models of authority.[12]

Forms of trust and reciprocity that had characterized much of the conversation between the British and Africans before formal colonial rule began to disappear once the British began demanding in the second half of the nineteenth century, and then commanding for much of the twentieth century, what they formerly had to negotiate. As a result, the ways in which blacks negotiated with the British altered. A certain amount of mutual cheating had characterized trading relations between Europeans and Africans during the trans-Atlantic slave trade, but in twentieth-century Africa, many black inter-

[11] Terence Ranger, 'The Invention of Tradition in Colonial Africa', in Eric Hobsbawm and Terrence Ranger, eds., *The Invention of Tradition* (Cambridge, 1983), pp. 230–36.

[12] See, Chap. by Bickford-Smith.

mediaries responded to the one-way tone of the conversation by practicing theft, extortion, bribery, and other forms of larceny. Clerks and interpreters, unlike the intermediaries and brokers of eighteenth-century West Africa, exploited their positions for their own benefit, at the expense of the general population, with whom they had no necessary connection. In West Africa clerks were known for standing up for their rights. Unlike 'native authorities', they were not prone to professing allegiance to the Empire they served.[13]

Imperial Racism

The relationship between blacks and whites, colonized and colonizers, oscillated between inclusion and exclusion. As Ann Stoler and Frederik Cooper point out, 'The tensions between the exclusionary practices and universalizing claims of bourgeois culture were crucial to shaping the age of empire'. Freedom and capitalism, part of these universalizing claims, were attractive to some blacks especially those at the bottom and top of black societies, such as slaves and women or members of black élites. But much of the time, the Empire kept blacks at arms' length and engaged in a series of exclusionary practices.[14]

The main, but not the only, form of exclusion was racial. In the Caribbean during the period of slavery, the racial animosity of whites toward enslaved blacks (with notable exceptions such as Edward Long) was inchoate, for the obvious reason that the institution more than accomplished the job of keeping blacks in an inferior position. Whites' racial hatred tended to focus on the minority of free blacks and free coloureds. During the Revolutionary era of the late eighteenth and early nineteenth centuries, the expansion of freedom intensified racism, which became much more coherent and virulent. By the middle of the nineteenth century pseudo-scientific thinking was fully developed and the emergence of Social Darwinian ideas reinforced belief in white domination as well as the subordination of blacks. Informal segregation became the norm: 'keeping the niggers out' was the mantra for most West Indian whites. The result was that the majority of the black middle class in most British Caribbean societies at the end of the nineteenth century were the descendants of the 'free people of colour'.[15]

[13] See Chaps. by T. C. McCaskie and Timothy H. Parsons.

[14] Ann Laura Stoler and Frederick Cooper, 'Between Metropole and Colony: Rethinking Research Agenda', in Frederick Cooper and Ann Laura Stoler, eds., *Tensions of Empire: Colonial Cultures in a Bourgeois World* (Berkeley, 1997), p. 37.

[15] Winthrop D. Jordan, *White Over Black: American Attitudes Toward the Negro, 1550–1812* (Chapel Hill, NC, 1968); see Chaps. by Heuman and Johnson.

The principal means of entering the middle class for most blacks in the Caribbean was through education and employment as either schoolteachers or clergymen. 'Educational opportunities created a middle-class elite whose members were able to manipulate English culture and were separated from lower-class blacks by their putative cultural "refinement".' The black lower classes 'retained a strong identification with Afro-creole culture'. Even as late as the 1960s limited access to colonial education meant that only a minority of blacks had received a secondary education, and fewer still a university education. As Austin Clarke, the Canadian–Barbadian novelist, noted, prospects for a secondary school leaver were limited in the 1940s. If he did well, he could become a civil servant, less so, then sanitary inspector, and, if even worse, a bookkeeper.[16]

In Africa, particularly in Sierra Leone and the Cape Colony, metropolitan racism spread more slowly and found itself in contention with a well established tradition of successful acculturation. Under Governor MacCarthy (1814–24) of Sierra Leone, Recaptives learned English, assumed European names, dress, habits, and tastes, and embraced both Christianity and education. 'Although their culture retained "specifically African cultural initiatives and components", Sierra Leone Creoles regarded themselves as "Black English" and became agents for the spread of British culture throughout West Africa.'[17]

By the middle of the nineteenth century, this highly dynamic culture produced many eminent leaders, people who had successfully negotiated their way into middle-class British society, having mastered its cultural norms and professional qualifications. Such were Samuel Crowther, the first black bishop in the Church of England, and J. A. B. Horton, the first black African to take a degree in medicine in Britain. When a British explorer witnessed this West African Creole culture in the 1860s, he condemned it as an 'inauthentic, offensive, comic mimicry of its British counterpart'. What it had become, in the increasingly exclusionary atmosphere of white supremacist thought, was a manifest denial of black inferiority—and it was this that gave offence. Not until the late nineteenth century did the bite of such ignorance make itself felt in Sierra Leone as well as in the Cape Colony. Only then would 'Anglicized Africans' become critical of the contradiction between a culture they admired and an experience they rejected, between Empire's universalizing claims and exclusionary practices. For many, this

[16] Chap. by Johnson.

[17] Chaps. by McCaskie and Bickford-Smith

experience would be a signal of the beginning of the formation of a distinct identity.[18]

This development was similar to the cultural identity that black slaves had created for themselves in eighteenth-century plantations in the Caribbean out of a process of creolization, but it was their descendants who would politicize it and join with many African Creoles in creating a Pan-African movement at the beginning of the twentieth century that was largely Anglophone and included African–Americans—the descendants of those blacks who had lived in the British Empire before the American Revolution.[19] The first Pan-African conference, which was held in London, was convened by the Trinidadian lawyer Henry Sylvester Williams in 1900, but it was the series of truly international congresses first organized by W. E. B. DuBois that are most closely associated with the idea of Pan-Africanism. These were held in 1919 (Paris), 1921 (London and Brussels), 1923 (London and Lisbon), 1927 (New York), 1945 (Manchester), and 1974 (Dar es Salaam). However, these were relatively small meetings of highly educated intellectual and political leaders aimed at affecting imperial attitudes. The 1921 Congress, which was the most radical, called upon England, 'with all her Pax Britannica', to 'train black and brown men in real self-government, to recognise civilised black folk as civilised, [and] to grant to coloured colonies those rights of self government which it freely gives to white men'. Other forms of Pan-Africanism, especially as espoused by the Jamaican political leader Marcus Garvey, had a much wider audience. Along with his second wife, Amy Ashwood Garvey, he founded the United Negro Improvement Association in 1914, moving its headquarters only two years later to Harlem. From there his ideas about African unity, which were much more radical and oppositional than those espoused at international congresses, came to reach a much wider audience than those of many more famous Pan-Africanists, not only within the United States and the Caribbean, but also in South Africa and throughout West Africa.

At the end of the day, however, it was at the Manchester Congress of 1945, which abandoned ideas of imperial reform in favour of an anti-imperialist ideology of independence and autonomy, that the successful post-war battle for black liberation began—a struggle that would no longer be based in the

[18] Chaps. by McCaskie and Bickford-Smith

[19] Chap. by Philip D. Morgan; J. Ayodele Langley, *Pan-Africanism and Nationalism in West Africa 1900–1945* (Oxford, 1973), p. 379; Vincent Bakpetu Thompson, *Africa and Unity: The Evolution of Pan-Africanism* (Harlow, Essex, 1969).

metropole, but which moved back to the colonies, and which could no longer be the preserve of educated blacks, but depended on mobilizing the masses. There, Kwame Nkrumah, the future leader of the first black colony to win independence from Britain, met W. E. B. DuBois, who was later to retire to Ghana where he died and is buried. The 1945 Congress affirmed the militant spirit of Garvey's ideas; even DuBois, once a strong critic of Garveyism, lent his support. Ironically, Garvey never went to Africa, even though he founded the Black Star shipping line, whose symbol adorns the Ghanaian flag when it was first hoisted in 1957, inaugurating the era of political independence for all African and Caribbean people that was to follow.

The exception to this enthusiasm among élite blacks for a Pan-African identity occurred in the Cape. Here a sizeable number of Creoles resisted any identification with ordinary Africans. But this stand-offish-ness was because many Cape Creoles could escape the worst of British and settler racism by claiming to be different—to be Coloured rather than 'Bantu'. Although 'people of colour' differentiated themselves from other blacks in the Caribbean from the time when they were a privileged élite within a slave society through the twentieth century when they were the core of the black middle class, they were never recognized under the law as being separate. Because Bantu-speaking 'natives' in South Africa were treated as a distinct group within a ranked set of racial identities, 'pragmatic self-interest' meant that most Cape Creoles chose to accept the privileges of an officially recognized 'Coloured' identity. At the same time, as race almost entirely eclipsed culture as the basis of full membership in the British Empire, most Creoles were forced to live with the reality that they had been rudely excluded.[20]

By calling people black, the British hoped to create boundaries between themselves and these 'Others.' What 'blackness' meant to the British changed over time, as it did to those so designated, but as with a range of other imperial dichotomies—such as ruler and ruled, colonizer and colonized, native and non-native—these distinctions were, in Stoler and Cooper's words, difficult to 'sustain, precariously secured, and repeatedly subverted'.[21]

Subversion was most obvious when it came to military service. Slaves had long served as auxilaries to the British military, but at the end of the eighteenth century the terms of their service changed significantly starting with the American Revolution. These ' "slaves in red coats" became the

[20] Chap. by Bickford-Smith.

[21] Stoler and Cooper, 'Between Metropole and Colony', p. 34.

"sable arm" of British authority' in the circum-Atlantic world. Although still slaves, black soldiers were armed, placed on an equal footing with white soldiers, and sometimes even commanded whites. After emancipation, the British policed their Empire from the Caribbean to the West African coast and the Cape Colony with free black soldiers. In the age of high imperialism, they conquered most of Africa, with the exception of the Afrikaners during the South African War, with black soldiers. For much of the nineteenth century they did not experience difficulty in finding soldiers. During both World Wars, however, they needed to attract black soldiers on a much wider scale, often invoking loyalty to Empire as a recruiting tool. But such service to Empire created expectations of equality and reciprocity that quickly led to disappointment and disillusionment—as a result of the racism black soldiers encountered from white officers and soldiers alike as well as because of the failure of colonial governments to acknowledge their service after their return. Many of those who joined nascent political organizations in the Caribbean were veterans from the First World War, 'whose wartime experiences of racial discrimination made them sensitive to racial and class injustice'. One Tanganyikan veteran of the Battle of Kalewa in Burma during the Second World War, where the King's African Rifles succeeded after the British and Americans had failed, remembered: 'We scorned the British, for we saw that a Briton's bragging was based on the deeds of others, especially we Africans. We saw that—given a rifle—we could be better than a European.'[22]

Yet, no amount of subversion could overcome racism, which was the typical medium through which Empire was experienced in the twentieth century. It sought to relegate blacks to a world that was clearly defined and impossible to escape. The Enlightenment had introduced new ways of looking at peoples based on separation and otherness, as David Cannadine notes. It did not wholly subvert earlier analogical ways of thinking, based on observation of status similarities and cultivation of affinities, just as he maintains, but it is far too optimistic to claim that only when the British thought collectively did they employ crude stereotypes and always when they thought individualistically they did so in terms or rank rather than race.[23]

[22] Chaps. by Brown and Johnson; John Iliffe, *A Modern History of Tanganyika* (Cambridge, 1979), p. 377.

[23] David Cannadine, *Ornamentalism: How the British Saw their Empire* (Oxford, 2001), pp. 8–9, 123–25.

After race, gender was the most common category of exclusion. It increasingly became the basis of participation within the Empire in the aftermath of slave emancipation in the Caribbean. Although emancipation improved the status of the majority of blacks within the Caribbean, it also represented a decline in status of a majority of those former slaves, who found that their subjecthood was conditioned not only by imperial ideologies of race, but also by ones of gender. Where once black women had been a significant force in slave societies, and in leading protests against apprenticeship as well as in the exodus from plantations, after 1838 they were increasingly forced into subsidiary roles in terms of political power. Ironically, as they faced exclusion from the public sphere, female-headed households became increasingly common throughout the islands. Ideas of male privilege in post-emancipation society had their origins in British gender stereotypes rather than ideas that had survived from Africa, where women enjoyed considerably more autonomy than did white middle-class British women. In nineteenth-century West Africa, patriarchal British culture often proved attractive to Creole men who embraced the ideology of Victorian marriage and the bourgeois family. Creole women found themselves with far less economic and political power than most women in the indigenous societies of the coast.

Worse still was the plight of many African women in the twentieth century, the result, in the first instance, of the attitudes of British officers, who saw women as belonging not only to an inferior race, but also to an inferior gender. Patriarchal ideologies in Africa, which eventually spread from white administrators, missionaries, and settlers to black men, had much in common, but elaborate attempts were made to pretend that these were African rather British ideas. Women had always been important farmers in Africa and became important producers of cash crops, yet Colonial Officers used euphemisms, such as calling a woman's farm her 'garden', in order to hide what they could not imagine—a world where gender roles were radically different from what they knew. Despite attempts by British feminists to shape imperial policy in ways that would be advantageous to African women, colonial officers worked with African men to create a system of patriarchy enshrined in 'native custom' and administered by 'native courts'. But 'native' was often just a euphemism for colonial, and colonial was itself a disguise for an alliance of black men and British officers.

No amount of gendered myopia, however, could disguise the importance of black women to the colonial African economies of the British Empire. As these economies demanded more migrant male labour, African women who remained in rural areas perforce assumed many of the roles and did much of the work of absent men. They bore the brunt of a labour system that did not rely on the incentive of attractive, or even adequate, wages, but the less subtle instruments of the law and taxation. Not all African women suffered a decline in power within the British Empire. In some instances, such as in areas where cash crop production was attractive, and in colonial cities, where new opportunities beckoned and older ones, such as marketing, persisted, some women prospered.[24]

Blacks as Subjects and Workers

Until emancipation, arguably most blacks were not part of the British Empire even though they lived within it, were a majority of the population in many places, and did most of the work. Until then, the vast majority of blacks were slaves working on plantations. Few whites shared the views of a small group of metropolitan reformers who, in the American Revolutionary era, believed that slaves should be treated as subjects, and so accorded the protection of the law and the Empire from the often inhumane treatment of their masters. In practice, as in law, the enslaved had no access to the customary rights, liberties, and protections enjoyed by the free. Yet slaves were subject to the law, if not subjects within the Empire. Throughout the Caribbean and the American colonies, elaborate slave codes were developed institutionalizing the relationship between the free and unfree. Unauthorized movements, large congregations, possession of weapons, drumming and the playing of horns, and the practice of secret rituals were all prohibited and punishments were severe.[25]

A very real difficulty—how to define Empire as a practical reality rather than merely as an ideological claim—existed. For those enslaved Africans held in British colonies, their bondage was neither sanctioned nor enforced by direct imperial intervention, but exercised and maintained within different colonies because of imperial connivance and neglect, lack of metropolitan authority, and settler autonomy. Nevertheless, slavery and Empire were in many ways synonymous. In the eighteenth century, it was impossible for all but a few whites to imagine a British Empire without slavery, and when

[24] Chap. by Diana Jeater; Jean Allman, '"England Swings Like a Pendulum Do?...". Africanist Reflections on Cannadine's Retro-Empire', *Journal of Colonialism and Colonial History*, III, 1 (2002), p. 7.

[25] Chaps. by Brown and Morgan.

more people saw the wisdom of separating Empire from slavery in the early part of the nineteenth century, the economic decline of plantations proved just how dependent Empire had been on slavery. The abolitionists' plans for emancipation, predicated on the possibility and desirability of more rational, humane, and, indeed, profitable use of black labour, were often motivated as much or even more by political and ideological considerations—reigning in settler independence and defending the good name of Empire.[26]

After emancipation the fundamental experience of most black men and women in the empire changed dramatically. Still, just because they were now recognized as British subjects and no longer under the exclusive authority of the planter, did not mean that blacks enjoyed the freedom they expected, since their lives were still very much tied to an economy that continued to depend upon their labour. For former slaves freedom meant autonomy, for planters and policy-makers alike it meant continuity of the plantation system and sugar production, with its 'established order and existing hierarchies'. Wages were supposed to do the work of the whip, as abolitionists hoped that incentive could replace coercion, but many former slaves looked for means of escaping the labour market instead of joining it because the terms of employment were often onerous and undesirable. Blacks in the Caribbean lacked land, and without land, autonomy. European missionaries responded to the plight of ex-slaves by setting up free villages on land purchased from planters in Jamaica, whereas ex-slaves organized their own in British Guiana, through co-operatives that purchased land from planters. As the withdrawal of labour increased, planters sought alternative sources from India, which only exacerbated the plight of ex-slaves as wages were depressed and the possibility of working on plantations during difficult times disappeared. Land continued to be a source of contention, along with other labour-related concerns, which resulted most famously in the 1865 Morant Bay Rebellion in Jamaica.[27]

The labour market that ex-slaves were trying to distance themselves from during the first generation of general emancipation, quickly deteriorated during the long depression of the late nineteenth century, thereby creating great want—'unemployment, underemployment and depressed wages'—among the poor blacks of the Caribbean. This poverty eventually gave impetus to labour migration from the Caribbean to other markets:

[26] Chap. by Brown. [27] Chap. by Heuman.

South Florida, the Dominican Republic, Panama, Costa Rica, Spanish Honduras, and Cuba, from the beginning of the twentieth century until the Great Depression. No longer a destination for labour, the British West Indies became a labour exporter, and no longer within the British Empire.[28]

For so many blacks in the British Empire, both before and after emancipation, work was their dominant experience. Their primary role even as subjects was as workers. This dependence was brought home acutely in the aftermath of the Second World War, when Britain needed workers to help with its post-war reconstruction. The Nationalities Act of 1948 specified the legal right of West Indians to enter Britain and between 1951 and 1961, about a quarter of a million did so. The subjects of Empire came 'home' for the first time in any large numbers.[29]

The shift from slavery to wage labour had never been well thought-out in the Caribbean, and the thinking that informed British plans in Africa was no better. Imperial pretensions led both officials in London and administrators in colonies to over-estimate their power to create a capitalist labour market in Africa. The first obstacle was seen to be slavery within conquered African territories, but the first problem was that colonial revenues often came from exports of crops grown by slaves, as well as peasants, and, secondly, that the colonial officials' tenuous political hold in many parts of Africa was through alliances with African leaders who were slave owners. Furthermore, the democratization of Britain and the racialization of science in the period between emancipation in the Caribbean and the conquest of Africa had introduced new distinctions between types of subjects that severely altered the implications of subjecthood for Africans.

Whereas the distinction between the free and unfree had been an important boundary of inclusion and exclusion in the Caribbean before emancipation, in Africa both slaves and slave-owners became British subjects once they were incorporated within the empire. Black slave-owners in Africa at the beginning of the twentieth century found themselves in a much different position than white slave-owners in the Caribbean at the beginning of the nineteenth century. In both instances, slavery was under threat, but black slave-owners, unlike their white predecessors, had no political rights; they were subjects as white planters had been, but they were not citizens. On the other hand, black slave-owners were not seen as a threat to empire, indeed, their co-operation was crucial to its stability. Freedom no longer defined

[28] Chaps. by Heuman and Johnson.

[29] Chaps. by Johnson and James.

what it meant to be a British subject simply because in the aftermath of Caribbean emancipation powerful and invidious forms of exclusion, those of race and gender, had created different types of subjects.[30]

For most blacks in Africa, subjecthood was not an escape from slavery—first, because, unlike in the Caribbean, most Africans were not slaves; second, in most instances enslaved Africans became subjects before they were emancipated. Because it was not experienced as freedom from something, for most Africans subjecthood was very different from what it had been in the Caribbean. African Creoles could strategically declare their allegiance to the Empire, but for most Africans, there was little that the British could do to command their loyalty. Imperial rule did allow slaves to free themselves from their former masters, but emancipation was never a single and decisive act in Africa, coming as it did at different times in different places, and by the time it had been formally declared in many places, former slaves had often already fled their servitude. For colonial intermediaries, Empire offered opportunities for accumulating small amounts of personal wealth and power, but few regarded the British monarch and the imperial state with genuine affection or gratitude. During the period of the British Empire in Africa, not all Africans suffered. New opportunities certainly arose for some Africans to sell everything from their voluntary labour to attractive cash crops (such as cocoa). As a result a sizeable minority benefitted, but because there was much more that British administrators and their intermediaries commanded that the majority of African subjects give to the Empire—through forced labour, taxation, and production of unattractive cash crops (such as cotton)—the benefits of Empire were difficult to sell.

The story of African labour during the twentieth century was largely about the struggle to be recognized as workers. Although the British eventually abolished slavery in law, yet often not in practice, in all of their African colonies by 1928, their appetite for transforming Africa was already diminished. Instead, by the First World War, the unreformed nature of African society was being proclaimed as a virtue of British colonial rule. Through the ideology of Indirect Rule, which was fully developed after the First World War and applied throughout British colonies in Africa, many Africans were relegated not only to the literal space of labour reserves, but also to the metaphorical space of tradition—a place of apparent timelessness according to British thinking. Because of these shifts in thought, British officials could

[30] Chap. by Frederick Cooper.

acknowledge that Africans could work, 'but not', as Cooper puts it, 'that they could be workers'. They became 'natives'.[31]

Migrant labour was endemic across British Africa. By the 1930s there were calls for 'stabilization' of the African workforce. What this meant was creating the economic conditions for sustaining rural life and to turn the labour force into a permanent, self-reproducing one. Labour disturbances throughout the Caribbean in the 1930s spread to Africa, and made London focus on the labour question. As war was looming with Germany, colonial labour disorder was seen as something that had to be addressed. The answer that emerged from London was the Colonial Development and Welfare Act of 1940. For the first time, Africans and West Indians were seen as part of the same colonial people and the social existence of workers in both areas was finally acknowledged; this, in turn, was identified as the key to their participation in the labour market. Education, housing, and nutrition were suddenly factors that the Colonial Office concluded were crucial to a modern labour market. But before the plan could be implemented in 1945, labour unrest spread throughout Africa.

All of these labour disruptions had the same cause: workers unwilling to work without the 'the social conditions to sustain themselves' in cities, mines, and ports. 'The British Empire was discovering that the worker was not just a unit of labor power, but a human being living in specific conditions.' The strikes of black workers in the 1940s and after drove home a message in Africa that black slaves had made in the Caribbean several centuries earlier, when they had forced whites to recognize their humanity by creating their own culture. Paradoxically, although nineteenth-century abolitionists had recognized the humanity of slaves, few had cared about them as workers in the aftermath of abolition.[32]

Cultural Encounters and Exchanges

If one theme dominates the black experience, it is migration—from the forced migration of the slave trade across the Atlantic to the internal migration of workers within Africa. It was a constant feature of the British Empire and therefore a common experience for blacks living within it. This world of

[31] Chap. by Cooper; Mahmood Mamdani, *Citizen and Subject: Contemporary Africa and the Legacy of Late Colonialism* (Princeton, NJ, 1996), pp. 40, 48.

[32] Mamdani, *Citizen and Subject.*

maritime connections has been christened the 'black Atlantic'. By this term Paul Gilroy does not mean the literal Atlantic, but a figurative one of memory and motion, for which the ship is a powerful symbol. It is a world that exists between Africa, Europe, America, and the Caribbean and that emerged from 'transnational and intercultural' processes that always have operated outside of conventional boundaries and definitions of space. After the slave trade, the peoples of the Caribbean continued to move in large numbers within the region and, later, to and from Britain. Within Africa, colonial governments moved labour with great frequency: workers from rural areas to mines, plantations, and ports, as well as from colony to colony (most notably to South Africa); colonial troops were deployed throughout the continent (and during the Second World War outside Africa); policemen and clerks were often stationed away from their areas of birth. The large and small movements of blacks within the Empire brought people into contact with other cultures in ways that might not ever have happened, and it also necessitated both a cultural and linguistic lingua franca, of which elements of British culture, from consumer products to fashion styles, and English vocabulary were important aspects.[33]

As well as a lingua franca, imperial encounters and exchanges generated a remarkable array of languages—forms of black English—from pidgin and creole languages of the ports and plantations to elegant literary forms of eighteenth-century black abolitionists and the inventive and challenging novels of post-colonial writers. English is an important 'marker of a cultural legacy', but even in its least creolized forms it should not necessarily be seen as a sign of imperial domination or colonial control. Certainly in Africa, where there was only 'shallow penetration by the colonizers', English was appropriated very much on African terms. In the early eighteenth century, a merchant of the city-state of Bonny was tellingly described as a 'mighty talking Black'. Linguistic play and subversion were also at the centre of the cultural resistance of slaves in the Caribbean, just as they were found in the popular culture of anti-colonialism in Africa, and continue into the contemporary period as the former colonies are 'writing back' to the imperial metropole, both from outside and within Britain.[34]

Black naming patterns too reveal a range of possibilities and some underlying similarities. The Sierra Leone Creoles demonstrated their loyalty

[33] Paul Gilroy, *The Black Atlantic: Modernity and Double Consciousness* (Cambridge, Mass., 1993).

[34] Chap. by Northrup; John Holm, *An Introduction to Pidgins and Creoles* (Cambridge, 2000).

during Queen Victoria's Golden and Diamond Jubilees when they named many of their female children 'Jubilee' and 'Victoria'. Similarly in the Caribbean, Learie Constantine, the cricketer, noted that, in the 1920s and 1930s, when visiting MCC teams toured the West Indies 'so great is the admiration for their prowess that hundreds of little black babies are named after them, sometimes using the white players' Christian names, but often using their whole name'. A long line of West Indian sportsmen have been named after this or that British general or politician: the Jamaican fast bowler Balfour Patrick Patterson, Gladstone Small of Barbados, and the Canadian-Jamaican sprinter Attlee Mabon Clement. But in the Caribbean, blacks' playfulness with names and onamastic delight encompass the self-assertive 'Kikuyu', 'Kenyatta', and 'Marcus Garvey', the angry 'Black and Hungry', to the Maroon name for a local site, 'Me No Sen' You No Come'. A name meant to reveal a bearer's essence has been labelled an African trait (one thinks of the prophetic quality of Equiano's four names in this connection) but equally, or even more so, it speaks to creolized inventiveness. As Richard Burton argues, this is not a culture of resistance but rather an oppositional culture, a subaltern culture, which engages the dominant culture by manoeuvre, manipulation, and mimicry.[35]

Sport is another arena in which British values were instilled, and an oppositional culture arose, and it is best evident in the Caribbean where colonialism was so intense and long-lasting. Cricket, with its restraint, intricate rules, unwritten codes, difficult technique, and its ritualism was an almost perfect expression of bourgeois civility, public-school morality, and quintessential Englishness, as C.L.R. James acknowledges in his *Beyond a Boundary*. He learned to play for the team, keep a stiff upper lip, and act generously to opponents. The élite island schools introduced the game to the coloured middle class and soon the black working class took it up in the streets, yards, and beaches. After the Second World War West Indians revealed that they had not only mastered the game but could beat their former masters at it, a ritual of inversion celebrated by James. A form of resistance ('liberation cricket'), the game can also be seen as an even more subtle form of domination, a testament to the power of an imperial sport at instilling alien values—James, for example, recognized that 'the British tradition soaked deep' into him, even down to his 'instinctive

[35] Chap. by Bickford-Smith; Richard D. E. Burton, 'Names and Naming in Afro-Caribbean Cultures', *Nieuwe West-Indisches Gids*, LXXIII (1999), pp. 35–58.

responses', and described himself, even as a young boy, as 'an alien in my own environment'.[36]

Christianity was a vital part of the black experience of Empire. Admittedly, under slavery, exposure to Christianity often took the form of an explanation and justification of servitude—and blacks thereby rejected it. Yet, when blacks heard a different message, particularly when conveyed by indigenous catechists rather than white missionaries, the effects of Christianity changed dramatically. Sam Sharpe, the leader of 'the Baptist War', the 1831 slave rebellion in Jamaica that helped shorten the timetable for emancipation, understood the Scriptures as demanding freedom and justice. Throughout the nineteenth century, blacks increasingly embraced the potentially liberating message of Christianity, because, among other attractions, it offered answers to questions about evil, misfortune, and death. As well as encouraging direct protest against the injustices of Empire, other practical advantages followed. In the late nineteenth century and early twentieth, Christian churches became the main providers of education in the Caribbean and had an important influence on ideas of freedom and liberation espoused by George Padmore and Marcus Garvey, among others. Yet, even as the middle class gained advantages from mainstream churches, the lower classes often gravitated to syncretic Afro-Christian religious cults.[37]

The story of Christianity in Africa also includes the formation of a culture that challenged important aspects of imperialism. In the nineteenth century Sierra Leonean Creoles, 'Christianized and in a way Anglicized yet not de-Yorubaized', had the greatest missionary successes when they returned to southwestern Nigeria. Their style of Christianity, full of inflections derived from the natal culture of the Recaptives, appealed to the Yoruba. By the end of the nineteenth century, racism within the various white missionary communities and issues of political autonomy led to the secession of many congregations in West Africa and southern Africa, and the formation of independent churches that signaled the birth of self-consciously African

[36] James, *Beyond a Boundary*, pp. 18, 66, 154; Gikandi, *Maps of Englishness*, pp. 9–13; Hilary McD. Beckles and Brian Stoddart, *Liberation Cricket: West Indies Cricket Culture* (Manchester, 1995); Richard D. E. Burton, *Afro-Creole: Power, Opposition, and Play in the Caribbean* (Ithaca, NY, 1997), pp. 177–86.

[37] Chaps. by Heuman and Johnson; Mary Turner, *Slaves and Missionaries: The Disintegration of Jamaican Slave Society, 1787–1834* (Urbana, Ill., 1982), esp. pp. 148–178; Arthur Charles Dayfoot, *The Shaping of the West India Church 1492–1962* (Kingston, Jamaica, 1999); Hemchand Gossai and Nathaniel Samuel Murrell, eds., *Religion, Culture, and Tradition in the Caribbean* (New York, 2000).

forms of Christianity. Even within the white mission churches at this time, converts were also inculturating, or domesticating, Christianity by infusing it with elements of their own cultures, albeit in ways most missionaries were unaware of. However, independent churches, such as the Ethiopian Church of Mangena Mokone in Johannesburg or the Native Baptist Church of Mojola Agbedi in Lagos, both established in the 1890s, allowed blacks to experience the self-government that colonialism was eroding and encouraged them to explore their own identities, often abandoning English baptismal names for African ones. Throughout British Africa many blacks borrowed elements from the evangelists' culture and mixed them with parts of their own culture so as to create not just independent churches but new forms of Christianity that were often both prophetic and political, such as that founded by Elliot Kenan Kamwana who preached that the British would be driven from Nyasaland (Malawi), the Hut Tax would end, and Christ would return by 1914. Between 1908 and 1909, the year he was deported from the colony and sent into exile, he attracted almost ten thousand followers. Other movements were more concerned with healing, which explains much of the success of Zionism in southern Africa or the growth of the Aladura movement in the 1920s in south-western Nigeria.[38]

In all these instances, Christianity resonated with Africans because they translated it into vernacular terms that had meaning to them, regardless of what missionaries thought these meanings should be. The success of Christianity in taking hold of the imaginations of blacks as well as their creativity in mixing that message with local concerns, experiences, and ideas is a story that began even before the British Empire in Africa, was greatly intensified during colonial rule, and then flourished after the Empire ended. In this sense the story of African Christianity, even though an important part of the black experience of Empire, is a somewhat different and larger story. In much the same way that imperial authorities attempted to control who in the Empire could call themselves British, missionary authorities attempted to regulate who could call themselves Christian. The missionary project, however, was overwhelmed by the vibrancy and inventiveness of African religious thought and practice. Missionary endeavours and black responses were part of a shift in the centre of Christianity from the First to the Third

[38] Chapters by McCaskie and Bickford-Smith; Adrian Hastings, *The Church in Africa, 1450–1950* (London, 1995), p. 341; J. D. Y. Peel, *Religious Encounter and the Making of the Yoruba* (Bloomington, Ind., 2000); John L. Comaroff and Jean Comaroff, *Of Revelation and Revolution: The Dialectics of Modernity on a South African Frontier* (Chicago, 1997).

World. In 1900 there were only 10 million African Christians, but today there are almost 400 million according to some estimates, constituting approximately a fifth of the Christian world, with most living in what was once the British Empire. Empire was an important part of this success, but the dissolution of Empire has not impeded the endurance and growth of Christianity.

While today there are more practising Anglicans in Uganda alone than in England, and the Anglican population of Africa is almost equal to the total population of England, the Caribbean should not be overshadowed by Africa. Although much fewer in number, the percentage of Christians in the Caribbean—usually above 90 per cent in all countries, with the exceptions of Guyana, where only half of the population are Christian, and Trinidad and Tobago, where two-thirds of the people follow one of several different churches—is much higher than in Africa, where indigenous beliefs and ritual as well as Islam have always been much stronger competitors for the faithful.[39]

Perhaps popular music is the best idiom through which to apprehend the interconnectedness of black Atlantic culture because, as has been said, the record album displaced the ship as 'the most important conduit of Pan-African communication'. From Calypso to Chimurenga, via Jazz, Highlife, Afro-beat, and Reggae, the circulation of music within the black Atlantic has produced an astounding number of new musical styles—and the antecedents go back much further in time. Trinidadian Calypso, for example, seems to have originated in the dance-drumming tradition known as *bamboula* along with the drum rhythms of *kalinda* stick-fighting, and would later incorporate the tuned steel pan, fashioned from discarded oil drums. Jamaican reggae drew inspiration from *ska*, *mento*, and the Rastafarian drumming tradition known as *nyabingi*. The importance of music in everyday black life can be traced ultimately to Africa—and learned traditions emphasizing complex rhythms, percussion, syncopation, and antiphonal patterns—but also to a world of restriction where music was one of the few cultural opportunities offered as a surrogate for other forms of individual autonomy denied by the plantation, the barracoons, and the colonial regime. These

[39] Peel, *Religious Encounter*, p. 1; Elizabeth Isichei, *A History of Christianity in Africa: From Antiquity to the Present* (London, 1995), p. 1; David B. Barrett, George T. Kurian, and Todd M Johnson, eds., *World Christian Encyclopedia: A Comparative Survey of Churches and Religions in the Modern World* (London, 2001).

connected musical traditions are extraordinarily rich and varied; their influence on world music has been immense.[40]

What was most distinctive, most unifying, and most dynamic about these cultures were their constant disposition to change and movement, constantly innovating through their embrace of hybridity and their syncretic practices. Some of this inventiveness was the product of Africa's open frontiers, where cultural pluralism and linguistic multilingualism were part of the landscape of historical interaction and where cultural encounters had long been punctuated more by affirmation than by disavowal. But much can also be attributed to the nature of the black engagement with the British Empire, which was a maritime encounter, with people crossing boundaries, contesting authority, negotiating identities, synthesizing disparate elements, continually inventing and reinventing themselves. With shared dispositions and sensibilities, they created distinct local black cultures, dizzying in their array and fascinating in their complexity. Attempts to unravel these likenesses will never be easy, but these fractured patterns of similarity must not be confused for endogenous, essentialist, or metaphysical signs of identity. 'Where there is commonality between cultures it is not through an "African" connection', Appiah writes with particular relevance to the continent, 'but through a "black", that is, colonial, [and, we might add, an imperial] connection'.[41]

The slave cultures of the New World created a synthesis out of a mixture of cultural fragments that survived the Middle Passage, using them for new purposes and imbuing them with new meanings. Out of this cultural bricolage came the seeds of recognition of a common African identity in the New World—a unity created out of the fragmentation and dislocations of the slave trade—and something that Equiano was one of the first to publicize. This shared basis for identity, that is, this creole and syncretic African culture of the New World, fed back to Africa in the nineteenth century when West Indians and African-Americans brought the idea of an African identity to Africans. There is of course an irony here: the educated élites of the Caribbean assiduously avoided much contact with the Afro-Creole culture of the majority of blacks well into the twentieth century, yet it was among their ranks that the idea of Africa as a label of identity first resonated. This

[40] Gilroy, *Black Atlantic*, p. 13; Chap. by Morgan; Kenneth M. Bilby, 'The Caribbean as a Musical Region', in Sidney W. Mintz and Sally Price, eds., *Caribbean Contours* (Baltimore, 1985), 181–218.

[41] Chap. by Kwame Anthony Appiah.

identity was first taken up by Creoles of Sierra Leone who, because most of them were actually born elsewhere in Africa (or were brought up by parents who were), often Africanized what they adopted from bourgeois British culture. Later, as they found themselves excluded from Empire by racism, they proudly asserted their claim to be African rather than British, while at the same time never rejecting those things they shared with a wider, imperial British culture.

Conclusion

Although there is no twentieth-century counterpart to Equiano, the most obvious successor is Chinua Achebe. Both are the best selling black writers in English of their times. Although today there is some question over whether the author of Equiano's narrative was really born in Africa, for Achebe there was never any question from the very first time he read the text as to whether its author was, like himself, Igbo. Moreover, within the narrative he claims to have found the clues necessary to pinpoint the exact village where Equiano was born, and in so doing repatriate his lost countryman to Africa and make him a progenitor of Nigerian literature.

Achebe's identity is not ambivalent or fluid like Equiano's. Unlike Equiano, Achebe's life was not the product of a hybrid Atlantic world of movement, but of contestation between Igbo culture and British colonialism. Born in 1930 to evangelical Christian parents in south-eastern Nigeria, Achebe was christened Albert, after Prince Albert, but later chose to drop 'the tribute to Victorian England' and to be known instead by a contraction of his Igbo name, which means 'God will fight my wars'. The trajectory of Achebe's life is in some way the opposite of Equiano's, who began with an Igbo name and later adopted a Western one; the former set out to recover his Igbo culture by rejecting the ethnocentric culture of late British colonialism, whereas the latter navigated his way through life with multiple identities, adopting new names as he encountered new circumstances. Equiano, of necessity, looked outward, while Achebe, out of firm cultural commitment, looked inward.

What some might take as signs of adaptability and hybridity in Equiano's life, Achebe regards as a form of alienation; his eighteenth-century countryman was too immersed in European culture to maintain but a 'fragmented memory' of his ancestral land and its culture. Whereas Equiano's alienation from Africa was fundamentally physical, the alienation that Achebe has tried to overcome through the act of writing, an alienation that for him was experienced through reading British writers—from John Lok to Joyce Carey—who described Africa and Africans in derogatory terms, was psychological. Achebe turned to the novel as a means of literally 'writing back' against the legacy of these texts. For Achebe, 'strong language is in the very nature of the dialogue between dispossession and its rebuttal'. Achebe's rebuttal took the form of novels that were instrumental in creating a new African literature, 'for and about' Africans, that had 'profound political significance' in the struggle against Empire and its legacies. However, as Appiah notes, one legacy of Empire that writers such as Achebe were not willing to repudiate was the English language. Even though he felt that the language was tied to a 'racial arrogance and prejudice'. Achebe has cautioned against a wholesale repudiation of English and other parts of the imperial 'package deal': 'Let us not in rejecting the evil throw out the good with it.' As a reminder of the effectiveness of English as a second language as well as a lingua franca for African literature, Achebe points to Equiano's 'beautifully written document', one that repudiated 'the lies and slander invented by some Europeans to justify the slave trade' very much in the language of eighteenth-century England. Two hundred years later, Achebe argues that the language of Empire should change to suit the needs of African writers; postcolonial writers should not have to change to suit the English language. He envisages a 'new English, still in full communion with its ancestral home but altered to suit its new African surroundings'. Just such a communion was not available to Equiano, who assumed a new identity to write in a received language, causing his connection to his ancestral home to become fragmented.[42]

Although Achebe and Equiano are linked by their shared positions of literary prominence, and possibly by a common natal culture, another writer, Caryl Phillips, is a more exemplary successor to Equiano's experiences after the latter was enslaved and taken from Africa. Both have written travelogues and autobiographical reminiscences; both are familiar with an Atlantic world; both have grown up, in Phillips's words, 'riddled with the cultural confusions of being black and British'; both are products, again in his words, 'of British imperial adventures'. Born in St Kitts in 1958, Phillips's family almost immediately emigrated to England. Phillips recalls as a seven-

[42] Chinua Achebe, *Morning Yet on Creation* (London, 1975), pp. 58, 59, 67; *Home and Exile* (Oxford, 2000), p. 77; Chap. by Appiah.

year-old (roughly the same age as Equiano when he arrived in England) listening 'to the turgid tones of "God Save the Queen" ' in a Leeds cinema and then walking back to his 'home'. He did not feel he belonged. 'I am of, and not of, this place', he remembers; he was 'too late to be coloured, but too soon to be British'. He observes that: 'History dealt me four cards; an ambiguous hand'. The four cards he has in mind are Africa, the Caribbean, Britain, and the United States—an Atlantic world—that has shaped Phillips in some of the same ways it did Equiano. Phillips has experienced the loneliness of an Atlantic crossing, getting attuned to the rhythm of life on the ocean, reliving his parents' experience in emigrating to England. He has visited Liverpool, the most successful slave port of the Atlantic world where the Town Hall, 'a spectacular repository of marble, crystal, oil paintings and gilt', and St George's Hall, 'an enormous neo-classifical edifice' meant to rival Athens's Acropolis, are monuments to the immense wealth generated by the city's trading in human lives. He has examined historical figures, such as Reverend Philip Quaque, born in the same decade as Equiano, another man of two worlds—born on the Gold Coast and educated in England—at home in neither, not able to identify with the terrible indignities visited upon his fellow Africans when he returned home to evangelize them, yet not fully accepted by the British either as their chaplain of Cape Coast Castle. As Phillips notes, 'The ambivalence, pain, and pathos of [Quaque's] letters signify loss. Loss of home, loss of language, loss of self, but never loss of dignity'. Phillips has gone to Ghana, where he too finds no home, envying people's rootedness, their not having to 'flinch at *the* question, "Where are you from?" ' For Phillips, much like Equiano, 'Our identities are fluid. Belonging is a contested state. Home is a place riddled with vexinq questions'.[43]

[43] Caryl Phillips, *The European Tribe* (1987; New York, 2000), p. 2; Caryl Phillips, *The Atlantic Sound* (New York, 2000), pp. 104–05, 126, 180; and *A New World Order: Essays* (New York, 2001), p. 6.

Select Bibliography

CHINUA ACHEBE, *Morning Yet on Creation* (London, 1975).

—— *Home and Exile* (Oxford, 2000).

RICHARD D. E. BURTON, *Afro-Creole: Power, Opposition, and Play in the Caribbean* (Ithaca, NY, 1997).

David Cannadine, *Ornamentalism: How the British Saw their Empire* (Oxford, 2001).

Vincent Carretta, *Equiano, the African: Biography of a Self-Made Man* (Athens, GA, 2005).

Jean Comaroff and John Comaroff, *Of Revelation and Revolution: Christianity and Consciousness in South Africa* (Chicago, 1991).

John L. Comaroff and Jean Comaroff, *Of Revelation and Revolution: The Dialectics of Modernity on a South African Frontier* (Chicago, 1997).

Olaudah Equiano, *The Interesting Narrative and Other Writings*, Vincent Carretta ed., (New York, 1995).

Toyin Falola and A. D. Roberts, 'West Africa', in Judith M. Brown and Wm. Roger Louis eds., *The Oxford History of the British Empire*, vol. IV, *The Twentieth Century* (Oxford, 1999).

Simon Gikandi, *Maps of Englishness: Writing Identity in the Culture of Colonialism* (New York, 1996).

Paul Gilroy, *'There Ain't No Black in the Union Jack': The Cultural Politics of Race and Nation* (London, 1987).

—— *The Black Atlantic: Modernity and Double Consciousness* (Cambridge, Mass., 1993).

Catherine Hall, *Civilising Subjects: Metroloe and Colony in the English Imagination 1830–1867* (Chicago, 2002).

C. L. R. James, *Beyond a Boundary* (1963; Durham, NC, 1993).

John Lonsdale, 'East Africa', in Judith M. Brown and Wm. Roger Louis eds., *The Oxford History of the British Empire*, vol. IV, *The Twentieth Century* (Oxford, 1999).

Mahmood Mamdani, *Citizen and Subject: Contemporary Africa and the Legacy of Late Colonialism* (Princeton, 1996).

Shula Marks, 'Southern Africa', in Judith M. Brown and Wm. Roger Louis eds., *The Oxford History of the British Empire*, Vol. IV, *The Twentieth Century* (Oxford, 1999).

J. D. Y. Peel, *Religious Encounter and the Making of the Yoruba* (Bloomington, Ind., 2000).

Caryl Phillips, *The European Tribe* (1987; New York, 2000).

—— *The Atlantic Sound* (New York, 2000).

—— *A New World Order: Essays* (New York, 2001).

Andrew Roberts, ed., *The Colonial Moment in Africa: Essays on the Movement of Minds and Materials, 1900–1940* (Cambridge, 1990).

Mary Turner, *Slaves and Missionaries: The Disintegration of Jamaican Slave Society, 1787–1834* (Urbana, Ill., 1982).

2

West Africans and the Atlantic, 1550–1800

DAVID NORTHRUP

In 1553 word of the arrival of English trading ships reached the capital of the kingdom of Benin in the Niger Delta (Map 2.1). Messengers were dispatched to the port town and escorted the English merchants and their Portuguese guide to the capital, also called Benin. In an audience chamber of his large palace the *oba* (ruler) welcomed them in Portuguese, a language he had learned as a child, and asked what had brought them to his kingdom. After the English explained their interest in purchasing a large quantity of Benin's pungent pepper, which the Portuguese had earlier introduced to Europe, the *oba* arranged for the visitors to inspect the sacks of peppercorns in a nearby warehouse. He also requested samples of the goods the English had brought so that his commercial agents might assess their value. So pleased was the *oba* of Benin with the prospect of opening trade with a second European country (the Portuguese having traded there since 1486) that he offered to sell pepper on credit to be repaid on the next voyage, should the English lack sufficient trade goods. In short order eighty tons of pepper were loaded aboard the English ships anchored offshore.[1]

Coastal West Africans in smaller and less centralized states than Benin also welcomed English traders and showed similar enthusiasm for incorporating new Atlantic trade into their commercial networks. Before reaching Benin, the same English ships had called at the Gold Coast, where Africans exchanged 2,400 ounces of gold for cloth, metals, hardware, and other goods that the English had brought. Even though the Atlantic coast of tropical Africa had been more isolated than regions closer to the Sahara or along the Indian Ocean until the arrival of the Portuguese, West African societies there had developed marketing networks, professional merchants, systems of

[1] Richard Eden's memoir of Thomas Windham's voyage to Guinea and Benin, 1553, in Richard Hakluyt [the younger], *The Principal Navigations, Voyages, Traffiques and Discoveries of the English Nation*, 10 vols. (London, 1927), vol. IV, pp. 39–45.

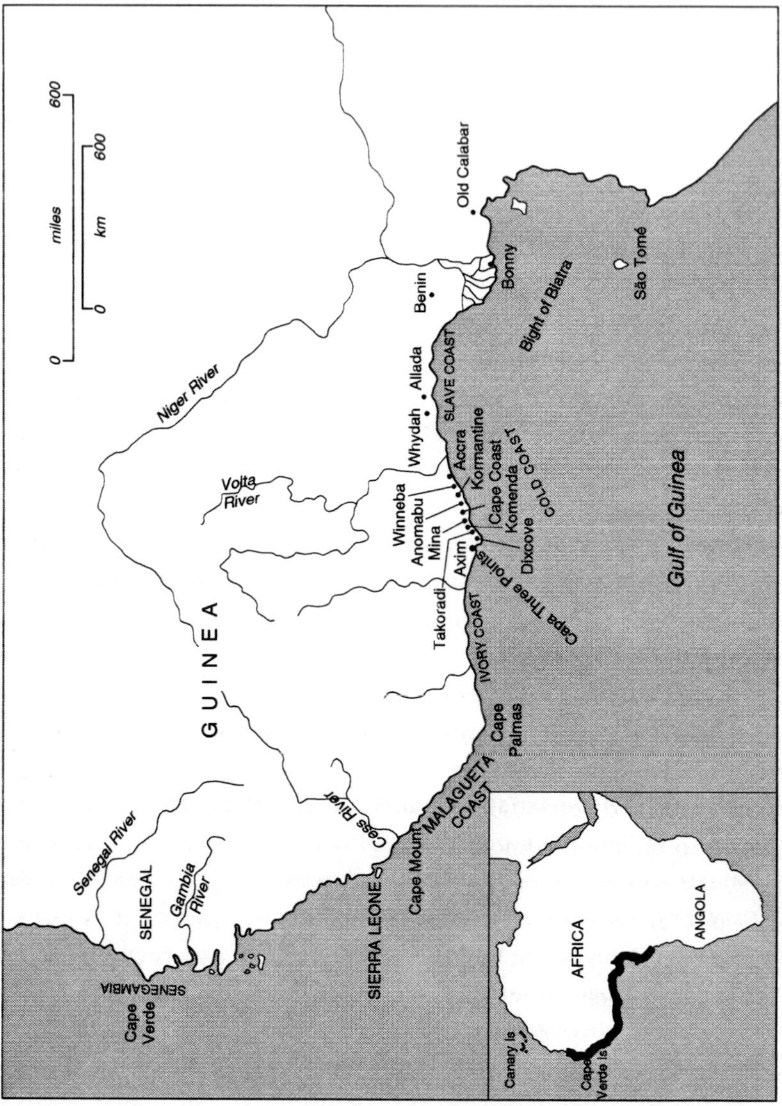

MAP 2.1: European Trade with West Africa.

Source: Nicholas Canny, ed., Oxford History of the British Empire, Vol. I, The Origins of Empire (Oxford

transport, and currencies through participation in local and regional trade. Before the arrival of the Portuguese, Benin had conducted inter-coastal trade with the Gold Coast, whose inhabitants prized the kingdom's high quality cotton cloths and stone beads. There is also evidence that Benin and other coastal West African societies had a long history of involvement in trade across the Sahara. For example, the copper used in the exquisite bronze and brass castings of lower Niger societies must have come from Saharan mines before 1500. West African rulers were accustomed to treating long-distance trade as a royal monopoly, and, as the first English visitors to Benin discovered, officials in charge of trade had made considerable progress in understanding European culture and languages since Benin sent its first trade delegation to Portugal in 1486.

The early English could also draw on a rich trading history, but it would take them more than a century to put their trade in West Africa on a solid footing. The commercial success of the 1553 voyage to Benin could not disguise its disastrous shortcomings. Only a month after anchoring in the Benin River, the ships fled in such haste that some of the English merchants were left behind at the capital. The panicked departure was to escape the tropical fevers that had sickened and killed so many of the officers and crew. One of the two English captains died at Benin and a hundred other members of the expedition perished there or on the voyage back to Plymouth.[2] The high mortality at Benin kept English traders away for three decades, but their trade on the Gold Coast developed more quickly. John Lok of a prominent London merchant family conducted a trading expedition there in 1554. His account described how Gold Coast Africans richly adorned themselves with ivory and gold and noted their skill and care in weighing gold, but Lok felt it necessary to inform his English readers what an elephant looked like and from which part of its anatomy ivory was obtained. In time, an elephant motif would adorn a new English coin, the golden Guinea, but to get to that point the English needed to ground their West African trade on a firmer basis and to improve their competitive advantage over their European rivals.[3]

Despite some royal opposition at home to interfering with Portugal's African trading monopoly, English merchant-adventurers persisted with their African adventures. In 1555 Lok brought five African men to England

[2] Alan Ryder, *Benin and the Europeans, 1485–1897* (London, 1969), pp. 76–84, 339–43.

[3] John Lok, 'The Voyage to Guinea in the Year 1554', in Hukluyt, *Principal Navigations*, IV pp. 54–57.

from the Portuguese outpost of Shama at the western end of the Gold Coast so that they might learn English and serve future English merchants as interpreters. At least three of the men later returned and became brokers and intermediaries in the trade, roles that Africans would dominate for the next three centuries.[4] During the next decade, John Hawkins's three voyages to Upper Guinea began the English participation in transatlantic slave trading, but his methods were those of a pirate rather than a merchant. On the 1564 expedition, the supposedly defenceless village he raided put up such effective resistance that Hawkins ended up with only ten captives at a cost of 'seven of our best men' with twenty-seven others on the casualty list. Four years later two similar raids produced comparable deaths and injuries but no captives. An attack on a third town was more successful, but, Hawkins noted, the African ruler who had joined forces with him in the attack had also cheated him out of most of the prisoners.[5]

Hawkins's rough methods and his interest in slaves were not typical of English ventures in that era. More commonly English merchants sought to improve their techniques for peaceful trading. Thus an English merchant prepared a detailed set of instructions for trading in pepper at Benin in 1582 that included information on the healthiest time of the year to go (the dry season at the beginning of the calendar year) and the more doubtful recommendation that one could ward off illness by consuming four or five heads of garlic with a pint of wine each morning. As late as 1620, Richard Jobson could still reject a Gambian's offer of slaves, affirming that the English 'were a people who did not deale in any such commodities, neither did wee buy or sell one another, or any that had our owne shapes'.[6] However, this aversion to dealing slaves eroded thereafter as a market for slaves developed in English colonies in the Americas.[7]

Despite these changes, there is no hint before 1800 of the British colonization and conquest of the Gold Coast that would come in the nineteenth century or of the expedition that would loot the palace at Benin in 1897. Two important differences in West Africa kept relations there from following the

[4] Peter Fryer, *Staying Power: The History of Black People in Britain* (London, 1984), pp. 5–7.

[5] Hakluyt, *Principal Navigations*, Vol. VI, pp. 17–18, 54.

[6] Randall Shawe to E. Cotton, PRO *State Papers* 12, no. 153, in Ryder, *Benin*, pp. 339–43; Richard Jobson, *The Golden Trade, or a Discovery of the River Gambia* (1623; London, 1932), p. 120.

[7] P. E. H. Hair and Robin Law, 'The English in Western Africa to 1700', *The Oxford History of the British Empire* (hereafter *OHBE*), Vol. I, *The Origins of Empire*, ed. Nicholas Canny (London, 1998), pp. 250–55.

pattern of European conquest and colonization in the Americas. First, early Europeans introduced no new diseases, sparing West Africans the demographic collapse suffered by the inhabitants of the Americas, while tropical diseases remained a formidable impediment to European penetration of most of sub-Saharan Africa and a significant cost of doing business there. Only when quinine came into use against malaria in the mid-nineteenth century did West Africa cease to be 'the white man's grave'.[8] Even had Europeans been willing to endure appalling loses of life, there was a second reason why the conquest of tropical Africa would have been extraordinarily difficult. As Hawkins had learned, African societies in these centuries possessed formidable fighting skills and weaponry.[9] These impediments and West Africans' ability and eagerness to engage in Atlantic exchanges made peaceful commerce a sounder policy .

The trade was not without friction, as each side sought to drive the best bargain by both fair means and foul. Once stung by European sharp dealing, West African buyers learned to scrutinize linens for flaws, check basins for holes and knives for rust, and, Europeans complained, count every bead. By the 1660s a German reported, Gold Coast traders could tell at a glance the difference between good quality Dutch or Indian textiles and the cheaper imitations made in England and Germany. Worse yet, he lamented, they had devised ingenious ways to cheat the European buyers by mixing gold with lesser substances and no longer permitted Europeans to seize such adulterated gold and punish would-be cheaters. In addition, European price-fixing efforts had collapsed as competing European companies and growing numbers of private traders sought to win over African trading partners with 'sweet words and presents'.[10] If some Europeans were inclined to denounce Africans as thieving, deceitful, and unprincipled, many Africans held similar views of European traders—and with equally good reasons. In one case, Africans denounced suppliers of inferior copper rings as white

[8] Reliable statistics, available only from the early nineteenth century, show that British troops stationed in the small West African colony of Sierra Leone died at an average rate of 483 per thousand per year in the years 1817–36—giving West Africa the worst mortality in any tropical part of the Empire. Philip D. Curtin, *Death by Migration: Europe's Encounter with the Tropical World in the Nineteenth Century* (Cambridge, 1989), p. 8. For the changes that made conquest feasible at the end of the century see Curtin's *Disease and Empire: The Health of European Troops in the Conquest of Africa* (Cambridge, 1998).

[9] John K. Thornton, *Warfare in Atlantic Africa, 1500–1800* (London, 1999).

[10] Wilhelm Johann Müller, 'Description of the Fetu Country, 1662–1669' in Adam Jones, ed., *German Sources for West African History, 1599–1669* (Wiesbaden, 1983), pp. 248–53.

devils; in another, an African accused of dishonesty, retorted indignantly, 'What! Do you think I am a white man?'[11] Despite such cross-cultural tensions and prejudices, the Atlantic trade thrived.

Thus by the mid-seventeenth century, there is little reason to see West Africans' commercial relations with the Atlantic as weak or coerced. Recent historians have argued that Africans participated in the Atlantic trade willingly and from a position of strength. They suggest that the trading relations between coastal Africans and Europeans need to be viewed as a partnership. When one takes into consideration that Europeans were unable to colonize tropical Africa in this era and were thus compelled to purchase and transport a labour force from Africa to the Americas, David Eltis argues, 'the slave trade was a symptom of African strength, not weakness'.[12]

No one argues that those shipped in chains from Africa can be counted as anything other than victims, though their powerlessness in shaping New World events is no longer assumed. No African or European trader uniformly made a profit, nor did individuals who profited financially use their gains to uniformly beneficial ends in the long or short run. Whether one considers the African rulers and merchants who grew rich from the trade as successful entrepreneurs or as class exploiters depends on one's interpretative perspectives even more than on the details. The horrific and wrenching experience of those who were taken away from their homes and families into slavery are the subject of other chapters in this volume. The task here is to examine the experiences of those Africans who remained at home (and some who went to Europe), as they sought to profit from the Atlantic trade and the cultural contacts that it brought.

Commercial Relations, 1660–1800

As the volume of the trade shot upwards and slaves became the dominant export, commercial relations between West Africans and Europeans showed both strong continuity and adaptive change over time. On the Gold Coast, Europeans of all nations adopted the early Portuguese approach of seeking

[11] 'Andreas Josua Ulsheimer's Voyage of 1603–4', in Jones, ed., *German Sources*, p. 27; John Newton, The *Journal of a Slave Trader (John Newton), 1750–1754* (London, 1962), pp. 106–7.

[12] David Eltis, *The Rise of African Slavery in the Americas* (Cambridge, 2000), pp. 149. For similar analyses see John K. Thornton, *Africa and Africans in the Making of the Atlantic World, 1400–1800*, 2nd edn. (Cambridge, 1998), pp. 43–57; David Northrup, *Africa's Discovery of Europe, 1450–1850* (New York, 2002), pp. 50–72.

local African consent to construct a fortified shore facility (called a 'factory'). By 1700, Portuguese, Dutch, English, Scandinavian, and German trading companies operated some twenty-five major factories and a about as many smaller trading posts along the 250-mile coast. By then English trade in West Africa was on firmer footing than it had been during the century before 1660. In 1663, the Royal African Company (RAC) took over the English factories on the Gold Coast that the underfunded Guinea Company of London had established between 1632 and 1650, along with a successful outpost on James Island in the Gambia River that the RAC's predecessor, the Company of Royal Adventurers, had opened in 1661. Bolstered by monopoly rights over all English trade with Atlantic Africa, the RAC moved to fortify its six major Gold Coast outposts against attacks by other Europeans and established its headquarters in the 'castle' it erected at Cape Coast.

The many wars among the Europeans in the seventeenth century for access to the African trade are in striking contrast to the largely peaceful relations between Europeans and their African hosts. The Gold Coast forts were not European colonies or bases for penetration of Africa, but sites of joint enterprises. The African ruler who had authorized the Portuguese to erect their first outpost in 1472 had perceptively emphasized the importance of good relations when he warned that, should the Europeans attempt anything underhanded, he could bring them to their knees simply by withdrawing his trade and the local labourers on whom the factory depended. In the seventeenth and eighteenth centuries, the small staff of Europeans stationed on the Gold Coast still relied heavily on local Africans for labourers, soldiers, and brokers, as well as wives and lovers. Aside from fort slaves who supplied some of the menial labour, most were persons freely pursuing their own interests in a symbiotic relationship with the foreign residents.

Both sides underwent changes as the volume and value of the Atlantic trade increased six-fold between the 1680s and the 1780s, largely as a result of the rapid expansion of the slave trade. On the European side, chartered national companies lost their monopolies and, saddled with high fixed costs and inefficient practices, eventually slid into bankruptcy. The RAC continued to operate until 1752, but private traders dominated English maritime commence with Africa after the Company lost its monopoly in 1698. In contrast to the growing competitiveness among Europeans, the most notable changes on the African side involved greater centralization of the trade. The powerful new kingdoms of Asante and Dahomey consolidated their control over the trade flowing through the hinterlands of the Gold Coast and the western Slave Coast respectively, while alliances of professional traders consolidated their economic power in the hinterland of the Bight of Biafra and Senegambia.

Yet there was also notable continuity in the overall structure of the trade. European remained confined to the coastal entrepôts. African merchants brought them slaves from local and distant wars, just as they had once brought gold, ivory, and other products. The relatively minor changes in the nature of imports into Africa were far less significant than was the huge increase in the quantity of trade goods that moved through ever expanding inland regions. At the coast, the greater volume of trade greatly increased the importance of maintaining peaceful relations between Africans and Europeans. An RAC agent advised his employers in 1705 that trade at the African coast required 'the same good sense, the same usage, the same cautions, the same harmony... as [trade] in Europe' and stressed the need to treat powerful Africans with kindness and gentleness, to pay them the fees and ground rents that had by then become customary.[13] In 1752 the Board of Trade reaffirmed that 'in Africa we were only tenants of the soil which we held at the good will of the natives'.[14] The Gold Coast was healthier for European residents than the rain forests of Benin, but death rates of 20–30 per cent a year remained a price of doing business for the English in the mid-1680s. As a consequence, high salaries were necessary to tempt competent European men to serve as agents-general, chief merchants, factors, and chaplains. Another problem was that the irregular arrivals of ships from Europe often left the factories short of appropriate trading goods.

A major change was that the Gold Coast declined in relative importance as the trade shifted eastward in the eighteenth century to ports that specialized in the slave trade. The Bight of Benin became known as the Slave Coast because of its prominence in the trade during the first half of the eighteenth century and the Bight of Biafra became dominant in West African coastal trade during the second half of the century. Africans did not allow Europeans to erect substantial shore facilities on these coasts, so the trade was conducted from the ships or in on-shore trading shanties. As a result, Europeans depended even more heavily on their African hosts for security and for the extensive labour forces they needed to load and unload their ships. Some

[13] John Snow quoted in K. G. Davies, *The Royal African Company* (New York, 1970), pp. 367–71.

[14] Commissioners for Trade cited in Hair and Law, 'English in Western Africa', p. 261.

African rulers appointed officials to oversee the commercial relations with Europeans. For example, by the 1720s the post of *Yevogan*, or 'Chief of the White Men' at the important port of Whydah, had evolved into three separate offices, one for the French, one for the English, and one for the Portuguese. In time there would be six such 'Captains of Trade'.

Before a ship could begin to trade in any of these ports, European merchants had to pay elaborate customs fees or 'comey' as well as make expensive gifts to the ruler and to his chief commercial agents. In 1700 Whydah's ruler exacted comey equal in value to ten slaves from each European slaver to open the market and required them to purchase his own slaves at a premium price before he would let them begin general trading with his subjects. Two decades later, when Whydah had become the greatest trading port along the West African coast, visited by forty to fifty ships a year, the comey had been refined to give the king the value of twenty slaves per ship, first refusal on all goods, and the right to sell his own slaves at a premium. The incorporation of Whydah and other ports into the inland kingdom of Dahomey ensured Europeans a rising number of slaves from the expanding kingdom's wars during the second half of the century, but they also had to deal with a more powerful state.[15]

At the eastern end of the Slave Coast, the rulers of the kingdom of Benin continued to exercise a tight control over the trade and its profits in the eighteenth century. The Dutch West India Company's agent in Benin wrote a long letter in 1724 complaining how difficult it was to conduct the trade there, partly because of rising competition from the English, but particularly because of Benin's resoluteness:

> the natives here so carefully regulated the trade at the time the factory was established, that it is now impossible to move them to pay more for the merchandise. For if I tell them that the merchandise now costs more [in Europe], they answer me that it does not concern them, that they concluded the trade on those terms at the time, and that they will now continue to trade in the same manner. They say too that they would rather do no trade than to be forced to abandon their old rights and customs.[16]

These conditions led the Dutch to withdraw from Benin, but French, English, and other European merchants continued to submit to a system

[15] Robin Law, *The Slave Coast of West Africa: The Impact of the Atlantic Slave Trade on an African Society* (Oxford, 1991), pp. 261–344.

[16] Gerrit Ockers to Pieter Valckenier, Director-General of the Dutch West India Company, Ughoton, Nov. 1724, in Ryder, *Benin*, pp. 331–34.

in which Benin officials unilaterally set the value of all imported goods and exports. Although state-management kept the price of slaves from rising as rapidly as elsewhere in West Africa, the cost of 'customs' and gifts to the *oba* and senior palace officials skyrocketed during the eighteenth century.

Benin had a modest share of the slave trade compared to the city-states on the eastern side of the Niger Delta. What these coastal societies lacked in size they made up for in entrepreneurial skills and in good inland connections. The merchant-princes who controlled the trade became rich and powerful. At the end of the seventeenth century, the merchant known as Captain Pepple of the city-state of Bonny was described in a French account as 'a sharp blade, and a mighty talking Black'. For his part, Captain Pepple proclaimed his 'great esteem and regard for the Whites, who had much enriched him by trade', but still drove a hard bargain. To open the trade, Europeans had to give Pepple two muskets, eight hats and nine lengths of cloth as well as other 'dashes'. Several other Bonny notables got the same and the king of Bonny and his principal men exacted loans of goods valued at 300 iron bars (about £40 in contemporary terms). By the late eighteenth century, when the Bight of Biafra was the centre of the West African slave trade and Bonny its premier port, comey at Bonny had risen to £150. At the port of Old Calabar to the east the price of opening the trade might be as much as £250.[17]

Even after all the preliminaries were satisfied, the conduct of the actual trade took careful planning and skill. According to John Atkins, a British naval surgeon who visited the African coast in the 1721–23 period, a successful voyage to West Africa required a refined knowledge of African tastes and practices on each part of the coast and the cordial treatment of African middlemen.[18] The first step was to assemble a cargo that was suited to African needs and tastes at the intended port of call. Cloth and metals were always in demand, but the colours and patterns of the textiles varied as did the preference for copper, brass, or iron. Coastal Africans assigned each trade item a value in terms of their perception of its desirability and Europeans regularly kept trading accounts in the trading currencies used by their African partners. West African valuations made some trade items, such as

[17] From the Journal of James Barbot, in *Barbot on Guinea: The Writings of Jean Barbot on West Africa 1678–1712*, ed. P. E. H. Hair, (London, 1992), vol. II, pp. 688–89; Captain Heatley, in Basil Davidson, ed., *African Civilization Revisited* (Trenton, NJ, 1991), p. 267; Capt. John Adams, *Sketches Taken during Ten Voyages to Africa between the Years 1786 and 1800* (London, 1822), cited in G. I. Jones, *The Trading States of the Oil Rivers* (Oxford, 1963), p. 46.

[18] John Atkins, *A Voyage to Guinea, Brasil, and the West-Indies* (London, 1735), pp. 158–69.

French brandy or gunpowder, more profitable for the Europeans, while other items, such as textiles, might be less profitable. Because Africans insisted on a mixture of goods, however, it was hard for Europeans to take advantage of such disparities. Some African currencies had been in use before the Atlantic contacts began, such as the gold ounces of the Gold Coast and the cowry shells in use on the Slave Coast, while other currencies of account, such as the currencies based on iron bars in Bonny and the Gambia, evolved around trade items supplied in quantity from overseas.

Once forced to peddle domestic imitations of Dutch textiles, the British attracted African buyers with a larger variety of desirable textiles from their East Indian partners than were available to other European merchants. In addition, Britain's highly productive domestic smelters and armourers were able to supply Africans with great quantities of low cost iron, guns, and gunpowder, which became a crucial part of the trade in the eighteenth century. African imports of copper and brass from England also rose from an average of 325 tons a year in the period 1701–10 to 2,860 tons a year in 1791–1800. Overall, English exports to Africa increased 780 per cent during the eighteenth century. Yet it would be misleading to see this tremendous increase in the volume of the trade as an expansion of European dominance in Africa. As important as Europeans' capital, colonies, and control of ocean shipping were in creating the Atlantic economy, such factors did not give them an upper hand in the tough bargaining that took place along the West African coast. Instead, as economic historians have demonstrated, the terms of trade shifted sharply in the African traders' favour during the eighteenth century, as the prices of slaves and other African exports rose more rapidly than the prices of the goods received in return. By one calculation, this shift in the terms of trade meant that a slave cost the English twice as much at the end of the century as at its beginning.[19]

Just as British traders' success in garnering the lion's share of the eighteenth-century slave trade depended on satisfying African commercial demands, the most successful African ports were those best able to sell European traders a large volume of slaves under predictable trading conditions. Dahomey's military expansion was a part of the port of Whydah's success, but other ports along the Bights of Benin and Biafra that were not

[19] Eugenia W. Herbert, *Red Gold of Africa: Copper in Precolonial History and Culture* (Madison, Wisc., 1984), pp. 125–53, 179–82; H. A. Gemery, Jan Hogendorn and Marion Johnson, 'Evidence on English/African Terms of Trade in the Eighteenth Century', *Explorations in Economic History*, XXVII (1990), pp. 157–77.

part of any large state also found ways to deal effectively with the merchants of powerful European states. Despite its reputation for tough bargaining and decentralized political organization, the city-state of Bonny in the eastern Niger Delta became one of the most important trading ports in West Africa because of its close ties to inland trading networks that ensured its steady supply of slaves. Further east, the cluster of Efik lineage groups the Europeans called Old Calabar was also successful in forging ties with a variety of inland trading groups and in transforming a traditional graded secret society known as Ekpe into an organization that was able to settle disputes between trading partners thus minimizing interruptions in the flow of slaves and trade goods. In time, British traders found joining Ekpe was an aid in collecting debts.[20]

Such debts were a growing feature of the trade. In contrast to Benin's offer of credit to the first English traders, eighteenth-century African traders often insisted on receiving goods on credit and, as European accounts make clear, frequently defaulted on such loans. To curtail their losses at Old Calabar and other West African ports, European traders increasingly made use of the West African custom of pawning. African merchants receiving goods on credit handed over human pawns to European slavers in pledge of repayment. The pawns might be domestic slaves, other members of their households, or even their own children. If the debt was not repaid before the ship sailed, the pawn became a part of the slave cargo. Last minute efforts to avert such eventualities were not always successful.[21]

In this case time worked against the African pawns and pawners, but the time was running out for the European slavers. The sooner a vessel could obtain a cargo, the lower the losses of life among both slaves and crew. Thus, while Europeans bargained hard over prices and inspected slaves carefully for any disease or defect that might reduce their value, as their time on the coast lengthened, they were constrained to make compromises that would hasten their departure. Whereas it was once assumed that the age and sex distribution of slave cargoes was entirely determined by European preferences, modern research on the notable variations among African ports strongly suggests a more complex explanation. As David Eltis puts it: 'Africans, as

[20] David Northrup, *Trade Without Rulers: Pre-Colonial Economic Development in South-Eastern Nigeria* (Oxford, 1978), pp. 85–145; A. J. H. Latham, *Old Calabar, 1600–1891: The Impact of the International Economy upon a Traditional Society* (Oxford, 1973), pp. 35–41, 80.

[21] Paul E. Lovejoy and David Richardson, 'The Business of Slaving in Africa: Pawnship in Western Africa, c. 1600–1810', *Journal of African History*, XLII (2001), pp. 67–89.

much as Europeans, shaped who entered the trade, the geographical patterns of the traffic, the conditions under which slaves travelled to the New World, and, indeed, what slaves did when they arrived in the New World.'[22]

Effects in Inland Africa

The Atlantic trade's operations along coastal West Africa are reasonably well documented, but the absence of observations of its impact makes its effects in inland Africa much harder to assess. Still one can safely assume that the impact of Atlantic imports was much more diluted there than at the coast. Most of luxury goods the coastal big men received as comey and presents went no further than their own households, and the considerable mark-up on the luxury goods that West African traders carried inland would have limited their market to a few notables. However, the composition of the trade goods received from the Atlantic suggests that there was a large inland market for the ordinary textiles, metals, and manufactures. Despite the rapid growth of these imports during the eighteenth century, recent analysis casts considerable doubt on the once common assertions that they damaged local manufactures. Atlantic imports supplemented rather than displaced locally made products in the inland regions. The quantity of the imports was not large on a per capita basis before 1800 and transportation and distribution costs would have reduced their competitiveness as the moved away from the coast. Only as industrialization caused a much sharper drop in prices during the nineteenth century did the per capita consumption of such imports and their geographical reach begin to affect local production. Improved transportation systems under colonial rule in the twentieth century lowered prices and increased sales still more.[23]

For those millions who were victims of the slave trade from Africa the consequences of the Atlantic contacts were obviously dire as several later chapters in this volume detail. The impact of their loss within Africa, however, is harder to calculate. It has long been understood that the majority of slaves were captured in wars, but where it was once common to blame most wars in West Africa on the slave trade, modern historians recognize that

[22] Eltis, *Rise of African Slavery*, pp. 146–47.

[23] David Eltis, 'Precolonial Western Africa and the Atlantic Economy', in Barbara Solow, ed., *Slavery and the Rise of the Atlantic System*, (Cambridge, 1991), pp. 97–119; Northrup, *Africa's Discovery*, pp. 77–106.

such an assumption greatly exaggerates the influence of Atlantic trade on West African statecraft. Warfare and enslavement had accompanied the rise and fall of states well before the Atlantic slave trade arose and continued to be prominent after the overseas slave trade declined. While it is reasonable to assume that the Atlantic slave trade had some effect on inland conflicts, objective measurement is impossible. Nor is subjective assessment any clearer. African rulers were as likely as monarchs in Europe to claim their wars were just and not fought for base motives. The Asante ruler Osei Bonsu, for example, insisted to a British visitor in 1820 that he and his predecessors went to war for the highest reasons of honour and statecraft and did not 'make war to catch slaves in the bush, like a thief'.[24] Still, his statement implies that less honourable men would have succumbed to the temptations brought by the Atlantic economy.

Speculation on the Atlantic slave trade's consequences has long assumed that larger states were able to defend their interests much better than the smaller chiefdoms and village groups that contained most of West African's population during these centuries. However, recent research has questioned whether such 'stateless' societies were really unduly vulnerable. Although examples of extreme vulnerability can be found, *as a group* the inhabitants of small and decentralized polities do not appear to have been more victimized than those who inhabited larger states. Small communities would have been as capable of defending themselves against attacks by their African neighbours as they were against Hawkins's raids. Moreover, some of their members were quite successful in profiting financially from the trade. Martin Klein concludes his recent survey of this issue with the telling observation: 'The logic of the state was not as irresistible as the logic of the market.'[25] From that perspective, the customary emphasis on the effects of the slaves exported from Africa misses the possibly more important effect of the goods imported. These imports required greater carriage, achieved wider distribution, and involved far more numerous transactions as they moved inland from the coast than did the export of slaves. Combined with the expanding internal trade in African produce and manufactures, the imports were part of a general expansion of markets and trade routes. Thus the trade in slaves deserves to be seen as a piece, rather than the centrepiece, of the economic changes underway in West Africa.

[24] Joseph Dupuis, *Journal of a Residence in Asantee* (London, 1824), pp. 162–64.

[25] Martin A. Klein, 'The Slave Trade and Decentralized Societies,' *Journal of African History*, XLII (2001), pp. 49–65.

Although the political and social impact of the slave trade within Africa are now seen in more complex terms than was once the case, modern research on the volume of the Atlantic slave trade has facilitated the calculation of its probable effects on Africa's population. A sophisticated demographic model developed by Patrick Manning finds that while losses varied considerably over time and place, the regions of the tropical Atlantic Africa most affected would have seen their populations stagnate as the slave trade rose in the first half of the eighteenth century and then would have experienced a steady decline in population during the peak centuries of the slave trade. By 1850 the population of the western coastal region of Africa would have been between a sixth to a quarter lower than it had been in 1700—a severe population loss by any measure, but it would have recovered quickly thereafter.[26] Manning's work has found general acceptance among historians, but because such modelling is based on assumptions about population size and normal birth and death rates rather than hard evidence, its conclusions are only a reasonable hypothesis.

Personal and Cultural connections

Commercial interests created the Atlantic exchanges in West Africa, but some Africans and Europeans found more in these exchanges than a pursuit of profit. Some individuals had cross-cultural experiences that were richer than the conduct of the trade itself necessitated. A few Europeans became interested enough to write books about Africa. Some Africans also wrote about their experiences, but it is notable that both their literacy and the fact that they wrote in European languages were products of cultural changes occasioned by Atlantic contacts. Other cross-cultural contacts were more intimate. Some Europeans whose commercial duties kept them in Africa for years on end took African lovers and raised Eurafrican families, just as some Africans who lived in Europe fathered families by European wives.

At the most basic level, Africans and Europeans needed to communicate effectively if they were to succeed commercially. As was related earlier, John Lok had followed the early Portuguese practice of taking a few Africans back to Europe and training them as translators, but compulsion soon became unnecessary. Recognizing the advantages to be gained, West Africans soon

[26] Patrick Manning, *Slavery and African Life* (Cambridge, 1990), pp. 60–85.

seized the initiative in learning Europeans' languages and national traits. The precedent set by the *oba* of Benin in greeting the first English visitors in a European language was followed everywhere. As the trade grew, coastal African rulers and merchants learned to converse with European visitors in their own languages, whereas it was a rare European who learned more than a few words of any African language.

The key African employee in Gold Coast forts was known as the 'linguist', even though his diplomatic skills were as important as his skills in European and African languages. Linguists conducted delicate negotiation with African rulers and merchants on behalf of the Europeans and were accordingly well compensated. For example, Quacounoe Abracon (as the English spelled his name) functioned as the RAC's chief broker at their Little Komenda 'factory' from 1681 to about 1683 and represented the RAC in its dealings with the settlement's political leaders. In addition to profits from his personal trading, he received an annual stipend of 3 ounces in gold and commissions on sales for the RAC that may have garnered him 40 ounces a year—enough to make him a wealthy man locally.[27]

As the British became dominant in the Atlantic trade in the eighteenth century, a new trading pidgin using English words developed, overlaying and displacing an older pidgin based on Portuguese vocabulary. Along with standard European languages, pidgin English was widely used in communication between Africans and Europeans and in some parts of West Africa it became a lingua franca among Africans as well. Some of the most successful Africans acquired a good command of standard European languages and customs through formal education in Africa or in Europe. The first English-medium school in sub-Saharan Africa was opened by the RAC in 1694 to educate the African and Eurafrican children living around its headquarters at Cape Coast Castle. Britain's first missionary to West Africa established a new school at Cape Coast Castle in 1752 at the request of the official linguist, Cudjo. Among its first pupils was Cudjo's relative Philip Quaque, who continued his studies in England, where he was eventually ordained an Anglican priest. Upon his return to Cape Coast in 1765, Quaque became the official chaplain to the English traders stationed there and also served as

[27] Per O. Hernæs, 'European Fort Communities on the Gold Coast in the Era of the Slave Trade', in J. Everaert and J. Parmentier, eds., *International Conference of Shipping, Factories and Colonization* (Brussels, 1996), pp. 167–80; Ray A. Kea, *Settlements, Trade, and Politics in the Seventeenth-Century Gold Coast* (Baltimore, 1982), pp. 223–26, 229–36.

catechist and schoolmaster to the African population. John Currantee, the chief caboceer (headman) at the English fort of Anomabu, sent his son William Ansah to Britain to study in the late 1740s. During the decade Ansah spent there, the English lavishly entertained and lionized him. King George II sent him back in 1750 in the British warship, *HMS Surprise*, richly clothed as an English gentleman. William Ansah readapted to coastal life and worked as a clerk and linguist at the Anomabu fort.[28] Ansah was not the first West African to be received at court. In the 1730s a Gambian Muslim named Ayuba Suleiman had been similarly treated by English notables, received by King George, and despatched back to his home with rich presents in an RAC ship.[29] Along the Bight of Biafra, some Old Calabar traders also sent their sons to be educated in England and when they returned some of these scholars tutored children of élite families in spoken and written English. A leading African merchant of Old Calabar in the 1780s even kept a diary in a rough form of English.[30]

Some late eighteenth-century rulers in Sierra Leone also pursued trading advantages through formal education. One sent a son to study with the English Christians and another inland to study with African Muslims. In the 1790s a prominent Sierra Leone chief named Naimbana went one better by educating one son locally as a Muslim, sending a second abroad to France, and a third, John Frederic, to London. There John Frederic mastered the intricacies of reading English in eighteen months and progressed rapidly in a range of studies. Although he became a sincere Christian, John Frederic was quick to take offence at anyone impugning his homeland. On one occasion, he became enraged when a Member of Parliament, in defending slavery, made disparaging remarks about Africans. John Frederic declared that while he could forgive someone who robbed him, shot at him, or even sold him into slavery, but not someone who made racist and disparaging remarks about Africans, for 'if anyone takes away the character of black people, that man injures black people all over the world'.

[28] Davies, *Royal African Company*, p. 280; Margaret Priestley, *West African Trade and Coast Society: A Family Study* (London, 1969), pp. 16, 19–23; F. L. Bartels, 'Philip Quaque, 1741–1816', *Transactions of the Gold Coast and Togoland Historical Society*, I, 5 (1955), pp. 153–77.

[29] Philip D. Curtin, 'Ayuba Suleiman Diallo of Bondu', in Philip D. Curtin, ed., *Africa Remembered: Narratives by West Africans from the Era of the Slave Trade*, (Madison, 1967), pp. 17–59.

[30] Daryll Forde, ed., *Efik Traders of Old Calabar* (Oxford, 1956), pp. 79–115. A new edition of the diary is in preparation

Nothing justified enslaving and abusing people because of the colour of their skin.[31]

By the late eighteenth century, other West Africans in Britain were taking the defence of their homeland into a spirited campaign against the slave trade. In 1787 Ottobah Cugoano, son of a Gold Coast chief, published *Thoughts and Sentiments on the Evils of Slavery*, in which he called for a naval patrol to suppress the slave trade from Africa and for the emancipation of all slaves in the Americas. The book denounced the inhuman and unchristian enslavement of Africans as 'an injury and robbery contrary to all law, civilization, reason, justice, equity, and charity'. His prediction that slaves might well rise up and overthrow the institution was remarkably prescient of the events that would unfold in Saint Domingue (Haiti) in the next decade. Cugoano's friend and fellow Afro-Briton Gustavus Vassa added to the campaign in 1789 with the publication of his remarkable and highly literate autobiography *The Interesting Narrative of Olaudah Equiano*. In this more subtle attack on the slave trade, Vassa (as he almost always identified himself outside the autobiography) described his early life in the hinterland of the Niger Delta, his kidnapping, and transportation in the Middle Passage. Although this early part of the book may have been fictionalized, the verifiable details of his subsequent life in slavery, his emancipation and resettlement in Britain, and his mastery of English and embrace of Christianity, and his other personal achievements were a moving indictment of the false image of Africans as inferior and destined for slavery. Both works found a wide and sympathetic audience, Vassa's going through eight more editions in Britain before his death in 1797.

Although a few eighteenth-century West Africans used their education and talents to pursue clerical and literary careers in the Anglophone world, most Africans were motivated by the commercial advantages they hoped to gain in bridging cultural barriers. Brandy, Dutch gin, and other distilled spirits introduced from Europe lubricated the trade negotiations and continued commercial success required resolving the details amicably. Three different English agents were discharged by the RAC for failing to stay on good terms with John Kabes, a prosperous African middleman known for his success in playing off the English and Dutch on the Gold Coast from 1688 to

[31] Zachary Macaulay, *The African Prince* [1796] in Paul Edwards and James Walvin, eds., *Black Personalities in the Era of the Slave Trade* (Baton Rouge, La., 1983), pp. 204–10; Christopher Fyfe, *A History of Sierra Leone* (London, 1962), pp. 11, 30, 54; Gretchen Holbrook Gerzina, *Black London: Life Before Emancipation* (New Brunswick, NJ, 1995), pp. 174–78.

1722.[32] In some cases European and African traders became genuine friends. For example, a leading trader in eighteenth-century Bonny known as John Africa was highly regarded by English traders for his honesty and generosity. On one occasion, he bestowed a rich gift of ivory tusks on one of his English partners 'in so delicate a manner, as would have done honour to an European of refined sentiment'.[33] The need to stay on good terms was mutual.

Some commercial relations in West Africa were also sexual. In contrast to the coerced favours and rapes that took place on some slaving ships, sexual contacts on African territory had to be consensual or there would be big trouble with local authorities. Some encounters were casual, but many European men who took up residence in Africa developed long-term relationships with African women. Under European law some of these 'country marriages' were bigamous, for the men might have another wife in Europe, but polygyny was permitted under African law. It is impossible to say if Englishmen entered into these relationships with the same frequency as the French and Portuguese, but prominent examples are not hard to find. RAC officials and ship captains in Sierra Leone built houses next to the official buildings for their country wives, whom they clothed in silk gowns. Circumstances were similar on the Gold Coast, where the Director-General of Cape Coast Castle in the early eighteenth century had four children by a local wife. He was a kind father and so devoted to his wife that at her urging he openly wore protective charms and amulets to safeguard his health. She, however, steadfastly refused to leave her homeland (lest she be seen as a slave) but did yield to his entreaties to allow their children to be educated in England. The head of the English factory at Tantumkweri in about 1770, John Cockburn, had several children by his African wife Ambah.[34]

Like the business friendships, 'country marriages' often had commercial benefits for both partners. Prominent African men sometimes promoted ties between female family members and resident European traders as a way of

[32] Kea, *Settlements*, pp. 223–26, 229–36; David Henige, 'John Kabes of Komenda: An Early African Entrepreneur and State Builder', *Journal of African History*, XVIII (1977), pp. 1–19.

[33] John Adams, *Remarks on the Country Extending from Cape Palmas to the River Congo* [London, 1823], in Thomas Hodgkin, ed., *Nigerian Perspectives: An Historical Anthology* (London, 1975), p. 234.

[34] Von der Groeben in Adam Jones, ed., *Brandenburg Sources for West African History, 1680–1700* (Wiesbaden, 1985), p. 27; Atkins, *Voyage*, pp. 94–95; George Metcalf, 'A Microcosm of Why Africans Sold Slaves: Akan Consumption Patterns in the 1770s', *Journal of African History*, XXVIII (1987); p. 392.

gaining better access to Atlantic goods. Similarly, European men sought not just a sexual partner but someone who could interpret local African speech and customs and had connections to African trading families and networks. There is only limited information about how the African women felt about such relationships, but they and their relatives seemed to have been pleased with the presents and other benefits they received. There were often long-term financial advantages for the woman as well, since she might inherit considerable sums in the likely event that tropical diseases made her a widow. Ambah Cockburn lived simply after her husband's death, but some other widows and daughters inherited sufficient wealth to become important in their own right. For example, Betsy Heard, the daughter of an African woman and an English merchant, who had sent her to England for her education, used her considerable talent and inherited wealth to become a major trader in Upper Guinea in the 1790s and 1800s. In the same region, another upwardly mobile woman, Elizabeth Frazer, was the daughter of an African-American settler and one of his African wives. After her marriage, in 1826, to William Skelton, Jr., the son of an African mother and an English father, she became wealthy in slave trading in the Rio Nuñez. Yet another prominent *entrepreneuse* was Mary Faber, the daughter of African-American settlers and wife of an Anglo-American ship captain.[35]

Children born to these unions tended to be comfortable in the cultures of both parents and often played important roles as culture brokers. Some mixed marriages founded important dynasties. The prominent Corker-Caulker family of Sierra Leone traces its origins to the union of an RAC official and Seniora Doll, Duchess of Sherbro. The locally influencial Brews of the Gold Coast are descended from Richard Brew, an Irish trader and official in the mid-eighteenth century, and Effua Ansah, the daughter of the African caboceer John Currantee and sister of William Ansah. Their two daughters were baptized in 1767 by the Revd Philip Quaque and a son later married a member of Quaque's family.[36]

These country marriages in Africa have an interesting parallel in the unions African men in Europe formed with European women. Most African students and visitors may have remained celibate or had casual affairs, but those who stayed on regularly chose brides from among local women.

[35] Bruce Mouser, 'Women Slavers of Guinea-Conakry', in Claire C. Robertson and Martin A. Klein, eds., *Women and Slavery in Africa* (Madison, W.sc., 1983), pp. 321–33.

[36] Fyfe, *History of Sierra Leone*, p. 10; Priestley, *West African Trade*, pp. 106–09, 121–26.

Perhaps the most famous was Gustavus Vassa, who after thirty-five years of residence in Britain married Susanna Cullen in 1792. Four years earlier the successful author and abolitionist had published his views on mixed marriages:

> If the mind of a black man conceives the passion of love for a fair female, [it should not be that] he is to pine, languish, and even die, sooner than an intermarriage be allowed, merely because ... [of] foolish prejudice ... God looks with equal goodwill on all his creatures, whether black or white—let neither, therefore, arrogantly condemn the other.[37]

In a thoughtful essay, historian Seymour Drescher argues that British people in this era exhibited 'tolerance of many black people ... as socially acceptable marriage partners' despite some vocal opposition.[38] Intermarriage was at least equally acceptable in West Africa, where it would be difficult to find any voice raised against the practice. Such toleration, of course, did not extend to British colonies in the Americas.

Conclusion

While promoting European colonies in the Americas, Atlantic contacts created cultural and economic opportunities for some coastal Africans. Although those in a position to benefit were fewer in number than those shipped into slavery from these shores and made up only a very small percentage of West Africa's population, their lives illuminate two important themes that deserve to be understood apart from the miseries of the slave trade and slavery detailed in the chapters that follow.

In the first place, their lives show that coastal West Africans were eager to participate in the Atlantic economy and succeeded in doing so effectively before, during, and after the transatlantic slave trade. The early part of the Atlantic connection was not dominated by the slave trade and whatever destruction that trade brought during its peak centuries; historians largely agree that its long-term effects in Africa were limited. The consumer goods Africans received did not produce an economic transformation in Africa comparable to those taking place in the Atlantic world as a whole. Neither

[37] *Public Advertiser*, 28 Jan. 1788, in Olaudah Equiano, *The Interesting Narrative and Other Writings*, ed. Vincent Carretta (New York, 1995), p. 329.

[38] Seymour Drescher, *From Slavery to Freedom: Comparative Studies in the Rise and Fall of Atlantic Slavery* (New York, 1999). pp. 283–84.

were the imports of sufficient quantity to undermine indigenous industries. Manning's model also suggests that the population loss occasioned by the export of so many millions of people would have been reversed a few decades after the Atlantic slave trade's peak. However, West African desire for imported goods from Europe, Asia, and the Americas guaranteed that African participation in the Atlantic trade did not cease with the exports of slaves. As the British-led campaign reduced the export of slaves, West Africans quickly developed new exports. Indeed, the 'legitimate trade' of the nineteenth century far surpassed the commerce of all previous centuries in its importance.

The second theme of these early encounters, Africans' cultural discovery of Europe, also continued and expanded after 1800. Though the impact of European culture had been confined to coastal communities in Africa and a few Africans in Europe, later chapters in this volume show that the influence of European languages, educational systems, religions, and racial ideas grew stronger and more widespread in Africa and in the African diaspora during the centuries that followed 1800. As in the early centuries, African people's individual decisions shaped these enduring legacies.

Select Bibliography

GEORGE E. BROOKS, *Landlords and Strangers: Ecology, Society, and Trade in Western Africa, 1000–1630* (Boulder, Colo., 1993).

PHILIP D. CURTIN, ed., *African Remembered: Narratives by West Africans from the Era of the Slave Trade* (Madison, 1968)

K. G. DAVIES, *The Royal African Company* (London, 1957).

DAVID ELTIS, *The Rise of African Slavery in the Americas* (Cambridge, 2000).

PETER FRYER, *Staying Power: Black People in Britain since 1504* (London, 1984).

GRETCHEN HOLBROOK GERZINA, *Black London: Life before Emancipation* (New Brunswick, NJ, 1995).

P. E. H. HAIR and ROBIN LAW, 'The English in Western Africa to 1700', in *The Oxford History of the British Empire*, Vol. I, *The Origins of Empire*, ed. Nicholas Canny (Oxford, 1998), pp. 241–63.

RAY A. KEA, *Settlements, Trade, and Politics in the Seventeenth-Century Gold Coast* (Baltimore, 1982).

ROBIN LAW, *The Slave Coast of West Africa: The Impact of the Atlantic Slave Trade on an African Society* (Oxford, 1991).

PAUL E. LOVEJOY, *Transformations in Slavery: A History of Slavery in Africa*, 2nd edn. (Cambridge, 2000).

DAVID NORTHRUP, *Africa's Discovery of Europe, 1450–1850* (New York, 2002).
—— *Trade Without Rulers: Pre-Colonial Economic Development in South-Eastern Nigeria* (Oxford, 1978).
MARGARET PRIESTLEY, *West African Trade and Coast Society: A Family Study* (London, 1969).
EDWARD REYNOLDS, 'Human Commerce', in *Captive Passage: The Transatlantic Slave trade and the Making of the Americas* [exhibition catalogue] (Washington, 2002), pp. 13–33.
ALAN RYDER, *Benin and the Europeans, 1485–1897* (London, 1969).
JOHN K. THORNTON, *African and Africans in the Making of the Atlantic World, 1400–1800* (Cambridge, 1998).
—— 'Africa: the Source', in *Captive Passage: The Transatlantic Slave trade and the Making of the Americas* (Washington, 2002), pp. 35–75.

3

Through a Looking Glass: Olaudah Equiano and African Experiences of the British Atlantic Slave Trade

DAVID RICHARDSON

Over forty years after his enslavement, Olaudah Equiano or Gustavus Vassa, 'The African', published in 1789 his *Interesting Narrative* of his life.[1] In it, Equiano recounted his kidnapping in Africa, his journey to the coast and then to America, his subsequent employment as a sailor, his manumission in the West Indies, and his life and conversion to Methodism in England. Conceived as an anti-slavery work, his narrative was a major publishing success, going through several editions before his death in 1797. A 'memorandum-book' of the horrors of the slave trade and its impact on Africa and Africans, the *Narrative* is also a chronicle of African potential and redemption at a time when British participation in the slave trade was under challenge.[2] As a personal history, Equiano's autobiography may not be wholly reliable and its representation of African experience of enslavement and freedom is not easy to gauge. Britons, after all, shipped over three million slaves from Africa during the three and a half centuries of the Atlantic slave trade, and the vast majority of those who survived the Atlantic crossing died as illiterate slaves after a miserable life of unremitting labour on American plantations. Equiano's life *in toto*, therefore, can hardly be seen as representative, a problem that besets all surviving personal narratives of

[1] *The Interesting Narrative of the Life of Olaudah Equiano or Gustavus Vassa, The African, Written by Himself* (London, 1789), reprinted in *Olaudah Equiano: The Interesting Narrative and Other Writings*, ed. Vincent Carretta (London, 1995). The version included in Carretta's volume is the ninth edition, published in 1794.

[2] In *Through the Looking-Glass*, Alice describes how the King used a 'memorandum-book' to record the details of 'the horror' of a moment that he wished 'never, *never*' to forget (Lewis Carroll, *Alice's Adventures in Wonderland and Through the Looking-Glass*, ed. Hugh Haughton (London, 1998, Centenary Edition), p. 130).

enslaved Africans.[3] To use personal narratives of Africans or African-Americans to 'individualize' the slave trade may thus be of doubtful value.[4] Relating such narratives to larger bodies of data on the Atlantic slave trade, however, can yield insights into the collective experiences of Africans of transatlantic slavery within the British Empire.

This chapter focuses on the movement of Africans to America on British slave ships. The exact number of British ships that participated in the slave trade will probably never be known, but in the 245 years separating the first known English slaving voyage to Africa in 1562 and the abolition of the British slave trade in 1807 merchants in Britain despatched about 10,000 voyages to Africa for slaves, with merchants in other parts of the British Empire perhaps fitting out a further 1,150 voyages.[5] Altogether, the ships involved in these British and British Empire voyages were responsible for carrying possibly 3.4 million or more enslaved Africans to the Americas, or one in three or four of all enslaved Africans entering the Atlantic slave trade during its history.[6] Only the Portuguese, who entered the slave trade before the British and remained in it for almost half a century after Britain abolished its slave trade, carried more enslaved Africans to America than the British.[7]

[3] For one recently published example, see Robin Law and Paul E. Lovejoy, eds., *The Biography of Mahommah Gardo Baquaqua: His Passage from Slavery to Freedom in Africa and America* (Princeton, NJ, 2001).

[4] On 'individualizing' the Atlantic slave trade, see Robin Law, 'Individualising the Atlantic Slave Trade: The Biography of Mamommah Gardo Baquaqua of Djougou (1854)', *Transactions of the Royal Historical Society*, Sixth Series, 12 (2002), pp. 113–40. Similar problems also arise with interpreting the significance of individual slave voyages, such as that of the French ship *Diligent* in 1731–32; see Robert Harms, *The Diligent: A Voyage through the Worlds of the Atlantic Slave Trade* (New York, 2002).

[5] All figures are from David Eltis, Stephen D. Behrendt, David Richardson, and Herbert S. Klein, eds., *The Trans-Atlantic Slave Trade: A Database on CD-Rom* (Cambridge, 1999). The figures on colonial ships include some British-owned ships that returned direct to Africa from America after completing a voyage from Britain to Africa and America, but most were ships owned in the colonies. Hereafter British Empire ships refers to British and British colonial ships.

[6] The figures given here include ships despatched from colonial ports and are thus higher than those given in the most recent estimates of the volume of the Atlantic slave trade and Britain's share of it; see David Eltis, 'The Volume and Structure of the Transatlantic Slave Trade: a Reassessment', *William and Mary Quarterly* (hereafter *WMQ*), Third Series, LVIII (2001), pp. 17–46. On-going research may result in some further revision of all these estimates, but the broad magnitudes suggested here are unlikely to change significantly.

[7] The most recent estimate suggests the Portuguese shipped 5.07 million slaves between 1519 and 1867, the peak of such shipments occurring after British abolition in 1807 (Eltis, 'Volume', p. 43).

The level of British slaving activity varied substantially through time. Although data on British slaving before the Stuart Restoration in 1660 are very patchy, British ships probably carried no more than 25,000 enslaved Africans to America in the century after John Hawkins initiated the British slave trade in 1562.[8] While not insignificant, the scale of British slave trading at this time remained modest relative to that of the Portuguese and Dutch, who dominated slave shipments to Brazil, the largest American market for slaves before 1650.[9] After the Stuart Restoration, however, British involvement in slaving expanded rapidly in response to West Indian demand for labour to cultivate sugar in Barbados and other British West Indian islands. In the 1660s the number of slaves taken from Africa in British ships averaged perhaps 6,700 a year, more than matching in this single decade the total number shipped by the British in the preceding century. Moreover, continuing expansion of West Indian sugar cultivation and the extension of slave labour to other parts of British America ensured that the scale of British slaving continued to grow during the succeeding century, with annual numbers of enslaved Africans carried away in British ships rising six-fold to reach 42,000 a year in the 1760s.[10] By this time, the British were the preeminent slave traders of the Western hemisphere, comfortably eclipsing their nearest competitors, the Portuguese and French, and accounting for probably more than one in two of all enslaved Africans carried to America. Thereafter, the scale of British slave trading levelled out or, especially in

[8] Based on Larry Gragg, ' "To Procure Negroes": The English Slave Trade to Barbados, 1627–60', *Slavery and Abolition* (hereafter *S & A*), XVI (1995), pp. 68–69. Relying on demographic data for Barbados, Joseph Inikori (*Africans and the Industrial Revolution in England: A Study in International Trade and Economic Development* (Cambridge, 2002), pp. 218–19) argues that 'the early British slave trade up to the beginning of 1662 may not have transported less than 100,000 slaves from Africa'. This figure is difficult to reconcile with evidence from shipping records, normally considered the most reliable source for computing slave shipments. Eltis, 'Volume', p. 43, suggests the British shipped 23,000 slaves from Africa in 1601–50.

[9] For data on Brazilian imports of slaves in the first half of the seventeenth century see C. R. Boxer, *Salvador da Sa and the Struggle for Brazil and Angola* (London, 1952), p. 225; and Boxer, *The Dutch in Brazil 1624–1654* (Oxford, 1957), p. 138. For Dutch slave shipments in the same period, see Ernst van den Boogaart and Pieter C. Emmer, 'The Dutch Participation in the Atlantic Slave Trade, 1596–1650', in Henry A. Gemery and Jan S. Hogendorn, eds., *The Uncommon Market: Essays in the Economic History of the Atlantic Slave Trade* (New York, 1979), pp. 353–77.

[10] For decennial estimates of the scale of the British Empire slave trade between 1662 and 1807, see David Richardson, 'The British Empire Slave Trade 1660–1807', in P. J. Marshall, ed., *The Oxford History of the British Empire* (hereafter *OHBE*), Vol. II, *The Eighteenth Century* (Oxford, 1998), p. 442. The total implied by these figures differs slightly from that presented in Eltis, 'Volume'.

war years, even declined, but it nevertheless remained at historically high levels up to British abolition in 1807. Olaudah Equiano's life, which began in 1745, thus straddled the years when the British were unsurpassed as slave traders, giving his narrative added value as an account of African experience of the British slave trade at its height.

The basic facts of Equiano's personal story of slavery and freedom are well known. An Igbo, Equiano was born in 'a charming fruitful vale named Essaka', an as yet unidentified place in the interior of modern south-east Nigeria some 'very considerable' distance 'from the sea coast'. Kidnapped at the age of ten, he was resold on several occasions in Africa before reaching the coast six or seven months after being seized. Sold to English traders, he was shipped first to Barbados, where he was offered for sale with the rest of the ship's loading of slaves. Not being 'saleable among the rest, from very much fretting', he was soon reshipped to and sold in Virginia, where he was employed for a short while on a plantation before being resold to an English shipmaster and carried to England. After service for his new master on naval and other ships during the Seven Years War, he was then sold to the master of a West Indian-bound ship and then resold in Montserrat, whence he served as a sailor on ships trading between the islands and mainland North America before purchasing his freedom in July 1766 at the age of twenty-one. Thereafter he travelled widely, converted to Methodism, and by the 1780s was settled in England where he published the first edition of his narrative in 1789. Married three years later, his wife predeceased him, but two daughters survived him when he died in March 1797.

Drawn from his *Narrative*, this précis of Equiano's life fails to capture the pleasure with which he remembered his early life in Africa and the trauma and sorrow he experienced during enslavement. Indeed, he suggests that the horrors of the latter 'served only to rivet and record' in his mind the former.[11] The *Narrative* relates the brutality with which his kidnappers treated him, hiding him in sacks, force-feeding him, stopping his mouth to prevent cries for help, and—the greatest sorrow of all—separating him from the sister who was simultaneously kidnapped with him. In describing his arrival at the coast, he writes of his 'astonishment, which was soon converted into terror' on seeing and boarding a slave ship. Entering the ship, he was 'immediately handled, and tossed up, to see if I were sound', a reception that convinced him that he was in 'a world of bad spirits' and was about to be killed and

[11] Equiano, *Narrative*, p. 46.

eaten, especially when he saw a 'large furnace of copper boiling' and the dejected faces of his fellow captives. He continues by recounting being flogged while held and stretched over the windlass for not eating. Recalling that 'I had never experienced any thing of this kind before', he contemplated trying to jump overboard to drown, even though 'not being used to the water, I naturally feared that element the first time I saw it'. He was prevented from doing so by the netting encasing the ship and by the severity of the punishment inflicted on those who tried unsuccessfully to scale it. When describing conditions in the Atlantic crossing, Equiano notes his sorrow at the 'absolutely pestilential' situation below deck, the crowding of people being almost suffocating and the resulting 'loathsome smells' causing sickness among the slaves, 'of which many died, thus falling victim to the improvident avarice, as I may call it, of their purchasers'. Although, as a child, Equiano was unchained, he claims that the 'galling of the chains' and 'the filth of the necessary tubs', combined with the 'shrieks of the women, and the groans of the dying', rendered the whole 'a scene of horror almost inconceivable' and a breeding ground for suicide. Thus, he notes, 'two of my wearied countrymen, who were chained together' successfully escaped and drowned, 'preferring death to such a life of misery', while a third, who was sick, attempted unsuccessfully to follow suit and was flogged 'unmercifully' for doing so. Arrival in Barbados brought no respite from the misery of the enslaved, the 'noise and clamour' of the sale serving 'not a little to increase the apprehensions of the terrified Africans' and the separation of families—'a new refinement in cruelty'—adding 'fresh horrors even to the wretchedness of slavery'. Against this catalogue of horrors, the conversations he had enjoyed 'with my countrymen' and the care he had received during the Atlantic voyage from the women slaves—now 'all gone different ways'—were but 'small remains of comfort'.[12]

The authenticity of Equiano's *Narrative* has received mixed reports. One authority claims that archival research shows 'his memory of events and details of thirty years earlier', when Equiano was a seafarer, to be 'remarkably accurate'.[13] The same authority, however, also identified inaccuracies in Equiano's chronology of his initial voyages to America and England and, more recently, has even raised doubts about whether Equiano was actually born in Africa.[14] His account of both his early life in Africa and his enslave-

[12] Ibid, pp. 46–62 (quotations, pp. 55–6, 58–59, 61–62). [13] Ibid, p. xxii.

[14] Carretta notes, for example, that Equiano's name (or, more accurately, his adopted one of 'Gust. Vasa') appeared on the muster roll of a British ship on 1 Jan. 1756, a year before he

ment and shipment to America therefore may be fictional, perhaps drawing on the memory of other enslaved Africans rather than direct personal experience. This possibility does not mean, of course, that, as an Anglo-African, Equiano's emotional reaction to enslavement and to British traders can be dismissed as overdrawn and unrepresentative. On the contrary, it should encourage efforts to use such narratives as a prism through which to focus on key issues in understanding African experiences of the British Atlantic slave trade. In particular, narratives such as Equiano's remind us of the need to understand how the enslaved were taken and where they came from, what happened to them on the Middle Passage and how they reacted to it, and where they landed in America and spent the rest of their lives. In other words, we need to retrace Equiano's own journey into American slavery, but on this occasion to use a collective rather than an individual lens in doing so.

When Hawkins sailed to Sierra Leone and other parts of Upper Guinea between 1562 and 1568, he procured, in Richard Hakluyt's words, 'partly by the sword, and partly by other means', perhaps a thousand enslaved Africans for shipment to America.[15] Characteristic of the Age of Discovery and perhaps understandable in the absence of established commercial relations, Hawkins' opportunism and predation to procure slaves in Africa had long since given way to organized Anglo–African trade by the time that Equiano boarded ship for America nearly two centuries later. Indeed, as British contemporaries of Equiano such as Adam Smith recognized, orderly trade relations with Africans, not British-led raiding, was crucial to the expansion of the British slave trade in Africa and, thereby, to the satisfaction of demand for coerced labour in America. Such order, in turn, rested, on the British side, on an appreciation of and respect for local African political authority and right to control and regulate slave supply. On the African side, it relied on protection of the property rights of British traders and on local enforceability of contracts. The outcome of such arrangements was an Anglo–African commercial exchange in which the scale and composition of slaves shipped

recounted in the *Narrative* arriving in England (Ibid, pp. ix, 67). On doubts about Equiano's African birth, see Vincent Carretta, 'Olaudah Equiano or Gustavus Vassa? New Light on an Eighteenth-Century Question of Identity', *S & A*, XX, (1999), pp. 96–105.

[15] Clement R. Markham, ed., *The Hawkins' Voyages*, Hakluyt Society, Vol. LVII, (London, 1878), p. 6. The reference is to the first of the three voyages made by John Hawkins to Guinea between 1562 and 1568.

by the British was primarily shaped by the interaction of market conditions in Africa and America. In terms of its impact on Africa and Africans, the policing and ordering of external trade relations ensured that some Africans could share, often disproportionately, in the profits or economic rents that such trade generated, while at the same time helping to determine the selection of those shipped to America.[16] In this respect the experience of Africans of the British slave trade was not always negative, a point highlighted by the remark in 1805 by a leading slave trader of Old Calabar in the Bight of Biafra to a visitor from the British African Association that if he 'came from Mr Wilberforce', the local traders would kill him.[17] Co-operation with the British ensured that some Africans grew wealthy from the export slave trade, personally investing their wealth in stocks of European goods, in wives, and in enslaved Africans. Without their participation, the British traffic in slaves could not have reached the scale that it did.

The principal methods of enslaving Africans for export to America were warfare, raiding, and kidnapping, though people were also enslaved through judicial processes, debt, and, in regions with unstable rainfall levels, drought and famine. The degree of violence involved in enslaving people varied between regions and through time. Warfare was quite commonly a source of slaves in Senegambia, the Gold Coast, the Slave Coast (or Bight of Benin), and Angola, while raiding and kidnapping seem to have predominated in the Bight of Biafra, whence Equiano was exported. The weak and vulnerable such as Equiano were the principal victims of kidnappers, judicial processes and drought. Relative to other regions, women and children constituted larger proportions of the slaves normally shipped from the Bight of Biafra. But males generally, and male adults in particular, almost invariably constituted the largest single category of slaves taken by British ships from Africa,

[16] E. W. Evans and David Richardson, 'Hunting for Rents: The Economics of Slaving in Pre-Colonial Africa', *Economic History Review* (hereafter *ECHR*), Second Series, XLVIII (1995), pp. 665–86. The point was also made in 1778 by Ignatius Sancho, who was born in 1729 to captive Africans on board a slave ship and subsequently lived most of his life in England: according to Sancho, 'In Africa, the poor wretched natives—blessed with the most fertile and luxuriant soil—are rendered so much the more miserable for what Providence meant as a blessing:—the Christians' abominable Traffic for slaves—and the horrid cruelty and treachery of the petty Kings—encouraged by their Christian customers—who carry them strong liquors, to enflame their national madness—and powder and bad fire-arms, to furnish them with the hellish means of killing and kidnapping'; *Ignatius Sancho: The Letters of the Late Ignatius Sancho, An African*, ed. Vincent Carretta (1802; New York, 1998), p. 131.

[17] Robin Hallett, ed., *Records of the African Association, 1788–1831* (London, 1964), p. 198.

the proportions of males usually varying between 55 per cent and 70 per cent and the proportions of adult males varying between 45 per cent and 60 per cent.[18] In this respect, Equiano, who was aged ten when seized, was from a minority group of enslaved Africans who were deported. Those shipped to America may also have been a minority of the total numbers of people enslaved as a result of violence, drought and other means. Most so enslaved may well have joined the ranks of those born into slavery and retained in Africa or who died en route to market. Precisely how those sent to the coast were selected from among the totality of those who survived enslavement processes has yet to be fully resolved, but is likely to have been determined by various factors. Prominent among these were domestic African preferences for female slaves, exporters' preferences for adult males, and the costs of moving slaves to the coast relative to coastal prices for slaves. Although some of the enslaved were forced to travel long distances to reach the coast, possibly passing, like Equiano, through several owners' hands before doing so, the costs of moving slaves, including risk of mortality, probably dictated that the homeland of the majority of enslaved Africans taken away by the British lay within a few hundred kilometers at most of the Atlantic coast of Africa. While few doubt, on balance, the destructive impact of the export slave trade on Africa, the extent to which this impact was seriously felt in societies more than a modest distance from the coast remains a contentious issue.[19]

The enslaved Africans shipped by the British comprised a mixture of ethnic groups, as British Empire ships took slaves from all parts of Atlantic Africa between Senegal in the north and the Congo River in the south, occasionally even venturing to take slaves from south-east Africa. Some

[18] David Eltis and Stanley L. Engerman, 'Fluctuations in Age and Sex Ratios in the Transatlantic Slave Trade, 1663–1864', *ECHR*, Second Series, XLVI (1993), pp. 308–23.

[19] One indicator of the extent of 'Atlantic' influences on African societies away from the coast may be found in patterns of slave prices. At the coast there was a premium on prices of males, especially adults, which may have been as high as 30 per cent, whereas at places several hundred kilometers inland, a premium was normally paid for females, reflecting African preferences for such slaves. Arguably, the 'line' of transition in price relativities may be seen as the frontier at which external influences on local slave prices became overshadowed by internal ones. The distance of this frontier line from the coast was likely to vary in accordance, among other things, with transport costs, and thus may have been greater where river transport routes existed. On interior slave prices and comparisons with coastal prices, see Paul E. Lovejoy and David Richardson, 'Competing Markets for Male and Female Slaves: Slave Prices in the Interior of West Africa, 1780–1850', *International Journal of African Historical Studies*, 28, 2 (1995), pp. 261–93.

ships loaded slaves at various localities, particularly ones trading at Upper Guinea and the Gold Coast, with some resulting mixing of ethnicities on board. Most—quite likely an increasing majority—tended to acquire the bulk of their slaves in one region or even one venue in Atlantic Africa. Evidence relating to the geography of British slave trading in Africa before 1662 is sketchy, but is much better for the last century-and-a-half of the British slave trade. The evidence for this later period is presented in Table 3.1. The table highlights two features of the distribution of British trade in *c.*1662–1807. The first is that the proportion of slaves taken from some regions of the coast was much higher than at others. Two thirds of the slaves carried away came from just three regions—the Bight of Biafra, the Gold Coast, and Central Africa—with the remainder being taken from Senegambia, Sierra Leone, the Bight of Benin (or Slave Coast), and South East Africa.[20] Overall, the British took fewer slaves from the three smallest suppliers in Atlantic Africa than the Bight of Biafra alone. Within the Bight of Biafra, moreover, just two venues—Old Calabar on the Cross River and Bonny in the Niger Delta—supplied the great majority of slaves entering British ships, a pattern of concentration of loading of enslaved Africans replicated in some, though not all, other regions. Overall, Igbos from the Bight of Biafra constituted probably the largest single ethnic group of Africans entering the British slave trade in 1662–1807, with Akan from the Gold Coast and Bantu from Central Africa providing other large proportions. By contrast, groups such as Aje-Fon and Yoruba of the Slave Coast and Mandinga of Upper Guinea were rather less prominent among deportees on British ships.

Table 3.1 also reveals that the proportions of slaves from individual regions—and thus the relative importance of different ethnic groups—varied greatly through time, with some of the less important sources overall becoming at times major suppliers of slaves to British ships. Thus, while the Bight of Biafra was the principal source of slaves for the British in the 1660s, it was soon eclipsed by the Bight of Benin and Central Africa, which became the major sources of slaves for British ships in the following two decades, as shipments from the Bight of Biafra declined. The Bight of Benin continued to be an important source of slaves for British ships through the 1720s but

[20] The regional definitions used in constructing this table are based on Curtin (P. D. Curtin, *The Atlantic Slave Trade: A Census* (Madison, 1969), pp. 128–30) and combine Sierra Leone and the Windward Coast.

TABLE 3.1: *Estimated Slave Exports from Africa, British Empire Ships, 1662–1807 (nearest 00)*

	Senegambia	Sierra Leone	Gold Coast	Bight of Benin	Bight of Biafra	Central Africa	South-East Africa
1662–1670	1,100	400	8,000	13,700	32,500	4,100	100
1671–1680	3,800	1,300	17,500	17,200	22,900	8,300	300
1681–1690	8,000	2,700	12,700	40,100	18,200	19,800	5,400
1691–1700	9,800	3,300	17,100	33,400	10,500	17,200	200
1700–1709	7,800	2,600	47,100	43,500	15,400	9,300	–
1710–1719	11,200	5,000	91,100	47,600	24,500	17,500	11,000
1720–1729	22,900	8,300	78,900	50,200	44,700	61,500	9,400
1730–1739	40,300	5,300	32,000	25,200	53,300	136,500	–
1740–1749	6,500	4,400	51,100	6,700	95,300	45,100	–
1750–1759	30,100	41,000	62,600	14,800	91,300	33,600	500
1760–1769	40,300	94,200	79,300	27,100	145,500	38,200	–
1770–1779	38,100	77,200	84,800	24,700	120,400	16,000	–
1780–1789	6,700	34,700	71,800	19,000	157,700	16,600	–
1790–1799	5,200	37,400	53,100	20,600	133,900	100,000	–
1800–1807	3,800	19,400	46,000	12,500	101,100	72,500	–
1662–1807	235,600	337,200	753,100	396,300	1,067,200	596,200	26,900
% shares	6.9	9.9	22.1	11.6	31.3	17.5	0.8

Sources: decennial totals, Richardson, 'Slave Trade', p. 442; African regional shares, based on David Eltis, Stephen D. Behrendt, David Richardson, and Herbert S. Klein, eds., *The Atlantic Slave Trade: A Database on CD-Rom* (Cambridge, 1999). Sierra Leone includes the Windward Coast.

much of the growth of British slave shipments between the 1690s and 1730s depended on a resurgence of activity in the Bight of Biafra and expansion of activity in other regions, notably Senegambia, the Gold Coast and Central Africa. By the 1730s, however, British slave shipments from the Bight of Benin had entered into a long-term decline absolutely and proportionately, and within a decade a similar fall in shipments from Central Africa had begun, only being arrested in this case by a belated resurgence of British trade there in the decade or so before abolition in 1807. At the same time the contribution of the Gold Coast to British slave exports tended to stabilize, while that of Senegambia continued to grow to the 1770s but then declined sharply. Table 3.1 shows, therefore, that most of the burden of sustaining renewed growth of British slave trading from the 1730s onwards was met by increasing intensity of trade in the Bight of Biafra and by a meteoric expansion of trade with Sierra Leone in 1750–80. As a result, in 1760–90 these two regions supplied over half of the slaves taken from Africa by British Empire ships, with the Gold Coast supplying a large share of the rest. Just as in Equiano's lifetime Igboland was being ever more actively exploited by the British as a source of enslaved Africans, British traders were also eagerly opening up new sources of slave supply further west along the Guinea Coast, thereby further extending the range of African ethnic groups entering the British slave trade.

Continuities and shifts in the ethnic structure of British slave shipments were the outcome of a complex set of factors that included inter-ethnic divisions and rivalries within the interior of coastal supply centres, the economic attractiveness of such centres to external traders, and the strength of British competitiveness in different African markets. Of these factors, the first two were largely shaped by conditions within Africa, particularly the balance of power between rival African states, which helped to dictate who might or might not be enslaved, and the nature of political authority in coastal trading venues, which helped to determine the efficiency and security with which Afro–European transactions were conducted. Because the slave trade is often compared to an ocean fishery, with potential for 'over-fishing', much attention has been given to variations in local population densities and to the incidence of depopulation as determinants of coastal patterns of trade.[21] The relevance of the fisheries model to slave trading, however, is open to question, as is the alleged linkage between population levels and the

[21] Robert P. Thomas and Richard N. Bean, 'The Fishers of Men: The Profits of the Slave Trade', *Journal of Economic History*, XXXIV (1974), pp. 885–914.

capacity of African traders to sustain high-volume slave exports in the long run.[22] Demographic factors cannot be ignored, but other factors within Africa were important in determining the relative attractiveness of competing African trading venues to British or other traders. Particularly important was the politics of the coastal trading states that served as a conduit between interior suppliers of slaves and European traders. A correlation appears to have existed between levels of local political order and slave exports, with economic security and rates of turnaround of ships serving as a bridge between the two. Thus, regions where political institutions came to provide mechanisms to protect the property of visiting traders and to expedite transactions were able consistently to attract traders, whereas those unable to provide such facilities were less able to do so. This dichotomy may help to explain why more distant regions from Britain and British America such as the Gold Coast and Bight of Biafra, where relatively efficient local mechanisms for safeguarding the property of external traders evolved, generally attracted more traders than places in Upper Guinea, where political disorder and instability and violence in Afro–European trade relations seem to have gone hand in hand. Only at the height of their slave trade in 1750–93—when markets for slaves throughout Atlantic Africa were stretched—were the British willing to trade in large numbers in Upper Guinea. On the whole, politically shaped order and efficiency in local processes of trade, more than demography or geography, dictated the relative attractiveness to the British of different slave supply venues in Atlantic Africa.

As the leading slave traders in 1660–1807, the British may appear to have been the most competitive in most regions in Africa. Evidence on the shares of different national carriers of slave exports from Africa paints a rather different story. It is true that the British were consistently the leading European traders in the Gambia, the Gold Coast and the Bight of Biafra in the eighteenth century. In tandem with merchants from mainland North America, they also dominated the trade of Sierra Leone once that region became a major source of slaves after 1750. Elsewhere, however, the situation was different. Rarely did British traders venture south of the Congo River, where the Portuguese maintained an almost complete stranglehold on trade, nor, except in 1759–79, when they controlled St Louis at the mouth of the River Senegal, did they succeed in breaking French domination of trade in that area. Normally excluded from trading with the most northern and

[22] Evans and Richardson, 'Hunting for Rents'.

southern slave-supply venues in Atlantic Africa, the British also lost ground to the French and Portuguese in the Bight of Benin from the 1720s onwards and on the Loango Coast north of the River Congo to the Dutch and French between the 1740s and early 1790s. Only in the 1793–1807 period, when war in Europe forced the French to abandon slave trading, did British traders return in large numbers to the Loango Coast. Otherwise failing after the 1730s to maintain their share of trade in the Bight of Benin and the Loango Coast, the British and British-colonial traders depended on enlarging ties with the Bight of Biafra and opening up Sierra Leone in order to expand their slaving activities between the 1740s and 1790s.[23]

The geography of the winds and ocean currents of the south Atlantic was a major factor in allowing Portuguese traders, many of whom sailed from Brazil, to monopolize trade south of the River Congo. Elsewhere in Atlantic Africa, however, variations in British influence over slave exports seem largely to have reflected levels of investment by different national carriers in building relations with local African traders as well as shifts in the balance of control over British trade to Africa among British ports. British control of slave exports from the Gambia and the Gold Coast mirrored continuing British investment in forts and factories in both regions from the late seventeenth century onwards. At the same time, the loss of British influence over trade with the Bight of Benin after the 1720s and the subsequent intensification of British activity in the Bight of Biafra and Sierra Leone were probably related to shifts of control of British slave trading from London to Bristol and Liverpool traders, who, armed with different mixtures of trade goods from their London counterparts, were also prepared to invest in fostering commercial alliances with Bonny, Old Calabar, and Sierra Leone.[24] However one explains variations in the intensity of British slave-trading activity, their impact on the experiences of enslaved Africans was clear. If one were Aje-Fon or Yoruba boarding ship in the Bight of Benin, it was, from the 1720s at least, much more likely that one would enter a French ship than a British one and, assuming one survived the Atlantic crossing,

[23] On Cameroons, in the eastern Bight of Biafra, see David Richardson, 'Profits in the Liverpool Slave Trade: The Accounts of William Davenport, 1757–1784', in Roger Anstey and P. E. H. Hair, eds., *Liverpool, the African Slave Trade, and Abolition* (Liverpool, 1976), p. 66.

[24] For an example of investment in personal relations between Liverpool and Old Calabar traders, see Paul E. Lovejoy and David Richardson, 'Trust, Pawnship and Atlantic History: The Institutional Foundations of the Old Calabar Slave Trade', *American Historical Review*, 104 (1999), pp. 339–47.

thus spend the rest of one's life under French rule. By comparison, if, like Equiano, one were an Igbo from neighbouring Bight of Biafra, there was a very high probability from the 1730s onwards that one would board not only a British, but even more particularly, a Liverpool ship and, assuming one survived, be sold in British America. The same would also apply to those taken from Gambia, Sierra Leone and even the Gold Coast at the same time that Equiano was deported. When and where enslaved Africans were loaded on board ship in Africa thus had potentially profound implications for where enslaved Africans surviving the crossing to America would live the rest of their lives. In this respect, Equiano's claim to be an Igbo predictably had him boarding a British ship bound for British America. It remains to be seen whether his reported experience of the Atlantic crossing comports with other experiences.

Ever since abolitionists in the 1780s alerted contemporaries to the intensity with which enslaved Africans were packed on board ship and the levels of their mortality in transit, the Atlantic crossing or 'Middle Passage' has served as a metaphor for the horrors of the slave trade. Although some merchants testifying to Parliamentary inquiries in 1788–90 into the slave trade calculated how restrictions on loading rates of slaves on board ship might affect voyage profits, other witnesses, including several ship surgeons, focused on shipboard conditions and the treatment of slaves, reminding us, as one historian has remarked, that the Middle Passage is properly 'considered in terms other than economic'.[25] Unfortunately, none of the witnesses to Parliament was African. As a result, Equiano's *Narrative* remains alone among contemporary writings to provide an African perspective on the Atlantic crossing. His sympathy for abolitionism makes his comments on this matter open to charges of exaggeration. Moreover, his commentary is unspecific about the number of slaves on board ship, their foodstuffs, health and mortality, and the length of the crossing, issues that have dominated historical research in this area. Nevertheless, Equiano's observations on the Middle Passage provide a platform for quantitative investigation of some aspects of the trauma experienced by Africans in the ocean voyage to America. Many aspects of that experience remain, of course, beyond quantification and two centuries after Equiano lived can barely be imagined.

[25] K. G. Davies, *The Royal African Company* (London, 1957), p. 292.

Ranging in size from 50 to 200 tons, most British slave ships carried probably three or more slaves per ton when they departed from Africa. Excluding those dying before ships departed Africa, the number of enslaved Africans on board ship at the start of the middle passage typically varied therefore between 150 and 600, with most ships carrying some 200–400 victims. Compared to other contemporary or later oceanic voyages involving the movement of people, these represented exceptionally high rates of packing, a finding that casts doubt on the value of arguments about the impact of slave per ton ratios or 'tight packing' on slave mortality. It also raises questions about the efficacy of such measures as the Dolben Act of 1788 to restrict the carrying capacities of ships and thereby lower slave mortality. Be this as it may, the transport of such concentrations of enslaved Africans on board ship demanded organization, aspects of which were revealed by both Equiano and other evidence, and helped to turn slave ships into what one former shipmaster called 'floating prisons'.[26] Equiano, for instance, describes how, on leaving the coast, 'we were all put under deck, so that we could not see how they managed the ship'; how slaves, notably men, were often chained; and how men tended to be held in apartments separate from the women and children.[27] Other evidence corroborates Equiano's observations, but also reveals that preparations for the incarceration and management of slaves on board ship were well advanced long before ships reached Africa. The number of crew enlisted in Britain was specifically linked to the anticipated number of slaves to be loaded, a ratio of one crew to ten slaves being the norm. The crew normally included a surgeon, and sometimes an assistant, armed with medical supplies. Ships sailed from Britain with 'negro provisions', principally beans and peas, as well as 'recreational' items such as tobacco and pipes. They were also usually expected to buy water and supplementary stocks of foods such as rice and yams in Africa, thus becoming 'floating' larders and reservoirs, often before loading slaves.[28] Carpenters, coopers, and their assistants were normally employed en route to the coast in building slave accommodation and preparing casks for water and latrines (or

[26] John Adams, *Remarks on the Country Extending from Cape Palmas to the River Congo* (1823; London, 1966), p. 133.

[27] Equiano, *Narrative*, pp. 58–61.

[28] Data on the quantities of foods and water carried on British slave ships in the 1780s are given in David Richardson, 'The Costs of Survival: The Transport of Slaves in the Middle Passage and the Profitability of the Eighteenth-Century British Slave Trade', *Explorations in Economic History*, 24 (1987), p. 185.

'necessary tubs'). Routines for handling, controlling, and ultimately dehumanizing enslaved Africans (described by one ship captain as 'black cattle'), while simultaneously trying to ensure their survival, had been well rehearsed on British slave ships by the time that Equiano was deported from Africa in 1750s.[29]

The most quantifiable experience of enslaved Africans on board British ships—their mortality rate—has been the subject of much investigation.[30] The most recent calculations suggest that, of the 3.4 million enslaved Africans deported in British Empire ships, some 450,000, or about one in seven, died in the Atlantic crossing. Because those enslaved were predominantly aged below 30 and because the ocean crossing normally lasted no more than three months, such losses represented an extraordinary age-specific mortality rate for such a population. It was more than equal to those experienced in mortality crises in Africa and Europe before 1800. It may thus be seen as testimony to Equiano's observation about the impact of the 'improvident avarice' of British traders on the health and mortality of the enslaved.[31] The alleged effects of such avarice, whether or not true, seem to have been tempered by various improvements in medical and health practices, ship design, and other factors that contributed to a halving or more of slave mortality levels on British ships in the eighteenth century.[32] Even with these falls in mortality, however, the spectre of death continued to hang heavily over the enslaved on British ships in the late eighteenth century, most shipowners or regulators of British ships assuming some loss of slaves in transit as being inevitable.[33] Only a tiny minority, at most, of ships seems to have reached America without any loss of life, while 20 per cent or more of the enslaved on perhaps one in ten of British ships died during the Atlantic crossing from 1751 to 1800. Disproportionately represented among the latter were ships that, like the one carrying Equiano, traded to the Bight of Biafra. Though the pattern varied from port to port, British ships leaving this region tended to lose, on average, some 15–20 per cent of their human cargo in the

[29] For the reference to 'black cattle', see Suzanne Schwarz, ed., *Slave Captain: The Career of James Irving in the Liverpool Slave Trade* (Wrexham, England, 1995), p. 113.

[30] For one recent discussion, with other references, see H. S. Klein, *The Atlantic Slave Trade* (Cambridge, 1998), pp. 130–61.

[31] Equiano, *Narrative*, p. 58.

[32] Robin Haines and Ralph Shlomovitz, 'Explaining the Mortality Decline in the Eighteenth-Century British Slave Trade', *ECHR*, Second Series, LIII (2000), pp. 262–83.

[33] The Dolben Act, for example, allowed payment of bonuses to shipmasters and surgeons where losses of slaves were less than 3 per cent of those shipped.

late eighteenth century, or twice as many as those leaving other parts of Africa. Observing that 'sickness among the slaves, of which many died' occurred on the ship that carried him from Africa, Equiano was therefore reflecting a common African experience on British ships leaving the Bight of Biafra.[34] Sadly, he was also reflecting an only moderately less common experience of enslaved Africans on British ships generally, especially before 1750.

The enslaved who died in the Atlantic crossing were largely victims of respiratory, intestinal or epidemic diseases. Some of these diseases were the product of conditions experienced by the enslaved before boarding ship, but shipboard conditions undoubtedly exacerbated such disorders and proved a breeding ground for additional ones. While disease was the principal killer of slaves, a small, but perhaps growing, proportion of shipboard deaths were caused by white action. Some slaves fell victim to international conflicts that resulted in attacks on British slave ships by enemy vessels or pirates. Though many ships were taken without slaves on board, a proportion was seized in the Atlantic crossing, with slaves sometimes being killed in the process. Other slaves were victims of behaviour by the crew of ships. Some, like those thrown overboard by Luke Collingwood, master of the Liverpool ship, *Zong*, in 1781–82, were victims of a mistaken assumption that insurance would compensate ship owners for slaves jettisoned during a food crisis.[35] Collingwood's heartless action was matched by other crew who physically abused slaves on board ship, notwithstanding instructions by owners of ships banning such behaviour. Typically motivated by sex and overwhelmingly directed against female slaves, such abuse sometimes resulted in the premature death of those who sought to resist the unwanted advances of ruthless and sadistic masters or other crew.[36] For women, therefore, to the risk of

[34] Equiano, *Narrative*, p. 58.

[35] For a discussion of the case of the *Zong*, see James Walvin, *Black Ivory: A History of British Slavery* (London, 1992), pp. 16–21.

[36] For examples on Bristol ships in the late eighteenth century, see Madge Dresser, *Slavery Obscured: The Social History of the Slave Trade in an English Provincial Port* (London, 2001), pp. 152–53. One local Bristol newspaper reported that on some ships 'the common sailors are allowed to have intercourse with such of the black women whose consent they can procure... [and] the officers are permitted to indulge their passions among them at pleasure'; cited by Dresser, p. 163. In the first wave of abolitionism in 1788–93, John Kimber, master of a Bristol ship, was tried in 1793 for assaulting and killing a fifteen year old girl on board his ship, but was acquitted.

death from disease was added rape and murder, a feature of female slave existence that was to continue beyond the ocean crossing.

Female resistance to white abuse was one element in a spectrum of forms of resistance by enslaved Africans on board ship that, in some cases, resulted in death. Some slaves chose passive resistance, refusing, for example, food or water, a form of resistance met by forced feeding. Others resisted their enslavement by more violent and destructive means, thereby threatening the security of the voyage. Some chose suicide, a form of escape from slavery particularly identified by some contemporaries with Igbos, and therefore a not uncommon occurrence on British ships. Consistent with this belief, Equiano noted in his *Narrative* the suicide at sea of two of his 'wearied countrymen', who jumped overboard and drowned. A third failed in a similar attempt and, Equiano reports, was flogged 'unmercifully' for 'attempting to prefer death to slavery'.[37] Suicide as a form of resistance, however, was not confined to Igbos. Nor was it the only, or even preponderant, form of resistance through violence by enslaved Africans, Igbos or otherwise, on British ships. More common, and more dangerous in terms of ship security, was armed rebellion by groups of enslaved Africans.[38] Enslaved Africans united to rise up against their captors in perhaps one in ten British slaving voyages. On voyages to Senegambia and Upper Guinea, to which British traders resorted in greater numbers after 1750 than earlier, the incidence of rebellion was much higher than elsewhere.

Various factors conspired to encourage slaves to rebel. Some historians suggest that the propensity for such action was greatest while ships were at the African coast and the chance of an uprising allowing the enslaved to return to their homeland remained conceivable.[39] Such claims are, however, contradicted by evidence showing that slaves seized the opportunity to rebel wherever and whenever they were held on board ship. Like the acts of suicide described by Equiano, therefore, revolts on British ships by enslaved Africans seem to have been driven, more than anything else, by an unqualified ambition for freedom from slavery or at least from enslavement by white

[37] Equiano, *Narrative*, p. 59.

[38] What follows draws on Stephen D. Behrendt, David Eltis and David Richardson, 'The Costs of Coercion: African Agency in the Pre-Modern Atlantic World', *ECHR*, Second Series, LIV (2001), pp. 454–76.

[39] D. P. Mannix and M. Cowley, *Black Cargoes: A History of the Atlantic Slave Trade* (New York, 1962), p. 111; Darold D. Wax, 'Negro Resistance to the Early American Slave Trade', *Journal of Negro History*, 51 (1966), p. 9.

captors. As acts of self-liberation, shipboard revolts by enslaved Africans were rarely completely successful. Most revolts were repressed, often with heavy bloodshed among both the slaves and their captors, and the ships involved went on to complete their voyages to America. Nevertheless, the fear of slave uprising remained constant among the owners and crews of British slave ships, helping to drive up the cost and thus lower the number of enslaved Africans carried to America.

The anxiety of enslaved Africans boarding ship bound for America was frequently ascribed by contemporaries to a belief that they were to be eaten by their white captors, a sentiment reinforced by the failure of any enslaved to return home. The reality, of course, was otherwise, but methods of shipboard confinement, high mortality, unchallenged abuse, and the unceremonious way in which the deceased where thrown overboard reinforced the impression that the enslaved were being consumed. Resistance and rebellion, however, demonstrated that the spirit and humanity of enslaved Africans was not crushed by their experience of the Middle Passage. On the contrary, erstwhile strangers among the enslaved formed bonds and new identities during the Atlantic crossing, sometimes drawing on recollections of their African homeland. Equiano, for example, claims that amongst 'the poor chained men' on board ship, he 'found some of my own nation, which in a small degree gave ease to my mind', and highlights the comfort he derived from the women slaves 'who used to wash and take care of me'.[40] He notes too, however, how on reaching America friends and relatives among the enslaved 'were sold in different lots' and were thus denied the solace of companionship to relieve 'the gloom of slavery'.[41] The spirit of resistance evident among the enslaved on board ship transcended the movement of Africans from ship to shore in the Americas, but whether bonds nurtured by memories of homeland and by the shared brutality of the Atlantic crossing were so easily dissipated as Equiano implies remains a more open question. To begin to explore this issue, we need to place Equiano's description of his arrival in Barbados and subsequent reshipment to Virginia in the mid-1750s in the context of the broader pattern of enslaved African arrivals in America in British Empire ships.

The history of slavery in British America was largely dominated by sugar, with the vast majority of the slaves arriving from Africa in British Empire

[40] Equiano, *Narrative*, p. 62. [41] Ibid, p. 61.

ships disembarking first in the West Indies. Barbados, the home of the mid-seventeenth century 'sugar revolution' in British America, was the principal destination of most British slave ships before 1700, but by the 1680s Jamaica and the Leeward Islands had also become important markets for slaves as the sugar revolution swept through the British Caribbean.[42] The dominance of these colonies over British American slave imports continued through to the time of Equiano's arrival in Barbados in the mid-1750s, though by then Barbados had been eclipsed by Jamaica and the two larger Leeward Islands of Antigua and St Kitts as disembarkation points for slaves. By this time, too, the hold of sugar over British American imports had also been loosened, with first Virginia and then South Carolina emerging as important destinations for British ships reaching America with slaves. In the 1720s and 1730s, the mainland colonies together received about one in six of all the slaves reaching the Americas in British ships. This represented, however, the peak of the mainland influence over British American slave imports. Unlike the West Indian sugar islands, which depended wholly on imports of Africans to expand their slave populations, natural reproduction of slaves meant that, in Virginia, dependence on imports from Africa had eased by the 1750s. This pattern was repeated in South Carolina, even though the buoyancy of the colony's demand for labour ensured it continued to attract large numbers of new slaves from Africa up to 1775. Yet, South Carolina's slave imports paled in comparison with those in the period 1763–75 to the British Caribbean, where the acquisition of new territories at the Peace of Paris in 1763 combined with buoyant demand for sugar in Britain to generate unprecedented demands for new slaves in the British islands. Moreover, the independence of the thirteen mainland colonies consolidated the stranglehold of the sugar colonies over the British slave trade after 1783, the only significant change in slave imports in British America in 1783–1807 being a shift in the balance of imports from old to newly conquered sugar colonies. From first to last, therefore, sugar dictated patterns of slavery in British America and the traffic in enslaved Africans on which it depended. For Equiano to have landed anywhere in British America other than in a sugar colony would thus have been unusual. That he landed in Barbados was emblematic of sugar's influence over British slavery.

[42] The patterns of slave arrivals in the Americas in British Empire ships described in this paragraph draws on data presented in Richardson, 'Slave Trade', p. 456.

After disembarking at Barbados, Equiano's experience of slavery was far from typical, though some aspects of it may not have been as exceptional as one might expect. If, as he initially anticipated after meeting a group of enslaved Africans that came to his ship, he had been put to work in sugar cultivation, his experience could well have been brutal and short. Sugar cultivation consumed enslaved labour; in most British sugar colonies, deaths of slaves consistently exceeded births, some times by as much as 4 per cent a year.[43] A proportion of newly imported slaves thus took the place of those whose lives were cut short by producing sugar to meet the 'sweet tooth' of British consumers. There were, however, escapes from the brutality of sugar cultivation other than an early, unmarked grave. Some slaves chose to run away, usually on pain of a public whipping if recaptured, but successful escapees, such as the maroons of Jamaica, were able to form free communities capable of continuing the resistance to white domination first evinced by enslaved Africans on board ship. Others, including some recaptured runaways, found respite from the harshness of sugar cultivation by being reshipped and sold on the mainland, where the survival chances of slaves were higher, at least by the mid-eighteenth century, while for some of those who remained in the islands relief came through being employed in activities other than sugar cultivation. Equiano's life offers insights into both the last two. Together with many others before and after, he was reshipped to another colony soon after landing in Barbados. For many, the experience of further dislocation did not mean any change in their working conditions and could only have added to the anxieties they had already faced during their passage from Africa. This was especially so of the many newly arrived Africans relocated from British to Spanish or French rule in the eighteenth century.[44] Equiano, however, followed a longstanding, though numerically modest, stream of enslaved Africans reshipped from Barbados or other British West

[43] On the demographic 'deficit' of slaves in British America, especially the West Indies, see B. W. Higman, 'The Economic and Social Development of the British West Indies, from Settlement to ca. 1850', in Stanley L. Engerman and Robert E. Gallman, eds., *The Cambridge Economic History of the United States: the Colonial Era* (Cambridge, 1996), pp. 307–09; J. R. Ward, 'The British West Indies in the Age of Abolition, 1748–1815', in Marshall, ed., *OHBE*, Vol. II, p. 431.

[44] Detailed estimates of the numbers of enslaved Africans resold across national colonial boundaries remain to be made, but some indication of possible numbers sold from British colonies to other parts of the Americas are to be found in Richardson, 'Slave Trade', p. 456, where it is suggested that 25–35 per cent of slaves arriving in British ships in the Americas between 1720 and 1807 may at times have been destined for non-British, notably Spanish and French, territories.

Indian islands to Virginia, where he quickly became employed as a domestic before being resold again to a British sea captain in the early stages of the Seven Years War.[45] After visiting England, he was later resold and reshipped to the West Indies, where, as a young adult, he was employed not in sugar but as a seaman on ships engaged in inter-colonial trade. Increasingly recognized, together with other service activities, as a not uncommon form of employment among enslaved Africans, Equiano's escape from sugar cultivation into a career at sea may well have prolonged his life. Whether it proved as advantageous to others in escaping from slavery itself as it did to Equiano has yet to be established.

As a story of re-invention of identity in the face of spatial dislocation and personal trauma, does Equiano's narrative shed any light on the wider issue of the impact of the Atlantic slave trade on the reconstruction of the identities of enslaved Africans removed to America? As noted earlier, the narrative offers mixed messages on this issue; Equiano claimed that identities and bonds created on board ship were subsequently destroyed by separation through the slave marketing process. Despite such observations, however, after arriving in Barbados Equiano evidently successfully reconstructed his own identity through a successive series of adaptations to new circumstances, drawing on his entrepreneurial skills, on his personality, and on his memory of Africa to do so. His life reminds us, therefore, that identities are unstable and mutable, 'always unfinished, always being remade'.[46] Even though he came eventually to acquire the characteristics and lifestyle of an English Christian and family man of letters, he nevertheless continued at the end of his life to insist in referring to himself as 'the African', a label used by others in similar circumstances.[47] In effect, Equiano became an Anglo-African Creole, a cultural hybrid, appropriating important attributes of the new American and British environments in which he found himself while self-consciously retaining memories of his own African-ness and remaining an advocate for Africa and enslaved Africans. In doing so, of course, Equiano acquired an exceptional position. Few enslaved Africans in the British Empire managed to liberate themselves by non-violent means and hardly any achieved the social standing in British society that Equiano

[45] For data on the Barbados–Virginia link, see H. S. Klein, *The Middle Passage: Comparative Studies in the Atlantic Slave Trade* (Princeton, NJ, 1978), pp. 121–41.

[46] Paul Gilroy, *The Black Atlantic: Modernity and Double Consciousness* (Cambridge, Mass., 1993), p. xi.

[47] Ignatius Sancho was referred to as 'an African' by the editor of his letters, Joseph Jekyll.

attained. But to focus so much, as Equiano does, on the destructiveness of the enslavement process for the mass of Africans taken from their homeland would be to understate their adaptability and resilience in forging, if perhaps in more modest yet personally meaningful ways, new identities and social relationships in British America.

If work was, according to Gaspar, 'the dominant force in the lives of slaves', this does not mean that they were unable to form durable personal relationships or marital unions, to create new institutions or languages, to develop autonomous economic and recreational activities, or to devise individual or collective forms of resistance.[48] Within the English-speaking world, evidence relating to the world that the slaves made is most abundant for the US antebellum South and for early nineteenth-century Jamaica, but glimpses into the longevity of slave unions or partnerships or other social arrangements of slaves in British America before 1807 are increasingly possible. The same applies, too, to other facets of slave life such as provision ground cultivation, the independent marketing of such produce, recreational and religious behaviour, and health and burial practices.[49] The defence by enslaved Africans of customary rights to 'free' time in order to pursue such matters became an important aspect of master–slave relationships, anticipating in important ways the future of employer–employee relationships in other contexts.[50] None of this should be seen to deny that slaves had few, if any rights, before the law or were free from abuse of various kinds from their owners and their agents. But it does mean that, in addition to being labourers in production systems, enslaved Africans emerged, among other things, as marital partners, doctors and spiritual leaders (or obeahmen), and hucksters and dealers in goods. As in other contexts, the identities forged by slaves were shaped by the wider socio-demographic conditions of the particular societies in which they lived. They were also subject to constant renegotiation in the face of changing local or individual circumstances, some of which were

[48] The quotation is from David Barry Gaspar, 'Sugar and Slave Life in Antigua before 1800', in Ira Berlin and Philip D. Morgan, eds., *Cultivation and Culture: Labor and the Shaping of Slave Life in the Americas* (Charlottesville, Va., 1993), p. 101.

[49] See for example, G. M. Hall, *Africans in Colonial Louisiana: the Development of Afro-Creole Culture in the Eighteenth Century* (Baton Rouge, Lou., 1992); Berlin and Morgan, eds., *Cultivation*; Lorena S. Walsh, *From Calabar to Carter's Grove: The History of a Virginia Slave Community* (Charlottesville, Va., 1997); P. D. Morgan, *Slave Counterpoint: Black Culture in the Eighteenth-Century Chesapeake and Lowcountry* (Chapel Hill, NC, 1998).

[50] Mary Turner ed., *From Chattel Slaves to Wage Slaves: the Dynamics of Labor Bargaining in the Americas* (London, 1995).

beyond the control of slaves themselves. Equiano was, nevertheless, plainly far from being alone among the slave population of British America to regain some control over his life after crossing the Atlantic.[51]

The acculturation of slaves in the Americas was a syncretic process in which, from the slaves' perspective, harsh, often uncontrollable, realities of existence in the Americas fused with African forms of resistance to slavery and the cultural heritage of the enslaved to foster new Creole cultures. This development embraced all aspects of slaves' lives, material and non-material, including language, naming practices, foodstuffs, dress, aesthetics, and spirituality. Articulation of new cultures was linked to demographic change on plantations, where, notwithstanding age and gender imbalances in slave imports, sufficient slaves born in the Americas survived and reproduced to ensure a more normal population structure in time. This process occurred faster in the mainland British North American plantation colonies than in the West Indies, but was evident even in those islands, such as Jamaica, where the growth of the slave population depended on imports from Africa through to 1807.[52] For some historians, however, the very dependence of slavery in British America on a constant infusion of newly imported labour allowed African ethnicity and heritage to dictate patterns of cultural adjustment by the enslaved to life in the Americas. Thus it has been argued that marriage between 'people of the same nation' encouraged the development of a 'national culture in the next generation', and, more specifically, that the 'Igboization of enslaved African-American communities' ensured the 'essential reality of Igbo as a nation in the diaspora'.[53] Such arguments have been

[51] We have growing information, based largely on plantation records, about the lives of some individual slaves, though nothing to match that for Equiano. See, for example, Richard S. Dunn, 'Slave Production and Slave Women in Jamaica', in Berlin and Morgan, eds., *Cultivation*, pp. 49–72; and 'The Story of Two Jamaican Slaves: Sarah Affir and Richard McAlpine of Mesopotamia Estate', in Roderick A. McDonald, ed., *West Indian Accounts: Essays in the History of the British Caribbean and Atlantic Economy in Honour of Richard Sheridan* (Kingston, Jamaica, 1996), pp. 188–210, which examine the lives of certain slaves on Mesopotamia plantation, Jamaica.

[52] Dunn, 'Slave Production', p. 51; Barry Higman, *Slave Population and Economy in Jamaica 1807–1834* (Cambridge, 1976); Higman, *Slave Populations of the British Caribbean 1807–1834* (Kingston, Jamaica, 1995).

[53] John K. Thornton, *Africa and Africans in the Making of the Atlantic World, 1400–1800*, 2nd edn. (Cambridge, 1998), p. 201; Douglas B. Chambers, ' "My own nation": Igbo Exiles in the Diaspora', in David Eltis and David Richardson, eds., *Routes to Slavery: Direction, Ethnicity and Mortality in the Atlantic Slave Trade* (London, 1997), p. 90.

criticized both by historical anthropologists, who challenge the impact of African heritage on the artifacts or practices of slave life in the Americas, and by cultural historians, who question the use of the concept of nationality in this context and emphasize discontinuities of slave supply from particular parts of Africa and the intermixing of slaves from different ethnic backgrounds as realities of slavery in the Americas.[54] The last is seen as diluting the impact of the specifics of heritage and ethnicity on the cultural adjustment of the enslaved in the Americas, and underlining the importance of heterogeneity, of 'mangled pasts', and of 'precarious and permeable zones of interaction...where cultures jostled and converged in combinations and permutations of dizzying complexity'.[55]

If adaptability rather than purity or pedigree should be given greater weight in understanding cultural adjustments of Africans to life under slavery in the Americas, it is perhaps still misleading to underplay continuities in transatlantic links between Africa and British America in shaping the menu of African influences on such adjustments in particular localities. Take, for example, the African regional origins of the slaves arriving in Barbados at the time when Equiano landed there in the mid-1750s. Of some 90,000 Africans disembarking in the island in 1751–75, no less than 44 per cent (or 40,000) came from the Bight of Biafra and thus were predominantly of Igbo origin. The next largest group, accounting for 15 per cent of arrivals, was from the Gold Coast. Put another way, when Equiano landed in Barbados over 1,500 Igbos were being added each year to a Barbados slave population that totaled 69,000.[56] Moreover, lest it be thought that the Igbo component of new slave arrivals in Barbados at this time was exceptional, it is worth noting that links between Barbados and the Bight of Biafra began in the mid-seventeenth century, at which time nearly half the slaves entering the island embarked there. In common with some other contemporaries, Equiano was subsequently reshipped elsewhere, in his case to Virginia, where, as it happens, the Bight of Biafra had been the principal source of

[54] See, for example, David Northrup, 'Igbo and Igbo Myth: Culture and Identity in the Atlantic World, 1600–1850', *S & A*, XXI (2000), pp. 1–20.

[55] Philip D. Morgan, 'The Cultural Implications of the Atlantic Slave Trade: African Regional Origins, American Destinations and New World Developments', in Eltis and Richardson, eds., *Routes to Slavery*, p. 142, where the term 'mangled pasts' is attributed to Sidney Mintz.

[56] Patterns of slave imports into Barbados are based on Eltis et al, *Database*. For estimates of the slave population of Barbados, see J. R. Ward, 'The British West Indies in the Age of Abolition, 1748–1815', in Marshall, ed., *OHBE*, II, p. 433.

slave arrivals direct from Africa in the preceding half century.[57] If his stay in either Barbados or Virginia had been longer, therefore, it is likely that Equiano would have had, in Thornton's words, 'no trouble finding members of [his] own nation with whom to communicate'.[58] Indeed, he and his fellow travellers probably quickly met other slaves of Igbo origin in Barbados, since he reports that, soon after arriving in the island, 'the white people got some old slaves from the land to pacify us'.[59] A not unique experience, it seems, for newly arrived slaves, the party of 'old slaves' that Equiano met almost certainly included some of Igbo origin.[60] Even, therefore, as Equiano and his fellow Igbos were faced with a vision of their own future, they—and their enslaved visitors—were simultaneously being re-acquainted with their past. The dialectic between the socio-demographic realities of plantation life and recollections of homelands that underlay the cultural adjustments of Africans to American slavery began as soon as the enslaved disembarked ship.

Olaudah Equiano's life as a slave in the British Empire can hardly be described as archetypical. Allegedly enslaved and taken as a child from Africa to America, he managed through a combination of chance, determination, and personal ingenuity to purchase his freedom at the age of perhaps twenty-one. Thereafter, he travelled widely, before settling in Britain, where he married and had children, accumulated a modest fortune, and became a prominent figure in the abolitionist movement before his death in 1797. To see Equiano's story as anything other than exceptional would be misleading. His narrative, however, does highlight features of African experiences of the British slave trade of more than personal significance. As someone who apparently lived under slavery or its shadow in Africa, America, and Britain,

[57] On the Chesapeake, see Walsh, *From Calabar to Carter's Grove*; also Walsh, 'The Chesapeake Slave Trade: Regional Patterns, African Origins, and Some Implications', *WMQ*, LVIII (2001), pp. 139–170.

[58] Thornton, *Africa and Africans*, p. 199.

[59] Equiano, *Narrative*, p. 60.

[60] For another example of a similar episode, see Robin Dizard and Mark N. Taylor, ' "The African Daughter: a True Tale"; a New Edition', *S&A*, 23 (2002), pp. 125, 133. The British-born West Indian slave factor and planter, James Baillie, who took up residence in Grenada in 1755 at about the time that Equiano is believed to have landed at nearby Barbados, reported in evidence to Parliament in February 1790 that it was customary on the arrival of Guineamen 'to carry some of their countrymen on board, in order to inform the slaves of the purposes for which they are carried to the West Indies' (Sheila Lambert, ed., *House of Commons Sessional Papers of the Eighteenth Century*, 145 vols. (Wilmington, Del. 1975), 71, p. 193).

Equiano's life encapsulated the trilateral nature of transatlantic slavery, with events at each point of the numerous triangles linking the three continents and potentially influencing events elsewhere. As an Anglo-African, Equiano's story reflected the growing integration of a British Atlantic world that profoundly shaped the lives of millions of his fellow enslaved Africans. His story also reminds us, however, that Africans were far from passive in accepting slavery and that, notwithstanding the power of slave traders and American slave masters and the exceptional mortality rates of the enslaved, those who survived the Atlantic crossing were often able to rebuild some form of meaningful life under slavery. In doing so, they tempered the harsh realities of life and premature death, notably on sugar plantations, by sometimes escaping but more often by creating new communities, drawing, as Equiano's narrative acutely reminds us, on shared experiences and memories of African homelands. British traffickers in and owners of Africans may have sought to erase the identity of those they enslaved, even giving them adopted names such as Gustavus Vassa, but, if Olaudah Equiano's story tells us anything, it is surely that, for all its cruelty and inhumanity, the experience of enslaved Africans in the British Empire could certainly not be described as social death.

Select Bibliography

IRA BERLIN and PHILIP D. MORGAN, eds., *The Slaves' Economy: Independent Production by Slaves in the Americas* (London, 1991).

IRA BERLIN and PHILIP D. MORGAN, eds., *Cultivation and Culture: Labor and the Shaping of Slave Life in the Americas* (Charlottesville, Va., 1993).

W. JEFFREY BOLSTER, *Black Jacks: African American Seamen in the Age of Sail* (Cambridge, Mass., 1997)

VINCENT CARRETTA, ed., *Olaudah Equiano's Interesting Narrative and Other Writings* (London, 1995).

VINCENT CARRETTA, ed., *Unchained Voices: An Anthology of Black Authors in the English Speaking World of the 18th Century* (Lexington, Ky., 1996).

PHILIP D. CURTIN, *The Atlantic Slave Trade: A Census* (Madison, 1969).

RICHARD S. DUNN, *Sugar and Slaves: The Rise of the Planter Class in the English West Indies, 1624–1713* (Chapel Hill, NC, 1972).

DAVID ELTIS, *The Rise of African Slavery in the Americas* (Cambridge, 2000).

DAVID ELTIS and PHILIP D. MORGAN, eds., *New Perspective on the Transatlantic Slave Trade*, special edition of *The William and Mary Quarterly*, Third Series, LVIII, no.1 (Jan. 2001).

DAVID ELTIS and DAVID RICHARDSON, eds., *Routes to Slavery: Direction, Ethnicity and Mortality in the Atlantic Slave Trade* (London, 1997).

HERBERT S. KLEIN, *The Atlantic Slave Trade* (Cambridge, 1999).

PAUL E. LOVEJOY, *Transformations in Slavery* (Cambridge, 1983, 2nd edn., 2000).

JOHN K. THORNTON, *Africa and Africans in the Making of the Atlantic World, 1400–1800* (Cambridge, 1992, 2nd edn., 1998).

LORENA S. WALSH, *From Calabar to Carter's Grove: The History of a Virginia Slave Community* (Charlottesville, Va., 1997).

JOHN R. WARD, *British West Indian Slavery, 1750–1834: The Process of Amelioration* (Oxford, 1988).

4

The Black Experience in the British Empire, 1680–1810

PHILIP D. MORGAN

During the 'long' eighteenth century, the black[1] presence in the Empire assumed formidable proportions. Between 1680 and 1810 the Empire's black population rose elevenfold. By the latter date, almost 1 million blacks lived in British territories, in spite of the loss of the 500,000 blacks who in 1776 became residents of the United States (and who in 1810 numbered 1.4 million people). In 1680 blacks in the Empire were largely confined to a few small islands in the Caribbean; a century later blacks were present everywhere along the North American seaboard and formed majorities in county and parish populations from Maryland to East Florida on the mainland and from the Bahamas to Tobago (and in another twenty years, to Trinidad and British Guiana) in the Caribbean. In Britain itself, a small but growing black population emerged not just in London but in provincial seaports and outlying countryside. By 1680 British traders had established secure bases on the African coast, and were already carrying more slaves from Africa than all the other Europeans put together. For as long as they participated in the trade, the British were the major carrier of slaves. From 1680 to 1807 approximately 3 million Africans—over three times the number of Europeans—left their native lands in British ships for the New World. In sheer number of

This chap. was published in P. J. Mashall, ed., *The Oxford History of the British Empire*, Vol. II, *The Eighteenth Century* (Oxford, 1998).

[1] *Black* is clearly an imprecise word. In most eighteenth-century contexts, it refers to indigenous peoples of Africa and their descendants. It therefore includes most *mulattoes* and *coloureds*, used in the sense of people of mixed European and African origins, many of whom of course looked quite white. It also excludes peoples of other continents and their descendants who are often referred to as black, such as East Indians, lascars (Asian seamen), most slaves in the Cape Colony (who were predominantly Madascagan and Asian in origin), and Australian aborigines. In none of these ascriptions, of course, am I assuming that race is an immutable biological fact.

emigrants, British America was actually more black than white, more an extension of Africa than of Europe.

Although most Africans arrived in the British Empire as slaves, their experiences were not uniform. The Caribbean was the heart of their story, for most blacks lived there, but that regional experience varied from an 'old' colony like Barbados to a 'new' colony like Trinidad, from the 4,411 square miles of Jamaica to the 35 square miles of Anguilla, from a sugar estate to a seaport, from working as a field-hand to serving in a British West India regiment, from a Maroon in the cockpit country of Jamaica to a concubine in the master's great house. In the third quarter of the eighteenth century North America challenged the Caribbean as the central black experience in the Empire. In 1750 50,000 more blacks lived on the islands than on the mainland; on the eve of the American Revolution 30,000 more blacks lived on the mainland than on the islands. In the space of a generation, the black population's centre of gravity had shifted from island to mainland. The North American experience was even more varied than its Caribbean counterpart: the contrast was huge between a New England farm and a Virginia tobacco plantation, between freedom in Nova Scotia and bondage on a South Carolina rice plantation, between Philadelphia and Savannah. Beyond the two heartlands of the black experience in the eighteenth-century British Empire—the Caribbean and North America, each of which had its own centres and peripheries—there were numerous other margins. In eighteenth-century Africa, blacks lived in the forts and factories under British control and increasingly others came under British jurisdiction—in the Crown colony of Senegambia between 1765 and 1783, in Sierra Leone from 1787 onward, and in the Cape Colony from 1795 onward (except for a brief return to Dutch rule between 1803 and 1806). Other marginal areas include Britain, Bermuda, even Australia. Mauritius, which was occupied by Britain in 1810, was marginal only in the sense of location, for it had a large slave population and a functioning plantation system.

To explore the black world in the British Empire, then, is to traverse continents, archipelagos, and an incredible kaleidoscope of experiences. Naturally, the majority—those slaves who lived on Caribbean and North American plantations—will garner most attention. But the many minorities—those who lived in Africa, Britain, or further afield, those who resided in towns and on farms, and those who were free—must also be encompassed. As a way of capturing the normal and the exceptional, this chapter will explore in turn the size and growth of the black population, work patterns,

TABLE 4.1 *Black Population of the British Empire (000s)*

	1680	1750	1810
Caribbean	76	295	824
Old Colonies	55	146	165
Jamaica	20	145	376
New Colonies	–	–	265
Marginal	1	4	18
North America	9	247	11
Chesapeake	4	151	–
Lower South	*	60	–
Mid-Atlantic	2	21	–
New England	*	11	–
Canada	–	–	6
Bermuda	2	4	5
Britain	*	8	10
Africa	*	5	50
Forts, factories	*	5	15
Sierra Leone	–	–	4
Cape Colony	–	–	31
Other			65
Mauritius	–	–	65
Australia	–	–	*
Total	86	555	960

Notes: * less than 1000. *Old Colonies* = Antigua, Barbados, Montserrat, Nevis, St. Kitts, and Virgin Islands. *New Colonies* = Berbice, Demerara, Essequibo, Dominica, Grenada, St. Lucia, St. Vincent, Tobago, and Trinidad. *Marginal* = Anguilla, Bahamas, Barbuda, Belize, and Cayman Islands. *Chesapeake* = Maryland and Virginia. *Lower South* = Georgia, North Carolina, and South Carolina. *Mid-Atlantic* = Delaware, New Jersey, New York, and Pennsylvania

Bermuda is included as part of North America because of geographic proximity, although it had close ties to the Caribbean.

African forts and factories: although technically not part of the empire because these were rented settlements not colonies, their black inhabitants and neighbours—the *grumetes*, free laborers, and mulatto traders—were *de facto* participants within the Empire.

Cape Colony: as black, are included Khoisan (15,000), the so-called 'free blacks' (2,000), a guess at the number of African-descended slaves (8,000 of 30,000), another guess at the number of Xhosa that might have been in the colony ca. 1810 (5,000), and Griqua (2,000). The resulting total is obviously an approximation.

Sources: Stephen J. Braidwood, *Black Poor and White Philanthropists: London's Blacks and the Foundation of the Sierra Leone Settlement 1786–1791* (Liverpool, 1994), pp. 22–23; Richard Elphick and Hermann Giliomee, eds., *The Shaping of South African Society, 1652–1840* (Middletown, Conn., 1988), pp. 43, 330, 379, 524; B. W. Higman, *Slave Populations of the British Caribbean 1807–1834* (hereafter *Slave Populations*) (Baltimore, 1984), p. 77;

family structures, social relations, cultural development, and political experiences. Many strands and some common threads fashioned the black experience.

A survey of the black population at the beginning, middle, and end of the long eighteenth century highlights the changing distribution of blacks throughout the Empire. In 1680 almost nine out of ten blacks lived in the Caribbean and half resided on the small island of Barbados. By contrast, the black population of Britain's North American colonies was extremely small; the mainland was predominantly white. Seventy years later blacks were much more widely dispersed. Jamaica had surpassed Barbados as the colony with the largest black population. Most of the Empire's blacks still lived in the Caribbean, but now the region only accounted for just over half of British blacks. What had changed was the enormous increase of blacks in North America, particularly in the Chesapeake. In 1750 four of every ten blacks in the Empire lived on the mainland. Another sixty years later the Caribbean was once again the centre of black life. The loss of the thirteen mainland colonies meant that hardly any British blacks lived in the remaining North American colonies. Within the Caribbean, Jamaica's black population had tripled, but most striking was the enormous increase of blacks in the new sugar colonies. In 1810 one-and-a-half times more blacks lived in the 'new' than in the 'old' West Indian colonies. The other change, although involving smaller numbers, was no less dramatic and even more portentous. In 1810 100,000 blacks lived under British jurisdiction where essentially none had before: either on the African continent—at the two major beach-heads of Sierra Leone and the Cape respectively—or on the western Indian Ocean island of Mauritius. By 1810 a few blacks had even been transported to Australia. The westward thrust of British slavery had now taken an eastward tack (see Table 4.1).

John J. McCusker, *The Rum Trade and the Balance of Payments of the Thirteen Continental Colonies, 1650–1775* 2 vols. (New York, 1989), I, pp. 548–712; John J. McCusker and Russell R. Menard, *The Economy of British America, 1607–1789* (Chapel Hill, NC, 1985), pp. 103, 136, 153, 203; Cyril Outerbridge Packwood, *Chained on the Rock: Slavery in Bermuda* (New York, 1975), p. 81; Walter Rodney, *A History of the Upper Guinea Coast, 1545–1800* (Oxford, 1970), p. 216; James W. St. G. Walker, *The Black Loyalists: The Search for a Promised Land in Nova Scotia and Sierra Leone 1783–1870* (New York, 1976), pp. 32, 40, 128; Robert V. Wells, *The Population of the British Colonies in America before 1776: A Survey of Census Data* (Princeton, NJ, 1975), p. 173; Robin W. Winks, *The Blacks in Canada: A History* (New Haven, 1971), pp. 9, 33, 34–45, 37–38, 45; Nigel Worden, 'Diverging Histories: Slavery and its Aftermath in the Cape Colony and Mauritius', *South African Historical Journal*, XXVII (1992), pp. 3–25.

The demographic experience of blacks in the British Empire varied most crucially between those populations that grew by natural increase, that is, by births exceeding deaths, and those that grew only by imports. The great success story was the North American mainland where, by 1720, the annual rate of natural increase of the slave population was greater than the annual increase due to importations. Virginia's black population grew naturally much earlier than South Carolina's, and some northern towns such as Philadelphia contained black populations that failed to reproduce, but overall the mainland slave population from the 1720s onward grew faster from natural increase than contemporary European populations. By contrast, throughout most of the British Caribbean, slave populations registered high rates of natural decrease. Had it not been for the swelling numbers of Africans imported into the region, island populations would have declined. By 1750 the British Caribbean had imported almost 800,000 Africans, but deaths had so far exceeded births that the slave population then stood at less than 300,000. Only slave populations in marginal colonies such as the Bahamas were able to increase naturally during the eighteenth century, although the Barbadian slave population was close to doing the same by the end of the century. The small Maroon population of Jamaica was another exception, as it grew by natural increase after 1750. The small black populations scattered throughout the rest of the Empire exhibited less severe variations of the general Caribbean pattern: the small black population of Britain, living mostly in towns and heavily male in composition, probably failed to grow by natural increase; and the black populations in the castles and later colonies in Africa were also subject to heavy mortality.

The reasons why the Caribbean was a graveyard for slaves and the mainland a breeding ground are difficult to disentangle. The Caribbean slave population's general inability to grow naturally has usually been attributed to high mortality, not low fertility. In early nineteenth-century Jamaica and Trinidad, for example, slave fertility was not unusually low but slave mortality was exceptionally high. But when the demographic performance of Caribbean slaves is compared to that of their North American counterparts, the critical difference seems to be fertility. Thus, in a comparison of the Jamaican and North American slave population in the early nineteenth century, mortality rates were similar but the fertility of mainland slaves was about 80 per cent higher. In a comparative context, a modest birth rate seems the key to the demographic failure of Caribbean slaves.

A variety of forces shaped these fertility and mortality rates. Perhaps the most important was the work environment. The onerous labour of sugar plantations explains why about half British West Indian slave women never bore a child in the mid-eighteenth century, why those women who did bear children suffered from infertility by their mid-thirties, and why death rates were much lower on all other types of holdings. Wherever slaves were not engaged in sugar production, their chances of living and reproducing were better. Closely related to work demands was the number of Africans and creoles in a population. The higher the labour demand, generally the more Africans were imported. African-born slaves experienced higher age-specific mortality rates and lower fertility rates than creoles born in the colony. Africans lost valuable child-bearing years in their transfer to the New World, often had difficulty in finding mates, may have been reluctant to bear children, and generally breast-fed for quite long periods, which depressed fertility. Also related to the intensity of a sugar economy was nutrition. Slaves engaged in sugar cultivation experienced seasonal hard times when provisions were in short supply. Menarche occurred one to two years later among Caribbean than North American slave women. Deficient in protein and low on fat content, the Caribbean slave diet delayed women's sexual maturity, disrupted menstrual function, and hastened the onset of menopause. Finally, the relative fragility of family life affected fertility. Although a significant minority of the Caribbean slave population did succeed in establishing conjugal ties, the nuclear family was weaker in the sugar islands than among the slaves of North America. Furthermore, white men on the mainland were less likely than in the Caribbean to engage in miscegenation because of the readier availability of white women. The higher the proportion of slave children fathered by whites, the weaker was the nuclear family and the lower the birth rate.[2]

The dominant economic experience of most blacks in the British Empire was work on a sugar plantation. Not until the factory system in Europe was it possible to regiment and discipline workers like the slave gangs on sugar

[2] Stanley Engerman and B. W. Higman, 'The Demographic Structure of the Caribbean Slave Societies in the Eighteenth and Nineteenth Centuries', in Franklin W. Knight ed., *UNESCO General History of the Caribbean*, Vol. III, *The Slave Societies of the Caribbean* (London, 1997), pp. 45–104; Robert William Fogel, *Without Consent or Contract: The Rise and Fall of American Slavery* (New York, 1989); Higman, *Slave Populations;* Allan Kulikoff, *Tobacco and Slaves: The Development of Southern Cultures in the Chesapeake, 1680–1800* (Chapel Hill, NC, 1986); and J. R. Ward, *British West Indian Slavery, 1750–1834: The Process of Amelioration* (Oxford, 1988).

estates, where the working conditions were more severe than for any other crop. In the late seventeenth-and eighteenth-century Caribbean, about 90 per cent of all slaves worked—probably one of the highest labour participation rates anywhere in the world. Children under the age of 6 and a few aged and invalids were the only people exempt from labour. Furthermore, few other regions of the world were more exclusively committed to a single economic activity than was the Caribbean. Some islands were little more than one vast sugar plantation. By the early nineteenth century nine in ten slave workers in Nevis, Montserrat, and Tobago toiled on sugar estates. In general, sugar became more important over time, displacing alternative export crops such as tobacco, indigo, and cotton. To be sure, coffee became an important secondary crop on some British Caribbean islands by the late eighteenth century, but the overall trend in most places (especially when viewed over a 'long' eighteenth century) was not away from, but towards, sugar monoculture. The major exception to this generalization was Britain's largest sugar island, which was always diversified and became somewhat more so over time. In the late eighteenth century the proportion of Jamaica's slaves on sugar estates was about 60 per cent and declining.

Although sugar was the greatest of the slave crops, many Caribbean slaves worked at other activities. A few British Caribbean territories—the so-called marginal colonies—grew no sugar. In Belize most slaves were woodcutters; in the Cayman Islands, Anguilla, and Barbuda, a majority of slaves lived on small diversified agricultural holdings; and on the Bahamas cotton cultivation was important for some decades, and fishing and shipping occupied a significant minority of slaves. Even in a monocultural economy like that of Barbados, about one in ten slaves produced cotton, provisions, ginger, arrowroot, and aloes. Livestock ranching was important on Jamaica, where specialized pens emerged. But the major secondary, and in some cases primary, crop at least by the second half of the eighteenth century was coffee, which employed a sizeable number of slaves on Jamaica, Dominica, St Vincent, Grenada, St Lucia, Trinidad, and Demerara-Essequibo, and Berbice. Coffee plantations tended to be more diverse and smaller than sugar estates, provided less occupational diversity, and because of their highland locations were more isolated. The single most important advantage possessed by slaves on coffee, cotton, cocoa, pimento, or provisions plantations was a less arduous work regime than sugar estate slaves.

On the mainland there was never the same concentration on one crop nor quite the same labour participation rate as on the islands. In the early eighteenth century there was a noticeable diversity in slave labour in British North America: in the north most slaves farmed or were domestics; in the Chesapeake most slaves cultivated tobacco, but also tended corn and raised livestock; and in the lowcountry, they acted as graziers, cut wood, and engaged in a whole array of pioneering activities. By the 1730s tobacco and rice occupied about four out of ten of the mainland's hands, but still the majority were employed in general farming, in domestic service, in crafts, or in other non-farm work. Not until the 1760s did about half of the mainland's slaves grow the three main staples—tobacco, rice, and indigo—but even then wheat farming was occupying the time of more and more slaves in the Chesapeake. As the eighteenth century proceeded, and children and the elderly constituted an ever higher proportion of the mainland slave population, the labour participation rate fell. By the time of the Revolution about 80 per cent of British North America's slaves were active in the labour force.

In other parts of the Empire, where slavery was more marginal than in the plantations of the Caribbean and North America, the work of blacks was far more wide-ranging. In Britain most blacks, even though slaves, occupied a position intermediate between chattel slavery and the domestic service of white servants. Most were household servants, working as pages, valets, footmen, coachmen, cooks, and maids. A significant minority were sailors, some plied a trade or worked as agricultural labourers. A few even gained employment as circus artists, singers, actors, musicians, boxers, prostitutes, as well as bizarre freaks at travelling shows. In late eighteenth-century Canada blacks worked as millwrights, blacksmiths, sawyers, caulkers, coopers; a few were printers; others carved gates and fences, drove carriages, and went to sea. In the forts and castles of Africa the *grumetes* or local slaves were often skilled and earned wages, and skilled canoemen and fishermen who were free also worked for the British; in Sierra Leone the black settlers turned to trade to survive; and in the Cape Colony most blacks were either urban domestics, pastoralists, arable farmers, or worked in the burgeoning early nineteenth-century vineyards.

Even on the plantations many slaves escaped field labour because they practised a trade, supervised other slaves, or worked in domestic capacities. In the late seventeenth and early eighteenth centuries slaves gradually replaced whites as skilled workers, as overseers, and as house servants.

The extent of the replacement depended on the type of crop, black-white ratio, and size of slave-holding. It was therefore most complete in a heavily black, large plantation, sugar colony like Jamaica and least complete in a predominantly white, small plantation, tobacco colony like Virginia. Mature slave societies generally distributed their employed slaves in the following rough proportions: 70–85 per cent field-hands; 10–20 per cent in skilled, semi-skilled, and supervisorial positions; and about 5–10 per cent in domestic service. These proportions varied considerably from place to place. Sugar plantations, for example, often had twice as many skilled personnel but only half as many domestics as did coffee or cotton plantations. On the mainland, opportunities for skilled work were about one-and-a-half times greater in the low-country than in the Chesapeake. Individuals were allocated jobs according to gender, age, colour, strength, and birthplace. Men dominated skilled trades, and women generally came to dominate field gangs; age determined when children entered the work-force, when they progressed from one gang to another, when field-hands became drivers, and when field-hands were pensioned off as watch-men; slaves of colour were often allocated to domestic work or, in the case of men, to skilled trades; drivers were taller and often stronger than the men and women who laboured in the gangs; creoles were more likely to fill craft slots than Africans, and some African ethnic groups had greater success in avoiding field work than others.

Those slaves in plantation societies who lived in towns and cities also escaped field labour. By the late eighteenth century the percentage of slaves living in urban places ranged from 5 per cent in most North American colonies to 10 per cent in most British Caribbean territories. Unlike most plantation slaves, urban slaves were often outnumbered by whites and freed people, lived on extremely small units, and under the close watch of a resident master who was often female. Within the urban slave population women usually outnumbered men, and coloured slaves were often prominent, as, more surprisingly, were Africans. Most urban slaves worked as domestics, but hawkers, higglers (many of whom were women), and transport workers were far more numerous in town than countryside, and roughly twice as many skilled tradespeople, fishermen, and general labourers lived in urban than in rural settings.

Slaves not only worked for their masters but also for themselves. This ability, however, varied greatly. It was probably most extensive on marginal islands like Barbuda and Great Exuma in the Bahamas, where slaves were virtual peasants, farming extensive provision grounds, owning much livestock, and spending a good deal of time hunting and fishing. Somewhat less advantaged were those slaves who had access to large provision grounds and owned livestock on the larger sugar islands like Jamaica and St Vincent. Even less advantaged were those low-country slaves on the North American mainland who worked by task and had to finish their jobs before being able to raise stock and tend crops on their own grounds. The ability to work for one's self was least extensive on small islands like Antigua and Barbados, in mainland areas like the Chesapeake, or in a diversified farming colony like the Cape, where slaves had little time to themselves and were permitted only garden plots. The impact of the slaves' economy was double-edged. The drawbacks were the lack of time slaves often had to tend their provision grounds, the distance separating slave huts from outlying grounds, the pressures on the aged, infirm, and young slaves, the extra burdens that provision grounds entailed, the greater ill health, lower life expectancy, and lower fertility that usually accompanied provision ground rather than ration systems. The benefits were the variety of the slaves' horticultural repertoires, the material benefits that accrued to slaves from selling and bartering their produce, the increased average size of provision grounds in many places over time, and the firm foundation that independent production gave to the slaves' domestic, religious, and community life.[3]

No longer can it be argued that the family was unthinkable or that the nuclear unit was unknown to most British American slaves. Slavery obviously subjected slaves' familial aspirations to enormous stress, often to breaking point: owners generally recognized only the mother-child tie, bought mostly men who then had difficulty finding wives, separated slave families by sale and transfer, and committed their own sexual assaults on slave women. Yet an emphasis on the instability, promiscuity, casual mating, disorganization, or near anarchy of slave family life is over-drawn. Historians now emphasize the resilience of slave families, the strength of kinship bonds, and the depth of parent-child affection. Nevertheless, it must be admitted that this more positive view of slave family life rests on fragmentary evidence; that much more is known of the structure of slave families than the quality of family relations; and that the information is invariably cross-sectional, providing snapshots of slave families at a point in time, rather than the serial

[3] Ira Berlin and Philip D. Morgan, eds., *Cultivation and Culture: Labor and the Shaping of Slave Life in the Americas* (Charlottesville, Va., 1993).

life-cycles of slave families. In short, much is unknown about slave family life, and it is best to emphasize the formidable obstacles facing slaves as they struggled to create and then maintain families.

The possibilities for family life varied enormously over time. Wherever Africans were in the majority, family life was extremely tenuous. In slave populations dominated by Africans, about a half or more lived with friends or other solitaries, not relatives. Nevertheless, Africans often practised a form of 'fictive kinship' particularly toward shipmates, who looked upon each others' children as their own. In early nineteenth-century Trinidad the fortunate Africans who found mates generally found other Africans, but not often from their own ethnic group or even region. Ethnic identity therefore probably dissolved rapidly. When Africans formed families they tended to be nuclear in form. In fact, in early nineteenth-century Trinidad Africans were more likely to be grouped in nuclear families than creoles. Africans probably saw the two-parent family form as the essential building-block of extended or polygamous family types rooted in lineage and locality. As the creole population grew, the larger plantations often became vast kinship networks. The typical slave dwelling comprised a man, woman, and her children, but kinship networks expanded as cross-plantation mating became common, so that many creoles tended to live in mother-children units (with a mate living at a nearby plantation) or in extended units. Family life often centred less on the household or nuclear family than on networks of relationships involving various relatives and spouses.

By the end of the eighteenth century a wide spectrum of family possibilities existed among blacks in North America and the Caribbean. The family, and particularly the nuclear family, was generally stronger among mainland than island slaves. The creolization of the slave population, which occurred earlier in North America than anywhere else, meant that slaves could find partners more readily and have kin around them. It is hard to imagine many slaves in the British Empire matching the experience of one Chesapeake woman who, as early as the 1770s, lived on a quarter surrounded by her five children, nineteen grandchildren, nine great-grandchildren, four children-in-law, and three grandchildren's spouses. She lived enmeshed in one large kinship web. Yet the advantages of mainland slaves should not be exaggerated. Because the presence of slave families generally increased with plantation size, there were likely to be more families on the sugar islands. Furthermore, the prospects of sale and transfer were undoubtedly less on the islands than on the mainland, where a rapidly expanding frontier led to many family disruptions.[4]

In other parts of the Empire the black familial experience was even more varied. In Britain, for example, black men so outnumbered black women that they had to marry white women if they wanted to form families. Many did, as was most graphically displayed when seventy white women, most of them wives to black men, accompanied the so-called Black Poor to Sierra Leone in 1787. In the castles and forts dotted along the African coast the shoe was on the other foot, and many white men took black women as their wives. The most complex permutations occurred along the Cape frontier.[5]

The family was the key social institution formed by blacks, but it of course cannot be divorced from the broader social setting. Relations in slave societies can be divided into those social forms that regulated the encounters between the free and the unfree, and those that linked and divided slaves. In the highly polarized world of a slave society, standardized patterns of interaction and carefully defined codes of behaviour arose quickly to govern relations both between whites and blacks and among blacks themselves.

The law was one vital means of institutionalizing interactions between the free and unfree. The British Caribbean territories, with Barbados the prototype, were the first to develop elaborate slave codes; the mainland colonies, with South Carolina taking the lead, began to follow suit in the late seventeenth and more commonly early eighteenth centuries. Police regulations lay at the heart of the slave system. Thus, common features of the black codes were the prohibition and suppression of the unauthorized movement of slaves, the large congregation of slaves, the possession of guns and other weapons, the sounding of horns and drums, and the practice of secret rituals. The punishment for actual or threatened violence against whites was severe. Special slave-trial courts were established in most colonies to provide summary and expeditious 'justice'. Within the Caribbean, Jamaica's penal code was the most savage; South Carolina's was the most severe on the continent.

[4] Michael Craton and Gail Saunders, *Islanders in the Stream: A History of the Bahamian People*, Vol. I, *From Aboriginal Times to the End of Slavery* (Athens, Ga., 1992), pp. 318–29; B. W. Higman, *Slave Population and Economy in Jamaica, 1807–1834* (Cambridge, 1976), pp. 156–75 and Highman, *Slave Populations*, pp. 364–77; Kulikoff, *Tobacco and Slaves*, pp. 352–80; Morgan, *Slave Counterpoint*, chap. 10.

[5] Braidwood, *Black Poor and White Philanthropists*, pp. 280–88; Margaret Priestley, *West African Trade and Coast Society: A Family Study* (London, 1969); Elphick and Giliomee, eds., *Shaping of South African Society*, pp. 201–02, 358–84, 454–60.

In the late eighteenth and early nineteenth centuries the legislation tended to become a little less terroristic. The murder of a slave by a white man, for example, generally became a crime, but ameliorative legislation was always limited by the sheer fact of planter power.[6]

Furthermore, in all colonies custom was as important as law in shaping the black experience. The way in which slave-owners ruled their slaves varied from person to person, and from society to society, but certain common features held true. One of the most important, a defining characteristic of slavery, was the highly personal mechanisms of coercion; the whip, rather than resort to law, was the institution's indispensable and ubiquitous instrument. On the plantation or in the household, the master and his delegates used a variety of methods of physical coercion without recourse to, and usually unchecked by, any external authority. Brutality and sadism existed everywhere, but the Caribbean and newly settled areas, where masters felt most isolated and insecure, gained the worst reputations. On the mainland, lowcountry masters were thought to be more callous than their Chesapeake counterparts. Of other British territories, the Cape Colony was noted for its cruelty, symbolized by the widely used rhinoceros-hide *sjambok*. But the use or threat of force faced blacks everywhere. A black woman in late eighteenth-century Shelburne, Nova Scotia—hardly a place that needed to terrorize blacks—suffered a total of 350 lashes for two acts of petty larceny.[7]

Masters hoped that rewards would offset punishments. Over time, a number of allowances and privileges became entrenched in both custom and even law. Granting slaves half-days or full days to tend their provision plots became commonplace in some societies. Allowing slaves to attend extraordinary social functions such as a neighbourhood funeral became a standard practice. Masters generally allowed slaves time off during the Christian holidays. Christmas, in particular, became a time for permissiveness and even social inversion in some slave societies—a black Saturnalia. Special gratuities became routine: an extra allowance of food here, some tobacco there, a ration of rum for completing the harvest, cash payments for Sunday work. Favours and indulgences were disproportionately allocated: concubines, domestics, drivers, and tradesmen were the primary benefici-

[6] Elsa V. Goveia, *The West Indian Slave Laws of the Eighteenth Century* (Kingston, Jamaica, 1970); William M. Wiececk, 'The Statutory Law of Slavery and Race in the Thirteen Mainland Colonies of British America', *William and Mary Quarterly* (hereafter *WMQ*), Third Series, XXXIV (1977), pp. 258–80.

[7] Walker, *Black Loyalists*, p. 56.

aries. Incentives tended to be most elaborate where plantations were large; the privileges of position within a specialized labour force based on rank and seniority generally did not apply to small-scale farms, common in the northern colonies of North America, parts of the Chesapeake, and the Cape colony.[8]

Although masters and slaves were locked into an intimate interdependence, blacks were not just objects of white action but subjects who regulated social relationships among themselves. A crucial distinction was geographical origin. Sometimes Africans from a particular region dominated the forced immigrants into a particular British American colony—in the 1730s three-quarters of slaves imported into South Carolina were from Angola; between 1750 and 1790 Jamaica took a disproportionate share, about 80 per cent, of slaves exported from the Gold Coast. It should be no surprise, therefore, that 'Angolans' were prominent in South Carolina's Stono Revolt of 1739 and 'Koromantis' in Tacky's Rebellion of 1760. Africans from the same coastal region or of a similar ethnic background sometimes absconded together. Nevertheless, for most of the time ethnic heterogeneity characterized the provenance of any British American slave population. Africans from one background had to find ways to communicate and deal with other Africans. Over time, Africans increasingly ran away with members of other ethnic groups, and intermarried with one another. An African identity among blacks emerged from their involuntary and voluntary associations in America.[9]

Creoles and Africans did not always get along. In the early years of almost all settlements, often extending many decades in most Caribbean territories, the numerically superior Africans often mocked creoles. But as creoles grew more populous, the targets of derision tended to shift. Self-confident creoles

[8] Richard Pares, *A West-India Fortune* (London, 1950), pp. 131–32; Robert Dirks, *The Black Saturnalia: Conflict and its Ritual Expression on British West Indian Slave Plantations* (Gainesville, Fla., 1987); Higman, *Slave Populations*, pp. 202–04.

[9] Peter H. Wood, *Black Majority: Negroes in Colonial South Carolina from 1670 through the Stono Rebellion* (New York, 1974); Orlando Patterson, *The Sociology of Slavery: An Analysis of the Origins, Development and Structure of Negro Slave Society in Jamaica* (Rutherford, NJ, 1969), pp. 113–44; Philip D. Curtin, *The Atlantic Slave Trade: A Census* (Madison, Wisc., 1969), p.160; John K. Thornton, *Africa and Africans in the Making of the Atlantic World, 1400–1680* (Cambridge, 1992); Michael Mullin, *Africa in America: Slave Acculturation and Resistance in the American South and the British Caribbean, 1736–1831* (Urbana, Ill., 1992), pp. 13–74; Sidney W. Mintz and Richard Price, *The Birth of African-American Culture: An Anthropological Perspective* (1976; Boston, 1992).

often looked down on those directly from Africa, derogatively labelling the newcomers 'Salt-water Negroes' or 'Guineabirds'. Whereas newly enslaved Africans often fled in groups, creole fugitives usually absconded alone. Creoles sometimes took pity on or took advantage of Africans. In some Caribbean societies creoles took Africans into their houses and made them work on their provision grounds. Where creoles constituted a majority, they set the tone and tenor of slave life remarkably early. Africans learned the ropes from them. In the Chesapeake, for example, African newcomers adjusted remarkably quickly to their new surroundings, attributable in large part to their close association with the more numerous creoles.[10]

The emergence of a creole majority in many ways facilitated cohesiveness among slaves, but over time gradations of colour, often closely linked to occupational differentiation, divided slave communities. By 1810 coloured slaves comprised about 12 per cent of the slave populations in the older sugar islands such as Barbados, Jamaica, and the Leeward Islands, 10 per cent in the marginal colonies, and 8 per cent or less in the newer sugar colonies. On the mainland, 8 per cent of Maryland's slaves in 1755 were listed as mulattoes and, by all accounts, mulattoes then formed a higher proportion of the black population in the Chesapeake than in the low-country. Although mainland planters tended to think in terms of just white and black and island planters in terms of white, coloured, and black, slaves of mixed race were often privileged in both regions. To be sure, island planters would almost never work mulattoes in the field, whereas mainland planters often did, but many domestics and skilled slaves in both places were coloured. The Hemings family, who arrived at Thomas Jefferson's Monticello in 1774, serve as a classic example of the privilege that came from mulatto status: they assumed all the primary roles in the household. The most privileged mulatto group in the British Empire were the mixed-race traders—the Caulkers, Clevelands, Tuckers, Rogers, and Brews—who rose to prominence on the African coast. They were the children of white men and their African common-law wives.[11]

[10] Edward Brathwaite, *The Development of Creole Society in Jamaica, 1770–1820* (Oxford, 1971), pp. 164–66; Gerald W. Mullin, *Flight and Rebellion: Slave Resistance in Eighteenth-Century Virginia* (New York, 1972), pp. 34–123.

[11] Higman, *Slave Populations*, pp. 147–57; Winthrop D. Jordan, 'American Chiaroscuro: The Status and Definition of Mulattoes in the British Colonies', *WMQ*, Third Series, XIX (1962), pp. 183–200; Joel Williamson, *New People: Miscegenation and Mulattoes in the United States* (New York, 1980); Lucia C, Stanton, ' "Those Who Labor For My Happiness": Thomas Jefferson and

Coloured slaves were the most likely of any to be freed, thereby producing the greatest divide among blacks and the slave system's greatest anomaly, a third party in a structure built for two. Freed persons often signalled their freedom by assuming a new name, by changing location, by putting their families on a more secure footing, by creating associations to strengthen community life, by actively buying and selling property, even slaves, and resorting to courts to protect their hard-won gains. But throughout the eighteenth century freed persons were too few to separate themselves markedly from slaves, and many of their closest contacts were still with slaves. In the 1770s free coloureds and blacks were just 2 per cent of the black populations of Jamaica and Virginia, less than 1 per cent of Barbados's and South Carolina's. As the free black population grew the chances for a separate identity expanded, but it was an uneven process. Thus, by 1810 one in four blacks in Belize, one in five in Trinidad, one in ten in Dominica and the Bahamas, one in twelve in Jamaica, one in twenty-eight in British Guiana, and one in thirty-three in Barbados were free. By 1810, then, in Belize and Trinidad a three-tiered caste system had arisen, with free blacks and coloureds playing a buffer role between white masters and black slaves; in Barbados and British Guiana most notably, free blacks and coloureds were still a tiny minority and the society was predominantly two-tiered. There were also gradations among freed persons, with the free coloured identifying most closely with whites and free blacks more oriented toward black slaves.[12]

Through various forms of social interaction, blacks in the British Empire created cultures and subcultures, the most fundamental building block of which was a language. The array of languages spoken by blacks was enormous. Along the belt of territories that supplied slaves to British America, Africans spoke about 1,000 languages; in late eighteenth-century British Africa blacks employed modes of communication that ranged from the

His Slaves', in Peter S. Onuf, ed., *Jeffersonian Legacies* (Charlottesville, Va., 1993), pp. 147–80; Walter Rodney, *A History of the Upper Guinea Coast, 1545–1800* (Oxford, 1970), pp. 200–22; Priestley, *West African Trade.*

[12] Ira Berlin, *Slaves without Masters: The Free Negro in the Antebellum South* (New York, 1974), pp. 3–50; David W. Cohen and Jack P. Greene, eds., *Neither Slave nor Free: The Freedman of African Descent in the Slave Societies of the New World* (Baltimore, 1972); Higrnan, *Slave Populations,* pp. 76, 107–09, 112; Arnold A. Sio, 'Marginality and Free Colored Identity in Caribbean Slave Society', *Slavery and Abolition,* VIII (1987), pp. 166–82; Gad J. Heuman, *Between Black and White: Race, Politics and the Free Coloreds in Jamaica, 1792–1865* (Westport, Conn., 1981).

tonal subtleties of Wolof to the implosive consonants or 'clicks' of the Khoisan. In time many African cultural brokers emerged who spoke more than one African language and an English-based creole. In the Cape Colony there were in fact two lingua franca: creolized Portuguese and an evolving form of Dutch, developed in the interaction between settlers, Khoisan, and slaves, which became Afrikaans. Some African languages or forms of them migrated to the New World. In the interior of Jamaica the Trelawny Maroons, while employing English, also held to a form of their Akan language, making use of their own linguistic brokers. In those plantation regions where Africans and blacks were most numerous some Africans for a time would be able to continue speaking their native languages, although they would also more than likely speak a pidgin and, over time, creole languages, perhaps even Standard English. In the towns, among privileged rural slaves, and in societies where Africans and blacks were not numerous, most blacks probably spoke a language undergoing rapid de-creolization, and some no doubt spoke Standard English. Small numbers of slaves spoke predominantly German, as in parts of Pennsylvania; Dutch, as in New York; French, as in Quebec, and the many Caribbean islands captured by the British; and even Gaelic, as in the North Carolina highlands. Without a doubt, blacks were the most linguistically polyglot and proficient of any ethnic group in the British Empire.

In spite of the bewildering variety, the norm was that most blacks in the British Empire spoke a creole language, which derived much of its vocabulary from English, but the phonology and syntax of which owed much to a prior West African creole or pidgin, and beyond that, to various African languages. In other words, Africans grafted a European vocabulary on to West African grammatical structures that had much in common. Although these Atlantic creole languages shared many structural features attributable to the substratum of African languages, they were separate languages. Blacks in the British Empire spoke at least twenty-five identifiable creoles: eighteen English-based (from Bahamian to Krio, from Belizan to Guyanese, from Caymanian to Gullah); two Dutch-based (Berbice and Afrikaans); and four French-based (Lesser Antillean in Dominica and St Lucia, Grenadan, Trinidadian, and Mauritian). Some creoles were profoundly influenced by various African languages. Everyday words in Jamaican creole, for example, can be traced to specific African languages, most particularly Twi. Most words in regular use among Gullah speakers in South Carolina derived from Angola, Senegambia, and Sierra Leone, although languages from southern Nigeria and the Gold Coast formed its central syntactic core. On the other hand, on most of the mainland and an island like Barbados where whites were relatively numerous, the African influence on the creole language was much reduced. Moreover, in almost all the mainland territories and on islands such as Barbados and the Caymans, the forces propelling rapid de-creolization were powerful. By the late eighteenth century most slaves in the Chesapeake region—the largest congregation of slaves on the mainland—probably spoke a non-standard English dialect.[13]

In much the same way as a broad spectrum of linguistic forms existed among blacks, a continuous scale of musical expression, ranging in inspiration from Europe to Africa, also unfolded. The variety began in Africa where, for example, peoples of a large section of Dahomey eschewed harmony in their music, while the Ashanti in the neighbouring Gold Coast employed at least two-part and frequently three-and four-part harmony for almost all their music. The variety expanded out of Africa. At one extreme stood George Augustus Polgreen Bridgetower, the virtuoso violinist for whom Beethoven composed the *Kreutzer* Sonata. Brought to England from the European continent by his African father, the 10-year-old gave recitals in the salons of Brighton, Bath, and London. Of lesser renown, but just as popular, were those blacks who became integral members of European military bands. Some black musicians became street players: Billy Waters, for example, a one-legged black ex-navy man, claimed to earn an honest living by the scraping of catgut on London streets. At the other extreme were Africans in the plantation colonies who danced their ethnic dances to their own homeland musical accompaniments—whether banjos, balafos, harps, lutes, gourd rattles, or various kinds of drums. In the Caribbean musical styles were ethnically identifiable, but so-called 'Angolan' and 'Koromanti' music already involved syncretism. Everywhere, blacks invented new music.

Black music developed in ways akin to the formation of creole languages. A basic musical grammar, as it were, with an emphasis on the importance of music and dance in everyday life and the role of rhythm and percussion in musical style, survived the middle passage. Even complex musical instruments made the crossing, although more notable is how slaves adapted traditional instruments, invented new ones, and borrowed Euro-American

[13] Mervyn C. Alleyne, *Comparative Afro-American: An Historical–Comparative Study of English-Based Afro-American Dialects of the New World* (Ann Arbor, 1980); John A. Holm, *Pidgins and Creoles*, 2 vols. (Cambridge, 1988).

ones. These adaptations, inventions, and borrowings were interpreted and reinterpreted according to deep-level aesthetic principles drawn from different African musical traditions. Blacks retained the inner meanings of traditional modes of behaviour while adopting new outer forms. In musical terms, the key elements of the inner structure were complex rhythms, percussive qualities, syncopation, and antiphonal patterns.[14]

Black religious expression also spanned a large continuum. There were major differences in the ways in which African societies explained evil, in the role allocated to a creator divinity, in the absence or presence of prophetism or spirit possession. Some slaves, particularly from the Upper Guinea coast, were Muslim; some from Kongo had been exposed to Catholicism; in most other places a variety of traditional religions existed. Nevertheless, an extraordinary diversity of religious forms coexisted with certain widely shared basic principles. Most eighteenth-century Africans, for example, drew no neat distinction between the sacred and the profane, shared assumptions about the nature of causality, believed in both a High God and many lesser gods as personifications of the forces of nature and of destiny, thought the dead played an active role in the lives of the living, and saw a close relationship between social conflict and illness or misfortune. In the New World there was enormous variety in black religion: Muslim slaves became particularly noted for the power of their magical charms; in the islands, African-style cults emerged such as Jamaican Myal; some South Carolina slaves may have fled to the Spanish because they were Catholic; and slaves embraced every form of Protestantism.[15]

Perhaps *the* major development that took place in the metaphysics of most slave communities was a shift from the benevolent lesser spirits, the unobservable personal beings so prominent in traditional African cosmologies, to sorcery, the harming of others by secretive means. Because of enforced coexistence with other African groups and because of the serious, everyday problems of dealing with harsh taskmasters, slaves turned to those spirits deemed useful in injuring other people. The most common term for sorcery

[14] Dena J. Epstein, *Sinful Tunes and Spirituals: Black Folk Music to the Civil War* (Urbana, Ill., 1977); Kenneth M. Bilby, 'The Caribbean as a Musical Region', in Sidney W. Mintz and Sally Price, eds., *Caribbean Contours* (Baltimore, 1985), pp. 181–218; Richard Cullen Rath, 'African Music in Seventeenth-Century Jamaica: Cultural Transit and Transmission', *WMQ*, Third Series, L (1993), pp. 700–26.

[15] Albert J. Raboteau, *Slave Religion: The 'Invisible Institution' in the Antebellum South* (New York, 1978); Jon Butler, *Awash in a Sea of Faith: Christianizing the American People* (Cambridge, Mass., 1990), pp. 129–63.

was *obi* or *obia* or *obeah*, which had multiple African origins, including Efik *ubio* (a charm to cause sickness and death) and Twi *o-bayifo* (sorcerer). The term was current among both North American and Caribbean slaves, although on the mainland 'conjuring' and 'conjurer' were more common. While the boundary between sorcery, folk medicine, and divination was porous, the dominant trend was a powerful concentration on those means for injuring people.[16]

The religious world view of early Anglo-American slaves was primarily magical, not Christian. In general, Anglican ministers were not zealous proselytizers of black slaves. The few who were sympathetic to the slaves' needs faced almost insurmountable odds, ranging from the vast extent of many parishes to the institutional weakness of their own church. But the most formidable barrier to the Christianization of blacks was the resistance posed by masters and slaves alike. At any time throughout the eighteenth century there were never more than a few Christian blacks on the Society for the Propagation of the Gospel's own trust estate in Barbados where successive catechists ministered. Even Philip Quaque, born on the Gold Coast in 1741, sent to England, where he was the first African ordained by the Church of England, and returned home in 1766 as a missionary to his own people, had little success over the succeeding half-century when confronted by a deeply entrenched Akan religion. Nevertheless, traditional religious beliefs were not static. Faced with the interpretative challenge of large-scale social change, many blacks in both Africa and America developed a more elaborate and active role for a supreme being, the formerly otiose High God of many traditional cosmologies. When blacks accepted Christianity or Islam, it often owed as much to the evolution of traditional religious beliefs as to the activities of missionaries.[17]

This syncretic process can help explain how and why blacks infused elements of their traditional religion into Christianity. They did not just accept Christianity wholesale but did so selectively. Nowhere is this better displayed than in beliefs about the role of the dead among the living. For

[16] Patterson, *Sociology of Slavery*, pp. 182–206; Mullin, *Africa in America*, pp. 175–86; Thomton, *Africa and Africans*, pp. 235–71.

[17] J. Harry Bennett, *Bondsmen and Bishops: Slavery and Apprenticeship on the Codrington Plantations of Barbados, 1710–1838* (Berkeley and Los Angeles, 1958), pp. 75–87; Margaret Priestley, 'Philip Quaque of Cape Coast', in Philip D. Curtin, ed., *Africa Remembered: Narratives by West Africans from the Era of the Slave Trade* (Madison, 1967), pp. 99–139; Robin Horton, 'African Conversion', *Africa*, XLI (1971), pp. 85–108 and 'On the Rationality of African Conversion', ibid., XLV (1975), pp. 219–35 and 373–99.

Africans, the funeral was the true climax of life. In Anglo-America many slaves thought death brought a return to Africa. Their common funeral practices included the accompaniment of drumming, dance, and song; feasting and drinking, with liquor and food thrown into the grave; treasured possessions buried with the corpse; broken crockery, upturned bottles, and seashells marking black graves.[18]

Highly expressive funeral practices were not far removed from the typical behaviour of eighteenth-century evangelicals, and it was this form of Christianity that began to appeal to blacks from about mid-century onward. Evangelical Christianity spread at different rates and in different forms. In South Carolina and Georgia the first inroads were made in the late 1730s by John Wesley and George Whitefield; in Virginia in the 1750s by Presbyterians, and in the 1760s by New Light Baptists; in Jamaica by Moravians in 1754; in Antigua by Moravians in 1756, and by Methodists in the 1760s; and in the Cape by Wesleyan missionaries who joined Moravians from 1798 onward. There were many black evangelicals; by 1776 perhaps a third of Virginia's Baptists were black; by 1790 a quarter of Nova Scotia's Methodists were black; by 1800 28 per cent of the Leewards Islands' 83,000 slaves had been converted by Moravian, Methodist, and Anglican missionaries; and between 1795 and 1815 the intensity of the coverts' zeal among thousands of Khoisan was striking. The evangelical appeal lay in a message of universal salvation through divine grace, an intensity of feeling and physical expressiveness, and a church structure that was quite egalitarian.[19]

Creating a distinctive language, music, and religion—in short, a culture—had political implications, but of profound ambivalence. On the one hand, it was an act of resistance, perhaps the greatest act of resistance accomplished by blacks in the British Empire. By carving out some independence for

[18] Brathwaite, *Development of Creole Society*, pp. 216–18; Jerome S. Handler and Frederick W. Lange, *Plantation Slavery in Barbados: An Archaeological and Historical Investigation* (Cambridge, Mass., 1978), pp. 171–215; Robert Farris Thompson, *Flash of the Spirit: African and Africo-American Art and Philosophy* (New York, 1983).

[19] Harvey H. Jackson, 'Hugh Bryan and the Evangelical Movement in Colonial Soutlt Carolina', *WMQ*, Third Series, XLIII (1986), pp. 594–614; Mechal Sobel, *The World They Made Together: Black and White Values in Eighteenth-Century Virginia* (Princeton, 1987), pp. 178–203; Elsa V. Goveia, *Slave Society in the British Leeward Islands at the End of the Eighteenth Century* (New Haven, 1965), pp. 263–310; Mary Turner, *Slaves and Missionaries: The Disintegration of Jamaican Slave Society, 1787–1834* (Urbana, Ill., 1982); Clifton C. Crais, *White Supremacy and Black Resistance in Pre-Industrial South Africa: The Making of the Colanial Order in the Eastern Cape, 1770–1865* (Cambridge, 1992), pp. 82–84, 100–105; G. A. Rawlyk, *The Canada Fire: Radical Evangelicalism in British North America, 1775–1812* (Kingston and Montreal, 1994).

themselves, by creating something coherent and autonomous from African fragments and European influences, by forcing whites to recognize their humanity, slaves triumphed over their circumstances. They opposed the dehumanization inherent in their status and demonstrated their independent will and volition. On the other hand, their cultural creativity eased the torments of slavery, gave them a reason for living, and made them think long and hard before sacrificing everything in an attempt to overthrow the system. It thereby encouraged accommodation to the established order. This ambivalence is at the heart of the political experiences of blacks in the British Empire.

It is apparent in slave resistance. List all the plots and rebellions in chronological sequence, and slave resistance appears structurally endemic. Recall the bitter fact that the vicious system of Anglo-American slavery lasted for hundreds of years without serious challenge, and its stability seems paramount. No Anglo-American mainland region faced a large-scale slave insurrection in the eighteenth century. No white person was killed in a slave rebellion in the colonial Chesapeake. The most notable incident on the mainland was South Carolina's Stono Revolt in which about sixty slaves killed approximately twenty whites and destroyed much property, but this was small-scale and of short duration. By contrast, the islands were always more brittle, even if (until 1816) Barbadian slaves never mounted a serious slave rebellion. In 1736 Antigua endured a harrowing slave plot in which well over a hundred slaves were put to death or banished. Jamaica experienced many rebellions, none more serious than the island-wide insurrection of 1760 that resulted in the deaths of 90 whites, 400 blacks, and the exile of another 600. Just as slave rebellions varied across space, so they did over time: from events inspired by Africans to events dominated by creoles, from attempts to secure freedom to attempts to overthrow slavery, from acts of rage to forms of industrial action. Slave resistance was also more than collective violence; it encompassed flight, sabotage, and individual murders. But as has been noted, the cook who put ground glass in the master's family food had first to get the job. The slaves who plotted in the market-places had first to produce for the market. There is no simple unilinear gradient from accommodation to resistance.[20]

[20] Sidney W. Mintz, 'Toward an Afro-American History', *Cahiers d'histoire mondiale*, XIII (1971), p. 321; Edmund S. Morgan, *American Slavery, American Freedom: The Ordeal of Colonial Virginia* (New York, 1975), p. 309; Michael Craton, *Testing the Chains: Resistance to Slavery in the*

Even Maroons, the ultimate symbol of rebellion, were forced to accommodate. They emerged almost everywhere: in lowcountry swamps, on the high seas, on mountains, as in Dominica and St Vincent, even in the Australian outback in the person of John Caesar, prototypical bushranger. By far the most significant set of Maroons in the Empire established themselves in Jamaica, where at mid-century about 1,000 persons, just under 1 per cent of the slave population, lived under the jurisdiction of two bands. By 1739, when the colonial government of Jamaica recognized their free and separate existence, the Windward Maroons in the eastern mountains and the Leeward Maroons in the western interior had been waging war against whites for more than eighty years. For the most part, the post-treaty Maroons proved effective allies, tracking down slave runaways and rebels, adopting the military hierarchy of the establishment, living in an uneasy symbiosis with their white neighbours, seeking arms, tools, pots, and cloth as well as employment. The white establishment never rested secure, and in 1795 their fears were realized when the Maroons of Trelawny Town engaged in one last two-year war with government troops. When these Maroons finally surrendered, apparently on the understanding that the government would listen to their grievances, they were transported to Nova Scotia before moving on to Sierra Leone. When they arrived in their new homeland in 1800 their first action was to quell a rebellion by many of Sierra Leone's black settlers, as if to illustrate how rebellion and accommodation went hand in hand.[21]

Blacks were, in fact, found on opposite sides of most political disputes. In the early years of many settlements slaves were often used as soldiers, but as their numbers grew opposition arose to arming them. However, in emergencies—a local rebellion or a foreign invasion—slaves thought to be loyal were periodically placed under arms. Moreover, throughout the century slaves continued to be used as auxiliaries and pioneers; in the islands free blacks became an important part of the militia; during the Revolutionary War the British army raised a black unit, the Carolina Corps; and the Anglo–French War of 1793–1815 made the use of black troops imperative. In 1795 the effectiveness of black troops and the shortage of white manpower led Imperial officials to form

British West Indies (Ithaca, NY, 1982); David Barry Gaspar, *Bondmen and Rebels: A Study of Master–Slave Relations in Antigua with Implications for Colonial British America* (Baltimore, 1985).

[21] Richard Price, ed., *Maroon Societies: Rebel Slave Communities in the Americas* (1973; Baltimore, 1979); Barbara Klamon Kopytoff, 'The Maroons of Jamaica: An Ethnohistorical Study of Incomplete Politics, 1655–1905', unpublished Ph.D. dissertation, Pennsylvania, 1973; Mavis C. Campbell, *The Maroons of Jamaica, 1655–1796: A History of Resistance, Collaboration, and Betrayal* (South Hadley, Mass., 1988).

black regiments. Eventually twelve black West Indian regiments were raised, and 30,000 black regulars recruited. Their commanders were generally complimentary about their character and conduct. In Africa Britain engaged in its first war against black men (an alliance of Khoikhoi and Xhosa)—the Third Frontier War (1799–1803)—with the assistance of the so-called Hottentot Corps, founded in 1793 by the Dutch, subsequently expanded, strengthened, and ultimately renamed the Cape Regiment.[22]

The eighteenth-century black world was multi-faceted. There was a majority experience—located on plantations—where in many ways slaves suffered a similar fate. They lived short and impoverished lives, worked most of the time, created fragile families, encountered great brutality, spoke creole, developed a distinctive musical style, believed in magic, and generally accommodated themselves to the system of slavery. But this description is a monochrome caricature, not a richly coloured portrait. It fails to do justice to the variations, the subtleties, the many temporal, spatial, and status distinctions in black life. The black experience varied most fundamentally depending on the nature of population growth, the type of employment, the size of the slave-holding unit, the level of material well-being, the quality of family life, encounters with whites, patterns of interaction among blacks, the extent of cultural autonomy, and the degree of resistance and accommodation to the system. There was no single black experience in the British Empire. There was, however, a core to the experience: drawing upon some shared principles and passing through the fires of enslavement, blacks everywhere forged a new culture.

[22] Peter M. Voelz, *Slave and Soldier: The Military Impact of Blacks in the Colonial Americas* (New York, 1993); Roger Norman Buckley, *Slaves in Red Coats: The British West India Regiments, 1795–1815* (New Haven, 1979); Elphick and Giliomee, eds., *The Shaping of South African Society*, pp. 35–38, 444–47.

Select Bibliography

IRA BERLIN and PHILIP D. MORGAN, eds., *Cultivation and Culture: Labor and the Shaping of Slave Life in the Americas* (Charlottesville, Va., 1993).

ROBIN BLACKBURN, *The Making of New World Slavery: From the Baroque to the Modern 1492–1800* (London, 1997).

MICHAEL CRATON, *Testing the Chains: Resistance to Slavery in the British West Indies* (Ithaca, NY, 1982).

David Eltis, *The Rise of African Slavery in the Americas* (New York, 2000).

Leland Ferguson, *Uncommon Ground: Archaeology and Early African America, 1650–1800* (Washington, 1992).

Robert William Fogel, *Without Consent or Contract: The Rise and Fall of American Slavery* (New York, 1989).

David Barry Gaspar, *Bondmen and Rebels: A Study of Master-Slave Relations in Antigua with Implications for Colonial British America* (Baltimore, 1985).

Elsa V. Goveia, *Slave Society in the British Leeward Islands at the End of the Eighteenth Century* (New Haven, 1965).

Douglas Hall, *In Miserable Slavery: Thomas Thistlewood in Jamaica, 1750–86* (London, 1989).

Jerome S. Handler and Frederick W. Lange, *Plantation Slavery in Barbados: An Archaeological and Historical Investigation* (Cambridge, Mass., 1978).

B. W. Higman, *Slave Population and Economy in Jamaica, 1807–1834* (New York, 1976).

—— *Slave Populations of the British Caribbean, 1807–1834* (Baltimore, 1984).

Kenneth F. Kiple, *The Caribbean Slave: A Biological History* (Cambridge, 1984).

Franklin W. Knight, ed., *General History of the Caribbean, Vol. III: The Slave Societies of the Caribbean* (London, 1997).

Allan Kulikoff, *Tobacco and Slaves: The Development of Southern Cultures in the Chesapeake, 1680–1800* (Chapel Hill, NC, 1986).

Sidney W. Mintz and Richard Price, *The Birth of African-American Culture: An Anthropological Perspective* (1976; Boston, 1992).

Philip D. Morgan, *Slave Counterpoint: Black Culture in the Eighteenth-Century Chesapeake and Lowcountry* (Chapel Hill, NC, 1998).

Michael Mullin, *Africa in America: Slave Acculturation and Resistance in the American South and the British Caribbean. 1736–1831* (Urbana, Ill., 1992).

Richard B. Sheridan, *Doctors and Slaves: A Medical and Demographic History of Slavery in the British West Indies, 1680–1834* (Cambridge, 1985).

Mechal Sobel, *The World They Made Together: Black and White Values in Eighteenth-Century Virginia* (Princeton, 1987).

Mary Turner, *Slaves and Missionaries: The Disintegration of Jamaican Slave Society, 1787–1834* (Urbana, Ill., 1982).

J. R. Ward, *British West Indian Slavery, 1750–1834: The Process of Amelioration* (Oxford, 1988).

Peter H. Wood, *Black Majority: Negroes in Colonial South Carolina from 1670 Through the Stono Rebellion* (New York, 1974).

5

From Slaves to Subjects: Envisioning an Empire without Slavery, 1772–1834

CHRISTOPHER L. BROWN

Few events matter more to the history of blacks in the British Empire than their transformation from British slaves to British subjects during the first half of the nineteenth century. This is not because emancipation in 1834 ended the exploitation of black labour, nor because it inaugurated a new era of racial equality. To the contrary, in key respects, the political and social order that emerged in the sugar colonies after emancipation perpetuated the iniquities that originated in plantation slavery. Emancipation mattered to the black experience in the British Empire because it reordered relations between captive Africans, colonial élites, and the British state. It established the metropolitan government as the ultimate arbiter of social and labour relations in the colonies. By outlawing private property in persons, it severely proscribed the traditional rights and liberties of colonial employers. And for peoples of African descent, it provided, in varying degrees, independence from white control, and leverage in the colonies against the most extreme manifestations of white supremacy.

Emancipation has sometimes been characterized as an instance of British humanitarianism. And there can be no doubt that the abolitionists believed themselves to be acting in the best interests of enslaved Africans. Yet the emergence of an emancipationist ethos depended as much upon a metropolitan reconsideration of imperial interests as a deepening concern with the situation of enslaved men and women. That reassessment—and its characteristic preoccupation with the promotion of imperial power, authority, and the rule of law—conflicted with the more restricted interests of the slaveholders who, in their dominions, saw themselves as rulers not colonists, and their labourers as chattel slaves not British subjects. As early as the era of the American Revolution, a small circle of thinkers interested in imperial questions had described the ways that gradual emancipation might serve the broader end of enhancing state power; much of this chapter is concerned with the origins, character, and legacy of these ideas. It would take the pressure of events, however, especially war, and the reactions of enslaved men and women to make subjectship for blacks a compelling alternative for authorities in England.

The Problem

Of the obstacles that would face those Britons in the eighteenth century who hoped to bring the injustice of slavery or the slave trade forward for public debate, few presented greater difficulties than the customary association of slavery with imperial wealth and power. To the many with an investment in the colonial economy or concerned with Britain's standing among European rivals, an Empire without slavery was simply unthinkable. And even those inclined to denounce slavery publicly often conceded that human bondage made Atlantic commerce and overseas settlement possible. When British chroniclers of American colonization, for example, reflected during the 1770s on the failed experiment to prohibit slavery in the infant colony of Georgia several decades earlier, they emphasized the folly of attempting to produce export crops without slaves. However humane the motives, William Russell maintained, banning slavery in the fledgling colony was 'a species of oppression'. John Huddleston Wynne found slaveholding distasteful, thought it corrupted the morals of British settlers, and feared it would end in bloody insurrections. Yet, even with his misgivings, Wynne could not bring himself to advocate slave trade or slavery abolition. The 'very short experience' in Georgia showed a ban on slavery to be 'an impractical measure'. 'The want of hands to cultivate the southern plantations' made slavery 'a necessity'.[2]

[1] This is a substantially revised and expanded version of an essay first published as 'Empire Without Slaves: British Concepts of Emancipation in the Age of the American Revolution,' *William and Mary Quarterly*, Third Series, LVI (April, 1999), pp. 273–306. My thanks to the editors for their suggestions for revisions.

[2] William Russell, *The History of America, From Its Discovery By Columbus to the Conclusion of the Late War, With an Appendix, Containing an Account of the Rise and Progress of the Present Unhappy Contest Between Great Britain and Her Colonies*, 2 vols. (London, 1778) II, p. 305. John Huddleston Wynne, *A General History of the British Empire in America: Containing, An Historical, Political, and Commercial View of the English Settlements; including all the Countries in North-America, and the West Indies, ceded by the Peace of Paris. In Two Volumes.* (London, 1770) II, pp. 540, 541, 545.

For the early British opponents of slavery, the challenge lay not only in the power of vested interests, but also in the limited ways that those troubled by slavery could imagine the future development of the American colonies. The fruits of long-standing practice and the imperatives of international competition made a strong case for resisting radical change. As best as anyone in Britain could judge, an Atlantic Empire required human bondage, a conviction that inhibited the possibility of organizing concerted action for change. For how does one rally support for an objective—Empire without slaves—which very few could conceptualize or articulate, which even fewer thought viable, and which, as it must have seemed to even the most idealistic, resided in the realm of fantasy?

Many in Britain could accept the moral argument against slavery. The real burden lay in rethinking the relationship between Empire and coerced labour, disassociating slavery from prevailing assumptions about the purposes of Empire, and developing practical, attainable, compelling alternatives. But what would an alternative to colonial slavery entail? To pose the question hints at the complexity of the task. Not only would reformers have to devise new schemes for the recruitment, organization, and management of labour. They also would have to uproot customs fundamental to enterprise in the British Atlantic. A programme to end slavery, for example, either would have to lure slaveholders into surrendering their slaves voluntarily, or would have to divest slaveholders of their human chattel through force. The latter strategy, of course, would require from the state an unprecedented invasion of customary, nearly sacred rights in property, an undertaking that would present daunting, if not insurmountable, constitutional, political, and logistical hurdles. Indeed, any plan for emancipation presented the spectre of enhanced imperial authority, if not a formal shift of power from the colonial Assemblies to Parliament. Even a scenario involving a gradual voluntary end to slavery would demand institutions empowered to mediate between freedmen and former slaveholders. How else, in the absence of mass revolt by the enslaved, could emancipation be secured and enforced throughout the colonies?

Furthermore, in addition to threatening to dispossess colonists of their property and to aggrandize the imperial state, emancipation promised revolutionary social change. Slavery established status in British America, as well as a scheme for labour. If the enslaved would no longer be slaves, what exactly, in civic terms, would they be? Abolishing slavery would seem to present one of two prospects: an incorporation, in some form, of liberated slaves into colonial society; or, alternatively, relocation of hundreds of thousands of freed slaves to the frontiers of the British Empire or outside the realm. A genuine challenge to slavery entailed, then, far more than a challenge to slave labour. It necessitated, as well, an engagement with fundamental questions regarding property, imperial governance, and social organization. At bottom, those who would abolish slavery required an alternative concept of Empire.

Slaves, Strangers, and Subjects

'These papers will contain a proposal for the extension of the future power and commerce of Great Britain'. This unlikely introduction opened an anonymously published essay printed in 1772 with the title *A Plan for the Abolition of Slavery in the West Indies*, the first British publication to offer a concrete, if quixotic, emancipation scheme. The author, Board of Trade adviser Maurice Morgann, suggested that the state purchase each year several dozen African boys and girls from the slaving forts along the eastern Atlantic coast, instruct and train the children in England, and, at the age of sixteen, settle them as colonists in the Pensacola district in the new British province of West Florida. The resulting colony of free Africans, Morgann argued, would encourage manumissions by providing British settlers with a place to send liberated slaves, while inducing 'a spirit of industry and achievement' among the enslaved by opening the prospect for freedom. Furthermore, the West Florida settlement would present, for southern climes, a competing model of labour and social relations.

Customary practices are hard to change in established colonies, Morgann conceded. By contrast, new and (from a British perspective) underpopulated provinces offered unusual opportunities for experimentation, perhaps 'a nursery of some good intentions, which may hereafter be extended with facility into the other colonies, or into Great Britain itself'. The Pensacola colonists could demonstrate that free labour would cultivate export crops and that Africans would produce them even if not held as slaves. Eventually, by necessity, the older colonies would abandon slavery to compete with their more successful neighbour. Over time, in Pensacola, 'the settlers will increase, they will cultivate, they will trade, they will overflow; they will become labourers and artizans in the neighbouring provinces; they will, being freemen, be more industrious, more skillful, and, upon the whole, work cheaper than slaves . . . and slavery will thereupon necessarily cease'. This, then, was an imaginative, if ingenuous plan to 'check the progress of slavery' by exposing its disadvantages, by displaying the merits of free labour and the capacities of Africans, and by allowing 'time and management', not a sudden shift in policy, to effect change. Through prudent, incremental steps, co-operation between blacks and whites in the Americas would replace the enmity bred by racial slavery.[3]

Several writers had proposed amelioration of slavery and many had denounced the institution on principle, but, before Maurice Morgann wrote in 1772, no one in England had devised a scheme for gradual abolition. Although published in 1772, he hatched the idea of colonizing free Africans in Pensacola nine years earlier, in the months following the Seven Years War. Morgann's manuscript addressed problems of administration, revenue, and defence. A settlement for freed Africans in the heart of the British Empire, he added, would further long-standing objectives: expanding trade, fortifying America's southern border, settling barren territories without the loss to England of productive labourers, enlarging the pool of consumers for British products, and developing a channel through which to funnel trade with the Spanish colonies. Africans could serve the Empire better, Morgann hypothesized, if not held as slaves.

He offered, instead, a novel ideal for social relations within the British Empire. Racial difference resulted from environment Morgann explained and as a consequence had utility. He accepted that Europeans perished in tropical climates and that in those regions, therefore, only Africans and their descendants could cultivate the land. But, to him, these 'facts' recommended the incorporation of Africans into civil society, not enslavement and social death. If the frontier imposed by climate marked the perimeter of British power, it also indicated where Africans could best serve as agents of British expansion. African allies and auxiliaries, if encouraged to settle the underdeveloped territories in the Floridas and the Caribbean, Morgann insisted, could themselves produce staple crops for European markets and conduct trade, on behalf of the British Empire, with Spanish America. Similarly, if nurtured and adequately supported, alliances with sovereigns along the coast of Africa could help extend commerce 'through the very heart' of the continent, where Britons lacked the capacity and constitution to settle.

[3] Maurice Morgann, *A Plan for the Abolition of Slavery in the West Indies* (London, 1772), pp. 7, 4, 25, 13, 15; Daniel Fineman, ed., *Maurice Morgann, Shakespearean Criticism* (Oxford, 1972), pp. 4–9.

Abolition of slavery, then, rather than compromising Empire, was the proper measure for a 'free and generous government' inclined to 'views of empire and domination' that were 'worthy of ambition'. Unleashed from the disgrace of slavery and no longer 'restrained by climate', the British Empire would stand upon 'the sure foundations of equality and justice'. Morgann envisaged an absorption of the 'black subjects of Britain' into the imperial corpus. In due time, Morgann assured, the former slaves would 'talk the same language, read the same books, profess the same religion, and be fashioned by the same laws'. Through marriages with Europeans in the new settlements, variations in skin colour would 'wear away' by steady, imperceptible 'degrees'. 'The whites will inhabit the northern colonies', and 'to the south, the complexions will blacken by regular gradation'. Then, with 'one tongue', a 'united people' would 'commemorate the auspicious aera of universal freedom' while 'the sable arm' of British authority would reach 'through every region of the Torrid Zone', 'shake the power of Spain to its foundations', and elevate Great Britain 'to the seat of unenvied and unlimited dominion'.[4]

After the Jacobite rebellion of 1745, to discourage further uprisings in the North, Parliament enacted legislation that would transform 'savage' Scottish highlanders into assimilated, productive, loyal Britons.[5] With a similar end in view, Morgann's plan gradually would acculturate Africans, award them a stake in the Empire and thereby discourage insurrections and the threat of what he predicted to be 'a general' and 'merited carnage'. And just as Scottish manpower helped make possible the conquests of the Seven Years War, blacks would help secure British supremacy in the Americas. Civilize, liberate, incorporate, and unite. This was Morgann's formula for achieving uncontested rule in the Americas, ending slavery, and in the process 'restoring the integrity of the British government, and vindicating the credit and honour of our common nature'.[6] In viewing Africans as potential allies rather than internal enemies, as subjects of the Crown rather than the property of slaveholders, Morgann pictured an empire defined by neither ethnicity nor religion—in fact, on nothing more than allegiance.

[4] *Plan for the Abolition*; citations on pp. 27, 33, 27, 26, 25, 33, 27. 17.

[5] Linda Colley, *Britons: Forging the Nation, 1707–1837* (New Haven, Conn., 1992), pp. 119–120. See also Eric J. Richards, 'Scotland and the Uses of the Atlantic Empire', in Bernard Bailyn and Philip D. Morgan, eds., *Strangers Within the Realm: Cultural Margins of the First British Empire* (Chapel Hill, NC, 1991), pp. 106–12.

[6] *Plan for the Abolition*, p. 32.

Maurice Morgann wrote creatively about slavery because, in part, as a matter of employment, he ruminated routinely on imperial policy. And his emphasis on regarding enslaved Africans as imperial subjects reflected a characteristic and growing concern among British administrators after the Seven Years War to enhance the presence and extend the influence of the Crown in the American territories. The cessions of the 1760s brought an unprecedented number and variety of peoples within British dominions. Never had England or Britain seized more land at once. 'In the multitude of people is the king's honour', the Book of Proverbs taught. Assessed in more utilitarian terms, the Crown had acquired an almost countless number of new cultivators, consumers, and dependants. By contemporary estimates, in 1763, the 25-year-old George III could now claim authority over an additional 75,000 French Canadians, approximately 30,000 planters, slaves, and Caribs in the Ceded Islands, perhaps one hundred thousand Native Americans, a smattering of Spanish colonists in the Floridas, and, it was believed, anywhere between 10 and 20 million people in Bengal.[7] In theory, by conquest or capitulation, each had become subjects of the Crown, as the propagandists of Empire repeatedly averred. Foreigners settling in British dominions 'are to be considered in the same light of obedience as natural born subjects', asserted scribe and agriculturist Arthur Young. 'The inhabitants [of India]', wrote William Knox, 'are British subjects, tho' governed by their own laws, or laws framed by the East India Company'. In the aftermath of British incursion on Carib lands in St Vincent's, John Campbell insisted that the natives were still 'intitled to Justice and Humanity when considered as subject of the crown of Great Britain'. To Campbell, the point was important enough to repeat: the Caribs must be 'trusted with Justice and Lenity, to which as Men, and subjects of the Crown of Great Britain, they are surely entitled'.[8]

[7] Contemporary estimates of population presented in P. J. Marshall, 'Empire and Opportunity in Britain, 1763–1775', *Transactions of the Royal Historical Society*, 6th series, V, p. 112, and, for the Ceded Islands, Lawrence Henry Gipson, *The Triumphant Empire: New Responsbilities Within the Enlarged Empire, 1763–1766* (Vol. IX in Gipson's series *The British Empire Before the American Revolution*) (New York, 1956), pp. 238, 240, 255–56.

[8] [Arthur Young], *Political Essays Concerning the Present State of the British Empire; Particularly Respecting I. Natural Advantages and Disadvantages. II. Constitution. III. Agriculture. IV. Manufactures. V. The Colonies. VI. And Commerce* (London, 1772), p. 36; [William Knox], *The Present State of the Nation: Particularly with Respect to its Trade, Finances, &c. &c. Addressed to the King and both Houses of Parliament* (London, 1768), p. 85; John Campbell, *A Political Survey of Britain: Being A Series of Reflections On the Situation, Lands, Inhabitants, Revenues, Colonies, And Commerce of This Island. Intended to Shew That we have not yet approached near the Summit of Improvement, but that it will afford Employment to many Generations before they push to their*

In the eighteenth century, the meaning of subjectship retained the quasi-medieval connotations of a personal bond between individual and lord. Subjectship could be natural or acquired, that is, a consequence of birth within the sovereign's domain or of absorption through naturalization or conquest. In either case, subjectship was understood as natural, perpetual, and immutable, a civic analogue of the relation between parent and child. The relationship entailed obligations: the monarch owed the subject protection, while the subject owed allegiance. The relationship also conveyed privileges: although subjects could and did hold different ranks, in theory, each could rightfully claim certain rights, not the least of which was the right to hold real property and the right to equal consideration under the law.[9] In this respect, the suddenly multiethnic, polyglot Empire presented difficult if not unfamiliar questions, specifically, the extent to which the new subjects would affirm their subordination by avowing allegiance to the Crown, and the extent to which those who pledged their allegiance should enjoy the same rights as natural-born subjects.

The inclination to describe conquered foreigners as imperial subjects reflected, in part, the paternalism fundamental to the monarchical ethos. To the new subjects, the step-children in the imperial family, the King owed and chose to provide protection. But honouring the property of conquered peoples and tolerating institutions and practices alien to British law represented even more a politic accommodation to circumstance. In some regions, imposing the British constitution, as a practical matter, was out of the question; this was certainly the case in Bengal and nearly so in Quebec. Elsewhere, the expense required to support effective administration was prohibitive, as Whitehall would learn between 1764 and 1768 when ministers attempted imperial regulation of the nominally British possessions west of the Appalachians and east of the Mississippi. Even more importantly, permitting British colonists to seize the property and land of existing residents risked inciting armed conflict. Recurring warfare threatened both to invite the interference of European rivals, especially in the Caribbean, and generate further costs to maintain peace. It made more sense to assuage and incorporate potential enemies living within British dominions. There was nothing

utmost extent the natural Advantages of Great Britain. In Two Volumes (London, 1774), II, pp. 682 fn., 684 fn.

[9] James H. Kettner, *The Development of American Citizenship, 1608–1870* (Chapel Hill, NC, 1978), pp. 3–8, 51.

new about attempts to pacify and acculturate American Indians. But in the 1760s, an assimilationist strategy could also answer the imperatives resulting from territorial expansion. When John Stuart, His Majesty's superintendent for the southern district, proposed to the Board of Trade in 1764 strict imperial regulation of colonists who traded with Indians, a bureaucracy to ensure enforcement of the new laws, and, in the words of historian J. Russell Snapp, 'a color-blind judicial system', he hoped to prevent settlers from fomenting a backcountry war.[10] With Native Americans, with Canadians, with French planters in the West Indies, with the peoples of Bengal, with Scottish Highlanders, and perhaps too with Africans as Maurice Morgann suggested, accommodation, absorption, and metropolitan supervision seemed the best way to further trade, decrease expenditures, and preserve peace.

These developments, the addition of new peoples to the Empire, and the disposition to conceive the relation in terms of allegiance and protection, help make sense of otherwise incongruous moments when writers treating imperial affairs, such as Maurice Morgann, cast slaves as subjects of George III. Absentee slaveholder William Knox presents the most unlikely case. Former Provost-Marshal of Georgia, briefly London agent for Georgia and East Florida, sometime adviser to the Society for the Propagation of the Gospel, Undersecretary-of-State in the American department from 1770 to 1782, Knox would emerge during the first years of the British anti-slavery movement of the late 1780s and early 1790s as a stalwart defender of the slave trade.[11] Yet, if Knox thought slavery necessary to Empire, he could not approve, in 1768, cruel treatment of 'so vast a multitude of his [majesty's] own subjects'. In his view, British colonists' property right in slaves was local, not absolute, because the legislatures granting the right themselves were subordinate to the 'supreme magistrate' of King-in-Council. Slaveholders may have a legal claim to a slave's service, but, as British subjects, as with

[10] P. J. Marshall, 'Empire and Authority in the Late Eighteenth Century', *Journal of Imperial and Commonwealth History*, 15 (1987), pp. 105–22; and Marshall, 'A Nation Defined by Empire, 1755–1776', in Alexander Grant and K. J. Stringer, eds., *Uniting the Kingdom? The Making of British History* (London, 1995), pp. 208–22; Snapp, *John Stuart and the Struggle for Empire on the Southern Frontier*, p. 63.

[11] Leland J. Bellot, *William Knox: The Life and Thought of an Eighteenth-Century Imperialist* (Austin, Tex., 1977). For Knox's support of the slave trade see: NA, Historical Manuscripts Commission, *Report on Manuscripts in Various Collections*, Vol. VI (Dublin, 1909), pp. 202, 203, 222, 291–292; [Knox], *A Letter to from W. K., Esq. to W. Wilberforce, Esq.* (London, 1790).

apprentices in England, slaves had a claim to 'an impartial dispensation of the laws'. In this argument, Knox was as interested in underscoring imperial sovereignty, specifically the authority of Parliament to legislate for the colonies, as ensuring humane treatment of the enslaved. But pertinent here is the off-handed, casual way with which Knox identified slaves as subjects and, in this designation, allowed a right to protection from the Crown. '[I]t is most reproachful to this country', he declared, 'that there are more than five hundred thousand of its subjects, for whom the legislature has not shewn the least regard'. He hoped ministers would examine the slave codes and require the colonies to report on measures taken to ensure the slaves 'legal rights'.[12]

Few adopted William Knox's notion of slaves as subjects, it should be emphasized. In this period, Britons rarely paused to reflect on the civil status of enslaved Africans, or to consider slaves as any more than the property of British colonists. In practice, as in law, the enslaved had no access to the customary rights, liberties, and protections enjoyed by the free.[13] But when Maurice Morgann proposed enlisting liberated Africans in imperial expansion, or when, several years later, James Ramsay characterized slaves as industrious, 'valuable subjects' deserving succour and patronage, or in 1775 when Lord Dunmore promised freedom to Virginia slaves willing to assist the Crown suppress an incipient colonial rebellion,[14] they each drew upon concepts of inclusion, allegiance, and protection that were strengthened, if not generated, by the accession of hundreds of thousands of aliens to the British Empire. Indeed, the idea of slaves as subjects perhaps only could have suggested itself when, more generally, as a consequence of the Seven Years War, the governance and incorporation of strangers had become, inescapably, the subject of extensive discussion, when the increasingly troublesome weakness of the imperial state made evident the potential strategic value of religious, racial, and ethnic minorities.

[12] William Knox, *Three Tracts Respecting the Conversion and Instruction of the Free Indians and Negro Slaves in the Colonies Addressed to the Venerable Society for the Propagation of the Gospel in the Foreign Colonies* (London, 1768), pp. 14–39; citations drawn from pp. 29, 31, 25, 31.

[13] Elsa V. Goveia, *The West Indian Slave Laws of the Eighteenth Century* (Barbados, 1970), pp. 20–21.

[14] James Ramsay, *An Essay on the Treatment and Conversion of African Slaves in the British Sugar Colonies* (London, 1784), pp. 113–14. For Dunmore, see Benjamin Quarles, *The Negro in the American Revolution* (Chapel Hill, NC, 1961), pp. 19–32.

Emancipation as Imperial Reform

As it happens, Morgann's *Plan for the Abolition of Slavery in the West Indies* was the first of several British emancipation schemes circulated in the 1770s. In 1776, Granville Sharp publicized what he called the 'Spanish Regulations', the colonial custom of *coartacion*, which enabled and encouraged Spanish Caribbean slaves to purchase their freedom in installments. In 1778, a Newcastle essayist appended a similar proposal to a pamphlet assaying prospects for retaining the North American Empire. That same year, the Reverend James Ramsay from the island of St Christopher in the Leeward Islands submitted to the Bishop of London and the Archbishop of Canterbury a memorial outlining 'a plan for the education and gradual emancipation of slaves in the West Indies'. In 1780 Edmund Burke composed a seventy-two point 'Negro Code' that provided for metropolitan oversight and administration of the British slave trade and slavery in the American colonies. Less than a year later, John Hinchliffe, Bishop of Peterborough, drafted a bill based upon the 'Spanish Regulations' that would 'soften & gradually reduce the Slavery in the West Indies'.[15]

[15] Granville Sharp, *The Just Limitations of Slavery in the Laws of God, Compared with the Unbounded Claims of African Traders and British American Slaveholders, With a copious Appendix: containing, An Answer to Rev. Mr. Thompson's Tract in Favor of the African Slave Trade.—Letters containing the lineal Descent of the Negroes from sources of Ham.—The Spanish Regulations for the gradual enfranchisement of Slaves. A Proposal on the same Principles from the gradual Enfranchisement of Slaves in America. Reports of Determination in the several Courts of Law Against Slavery, &c.* (London, 1776), pp. 54–55; Maurice Morgann, *Essays, Commercial, and Political, on the real and relative interests of imperial and dependent states, particularly those of Great Britain, and their Dependencies Displaying the Probable Causes of, and a Mode of Compromising the present Dispute between this Country and the American Colonies: To which are added an Appendix, on the means of emancipating slaves, without loss to their proprietors* (Newcastle, 1777); 'Memorial suggesting motives for the improvement of the sugar colonies particularly of the slaves employed in their culture, and offering reasons for encouraging the advancement of these last in social life and their conversion to Christianity; extracted from a manuscript composed on that subject by James Ramsay, Minister in the Island of St. Christopher, and Author of a Plan of Reunion between Great Britain and her Colonies published by Murray No 32. Fleet Street', Catalogued as: 'Memorial on the Conversion of Slaves in the Sugar Colonies by James Ramsay', London, Lambeth Palace Library, Fulham Papers, XX, f. 80 (for the copy addressed to the Bishop of London see, Lambeth Palace Library, Society for the Propagation of the Gospel Papers, XVII, ff. 221–3); Edmund Burke, 'Sketch of a Negro Code', in Warren M. Elofson, ed., *The Writings and Speeches of Edmund Burke*, Vol. III, *Party, Parliament, and the American War, 1774–1780* (Oxford, 1996), pp. 562–81. Evidence concerning Hinchliffe's scheme is preserved in Granville Sharp's diaries, although the document itself appears not to survive. Diary G (7 Feb., 12 March, 19 March, 7 April) ff. 106, 108, 110, the Gloucestershire Record Office, Granville Sharp Papers, D3549 13/4/2.

Why did several writers in these years promote emancipation, when no one in Britain had thought to do so before? Each possessed an acute hostility to human bondage, of course, and they wrote at a time when intellectuals elsewhere in Europe and the Americas also toyed with plans for fundamental reform to colonial slavery. In 1765, two years after Maurice Morgann composed his sketch for a free colony in Pensacola, the French political economist Abbé Baudeau suggested sending liberated Africans to till the vast tracts of land west of the Mississippi. Several years earlier, in 1758, a Lisbon-born lawyer residing in Bahia advocated abolishing slavery in Brazil in favour of indentured labour. Pennsylvania Quaker Anthony Benezet in 1771 recommended abolition of the British slave trade, a limited time of servitude for those already held in slavery, oversight of freed slaves by county supervisors, substitution of white indentured servants for slaves, and the establishment of a free colony for blacks west of the Appalachians. More generally, the burgeoning revolution against imperial rule in North America occasioned a variety of proposals for a comprehensive emancipation.[16]

Yet, in most instances, these contemporaneous initiatives, which sometimes received limited circulation even in their original languages, appear not to have informed British writings. Instead, the British emancipation schemes arose, in part, from the broader tendency among European thinkers to apply in theory the lessons drawn from the emerging science of human society. The would-be emancipators chose to exploit cultural assumptions prevailing among very many of the late eighteenth-century intelligentsia. British reformers assumed that individuals worked more productively if moved by incentive rather than force. They thought the right to self-possession sacred. And they held an unshakable confidence in the human capacity for moral development. In important respects, these writers aimed to bring colonial practice in line with what they thought to be universal truths about humanity and the good society. So, to a degree, the late eighteenth-century idea of emancipation reflected an

[16] David Brion Davis, *The Problem of Slavery in Westurn Culture*, pp. 429–30; A. J. R. Russell-Wood, 'Iberian Expansion and the Issue of Slavery: Changing Portuguese Attitudes, 1440–1770,' *American Historical Review*, LXXXIII, 1 (Feb, 1978) p. 38; Anthony Benezet, *Some Historical Account of Guinea, Its Situation, Produce and the General Disposition of its Inhabitants with an Inquiry into the Rise and Progress of the Slave Trade, its Nature and Lamentable Effects...* (Philadelphia, 1771), pp. 139–41.

'enlightened' interest in guiding American plantation societies into conformity with 'civilized' norms.[17]

Yet if the idea of an Empire worked by free labour was informed by an optimistic ambition to make the world anew, emancipationism in Britain took shape under the tangible pressures of a specific juncture in imperial history. Like Maurice Morgann, those who would reform slavery had in view the ways emancipation could sustain, and even advance, colonial enterprise. Rather than abstract and vague expressions of principle or fantastic projections of future change, the schemes, on the whole, exhibited concrete ways to generate accord and security within the Empire at a moment of threatened dissolution, an agenda most evident when the sum effect of shared principles comes into view.

Consider the proposed work regimes. British emancipationists accepted the need to sustain the productivity of colonial plantations. They questioned, however, the labour model upon which those economies relied. Implicit in the dependence on slavery was the assumption that only force, or the threat of force, could drive black men and women to work. This inability to control or influence the situations or manner in which one worked, in key respects, defined the experience of blacks in the British colonies. To the emancipationists, apparently successful practices customary in the British Isles seemed to establish axiomatic truths about human psychology applicable to workers in every society, truths enshrined in Adam Smith's influential passage on the advantages of wage labour in book three of *The Wealth of Nations* (1776). James Ramsay urged slaveholders to consider 'the state of workers in free countries', who, he asserted, execute 'in the same time, thrice the labour of slaves'. Consider, too, the work slaves and free labourers actually performed, the Newcastle essayist observed: 'men conscious of being free, will, even for moderate wages, engage themselves in labour that appear the most intolerable to slaves'. That colonial experience failed to verify such propositions worried these reformers not at all. Planters may require African labour, Morgann and others agreed, but they did not require slave labour. How, then, to effect a transfer from slavery to liberty without infringing the property rights of slaveholders? Permit slaves to purchase their freedom

[17] David Brion Davis, *The Problem of Slavery in Western Culture*, pp. 400–38; Steven Mintz, 'Models of Emancipation During the Age of Revolution', *Slavery and Abolition*, XVII (Aug., 1996) pp. 1–21.

from their owners by allowing wages for work completed during, as the Newcastle pamphleteer put it, 'leisure hours'. Schemes for self-purchase, as established by customs such as the 'Spanish Regulations', 'give such encouragement to industry', enthused Granville Sharp, 'that even the most indolent are tempted to exert themselves'.[18] In this arrangement, slaves gradually would acquire freedom, plantations would retain their work force, and slaveholders would take a dual return on their investment—receiving both labour and a refund on the price paid for the freed slave. In effect, in exchange for liberty, slaves would bear the cost of their initial purchase and, presumably, perform the same work with greater efficiency. The emancipators did not intend simply to set slaves free. Instead, they would have the manumitted labour as before, but to draw wages rather than at the instigation of the whip.

To this end, emancipationists sought to protect slaves' earnings and to ensure them of their control over the money.[19] Edmund Burke's code, for example, would have allowed the enslaved to bequeath property to descendants and to prohibit its seizure or appropriation by slaveholders. Such provisions would initiate, even where bondage remained, transfer of proprietorship from the slaveholder and towards the slave. In this transition to self-possession, the reformers thought an inviolable right to family relations fundamental. The Newcastle essayist would require slaveholders to sell enslaved children to their free parents who presented sufficient funds. Burke's code contained several provisions designed to recognize, encourage, and protect slave marriages. Similarly, the various proposals would vest slaves with claims to land. Granville Sharp would have 'spare' lands divided into '*compact little farms*' and slaves settled as peasants. In Burke's regime, married slaves resident on a plantation for more than twelve months could

[18] Ramsay, 'Memorial suggesting motives for the improvement of the sugar colonies', f. 79; Morgann, *Essays, Commercial, and Political*, pp. 143, 137; Granville Sharp, *Just Limitation of Slavery in the Laws of God*, p. 55.

[19] In nearly every instance, metropolitan commentators appear to have assumed, perhaps understandably, that slaves in British America always lacked claims to property. Generally, British anti-slavery writers knew nothing of the variety of labour systems embraced by the institution of slavery. Specifically, they were wholly unaware of the prevalence of task labour in the North American lowcountry. Nor did they know of the existence or character of the internal economies in slave societies in British America or elsewhere. For an introduction to these topics, see Philip D. Morgan, *Slave Counterpoint: Black Culture in the Eighteenth-Century Chesapeake and Lowcountry* (Chapel Hill, NC, 1998).

not be sold away.[20] In addition, then, to a right of self-purchase, the projectors would establish for slaves a prior right to property and family, in effect, delineating a civil and domestic sphere for the enslaved where slaveholders could not intrude. If the emancipation schemes resisted ceding the enslaved full autonomy, they chipped away at the custom of slaves as alienable chattel. Masters would retain, for a time, rights to their human property, but not the unlimited discretion to dispose of that property as they saw fit.

For the enslaved, compliance with prescribed cultural norms would be the price of the ticket to self-possession. If slaves were to be freed, the emancipators concurred, they would have to adopt British mores. The relative cultural autonomy enslaved men and women enjoyed in much of British America would have to be crushed. What the enslaved may have wanted for themselves scarcely figured in the emancipationists calculations. Reform schemes espoused slave marriages, for example, less to honour slaves' desires than to foster civility. Admission to society required adhering to the patriarchal ethos. Because, in Burke's words, 'the state of matrimony and Government of family' best formed 'men to a fitness for freedom, and to become good Citizens', he made marriage a precondition of liberty. Indeed, in his plan, slaveholders would provide 'a Woman' to enslaved men over the age of twenty-one upon the 'requisition' of Crown-appointed colonial officials. Those male slaves 'fitted' for 'the Office of Freemen' would have reached thirty years, fathered no less than three children 'born in lawful matrimony' and earned a certificate from a parish minister attesting to 'regularity in the duties of Religion, and of... orderly and good behavior'. James Ramsay also positioned proper morals and manners as the bridge to liberty. To Ramsay, absolute dependence in slavery left the unfree worse than savages: 'A savage in all his efforts, acts for himself, and the advancement of his proper concerns; but a slave is the bare appendage of a man, he has nothing to call his own.' To free slaves without moral instruction, he reasoned, would leave them without the facility for self-advancement, which, to Ramsay's way of thinking, entailed fidelity to 'the good of the community'. To instill the values of social responsibility, Ramsay would have slaves judge each other's conduct 'in the manner of juries'.[21] In this way, slaves would grasp the importance of

[20] Edmund Burke, 'Sketch of a Negro Code,' pp. 577–79; John A. Woods, 'The Correspondence of Benjamin Rush and Granville Sharp, 1773–1809', *Journal of American Studies*, I, 1 (1969) p. 15.

[21] Burke, 'Sketch of a Negro Code', pp. 578, 580; Ramsay, 'Memorial suggesting motives', f. 79.

normative behaviour and thereby acquire a stake in preserving the social order.

A persisting concern for stability, commerce, and civic harmony, then, figured prominently in these schemes. The emancipationists envisioned an ordered and orderly transition to freedom, a transition which, they optimistically presumed, would bring extensive benefits at negligible costs. Replacing slave labour with free labour would increase wealth because slave labour was inefficient. It would bring, they contended, an explosive growth in colonial consumption, as freedmen able to earn and acquire would purchase British manufactures in greater quantities. Best of all, slave labour would transform mutual contempt and violence among black and white in British America into a perpetual, fraternal peace. 'To the public', Ramsay aphorized, 'the difference between the slave and the citizen is immense, the one being the strength, the other being the weakness of the state'. 'Should we continue to keep nearly the whole race as slaves, and not encourage and assist them to liberate themselves', the Newcastle essayist warned, 'the epoch of their universal freedom, and ruin of their present masters, may be at no very distant period'. How foolish was this, when emancipation, properly administered, could serve '*state policy*?' In a scheme that expedited self-redemption, Africans '*must either be looked on as an accession of so many subjects, or as the means of such a national acquisition of property as they have paid for their emancipation*'.[22] For the first time, the argument from necessity was being turned on its head. Understood correctly, the gradual extension of liberty held the best prospects for preserving imperial wealth and power. 'Police and public utility', Ramsay professed, 'join their voices with religion and humanity'.[23] The interests of slaves are the interests of masters. The interests of both are the interests of Empire.

This notion, implausible and to most contemporaries demonstrably false, issued from a variety of sources, not from a coherent movement. The authors were largely unknown to each other and, evidently, drafted their schemes independently. What they shared—by virtue of experience, employment, or disposition—was an active engagement with imperial policy. The first proponents of emancipation not only factored imperial interests into their proposals. They were themselves active in debating and rethinking the governance and administration of the colonies. British slavery and the

[22] Burke, 'Sketch of a Negro Code', f. 80; Morgann, *Essays, Commercial, and Political*, pp. 143–44.
[23] Ramsay, 'Memorial for suggesting motives', f. 79.

British slave trade remained far less vulnerable to attack while agreement prevailed on the means and ends of Empire, as long as custom validated established practice. While priorities remained fixed, few opportunities arose to question the apparently neccesary tie between slavery and Empire. The American Revolution, however, put the imperial project to question and inspired a panoply of creative and sometimes comprehensive plans to rework its structure. To an unusual degree, in the 1770s, the British chose to examine received premises about overseas dominion, about its peoples, and about their relationship to each. Revolt in the North American colonies opened a space for the reconsideration of imperial policy. And in this space those who intensely disliked slavery had an unprecedented opportunity to not only express anti-slavery sentiment but to develop novel alternatives.

The Limits of Imperial Authority

The emancipation schemes of the 1770s, as an intellectual exercise, represented a sharp break from customary ways of conceiving the relationship between slavery and Empire. As potential policy initiatives, they raised provocative questions regarding the exercise of power. Reducing the power masters held over slaves required, in some way, reducing the power slaveholders possessed in the governance of colonial societies. It was one thing to propose alternatives to slavery but something else to force those schemes on colonial planters. The first anti-slavery crusaders considered the political strength of the West India interest nearly insurmountable. The more fundamental problem was, however, constitutional, not political. Even if emancipationists could generate momentum for slavery reform, did the Crown or Parliament have the standing and resources to make such measures enforceable law? To frame the question in more general terms, who, if anyone, possessed the requisite authority to abolish slavery and how, as a practical matter, could the proper authorities implement and sustain substantive change to colonial practices?

In the eighteenth-century British Empire, there was no precedent for imperial management of colonial slavery and no infrastructure to give such a design administrative life. Indeed, metropolitan officials capable, in theory, of shaping slavery in British territories had chosen, in effect, to ignore human bondage in America. From the first years of colonization onwards, legal historian Jonathan Bush has stressed, neither the Privy Council, Parliament, nor the common law courts at Westminster attempted to author slave laws for the colonies or revise the codes enacted by colonial Assemblies. This neglect followed from the broader custom of conceding to British settlers extensive autonomy in governing their internal affairs.[24] The Privy Council did negate prohibitive duties on slave imports and instruct Royal Governors to secure legislation protecting slaves from murder and 'inhumane' severities.[25] But, in practice, imperial sovereignty proved less decisive than the consistency with which British ministers honoured colonial legislation that provided for property in and the governance of slaves. Metropolitan officials proceeded as if the local custom of slavery established an inviolable private right. And this tradition of near purposeful neglect instilled an unspoken belief among American slaveholders that imperial administrators *could not* interfere in the possession and management of slaves in the British colonies. Paradoxically, then, colonial slavery, with the almost feudal autonomy it granted British settlers, resided *sub silentio*. It lay outside of imperial oversight, while still, in principle, within the realm of imperial authority. For blacks residing within the British Caribbean and British North America, this meant that, in practice, the laws of the colonies and the will of an owner were the only laws that mattered.

Thus, the custom of colonial autonomy presented a formidable block to prospects for emancipation, as it did more generally to the exercise of imperial authority. A metropolitan attempt to seize and manage an institution traditionally administered exclusively by the colonial legislatures threatened, by necessity, profound constitutional change. Predictably, the tentative emancipation schemes of the 1770s arose with and complemented the new priorities that took shape after the Stamp Act crisis, after British Americans explicitly challenged Parliament's authority to legislate for the colonies. To the few inclined to muse at length on the subject of colonial slavery, the apparently unlimited, inviolable right in British America to property in persons proved that the colonists possessed, already, far too much independence. Even evident, egregious abuses lay beyond the power of

[24] Jonathan A. Bush, 'Free to Enslave: The Foundations of Colonial American Slave Law' *Yale Journal of Law and the Humanities*, V (1993) pp. 417–70; Jack P. Greene, *Peripheries and Center, Constitutional Development in the Extended Polities of the British Empire and the United States of America, 1607–1788* (Athens, Ga., 1986), pp. 1–76; Greene, 'Negotiated Authorities: The Problem of Governance in the Extended Polities of the Early Modern Atlantic World', in his *Negotiated Authorities: Essays in Colonial Political and Constitutional History* (Charlottesville, Va., and London, 1994), pp. 1–24.

[25] W. E. B. Dubois, *The Suppression of the African Slave-Trade to the United States of America, 1638–1870* (1898; New York, 1969), pp. 7–37; Leonard W. Labaree, *Royal Instructions to British Colonial Governors* (1935; New York, 1967) II, pp. 505–08.

the British state to prevent. For those opponents of slavery who believed Parliament should legislate aggressively on colonial questions, anti-slavery measures promised not only to redress moral wrongs; they promised as well to assist in the rehabilitation of metropolitan authority.

No writer defined this agenda with greater clarity than Reverend James Ramsay, a pamphleteer long recognized by historians as a forceful anti-slavery campaigner in the 1780s, but less frequently as a rabid opponent of colonial rebellion in the decade before.[26] Ramsay discerned that slavery reform could occur only by centralizing sovereign power in the British Empire, a step which, anyway, he thought urgent to preserving command of the North American colonies. Two decades of residence in the British Caribbean left Ramsay hostile toward its ruling oligarchs. He took issue with the way colonists placed what he called the 'Kingdom of I' above the interests of society as a whole. Slavery in British America displayed the consequences of such an ethos. Here was evidence of the tyranny unrestricted freedom spawned. 'Every where in every age', Ramsay noted, 'the chain of slavery has been fashioned by the hand of liberty'. Although positioned to bring slavery within the compass of law, the culprits, the colonial Assemblies that licensed oppression were 'neither competent, or inclined, to introduce such reformation as humanity solicites'. Indeed the slave codes the Assemblies enacted led to 'the negation of the law', since the end of law, Ramsay wrote, was to secure 'the equal protection of its citizens'.[27] That slaves were not citizens was irrelevant to Ramsay where the right to legal protection was concerned. As labourers for the British state, slaves were members of society; and as members of society, slaves had a claim to the rights upon which society, as such, existed to guarantee. Those colonial Assemblies that refused to honour the rightful claims of each member to legal protection had forfeited, in principle, their right to legislate. For Ramsay, the wickedness of British American slavery clinched the case against colonial self-governance.

If the problem, then, lay with the imperial constitution, the self-evident solution was to 'unhinge the present method of managing the colonies', end 'the absurdity and contradiction of various, jarring legislators', recognize

[26] John A. Schutz, 'James Ramsay, Essayist: Aggressive Humanitarian,' in Samuel Clyde McCulloch, *British Humanitarianism: Essays in Honor of Frank J. Klingberg* (Philadelphia, 1950), pp. 145–65; Folarin O. Shyllon, *James Ramsay: The Unknown Abolitionist* (Edinburgh, 1977); and Sir James Watt, 'James Ramsay, 1733–1789: Naval Surgeon, Naval Chaplain and Morning Star of the Antislavery Movement', *The Mariner's Mirror*, LXXXI, 2 (May, 1995), pp. 156–70.

[27] 'Motives for Improvement of the Sugar Colonies', xiifn., 44fn, 27, 69, 39, 44.

parliament as the 'supreme legislature', and reduce the power of colonial Assemblies. A host of improvements to the sugar colonies, including a reformation of slavery, could follow, Ramsay explained. No longer should the colonies govern with minimal oversight from London. And no longer should the Privy Council have the responsibility of reviewing colonial legislation. Instead, Ramsay recommended, each measure authored in British America should be reviewed by a committee of Parliament, composed, in part, by delegates appointed by the several colonies. These procedural reforms would then clear the way for a substantive revision of colonial laws. 'Through a timely interposition of the legislature', Britain would 'acquire a considerable accession of strength; have its trade and taxes improved, and a large number of useful fellow subjects, now sunk in misery and bondage made happy here, and capable of happiness hereafter'.[28]

James Ramsay hated slavery, but he may have hated American rebels even more. He despised their leading men in Congress ('atheistical profligate bankrupts'), the actions of their army ('numerous scenes of horror, oppression, inhuman murders, and unrelenting cruelty in every possible dress'), their constitutional principles ('laid in profligacy, Atheism, ingratitude, and oppression'), and the 'consummate effrontery' of their friends in Britain, particularly the Rockingham Whigs. In the end Ramsay, would have to console himself with an attack on slavery alone.[29] Those efforts would bring him notoriety and influence; Ramsay would be the first to fix British attention on colonial slavery in a way that had lasting effect. With this success, though, he failed utterly in what he initially set out to do: assist in preserving and reconstructing the British Empire in America.

Nascent British interest in slavery reform during the era of the American Revolution must not be divorced from the ultimately unsuccessful metropolitan efforts to reconstitute imperial authority. When William Knox suggested that slaves, like indentured servants, should be eligible for an 'impartial dispensation of the laws', he stressed that 'no authority, but that of Parliament', could institute such a measure. Of slavery, Maurice Morgann wrote, 'the evil is wholly imputable to the state; and the remedy can be obtained only by its assuming different maxims and a better policy' for the Empire as a whole. Provide America with a new constitution, Methodist minister Thomas Vivian advised Lord Dartmouth, the former Secretary of State for America, and let that constitution 'be similar to our own' under 'the

[28] 'Motives for Improvement of the Sugar Colonies', pp. 72–93, 154–68.

[29] *Ibid.*, pp. 52n., 53n., 135n.

same Supreme Legislature'. The price of political equality, Vivian added, should be conformity with metropolitan standards of civility and justice: 'Why not compleat the resemblance or union as much as possible by abolishing slavery among them?' Moreover, Vivian stated, emancipation would rescue enslaved Africans from oppression, contribute to uniting the Empire under uniform laws, and, importantly, ensure the dependence of the colonies. Even if Americans surrendered their arms, he observed, 'they would still be glad to embrace the opportunity of becoming independent'. Only divesting Americans of their bondsmen would permanently 'weaken' their strength.[30]

The self-styled British friends of American liberty who favoured slavery reform hid from the authoritarian implications of the anti-slavery measures they espoused at the cost of coherence. David Hartley wanted Parliament to enact a law protecting slaves from their owners but opposed metropolitan attempts to legislate for the colonies. Granville Sharp campaigned ardently early in the Revolutionary war on behalf of colonial autonomy yet hoped the Crown would prevent colonists 'from oppressing their poor Brethren'. This, he declared, was an 'essential purpose of royal government'.[31] Edmund Burke too wrestled with conflicting principles. In 1778, he renounced the imperious maxims enshrined in the Declaratory Act of 1766, which he had a hand in producing. Yet the provisions of his 1780 Negro Code would have designated an army of administrators, in England, West Africa, and the Caribbean to police each component of the slaving network in the British Atlantic. Indeed, if enacted, it would have established a colonial bureaucracy more extensive than even the most ambitious plans of imperial administration for North America proposed to date.[32] Burke, like Knox and Ramsay before him, championed the 'indiscriminating supremacy of law' throughout British dominions, law which, he and others were coming to believe, should admit the claims of the enslaved.

[30] William Knox, *Three Tracts*, p. 25; [Morgann] *Plan for the Abolition of Slavery in the West Indies*, p. 13; Thomas Vivian to the Earl of Dartmouth, 16 Jan. 1777. Staffordshire Record Office, Dartmouth Papers D(w) 1778/II/1733:

[31] George Herbert Guttridge, *David Hartley, M. P. An Advocate of Conciliation 1774–1783* (Berkeley, 1926), pp. 327–28; Prince Hoare, ed., *Memoirs of Granville Sharp* (London, 1820), pp. 78–80: Granville Sharp to Lord North, 18 Feb. 1772; Granville Sharp, *The Law of Retribution; or, A serious warning to Great Britain and her Colonies, found on unquestionable examples of God's temporal vengeance against tyrants, slaveholders, and oppressors...* (London, 1776), p. 183 fn.

[32] 'Speech on Repeal of the Declaratory Act', and 'Sketch of a Negro Code', in *The Writings and Speeches of Edmund Burke*, III, pp. 373–74, 563–81.

The proposals to superintend colonial slavery through new bureaucracies comported with wider attempts to fortify and extend in the Americas the administrative machinery of the state. They marked a faith in the advantages of centralizing power within the Empire. And they reflected an emerging preference to assert greater control over the far-flung settlements and conduct policy in a way that assuaged and 'improved' the diverse peoples residing within. But dissolution of the North American Empire during the American Revolution interrupted efforts to strengthen imperial rule. With faith lost in the ability of the government to command consent in the Western Atlantic, interest in concrete measures for slavery reform waned along with broader attempts to strengthen metropolitan control in colonies governed by representative Assemblies. In their initial, unguarded incarnations, the innovative schemes for gradually abolishing slavery composed by John Hinchliffe, James Ramsay, and Edmund Burke would remain unpublished.

Blacks as Subjects before Emancipation

War, instead, would prove a more effective agent of change than the ambitions of reformers fixed upon radical innovations in imperial governance. Forty years of intermittent fighting in the Americas, from the beginning of the American Revolution through the end of the Napoleonic Wars recast the place of slaves and slavery within the British Empire. Confronted with the prospect of diminished authority in North America after 1775, the British government sometimes competed with slaveholders for the labours of black men and women to sustain power and influence in the colonies. In 1778 General Henry Clinton, expanding on Dunmore's stratagem, offered liberty and protection to enslaved men and women willing to desert from rebel slaveholders. During the final desperate months of the conflict, British commanders in the southern states discussed arming several thousand black soldiers to reclaim the former colonies for the Empire. Those proposals became the basis in 1795 for a new colonial policy as the opportunity to conquer Saint Domingue and the prospect of defeat elsewhere in the Caribbean, led the army to establish twelve regiments of slave soldiers. These 'slaves in red coats' served British forces throughout the Caribbean during the Haitian Revolution and its aftermath, and became in the early nineteenth century the primary defenders of the new British settlements just emerging on the West African coast.[33] During the Seven Years War, and before, slaves sometimes served as auxilaries during British military expeditions in the Caribbean, as Maurice Morgann probably knew. But only under the stress of consecutive American revolutions did black soldiers emerge, in several of the colonies, as the 'sable arm' of British authority.

No one in Britain or the colonies intended these expedients as a prelude to comprehensive emancipation. In most instances, the British armed slaves to defend slavery, rather than abolish it, to grant protection to some black men and women so as to better secure the enslavement of the rest. Slave soldiers in the West India Regiments policed the plantations to discourage slave revolts in the British Caribbean during the Haitian Revolution. They served in the British campaigns in San Domingue that aimed to capture the colony for the Crown and return the insurgents to slavery. And they contributed decisively to British victories in St Lucia, Trinidad, Tobago, Demerara, Essequibo, and Berbice, in the process increasing the number of enslaved men and women residing within the British Empire. The military's need for slave soldiers, historian Roger Norman Buckley has argued, may have helped delay slave trade abolition, which after 1787 became the central concern of the anti-slavery movement. In the last decade of the British slave trade, no one in the Empire owned more slaves than the state itself, which purchased more than 13,000 Africans from Atlantic merchants between 1797 and 1807 in order to man its Caribbean forces.

To the horror of West Indian planters, though, the British government was a different kind of slaveholder. Its agents in the colonies proved far less committed than the white residents to upholding the racial order. Not only did the state put weapons in the hands of slaves. It placed black and white soldiers on an equal footing, providing them with the same uniforms, rations, training, and pay. Black non-commissioned officers sometimes commanded white soldiers. And the Army tried to block colonial efforts to subject the West India Regiments to the authority of the West Indian legislatures, to make slave soldiers subject to the colonial slave codes. When those attempts to protect armed slaves from the West India legislatures failed, Parliament, in 1807, simply declared the more than 10,000 slave soldiers free. By 1815, as a consequence, service for the imperial state had transformed thousands of

[33] This paragraph and the two that follow draw primarily from Sylvia Frey, *Water From the Rock: Black Resistance in a Revolutionary Age* (Princeton, NJ, 1992); and Roger N. Buckley, *Slaves in Red Coats: The British West India Regiments, 1795–1815* (New Haven, Conn., 1979).

men and women from the private property of colonists and merchants into free subjects of the crown. If the British government, for a time, was the largest slaveholder in the Empire, it was also, before emancipation, the most significant liberator. In addition to the tens of thousands who escaped to British lines during the American Revolution, in addition to the 4,000 more that left the United States with British forces during the War of 1812, the British Navy seized between 50,000 and 100,000 enslaved men and women from illicit slave traffickers in the Atlantic between abolition in 1807 and emancipation in 1834.[34] In each case, the liberated were settled at the peripheries of the empire—in Nova Scotia, Sierra Leone, the Cape of Good Hope, Trinidad, or British Honduras—where, as colonists and labourers, they could help secure possession of newly claimed lands.

Taken together, these actions held out the prospect of an Empire defined by allegiance, rather than by race or nationality. Throughout the American colonies and beyond, Africans and the descendants of Africans seized the apparent opportunity by presenting themselves as loyal, and therefore deserving, British subjects. That initiative began in the 1760s, when runaway slaves in England sought at the Court of King's Bench protection from slaveowners who insisted on the right to ship fugitives back to the colonies. Those appeals led to the landmark 1772 case of *Somerset v. Steuart*, which allowed slaves in England the common law right to protection from involuntary exile. Black claims to subjectship multiplied during the 1770s as thousands of enslaved men and women in North America offered loyalty and service to the Crown during the American Revolution in exchange for liberty. In most instances, the black embrace of subject status was instrumental. Black loyalists in Nova Scotia deployed the language of subjectship to establish their rights to land. Sierra Leone settlers referenced their status as subjects to insist on a right to self-governance. In Barbados in 1816, in Demerara in 1823, and in Jamaica in 1832, slaves in rebellion sometimes described their resistance as an attempt to assist Crown efforts to promote emancipation. Free coloureds in the Caribbean made a show of their loyalty to win favour and preference from a government frustrated by recalcitrant

[34] Johnson U. J. Asiegbu, *Slavery and the Politics of Liberation, 1787–1861: A Study of Liberated African Emigration and British Anti-Slavery Policy* (New York, 1969), pp. 91–105; Alvin O. Thompson, 'African "Recaptives" under Apprenticeship in the British West Indies, 1807–1828', *Immigrants and Minorities*, IX, 2 (July, 1990), pp. 123–44; John McNish Weiss, 'The Corps of Colonial Marines, 1814–1816: A Summary', *Immigrants and Minorities*, XV, 1 (March, 1996), pp. 80–90.

white élites in the plantation colonies. What historian Carl Campbell has written about freedmen in the British West Indies applies, in many instances, more broadly to all descendants of Africans in the early nineteenth-century British Empire: 'they looked to the British government to deliver them from the oppression of whites'. The 'rights of British subjects' emerged as a key element in the political ideology of black resistance during and after the age of revolutions. In some instances, that ideology became a core component of collective identities. In 1787, five years after the British fleet departed from the independent state of Georgia, dozens of armed fugitives from slavery continued to harrass Savannah River plantations under the sobriquet of 'the King of England's Soldiers'.[35]

The appeals for British rights met with mixed results. If the British government acknowledged some blacks as subjects of the Crown during and after the American Revolution, it typically failed to provide what those subjects thought they had earned and deserved. The black loyalists received the smallest and least valuable plots in Nova Scotia. Black migrants to Sierra Leone lost the initiative in local politics to white administrators in 1800, after a failed attempt to establish rights to self-governance. The British government took no interest in the aspirations of the recaptives it liberated from the slave trade in the first half of the nineteenth century. Instead, it used 'the Prize Negroes' to solve labour shortages within the Empire. The Abolition Act of 1807 permitted the British Navy and the West India Regiments to conscript those suitable for military service. The state distributed the rest to employers in Sierra Leone, Cape Coast, and the British West Indies to serve as 'apprentices'. These apprenticeships, in theory, prepared liberated Africans to function as independent laborers and consumers. Like the first emancipation theorists writing in the decades before, officials assumed that the newly freed needed supervision and guidance to make the best of liberty. The government designated the Collector of Customs in each colony to monitor the welfare and progress of these wards of the state. In practice, though, the government simply abandoned the recaptives to their masters in the colonies, who, in most instances, treated their charges as if they were slaves.[36]

[35] James W. St. G. Walker, *The Black Loyalists: The Search for a Promised Land in Nova Scotia and Sierra Leone, 1783–1870*, 2nd edn. (Toronto, 1992); Carl C. Campbell, *Cedulants and Capitulants: The Politics of the Coloured Opposition in the Slave Society of Trinidad, 1783–1838* (Port of Spain, Trinidad, 1992), p. 248; Frey, *Water From the Rock*, p. 227.

[36] In addition to the works by Walker, Asiegbu, and Thompson cited above, see Howard Johnson, 'The Liberated Africans in the Bahamas', *Immigrants and Minorities*, VII, 1 (1988)

The enslaved themselves fared even worse. The increasingly familiar notion of blacks as subjects, brought little relief before the 1820s to men and women understood first and foremost as the property of British colonists.

The commitment to gradual emancipation came from the abolitionists, not the state. At a time when slave trade abolition, not emancipation, dominated the anti-slavery agenda, the new settlements populated by liberated black subjects helped revive otherwise dormant interest in free labour experiments. Sierra Leone and Trinidad particularly, like the new colony of Georgia a half century before, allowed abolitionists to explore alternative labour regimes without directly challenging established plantation colonies, without expropriating private property, and without threatening the constitutional rights of the assemblies. The first code of laws for Sierra Leone, as conceived by Granville Sharp in 1786, prohibited the engrossment of land and labour. The Sierra Leone Company, a coalition of abolitionists and merchants that took control of the colony in 1791, encouraged commercial exports from the coast to show that free labour in western Africa could and would produce staple crops for European markets. When these projects failed, successive British Governors reimagined the colony as a beachhead for 'civilization' that might, in time, discourage slaveholding in Africa.

Denied the representative institutions that elsewhere allowed slaveholders to dominate colonial society, Trinidad looked to be the ideal laboratory for anti-slavery projects, or, as one observer put it, 'a subject for an anatomy school... on which all sorts of surgical experiments are tried, to be given up if they fail and to be practiced on others if they succeed'. George Canning wanted to settle English colonists on small plots of land to discourage the creation of sugar plantations. James Stephen hoped in 1803 that the colony might be used to grow sugar with free labour. Four years later, Joseph Barham called for the importation of wage workers from China to show that sugar might be cultivated profitably in the West Indies without slavery and without Africans, a plan briefly tried and abandoned.[37] As with the new colony of Georgia several decades before, the expansion of Empire enabled

p. 16–40; Christopher Saunders, ' "Free Yet Slaves": Prize Negroes at the Cape Revisited', in Nigel Worden and Clifton Crais, eds., *Slavery and its Legacy in the Nineteenth Century Cape Colony* (Johannesburg, 1994), pp. 99–115;

[37] Seymour Drescher, *The Mighty Experiment: Free Labor Versus Slavery in British Emancipation* (Oxford, 2002), pp. 91–100, 106–10; Bridget Brereton, *A History of Modern Trinidad, 1783–1962* (Kingston, Jamaica, 1981), pp. 32–75.

schemers in the metropole to reconceive the means and ends of Empire without destabilizing existing settlements.

The free labour experiments, when tried, proved to be of little help to the abolitionists. They tended to show, as some had feared, that, in the Caribbean, free labour competed poorly with slave labour. As a consequence new approaches to imperial governance would make a greater impact on British ideas of emancipation than new ways to organize and motivate labour. Slavery reform became practical after 1815 because the imperial state, in the new colonies, enjoyed a greater leeway to act. Imperial administrators, such as Maurice Morgann and William Knox, had long fantasized about enhancing metropolitan control of the colonies. But only with the demands presented by an expanding war in the Caribbean did the Crown improve the infrastructure for the management of the colonies. A new Colonial Office, established in 1801, centralized expertise in imperial affairs, gave that expertise greater prominence, and encouraged the emergence of specialists inclined not only to review colonial legislation but to legislate for the colonies. This growing faith in the capacity of the state to govern in the Americas directly helped discourage the emergence of self-government in the new British colonies captured from European rivals in the 1790s and 1800s. Concerned about the prospects for colonial self-rule in a colony where British settlers constituted a small minority of the population, the state refused to grant Trinidad a colonial Assembly and instead reserved executive and legislative authority to itself. Encouraged in this and other instances by the abolitionists, who hoped to prevent the expansion of plantation slavery, British officials made similar arrangements for the other conquered colonies in the Caribbean, the Indian Ocean, and the Cape of Good Hope. As a consequence, in these places, ameliorative and anti-slavery measures could be drafted and instituted through Orders-in-Council prepared by the Colonial office, without securing an Act of Parliament and without having to cajole recalcitrant Assemblies.[38]

What emerged, then, during the first three decades of the nineteenth century, were two constitutional orders. In the older core colonies, planters retained their traditional political and economic supremacy, the imperial state accepted limits on its authority, and plantation slavery remained the

[38] D. J. Murray, *The West Indies and the Development of Colonial Government, 1801–1834* (Oxford, 1965); John Manning Ward, *Colonial Self-Government: The British Experience, 1759–1856* (Toronto, 1976), pp. 83–114.

preeminent mode of production. At the peripheries of the slaving empire, however, in the colonies acquired after the 1790s, liberated slaves often possessed a semblance of legal protection under the care of a paternalist state, which in various guises and with mixed success, permitted experiments in free labour, encouraged the amelioration of slavery and limited the conventional rights of the British colonial élite. Therefore, although apparently still secure in their constitutional rights, the slaveholders of the older colonies confronted a troubling new circumstance. Not only had an Empire without slavery become thinkable. In certain remote parts of the Empire, aspects of the emancipation agenda had begun to influence policy and practice.

This situation could have lasted longer than it did. The reluctance in official quarters to interfere with the customary rights of the colonial Assemblies was profound. The abolitionists sometimes protested the autonomy of the colonial legislatures, especially after the publication of Burke's *Negro Code* in 1792 publicized the range of interventions that gradual emancipation would require. The East India Company reformer Phillip Francis referred to Burke's ideas in 1796 when calling for a comprehensive reorganization of the West Indian establishment. Later activists tried to draw Parliament into assuming a more aggressive stance on colonial questions during the fits and starts of the British anti-slavery movement after 1807, during the effort to establish a register of West Indian slaves during the 1810s, and in the campaign for immediate emancipation after 1823. Among some officials within the new and increasingly influential Colonial Office, the younger James Stephen and Henry Taylor especially, direct intervention by Parliament had its advocates. But, with memories of the American Revolution still fresh, no one with the power to decide was willing to violate traditional colonial rights to property or self-governance.[39] Even as politicians came to agree that Parliament should abolish slavery, reservations remained about whether parliament could abolish slavery.

As a consequence, as pressure from the abolitionists intensified, successive British ministries decided to bully the West Indian Assemblies into reforming, and then abolishing, slavery themselves. The pressure was applied

[39] *Parliamentary History of England*, vol. 32, p. 944–87; Paul Knaplund, *James Stephen and the British Colonial System, 1813–1847* (Madison, Wisc., 1953), pp. 95–130; Robert Livingston Schuyler, *Parliament and the British Empire: Some Constitutional Controversies Concerning Imperial Legislative Jurisdiction* (New York, 1929), pp. 117–93.

in a variety of ways. Model ameliorative legislation drawn up for the Crown Colonies by the Colonial Office advertised the seriousness of the government's intent, and provided a standard to which the West Indian legislatures would be held. Repeatedly after 1815, British ministers threatened the sugar colonies with action by Parliament if they refused to enact ameliorative measures on their own. When not warning of parliamentary intervention, ministers sometimes threatened instead to remove the preferential sugar duties that kept West Indian planters in business.[40] Ultimately, the state offered both the carrot and the stick. By purchasing the freedom of the King's enslaved subjects for £20,000,000, Parliament bribed the West Indian legislatures into enacting emancipation on their own. In the end, in Britain, there was a greater concern to preserve the imperial constitution than colonial slavery.

The British Emancipation Act of 1834, like the emancipation schemes that preceded it, provided for reform without revolution, property without property in slaves, colonial self-governance without colonial independence, plantation labour without the apparatus of physical coercion, Empire without the embarrassment of slavery. It differed little, in its essentials, from the models of emancipation first conceived more than fifty years before. In one respect, the gradual recognition of black men and women as British subjects produced a fundamental change to their experience and position in the British Empire. Subjectship brought enslaved men and women out from under the exclusive authority of the planter. Winning the rights of the subject, however, did not free the liberated from the constraints of race, or the taint of their former status. Because land remained with the planters, because the Caribbean economy remained dependent upon sugar, blacks in the British West Indies would be free from slavery but not free to do as they chose. From the first emancipation schemes through emancipation itself, British reformers had conceived the end of slavery in such a way as to encourage economic liberalism and the rule of law in the British West Indies, and market discipline and dependence for black workers. A resolution to the problem of slavery would leave unresolved emerging questions about the rights free black subjects were due.

[40] Mary Turner, 'Modernizing Slavery: Investigating the Legal Dimension', *New West Indian Guide/Nieuwe West-Indische Gids*, LXXIII, 3–4 (1999), pp. 5–26.

Select Bibliography

JOHNSON U. J. ASIEGBU, *Slavery and the Politics of Liberation, 1787–1861: A Study of Liberated African Emigration and British Anti-Slavery Policy* (New York, 1969).

BRIDGET BRERETON, *A History of Modern Trinidad, 1783–1962* (Kingston, Jamaica, 1981).

ROGER NORMAN BUCKLEY, *Slaves in Red Coats: The British West India Regiments, 1795–1815* (New Haven, 1979).

EDMUND BURKE, 'Sketch of a Negro Code', in Warren M. Elofson, ed., *The Writings and Speeches of Edmund Burke, Volume III: Party, Parliament, and the American War 1774–1780* (Oxford, 1996).

JONATHAN A. BUSH, 'Free to Enslave: The Foundations of Colonial American Slave Law', *Yale Journal of Law and the Humanities*, 5 (1993) pp. 417–70.

SEYMOUR DRESCHER, *The Mighty Experiment: Free Labor Versus Slavery in British Emancipation* (Oxford, 2002).

SYLVIA FREY, *Water From the Rock: Black Resistance in a Revolutionary Age* (Princeton, 1992).

ELSA V. GOVEIA, *The West Indian Slave Laws of the Eighteenth Century* (Bridgetown, Barbados, 1970).

JACK P. GREENE, *Peripheries and Center: Constitutional Development in the Extended Polities of the British Empire and the United States, 1607–1788* (Athens, Ga., 1986).

P. J. MARSHALL, 'Empire and Authority in the Late Eighteenth Century', *Journal of Imperial and Commonwealth History*, 15 (1987) 105–22.

D. J. MURRAY, *The West Indies and the Development of Colonial Government, 1801–1834* (Oxford, 1965).

JAMES RAMSAY, *An Essay on the Treatment and Conversion of African Slaves in the British Sugar Colonies* (London, 1784).

ROBERT LIVINGSTON SCHUYLER, *Parliament and the British Empire: Some Constitutional Controversies Concerning Imperial Legislative Jurisdiction* (New York, 1929).

MARY TURNER, 'Modernizing Slavery: Investigating the Legal Dimension', *New West Indian Guide/Nieuwe West–Indische Gids*, 73, 3–4 (1999) pp. 5–26.

JAMES W. ST. G. WALKER, *The Black Loyalists: The Search for a Promised Land in Nova Scotia and Sierra Leone 1783–1870* (Toronto, 1976).

6

From Slavery to Freedom: Blacks in the Nineteenth-Century British West Indies

GAD HEUMAN

The nineteenth century witnessed significant changes in the British West Indies. Although slavery was abolished, former masters sought to maintain control of their freed slaves. Yet freed people had a different idea of freedom: where it was possible, they sought autonomy for themselves and their families. The riots and disturbances throughout the century were testimony to their continued resistance at attempts to regulate their labour and their mobility. At the same time, freed people sought to participate in politics and often opposed the policies of the planter class. Moreover, blacks developed ideas about race pride which were very different from those of the white value structure. While some of these ideas were congruent with the maintenance of Empire, they would ultimately lead to independence.

In the early nineteenth century, however, the majority of blacks in the British West Indies were slaves.[1] The institution of slavery is therefore crucial to understanding the nature of these societies. In general, a small planter class controlled a large number of slaves. The figures are revealing: at one end of the scale, British Guiana in 1823, the ratio of blacks to whites was 20:1. On the plantations of the colony, the numbers were even higher, often reaching figures of 60:1.[2] In the more settled colony of Jamaica, the preponderance of slaves was still significant; there, the ratio was closer to ten slaves for every white. The exception in the West Indies was Barbados, where a largely resident planter class remained in the island. Yet even here, the ratio of blacks to whites was 4:1.

[1] 'Blacks' is used here to mean all people of African descent, including the offspring of blacks and whites. It excludes people from India who came as indentured labourers to the West Indies in the aftermath of emancipation.

[2] Michael Craton, *Testing the Chains: Resistance to Slavery in the British West Indies* (Ithaca, NY, 1982), p. 269.

Although slaves did a variety of tasks, most of them worked on sugar plantations. In some of the colonies, sugar dominated the economy and the terrain. Several of the early colonies in the region had been producing sugar for almost 200 years; consequently, in islands such as Barbados, nearly all the land in the colony was devoted to sugar. Yet in some of the more recently acquired territories, such as Trinidad and British Guiana, sugar was a relatively new development. The differences between the colonies of the British West Indies would become even more marked during the nineteenth century, especially as a result of emancipation and its aftermath.

Not all slaves in the West Indies produced sugar. In Belize, for example, the export was timber, and the extraction of mahogany and logwood required a very different form of labour organization than the cultivation of sugar. Slaves in Barbuda grew provisions for the plantations in Antigua while many slaves in the Bahamas worked on salvaging shipping wrecks. Even in predominately sugar-growing colonies, such as Jamaica, slaves grew coffee and other commodities, which generally meant less onerous working conditions for the slaves. Whatever the crop, however, there was still considerable differentiation among the slaves.[3]

Blacks were affected not only by the work they did but also by the society around them. One of the significant characteristics of the West Indies was a marked degree of absentee ownership of the sugar estates and a relatively small number of whites. Many whites regarded the West Indies as a place to make money; their hope was to make their fortunes and return to England to live off their estates. Most whites did not achieve this aim, but a significant proportion of the sugar plantations were in the hands of absentee owners. These were generally the largest and the richest of the sugar plantations in the colonies. Although there were considerable white populations in parts of the British West Indies, the absentee *mentalité* had an important effect on blacks as well as whites.[4]

By 1815, another class in West Indian society, the free people of colour, had grown in importance. The free coloureds were an unintended by-product of slave society. As Arnold Sio has put it, they were 'a third party in a system

[3] Gad Heuman, 'The Social Structure of the Slave Societies in the Caribbean', in Franklin Knight, ed., *The Slave Societies of the Caribbean*, Vol. III, *General History of the Caribbean* (London, 1997), p. 142.

[4] J. R. Ward, *British West Indian Slavery, 1750–1834: The Process of Amelioration* (Oxford, 1988), p. 13.

built for two'.[5] Many free people of colour were the offspring of liaisons between white males and black (and subsequently brown) females, and whites sometimes freed their brown children as well as the slave women who produced them. These sexual relationships reflected the curiously skewed demography of most West Indian slave societies in which a minority of whites controlled a large majority of black slaves. Since the white population was often predominately male, relationships between white and black, free and slave quickly developed. The resulting population of free people of colour was therefore heavily coloured and female.

One of the most significant characteristics of the free people of colour in the West Indies was their rapid numerical growth, especially in the early nineteenth century. This was a striking development, especially in the face of an often sharply declining slave and white population. For example, in St Kitts, free coloureds outnumbered the whites by 1823; in Antigua, they had already done so more than a decade earlier and would, in the following decade, be more than double the number of whites. These figures become even more significant when placed in the context of the slave population, which heavily outnumbered that of the whites and the free coloureds. In St Lucia, for example, slaves in 1824 made up almost 75 per cent of the total population. Similarly, in Jamaica, although the free people of colour were more than double the population of whites, the free non-whites comprised just over 10 per cent of the slave population in 1834. The overwhelming predominance of slaves in these societies and the growing numerical importance of the free people of colour meant that it was possible for them to challenge the system which had discriminated against them for so long.[6]

The discrimination against the free people of colour in the West Indies included a variety of political and economic disabilities. Consequently, free coloureds could not vote, partake in political life or testify in court against whites; they were also barred from certain occupations, including working in supervisory posts on the plantations. The free people of colour therefore organized campaigns in the first few decades of the nineteenth century to improve their legal condition in these societies. While many whites were still

[5] Arnold A. Sio, 'Marginality and Free Colored Identity in Caribbean Slave Society', *Slavery and Abolition*, VIII, 2 (Sept., 1987), p. 166.

[6] Gad J. Heuman, *Between Black and White: Race, Politics, and the Free Coloreds in Jamaica, 1792–1865* (Westport, Conn., 1981), p. 7.

prejudiced against the free people of colour, others believed that it was important to respond to their demands, especially in the face of attacks on the slave system itself.[7]

Unlike the free coloureds, the slave population in the British West Indies generally continued to decline in the early nineteenth century. This was a considerable disappointment to the humanitarians, who believed that the abolition of the slave trade in 1808 would lead to an improvement in the condition of the slaves. The humanitarians argued that slaves would no longer be expendable as they had been during the era of the slave trade; consequently, planters would look after their slaves more carefully. Indeed, slavery itself might disappear since planters would realize that free labour was cheaper and more efficient than slave labour.[8]

The reality was very different. All of the British West Indian colonies, apart from Barbados and the Bahamas, failed to maintain a positive natural increase in the slave population in the period from 1816 to 1834. While there were some significant variations from colony to colony, the heaviest decreases occurred in those areas dominated by sugar plantations.[9] Barbados was an exception to this rule. There, the slave population was more creole than elsewhere in the British West Indies. While 44 per cent of the Trinidad slave population consisted of Africans in 1817, only 7 per cent of the Barbadian slaves had been born in Africa. By the turn of the nineteenth century, Barbadian planters were secure in the knowledge that their slave population was self-reproducing. Some Barbadian planters even supported the abolition of the slave trade, seeing African slaves as more problematical than creoles and more likely to rebel.[10]

In spite of their success in abolishing the slave trade, British humanitarians continued to monitor developments in the West Indies. Since they feared the possibility of illegal slave trading, the humanitarians succeeded in enforcing a system of public registration on the slave colonies. Beginning in 1817 and usually repeated every three years, the registration of slaves revealed that conditions for the slaves had not improved after 1808. As low birth rates and

[7] Ibid., pp. 3–51.

[8] Howard Temperley, *British Antislavery, 1833–1870* (London, 1972), p. 7.

[9] B. W. Higman, *Slave Populations of the British Caribbean, 1807–1834* (Baltimore, 1984), pp. 72–76.

[10] Hilary McD. Beckles, 'Emancipation by Law or War? Wilberforce and the 1816 Barbados Slave Rebellion', in David Richardson, ed., *Abolition and its Aftermath: The Historical Context, 1790–1916* (London, 1985), p. 86; Hilary McD. Beckles, *A History of Barbados: From Amerindian Settlement to Nation-State* (Cambridge, 1990), pp. 77–78.

high mortality rates continued to characterize the West Indian colonies, the abolitionists concluded that the planters were continuing their old patterns of mistreating their slaves and working them to death.[11]

The abolitionists therefore decided to establish a new organization and a new policy to deal with the problem of colonial slavery. In the spring of 1823, they founded the Anti-Slavery Society. It sought to develop a gradual plan for the ultimate abolition of slavery but also favoured an immediate improvement in the condition of the slaves. Through a series of compromises between the Anti-Slavery Society and representatives of the West India planters, the British government worked out a set of proposals designed to ameliorate slave conditions. Although moderate in tone, the proposals were greeted with defiance by the colonists in the West Indies. This resistance set the pattern for several years: the British government provided suggestions for amelioration which were met by strong opposition in the colonies.[12]

Angered by these delays, more radical members of the Anti-Slavery Society decided in 1831 to seek immediate emancipation. When news of the renewed anti-slavery drive reached the West Indies in the late spring and summer in 1831, the whites immediately protested. As in 1823, the protests in Jamaica were especially vehement. But now, because of the actions of the abolitionists as well as the support of the government for significant improvements in the conditions of the slaves, whites feared a slave rebellion. Some colonists even threatened to reconsider their allegiance to the Crown.[13]

The problem for the whites was that slaves were aware of the activities of the Anti-Slavery Society and the local resistance to it. This had already led to serious outbreaks elsewhere in the British West Indies. In 1816, Barbadian slaves had become agitated about the Assembly's resistance to Imperial legislation seeking the registration of slaves. Reports at the time equated the registration act with a plan for the emancipation of the slaves, and some slaves believed that freedom was being withheld from them. One literate domestic slave, Nanny Grigg, claimed that slaves were to be freed on Easter Monday, 1816, but 'the only way to get it was to fight for it, otherwise they would not get it; and the way they were to do, was to set fire, as that was the way they did in Saint Domingo'.[14] When the slave rebellion did break out on

[11] Temperley, *British Antislavery*, p. 7.

[12] Ibid., pp. 9–12; Beckles, *History of Barbados*, p. 86.

[13] D. J. Murray, *The West Indies and the Development of Colonial Government* (Oxford, 1965), p. 188; Heuman, *Between Black and White*, pp. 83–84.

[14] Craton, *Testing the Chains*, p. 261.

Easter Sunday, it spread to a third of the island. Its leaders timed the rebellion to coincide with the peak of the harvest season. The slaves turned to arson in an attempt to obtain their freedom; however, the rebellion proved short-lived and the repression was savage.[15]

There was a similar backdrop to the Demerara slave rebellion in 1823. Again, slaves believed that the local whites were withholding their freedom; in this case, the Imperial context of the rebellion was the formation of the Anti-Slavery Society and the beginning of the abolitionists' campaign in Britain. The rebellion broke out in August, involving thousands of slaves. Like the Barbados uprising, it was repressed severely, with the death of about 250 slaves. The planters linked the rebellion to the work of the humanitarians and, more specifically, to the chapel in Demerara of the Revd John Smith, a missionary for the London Missionary Society. He was found guilty of complicity in the rebellion and died in prison while awaiting a reprieve from the Crown.[16]

In 1831 slaves in Jamaica concluded that they, too, had been freed, in part because of the whites' resistance to the Order-in-Council that year which recognized slaves as legal witnesses. When the rebellion broke out just after Christmas, 1831, it was the largest outbreak Jamaica had seen. One report claimed that 20,000 slaves were involved in the uprising; it spread throughout western Jamaica and 226 estates sustained damages involving more than £1,000,000 sterling.[17]

In the Jamaican rebellion, as in Demerara, missionaries were implicated; the rebel, Sam Sharpe, was a leader in the Baptist Church as well as a 'Daddy' in the Native Baptist Church. Essentially, Sharpe used the organization of the church to organize the rebellion. As Mary Turner has suggested, 'the Baptist war... was essentially the Native Baptist war; its leaders shaped mission teaching to their own ends and used mission organization for their own purposes'. Sharpe planned a campaign of passive resistance for the period just after Christmas, 1831: the slaves would simply cease work until their owners paid their wages and thereby conceded that the slaves were free.

[15] Beckles, *History of Barbados*, pp. 79–81.

[16] Craton, *Testing the Chains*, chap. 21, but see also Emilia V. da Costa, *Crowns of Glory, Tears of Blood: The Demerara Slave Rebellion of 1823* (New York, 1994).

[17] Mary Turner, *Slaves and Missionaries: The Disintegration of Jamaican Slave Society, 1787–1834* (Urbana, Ill., 1982), chap. 6; Craton, *Testing the Chains*, chap. 22; and Thomas C. Holt, *The Problem of Freedom: Race, Labor, and Politics in Jamaica and Britain, 1832–1938* (Baltimore, 1992), pp. 14–15.

Sharpe, however, also developed an alternative strategy of armed rebellion in case passive resistance failed.[18]

In organizing the rebellion, Sharpe made use of oaths to exact loyalty from his confederates. The oaths varied: one promised not to 'raise any rebellion' while another vowed 'not to flinch till they had succeeded in getting their freedom'.[19] Although these oaths represented a fusion of religion and politics, political goals were dominant. 'The Baptist War', as the rebellion was called, was a political movement based around religious meetings. Moreover, the rebellion demonstrated 'some degree of political maturity among the slaves. They had created a protest movement... in which religion had been subordinated to political aims.'[20]

The suppression of the rebellion was savage. Soldiers and militiamen seem to have regarded all blacks in the affected areas as enemies and subject to immediate retribution. Running away from the soldiers was regarded as sufficient proof of guilt and alleged ringleaders were often executed without trial. The courts-martial were shams; in the Christmas Rebellion, out of ninety-nine slaves tried at Montego Bay, eighty-one were executed. Prisoners were sometimes executed for minor offences, such as killing estate stock, and whole slave villages on some of the rebel estates were destroyed. In addition, whites blamed missionaries for the rebellion and attacked missionaries and tore down their chapels.[21]

The Jamaican slave rebellion made it clear to many in Britain that slavery could not continue. The abolitionists were now seeking immediate emancipation, and, after 1832, the reformed House of Commons was likely to be more responsive to popular pressure. By 1833, it was apparent to the British government that slavery would have to be abolished; the issue was how it was to be done.

In the end, the Act to emancipate the slaves was a compromise worked out by the government with representatives of the Anti-Slavery Society and the West Indian planters. At its heart was the establishment of the Apprenticeship System: slaves would be freed but become apprentices. They would work for their former masters for up to forty-five hours a week, and less for those

[18] Turner, *Slaves and Missionaries*, pp. 153–54.

[19] Gad Heuman, *'The Killing Time': The Morant Bay Rebellion in Jamaica* (London, 1994), p. 37.

[20] Mary Reckord (née Turner), 'The Jamaica Slave Rebellion of 1831', *Past and Present*, XL (July, 1968), p. 123.

[21] Turner, *Slaves and Missionaries*, pp. 160–61.

who maintained themselves by provision grounds. The legislation separated field and skilled slaves, with skilled slaves ending their apprenticeship after four years while field slaves would do so after six. Children under the age of 6 were to be freed immediately, and special magistrates were to be appointed to oversee the workings of the system. Most important from the planters' point of view was a grant of £20 million compensation for the loss of their slaves. Although the legislative colonies were given the responsibility of passing the specific emancipation legislation, they did so readily since the compensation payments were dependent on it. Two colonies, Antigua and Bermuda, decided to opt for full freedom immediately. In Antigua planters believed they could control their freedmen without the intervening Apprenticeship; in Bermuda slaves worked in maritime occupations and Apprenticeship was therefore less applicable.[22]

At midnight on 31 July 1834, 750,000 former slaves in the British West Indies celebrated their freedom. In general, observers reported calm; missionaries described full churches and peaceful celebrations to mark the end of slavery. But there were problems. In St Kitts the labourers on the plantations had resolved not to return to work without pay. Some of the apprentices said that 'they would give their souls to hell and their bodies to the sharks rather than be bound to work as apprentices'. The authorities declared martial law, rounded up the striking apprentices who had fled and forced then back to work.[23]

The speedy suppression of the apprentices' strike in St Kitts had significant ramifications for neighbouring islands. The Lieutenant-Governor of Dominica, Sir Charles Schomberg, reported that there were close connections between the apprentices in Dominica and in St Kitts. Schomberg had heard that Dominican apprentices were proclaiming, 'We free; no bind; no work, as in St. Christopher's.' His view was that if the strike in St Kitts had not been put down quickly, there would have been 'a dire situation in Dominica'.[24]

As it was, there were disturbances on the island. In at least two districts of Dominica, apprentices refused to work; in the parish of St Peter, for example,

[22] William A. Green, *British Slave Emancipation: The Sugar Colonies and the Great Experiment, 1830–1865* (Oxford, 1976), chap. 5.

[23] Richard Frucht, 'From Slavery to Unfreedom in the Plantation Society of St. Kitts, W.I.', in Vera Rubin and Arthur Tuden, eds., *Comparative Perspectives on Slavery in New World Plantation Societies* (New York, 1977), p. 384. See also Robert S. Shelton, 'A Modified Crime: The Apprenticeship System in St. Kitts', *Slavery and Abolition*, XVI, 3 (1995), pp. 331–45.

[24] MacGregor to Spring Rice, 1 Jan. 1835, no. 216, encl: Schomberg to MacGregor, 2 Dec. 1834, *Parliamentary Papers* (hereafter *PP*) (1835) (278-II), no. 4, p. 635.

apprentices declared themselves as free as the magistrates, and one apprentice 'became so outrageous as to offer his breast to be shot rather than obey the law'. Elsewhere, it required a detachment of the 76th Regiment to put down the resistance of the apprentices. As in St Kitts, apprentices in Dominica claimed that the King had freed them and that it was the local authorities who were responsible for the Apprenticeship and for 'endeavouring to keep them in bondage'.[25]

Further afield in the Caribbean, there were also serious difficulties among the apprentices. In Trinidad, the apprentices vowed to strike and reiterated some of the same themes as the apprentices in St Kitts and in Dominica. According to one report, the Trinidad apprentices believed that the King had freed them outright and that Apprenticeship was a plan hatched by their masters and the Governor. For the apprentices, the planters were 'dam tief' and the Governor 'an old rogue'; after all, the King had enough money to buy them fully out of slavery and was not such a fool as to only make them half free.[26] Again, there was a problem with the logic of Apprenticeship. The apprentices could not understand how the King could call them 'free', and yet force them to work for their former owners. Parodying the concept of Apprenticeship, the apprentices also claimed that they already knew their work sufficiently and did not need an 'apprenticeship' of any kind.[27]

Apprentices in Jamaica shared these views and also reacted negatively to the Apprenticeship System. In the parish of St Ann, they went on strike, vowing not to work unless they were paid. Elsewhere on the island, they were disappointed by the behaviour of the planters who withdrew many of the privileges which the apprentices had enjoyed as slaves. These included forcing women who had formerly been excused from field labour (because of old age or because they had produced six children) back into the work gangs; not allowing mothers to suckle their children in the fields; and taking away all field cooks and nurses to watch the children in the fields. The Governor of Jamaica, Lord Sligo, was disturbed about the behaviour of the whites: he saw it as 'outrageous and oppressive' and believed that it was producing very negative effects among the apprentices.[28]

[25] The *Royal Gazette of British Guiana*, 11 Sept. 1834, citing *The Observer*, 6 Aug. 1834 and *The Colonist*, 9 Aug. 1834.

[26] *Supplement to The Royal Gazette*, 13–20 Sept. 1834.

[27] Hill to Spring Rice, 7 Aug. 1834, *PP* (1835) (278-II), L, no. 301, p. 736.

[28] *PP* (1835) (278-II) L, p. 151; Sligo to Bishop of Jamaica, 2 Sept. 1834, in ibid., p. 156.

Apart from the strikes and disputes across the island, there was another level of protest which was more generalized and more difficult to control. James Scott has described this behaviour of peasants in terms of 'hidden transcripts', using 'foot-dragging' or 'poaching' as part of an everyday form of resistance.[29] Apprentices in Jamaica employed such tactics. Governor Sligo commented on the reaction of many apprentices who were unhappy with the new system: they resorted to 'turning out late, irregularity to work, and idling of time'. To some degree, these 'delinquencies' were dealt with by the special magistrates, but there was the additional problem of what planters perceived as 'insolence and insubordination'. The use of language was significant in this context; a special magistrate, E. D. Baynes, reported that the apprentice was 'daily becoming more heedless of and more disrespectful to his manager'. According to Baynes, apprentices were no longer willing to accept the language of their former owners without an appropriate retort.[30]

Although this pattern of day–to–day resistance was not easy to manage, the more overt acts of resistance were suppressed quickly. In the most significant of the outbreaks, the problems in St Ann, Governor Sligo dispatched a steamship with 160 soldiers who were deployed throughout various parts of the parish. At first, the apprentices believed that the troops had come to protect them, but they soon realized that this was not the case. As one observer noted, the troops quelled 'that spirit of passive resistance' which the apprentices had adopted. Even then, the forces had to punish 'a vast number of the Negroes' by whipping and by putting them in the workhouse. In the face of this considerable show of force, the apprentices had little choice: 'finding the soldiers so close upon them in every direction', they returned to work.[31]

The reaction of the apprentices in the first year of the Apprenticeship was highly revealing. Their image of freedom differed substantially from those of the policy-makers in the Colonial Office as well as their former masters. For those in authority, it was critical to maintain the established order and the

[29] James Scott, *Domination and the Arts of Resistance: Hidden Transcripts* (New Haven, Conn., 1990), p. xiii.

[30] Sligo to Glenelg, 5 March 1836, no. 362; encl: Murchison to Nunes, 1 March 1835, CO 137/215; Sligo to Glenelg, 2 April 1836, encl: Report of E. D. Baynes, 28 March 1836, *PP* (1836) (166-I), XLVIII, p. 343.

[31] *Supplement to The Royal Gazette*, 9–16 Aug. 1834; *Postscript to The Royal Gazette*, 9–16 Aug. 1834; Sligo to Spring Rice, 13 Aug. 1834, CO 137/192, no. 16.

existing hierarchies in the Caribbean. Certainly, there was a recognized need to protect the apprentices, but it was also important to ensure the continuity of the plantation system and the production of sugar.

For the apprentices, and especially those who resisted the establishment of Apprenticeship, it was difficult to comprehend the new system. Like the apprentices in Trinidad, they felt that they needed no 'Apprenticeship'; they needed no training for freedom or for their work on the plantations. In fact, the nature of the slaves' own economy in the Caribbean, with its extensive provision-ground system and highly developed markets, meant that slaves were probably better prepared for freedom than were their former masters.[32] At the onset of Apprenticeship, ex-slaves wanted to be fully free; they sought 'unrestricted freedom' and not a system of forced labour, even for part of the week. Apprentices were prepared to work for wages, but many also believed that their houses and their provision grounds belonged to them and not to the planters.

One of the most noticeable aspects of the apprentices' resistance to the system was the role of women. They were prominent in the march on Government House in Trinidad and in several of the disturbances in Jamaica. The authorities repeatedly complained about the women apprentices; for example, Governor Sligo wrote home that 'it is notorious that they [the women] are all over the Island the most troublesome'.[33] There were good reasons why women were so prominent in the resistance to Apprenticeship. As Thomas Holt has pointed out, female apprentices formed the bulk of the field labouring force on the plantations, just as they had during slavery. Regulations about hours and about working practices would therefore have affected women more directly than men.[34]

The explanation for the role of women as ringleaders against Apprenticeship is, however, more complicated than simply numerical predominance. In a perceptive treatment of this issue, Mimi Sheller discusses women's role in Jamaica during this period as both workers and mothers. As Sheller suggests, 'unlike their male counterparts, female field labourers could make claims for improved working conditions not simply as free workers, but specifically as mothers who were struggling to support their families'. The planters' withdrawal of privileges during Apprenticeship and, specifically, those affecting

[32] For an important collection on this theme, see Ira Berlin and Philip D. Morgan, eds., *The Slaves' Economy: Independent Production by Slaves in the Americas* (London, 1991).

[33] Sligo to Spring Rice, 9 Dec. 1834, CO 137/194, no. 91.

[34] Holt, *The Problem of Freedom*, p. 64.

pregnant women, women with children, and the role of elderly matriarchs impinged directly on women. 'Female apprentices were punished in large numbers for trying to assert and protect the limited rights they had won as mothers of the slave labour force...' In the end, the harsh treatment of women rebounded against the planters and helped to discredit the whole Apprenticeship scheme and led to its premature abolition in 1838.[35]

Abolitionists in Britain, who had opposed the establishment of the Apprenticeship System, were aware of the problems associated with it and began an anti-apprenticeship campaign. Led by a wealthy merchant, Joseph Sturge, it gathered momentum after Sturge and one of his associates, Thomas Harvey, published an attack on the system, *The West Indies in 1837*. Although the government sought to improve the workings of the system in early 1838, the campaign against the Apprenticeship System continued. Bowing to this pressure, the Assemblies in the West Indies ended the system prematurely on 1 August 1838. Yet, even in its abbreviated form, the Apprenticeship System was not successful; it did not establish a useful basis for a free society. Instead, it frequently led to bitterness and controversy and made the working out of freedom that much more difficult.

Although the planters were willing to end the Apprenticeship System early, they did not envision emancipation altering either the hierarchical nature of society or their political dominance. More importantly, they sought to ensure a steady and cheap supply of labour. Faced with the possibility that ex-slaves might leave the estates, former masters turned to a variety of coercive measures to retain their labour. The most common method, known as the tenancy-at-will system, combined rents with wages and led to exorbitant charges for the rental of houses and grounds, often exceeding the wages paid to the labourers. With varying degrees of success, the system was used in Dominica, Nevis, Montserrat, St Lucia, Tobago, St Vincent, Antigua, British Guiana, Jamaica, and Barbados.[36]

Lionel Smith, the Governor of Jamaica, pointed out some of the consequences of these excessive charges. He had heard of many cases in which a labourer earned 5 shillings a week for his work but was charged 8s. for rent, leaving him in debt to the plantation and with nothing to maintain his

[35] Mimi Sheller, 'Quasheba, Mother, Queen: Black Women's Public Leadership and Political Protest in Post-Emancipation Jamaica, 1834–65', *Slavery and Abolition*, XIX, 3 (Dec. 1998), pp. 93, 94.

[36] Brian L. Moore, *Race, Power and Social Segmentation in Colonial Society: Guyana After Slavery, 1838–1891* (New York, 1987), p. 39.

family. A further problem arose when planters simply ejected their former slaves from the plantations. These 'ejectments' could arise over trivial offences. In Barbados, Betsy Cleaver, a labourer, was thrown off the plantation, had her house destroyed and her possessions thrown into the road because she had chosen to have her sugar cane processed at another estate. A magistrate in Jamaica concluded that the planters were to blame for the difficult state of labour relations after emancipation: 'what with demanding double rent, mulcting them of their pay, non-payment of wages due, the daily threat of turning them off and rooting up their grounds, and of still imbibing olden prejudices, and vaunting them; that punishment alone is the impetus by which they are to be made to labour'.[37]

Freed men and women reacted to these measures, often by leaving the plantations when it was possible to do so. This was precisely what the planters had most feared. In the case of Jamaica, where there was abundant land not controlled by the estates, thousands of ex-slaves left the plantations to establish freeholds and independent villages. Thomas Holt calculated that by 1845, seven years after full emancipation, over 20,000 freeholds of less than ten acres had been registered, encompassing a population of over 60,000 people. Over 20 per cent of the ex-slave population had settled on small freeholds. While many of these free people continued to work at least part-time on the estates, their freeholds provided them with a significant degree of independence from the planters. Other colonies also reported significant losses of labourers from the plantations. In Dominica, a survey of forty-one estates for the six month period after the onset of full freedom revealed a decrease in the plantation labour force of 39 per cent.[38]

While it was not possible in many cases for free people to purchase freeholds, they none the less made clear their views about the meaning of freedom. A magistrate in Jamaica writing about events in the western part of the island just over six months after emancipation complained about the labourers. They began work late, finished earlier than in the past, and had the idea that freedom meant they should work less than during slavery. As the magistrate put it, 'a foolish idea having got into the negroes' head that (to use his own words) he must not sell "his free" and he thinks that freedom ought

[37] Smith to Glenelg, 24 Sept. 1838, CO 137/232, no. 182; *Barbados Globe & Colonial Advocate*, 4 Nov. 1839; Smith to Glenelg, 23 March 1839, encl: Report of Hamilton, Port Royal, 25 Feb., CO 137/242, no. 65.

[38] Holt, *The Problem of Freedom*, pp. 144, 154; Michel-Rolph Trouillot, *Peasants and Capital: Dominica in the World Economy* (Baltimore, 1988), p. 78.

at all events to produce a diminution of his manual labor, or he would be undeserving such a boon'.[39]

Other free people elsewhere in the Caribbean expressed similar ideas about labour and freedom. When a magistrate visited some of the largest estates in Dominica soon after emancipation, he asked the ex-slaves for their views. One woman said that she 'had been a slave all her life, and would not work for anybody again'. Another asked if she could go to town for a week or two and then return to work on the estate. When the magistrate told her that she needed permission, she responded, 'Is this what you call free'? Writing nearly two months after emancipation, another magistrate on the island reported that the people had done little or no work on the plantations since 1 August. According to the magistrate, the free people believed that they had two months to rest and, as they put it, 'to refresh themselves'.[40]

Issues of gender and labour were also highly significant to the ex-slaves. After emancipation, women often withdrew from plantation labour in large numbers. Since women had formed the majority of the field labour force during slavery, this could have dramatic effects. Swithin Wilmot has detailed the decline in the female labour force on Golden Grove Estate in Jamaica: he found that of the 137 women working on the estate up to emancipation, only nineteen were at work in October, 1838. Across the island in St James parish, 60 per cent of the workers on estates were women up to the end of the Apprenticeship System; less than six months into full freedom, only one-third of the labourers were women.[41]

Although European ideas of gender had a role in the withdrawal of female labour from the plantations, there were also more important factors at work. Bridget Brereton has emphasized the family strategies pursued by many ex-slaves after emancipation. Rather than working on the plantations, women chose to work in the provision grounds and in marketing their produce. This

[39] Smith to Glenelg, 23 March 1839, encl: Report of Tho. Abbott, Westmoreland, 28 Feb., CO 137/242, no. 65.

[40] Colebrooke to Glenelg, 15 Oct. 1838, p. 390, encl no. 2: Phillips to the President, 1 Oct., p. 393, *PP* (1839) (107-V), XXXVII; Colebrooke to Glenelg, 15 Oct. 1838, encl: report of Howard Lloyd, stipendiary magistrate, 25 Sep., CO 71/87, no. 232.

[41] Swithin Wilmot,' "Females of Abandoned Character"?: Women and Protest in Jamaica, 1838–65' in Verene Shepherd, Bridget Brereton and Barbara Bailey, eds., *Engendering History: Caribbean Women in Historical Perspective* (Kingston, Jamaica, 1995), p. 280; Smith to Glenelg, 23 March 1839, no. 65, encl: Report on the actual state of the LABOURING POPULATION ... of Saint James between the abolition of the Apprenticeship System and the middle of February, 1839, *PP* (1840) (272), XXXV, p. 599.

decision made economic sense, but it also provided a greater degree of autonomy for ex-slaves after emancipation. The free people on an estate in western Jamaica reinforced this point, when they told a magistrate:

> that it was of no use being free, it was only the name '*so-so*' that when it was necessary their wives would assist *them*, by performing light work, but they could not give their consent, to make them work always, and at all sorts of work.

Independence from the plantation meant more than just autonomy; as Brereton has argued, freedom also included 'the right to control one's own body, the right to be free of violation and abuse'. This right extended to children as well: it was part of the family strategy after emancipation to keep young children out of field work and, if possible, to send them to school or to use the older children in domestic production.[42]

The ex-slaves' views about gender and labour as well as about freedom led to a series of strikes and riots in the immediate aftermath of emancipation. Across the region, free men and women resisted low wages and high rents. For example, in St Lucia, one report soon after emancipation claimed that 'two-thirds of the labouring population refused to work on the estates'. There were frequent strikes on the island and many clashes with the authorities. In Grenada, the authorities sought to eject an ex-slave from his house because he refused to accept the wages offered and also would not leave his home. But the attempt failed, as a large group of free men and women attacked the constables who sought to serve a warrant. The men and women regarded the houses as their own, 'given them by the Queen; and said, with violent oaths, they were determined to keep possession of [them]'. Writing from Tobago less than three weeks after emancipation, the Lieutenant-Governor (Glerely) described the reluctance of labourers to return to work for the wages on offer. He reported that 'there was as well organized a combination, from one end of the island to the other, to strike for wages as ever took place in England, but conducted with more secrecy'.[43]

[42] Smith to Glenelg, 3 Dec. 1838, encl: Report of J. A. Harris, 3 Dec., Lucea CO 137/232, no. 202; Bridget Brereton, 'Family Strategies, Gender, and the Shift to Wage Labour in the British Caribbean', in Bridget Brereton and Kevin A. Yelvington, eds., *The Colonial Caribbean in Transition: Essays on Postemancipation Social and Cultural History* (Kingston, Jamaica, 1999), pp. 98–99, 105. See also Mimi Sheller's article, which reinforces this point about women's resistance to labour on the plantations and describes it as 'part of a broader political strategy of strikes and labour solidarity aimed at breaking planters' power to control black families' (Sheller, 'Quasheba, Mother, Queen', p. 98).

[43] Michael Louis,' "An Equal Right to the Soil": The Rise of a Peasantry in St. Lucia, 1838–1900', unpublished Ph.D. dissertation, Johns Hopkins University, 1981, p. 25; MacGregor

Strikes and riots were one form of response of the ex-slaves to emancipation; another was challenging the political domination of the planters. This took the form of electing black and brown representatives to the local Assemblies. Although not forming a single political bloc, black and brown Assemblymen generally supported British government policies. Moreover, they could be significant: in Dominica, for example, coloured representatives formed a majority in the Assembly. Their presence prevented the passage of harsh legislation against the ex-slaves which characterized many other West Indian colonies.[44]

In Jamaica, the coloured and black members of the Assembly united to form the Town Party, a faction which opposed the predominately planters' Country Party. The coloureds favoured funds being spent on education, resisted expensive immigration schemes, and sought to counter planter attempts to restrict the franchise. Moreover, the coloureds also voted against measures to shift the burden of taxation almost entirely on small settlers. Brown and black representatives did remain a minority in the Jamaican House of Assembly, but as their numbers increased, the planters became increasingly alarmed about the possibility of being outnumbered.[45]

Coloured and black politicians were not the only group to oppose the planters. European missionaries, and especially the Baptists, were concerned about the plight of the ex-slaves. They attacked the harsh legislation emanating from the Jamaican Assembly and also wished to sever the connection between church and state in the colony. Led by William Knibb, the Baptists sought to organize the small settler vote; they wanted to elect Assemblymen committed to their programme. The Baptists therefore attempted to register large numbers of freeholders who would return suitable candidates to the Assembly. In the early 1840s, they were becoming a potentially important political force: Governor Charles Metcalfe regarded them as a political party with great influence over the ex-slave population. However, when his successor, Lord Elgin, called a surprise election in 1844, the Baptists were unable

to Glenelg, 18 Sept. 1838, *PP* (1839) (107-IV), XXXVI, no. 249, p. 503, encl. A: Richard & Munn to Captain Clarke, 24 Aug., *PP* (1839) (107-IV), XXXVI, no. 249, p. 503; MacGregor to Glenelg, 4 Sept. 1838, no. 242, p. 531, encl. 9: Darling to MacGregor, 18 Aug., *PP* (1839) (107-IV), XXXVI, no. 242, p. 531.

[44] Russell Chace, Jr., 'Protest in Post-Emancipation Dominica: The "Guerre Negre" of 1844', *Journal of Caribbean History*, XXIII, 2 (1989), p. 119.

[45] Heuman, *Between Black and White*, chap. 10.

to affect the results significantly and they declined thereafter as a political force in Jamaica.[46]

Missionaries also aided the process of setting up free villages after emancipation. Often helped by British philanthropists, missionaries bought land from the planters for the purpose. Some of the Jamaican free villages were established during the apprenticeship period: the first such village, Sligoville, was founded in 1835. During the next six years, Baptist missionaries settled more than 3,000 people in Baptist villages, some with evocative names such as Buxton, Wilberforce, and Victoria.[47]

It was not only missionaries who organized free villages; ex-slaves did so as well. In British Guiana, former plantation headmen bought up estates on behalf of a larger group of freed people. For example, in November 1839, sixty-three people, many of whom were headmen, bought Northbrook Estate for $10,000; this was subsequently subdivided. A few years later four headmen purchased Den Amstel estate on behalf of seventy field workers. Villages were also established in some of the smaller colonies: in Antigua, by 1842, there were twenty-seven independent villages containing over 1,000 homes and 3,600 people.[48]

The establishment of free villages and the withdrawal of labour generally from the estates meant that planters looked abroad for a new supply of labour. The most fruitful source of that labour proved to be India, and the number of immigrants was significant. Nearly 250,000 went to British Guiana, almost 150,000 to Trinidad, and over 36,000 to Jamaica. In each of these colonies, more than two-thirds of the Indians chose to remain rather than return to India.[49]

Although Indian immigration benefited the West Indian sugar industry, it did little to improve the condition of the ex-slave population. Instead, the planters' focus on importing labour meant that the problems of the freed people were often ignored. This oversight had serious repercussions. For example, in the aftermath of emancipation, there was a lack of doctors

[46] Robert J. Stewart, *Religion and Society in Post-Emancipation Jamaica* (Knoxville, Tenn., 1992), pp. 19–20.

[47] Philip D. Curtin, *Two Jamaicas: The Role of Ideas in a Tropical Colony, 1830–1865* (Cambridge, Mass., 1955), p. 115.

[48] Green, *British Slave Emancipation*, p. 302; Douglas Hall, *Five of the Leewards, 1834–1870: The Major Problems of the Post-Emancipation Period in Antigua, Barbuda, Montserrat, Nevis and St. Kitts* (Bridgetown, Barbados, 1971), p. 53.

[49] K. O. Laurence, *Immigration into the West Indies in the 19th Century* (Kingston, Jamaica, 1971), pp. 26.

available for the ex-slave population. Moreover, epidemics swept through the West Indies, often causing terrible loss of life. A cholera epidemic in Jamaica in 1850 cost 30,000 lives; it was followed by an outbreak of influenza as well as smallpox and then a return of cholera. The disease also spread through the Lesser Antilles and Barbados; in 1854, upwards of 15,000 people died from its effects.[50]

Ex-slaves did not passively accept their condition in the post-emancipation West Indies. There was a series of riots and protests throughout the region. In 1844 freed people protested violently in Dominica against the taking of a census. At first, enumerators were assaulted, but these incidents developed into attacks on estate property and managers. A conspiracy four years later in western Jamaica was accompanied by protests and riots in other parts of the island. Jamaica was also the scene of two riots in 1859, one of which was directed against toll-gates in several parts of western Jamaica. In 1862 a labour strike in St Vincent escalated into a riot: freed people assaulted estate managers and plundered planters' houses and shops over a wide area. The authorities killed four people and wounded at least seven others in suppressing the riot. There were two important riots in 1876, one in Tobago, the other in Barbados. In Tobago a policeman was killed, after fatally shooting a woman and injuring a man when a crowd resisted arrest. The Barbados riots were more serious: there, the issue was whether Barbados would be joined politically to the Windward colonies. The riots over Confederation led to the death of eight people.[51]

There were common grievances in many of these riots. One was the problem of low pay, made worse by patterns of irregular payments and arbitrary work stoppages. When linked to the truck system, in which estates had their own shops and created a type of debt peonage among their workers, the situation could become tense. Another serious grievance centred around the fear of re-enslavement; this was the motivating force behind the Dominica riots and was a factor in several others. In addition, the ex-slaves' desire for land was often an element in these disturbances. Freed people in Dominica believed that freedom implied more than a change in legal status; it also meant a grant of land.[52]

[50] Green, *British Slave Emancipation*, pp. 311–12.

[51] Gad Heuman, 'Post-Emancipation Resistance in the Caribbean: An Overview', in Karen Fog Olwig, ed., *Small Islands, Large Questions: Society, Culture & Resistance in the Post-Emancipation Caribbean* (London, 1995), pp. 123–34.

[52] Ibid.

Several of these factors were prominent in the Morant Bay Rebellion in Jamaica, the most important post-emancipation outbreak during this period. On 11 October 1865 several hundred blacks marched into the town of Morant Bay, the principal town in the sugar parish of St Thomas in the East. Led by Paul Bogle, a native Baptist deacon, the crowd attacked the police station before confronting the militia and the parish authorities. Firing began. In the subsequent mêlée, the crowd killed eighteen people. Over the next few days, local people killed two planters and attacked many plantations in the parish.

While there were specific tensions in the parish of St Thomas in the East, many of the local problems were symptomatic of difficulties across Jamaica. The common people were bitter about the continued political, social, and economic domination of the whites. Among other things, this meant a lopsided and partial judicial structure; for many blacks, the only solution was an alternative legal system which they themselves controlled. Another problem centred around land: the people believed that their provision grounds belonged to them and that they should not have to pay rent. Access to land was a symbol of freedom, a freedom which some believed might even be denied to them. In addition, there were repeated complaints about the low level of wages paid on the plantations.

The government's response to the rebellion was swift and brutal. The Governor, Edward John Eyre, declared martial law in the eastern part of Jamaica, despatched British troops to the parish, and organized the Maroons to deal with the outbreak. The month-long period of martial law resulted in the deaths of over 400 blacks. Because of the severity of the repression, the case because a *cause célèbre* in England. John Stuart Mill was among a group of radicals and Nonconformists who organized a campaign to try the Governor for his part in the suppression of the rebellion. In response, Thomas Carlyle, Charles Kingsley, and Charles Dickens helped to establish an Eyre Defence Committee. Although Eyre was never committed for trial, the controversy surrounding his case raised important issues about the nature of colonial rule and governmental accountability.[53]

In Jamaica, the Governor made use of the rebellion to push for constitutional change. Since the Colonial Office had wanted for some time to abolish the House of Assembly, Eyre convinced a frightened House that they should opt for Crown Colony government. Although there was some

[53] Heuman, '*The Killing Time*'.

opposition to this change, the legislators ultimately accepted it. This meant classic Crown Colony government, with a nominated Council, consisting of six officials and three unofficial members and the abolition of the 200–year–old House of Assembly. Apart from Barbados, the other legislative colonies in the West Indies followed suit, although it took nearly a decade for colonies such as Grenada and Tobago to make the change. By the mid–1870s, and with the continuing exception of Barbados, Crown Colony government was fully established in the British West Indies.[54]

Crown Colony government had certain advantages. Unlike the system of representative government, with its often fractious assemblies, there was less scope for serious political divisions in the legislature. Administration was smoother; there was effectively no opposition to the Governor. It was therefore possible to inaugurate administrative changes which were long overdue.

Nevertheless, there were also problems with Crown Colony government. In the case of Jamaica, for example, government reforms were expensive and taxes had to be increased. Neither the people nor their representatives were involved; one local newspaper, *The Falmouth Post*, described the system as one of 'paternal despotism'. During the 1870s, there was increasing hostility to Crown Colony government in Jamaica. Since the system was dominated by expatriate white officials, blacks and people of colour felt the loss of political offices which had previously been open to them. Yet local whites also resented Crown Colony government, since it excluded Jamaicans generally. Agitation against the system led to its modification: in 1884, the Legislative Council was altered to increase the number of elected members. In general, however, Crown Colony government remained largely unmodified until after the First World War. It was this political system which had to deal with the economic crisis of the late nineteenth century.[55]

The problem was caused primarily by European beet sugar producers increasing their production substantially during the second half of the century. By 1870 they produced nearly one-third of the total world sugar output. When Germany, the world's major producer of beet sugar, doubled bounties on its sugar exports in 1883–84, the effect on the British market was dramatic. There was a massive increase in the amount of beet sugar imported

[54] Heuman, '*The Killing Time*' p. 190; H. A. Will, *Constitutional Change in the British West Indies, 1880–1903* (Oxford, 1970), p. 11.

[55] Will, *Constitutional Change*, p. 3; Heuman, '*The Killing Time*', pp. 177–78; J. H. Parry and Philip Sherlock, *A Short History of the West Indies*, 3rd edn., (London, 1976), pp. 216–17.

into Britain and, consequently, a collapse in the sugar price. The position of West Indian sugar worsened further when the French and Germans doubled their bounties on beet sugar in 1896, leading to a further drop in sugar prices the following year. In the West Indies, the planters claimed that they were threatened with extinction.[56]

As in the crises of the late 1840s, a number of West Indian merchant houses collapsed, especially those involved in the smaller islands. The production of West Indian sugar was drastically affected: for example, Grenada's output of sugar dropped by more than a half as an immediate result of the crisis. In St Vincent, two-thirds of the sugar cultivation in the island had been abandoned by 1886. Jamaica's production was affected by the simultaneous exodus of thousands of labourers to work on the Panama Canal.[57]

A further consequence of the economic crisis of the late nineteenth century was the amalgamation of sugar plantations. Of the 150 estates in British Guiana in 1865, for instance, there were only fifty remaining by the turn of the century. In Trinidad, where the first central factories were established in the West Indies, there was also a reduction of the number of estates, from 110 in 1865 to half that number at the end of the century. The number of sugar estates in Jamaica continued to decline, with only about 140 remaining in 1896. Overall in the British West Indies, the number of estates declined by about a third between the time of emancipation and 1900.[58]

The prolonged economic depression in the late nineteenth century had repercussions for the working population in the West Indies. In response to the crisis, planters reduced wages, which created considerable hardship for sugar-cane workers. There were reports of widespread destitution and malnutrition after 1884, as well as an increase in the incidence of disease. As in the years following emancipation, the economic and social difficulties of the period were reflected in a large number of riots and disturbances.[59]

These riots spread throughout the region. Violence erupted in Grenada in 1895, in St Vincent in 1891 and Dominica in 1893. In 1896 strikes and

[56] Richard Lobdell, 'Patterns of Investment and Sources of Credit in the British West Indian Sugar Industry, 1838–1897', *Journal of Caribbean History*, IV (1972) p. 325; R. W. Beachey, *The British West Indies Sugar Industry in the Late 19th Century* (Westport, Conn., 1957), pp. 59, 148–49.

[57] Beachey, *British West Indies Sugar Industry*, p. 59.

[58] Ibid., pp. 121–27.

[59] Bonham C. Richardson, 'Prelude to Nationalism? Riots and Land Use Changes in the Lesser Antilles in the 1890s', in Wim Hoogbergen, ed., *Born Out of Resistance: On Caribbean Cultural Creativity* (Utrecht, 1995), p. 206.

demonstrations over the issue of lowered wages marked the beginning of the harvest season in St Kitts; during the subsequent riots, two people were killed and many others wounded. A plantation riot among Indian indentured workers in British Guiana later in the same year also led to the loss of life: five Indian workers were killed and another fifty-nine injured when the police opened fire on the crowd. In addition to smaller outbreaks in Montserrat and Dominica, there were serious riots in Montego Bay, Jamaica in 1902, largely because of high taxes but also because of difficult economic conditions. Montego Bay was the target of the rioters for two days, and it took British forces from across the island to quell the riots. The 1905 riots in British Guiana linked urban workers and sugar estate labourers and were also a response to the declining living standards of the workers at the end of the century. In many of these outbreaks, women in British Guiana had a significant role in the riots.[60]

The 1890s also witnessed the first organized workingmen's association in the West Indies. In Jamaica, skilled tradesmen created separate unions, beginning in 1898 with the establishment of the Artisans' Union. A decade later, two others, made up of cigar-makers and printers, were also formed. Elsewhere, the Trinidad Workingmen's Association sought to bring together various trades within one organization. Unlike the unions in Jamaica, the Trinidad union had political objectives, such as the reduction of taxes and constitutional reform. But these unions either foundered after unsuccessful strikes or simply ceased to function; it was not until after the First World War that more permanent unions were established.[61]

This period saw another important development: a reaction to the pseudo-scientific racism in British thought. One strand of British thinking in the mid-nineteenth century was reflected in the work of Thomas Carlyle, who regarded blacks as an inferior race and emancipation as the ruin of the West Indies. The Morant Bay Rebellion in Jamaica helped to strengthen these views, and the emergence of Social Darwinian ideas reinforced belief in white domination as well as the subordination of blacks. But not all blacks accepted these notions. A Trinidadian, J. J. Thomas, in a book entitled

[60] Ibid., pp. 208–09; Patrick Bryan, *The Jamaican People, 1880–1900* (London, 1991), pp. 271–74; Walter Rodney, *A History of the Guyanese Working People, 1881–1905* (Kingston, Jamaica, 1981), chap. 8.

[61] Richard Hart, 'Origin and Development of the Working Class in the English-Speaking Caribbean Area, 1897–1937', in Malcolm Cross and Gad Heuman, eds., *Labour in the Caribbean: From Emancipation to Independence* (London, 1988), pp. 43–50.

Froudacity published in 1888, called for united action to uplift blacks and for a recognition of the links between the New World and Africa. Although some middle-class blacks in Trinidad undoubtedly rejected their racial heritage, a significant number were strong proponents of race consciousness.

In Jamaica, such views were reflected in a black colonizing scheme. In 1899, Dr Albert Thorne, a Barbadian, held a meeting in which he proposed to settle West Indian settlers in Africa, with the intention of improving the status of the African race. Thorne had some influence on Marcus Garvey, a black Jamaican whose ideas about black capability and self-worth would be highly popular just after the First World War. It is important note that many of Garvey's ideas emerged out of the black intellectual milieu of the late nineteenth century.[62]

Another figure who prefigured Garvey was Robert Love, a Bahamian who lived in Jamaica from 1890 until his death in 1914. His biographer, Joy Lumsden, regards him as the outstanding black man in Jamaica at the end of the nineteenth century. According to Lumsden, Love had a vision of the future for blacks in the West Indies and also sought to highlight black accomplishments in the past. He lectured on topics such as the life of Toussaint L'Ouverture and also established a weekly newspaper for the blacks in the island. In addition, Love supported black candidates for seats on the Legislative Council and was himself elected to the Council in the early twentieth century.[63]

As with these black challenges to racism, many of the changes in the nineteenth and early twentieth centuries laid the groundwork for future developments. Politically, representative government gave way to Crown Colony administration, but there were already modifications to the system which would lead to a wider electorate. Attempts to maintain control of labour in the aftermath of emancipation met with considerable resistance; this not only led to riots and disturbances but also to the growth of a significant peasantry. Moreover, by the end of the nineteenth century, Colonial Office officials and policy-makers had shifted their views about the

[62] Bridget Brereton, 'The Development of an Identity: The Black Middle Class of Trinidad in the Later Nineteenth Century', in Hilary Beckles and Verene Shepherd, eds., *Caribbean Freedom: Society and Economy to the Present* (Kingston, Jamaica, 1993), pp. 281–82; Bryan, *Jamaican People*, p. 258–59.

[63] Joy Lumsden, 'A Forgotten Generation: Black Politicians in Jamaica, 1884–1914', in Brian Moore and Swithin Wilmot, eds., *Before and After 1865: Education, Politics and Regionalism in the Caribbean* (Kingston, Jamaica, 1998), pp. 117–20.

importance of the peasantry: sugar was no longer king and the idea of progress was not tied solely to sugar cultivation.[64] The position of blacks had changed significantly during the course of the century. Although many blacks continued to endure poor material conditions, the transformation from slavery to freedom had led to significant improvements in their position in West Indian politics and society. More fundamental changes, however, would have to wait until the coming of political independence.

[64] Richard A. Lobdell, 'British Officials and the West Indian Peasantry, 1842–1938', in Cross and Heuman, *Labour in the Caribbean*, pp. 199–202.

Select Bibliography

R. W. Beachey, *The British West Indies Sugar Industry in the late 19th Century* (Oxford, 1957).

Bridget Brereton, 'Family Strategies, Gender, and the Shift to Wage Labour in the British Caribbean', in Bridget Brereton and Kevin A. Yelvington, eds., *The Colonial Caribbean in Transition: Essays on Postemancipation Social and Cultural History* (Kingston, 1999), pp. 77–107.

Patrick Bryan, *The Jamaican People, 1880–1900* (London, 1991).

Michael Craton, *Testing the Chains: Resistance to Slavery in the British West Indies* (Ithaca, NY, and London, 1982).

Philip D. Curtin, *Two Jamaicas: The Role of Ideas in a Tropical Colony, 1830–1865* (Cambridge, Mass., 1955).

Emilia V. Da Costa, *Crowns of Glory, Tears of Blood: The Demerara Slave Rebellion of 1823* (New York and Oxford, 1994).

William A. Green, *British Slave Emancipation: The Sugar Colonies and the Great Experiment, 1830–1865* (Oxford, 1976).

Douglas Hall, *Free Jamaica, 1838–1865: An Economic History* (New Haven, 1959).

Gad Heuman, *Between Black and White: Race, Politics, and the Free Coloreds in Jamaica, 1792–1865* (Westport, Conn., 1981).

—— *'The Killing Time': The Morant Bay Rebellion in Jamaica* (London, 1994).

B. W. Higman, *Slave Population and Economy in Jamaica, 1807–1834* (Cambridge, 1976).

—— *Slave Populations of the British Caribbean, 1807–1834* (Baltimore and London, 1984).

Thomas C. Holt, *The Problem of Freedom: Race, Labor, and Politics in Jamaica and Britain, 1832–1938* (Baltimore, 1992).

BRIAN L. MOORE, *Race, Power and Social Segmentation in Colonial Society: Guyana After Slavery, 1838–1891* (New York, 1987).

WALTER RODNEY, *A History of the Guyanese Working People, 1881–1905* (Kingston, 1981).

MIMI SHELLER, 'Quasheba, Mother, Queen: Black Women's Public Leadership and Political Protest in Post-Emancipation Jamaica, 1834–65', *Slavery and Abolition*, XIX, 3 (Dec., 1998), pp. 90–117.

HOWARD TEMPERLEY, *British Antislavery, 1833–1870* (London, 1972).

MARY TURNER, *Slaves and Missionaries: The Disintegration of Jamaican Slave Society, 1787–1834* (Urbana, Ill., 1982).

DONALD WOOD, *Trinidad in Transition: The Years after Slavery* (London, 1968).

7

Cultural Encounters: Britain and Africa in the Nineteenth Century

T. C. MCCASKIE

Encounters between cultures are complex, ambiguous, and unstable transactions, simultaneously events in time and works of the imagination. Their leitmotif is a tangled knot of realities and representations. This is difficult to untie, for it clothes issues of cause and effect in projections and fantasies. Motive and purpose then become hard to tease out of an already complex factual record that reveals the process of encounter between cultures as a constantly shifting kaleidoscope of give and take. Tension is implicit in this quotidian incommensurability between cultures. Thus, imperatives to imposition and acculturation by one side invoke strategies of negotiation and acculturation by the other. The historical result is an ever evolving cultural hybrid in which imagined, willed, and contingent acts are densely interwoven.[1]

Irrespective of disparities in power, cultural encounters between Britain and Africa in the nineteenth century conformed to the model just described. It is important to acknowledge this, for it is all too easy—but profoundly misleading—to equate the achieved territorial substance of the British Empire in Africa with a hegemony in areas other than the geographical. The image conjured up by this misreading supposes a nineteenth-century retrospect in which an ascendant Britain stamped its cultural imprint ever more forcefully upon passive or otherwise cowed Africans. Leaving aside the

This essay originally appeared in Andrew Porter, ed., *The Oxford History of the British Empire* (hereafter *OHBE*), Vol. III, *The Nineteenth Century* (Oxford, 1999).

[1] Compare Gananath Obeyesekere, *The Apotheosis of Captain Cook: European Mythmaking in the Pacific* (Princeton, 1992), with Marshall Sahlins, *How 'Natives' Think: About Captain Cook, For Example* (Chicago, 1995). For the early history of the British in West Africa, see P. E. H. Hair and Robin Law, 'The English in West Africa to 1700' in Nicholas Canny, ed., *OHBE*, Vol. I, *The Origins of Empire* (Oxford 1998); and chap. by David Richardson above.

issue of Britain's purposes and her own understanding of them, this is simply untrue. The British encounter with African cultures in the nineteenth century—as indeed in the twentieth—was never a direct, one-way road leading from London. This is not to deny the potency of British influence. But it is to situate it in a dialogue. On both sides of this conversation, cultural encounters commonly led to unforeseen or unintended consequences. Britain assimilated readings and misreadings of Africa to her own concerns with the continent. Africa reciprocated, interpreting the historical substance of the encounter to its own purposes. Even when one partner in the dialogue raised its voice to an Imperial shout, no earlier than the mid-1870s, this changed the tone rather than the fact of conversation.[2]

This latitude of response on both sides needs to be seen in the light of a simple fact. Until the last quarter of the nineteenth century Britain encountered very few African cultures, because the British presence in tropical Africa was perfunctory and equivocal. For much of the century the British presence was confined to small coastal enclaves, to intermittent expeditions or embassies into an unknown interior, or to the offshore influence of the Royal Navy. Britain was a power only of the littoral, with an often precarious tenure and a limited commitment in—and to—Africa. The rest was imagination. In this dispensation the West African coast between the Senegambia in the west and the Niger delta in the east was of singular importance. Here, in West unlike East Africa, the British had an established physical presence—notably on the Gold Coast—going back to the seventeenth century. It was along this West African coast, the hub of British activity in the transatlantic slave trade, that interests were concentrated at the beginning of the nineteenth century. It is here, in what is now Sierra Leone, Ghana, and Nigeria, that we must start with the history of cultural encounter in the nineteenth century. The account given is necessarily complex, and involves much toing and froing between actions and ideas.[3]

[2] A readable overview is J. D. Fage, *A History of Africa*, 3rd edn. (London, 1995). On key aspects, John Lonsdale, 'States and Social Processes in Africa: A Historiographical Survey', *African Studies Review*, XXIV, 2/3 (1981), pp. 139–225.

[3] For western African societies in the era of the slave trade, Philip D. Curtin, *Economic Change in Precolonial Africa: Senegambia in the Era of the Slave Trade* (Madison, 1975); Boubacar Barry, *Senegambia and the Atlantic Slave Trade* (Cambridge 1997); Robin Law, *The Slave Coast of West Africa, 1550–1750: The Impact of the Atlantic Slave Trade on African Society* (Oxford, 1991); J. C. Miller, *Way of Death: Merchant Capitalism and the Angolan Slave Trade, 1730–1830* (London, 1988).

The ideas and ideologies that were in play between the epochal Mansfield decision in the Somerset case of 1772 (which prohibited the restitution of former slaves in Britain to their masters) and the emancipation of slaves in Britain's colonies in 1834, were of prime importance in redefining British attitudes and policies towards Africa. In the aftermath of the Mansfield decision the abolitionist Granville Sharp took the lead in organizing the repatriation to Africa of ex-slaves and black refugees from the War of American Independence. Sharp's impulse was evangelical and moral. It was also prescriptive. It presumed that Britain, having unilaterally liquidated slaving, knew what was best for the improvement of Africa. Sharp wanted a Christian colony in Africa, and to this end he and his associates drew up a constitution for a self-governing community of yeoman farmers. This 'Province of Freedom' was to be planted in Africa, a donation from the morally enlightened to the spiritually impoverished. It would act as beacon and inspiration, casting its Christian light and self-improving example over the surrounding darkness. Britain had abolished the slave trade but still knew best. The 'Province of Freedom' was to be sited in the Sierra Leone estuary (where the British had traded since the sixteenth century). Government fell in with this plan to export an undesirable black community from Britain, and in 1787 some 400 settlers reached Sierra Leone. Land was secured from the uncomprehending Temne of Koya by an agreement rich in irony. Britain's attempt to improve Africa had as its foundational act the first instance, in West Africa, in which sovereign rather than tenant rights were transferred by treaty.

The 'Province of Freedom' foundered. It was unable to sustain itself economically by farming, and mortality rates were high. Interested idealism had to compromise with harsh reality. The venture was taken over and refinanced by a shareholding company (1791–1808) and thereafter by government. In the process it lost its autonomous status and was administered by London bankers and then by the Secretary of State. Despite these vicissitudes numbers grew. In 1792 the company recruited 'Nova Scotians' (escaped American slaves), numbers of whom were already literate Christians, and in 1800 these were joined by Jamaican Maroons (runaway slaves, predominantly of Gold Coast Akan origin). All these repatriated communities joined together in forming a distinctive culture (sometimes termed Euro-African), albeit not exactly on the model formulated by Sharp. They were enterprising traders rather than subsistence or export farmers, urban rather than rural dwellers, but imbued with ideologies of Christian improvement and material advancement. Their settlement—Freetown—was laid out on the North American colonial grid model, with substantial European-style dwellings sited on large plots. This town became the fount and hub of an emergent culture that was to be replicated elsewhere in West Africa. Its citizens were certainly Christians who placed a premium on literacy and education, but they also modelled their consumption patterns after those of the British middle classes and saw their future in terms of commercial profits and reinvestment in urban property.

The Freetown population was much increased by British measures to implement the abolition of the transatlantic slave trade. After 1808 the Royal Navy patrolled West Africa in order to intercept slave ships under the provisions of a series of bilateral treaties. Captured slavers were arraigned before a Court of Mixed Commission in Freetown and their cargoes, known as Recaptives or Liberated Africans, were settled in Freetown and its peninsular hinterland. By 1820 these freed slaves greatly outnumbered the original settlers, and they continued to arrive until mid-century with a peak in the 1830s to 1840s. By birth Recaptives originated from the entire West African coast, from Senegambia down to the Congo and Angola. But the majority were Yoruba speakers (from present South-West Nigeria), enslaved as a result of the political anarchy, population movement, and endemic warfare that accompanied the protracted collapse (from the 1790s to the 1830s) of the Oyo empire. Recaptives were initially integrated into Sierra Leone's settler society as servants, soldiers, or smallholders. But Governor MacCarthy (1814–24) saw in their numbers an opportunity to revive something of Sharp's original vision of an exemplary Christian community that would cast its civilizing light over African peoples. In short, he proposed to Christianize them and then send them 'home' to serve as models for their countrymen. The Recaptives were settled in villages around Freetown and there exposed to missionary instruction from Anglicans (the Church Missionary Society, arrived 1804) or Methodists (the Wesleyan-Methodists, arrived 1811). Missionaries, always few in number, were joined in this enterprise by already established Freetown settlers.

The Christianizing of Yoruba Recaptives in Freetown was a decisive moment in the cultural encounter between Britain and Africa. Cast up on an alien shore and with a functioning model of a new society placed before them, the Recaptives adopted Christian salvation as a spiritual counterpart to their secular emancipation. Trauma and disorientation must have played a part in this, but so too did the willing embrace of a new life furnished by providence. Recaptives learned English, and took on European names, dress, habits, and tastes. They prized Christian education, the redemptive cornerstone of their own second chance in life, and insisted upon it for their children. But Recaptive Christianity and Westernization had specifically African cultural initiatives and components. Yoruba veneration of and identification with ancestors (as in the masked spirits of *egungun*), the spatialized notion of religion in the community (as in the sacred centre—*akata*—of a town quarter), the hierarchies of seniority and authority (as in the institution of the king—*oba*—and the mass of subordinate title-holders), and a host of other cultural signifiers were all assigned reformulated significance in the light of Christian belief. It is a moot point as to what extent Recaptive Yoruba were born again into a new life or familiarly encountered themselves in another guise in the pages of the Bible. Be that as it may, Recaptive cultural norms were syncretically fused together with evangelical precepts and the British understanding of the achieving individual. Important in this syncretism was the widespread concept of the 'big man'—found among Yoruba speakers, but also among the Igbo and the Akan—by which understanding a successful Christian was also required to manifest traditional, if modified, norms of attainment: the public accumulation, display, enjoyment, and conspicuous consumption of wealth; the possession of a following of clients, conferring esteem, prestige, and weight in the community; the scrupulous provision of goods in exchange for services from lineage kin and other dependants; and the fitting conclusion to the well-lived life in the form of elaborate funeral obsequies and fervent commemorations. To variable degrees all these customary norms shaped and informed Recaptive life. Some, such as competitive pieties in adherence and giving, chimed in with evangelical sensibilities. Others, such as the lavishing of money on big houses or on imports to furnish ostentatious weddings, offended them deeply. Recaptive Christianity was a mobile dialogue between cultures, an equipoise by turns sustained, interrogated, or overturned.[4]

[4] John Peterson, *Province of Freedom: A History of Sierra Leone, 1787–1870* (London, 1969); Arthur T. Porter, *Creoledom: A Study of the Development of Freetown Society* (London, 1963); Akintola Wyse, *The Krio of Sierra Leone: An Interpretative History* (London, 1989). On Yoruba cultural history, J. D. Y. Peel, *Ijeshas and Nigerians: The Incorporation of a Yoruba Kingdom, 1890s–1970s* (Cambridge, 1983), and *Religious Encounter and the Making of the Yoruba* (Bloomington, Ind., 2000); Karin Barber, *I Could Speak Until Tomorrow: Oriki, Women and the Past in a Yoruba Town* (Edinburgh, 1991). On Asante, greatest of the Akan states, Ivor Wilks, *Asante in the Nineteenth Century: The Structure and Evolution of a Political Order* (Cambridge, 1975; reprinted with a new 'Preamble', 1989); T. C. McCaskie, *State and Society in Precolonial*

Like their settler predecessors the Freetown Recaptives took to trade, forsaking farming. This disappointed British evangelicals and industrialists alike, for each interest hoped for an export agriculture, either to sustain settlement or to provide raw materials. But trade offered high returns and surpluses for reinvestment. In 1842, for example, the Nupe Recaptive and Methodist John Ezzidio visited Britain, established trading contacts there, and returned to Freetown to create an import–export business that eclipsed all of the British firms in the town. Money from trade was certainly spent on consumption and property, but *rentiers* also invested in Christian education. In 1827 the Church Missionary Society (CMS) established Fourah Bay College east of Freetown, intended to train missionary teachers for the purpose of spreading the Gospel throughout West Africa. Eventually supported by Society grammar schools, Fourah Bay College became the Christian educational forcing-ground of Freetown society. It had a particular impact on Recaptives and their children. In 1839 a group of Yoruba Recaptives, inculcated with the idea of proselytizing among their own people and wishing to see home again, sailed to Badagry, a major slaving port for the illicit Yoruba trade. Government refused their petition to establish a British colony there, but their example had important consequences. Other Yoruba Recaptives and Creoles, the term that came into use to identify the Freetown community, followed these pioneers. Returned Yoruba were known as Saro (a local corruption of Sierra Leone). They induced the CMS and Methodists to establish among them and they were at the cutting edge of bearing the Christian message—and their culture—into the Yoruba country. Outstanding among them was Samuel Ajayi Crowther, born at the Yoruba town of Osogun about 1806, enslaved in the war that destroyed his home, recaptured and landed at Freetown by the Royal Navy, and the first pupil of Fourah Bay College. In 1864 he was created Bishop in the Church of England, and thereafter headed a CMS Mission to the Niger peoples.

Freetown Saro opened the first Christian church in Lagos, and it was that coastal settlement that became the centre of Victorian Yoruba Christian life after intervention (1851) and annexation (1861) by the British. By 1870 approximately 1,500 Saro had made their homes in Lagos, involving themselves in the palm-oil trade and contributing to the building and governance

Asante (Cambridge, 1995). On Igbo, Richard N. Henderson, *The King in Every Man: Evolutionary Trends in Onitsha Ibo Society and Culture* (New Haven, Conn., 1972); Elizabeth Isichei, *A History of the lgbo People* (London, 1976).

of the town. The Saro impact on Yoruba culture generally was profound, but it is difficult to give a succinct evaluation. This is because, apart from their transplantation of Freetown cultural syncretism to the Niger, and their role in spreading Christianity, the Saro and those who followed them played a fundamental role in the (re)construction of a usable Yoruba 'national' identity in the second half of the tumultuous nineteenth century. If they are memorialized in the churches and dwellings of Victorian Lagos, then their devotion to a specifically Yoruba identity inclusive of Christianity and education is commemorated in their writings. Supreme among these, and indispensable to historians, is the monumental, late-nineteenth-century history by the Yoruba divine and 'nationalist' the Revd Samuel Johnson.[5]

As Creole society became embedded in Freetown its goals extended beyond the worlds of missionary Christianity and trade to encompass middle-class, professional education. In time Fourah Bay College came to accept students for general higher education; eventually it was affiliated to Durham University in 1876 so that it might confer British degrees. Secular education in Freetown, and increasingly in Britain herself for the wealthy, opened the doors to law, medicine, journalism, scholarship, and other professional opportunities. Thus, in 1859 the Creoles J. A. B. Horton and W. B. Davies qualified as doctors in Britain. Both served in the army in West Africa as medical officers, and Horton published books on scientific and political topics. The Freetown lawyer and politician Samuel Lewis was knighted for services to the colony. Behind these leading figures stood a host of others. Like their evangelizing counterparts they sought employment along the West African coast in towns where their skills were esteemed and remunerated. The flourishing of later-nineteenth-century Gold Coast and Nigerian newspapers had a significant Freetown Creole input. So too did the legal and medical professions in British West Africa. By the second half of the nineteenth century Freetown was at the centre of a diaspora extending from the Gambia to the Bight of Benin and to Britain herself. This linked together expatriate Sierra Leoneans in a network that also included the emergent Victorian middle classes of the Gold Coast and Nigeria.[6]

[5] Samuel Johnson, *The History of the Yorubas: From the Earliest Times to the Beginning of the British Protectorate* (London, 1921); J. F. Ade Ajayi, *Christian Missions in Nigeria, 1841–1891: The Making of a New Elite* (London, 1965); E. A. Ayandele, *The Missionary Impact on Modern Nigeria, 1842–1914: A Political and Social Analysis* (London, 1966); Kristen Mann, *Marrying Well: Marriage, Status and Social Change among the Educated Elite in Colonial Lagos* (Cambridge, 1985).

[6] An overview is Akintola Wyse, 'The Place of Sierra Leone in African Diaspora Studies', in J. F. Ade Ajayi and J. D. Y. Peel, eds., *People and Empires in African History: Essays in Memory of*

Developments on the Gold Coast paralleled but were distinct from those in Freetown and in the Yoruba country. Here the British presence was stronger than anywhere else in tropical Africa. Competition over the slaves and other resources of the Gold Coast led to the building of over thirty European castles and fortified posts between the fifteenth and eighteenth centuries. By the beginning of the nineteenth century the British, Dutch, and Danes were the only remaining European powers. The British headquarters at Cape Coast Castle was situated among the small trading polities created by the Fante, a Twi-speaking Akan people. The British were historically embroiled in local politics, and from 1807 onward this brought them into repeated conflict with the powerful inland Akan state of Asante. The British presence here, whether under trading-company or government authority, was configured in such a way that, despite equivocation, London found itself inexorably drawn ever deeper into local political affairs. The Anglo–Asante Treaty (1831) and the so-called Bond (1844) locked Britain into a vague Protectorate over, and rights of judicial interference in, the Fante states. This was extended to the eastern Gold Coast when the Danes quit (1850). The departure of the Dutch (1872) prefigured a British expedition against Asante (1873–74), following which British colonial control over an enlarged southern Gold Coast was formalized by direct annexation.

In the 1830s Methodist missionaries were invited to Cape Coast. This initiative came from the nominally Christianized urban mulatto élite that had originally risen to prominence under the aegis of the slave trade and that had then turned to other types of commerce. Under the dynamic leadership of the Revd T. B. Freeman, himself a West Indian mulatto, the Methodists proselytized among the Fante. As in Freetown and among the Yoruba, there swiftly emerged an evangelized, trading, property-owning, Victorian middle class. First confined to the British posts at Cape Coast and Anomabo, Christianity carried by British missionaries and a growing network of indigenous catechists then made inroads into the Fante hinterland. This was not without its problems. Resistance was offered by the *akomfo* ('priests') of Fante religion, but on the Gold Coast missionaries enjoyed the direct, if sometimes reluctantly given, sanction of British law. The world of the Fante

Michael Crowder (London, 1992), pp. 107–20. Also Johnson U. J. Asiegbu, *Sierra Leone Creoles in British Nigeria Revisited, 1857–1920* (Oxford, 1984). A pioneering biography is John D. Hargreaves, *A Life of Sir Samuel Lewis* (London 1958). The best overall guide to the Gold Coast is R. Jenkins, 'Gold Coast Historians and Their Pursuit of the Gold Coast Pasts, 1882–1917', unpublished Ph.D. thesis, Birmingham, 1985, 2 vols.

Christian bourgeoisie is portrayed at length in the pages of the British official Brodie Cruickshank's *Eighteen Years on the Gold Coast of Africa* (1853). The picture that emerges from Cruickshank, as from many other texts, is one that resonates with the experiences of Freetown or Lagos.

Fante Christianity was resolutely aspirational in terms of salvation, but also in the worldly spheres of status, wealth, education, and consumer modernity. The Fante conception of the Akan 'big man' (*obirempon*) laid emphasis on instrumental strategies of seeking advantage in status competition among peers. In a sense, trading wealth, Western education, the building of imposing houses, and the rest were simply added to the existing repertoire of Fante norms and values. In this environment Christianity itself, whatever the strength of personal belief invested in it, was a further token of individual attainment in its own right within this intensely competitive milieu. Broadly speaking, mission education among the Fante followed the path already described (although there was no equivalent of Fourah Bay College in the Gold Coast). Schools turned out catechists and government employees. The latter were much in demand, for British administration and commerce had more need for clerkly skills on the Gold Coast than in any other part of tropical Africa. After mid-century the Fante urban élite produced a notable intelligentsia of writers, journalists, and pamphleteers. These were bound together by Christianity, education, and modernity, but also by older patterns of proximity and intermarriage, given a new fillip by an increasingly self-conscious sense of belonging to an élite.[7]

Mid-nineteenth-century Sierra Leone, Nigeria, and the Gold Coast, with their confident élites, is a useful point to pause and take stock. The background to the developments just described was the quickening pulse of British industrial and financial power. This manifested itself in numerous ways. For present purposes we must look first to the growing capacity and desire—religious, economic, scientific—to replace the tropical Africa of the imagination, virtually a *terra incognita*, with a continent explored, explained, and domesticated to British ideals of Christian culture. However, caution is

[7] G. E. Metcalfe, *Maclean of the Gold Coast: The Life and Times of George Maclean, 1801–1847* (London, 1962); Edward Reynolds, *Trade and Economic Change on the Gold Coast, 1807–1874* (London, 1974); Mary McCarthy, *Social Change and the Growth of British Power in the Gold Coast, 1807–1874* (Lanham, Md., 1983); and the important K. Arhin, 'Rank and Class among the Asante and Fante in the Nineteenth Century', *Africa*, LIII, 1 (1983), pp. 2–22.

required, for it is only with hindsight that this impulse can be cast in the role of preamble to colonial overrule.

In 1841 a mission was despatched to the confluence of the Niger and Benue rivers in the interior of what is now southern Nigeria. Its purpose was to explore West Africa's greatest river, to root out slave-trading at source, to assess Christian prospects, and to establish cash-crop plantation agriculture. Grandiose plans, however, did not prevent its failure. This sounded the death-knell of the original abolitionist dream of African farmers organized and mobilized to support themselves by producing for the British market. West African exports—notably palm-oil—became the province of indigenous entrepreneurs rather than Christianized communities of yeomen. But if the Niger expedition was a failure, it was one with heroic resonances.[8] Anti-slavery and Christianization were inspired to a new urgency in tandem with the growing wish to explore and to cast light on the 'dark continent'. Sometimes these imperatives were joined together, sometimes they operated independently. The objective was the interior of tropical Africa. The greatest unknown of all was East and Central Africa, and it was there that the legacy of the Niger expedition found its fullest expression.

In the eighteenth century Europeans, including the British, rarely visited East Africa. The western end of the Indian Ocean trading network was an Omani Arab domain. An Islamic Swahili coastal élite brokered commerce between Gulf seafarers and the trading networks of East and Central Africa. The Yao and later the Nyamwezi traded ivory, slaves, and gold from the interior into Portuguese Mozambique and such long-established coastal entrepôts as Kilwa and Mombasa; until the 1850s cloth, beads, and copper were the most prized imports. A complex of developments drew Britain into this world in the nineteenth century. First, slaving in this area greatly increased after British abolition. Demand from the Gulf, Cuba, and Brazil, and from intensified sugar production on the Mascarenes (Réunion and Ile de France) all contributed to anti-slavery outrage in Britain. The East African slave trade became a moral crusade. Secondly, although the Royal Navy's anti-slavery presence in the Indian Ocean was limited by comparison with the Atlantic, Britain felt able to fix upon Zanzibar as the key to increased slaving. For economic reasons Sayyid Said ibn Sultan, ruler of Oman, transferred his court to Zanzibar in 1840, and when he died in 1856 the island

[8] Most recently, Howard Temperley, *White Dreams, Black Africa: The Antislavery Expedition to the River Niger, 1841–1842* (New Haven, Conn., 1991).

became independent. In addition to slaving wealth Zanzibar possessed an enticingly valuable export industry in cloves. Abolitionist and commercial interests saw a British Consul appointed to Zanzibar in the 1840s. Thirdly, although Britain lacked details it seemed clear that the East African slave trade was conducted with particular brutality. Zanzibari merchants, Indian financiers, Arab-Swahili caravans, and their predatory African partners extended the destabilizing trade far inland to the Bemba and beyond to the Lozi and Lunda of Central Africa. Accounts of savage cruelty reinforced British anti-slavery with an urgent wish to carry the saving grace of Christianity into the heart of Africa.[9]

The totemic figure in the Christian fight against the East and Central African slave trade was David Livingstone. An ambiguous and complicated individual, Livingstone traversed the continent (1853–56) and then sought to reach Central Africa via the Zambezi River (1858–64). He achieved heroic stature in Britain, and did more than anyone else to expose and keep before the public the horrors of slavery. To him belongs a deal of the credit for the British decision to impose an end to the Zanzibari slave trade in 1873, but his impact on African cultures themselves was less than was claimed by later imperial hagiographers. In addition to his Christian mission against slavery, his significance lay in his contribution to the collective British enterprise of exploring eastern Africa.[10] Here the prize—the Niger writ large—was the source of the Nile. The Royal Geographical Society presided over intense public interest in this question. The expeditions of Burton and Speke (1857–58), from East Africa to Lakes Tanganyika and Victoria, of Speke and Grant (1860–63) from East Africa via Lake Victoria, Buganda, and Bunyoro down the Nile to Cairo, and of Baker (1862–65), from Cairo via Khartoum, Lake Victoria, and Bunyoro to Lake Albert, explored vast, previously unknown areas but failed to resolve the Nile question. In 1866 the Society recruited Livingstone to settle the matter. His five-year journey, until his celebrated 'rescue' by Stanley in 1871, became an iconic representation of Victorian England's view of herself. But Livingstone died in 1873 and it was left

[9] E. A. Alpers, *Ivory and Slaves in East Central Africa: Changing Patterns of International Trade to the Later Nineteenth Century* (London, 1975); Frederick Cooper, *Plantation Slavery on the East Coast of Africa* (New Haven, Conn., 1977); Thomas Q. Reefe, *The Rainbow Kings: A History of the Luba Empire to 1891* (Berkeley, 1981); Abdul Sheriff, *Slaves, Spices and Ivory in Zanzibar: Integration of an East African Commercial Empire into the World Economy, 1770–1873* (London, 1987); Charles H. Ambler, *Kenyan Communities in the Age of Imperialism: The Central Region in the Late Nineteenth Century*, (New Haven, Conn., 1988).

[10] Consult Adrian Hastings, *The Church in Africa, 1450–1950* (Oxford, 1994).

to Henry Morton Stanley (1874–77) to conclude the quest for the source of the Nile. In the course of his journey he linked the Indian and Atlantic oceans, travelling from the interlacustrine region of eastern Africa down the Lualaba–Congo river system to its mouth on the coast of western Africa.[11]

The explorers Burton and Stanley were unusual individuals, but in their views and writings both gave pointed expression to shifting attitudes towards Africa and Africans. European ideas of African cultures were increasingly informed by new ideological currents against which Britain assessed herself and her experience of Africa. These included a burgeoning power and concomitant sense of a superior British destiny, reinforced by imperial gains elsewhere and underpinned by the sedulous rise of pseudo-scientific racism; a growing confidence that Africa might be civilized in its own interest, not simply by missionary enterprise and free trade, but also by exposing its peoples to all of the many ordering technologies and secular disciplines of modern bourgeois life. As corollaries, the failure to effect wholesale Christian conversion despite the expenditure of money, effort, and lives, the lack of success in fostering an export-oriented plantation economy, the continuing stain of the slave trade, despite abolition (now combined with more information—and misinformation—about the extent and nature of African domestic slavery), and the presumed barbarism of great African states and cultures (Asante, Dahomey, Buganda, the Congo) were all intimations that, perhaps, Africans were irredeemable if left to govern themselves. Such ideas were the prelude to the Imperial Age in Africa. They were first articulated and acted upon in West Africa.[12]

First, some indicative straws in the wind. The explorer Richard Burton served as Consul in the Bight of Benin (1861–64) and travelled again in West Africa in 1881. In his writings on West Africa he expressed (predictably enough) a prurient fascination with the barbaric splendour, as he saw it, of the Dahomean court. But he abhorred West African Creole culture, regarding it as no more than an inauthentic, offensive, comic mimicry of its British counterpart. As ever, Burton's opinions were highly coloured, but there is much evidence that by the 1860s many British commentators and officials shared his dismissive view of the ultimate outcome of early

[11] Clements R. Markham, *The First Fifty Years' Work of the Royal Geographical Society* (1881); Robert A. Stafford, 'Scientific Exploration and Empire', in Andrew Porter, ed., *OHBE*, Vol. III, *The Nineteenth Century* (Oxford, 1999).

[12] Philip D. Curtin, *The Image of Africa: British Ideas and Action, 1750–1850* (Madison, Wisc. 1964).

abolitionist hopes and policies.[13] Increasingly, this rejection assumed racial forms. Educated or westernized West Africans of whatever sort came to be widely viewed as mimic-men, legatees of a false, pre-colonial start in civilizing Africa. Racial tensions developed, even in mission circles. Thus, indigenous Africans complained of the rise of patronizing, racist attitudes within the Methodist mission to the Gold Coast, and looked back with longing to the more egalitarian ethos that had prevailed before mid-century. In 1879 the finances of the Church Missionary Society's Niger mission were entrusted to a European. Africans resigned or were dismissed in an atmosphere of racial division. When the celebrated Bishop Crowther died in 1891 he was replaced by a European.[14]

Policy mirrored these shifts. In 1868 J. A. B. Horton, the Freetown Creole army doctor long resident on the Gold Coast, published his *West African Countries and Peoples*. This distilled the widespread educated African aspiration for a part in government and offered blueprints for political participation. Horton directly inspired the creation of the Fante Confederation and its (second) 1871 Constitution, providing for a King or President and representative and national Assemblies, was based on his proposals. A Great Seal was struck and a Supreme Court convened. The Fante, historically disunited, banded together in confederacy around the issues of British impositions and high-handedness. Taxes, the lack of a right of consultation or voice in policy-making, and uncertainty over Britain's commitment to defend them against Asante were key concerns. Confederation failed, in part because of internal disagreements, but also because Britain was opposed to it. Ideas of governmental modernization along Western lines spread inland beyond the sphere of British jurisdiction. As early as 1865 the Abeokuta Egba on the western fringe of Yorubaland set up a United Board of Management with a President, a High Sheriff, a Supreme Court, and a postal system. The Sierra Leonian G. W. Johnson played a leading role in this experiment, but the Egba modernizers enjoyed only limited success. The larger significance of events among the Fante and Egba is that, just as British attitudes were hardening in

[13] Richard Burton, *Wanderings in West Africa: From Liverpool to Fernando Po*, 2 vols. (London, 1863), *Abeokuta and the Cameroons Mountains. An Exploration*, 2 vols. (London, 1863), and *A Mission to Gelele King of Dahome*, 2 vols. (London, 1864); Richard F. Burton and Verney Lovett Cameron, *To the Gold Coast for Gold*, 2 vols. (London, 1883). Cf. W. Reade, *Savage Africa* (London, 1863) and *The African Sketch-book*, 2 vols. (London, 1873).

[14] These changes can be traced in detail in the Wesleyan-Methodist Missionary Society Archives (School of Oriental and African Studies, London) and in the Church Missionary Society Archives (Birmingham University).

the manner described, westernized Africans—both under British jurisdiction and beyond it—were taking tentative first steps towards modern forms of political participation and autonomy.[15]

In 1865 a Parliamentary Select Committee recommended that Britain reduce her commitments in West Africa wherever possible. The Colonial Office favoured retrenchment on the grounds of expense and the vagueness of British jurisdiction. This last consideration, it was felt, had the potential to involve Britain in unwanted future conflicts and obligations.[16] In essence, and despite much equivocating argument, nothing was done. Eight years later in 1873–74 Britain found herself confronting an Asante invasion of Fante and then committing troops to advance 150 miles inland to burn the Asante capital of Kumasi. The politics of this first serious British military venture into the tropical African interior need not detain us here. More germane is the fact that this Anglo–Asante War was the first conflict to be fought in the aftermath of the Cardwell reforms. It was commanded by Sir Garnet Wolseley and officered by members of his 'ring'. These men rose to dominate British military thinking about Africa until the South African (Anglo–Boer) War (1899–1902), and directed military policy at the height of the colonial conquest. Famously self-promoting, the Wolseley 'ring' deluged the British public with accounts of its first success as a team. These writings concerned a sophisticated culture and great state in the interior of West Africa, and because of the later importance of the authors their views formed a powerful template for subsequent readings of other polities during—and beyond—the conquest.[17]

Several broad, complementary interpretations of Asante culture prevailed in the writings of the Wolseley 'ring', and were endorsed by journalists (including Stanley) who accompanied the expedition.[18] The first view was

[15] Francis Agbodeka, *African Politics and British Policy in the Gold Coast, 1868–1900: A Study in the Forms and Force of Protest* (London, 1971); Saburi O. Biobaku, *The Egba and Their Neighbours, 1842–1872* (Oxford, 1957); A. Pallinder, 'Adegboyega Edun: Black Englishman and Yoruba Cultural Patriot', in P. F. de Moraes Farias and Karin Barber, eds., *Self-Assertion and Brokerage: Early Cultural Nationalism in West Africa* (Birmingham, 1990), pp. 11–34.

[16] *Report fromt the Select Committee on Africa (Western Coast)*, Parliamentary Papers, (1865) 412, V.

[17] From a large choice, Henry Brackenbury, *The Ashanti War: A Narrative: Prepared from Official Documents by Permission of Major-General Sir Garnet Wolseley*, 2 vols. (London, 1874); William Francis Butler, *Akim-Foo: The History of a Failure* (London, 1875); E. Wood, *The Ashanti Expedition of 1873–4* (London, 1874).

[18] Henry M. Stanley, *Coomassie and Magdala: The Story of Two British Campaigns in Africa* (London, 1874).

a graphic enlargement of earlier missionary presumptions concerning an Asante—and African—predilection for 'human sacrifice'. Wesleyans such as T. B. Freeman in the 1840s condemned such practices but believed they would disappear with the advent of Christianity. The Wolseley 'ring' termed Kumasi 'the city of blood', and argued that 'human sacrifice' was a mode of government. That is, Asante needed humbling and conquest rather than empathy and conversion before it would change its ways. The second view was a crystallization of emergent British racial attitudes. As members of an inferior race the Asante required discipline rather than understanding in order to function as a culture. The current dispensation of bloodletting and 'human sacrifice' was inhumane, but any future British administration would have to adopt Draconian measures for Asante's own good. The equation of Africans 'in a savage state of nature' with wilful children underpinned this brisk recommendation. The third view was that, as all Africans were damned to an inferior place within the human family, then the 'natural' Asante, provided he was strictly ruled, was to be preferred to the abomination that was westernized Fante Creole culture. In extension of Burton's strictures the Wolseley 'ring' urged the sheer unnaturalness of any sort of hybridity. Cultures were fixed in rank, and any attempt to assimilate an African to Anglo-Saxon ideas and practices could only result in a displaced, pathetic caricature. The final view, much enlarged upon by Wolseley in later life, combined pseudo-scientific racism with fashionable canards about the influence of climate and ecology upon cultural history.'[19] The Asante were manly and warlike because they lived under iron discipline in an invigorating environment. The Fante were weak and cowardly because they were creolized residents of a debilitating milieu. Forests, deserts, and highlands were good; coasts, swamps, and lowlands were bad. These were all extreme, formalized versions of opinions in general circulation on the eve of Britain's subjugation of its African Empire. Repetitions, traces, or echoes of all of them are to be found in the literature of colonial conquest concerning Benin, Yorubaland, Igboland, and Sokoto in West Africa, or Zululand and the Sudan elsewhere on the continent.[20] They testify *inter alia* to the continuing potency of an imagined Africa in an era of greatly increased factual knowledge.

[19] General Viscount Wolseley, 'The Negro as a Soldier', *The Fortnightly Review*, New Series, CCLXIV (1888), pp. 689–703.

[20] For one aspect, C. Madge and R. Cline-Cole, 'The West African Forest Zone in the European Geographical Imagination', *Geography*, no. CCCLIII, 81 (1996), pp. 24–31.

The colonial conquest of East Africa was preceded by a period around and after mid-century when the informal advance of traders, missionaries, explorers, and the rest not only augmented Europe's store of information about Africa, but also exposed African cultures to an indiscriminate, eclectic barrage of new ideas, practices, and technologies. Nowhere did this development call forth a more complex response than in Buganda, most powerful of the interlacustrine kingdoms. By the early nineteenth century the *kabaka* (king) of Buganda controlled the western side of Lake Victoria. From there Buganda was linked into the long-distance trade network of eastern Africa, including the route that ran nearly 800 miles via Nyamwezi to the coast facing Zanzibar. Early in his reign the *kabaka* Mutesa (late 1850s–84) developed a strong interest in the culture, religion, and technology of the Zanzibari traders who visited his court. Advanced guns and consumer goods were his initial concern. These were conventional trade items, but Mutesa also had a consuming interest in theology. He became fascinated with the precepts of Zanzibari Islam, introduced the Koran, and rewarded youthful royal pages who learned Arabic. However, when Zanzibar failed to assist Buganda against threats from the Sudan, devout pages argued that this was because Mutesa's Zanzibari Islam was too lax. In 1876 the *kabaka* executed the most critical of his Muslim subjects. But having opened the door to foreign trade and ideas Mutesa found that he could not close it again. Protestant and Catholic missionaries were invited into Buganda to check Islam, and one another. When Mutesa died he had lost control of the situation. In 1886 his desperate successor martyred Christians in the name of the local spirit cults. But a Muslim, Protestant, and Catholic alliance deposed and then reinstated him on their own terms. Thus far these developments had been matters of court politics, barely affecting the countryside. But in the 1890s British troops arrived, Protestantism triumphed with their support, and religious fervour—exacerbated by the chaotic uncertainties of foreign conquest—spread to embrace all Buganda. As the world of the Ganda people was turned upside down many thousands embraced Christianity, looking to the Bible to explain what had happened.[21]

[21] M. S. M. Kiwanuka, *A History of Buganda* (London, 1971); M. Wright, *Buganda in the Heroic Age* (Nairobi, 1971); D. A. Low, *Religion and Society in Buganda, 1875–1900* (Kampala, n.d. [1957?]). Sir Apolo Kaggwa, *The Kings of Buganda*, English translation (Nairobi, 1971) is an insider account from the early colonial period.

The European 'scramble' for Africa was breathtaking in its rapidity.[22] As a result Britain and a host of African cultures and peoples suddenly found themselves confronting each other. The ostensible arrangement was one of rulers and ruled, but this simple equation in theory turned out to be subtly complex in practice. British conquest was accomplished with no clear idea of how particular areas should be governed nor any substantive knowledge of many subject cultures. The choice of responses open to Africans was bewilderingly complex, both between and—importantly—within cultures. They might 'collaborate' in an effort to secure British favour; they might 'resist' to the point of defeat or disintegration; they might submit in a process of bargaining the conditions of their subjection; they might equivocate, dissemble, change their minds, or simply await developments. Choices with longer-term implications surrounded the issue of European culture. Nowhere did Africans resolve this by polar responses of outright rejection or acceptance. Everything was shaded; thus, for example, Africans might embrace education but be sceptical about the mission Christianity of its bearers. In truth, cultural encounters between Briton and African during the late-nineteenth-century conquest, even where violence was involved, were on both sides matters of probing negotiation towards the equilibrium of a changed order rather than permanently binding choices between strategies of outright collaboration or resistance.[23]

Example rather than comprehensiveness must suffice to illustrate the theme of negotiated cultural contact during the colonial conquest. The object is to show something of the range and complexity of an encounter that was misleadingly assumed to be simple (even one-sided) before the development of modern African historiography. The examples of Asante and Sokoto in West Africa and the Ndebele in Central Africa serve to make the point.

The British invasion of Asante in 1873–74 was a punitive expedition. Asante retained its political autonomy, but was subject to increasing British pressure and influence thereafter. The British finally deposed the *asantehene* Agyeman Prempe in 1896, suppressed an uprising against them in 1900, and formally annexed Asante as a Crown Colony in 1901. Pre-colonial Asante was a culture in which the state exercised formidable controls over political office,

[22] See Colin Newbury, 'Great Britain and the Partition of Africa, 1870–1914', in Porter, ed., *OHBE*, III.

[23] See the chaps. by John D. Hargreaves and Terence Ranger in L. H. Gann and Peter Duignan, eds., *Colonialism in Africa*, 5 vols. (Cambridge, 1969–75), I.

access to wealth, and ingress or egress from the country. Weakened and laid open after 1874, Asante experienced a series of crises including a protracted dynastic conflict (1883–88). In the course of this numbers of Asante became alienated from a polity that monopolized wealth but no longer reciprocated with security. They voted with their feet and fled into the British Gold Coast. Once there, they were exposed to the acquisitive individualism of *laissez faire* capitalism, the dispositionary rights of the person under English common law, and the gamut of Western cultural influences. They supported British subversion and conquest of Asante, but in a particular way that sought to combine their acquisitive individualism with access to the prestigious chiefships of historic Asante culture. After 1901 the British relied on these people to implement colonial rule and supported and favoured them. Their example, and the unchecked access of European norms and values, swiftly fused historic Asante identity with an untrammelled capitalism. The uprising of the old order in 1900 was not repeated. It was capitalism—expressed in the rapid spread of cocoa as a cash crop—that reconciled Asante to British colonial overrule. Official records from the early colonial era show the significant extent to which administrators relied for support upon Asante who were ideologically reconciled to the new order. Nor was there a realistic alternative, for British personnel were few and their knowledge of Asante was very limited. Earlier British stereotypes of savage, warlike Asante survived into the colonial period but were soon replaced by admiration for a 'progressive' people devoted to making money.[24]

Sokoto (in present-day northern Nigeria) reveals another set of variations on the theme of cultural encounter during the conquest. Created by jihad (holy war) in the first decade of the nineteenth century, the Sokoto Caliphate was the largest West African Muslim polity annexed by the British. Due to its geographical remoteness from the coast it was little known by the British prior to the conquest of 1903. Extensive and presumed to be formidable, Sokoto puzzled the British by offering little concerted resistance. The immediate British explanation relied on the late-nineteenth-century European commonplace about the corruption, decadence, and weakness of Islamic polities. The truth was much more complex. Sokoto was constructed out of potentially volatile and conflicting components—Hausa, Fulani, and smaller

[24] Apart from works already cited, Thomas J. Lewin, *Asante Before the British: The Prempean Years, 1875–1900* (Lawrence, Kan., 1978); William Tordoff, *Ashanti Under the Prempehs, 1888–1935* (Oxford, 1965); and Jean Marie Allman, *The Quills of the Porcupine: Asante Nationalism in an Emergent Ghana* (Madison, Wisc., 1993).

ethnic groups, core and periphery, town and countryside, orthodox and popular Islam (syncretically fused with non-Islamic beliefs)—and the shock of British conquest brought latent cleavages between the ruling élite and its subjects into the open.

First, the urban, orthodox Islamic élite around the Caliph consulted Muslim precedents for guidance in dealing with infidels. A choice was made to practise canonically sanctioned dissembling; that is, to submit in body but not thought. The state's autonomy (a thing of this world) was surrendered so as preserve the integrity of Islam against any excess of British destructiveness provoked by military resistance. Secondly, the arrival of the British coincided with a rising tide of popular Islamic Mahdist expectation and acted to confirm the belief that the end of the material world was imminent. Accordingly, numbers of commoners began to move eastward to meet 'the expected one' (the Mahdi) and prepare for the last battle between good and evil. Throughout the nineteenth century the Sokoto élite had discouraged such radical views among its subjects. It was now alarmed by wholesale defections to the east, and particularly so as in the prevailing confusion the Caliph (willingly or not) was with his migrating subjects. British forces caught up with the Mahdists and the Caliph was killed in the fighting. Mahdist expectation survived, and in 1906 became centred on the insurrectionary village of Satiru near Sokoto. The British were caught unprepared. However, the Sokoto élite allied itself with its infidel rulers and suppressed its own rebel subjects on their behalf. This was a calculated act. The British administration had already guaranteed the survival of Islam and the precolonial emirate system. Indeed, Sokoto's conqueror Sir Frederick Lugard developed his concept of 'indirect rule' through historically sanctioned native rulers—*the* theory of British colonial rule in Africa—out of his experience governing these very emirates. The Sokoto élite for its part had opted for British support in maintaining its sway over its own historically disaffected subjects.[25]

The Ndebele were a creation of the *mfecane* or 'time of troubles', the revolutionary changes that convulsed southern Africa in the late-eighteenth

[25] D. Murray Last, *The Sokoto Caliphate* (London, 1967); R. A. Adeleye, *Power and Diplomacy in Northern Nigeria, 1804–1906: The Sokoto Caliphate and its Enemies* (London, 1972); Robert W. Shenton, *The Development of Capitalism in Northern Nigeria* (London, 1986); Paul E. Lovejoy and Jan S. Hogendorn, *Slow Death for Slavery: The Course of Abolition in Northern Nigeria, 1897–1936* (Cambridge, 1993); and John W. Cell, 'Colonial Rule' in Judith M. Brown and Wm. Roger Louis, eds., *OHBE*, Vol. IV, *The Twentieth Century* (Oxford, 1999).

and early-nineteenth centuries.[26] Fleeing before Shaka's Zulu, the Ndebele settled in the late 1830s as overlords among a part of the decentralized Shona people (in present-day Zimbabwe). The Ndebele kingdom preserved its own language and military arrangements, but it adopted the Shona territorial cult of *mwari* and other rituals. British missionaries arrived in 1859 but entirely failed to gain converts. In 1889 the British South Africa Company occupied Shona territory with little difficulty. Initially, the Ndebele opted for a policy of coexistence. But in 1893 a mix of British high-handedness and chafing resentment on the part of youthful Ndebele warriors provoked a limited war. Three years later, in 1896–97, a full-scale revolt occurred as the Ndebele came to realize, with the advice of their spirit cults, that pioneer British South Africa Company officials and gold-seekers were the advance guard of a wave of whites who planned to settle. Fearing massive land seizures, loss of cattle, and extinction as a culture, the Ndebele and their Shona clients conducted guerrilla warfare and besieged the nascent settlement of Bulawayo. The revolt, which the Ndebele were now convinced was a matter of national survival, was bitterly fought and bloodily suppressed. Defeat led to the dissolution of the Ndebele polity, to landlessness, to cultural disorientation, and personal anomie. The barrier to unrestricted white inroads into this part of Central Africa was removed and farmers flooded in after the gold-prospectors. The Ndebele were left to negotiate their place in the colonial order from a position of virtual powerlessness. Under the new dispensation they were reduced to labouring on white grain and tobacco firms.[27]

The cultures of Asante, Sokoto, and the Ndebele were organized around and arbitrated by complex state structures. But very many of the African peoples that succumbed to British conquest lived in acephalous, decentralized, small-scale societies. Statelessness posed special problems for the British conquerors. Often, and quite literally, there was no one with the authority to make formal submission. The imposition of colonial rule over such peoples was a slow osmotic process rather than a finite political event. Thus, in the occupation of south-east and central Nigeria the British sent military columns into Igboland and among the Tiv of the Benue river valley. Other than as a declaration of intent these were somewhat futile exercises. Resolving the cultural encounter between the British and such decentralized

[26] Carolyn Hamilton, ed., *The Mfecane Aftermath: Reconstructive Debates in Southern African History* (Johannesburg, 1995).

[27] The classic account is T. O. Ranger, *Revolt in Southern Rhodesia, 1896–7*, 2nd edn. (London, 1979).

peoples was something that took time. In the first stages of conquest British administrators were as much persuaders as conquerors. The Igbo or Tiv had to be won over to an understanding of the advantages and obligations of British rule. Tax-gathering by diktat in the absence of an indigenous chain of command would have required manpower resources that the British did not possess. Igbo or Tiv people responded to the perceived benefits and drawbacks of colonial rule on an individual and sectoral basis, a point complexly illustrated in the Igbo novelist Chinua Achebe's celebrated *Things Fall Apart*. In the cultural encounter with the Igbo the British ran the risk of subverting negotiation by radical innovation in the interests of a more structured, hierarchical, transparent administration. Thus, the eventual introduction among the Igbo of 'Native Administration' chiefs, a variant of Lugard's 'indirect rule', was a greatly resented mistake and acknowledged as such by experienced officials on the spot.[28]

Among the issues that preoccupied the British immediately following conquest none was of wider concern than that termed 'domestic slavery' by officialdom. This phenomenon was held to be endemic to Africa's cultures; certainly, very diverse forms of indigenous servitude and clientage existed on the continent together with other sorts of dependency barely understood but disapproved of by the British. Nineteenth-century abolitionists and missionaries deplored 'domestic slavery' but recognized its fundamental place in societies they could do little to change. Commercial interests took the sanguine view that 'domestic slavery' was functionally necessary to African economic production. In theory the moral responsibilities of colonial rule precluded the continuation of such indulgent attitudes. In practice matters were not so simple. The British abolished 'domestic slavery' by fiat in cultures where they wished to quash opposition or punish intransigence. In 1897 a British mission to the Edo kingdom of Benin (in present-day Nigeria) was virtually annihilated.[29] A punitive expedition then occupied Benin, but the capital had been abandoned. The British declared emancipation for any slave coming back to the town, and then freed the royal slaves to teach the Edo king a lesson. But the Edo experience was unusual. In most cultures the British swiftly learned the accuracy of nineteenth-century perception.

[28] Sir F. D. Lugard, *The Dual Mandate in British Tropical Africa* (London, 1922); A. F. Afigbo, *The Warrant Chiefs: Indirect Rule in South Eastern Nigeria* (London, 1972).

[29] P. A. Igbafe, *Benin Under British Administration: The Impact of Colonial Rule on an African Kingdom, 1897–1938* (London, 1979).

'Domestic slavery' was the existing mechanism for mobilizing labour, and British officials needed it as much as had African rulers. Practice diverged from theory. The British continued to abhor 'domestic slavery' but permitted its continued existence under one or another fictive legalism. Sometimes this caused conflict with zealous missionaries.[30] But 'domestic slavery' survived in parts of British Africa into the 1920s until such time as labour needs could be fully met from within the developed cash economy.

Slavery of another kind produced the first crisis in Britain's nineteenth-century involvement in another, quite distinct part of Africa. South Africa was a special case and needs to be treated as such.[31] Britain occupied the Cape in 1795 and established a permanent presence at the end of the Napoleonic Wars in 1815. Here, uniquely, Britain encountered after 1795 earlier European settlers of Dutch, German, or French Huguenot stock who first settled in 1652. These Boers (or Afrikaners) evolved their own, fiercely independent religion, language, and culture, based upon crop and livestock farming supported by indentured and African slave labour. In the century-long clash which developed between Briton and Boer, culminating in the protracted, bitterly fought war of 1899–1902 and the compromise of the Union of South Africa in 1910, the ultimate victims were the African peoples.

The Xhosa, borrowing from Christian missionary eschatology, killed their cattle in 1857 in an other-worldly attempt to expel Europeans once and for all. This extreme measure precipitated the destruction of Xhosa society by the British Cape government and Boer farmers. The Zulu kingdom—greatest of the states to emerge from the upheavals of the 1790s to 1830s among the Bantu societies of eastern South Africa (the *mfecane*)—finally went down to military defeat in 1879 after a victory over British forces at Isandhlwana. African 'resistance', whether cultural or military, was ultimately unable to stand against Boer and British imperialism.

Once drawn into the orbit of the white colonial societies, many Africans were confronted by new and difficult problems of adjustment. Others, however, initially adapted very successfully to the opportunities presented by change. In the early phases of mining development paid African labour was needed and offered better wages than those available on white farms. From mission stations like Lovedale in the eastern Cape numbers of Africans

[30] e.g. in Asante between British officials and Basel missionaries in Kumase.

[31] See Christopher Saunders and Iain R. Smith, 'Southern Africa', 1795–1910, in Porter, ed., *OHBE*; III.

took away an education that held out prospects of employment in the cash economy. African farmers and transport drivers took advantage of the commercial openings offered by colonial urban expansion; their output was vital, for instance, in feeding the Rand. However, African economic independence was no more acceptable than political. From the 1890s, and ever more rapidly after 1902 and 1910, the colonial government cut back African prospects to fit the demands of white enterprise, using the mechanisms of land control, labour legislation, and taxation. Thus, in the second half of the nineteenth century and beyond the African peoples of South Africa experienced political annexation, societal breakdown, and cultural anomie. Africanized Christianity with its numerically small, emergent middle class offered one of the few means of sustaining the seeds of a new African politics which was gradually to find its voice in the twentieth century.[32]

Deposited in all British—and European—archival records of the colonial conquest are maps, ranging from the nearly blank to the elaborately detailed. Maps are perhaps the most potent of all symbolic representations of the partition of Africa. Indeed, a familiar image of the Berlin Conference of 1884–85, at which Britain and the other imperial powers delimited their future African possessions, is of intent statesmen poring over a map of the continent.[33] The cartographic enterprise was pivotal to implementing conquest and embedding colonial rule—the siting of boundaries, ports, railways, roads, or towns and the labelling of forests, rivers, lakes, mountains, or plains were all referenced to map-making and sprang from it. Maps also symbolized the reconfiguration of cultural encounter. By 'filling in' Britain's map of Africa cartographical knowledge enabled the recasting of the continent's cultures in terms of colonial concepts of bounded spatial identities and

[32] From a huge literature, Richard Elphick and Hermann Giliomee, eds., *The Shaping of South African Society, 1652–1840*, 2nd revised edn. (Middletown, Conn., 1989); J. B. Peires, *The House of Phalo: A History of the Xhosa People in the Days of their Independence* (Johannesburg, 1981), and *The Dead Will Arise: Nongqawuse and the Great Xhosa Cattle Killing Movement of 1856–7* (Johannesburg, 1989); Jeff Guy, *The Destruction of the Zulu Kingdom: The Civil War in Zululand, 1879–1884* (London, 1979); Philip Bonner, *Kings, Commoners and Concessionaires: The Evolution and Dissolution of the Nineteenth Century Swazi State* (Cambridge, 1983); Peter Delius, *The Land Belongs to Us: The Pedi Polity, the Boers and the British in the Nineteenth-Century Transvaal* (London, 1984); Elizabeth A. Eldredge, *A South African Kingdom: The Pursuit of Security in Nineteenth-Century Lesotho* (Cambridge, 1993).

[33] See T. Bassett, 'Cartography and Empire Building in Nineteenth-Century West Africa', *Geographical Review*, LXXXIV, 3 (1994), pp. 316–35.

rigid territorial attachments. Much evidence exists to suggest that the majority of pre-colonial African societies annexed by the British construed themselves in terms of cultural indicators of belonging rather than geographical delimitations of territory. The 'great states' of pre-colonial Africa themselves operated with fluid notions of core, periphery, and influence rather than fixed ideas of demarcation, frontier, and foreignness. By labelling and fixing African cultures in space to define possession and expedite overrule the British—like other imperial powers—opened a Pandora's box. In particular, issues of ethnicity and identity referenced to spatial boundaries became contentious urgencies of the colonial era. The construction, content and nature of 'Yorubaness' within Nigeria, say, or 'Kikuyuness' within Kenya, or 'Gandaness' within Uganda, or 'Asanteness' within the Gold Coast, became pointed, contested questions that continue to trouble Africans in the post-colonial era.[34]

Some attempt at retrospect and prospect is offered here. At the start of the nineteenth century Britain's presence in tropical Africa was narrowly confined to the—mainly West African—coast. Systematic exploration of the interior occupied the entire nineteenth century (and extended in remoter areas into the twentieth), dating, perhaps, from the 1788 foundation of the African Association by the savant Joseph Banks and others.[35] The ideological grounding of this effort shifted over time. At its outset the British cultural encounter with African societies was dominated by inquiries dedicated to accumulating knowledge, to bridging the gap between imagination and reality. That this reconciliation might be reconfigured but never achieved is apparent in all nineteenth-century British reporting of Africa. The most generalized indication of this is the way in which—around and after mid-century—the imagined Africa of pseudo-scientific racial thinking became the optic through which an ever increasing factual knowledge was viewed. Bowdich's first eyewitness account of Kumasi (1817) is characterized by scientific curiosity, but none the less treats Asante culture as a complex achievement in its own right and on its own terms. Robert Baden-Powell's participation in the British occupation of Kumasi (1896) resulted in an account of Asante that enlarges on the views of the Wolseley 'ring'. In this,

[34] The best treatment (on Kenya) is Bruce Berman and John Lonsdale, *Unhappy Valley: Conflict in Kenya and Africa*, 2 vols.(London, 1991).

[35] See Stafford, 'Scientific Exploration'; and Richard Drayton, 'Knowledge and Empire', in P. J. Marshall, ed., *OHBE*, Vol. II, *The Eighteenth Century* (Oxford, 1998).

Asante is a blood-soaked despotism condemned to its fate by racial inferiority. Only Anglo-Saxon rule can redeem it from the excesses of its birthright.[36] This is an extreme distillation of a widespread climate of opinion. Even those dedicated to a humane tutelage of Africans by colonial overlordship shared implicitly in ideas of superiority and inferiority that were grounded in assumptions about race and destiny.[37]

It needs to be restated that the British missionary enterprise in Africa arose from a complex of ideas. Principled abolitionism and anti-slavery were accompanied by paternalist ideas of social improvement to be rooted in economic production for British markets. This is not to question the Christian sincerity of British missionaries. Africa was remote and unhealthy; many missionaries died but the supply of replacements never dried up. But missionary work, like exploration, requires ideological contextualization. Missionaries were products of British society and to a degree shared in its evolving values. Thus, it is scarcely surprising that the later decades of the nineteenth century saw an increasing racial awareness being added to early Victorian paternalism. Ironically, this development was greatly sharpened by the very real, if localized, success of missionaries among peoples such as the Fante and Yoruba. A latent contradiction existed between the ongoing Christianizing of Africans and the point at which an established African Christianity might be deemed ripe for emancipation from stewardship. Missionary writings of the later nineteenth century are replete with vexed—and vexing—discussions about autonomy and independence for African congregations. Issues of race certainly played their part in British reluctance to relinquish control, in African alienation from mission churches, and in the rise of the independent African church movement in the 1880s and 1890s.[38]

By then one of the guiding suppositions of the early abolitionists had long since proved false. The foundation of Freetown led to the emergence of a property-owning middle class and not a community of industrious agriculturalists. This pattern was repeated wherever urbanized societies emerged on the Sierra Leone model or out of the conditions of trade. Like their Creole

[36] T. E. Bowdich, *Mission From Cape Coast Castle to Ashantee* (London, 1819); R. S. S. Baden-Powell, *The Downfall of Prempeh: A Diary of Life with the Native Levy in Ashanti, 1895–96* (London, 1896).

[37] For some of the resonances, Thomas Richards, *The Imperial Archive: Knowledge and the Fantasy of Empire* (London, 1993).

[38] Hastings, *Church in Africa*, chap. 7.

counterparts, indigenous West or East African entrepreneurs (in palm-oil, timber, ivory, gum, etc.) who achieved economic success as individuals also came to take many of their cultural cues from bourgeois Victorianism. This westernized African society, fostered by abolitionists, missionaries, and a whole panorama of economic possibilities in commerce had a complex nineteenth-century history. Evolving racial attitudes again played an instrumental role. The 1850s and 1860s are sometimes spoken of as being an 'Indian summer' for this community. It was in these decades that it realized the British were opposed to granting it due political participation and that the source of this denial lay in shifting metropolitan attitudes towards the very idea of civilized, Anglicized Africans. In the second half of the century this community suffered a cultural ambivalence. On the one hand British civilization was an admirable thing; but on the other its representatives in Africa were increasingly rejectionist and contemptuous towards westernized Africans. Members of this community took to separating out the message from the messenger. Constitutionalism, the rule of law and a concern with asserting (and defending) juridical rights came to occupy a central place in their thinking and discourse. Britain was often said to be failing her own ideals. Obversely, the rhetoric and terms of encroaching British colonialism fed a reactive interest in the specificity of African cultures and history. Late-nineteenth and early-twentieth-century writing by Africans is shot through with these often contradictory impulses.[39]

In 1800 most Africans had seen few if any Europeans. In 1900 nearly all of Africa was ruled by Europe. The sheer number and diversity of African cultures that encountered the British in the course of the nineteenth century is bewildering. Exemplary cases have been discussed throughout, for generalization about such a range of societies risks relapse to levels of analysis that obtained before the emergence of a modern African historiography. Having entered that caveat, it remains important to draw attention to a theme that applies to African cultures generally in their encounter with the British, whatever the historical specifics of place and time. That theme is the conditions of the cultural encounter seen with hindsight from the perspective of African peoples. Early-nineteenth-century British sojourners in African cultures were supplicants of one kind or another. They *asked* for audience, consideration, protection, information, trade, diplomatic relations, con-

[39] e.g. J. E. Casely Hayford, *Gold Coast Native Institutions, with Thoughts upon a Healthy Imperial Policy for the Gold Coast and Ashanti* (London, 1903).

verts, and the rest. By corollary, African cultures maintained the capacity not only to accede to or deny such requests but also to control or expel British visitors. A vital element in the same configuration was that African cultures had considerable powers of arbitration in rejecting or accepting British ideas and artefacts. The record overall shows African cultures to have been aware of the notion of *caveat emptor.*

These conditions shifted after mid-century, and from the 1870s on African cultures found themselves increasingly unable to resist British penetration. By this reading colonialism can be contextualized as the culmination of a century long shift from a Britain that *asked* to one that *demanded* and at last *commanded.* The reasons for this change are to be sought in the politics of Europe, in Britain's evolving strategic view of herself, and—perhaps most directly for Africa's peoples—in the 'speeding up' of British cultural capacity; in the period from the 1860s to the 1890s a series of revolutions in bureaucratization, technology, weaponry, communications, medicine, and the rest conferred upon Britain (and Europe) a hugely augmented capacity for cultural transmission and imposition in the broadest sense. African cultures succumbed to the onslaught of a Britain (and Europe) now organized, translated, and mobilized through the ever accelerating pace of modernity. Max Weber is as trustworthy a guide, as ever Marx was presumed to be, to the British overcoming of African cultures. This is not at all to argue that African cultures lay supine and inert before Europe's insertions and subversions. In the final quarter of the nineteenth century numbers of African societies braced themselves against change, engaged with it, and even tried to bend aspects of it to their own purposes. But the conditions of the cultural encounter were running against them, and whatever negotiation they managed to achieve within the new dispensation must be seen against the background of a single, blunt fact. British and other European colonialisms incorporated African peoples into the ideological and materialist worlds of Western modernity. All African cultures are still negotiating dialogue with—and within—the implications of that fact.

Select Bibliography

J. F. Ade Ajayi and Michael Crowder, eds., *Historical Atlas of Africa* (London, 1985).

—— eds., *History of West Africa*, Vol. 1, 3rd edn. (London, 1985), and Vol. 11, 2nd edn. (London, 1987).

Ralph A. Austen, *African Economic History: Internal Development and External Dependency* (London, 1987).

P. J. Cain and A. G. Hopkins, *British Imperialism: Innovation and Expansion, 1688–1914* (London, 1993).

Jean Comaroff and John Comaroff, *Of Revelation and Revolution: Christianity, Colonialism and Consciousness in South Africa* (Chicago, 1991).

John L. Comaroff and Jean Comaroff, *Of Revelation and Revolution: The Dialectics of Modernity on a South African Frontier* (Chicago, 1997).

T. R. H. Davenport, *South Africa: A Modern History*, 4th edn. (London, 1991).

Christopher Fyfe, *A History of Sierra Leone* (London, 1962).

—— *Africanus Horton: West African Scientist and Patriot* (Oxford, 1972).

Jonathan Glassman, *Feasts and Riot: Revelry, Rebellion and Popular Consciousness on the Swahili Coast, 1856–1888* (London, 1995).

Robin Hallett, ed., *Records of the African Association, 1788–1831* (London, 1964).

John Iliffe, *Africans: The History of a Continent* (Cambridge, 1995).

Elizabeth Isichei, *A History of African Societies to 1870* (Cambridge, 1997).

David Kimble, *A Political History of Ghana: The Rise of Gold Coast Nationalism, 1850–1928* (Oxford, 1963).

Martin Lynn, *Commerce and Economic Change in West Africa: The Palm Oil Trade in the Nineteenth Century* (Cambridge, 1997).

Phyllis Martin and Patrick O'Meara, eds., *Africa*, 3rd edn. (London, 1995).

Roland Oliver and others, eds., *History of East Africa*, 3 vols. (Oxford, 1963–76).

J. D. Y. Peel, *Religious Encounter and the Making of the Yoruba* (Bloomington, Ind., 2000).

Ronald Robinson and John Gallagher, with Alice Denny, *Africa and the Victorians: The Official Mind of Imperialism*, 2nd edn. (London, 1981).

Nigel Worden, *The Making of Modern South Africa: Conquest, Segregation and Apartheid* (Oxford, 1994).

C. C. Wrigley, *Kingship and State: The Buganda Dynasty* (Cambridge, 1996).

8

The Betrayal of Creole Elites, 1880–1920

VIVIAN BICKFORD-SMITH

In 1897, the year of Queen Victoria's Diamond Jubilee, the *Cape Argus* contained a story of a visitor to Cape Town who asked a docker whether he was a 'native' of the colony. The dock worker replied that he was not, that he was English. Pointing to people the *Argus* report referred to as 'coal-carrying Kafirs', he said that they were the 'natives'.[1] The story is instructive. Notably it suggests that a crucial part of the black experience of Empire was the struggle over identity, and meanings and consequences associated with identity. The Comaroffs, in their magisterial study of the Tswana, support this contention. They argue that colonialism involved one common and distinctive experience for the colonized: 'the experience . . . of coming to feel, and to *re-cognize* [their italics] one's self as, a "native" '.[2]

We might quibble over whether this was indeed an experience common to all Africans. For instance those who came to think of themselves as 'Coloureds' in Cape Town, including no doubt the docker we have mentioned, largely resisted such 're-cognition' as we shall see. But the point is taken that the black experience of Empire was partly, but importantly, about categorization and self-categorization.[3]

[1] *Cape Argus*, 3 April 1897. I would like to thank Sean Hawkins, Sara Pienaar and Ruth Watson for reading draft versions of this chapter. Their comments have influenced the final version.

[2] John L. Comaroff and Jean Comaroff, *Of Revelation and Revolution: The Dialectics of Modernity on a South African Frontier* (Chicago, 1997), p. 19.

[3] Terminology: by using the terms 'black' or 'white', or 'African', 'Coloured', or 'Native', I do not wish to imply that that they are anything other than ethnic labels or racialized categories. I use the synonym 'African' for contemporary terms more obviously offensive today, such as 'Native', 'Negro', or 'Kaffir'. Although white was a common self-description used by Europeans in Africa, whether settlers or visitors, black was employed as a self-description by Africans somewhat less often. I have used black as a synonym for the British nineteenth-century term 'other than white'; thus black is used as a collective noun for people who have thought of themselves, for instance and at times, as African, Coloured, Creole or 'Native'.

Hence this chapter begins by asserting that in the 1880s many, if not most, members of creole élites throughout the British Empire in Africa saw themselves not as 'natives' but as 'black Englishmen'. In doing so they were staking a claim to equal social and political rights with 'white Englishmen' within this Empire. Members of creole élites wished to be treated as equal partners in the 'civilizing mission'.

Because of the actual experience of partnerships in trade and missionary work in West Africa, or because of the non-racial nature of laws and the franchise in the Cape, such expectations had seemed not only reasonable but also achievable for much of the nineteenth century. But by the 1880s, as we shall see, increasingly strident articulations of both metropolitan and white settler racism accompanied the period of high imperialism. In the 1890s and early 1900s, during the partition of Africa, this racism led to growing instances of discrimination against members of creole élites: be it in terms of job opportunities or through social and residential segregation.

Crucially, such discrimination culminated by the 1910s in political betrayal. The British abandoned creole élites—as actual or potential partners in Empire—in favour of recently defeated Afrikaners in South Africa and 'traditional' leaders in West Africa. An unintended consequence of racial discrimination and political betrayal was that many members of creole élites 're-cognized' themselves not only as 'natives' but also, in due course and fatefully, as nationalists.

Defining Creole Élites

By the late nineteenth century, westernized black élites existed in many parts of British Africa. They were the result of cultural encounters between Africa and Europe, as Tom McCaskie's chapter has outlined. We refer to such élites as 'creole' because this term—though used historically in different ways in different places—usefully suggests a high degree of cultural hybridity rather than a purely one-way process of acculturation.[4] In the case of some members of creole élites, notably 'Coloureds' in the western Cape, cultural hybridity was accompanied by 'racial' hybridity.[5]

[4] This and all subsequent references to McCaskie refer to his chapter in this volume. For discussion of some of the historical uses of the term creole—in the West Indies, South America and Sierra Leone—see Leo Spitzer, *The Creoles of Sierra Leone 1870–1945* (Madison, 1974), pp. 12–13.

[5] Gavin Lewis, *Between the Wire and the Wall: A History of South African 'Coloured' politics* (Cape Town, 1987), pp. 7–20.

The focus here is particularly on the relatively large creole élites of Sierra Leone in West Africa and those of the Cape Colony in South Africa: people who were called by whites, or called themselves, 'Creoles', 'Coloureds', 'Malays' or 'Natives'. Mention will also be made of those smaller groups elsewhere, especially the 'Saro' (Yoruba 'returnees' from Sierra Leone) in what became Nigeria. In whatever locale, it should be stressed that these élites were always a small minority of the population, numbering only a few thousand in the Cape and Sierra Leone, fewer in other places. But their significance lies in the leading role they played in responding to British policies and practices in the age of high imperialism and conquest, and the impact that these responses eventually had on the overall black experience of Empire beyond our period.

As the Comaroffs have demonstrated, creole élites emerged out of a process of 'long conversations' between Africans—or slaves brought to Africa in the case of some members of western Cape elites—and agents of European modernization. In this respect, the most important agents of change were missionaries, settlers, and businessmen rather than the colonial state. The Comaroffs argue persuasively that the colonial encounter was—one might add whether for Tswana in Kuruman (British Bechuanaland) or Creoles in Freetown—'first and foremost an epic of the ordinary'.[6] In other words it was experienced by black Africans—importantly in varying ways and degrees depending on factors such as gender, generation, class or the specific historical context of the society to which they belonged—at the level of the quotidian or everyday. Thus the black experience of cultural change (and exchange) was at the level of religious belief, dress, agricultural practices, domestic architecture, privately owned objects, diet, and the sense of self in relation to society.

The creole élites that form the focus of this chapter were, in general, the most changed. In McCaskie's phrase, they were the most 'incorporated into the ideological and material worlds of Western modernity', even if cultural encounters were always two-way conversations. Most had a number of characteristics in common by the 1880s. These spoke intimately to a shared experience of Empire. They also helped to forge a sense of cohesive identity both within and beyond particular urban settings.

Members of creole élites—whether in South or West Africa— were largely bourgeois or petty-bourgeois, with men employed mostly as missionaries,

[6] Comaroff and Comaroff, *Dialectics of Modernity*, p. 35.

regular clergymen, lawyers, teachers, and doctors, or in government service, commerce and particular trades. Elites, whether they were Coloureds in Cape Town, Saros in Lagos, Xhosa or Mfengu in the eastern Cape, Tswana in Bechuanaland or Creoles in Freetown, gained both the sense and reality of cohesiveness through shared educational and religious backgrounds, similar class positions, joint membership of social and political organizations, literary production and readership, and through consequent marriage ties and friendships.

Most were Christian, albeit that their Christianity might have varying degrees of syncretism; there were also important Muslim minorities in both the western Cape and many West Africa towns. Nearly all members of creole élites had a similar educational background. They had obtained a Western education at mission schools, superior Christian colleges such as Fourah Bay in Sierra Leone, or at universities in Britain or the United States. So most could speak, read, and write English well. Unsurprisingly many, as part of bolstering their own status but also from acquired belief, looked down on vernacular languages—including creolised vernaculars like Afrikaans (spoken in the Cape) and Krio (spoken in Sierra Leone)—even if they still used them.

Most, like the African petty bourgeoisie in Kimberley, believed in 'the possibility, indeed the obligation, of individual advancement through the medium of education' for both men and women, and through improving and respectable leisure activities.[7] The latter included the likes of chess, cricket, rugby, or cycling; 'dignified' dancing, free from 'savage' and suggestive 'gyrations'; public instructional lectures; debating; temperance, 'improvement' and Christian youth and 'ladies' associations; musical recitals and literary recitations; and, of course, reading appropriate literature—*Boswell's Life of Dr Johnson* and *English Journalism and the Men who have made it* were just two of the possibilities on offer in a Freetown bookshop in 1886.

Many believed that such advancement—symbolized by the adoption of aspects of European material culture—differentiated them from 'the savage', situated themselves on a 'putatively universal grid of difference' as 'civilized'. A number would probably have agreed that 'saving the savage meant teach-

[7] Brian Willan, 'An African in Kimberley: Sol T. Plaatje, 1894–1898', in Shula Marks and Richard Rathbone, eds., *Industrialisation and Social Change in South Africa* (London, 1982), p. 243.

ing the savage to save', though conspicuous consumption was certainly in evidence among the élite of Freetown.[8] Many believed that they were and should be 'respectable', and frequently reserved their fiercest denunciation of 'savagery' for lower-class members of what they, and others, perceived to be their own ethnic or racial group. Thus Sierra Leonean Creole prostitutes were referred to as 'Yoobas', or Buzzards; creole élites in Cape Town castigated Coloured prostitutes as 'picturesque filth' who were able to 'strut about the streets to the delight of the enemies of the race . . . but to the disgust of the decent and respectable citizen'.[9]

In brief, the majority among these élites had fashioned themselves along the lines of what they took to be the respectable, metropolitan, British middle-classes. As Patrick (sometimes known as Dele) Cole put it, Christmas among the creole élite of Lagos meant 'concerts and athletic sports, dinners, with the accessories of plump turkeys, minced pies, plum puddings, and Christmas trees'; all it lacked was snow.[10] In the early 1880s the town even had a musical merry-go-round. And one of Lagos's leading citizens, Herbert Macaulay who had studied surveying and civil engineering in England, was both 'a gifted pianist and violinist, and represented the West of England at chess'.[11] Macaulay was a founder-member of one of Nigeria's first political parties, the National Council of Nigeria and the Cameroons, and in modern times has been represented as the 'father' of Nigerian nationalism on the one Naira coin. Similarly, Sol Plaatje—future founder-member of the South African Native National Congress—had himself elected joint secretary of the Eccentrics Cricket Club in Kimberley in 1895, despite the fact that he was not particularly good at the game.

The point was that most creole élites wanted to be accepted as 'Black English', the name conferred by the British on grateful Sierra Leonian Creoles by mid-century, and acted accordingly.[12] They did so in part because this was about claiming a suitably distinct identity from a range of 'traditional' African identities which they had (at least temporarily) rejected, albeit that being both 'black' as well as 'English' meant for many an acknowledgement of their African heritage. But being 'Black English' was also about claiming

[8] Comaroff and Comaroff, *Dialectics of Modernity*, pp. 166, 408.

[9] Spitzer, *Creoles of Sierra Leone*, pp. 21–22. *South African Spectator*, 9 Feb. 1901.

[10] Cited in Elizabeth Isichei, *A History of Nigeria* (Harlow, Essex, 1983), p. 340.

[11] Isichei, *Nigeria*, pp. 340–41.

[12] Spitzer, *Creoles of Sierra Leone*, p. 39. Philip S. Zachernuk, *Colonial Subjects: An African Intelligentsia and Atlantic Ideas* (Charlottesville, Va., 2000), pp. 42–46.

social and political rights within the British Empire. Hence the countless protestations of loyalty to Britain that continued into the age of high imperialism, and despite the increasing 'cultural ambivalence' that Tom McCaskie has noted.

The Pursuit and Purpose of Patriotism

Loyalty was most obviously demonstrated on occasions of British royal celebrations as well as in numerous newspaper articles and editorials. Thus both Queen Victoria's Golden and Diamond Jubilees were enthusiastically celebrated throughout British Africa. Parades, fireworks, balls and a bewildering variety of additional entertainments were held in honour of 'the Great White Queen across the sea', or 'We Mammy' as she was nick-named in Sierra Leone. For example in Cape Town, in June 1887, 'the great mass of people of all colours, creeds and denominations gathered together to do homage to their sovereign lady', waving banners or flags to celebrate the Golden Jubilee.[13] At night 'even the poorest Malays in the back streets illuminated their tenements'.[14] In Sierra Leone, many female children born in the course of the year were named 'Jubilee' or 'Victoria'.

The Diamond Jubilee, held ten years later, was marked in similar fashion. During or after both Jubilees, statues were erected in honour of the Queen; roads, buildings and places named after her. Thus in Sierra Leone, Freetown gained 'Victoria Park, complete with benches and bandstand'.[15] Or, in the Cape, the Queen's Jubilee Commemoration Hall was opened in the 'Malay Camp', Kimberley.[16] In opening this hall, Isaiah Bud-M'belle, a High Court Interpreter, 'compared their [the 'natives'] present condition to what prevailed at the time of the accession of the Queen, and pointed out that though then scarcely a native could write his name and there were no Native ministers, now thousands could write, and there were about five hundred Native Ministers'.[17] Similarly there were numerous articulations of loyalty in journals produced and read by Creoles in Sierra Leone from the 1840s onwards. For instance, an article in the *Sierra Leone Weekly News* (*SLWN*) in 1885 asserted that: 'A few months residence in England among Englishmen will tend to round off those angularities in our character which only mixing

[13] *Cape Argus*, 22 June 1887. [14] *Excalibur*, 24 June 1887.

[15] Spitzer, *The Creoles of Sierra Leone*, p. 41. [16] Willan, 'Sol Plaatje', p. 243.

[17] *Imvo*, 18 Nov. 1897, cited in Willan, 'Sol Plaatje', p. 243.

with refined people can effect.'[18] Or as late as 1899 an editorial in the *SLWN* could state: 'We are largely indebted to England for material, intellectual, and it may be, ultimately, spiritual salvation.'[19]

Frequently pro-British newspaper articles or editorials either urged, or coincided with British military interventions aimed at enlarging or securing the Empire in Africa. The *Gold Coast Chronicle* argued in 1894 that 'we must go straight to Kumasi and occupy it or annex it declaring Ashantee a British protectorate'. The *Lagos Times* declared in 1891, 'We "black Englishmen"... cannot sit still and see her [England] robbed of the well-earned fruits of her sagacity, enterprise and goodwill.'[20] And according to the Cape newspaper *Izwi Labantu*, Britain had to triumph in the South African War (1899–1902) against 'the narrow, prejudiced and inhuman tyranny of Boer Republicanism' to preserve democratic ideals and ensure progress in South Africa.[21]

Such displays or protestations of loyalty 'should not be interpreted as the product of a simple, unmediated absorption of an imperial creed'. Rather 'own meanings' were imposed on patriotism.[22] The examples already cited begin to reveal such meanings. One was that creole élites thought of themselves as—and for much of the nineteenth century were seen by the British to be—partners in the 'civilizing mission' to Africa. The success of this mission was a major part of the 'progress' that Bud-M'belle believed had accompanied Queen Victoria's reign. And as the creole Bishop Crowther charged his West African clergy in 1869: 'If we have any regard for the elevation of Africa, or any real interest for the evangelization of her children, our own wisdom would be to cry to those Christian nations which have been so long labouring for our conversion to redouble their Christian efforts.'[23] In fact Crowther was being modest. 'Native agency', including his own, was a critical component of the success of evangelizing, and 'civilizing', efforts throughout Africa. But enthusiasm for the civilizing mission was in part a result of the assumption, if not exactly the condition, that it was a partnership between Britons and Africans, and a partnership of equals.

[18] Cited in Spitzer, *Creoles of Sierra Leone*, p. 40. [19] Ibid. p. 43.

[20] *Gold Coast Chronicle*, 30 Nov. 1894; *Lagos Times*, 14 Feb. 1891—both cited in J. B. Webster, 'Political Activity in British West Africa, 1900–1940', in J. F. Ade Ajayi and Michael Crowder, eds., *History of West Africa*, 2 vols. (London, 1974), II, pp. 569–70.

[21] *Izwi Labantu*, 20 Aug. 1901, cited in Andre Odendaal, *Black Protest Politics in South Africa to 1912* (Cape Town and Totowa, 1984), p. 31

[22] Bill Nasson, *Abraham Esau's War* (Cambridge, 1991), p. 62.

[23] Cited in Toyin Falola, ed., *Tradition and Change in Africa: The Essays of J. F. Ade. Ajayi* (Trenton, NJ, 2000), p. 78.

Enthusiasm for British rule among Coloureds in the western Cape, among the Creoles of Sierra Leone or the Saros of Nigeria also stemmed from the way that Britain was seen as the deliverer from slavery and the provider of 'freedom'. In the Diamond Jubilee parade in Cape Town, one group of Muslims represented the year 1837 as 'Slavery', another the year 1897 as 'Freedom'. But Britain and its colonial representatives had to earn such bouquets, had to remain guarantors of 'freedom'. Thus in 1878, when mainly Muslim fishermen in Cape Town felt their livelihoods threatened by local and central government interference, leaders of that community wrote to the town council: 'We were always under the impression that we were emancipated in the reign of our most Gracious Majesty Queen Victoria, and freed from tyranny, but it seems that we are mistaken, as our rulers (perhaps without intention) are depressing us [sic]; surely it is without the proper knowledge and extent of our misfortunes.'[24]

What underpinned loyalty to Britain by creole élites, in whatever part of Africa, was a mixture of practical partnerships and acceptable imperial practices. Among the Creoles of Sierra Leone or Saros of Nigeria, such partnerships had characterized, most notably, trade and missionary work, at least for the first three-quarters of the nineteenth century. Creole élites in West Africa were also allowed a limited, but promising, role in Legislative Councils and the civil service, even if they lacked representative governance.

In the Cape, religious and economic partnerships played a somewhat lesser role, not least because of the greater presence of white settlers, clerics, and businessmen. But this was partially compensated for by the existence of the 'Cape liberal tradition'. The 'great' tradition of Cape liberalism consisted of technical equality of all colonists, irrespective of colour, before the law (after 1838) and the low, (male) colour-blind franchises of 1853 and 1872 through which the British conferred Representative and Responsible Government, respectively. The 'small' tradition consisted of local political constituency alliances across the colour-line based on perceived mutual interests.[25]

[24] Cited in Vivian Bickford-Smith, 'Meanings of Freedom: Social Position and Identity among Ex-slaves and their Descendants in Cape Town, 1875–1910', in Nigel Worden and Clifton Crais, eds., *Breaking the Chains: Slavery and its Legacy in the Nineteenth-Century Cape Colony* (Johannesburg, 1994), p. 303.

[25] S. Trapido, ' "The Friends of the Natives": Merchants, Peasants and the Political and Ideological Structure of Liberalism in the Cape, 1854–1910', in Shula Marks and Anthony Atmore, eds., *Economy and Society in Pre-Industrial South Africa* (London, 1980), pp. 247–74.

'Partnership' in West Africa and 'liberalism' in the Cape were both the result of British pragmatism. Thanks in part to the ravages of tropical diseases, a paucity of whites in West Africa meant British reliance on creole élites for both economic and religious endeavours. A British parliamentary Select Committee in 1865 went as far as recommending self-government under their leadership in this region of the Empire. In turn, the great tradition of Cape liberalism was thought by the British to be the best way of maintaining peace and uniting inhabitants of the Colony across ethnic divides. Creole élites, in both the eastern and western Capes, qualified for the vote—another characteristic that marked élite status—and duly participated in such constituency alliances.

Most Creoles at the advent of the period of high imperialism were not only British patriots but also, as we have seen, enthusiastically espoused British culture. This enthusiasm was not the result of mere mimicry by 'colonized minds'. Rather adherence to British ideas and manners stemmed from a realization that these provided a source of power within a (often rapidly) changing African setting. But such enthusiasm was also conditional. It could wane, at least for some individuals. This is exemplified in the shifting views of Edward Blyden.

West Indian born, Blyden moved to Liberia in 1851, but from the late 1870s until his death in 1912 he made Freetown his home. Blyden's life and literary efforts epitomized more dramatically than most the cultural ambivalence and medial position of Creoles in the British Empire. Thus Blyden continually supported the extension of British rule over Africa, even if he criticized particular British colonial practices such as land appropriation. He served the British in a number of capacities, including that of 'Agent for Native Affairs' in Lagos. He initially saw the expansion of British-style education as essential for African upliftment. Yet Blyden ultimately became a critic of European values, a champion of the idea of a distinct, and more spiritual 'African personality' and destiny, and thereby a pioneer of African cultural nationalism; the fact that he did so had much to do with the growth of European racism.

The Growth of Racism and Segregation

Metropolitan and settler racism and discrimination grew rapidly in the late nineteenth century. The eventual outcome was the British abandonment of creole élites in favour of new partners in Empire: freshly created 'native' élites in West Africa and recently defeated Afrikaner settlers in South Africa. The sense of betrayal among creole élites was acute in both regions, even if those in West Africa may have felt that the perfidy in their case was greater, given the extent of British pre-colonial reliance on their services.

Metropolitan racism was fuelled by the popularization of 'scientific racism' and pseudo-Darwinist ideas about racial struggle in mid-century, as well as by the continuing close correlation in the Empire between class and colour. It was also encouraged by events—be they the Indian Sepoy Mutiny of 1857 or the Morant Bay rebellion in Jamaica in 1865—that seemed to cast doubt over the ultimate success of the 'civilizing mission' and coincided with, and partly fuelled, doubts about the imperial project itself. By the time of the 'scramble' for Africa in the last decades of the nineteenth century, a new enthusiasm for imperialism was accompanied by a new ideology. If African Empire had been seen by the British earlier in the century as 'a commercial and evangelical mission to potential equals', it had now become 'a mandate to develop and protect an inferior race'.[26]

Given the absence of a substantial settler population, metropolitan racism was of particular significance to creole élites in West Africa—even if such racism had less immediate political implications due to the lack of representative politics. Growing doubts about African capabilities was first fuelled for some in West Africa by competition between whites and Africans for particular posts in the missionary church. It was here that betrayal of creole élites began, rather than in the realm of colonial government itself.

Thus Henry Townsend, of the Church Missionary Society (CMS) in Abeokuta, questioned the appointment of Samuel Crowther as bishop of 'West Equatorial Africa in regions beyond the Queen's dominions' as early as the 1850s. This was an appointment that Townsend may well have expected to be given himself, and he wrote to Henry Venn, General Secretary of the CMS, suggesting that Africans needed white superiors: 'the Negro... feels a great respect for the white man, [and] God gives a great talent to the white man in trust to be used for the Negro's good... Shall we shift the responsibility? Can we do it without sin?'[27] The fact that Crowther was given no authority in, say, Sierra Leone, or even Lagos—despite the fact that his episcopal seat was there—says a great deal about the desire of the CMS not to offend Townsend, or white missionary susceptibilities in general. So does the fact that when

[26] Zachernuk, *Colonial Subjects*, p. 7.

[27] Cited in Falola, *Essays of J. F. Ade Ajayi*, p. 76.

another Saro, James Johnson, was considered for the position of Bishop of Yorubaland in the late 1870s, he had to undergo a trial period of three years as Superintendent of the Interior Missions; and at the end of this period white missionaries barred his promotion to the episcopacy.

Matters came to a head in the 1890s when Africans were effectively blocked from any positions of control within the Anglican church in West Africa. Notably Crowther resigned from a CMS finance committee in 1890 when it became clear that it had usurped his episcopal authority. When he died in 1893 he was not replaced by a fellow African. In the same year Johnson was again denied a see—this time of the Delta Pastorate—and insultingly offered instead the position of assistant bishop to the now white Bishop of West Equatorial Africa, a position which he understandably declined. Crowther was, then, the first and last African to be appointed a diocesan bishop in West Africa until the 1950s.[28]

The position of West African creole élites was being undermined in a number of other ways by the early 1900s. This was largely due to a combination of racism, expanded colonial conquest and commerce, and the fact that medical advances had made the region less of a white man's grave; medical advances between 1903 and 1913 halved the deaths among white officials.[29] For much of the nineteenth century creoles had held important positions in the colonial civil and medical services, and salaries had been paid on a colour-blind basis. European traders had seldom ventured much beyond the coast, leaving the hinterland as an area for creole enterprise. The late nineteenth century had seen creole traders being increasingly elbowed out by Europeans, however, a situation abetted by the fact that portions of the interior had recently been ceded to France. And by 1902, the upper echelons of the colonial administration had been reserved for white Britons. So was the recently formed West African Medical Staff, for whom candidates had to be 'of European parentage'; all members of this Medical Staff ranked above even the most senior 'Native Medical Officers', and salaries were higher for Europeans. By 1912, only seven of the 200 or so doctors employed in the West African medical service were creoles.[30]

[28] Cited in Falola, *Essays of J. F. Ade Ajayi*, pp. 76, 85–87, 93, 107, 112, 119–20.

[29] Toyin Falola and A. D. Roberts, 'West Africa', in Judith M. Brown and Wm. Roger Louis, eds., *The Oxford History of the British Empire*, Vol. IV, *The Twentieth Century* (Oxford, 1999), p. 517.

[30] Spitzer, *Creoles of Sierra Leone*, pp. 63–69; Falola and Roberts, 'West Africa', p. 519.

In mid-century there had been considerable social intercourse between creoles and Europeans in West Africa, particularly in Freetown, whether at balls, concerts, or 'at homes'. Yet this had largely ended by the early twentieth century. Freetown also witnessed the establishment between 1902 and 1904 of the European residential enclave Hill Station—echoes of India here—750 foot above the city. As with residential segregation in many other parts of the Empire, including the Cape, the ostensible motivation had been the protection of European health, what has been dubbed 'the sanitation syndrome'.[31] British officials hoped that Hill Station would be freer from malarial mosquitoes, as well as from African carriers of the disease. However Creoles in the town below were conscious of the fact that Hill Station also represented their social exclusion: thus the 'Mountain Railway', between the two, was *de facto* racially segregated, and not a single Creole was invited to join the Hill Station Club. In subsequent years, the housing developments that sprang up around Hill Station were also exclusively white. Together they stood as monuments 'to the deterioration of the British experiment in philanthropy and racial equality which had led to the original founding of Sierra Leone.'[32]

The future Nigeria witnessed similar creeping segregation. Africans were excluded from the Chamber of Commerce in 1897. In the next decade, Lagos witnessed the establishment of a white settler church, whites-only freemasons' lodge, and residential segregation. And, during the First World War, Port Harcourt was planned as a racially segregated town.

But the climax of the British betrayal of Creole élites came with the implementation of Indirect Rule in the newly conquered parts of West Africa, a policy confirmed by Lugard once he had become Governor of all Nigeria in 1912. The British had chosen 'traditional leaders' as partners in Empire rather than the Western educated élites. Indeed Lugard undermined the limited role that Creoles had been playing in local administration in Yorubaland, by ending Abeokuta's independence and excluding Creole advisers from courts in other states, including Ibadan. Creole élites were left with the sop of nominated unofficial representation on Legislative Councils. These had some powers over Lagos, the Gold Coast colony, and the colony and Protectorate of Sierra Leone. But even this representation was minimal, and it was seen by many creoles to be largely ineffectual.[33]

[31] Maynard Swanson, 'The Sanitation Syndrome; Bubonic Plague and Urban Native Policy in the Cape Colony, 1900–1909', *Journal of African History*, XVIII, 3 (1977), pp. 387–410.

[32] See Spitzer, *Creoles of Sierra Leone*, pp. 23–24, 55–63.

[33] Falola and Roberts, 'West Africa', pp. 518–19.

Settler racism was predictably of greater significance than metropolitan racism in explaining the growth of discrimination and the ultimate betrayal of creole élites in South Africa. Negative stereotypes of Africans were assembled in 'coherent theories' for English-speaking white Cape Colonists as early as the 1840s. Within a decade, books such as A. Cole's *The Cape and the Kafirs* were drawing on contemporary, metropolitan, ideas about a hierarchy of races, with 'Caucasians' at the top and 'Negroes', 'Hottentots', and Australian Aboriginals at the bottom.[34] By the 1860s, and particularly worrying for creole élites, numerous works were singling out 'ultra-civilized black loafers' for ridicule. As McCaskie has pointed out, the likes of Burton, Banbury, Ellis, Kingsley, and Mockler-Ferryman mocked educated West Africans as 'mimic-men'. Similar sentiments were expressed in the first popular novel to be published in Cape Town. *Sitongo*, written in 1884 by J. D. Ensor—significantly a shorthand writer for the Native Laws and Customs Commission of 1883—told the story of the eponymous, highly educated hero who ultimately failed to assimilate to European society despite his ability to 'pass for white'. The novel ended with Sitongo returning to being a 'native' in the remotest part of the Cape Colony: 'I was still a Kaffir at heart'.[35]

By the late nineteenth century British discourses about race were less harsh on supposedly more culturally—and 'racially'—pristine African societies as McCaskie has indicated. The application of social Darwinist ideas to the Cape in the 1880s and 1890s led to the harshest comments being reserved for the 'mixed race' inhabitants of the western Cape. Thus in 1887 the Reverend James Mackinnon saw what he termed the 'bastard Hottentots' as examples of racial 'retrogression', which he ascribed to the human tendency to 'absorb the bad and neglect the good'. Taking a specific swipe at the western Cape Coloured élite, he commented that they 'were mightily puffed up with their superiority as half-white and full blown British subjects'.[36]

The problem for creole élites in the Cape Colony was that they were subject not only to the racist rantings of temporary visitors to South Africa, or the occasional local white novelist—more easily rationalized or brushed aside perhaps—but also to continual racism in the local white press, racism

[34] Vivian Bickford-Smith, *Ethnic Pride and Racial Prejudice in Victorian Cape Town* (Cambridge, 1995), p. 79.

[35] J. D. Ensor, *Sitongo* (Cape Town, 1884), p. 166.

[36] J. Mackinnon, *South African Traits* (Edinburgh, 1887), pp. 66, 115–16. For similar comments see J. Ewing Ritchie, *Brighter South Africa* (London, 1892), p. 52; S. Cumberland, *What I think of South Africa: Its People and Its Politics* (London, 1896), p. 10.

informed both by metropolitan ideas about a hierarchy of 'races' as well as by the pragmatic self-interest of white settlers. Responsible Government in 1872 had effectively handed control of the Cape to its white inhabitants. Most blacks were still too poor to achieve the low property or wage qualification, despite gradually increasing black wealth and the concomitant size of the black vote during the 'mineral revolution', the economic expansion and change which accompanied the late nineteenth-century discovery of diamonds and gold in South Africa. Responsible Government predictably brought the beginnings of party political organization in the Cape along the interconnected lines of ethnicity and economic interests. Ethnic mobilization by Afrikaners and white English South Africans, struggling over the significantly increased resources of both central and local governments that came with the mineral revolution, was accompanied by considerable hostility to 'others', not least black Cape colonists. And these internal struggles were taking place against the backdrop of British imperial expansion that encouraged an increasingly assertive, and racist, Cape-settler Englishness.[37]

Racist rhetoric was followed by racist practice in both South and West Africa. In the Cape, segregation grew rapidly with white settler control of government. Before 1872 Cape liberalism had held out the assimilationist possibility to creole élites that class would matter more than race in the Cape's social order. In general, and doubtless in part because of the relatively small size of creole élites before the mineral revolution, social practice supported this view. Certainly in Cape Town class rather than colour was the more important factor determining admission, or where you were placed, in most social facilities and institutions be they hospitals, hotels, theatres, prisons or schools.

After 1872 racial segregation became the means used by the Cape Government and many white employers to solve four, linked, problems: what to do about newly conquered African societies in the eastern Cape; how to supply growing labour needs resulting from the mineral revolution; what to do about the significantly increased size of creole élites in both the eastern and western Capes; and how to cope with rapidly quickened urbanization and accompanying 'disorder'. The choice of segregation as the solution was obviously facilitated, and rationalized, by the arguments conveniently supplied by metropolitan 'scientific' racism. By the early 1900s, the need and

[37] Bickford-Smith, *Ethnic Pride*, pp. 91–125.

desire for complete racial separation between white and black had not only emerged as a dominant ideology among the Cape's ruling classes but had also prompted the introduction of segregation in many institutions and social amenities.[38]

Discussion about possible changes to the Cape franchise in the 1890s showed that the ideology of social separation threatened the maintenance of the 'great tradition' of Cape liberalism, a tradition still alive largely thanks to white political alliances with black voters at constituency level. Several articles that appeared in Cape newspapers now talked of the merits of black disenfranchisement, referred approvingly to its implementation in the southern United States, and cited the problem posed for white rule by the beginnings of nationalism in India. In the event, laws in 1887, 1892, and 1893 effectively limited the extent and efficacy of the black vote, and gave further cause for alarm among creole élites.

Another cause for concern was the contemporaneous erosion of economic opportunities, initially enhanced by the mineral revolution. White control of the colonial state meant that blacks were confined to the lower rungs of an expanding civil service. It also allowed, or actively promoted, the limiting of black accumulation in two key sectors of the economy: mining and commercial agriculture. In the course of the 1870s, white diggers effectively excluded blacks from mining claims in Kimberley, and in the ensuing decades a plethora of legislation ensured a rigid racial division of labour with blacks as unskilled workers. At the same time, and as part of supplying unskilled black labour to mines and white-owned farms, laws such as the Glen Gray Act (1894)—which limited African land holdings in parts of the eastern Cape—stifled the growth of a vibrant black peasantry.[39]

That the erosion of black political and economic rights went no further than it did before the beginning of the twentieth century was largely a result of both British settlers and the Imperial Government courting black support in the years leading up to, and during, the South African War. Both Cecil John Rhodes (leader of the predominantly British settler Progressive Party in the Cape) and Lord Milner (Governor of the Cape) promised equal rights for

[38] Precisely how and why this happened is discussed at length in Bickford-Smith, *Ethnic Pride*.

[39] Nigel Worden, *The Making of Modern South Africa* (Oxford, 1994), pp. 37–38, 47–49; Colin Bundy, *The Rise and Fall of the South African Peasantry* (London, 1979); William H. Worger, *South Africa's City of Diamonds: Mine Workers and Monopoly Capitalism in Kimberley, 1867–1895* (Johannesburg, 1987), pp. 244–46.

all 'civilized' men 'south of the Zambezi'.[40] In this context, the Treaty of Vereeniging (1902) which ended the war came as a bitter blow, all the more so for being delivered by the Imperial Government. The treaty allowed the white settlers in the defeated Boer republics the right to decide whether blacks should be included in the franchise in these areas after self-government had been regained.

In effect, the British had chosen rapprochement and partnership with Afrikaners, who formed the majority of white settlers, at the expense of creole élites. This was confirmed in the legislation that established the Union of South Africa in 1910. Although the non-racial franchise was retained in the Cape, it was not extended to other parts of the Union, and only those of 'European descent' were allowed to sit in the South African Parliament.[41]

This, then, was a betrayal almost on a par with the British abandonment of creole élites in West Africa in favour of 'traditional' rulers. Indeed creole élites in both West and South Africa had similar experiences of Empire in the late nineteenth and early twentieth centuries: increased white racism, discrimination, and segregation culminating in political abandonment. It is hardly surprising that there were also considerable similarities, as well as distinctions, in the way they responded.

Arguably there were three main, chronologically overlapping, responses. The first took the form of pleading the case against discrimination—whether in editorials (and some newspapers were established in part precisely so that the creole case could be put), letters to the press, or in petitions and delegations to the authorities. The second consisted of various forms of self-examination which often included the use of history to bolster self-esteem or enable self-assertion. Thirdly, creole élites created their own religious and overtly political organizations aimed at countering discrimination and furthering their interests. Such organizations were also an essential ingredient in the assertion of self-identity.

Appealing against Racism and Discrimination

Creole élite enthusiasm for one element of British culture, literacy in English, both encouraged and facilitated responses to racism that took literary form. In West Africa the readership of such writings, beyond fellow Creoles, was

[40] Lewis, *Between the Wire and the Wall*, p. 11.
[41] Ibid., pp. 19–63; Odendaal, *Black Protest Politics*, pp. 132–33.

assumed to be the imperial authorities, and beyond them a broader metropolitan intelligentsia. In the Cape, creole writers generally addressed white settlers and their governments.

Written pleas against discrimination varied in tone and form through time. For instance, in Sierra Leone the black-owned and edited newspapers generally reacted mildly before the twentieth century. They played down white racist rantings as the result of the overly brief acquaintanceship with Africa of 'Instant Experts', hoping no doubt—as creole élites hoped in the Cape—that partnership with Britain could be maintained, and with it assimilation into the imperial hierarchy or white colonial society. One editorial, in the *Methodist Herald* of 1885, even blamed white racism on the West African climate: 'The liver of foreigners in this climate is subject to such melancholy vicissitudes, that a great deal may be said in palliation of the execrating (and execrable?) proclivities of "roving" penny-a-liners.'[42] But by the 1900s, in the context of overt discrimination and segregation, the tone had changed. The immediate cause was the publication of a British White Paper that attempted to explain the inferior role given to Africans in the West African Medical Staff. An editorial in the *Sierra Leone Weekly News* read in part:

> We see many signs . . . which seem to indicate . . . a nefarious intention on the part of many Europeans serving on the W. Coast of Africa to lose no opportunity of creating the impression upon the minds of the British public, that Creoles—educated Africans—can never become qualified to occupy the superior, highly paid, or governing position in any one of the Governing Departments, and that, therefore, such positions should be reserved exclusively for Europeans . . . The Foundation of the nefarious intention is Race-Prejudice, which is against all human reason.[43]

Newspapers in the Gold Coast and Nigeria were issuing similar charges of racial discrimination by the close of the First World War.

There were no newspapers aimed specifically at a black readership in the western Cape before the twentieth century. Consequently creole élites in this part of South Africa used the letter pages of 'white' journals in an attempt to counter white racism. The first responses appear to have come as reactions to the growth of social segregation already experienced by the 1870s. Thus in 1879 Cape Town's only black doctor, Andrew Jackson—who was probably of

[42] *Methodist Herald*, 9 Dec. 1885, cited in Spitzer, *Creoles of Sierra Leone*, p. 49.

[43] *Sierra Leone Weekly News*, 6 Nov. 1909, cited in Spitzer, *Creoles of Sierra Leone*, p. 68.

West Indian origin and had been educated in Britain—wrote to the *Lantern* to complain against black exclusion from a recently opened roller-skating rink. In doing so he was one of the first among Cape Town's creole élite to express fears that the future lay in segregation rather than assimilation: 'We, the excluded, may soon expect to hear churches refuse us admission, theatre doors closed against us, the very side walks in the streets we dare not tread. In train and tram-car we'll be refused, because we are inferior.'[44]

In the course of the 1880s and 1890s Jackson was joined in the letter pages of local newspapers by other members of Cape Town's creole élite. They were responding to the racism that accompanied the rhetoric of English ethnic mobilization we have mentioned. Muslims—or 'Malays'—were initially in the vanguard. They defended themselves from white settler-conferred stereotypes. A recurring theme was that the whole 'community' should not be judged by the actions of a few. And if Muslims showed signs of not simply deferring to white susceptibilities then, according to Abdol Soubeyan, this should be expected: 'independence is the aim of everyone who is a little above groveling in the mud'.[45]

The first creole-run newspaper in Cape Town, the *South African Spectator*, took up the fight between January 1901 and December 1902. Its editor was Francis Peregrino who had been born in the Gold Coast, educated in Britain, and had already run a newspaper for African-Americans in the United States. Peregrino used his editorial position to reject white racism and campaign against any and every act of racial discrimination. So did the *A.P.O.* (the official journal of the African Political Organization), another more enduring Cape Town journal with a largely creole readership that ran from 1909 to 1923.

Given a history of relatively recent independence, as well as subsequent conquest by the British and local strident settler racism, it is hardly surprising that newspapers in the eastern Cape were quicker than their western Cape, or indeed West African, counterparts to suggest that strong arguments might be needed to claim rights under British colonialism as 'civilized' men. The British had not been deliverers from slavery, as they had been for creole élites in the western Cape or West Africa. Instead they were recent conquerors. Nor could educated Xhosa or Mfengu hope, as some 'mixed race' creoles could hope in the western Cape, to 'pass for white'.[46]

[44] *Lantern*, 23 Aug. 1879.
[45] *Lantern*, 23 Sept. 1882.
[46] Lewis, *Between the Wire and the Wall*, p. 13.

Actual or potential partnership with the British for educated Cape Africans rested not so much on past imperial benefits as on the fulfillment of missionary and liberal politicians' promises that conversion and education would lead to their acceptance and assimilation as 'civilized'. They wished to be distinguished from un-westernized, red blanket 'savages' who might well deserve inferior treatment. The breaking of this understanding was bitterly felt, and hard to accept even after discrimination on the basis of 'race' alone had become a well established practice. As D. D. T. Jabavu put it while addressing a mission conference in 1920: '[Railway] waiting rooms are made to accommodate the rawest blanketed heathen; and the more decent native has either to use them and annex vermin or to do without shelter in biting wintry weather.'[47]

A Lovedale missionary newspaper, the *Kaffir Express*—later renamed *Isigidimi Sama Xhosa*—had become the first forum for educated African opinion in 1870, and gained an African editor, Elijah Makiwane, in 1876. It was this journal that published a telling poem by an early Xhosa poet, I. W. W. Citashe:

Your cattle are gone my countrymen!
Go rescue them! Go rescue them!
Leave the breechloader alone
And turn to the pen.
Take paper and ink,
For that is your shield.
Your rights are going!
So pick up your pen.
Load it, load it with ink.
Sit on a chair.
Repair not to Hoho
But fire with your pen.[48]

A Western-educated Mfengu, John Tengu Jabavu, became the editor of *Isigidimi* in 1881, and subsequently of his own newspaper *Imvo Zabantsundu*, or 'Native Opinion'. *Imvo* became a medium for the airing of grievances against any and all anti-African—or 'Native'—legislation. And this legislation, including the pass laws, liquor laws and 'location' legislation, had

[47] Cited in Tom Lodge, *Black Politics in South Africa since 1945* (Johannesburg, 1985), pp. 2–3.

[48] Cited in Odendaal, *Black Protest Politics*, p. 6. Hoho was, following Odendaal, 'a mountain-forest stronghold where the Xhosa chief, Sandile, was shot and killed'.

become an important distinguishing marker by the early twentieth century between 'Natives' and Coloureds.

If editorials and letters to newspapers were the means for airing grievances or arguing with white racist rhetoric, petitions and delegations—whether to colonial governments, the British government, the CMS, or the Aboriginal Protection Society—were the preferred means of making direct appeals to the authorities. Creole petitioning seems to have been a method learnt from, or suggested by, missionaries. Hence in the Cape, it was missionaries and ex-residents of mission stations in the eastern Cape who combined to forward appeals to the colonial authorities against the introduction of a Vagrancy Act in the 1830s, fearing that the latter would effectively rescind emancipation legislation. A mission station in the western Cape, Genadendal, was the source of a petition to the Cape government in 1871, against Masters and Servants legislation. Similarly early petitioning in West Africa—for British intervention in the 1840s and 1850s against the slave trade for example—came from mission stations.

By the late nineteenth century, petitioning was an approach used independently by creole élites against what they saw as racist practices by British authorities. Hence Andrew Jackson, and 120 others whose names were not published, signed a petition in 1873 to the Cape government against a licensing board which intended to stop selling liquor on a Sunday to people it considered to be 'coloured'.[49] Likewise, in West Africa, creole élites wrote 'profuse petitions' to the Aboriginal Protection Society against British methods of conquest in Nigeria; and forty-one residents of Lagos signed a memorandum to the CMS against the shoddy treatment of Bishop Crowther in 1890.[50]

In attempting to get their views across to British authorities, the most direct strategy used by creole élites was the delegation. Cape Town Muslims had used this approach as early as the mid-1880s. The Cape government was set on closing Muslim cemeteries near the city centre for sanitary reasons. The Muslim delegation failed in its attempt to delay this action. In 1901, during the South Africa War, a delegation 'representing the coloured people of the Western Province' met the Cape Governor, Lord Milner, to ask that the British extend the Cape franchise to the ex-Afrikaner republics. Milner glibly

[49] 'Petition of Coloured Persons, Inhabitants of Cape Town and Neighbourhood', *Cape Parliamentary Papers*, A13–1873.

[50] Falola, *Essays of J. F. Ade Ajayi*, pp. 81, 101.

assured them that 'it was not race or colour, but civilization which was the test of a man's capacity for civil rights'.[51] But neither this delegation nor ensuing deputations—and there were direct appeals to the imperial government in 1906, 1909, 1914, and again in 1919—could prevent or undo the political betrayal enduringly 'enshrined' in South African Union.[52]

A delegation from all four colonies of British West Africa, which arrived in London in 1920, was not much more successful in attempting to undo the betrayal of creole élites that was integral to the implementation of Indirect Rule. This delegation requested, inter alia, improved educational provision and an end to racial discrimination in employment practices, as well as the introduction of representative political institutions in West Africa. Milner, now Colonial Secretary, rejected the petition on the grounds that the delegation did not represent 'the native communities on whose behalf it purports to speak' and that this had been confirmed 'by all the chiefs in the Gold Coast'.[53]

So pleas against discrimination, in whatever form, were usually ineffective. But, if creole élites wished to remain 'respectable'—and respectability was part of their defining characteristics in this period—there appeared to be few alternatives to this approach: 'revolution and anarchy were not just unobtainable', they were 'undesirable'.[54] This is not to say that merely pleading against discrimination was a futile pursuit. On the contrary, it was part of the process through which creole élites discovered their own voices and identities. It was also a necessary prelude, as well as partner, to political organization.

Self-examination and Self-assertion

Self-examination by creole élites was another early response to white racism, one that seemingly went further in West Africa than in the Cape. Some instances were cruelly self-critical. Thus Saros in Lagos on occasion concurred with racist British travellers, denouncing themselves as a 'community of counterfeit Englishmen' or 'mountebank exhibitionists of Western civilisation'.[55] One logical consequence of such conclusions was to search for an

[51] *Cape Times*, 9 Jan. 1901, cited in Lewis, *Between the Wire and the Wall*, p. 15.

[52] William Beinart, *Twentieth Century South Africa* (Oxford, 1994), pp. 86–7.

[53] Falola and Roberts, 'West Africa', p. 519.

[54] Lewis, *Between the Wire and the Wall*, p. 24.

[55] E. A. Ayandele, *The Educated Elite in Nigerian Society* (Ibadan, 1974), p. 47, cited in Isichei, *Nigeria*, p. 341.

alternative, African, identity as well as for African values that could guide the continent's future in a direction distinct from that of Europe. The difficulty was in reconciling this quest with any continued desire to modernize. Some reconciliation was achieved, if not always entirely successfully, by inventing African 'traditions' that were in keeping with modernization.

One of the pioneers and pre-eminent figures in the assertion of African distinctiveness, and thereby of African cultural nationalism, was Edward Blyden. When Blyden started writing, in the 1850s, he did so in an era when Europeans generally explained African distinctiveness in terms of historical and cultural difference. At this time Blyden seemingly agreed with the dominant European view that Africa was relatively 'backward'. Like many other creole thinkers, Blyden thereby internalized Eurocentric opinion of what constituted civilization. Consequently, and drawing in part on the Bible, Blyden—along with other creole writers such as James Africanus Horton and A. B. C. Merriman-Labor—argued that Africa had been the cradle of Greco-Roman civilization. The achievements of Babylon and ancient Egypt were ascribed to 'Negro-Africans', the direct ancestors of creole élites in West Africa. Africa's contemporary decline was seen as temporary, part of the cyclical nature of history.

In the last two decades of the nineteenth century Blyden felt compelled to respond to metropolitan 'scientific racism' that now ascribed African backwardness to permanent racial inferiority. He did so in unusual fashion. Instead of rejecting contemporary European ideas about the racialization of humanity, he drew deeply on them to argue that Africans were not inferior but merely racially distinct: 'The two races are not moving in the same groove, with an immeasurable distance between them, but on parallel lines ... They are not identical ... but unequal; they are distinct but equal.'[56] Blyden argued that 'each race is endowed with peculiar talents ... in the music of the universe each shall give a different sound, but necessary to the grand symphony'.[57] Consequently Africans should not attempt to become Europeans but should fulfil their own destiny. Yet in somewhat contradictory fashion he still insisted at this stage that creole élites should provide leadership for Africa, and that attributes they possessed—such as Christianity or an

[56] E. W. Blyden, *Christianity, Islam and the Negro Race* (Edinburgh, 1887), cited in Robin Law, 'Constructing "a real national history": A Comparison of Edward Blyden and Samuel Johnson', in P. F. de Moraes Farias and Karin Barber, eds., *Self-Assertion and Brokerage: Early Cultural Nationalism in West Africa* (Birmingham, 1990), p. 85.

[57] Cited in Spitzer, *Creoles of Sierra Leone*, p. 112.

education in the classics—were universal aspects of civilization which were 'everywhere applicable'.[58]

By the early twentieth century, and in tandem with the growth of white-imposed racial discrimination and segregation throughout British Africa, Blyden had gone further and argued that African peculiarities might actually be superior in some respects to those of Europe. In an enduringly influential way for subsequent African (and many African-American) intellectuals, he contrasted an innocent, spiritual, co-operative, and communal African culture with European individualism and competitiveness that had spawned the likes of poverty, inequality, and moral deprivation. Europeans might have to look to Africa to rediscover some spirituality and social equilibrium of their own. The corollary was that Africans should not copy either European culture or European institutions.

The problem for Blyden, and those that came to think as he did, was that creole élites, like those in Freetown and Lagos, had already affected 'habits and customs entirely out of keeping with their surroundings'; so that 'in the European settlements on the coast, there are visible the melancholy effects of the fatal contagion of a mimic or spurious Europeanism'.[59] As Blyden put it to the Freetown Unity Club in 1891: 'Your first duty is to be yourselves . . . You need to be told to keep constantly before yourselves the fact that you are African, not Europeans—black men, not white men.'[60] So instead of emulating Europeans, creole élites should seek role models in the supposedly vigorous 'personality' of Africans in the interior.

The question was how, in practical terms, to do this. Some creoles, whether in Lagos or Freetown, found the answer in Africanizing their names and dress. Thus one eminent Lagosian changed his name from Edmund Macauley to Kitoyi Ajasa; or the Freetown school teacher William Davis became Orishatukah Faduma. Some Lagosians also adopted 'Nigerian' dress, while in Freetown a Dress Reform Society was established in 1887 with Blyden and the Reverend James Johnson among its associates. The idea was to convert creoles from the 'religion of the Frock Coat and Tall Hat' to a newly invented pseudo-traditional African wardrobe that included, for men, under-tunics, gowns, and knee-breeches. But in the face of considerable scorn from both Europeans and other Creoles, dress reform and

58 Law, 'Blyden and Johnson', p. 87.

59 Cited in Spitzer, *Creoles of Sierra Leone*, pp. 112–14.

60 *Sierra Leone Weekly News*, 20 June 1891, cited in Spitzer, *Creoles of Sierra Leone*, p. 113.

name-changing initiatives had limited impact, as did the attempt to promote Krio ahead of English in Freetown schools. All were phenomenon of a particular generation and period, as a study of the May family of Freetown has demonstrated.[61]

The point was that most Creoles were not willing to follow Blyden to his logical conclusion and turn their backs on all things European. After all, they owed their position and power in British Africa largely to the extent of their successful westernization. Rather they chose largely to take from Blyden his enduringly important message of 'race' pride, a message also assimilated by African-American intellectuals such as W. E. B. du Bois. And it was the idea of race pride that ultimately reached creoles in the Cape through the columns of Peregrino's *South African Spectator.* Peregrino had absorbed the concept of race pride from du Bois while working in the United States. He was persuaded to travel to South Africa and establish the *Spectator* having attended the first Pan-African Conference in London in 1900. His paper's editorial line drew heavily on du Bois, and thus indirectly on Blyden, as well as on Booker T. Washington's emphasis on the need for black self-help and upliftment. The first edition noted that 'white men' were doing everything 'to build up their race . . . Coloured people! Take a lesson from him.' Peregrino attempted to follow his own advice by publishing 'some of the grand and noble achievements of the race in times past'.[62]

Suggesting that Africans had distinct personalities, and self-consciously Africanizing names (if not already African), dress, and language, does not seem to have been a policy undertaken by urbanized creole élites in South Africa at this stage; commercial pragmatism rather than ideology explains why some newspapers published columns in languages other than English.[63] Presumably, this was because such élites—like many 'Europeanizers' in Sierra Leone—desired to symbolize their similarity with the substantial white settler population in their midst, not their difference. They saw the need to do so as an essential part of being accepted as 'civilized'. It was left to a

[61] Isichei, *Nigeria*, p. 341; Spitzer, *Creoles of Sierra Leone*, pp. 116–20, 138–47. Leo Spitzer, *Lives in Between: Assimilation and Marginality in Austria, Brazil and West Africa 1780–1945* (Cambridge, 1989).

[62] *South African Spectator*, 14 Jan. 1901; 9 Feb. 1901. See also Lewis, *Between the Wire and the Wall*, pp. 16–18; and J. Ayodele Langley, *Pan-Africanism and Nationalism in West Africa 1900–1945* (Oxford, 1973), pp. 17–40.

[63] Mohammed Adhikari, ed., *Straatpraatjes: Language, Politics and Popular Culture in Cape Town, 1909–1922* (Cape Town, 1996), pp. 6–7.

largely rural strata beneath the élite, among Tswana Christian converts at least, to use 'cultural patchwork' in dress 'to speak back to the whites'.[64]

Most Creoles in West Africa also saw the need to emphasize similarities with Europeans rather than differences as a means of maintaining their relatively privileged medial position within the Empire. They rejected Blyden's conclusion, towards the end of his life, that there could only be 'sporadic examples' of successful African assimilation to European ways. Likewise they rejected Blyden's belief that official colonial policy should be: 'To encourage the development of the natives along the lines of their own idiosyncracies as revealed in their institutions.'[65] This, for Creoles, was all but complicity with the British imposition of Indirect Rule and thereby their abandonment.

Rather what they sought to do was to bolster self-esteem through inventing African 'traditions' they could both be proud of, not unlike the way in which rulers of the British Empire were busily inventing their own traditions. One of the ways that they embarked on this project was to produce historical studies that could be part of claiming, or reclaiming, an African identity not at odds with their modernizing ambitions. In the process they might, consciously or not, help to mark and perpetuate different black ethnicities or proto-nationalisms. One of the earliest examples of such efforts was J. O. George's 'Historical Notes on the Yoruba Country'. George was overtly concerned to show that: 'Yoruba people may not be properly called real savages; they are not quite ignorant of the elements and marks of civilization.'[66] Some Creoles in the Cape embarked on similar projects. Thus Sol Plaatje read a paper on 'The History of the Bechuana' to the South African Improvement Society in Kimberley in 1895. And creole élites were also behind public commemorations of black history: whether in the form of Blyden's historical pageant in 1887, marking the centenary of the founding of Sierra Leone, or John Tobin's celebrations of slave emancipation day in Cape Town in 1903.[67]

It was arguably left to Samuel Johnson, however, in his *History of the Yorubas*, to construct a history that most perfectly balanced the desire for

[64] Comaroff and Comaroff, *Dialectics of Modernity*, pp. 235, 271; Spitzer, *Creoles of Sierra Leone*, pp. 132–47.

[65] Cited in Law, 'Blyden and Johnson', p. 87.

[66] Cited Ibid., p. 91

[67] Spitzer, *Creoles of Sierra Leone*, p. 115, ftnote 26; Bickford-Smith, 'Meanings of Freedom', pp. 306–07.

pride in past African events, and consequently pride in an African identity, with the present concerns of most creoles for assimilation within the British Empire. Johnson stated in the Preface to his book that he embarked on the project because educated Yorubas knew a great deal about British history but little of that of their 'fatherland'. Writing the history of Oyo as though it were identical with the history of Yorubaland, he stressed its similarity with British history and culture. Nineteenth-century problems were only temporary: in Johnson's argument, the result of the slave trade and civil wars. Thus, unlike Blyden, Johnson was implicitly arguing for the likely success of assimilationist and modernizing colonial policies. For instance in Johnson's *History* the Yorubas, like the English, supposedly had a 'Love of independence, a feeling of superiority over all others, a keen commercial spirit, and... that quality of never being able to admit or consent defeat...'[68] He even argued that Yoruba religion was not only essentially monotheistic, but that Yoruba prophecies had foretold the coming of Christianity. And he was consistently enthusiastic about British conquest. Criticism was reserved for aspects of Yoruba tradition currently being reformed, such as bad sanitation, scanty clothes or certain elements of traditional religion. Thus Johnson's *History* offered creoles in Yorubaland precisely what they wanted in 'speaking back' to British doubters: pride in an African identity accommodated within an argument for the likelihood of successful assimilation

Religious and Political Organization

This quest for an African identity reminds us of the Comaroffs suggestion at the beginning of this chapter that the black experience of British imperialism was commonly about coming to 'feel, and to *re-cognize*' oneself as a native, even if this identity was subsequently more assertively (and acceptably) renamed 'African'. The same is true of the names and specified purposes of many of the creole religious and political organizations that emerged in the late nineteenth century. These organizations were another means by which creoles could claim or maintain an African identity. But the construction of such institutions itself allowed creoles a combination of existential and pragmatic self-assertion while enabling them to maintain overt patriotism to the British Empire.

[68] Law, 'Blyden and Johnson', p. 92

The creole institutions were established out of frustration: because white-dominated churches or political structures were seen as no longer meeting creole needs or ambitions, or actively denying them. Thus Christian separatist churches emerged throughout British Africa in the 1880s and 1890s and beyond as offshoots from white churches and missionary initiatives. They included the likes of the Native Independent Congregational Church in British Bechuanaland in 1885; the Ebenezer Baptist Church and United Native African Church in Lagos in 1888 and 1891 respectively; and the Ethiopian Church in Pretoria in 1892. Four years later, the Ethiopian Church affiliated to the (African-American founded) African Methodist Episcopal Church of the United States, which consequently became a major separatist presence in South Africa.[69]

The founders of these separatist churches all wished to bring about African control over ecclesiastical affairs and thereby, at least in part, their own lives. Some, whether from deep existential needs or persuaded by the arguments of cultural nationalists, felt that such control should go hand-in-hand with African content. There was predictably much debate as to the compatibility, or otherwise, between Christianity and 'traditional' religious beliefs and cultural practices such as polygamy or *lobola*.[70]

Many, in both West and South Africa, went further. They saw in the establishment of such churches a more fully-fledged nationalist agenda, the possibility, as Elijah Makiwane of the Ethiopian Church put it, of 'building up... the Africans as a people'.[71] For Blyden this was part and parcel of 'race organization and race consolidation'.[72] There was, then, a sometimes explicitly political dimension to separatist movements. There were also close connections—in terms of both ideology and personnel—between them and the early and overtly political organizations

Arguably it was the development of these political organizations that became the most important factor in helping creole élites to shape acceptable self-identities, as well as providing the means through which they could express their secular aspirations. Such organizations drew at least some of

[69] Odendaal, *Black Protest Politics*, pp. 23–29; Falola, *Essays of J. F. Ade Ajayi*, pp. 79–80; Isichei, *Nigeria*, p. 461.

[70] Zachernuk, *Colonial Subjects*, pp. 60–61.

[71] Cited in Odendaal, *Black Protest Politics*, p. 83.

[72] Cited in Zachernick, *Colonial Subjects*, p. 67.

their leading members from separatist churches. They drew others from pre-existing lay associations such as education or temperance organizations.[73]

In West Africa, as McCaskie has shown, Creoles had already both expressed an ambition for participation in government and attempted some experiments in this direction in the 1860s. Horton's *West African Countries and Peoples* had advocated 'the Self-government of Western Africa', and his writing helped creole élites to imagine West Africa as a potential national community.[74] Thereafter, and with political ambitions dampened by increased British racism in the 'period of pacification', creole élites appear to have put most of their energies into organizing separatist churches. One of the motivating factors was the belief that Christianity would be a major unifying factor within any future West African state. A couple of proto-political exceptions, explicable at a time of increased British military intervention and land-grabbing, were the Aborigines' Rights Protection societies established in the Gold Coast and in Lagos from 1897.[75]

Horton's idea of a West African state was kept alive in numerous newspaper articles and books by subsequent creole writers. One of them, J. E. Casely Hayford—author of *The Truth about the West African Land Question* and *United West Africa*—was a leading instigator of the proposal for a pan-West African conference. Before and during the First World War—which itself leant impetus to international debates on 'self-determination'—Casely Hayford wrote to both influential individuals and the Gold Coast Aborigines' Rights Protection Society in this respect. West African newspapers in all four British colonies enthusiastically espoused the cause, and the resulting National Congress of British West Africa (NCBWA) met in Accra in 1920. The Congress, as we have seen, sent a delegation to London urging the British to end discrimination in civil service appointments, ensure that half the members of legislative councils were elected, and to improve education.[76]

In South Africa, political organizations—often short-lived—appeared first among creole élites in the eastern Cape, in response to white ethnic political mobilization that followed 'Responsible Government'. One of the

[73] Odendaal, *Black Protest Politics*, p. 7; Lewis, *Between the Wire and the Wall*, p. 14.

[74] J. A. B. Horton, *West African Countries and Peoples: A Vindication of the African Race* (London, 1868), p. vii.

[75] Webster, 'Political Activity in British West Africa', pp. 575–76.

[76] Ibid; Langley, *Pan-Africanism and Nationalism in West Africa*, pp. 107–33; Spitzer, *Creoles of Sierra Leone*, pp. 169–79.

earliest was the Imbumba Yama Nyama, literally Hard Solid Sinew, formed in Port Elizabeth in 1882. Several more had appeared before the end of the decade. Issues discussed and promoted by these organizations included education, the need to retain the existing franchise, the importance of registering voters, and tax grievances.

Although most of these initial organizations had disappeared by the 1890s, a pro-British South African Native Congress (SANC) was established in the Cape on the eve of the South African War in 1898. The forming of this Native Congress had been instigated by the newspaper *Izwi Labantu*, which became the SANC's organ. The SANC and its newspaper became the major vehicles through which educated Cape 'Natives' continued to plead the case for equal rights to both the Cape and British governments.

These pleas became more desperate as British imperial policies and practices in South Africa gave less and less room for hope in the early 1900s. For example, a South African Native Affairs Commission—appointed by the Governor of the Cape, Lord Milner—recommended separate voters rolls for Africans throughout South Africa in 1905, which would have ended the non-racial franchise in the Cape. Similarly depressing was the way in which the British suppressed the so-called Bambatha rebellion against the imposition of a Poll Tax in Natal the following year: the death of two white police officers was followed by the killing of between 3,500 and 4,000 Africans. Disillusionment with Britain was all but complete when the terms of the Act of South African Union (1910) failed to extend the Cape franchise to the rest of the new country, and cemented white settler political supremacy despite protest delegations to London.[77]

The Act of Union did however succeed in promoting unity among educated Africans throughout South Africa. Thus the publication of the draft version prompted the formation in 1909 of a national convention of African political organizations, which had increased in number and membership since the war. It was in an attempt to maintain the 'Native Union' achieved by this convention that a national political party, the South African Native National Congress (SANNC), was formed in 1912. According to its draft constitution, the purpose of the SANNC was, *inter alia*, 'safeguarding the interests of the native inhabitants throughout South Africa' and promoting

[77] Odendaal, *Black Protest Politics*, pp. 8–12, 40–43, 66–68, 151–226.

their 'elevation'. By the 1920s, the SANNC—now known as the African National Congress—had largely failed in both respects.[78]

Not all creoles in British Africa had come to 're-cognize' themselves as 'Natives' by the 1920s; a sizeable section in the Cape had resisted doing so. Given that Bantu-speaking 'natives' were being singled out by the Cape Government for specific discrimination by the early twentieth century—including residential segregation and prohibitory liquor laws—pragmatic self-interest played a role in the choice, when possible, of a 'Coloured' identity. But in fact this identity had emerged out of a complicated dialectic between metropolitan and white settler divide-and-rule racialization on the one hand, and creole self-assertion on the other.

'Coloured' had been a term often used by whites in the Cape to refer to all people seen—and described in censuses—as 'other than white' after slave emancipation, but sometimes it was used more narrowly to describe people in the western Cape who were not Bantu-speaking Africans. The vast majority of 'coloured' people, in this narrower sense, were descended from a mixture of slave, Khoi, and white ancestry and spoke a creole-Dutch that developed into Afrikaans. 'Coloured' endured as a label for such South Africans not just because of white racialization and discrimination—though this was crucial—but also because as a self-description it stressed the fact that shade of pigmentation closely correlated with historical and contemporary experience. And in the late nineteenth century new divisions of labour were tending to confirm a tri-partite division of the western Cape's social formation into 'white', 'Coloured', and 'Native' as migration of the last group from other parts of South Africa increased.

By the early 1890s creole élites in places like Kimberley and Cape Town had established overtly Coloured, in the narrower sense, political organizations to fight white discrimination. By the early 1900s members of Cape Town's creole élite had founded a number of parallel social organizations which called themselves 'Coloured'. It was W. A. Roberts, the vice-president of one such organization—the Coloured Young Men's Christian Association—who founded the African Political Organization (APO) in 1902, prompted by the provisions of the Treaty of Vereneeging. Despite its name, the APO was

[78] Odendaal, *Black Protest Politics*, pp. 256–77; T. R. H. Davenport, *South Africa: A Modern History* (Basingstoke, Hampshire, 1991), p. 236; Beinart, *Twentieth Century South Africa*, pp. 54–55; Lodge, *Black Politics*, pp. 1–5.

established to defend specifically Coloured social, political, and civil rights, as its subsequent actions, membership, and newspaper made clear.[79]

Conclusion

Creole political organizations enjoyed strictly limited success in defending, let alone advancing, 'rights' by the 1920s. The demands of the NCBWA were all but ignored. Britain did introduce an elective element to legislative council in the 1920s, but elected members were outnumbered by traditional leaders. And if educational provision was slightly improved and some civil service jobs were desegregated, in the Gold Coast at least, educated Africans were still excluded from the 'political service'. In addition, particularly in Sierra Leone, they faced more commercial competition in the form of Lebanese traders, the so-called 'Syrians'.[80]

The SANNC and the APO fared little better in protecting their constituencies, beyond gaining the occasional sop such as (segregated) first class railway accommodation. The APO failed, before and after 1910, to get Coloureds recognized as 'of European descent', and so were unable to extend Coloured political rights or to halt educational segregation. The organization was all but moribund by the mid-1920s. It lost the backing of disillusioned supporters; but it also lost ground to Coloured politicians now willing to accept a permanent future for Coloureds as a separate 'race' from whites in return for a status well above the 'Native'.[81]

Equally the SANNC could not prevent the Natives Land Act (1913) and Natives (Urban Areas) Act (1923) extending segregation and control over Africans in countryside and town. African élites in the Cape (because they were voters) and Coloureds throughout the Union (because they were not 'Natives') were exempted from these laws. But the fear remained, particularly for educated Africans, that one day they would be 'measured with the same measure' as 'the raw man who comes from the kraals'.[82] As Sol Plaatje, the first General Secretary of the SANNC, wrote of the Land Act: 'the South

[79] See Bickford-Smith, 'Meanings of Freedom', pp. 308–09 and 'Black Ethnicities', pp. 445, 452–3, 458–62; Lewis, *Between the Wire and the Wall*, pp. 7–28.

[80] Falola and Roberts, 'West Africa', pp. 519–20.

[81] Lewis, *Between the Wire and the Wall*, pp. 29–91.

[82] John Makue's testimony to the *South African Native Affairs Commission* given in 1904, cited in Gwendolyn Carter and Thomas Karis, eds., *From Protest to Challenge: A Documentary History of African Politics in South Africa, 1882–1964*, 4 vols. (Stanford, 1971), Vol. I, *Protest and Hope, 1882–1934*, p. 20.

African Native found himself, not actually a slave, but a pariah in the land of his birth'.[83]

It might seem that Plaatje's words could stand as an epitaph for the experiences of most creole élites in British Africa by the 1920s. Existing historiography has seemingly overlooked the fact that betrayal and disillusionment were experiences common to creole élites in both equatorial and southern Africa.[84] Once able to perceive themselves as partners in Empire, Creoles had been sidelined by the British in favour of recently defeated Afrikaners in South Africa, and of traditional leaders in West Africa, many of whom had also been recently defeated. Political attempts to halt or reverse these developments had apparently ended in all but abject failure.

In retrospect one is able to see that these attempts were a turning point in that 'long conversation' which accompanied colonialism. Creole élites, through refashioned identities and political organization, had learnt to use decidedly new means of communication. Some were also beginning to experiment with new vocabularies: the SANNC in temporarily supporting popular anti-pass campaigns and striking workers in 1918–19; the APO in seeking common cause, however tentatively, with Africans over franchise and land issues in the 1900s and 1910s; and West African politicians in spearheading the diffusion of indigenous and African-American ideologies of 'race pride' and Pan-African unity to other parts of Africa, including the South.[85] The irony was that creole élites had learnt much of this vocabulary from the British. To borrow from Sudipta Kajirav's insights on India's rising subaltern class: the British imperial discourse had taught African creole élites 'how rationalism could be turned against the European colonizers themselves'.[86]

[83] S. T. Plaatje, *Native Life in South Africa* (Johannesburg, 1983), p. 17. The book was first published in 1916.

[84] Mahmood Mamdani's *Citizen and Subject: Contemporary Africa and the Legacy of Late Colonialism* (Princeton, NJ, 1996) reminds us of the need to overcome the artificial separation of South African history from the history of the rest of the continent.

[85] Lodge, *Black Politics*, pp. 3–4; Lewis, *Between the Wire and the Wall*, pp. 42, 50, 59–60, 77–80; Odendaal, *Black Protest Politics*, pp. 86–91, 110–11; Langley, *Pan-Africanism and Nationalism*.

[86] Sudipta Kaviraj, 'On the Construction of Colonial Power: Structure, Discourse, Hegemony', in Dagmar Engels and Shula Marks, eds, *Contesting Colonial Hegemony: State and Society in Africa and India* (London, 1994), p. 44.

Select Bibliography

MOHAMMED ADHIKARI, ed., *Straatpraatjes: Language, Politics and Popular Culture in Cape Town, 1909–1922* (Cape Town, 1996).

VIVIAN BICKFORD-SMITH, 'Black Ethnicities, Communities and Political Expression in Late Victorian Cape Town', *Journal of African History*, 36 (1995), pp. 443–65.

—— *Ethnic Pride and Racial Prejudice in Victorian Cape Town* (Cambridge, 1995).

JEAN COMAROFF and JOHN COMAROFF, *Of Revelation and Revolution: Christianity, Colonialism and Consciousness in South Africa* (Chicago, 1991).

JOHN L. COMAROFF and JEAN COMAROFF, *Of Revelation and Revolution: The Dialectics of Modernity on a South African Frontier* (Chicago, 1997).

P. F. DE MORAES and KARIN BARBER, eds., *Self-Assertion and Brokerage: Early Cultural Nationalism in West Africa* (Birmingham, 1990).

TOYIN FALOLA, ed., *Tradition and Change in Africa: The Essays of J. F. Ade Ajayi* (Trenton, NJ, 2000).

TOYIN FALOLA and A. D. ROBERTS, 'West Africa', in Judith M. Brown and Wm. Roger Louis eds., *The Oxford History of the British Empire*, Vol. IV, *The Twentieth Century* (Oxford, 1999).

ELIZABETH ISICHEI, *A History of Nigeria* (Harlow, Essex, 1983).

J. AYODELE LANGLEY, *Pan-Africanism and Nationalism in West Africa 1900–1945* (Oxford, 1973).

ROBIN LAW, 'Constructing "a real national history": A Comparison of Edward Blyden and Samuel Johnson', in P. F. de Moraes Farias and Karin Barber eds., *Self-Assertion and Brokerage* (Birmingham, 1990).

GAVIN LEWIS, *Between the Wire and the Wall: A History of South African 'Coloured' Politics* (Cape Town, 1987).

LEO SPITZER, *The Creoles of Sierra Leone, 1870–1945* (Madison, Wisc. 1974).

—— *Lives in Between: Assimilation and Marginality in Austria, Brazil and West Africa 1780–1945* (Cambridge, 1989).

BILL NASSON, *Abraham Esau's War* (Cambridge, 1991).

ANDRE ODENDAAL, *Black Protest Politics in South Africa to 1912* (Cape Town, 1984).

J. D. Y. PEEL, 'Between Crowther and Ajayi: The Religious Origins of the Modern Yoruba Intelligentsia', in Toyin Falola ed., *African Historiography: Essays in Honour of Jacob Ade Ajayi* (Harlow, Essex, 1993).

J. B. WEBSTER, 'Political Activity in British West Africa, 1900–1940', in J. F. Ade Ajayi and Michael Crowder eds., *History of West Africa*, Vol. II (London, 1974).

Brian Willan 'An African in Kimberley: Sol Plaatje, 1894–1898', in Shula Marks and Richard Rathbone eds., *Industrialisation and Social Change in South Africa* (London and New York, 1982).

A. J. G. Wyse, *The Krio of Sierra Leone, an Interpretative History* (London, 1989).

Philip S. Zachernuk, *Colonial Subjects: An African Intelligentsia and Atlantic Ideas* (Charlottesville, Va., 2000).

9

The British Empire and African Women in the Twentieth Century

DIANA JEATER

The authors of the official ideology of the British Empire were never particularly concerned with the ordinary lives of women, yet colonial agents—colonial administrators as well as British missionaries—spent a great deal of time and effort attempting to regulate and control their lives. For a long time, historians of the British Empire overlooked the practical preoccupations of colonial administrators, taking at face value the indifference of official ideology towards women when compared with men and thereby leaving the impression that women were largely invisible within the Empire. Today, however, few historians would deny that women's labour was crucial in generating cash-crop incomes, in sustaining rural communities and building urban centres, or that the Empire in Africa depended on the preservation of old and creation of new forms of female subordination, all of which explain why the subject of women commanded so much attention from Colonial Officers.

Women played a defining part in shaping colonial society. One important dimension of women's experience of Empire was their encounter with attempts to control and redirect their sexuality.[1] Controlling men's labour, always of paramount importance to the architects of Empire in Africa, was matched, if not at times surpassed, by colonial concerns over the sexuality of African women. As the nature of gender relations changed under the architecture of colonial administration, so the experiences of women were altered. Control over women's labour was also vital to the imperial project, and African women experienced major changes in the quantity, nature, and context of their work within the Empire.

[1] Nancy Rose Hunt, 'Placing African Women's History and Locating Gender', *Social History*, 14, 3 (1989), pp. 359–79; Nancy Rose Hunt, Tessie R. Liu, and Jean Quataert, eds., *Gendered Colonialisms in African History* (Oxford, 1997); James Giblin's review of Fiona D. Mackenzie, *Land, Ecology and Resistance in Kenya, 1880–1952* (Edinburgh, 1998), *Journal of African History* (hereafter *JAH*) XLI, 1 (2000), p. 156.

The British Empire affected African women differently than it did African men. Because of the assumptions that the agents of the British Empire made about gender in African, black women were discriminated against on two fronts—by virtue of race *and* gender. This outcome was partly, of course, because British society treated women differently from men. Imperial officials formulated different policies for African women than for African men, and introduced measures specifically intended to benefit men at the expense of women. Most notably in the period up to the Second World War, Colonial Officers across sub-Saharan British Africa consistently attempted to alter marriage practices, transform sexual relationships, and limit African women's economic and geographical freedom. Metropolitan ideas about marriage, prostitution, domesticity, the gendered nature of politics and public space, and the economic role of women *vis-à-vis* men and children produced policies that had direct effects on women. In addition, regulations that targeted men, such as forced labour, indirectly affected women.[2]

The Empire also affected African women differently than it did men because the sexes were *already* differently situated within African societies. They did not perform the same types of work, had distinct means of acquiring status, and exercised contrasting forms of power, so they were bound to experience the colonial interventions of the British Empire differently. This difference was not solely, or even primarily, in Africans' responses to imperial interventions, but in their responses *to each other* in the light of those interventions. Imperial power affected local gender relationships even without meaning to, and without passing new laws or enforcing new rules. As Allan Christelow observed about Kano, Nigeria, 'The early phase of British colonial rule... did not bring new laws, but rather a new "time", a new political and economic context in which traditional authority, laws, and legal mechanisms had to operate.'[3] In these 'new times', gender relationships continued, as before, to frame social relationships, and to be contested, transformed and defended. But now there was a new element—the Empire—affecting these processes.

As the British Empire made its major intervention into Africa at the end of the nineteenth century, Victorian imperialists had clear views about the areas of life in which gender was operative, and judged local African gender

[2] Luise White, *The Comforts of Home: Prostitution in Colonial Nairobi* (Chicago, 1990), p. 52.

[3] Allan Christelow, 'Theft, Homicide, and Oath in Early Twentieth-Century Kano', in Kristin Mann and Richard Roberts, eds., *Law in Colonial Africa* (London, 1991), p. 219.

relationships accordingly. During the high Victorian period, women were expected to support men's work by providing domestic services and raising children, but were not themselves expected to be publicly or economically active. These ideas about women did not transfer easily to the African context. In nineteenth-century Africa, women's economic activity was vital to local food production and distribution. Domestic and economic partnerships were more likely to be with co-wives, than with husbands. Imperial officers could accommodate women's farms within a European model of gender relations by renaming them 'gardens', but women's role in the market place, particularly in West Africa where they were often major entrepreneurs and traders, could not be glossed over so conveniently.

Although gender ideologies imported from Britain failed to describe African women's experiences accurately, colonial administrators found it difficult to develop more appropriate ways of thinking about local women. They had European notions about the spheres in which subordination was crucial for 'civilization', notably sexual propriety, marriage, the division of labour, and property. They tried to intervene in these areas to make African women 'civilized'. Sexual propriety seemed notably lacking in African society. A large part of the colonial administrators' thinking betrayed unease about African female sexuality, and a wish to introduce more European patriarchal models of women's sexual behaviour.

Female Sexuality and the Beginning of Empire in Africa

The late nineteenth and early twentieth century in Britain was characterized by a blanket silence concerning female sexuality. Victorian ideology sentimentalized marriage; popular art and literature heavily emphasized love and duty. Sexual restraint was integral to female respectability, and was enforced as a means of controlling women. Prostitution, social purity, and venereal disease dominated public gender discourses, and were either promoted or prohibited as ways to repress or deny female sexuality.

In African cultures, by contrast, control over women's fertility was more significant than control of their sexuality. Female sexuality was fully recognized, albeit often in overt attempts to control it through ritual and the authority granted to senior women. While this recognition did not produce sexual freedom for women, it did at least acknowledge them as sexual beings, something colonial officials in Britain's African colonies found hard to digest. They believed that it was their duty to 'civilize' social relationships by not only eradicating slavery, but also by requiring African women to behave like respectable, middle-class women in Britain. A genuine and serious policy debate, which straddled the late nineteenth and early twentieth centuries, questioned whether sexualized African women could become truly 'civilized'.[4]

Late nineteenth-century British patriarchal thought condemned sexualized women to an underclass existence, partly because prostitutes were associated with female sexuality, but also because sexual promiscuity became firmly linked to physical and mental inferiority. Eugenics gave new life to that link at the beginning of the twentieth century. Both poor and non-white women were seen as 'degenerate', that is, as falling below the full measure of humanity. Allegedly inappropriate and excessive sexual activity was deemed both the cause and effect of this degeneracy. London's prostitutes, and the poor in general, were urged to restrict their sexual activities, in the belief that promiscuity exposed the white race at best to venereal disease, and at worst to the risk of atavism.

African men and women were regarded as already belonging to a lesser race, which accounted for their 'uncivilized' recognition of sexuality in their societies. Some observers regarded Africans as incapable of sexual restraint. As one missionary, put it, 'The great curse of the Native men is licentiousness, and, I believe, it is the same with the women. We may say they are virtuous, but I believe they are not.'[5] Such arguments were often gendered, so that *women's* sexual activities were seen as the source of degeneration, not least through the spread of venereal disease. The Attorney General in Southern Rhodesia asserted, 'Disease is certainly spread by promiscuous intercourse, but the agent is the woman not the man.'[6] While both men and women in Africa were perceived as dangerously sexual, Victorian ideology found women's sexuality impossible to accept.

In Africa the openness towards female sexuality seemed almost to be threatening apocalypse. In the early decades of the twentieth century whole groups of Africans were thought to be facing 'extinction' as a result of 'premature debauchery'. Inspired by anxieties about labour shortages and declining tax revenue, colonial officials genuinely feared demographic

[4] Cherryl Walker, ed., *Women and Gender in Southern Africa to 1945* (London: 1990), p. 14.

[5] Revd. G. A. Wilder, evidence to the Southern African Native Affairs Commission, 30 Aug. 1904.

[6] Attorney General's Memo on Colonel Stanford's letter, 10 Feb. 1915, National Archives of Zimbabwe A3.21/50.1.

collapse in various parts of British Africa, which they explained as the result of VD-induced infertility. Colonial administrators blamed sexually transmitted diseases for a range of difficulties they faced throughout the period of British rule in Africa.[7]

Colonial worries about the perceived problem of African female sexuality, racial degeneration, and demographic disaster did not march in step with metropolitan ideas about female sexuality. During the early twentieth century, metropolitan ideas about women moved away from an interest in sexual restraint, venereal disease, prostitution, and 'racial extinction', and towards a greater sense of women's autonomy and place in the public sphere. By the late 1910s women in Britain were permitted to apply for jobs previously closed to them, although domestic service remained the most significant source of female employment even into the 1930s. Marriage bars, which had required women to resign on marriage, were removed from teaching and the civil service in the 1920s.

That most African cultures did not deny the existence of female sexuality resonated in the lives of European women. By the 1920s female sexuality re-entered public discourse in Europe, not least through the modernist art movements. The acknowledgement of female sexuality in Africa provided an outlet for its recognition within Europe, at a safely exoticized distance. The sexual aspects of African bodies, and particularly female bodies, became the subject of suitably 'ethnographic' discussion and observation.[8] By the 1920s a degree of sexual freedom was permitted in Europe, for upper class women at least. Women who were open to offering sexual favours began to

[7] Sir Harry Johnson's phrase, quoted in Nakanyike B. Musisi, 'Gender and the Cultural Construction of "Bad Women" in the Development of Kampala-Kibuga, 1900–1962', in Dorothy L. Hodgson and Sheryl A. McCurdy, eds., *'Wicked' Women and the Reconfiguration of Gender in Africa* (Oxford, 2001), p. 175; Bryan Callahan, ' "Veni, VD, Vici"? Reassessing the Ila Syphilis Epidemic', *Journal of Southern African Studies* (hereafter *JSAS*), XXIII, 3 1997, pp. 421–40; Carol Summers, 'Intimate Colonialism: The Imperial Production of Reproduction in Uganda, 1907–1925', *Signs*, XVI, 4 (1991), pp. 787–807; Megan Vaughan, *Curing Their Ills: Colonial Power and African Illness*, (Cambridge, 1991), esp. chap. 6.

[8] Sander L.Gilman, 'Black Bodies, White Bodies: Toward and Iconography of Female Sexuality in Late Nineteenth-century Art, Medicine and Literature', Henry Louis Gates Jr, ed, *'Race', Writing, and Difference* (Chicago, 1986); Julie English Early, 'Unescorted in Africa: Victorian Women Ethnographers Toiling in the Fields of Sensational Science', *Journal of American Culture*, 18, Winter (1995), p. 68; Barbara Bush, *Imperialism, Race and Resistance*, (London, 1999), p. 79; Patricia Hayes, ' "Cocky" Hahn and the "Black Venus": The Making of a Native Commissioner in South West Africa, 1915–46', in Hunt, Liu, and Quataert, eds., *Gendered Colonialisms*, pp. 42–70.

displace prostitutes, and the idea of a companionate marriage, in which women as well as men could enjoy sex, grew alongside birth-control campaigns. Prostitution began to fade as a public issue, and female singleness declined as a virtue. The 'respectable' single woman became suspect as a sexually frustrated spinster. Meanwhile, official policies in Africa increasingly attempted to limit women's mobility and autonomy. By the 1930s growing metropolitan tolerance towards female sexual independence was out-of-step with the dominant colonial ideas about what was good for African women, and what was good for Empire.

Early Missionary and Colonial Attempts at Regulate African Marriages

Beginning in the early decades of the twentieth century, colonial administrators had various reasons for gathering data on local marriage systems. Where a tax was levied on wives, it was important to have some definition of 'wife' that would stand legal scrutiny. Where Africans brought civil cases to white judicial officers, and where local marriage and inheritance systems had legal recognition, it was vital to know what constituted a marriage or defined an heir. Martin Chanock has commented that in Nyasaland and Northern Rhodesia: 'Over the whole of the colonial period cases concerning conflicts between men and women took up most of the time of the colonial courts. Indeed in terms of the time which officials claim to have spent on it this was one of the colonial government's most important interventions into African life.'[9] Alongside these practical considerations, there were also concerns about the morality of local marriage systems, debates about the equivalency of bridewealth payments to purchase or slavery, and questions about the legitimacy of polygyny.

In southern Africa legislation affecting the payment of bridewealth was framed as an attempt to protect women from predatory African men. Not all early colonial administrators blamed women for the 'curse of licentiousness' or tried to limit their freedom. In the settler colonies of South Africa and Southern Rhodesia, the late nineteenth century saw the birth of a hybrid version of Victorian views on female sexuality that was to have exactly the opposite effect that it did in Britain. Here, the emphasis was on women's freedom, and specifically the need to free them from unhappy and exploitative relationships with African men. Rather than the cause of licentiousness, women were presented as its victims.

[9] Martin Chanock, *Law, Custom and Social Order* (Cambridge, 1985), p. 145.

This alternative way of looking at African female sexuality was a product of the specific nature of the 'civilizing' mission in southern Africa. North of the Zambezi, criticism of female promiscuity by colonial officials reflected the belief that women whose sexuality was recognized must be without sexual restraint, and so could not be 'civilized'.

South of the Zambezi, the demand for a steady supply of regular waged labour, particularly in the mines, shifted interest from sexuality to polygyny and the exploitation of female labour by male household heads. Missionaries and patrician British Governors believed that, if African women were allowed greater marital choice, they would reject polygyny. By raising male sexual standards, but perhaps more importantly by forcing men to work themselves, rather than exploiting all their wives' labour, women would move the people as a whole towards the 'civilized' world. Domestic households could become integrated as consumers and labourers into the colonial economy.

The focus on African women's marital choices, rather than on their sexuality, exposed an alternative metropolitan view of African women, as the degraded victims of African men. Referring to African men, the traveller Stanley Hyatt claimed that they 'have had no idea of the love of woman, for woman to them is, first, a worker in the fields, secondly, a means of satisfying their purely animal lusts'.[10] Such paternalism was popular in the missions, particularly among the Nonconformist movements that had championed the abolition of slavery. Both missionaries and administrators widely misinterpreted bridewealth practices as a form of slavery. For people from societies where a 'farmer' was a man and his partner was the 'farmer's wife', not a farmer herself, the sight of wives working in the fields was considered exploitative. As a legislator in Southern Rhodesia explained, 'polygamy was, in the eyes of the native, a form of marital slavery. It had been invariably found to be the case that the native woman who had left her husband had done so on account of the system of slavery meted out to them, and to their being obliged to work as beasts of burden in the fields.'[11] These misunderstandings were compounded by the recognition that, in many regions, there were women and children with the status of slaves or pawns, including in the white settler communities of South Africa.

Under the influence of Christian missions and anti-slavery campaigns, African women came to be seen as in need of protection by the Empire.

[10] Stanley P. Hyatt, *Off the Main Track* (London, 1911), p. 24.

[11] *Debates*, Legislative Council of Southern Rhodesia, 3 May 1916.

Imperial expansion was justified in part by its concern for their welfare and protection. During the late Victorian period, missionary concerns about African women tended to emphasize their need for *liberation*, and to encourage an ideology of individualism and female independence. In parts of southern Africa, this viewpoint coincided with administrative interests in breaking the power of senior men. The submerged current of truly 'Victorian' limits on women's autonomy did not become prevalent within the region until the 1920s, long after its demise in the metropole.

Missions played a significant role in arguing for increased autonomy for women in marriage. Missionaries were generally both more interested in African marriage, and more able to intervene, than administrators. Missions needed to report successes in order to keep the funds flowing. They could not be seen tolerating the immorality of 'harems' or 'buying wives', and tended to evict families from 'their' land if they did not respect their rules. Many of the Christian missions in southern Africa at the turn of the century lobbied hard for what they saw as women's liberation. They attacked the patriarchal elders' power to arrange marriage alliances for their wards and junior kin, and offered refuge to women trying to evade unwanted husbands.

In general, white missionaries did not recognize that they shared with local male elders an interest in sexual propriety and stable marriage. The markers of ordered family life recognized by white missionaries—sober clothing, monogamy, domesticity, and silence regarding female sexuality—were absent, and so moral disorder was assumed. Real sources of wealth and status for African women, particularly as they aged, were barely noticed. Missions focused on the issues that seemed to them most oppressive to women. Symptomatic was one missionary's injunction to 'civilize' the African husband: 'Make him give up his polygamy, give up his "lobolo" [bridewealth], give up being supported by his wives, make him support his wife.'[12] Missionaries highlighted forced marriage, but also campaigned against pagan superstition, pledging, polygyny, and the payment of bridewealth. These institutions, which the missions excoriated for keeping women in bondage, were not often regarded as oppressive by local women, but as sources of wealth, security, and status.

Older married women were likely to defend existing institutions and express hostility towards the missions. Missionaries may have intended to

[12] Amanda Porterfield, 'The Impact of early New England Missionaries on Women's Roles in Zulu Culture', *Church History*, LXVI (1997), p. 71; Revd. G. A. Wilder, evidence to the Southern African Native Affairs Commission, 30 Aug. 1904.

'free' women, but often their assaults on alliance-based marriage systems, in which there were clear obligations towards women, left older women, whose status and security was assured by those systems, more vulnerable. Women also valued their access to religious status outside mission control. Zulu women, for example, defended their position as diviners, which had become an important female role in the nineteenth century.[13]

Some women welcomed the missions' interventions, and found ways to enhance their power *vis-à-vis* men by using mission resources. Women perceived mission stations differently from men, and those who attached themselves to missions did not do so for the same reasons as men. Men tended to view mission stations as material resources for training, land, and employment. For some women, missions offered a refuge from witchcraft accusations, albeit at the expense of being required to reject other claims to spiritual authority, such as divination. For others, missions provided a focus for concerns about health and fertility. The women's prayer unions that flourished in South Africa in the early twentieth century provided important new outlets for women's leadership and authority.[14]

In various ways, the 'female choice' message of the missions exacerbated existing tensions between senior men and subordinate women, which had been compounded by changes in access to land, status, and resources thrown up in the wake of war, white settlement, and British rule. The missions' position on forced marriage had a genuine appeal for many women, and significant numbers took advantage of the possibilities of refuge, often resulting in conflict between missionaries and local authorities, whether African or white. The ensuing social upheavals increased female insecurity, and made women receptive to ideas about individual autonomy, which played an important part both in Protestant and Nonconformist theology, and in the political ideology of many Catholic missions. John and Jean Comaroff have noted how the 'egalitarian rhetoric' of mission Christianity seemed to have more impact on women than on men.[15] Becoming a spiritual leader was already an established means by which women could exert power

[13] Sean Hanretta, 'Women, Marginality and the Zulu State: Women's Institutions and Power in the Early Nineteenth Century', *JAH*, XXXIX, 3 (1998), pp. 389–416.

[14] Porterfield, 'Early New England Missionaries', p. 74; Jean Allman and Victoria Tashjian, *'I Will Not Eat Stone': A Women's History of Colonial Asante* (Oxford, 2000), p. 223; Deborah Gaitskell, 'Devout Domesticity? A Century of African Women's Christianity in South Africa,' in Walker, ed., *Women and Gender*, pp. 251–72.

[15] Jean Comaroff and John Comaroff, *Of Revelation and Revolution: Christianity, Colonialism and Consciousness in South Africa* (Chicago, 1991), p. 240.

and transgress conventional gender boundaries. Christianity offered the double attraction of an egalitarian message and a route through which women could claim status and authority.

Missionary lobbyists, then, pressed hard for policies that were supposed to protect African women by transforming marriage practices. For some women, this insistence on their individual autonomy was welcome, but the 'female choice' ideology was double-edged. As well as offering opportunities for greater personal autonomy, it posed a threat to women's status and security, usually simultaneously. It did much to undermine social stability and elder women's authority. Many missionaries denigrated the institutions of bridewealth, kinship obligation, and divination, and dismissed evidence that women could have investments in these institutions. As far as women themselves were concerned, the interference with marriage arrangements, arising out of imperial perceptions of African women as victims, complicated rather than resolved gender struggles.

While missionaries fulminated against the immorality of polygyny, administrators in southern and eastern Africa were more interested in the payment of bridewealth. In most of West Africa, where there was no white settler population and administrators saw their job more as one of tax-collection rather than as the creation of a waged labour-force, there was little incentive to interfere in systems of social reproduction. In the white settler societies, however, where new social relationships were required, a greater degree of intervention occurred. There was no actual policy, however, and the principle of 'civilizing' African marriages was used in a fairly *ad-hoc* way to instigate, frame, and justify such intervention.[16]

Legislation on bridewealth rarely stayed consistent for long. Measures reflected changing administrative concerns, unexpected outcomes of legislation, and the inability of imperial agents to enforce measures. In Southern Rhodesia, for example, a limit on bridewealth was imposed in 1901, abolished in 1912, re-imposed in 1950, and abolished again in 1962. The 1901 legislation was primarily aimed at encouraging stable, European-style marriages

[16] The important exception was in late nineteenth-century Natal, where Theophilus Shepstone's work was influential. He encouraged a policy across southern Africa where local administrators insisted that Africans paid bridewealth, in a context where the original meanings of the transaction were distorted by ideas of 'ownership and control' over women. See Jeff Guy, 'The Destruction and Reconstruction of Zulu Society', in Shula Marks and Richard Rathbone, eds., *Industrialization and Social Change in South Africa: African Class Formation, Culture and Consciousness 1879–1930* (London, 1982), pp. 167–94.

guaranteeing female choice. It included a requirement to register marriages merely as a mechanism to check that the women had consented. Its successor in 1917 had lost the paternalist emphasis and was largely a bureaucratic measure to ensure that marriages were actually registered, at a time when the administration believed that monitoring what Africans were doing would help in controlling social transformation. In Buganda, where laws were made not by colonial officials, but by the local African Parliament, bridewealth rates were kept high by legislation in 1899, to benefit the Christian élite, and then lowered and limited by legislation in 1920, in an attempt to reduce the number of independent and unmarried women.[17]

None the less, these interventions could give impetus to new directions in African gender relationships. In early twentieth-century Southern Rhodesia, for example, transformations in bridewealth had almost nothing to do with legislation and everything to do with senior African men manipulating marriage transactions to their advantage. For women, the elders' strategy of demanding fewer, larger, often cash payments from their prospective husbands just meant more work and less freedom.[18]

Colonial policies on divorce, whatever their intentions, had diverse outcomes, depending on the local context. There was a much greater readiness to grant divorces to African women in Africa than there was to grant divorces to British women in Britain during the same period. Imperial agents were usually trying to introduce their own ideas of a better deal for 'downtrodden' African women when they got involved in these matters. In late-nineteenth-century Cape-ruled Basotholand, colonial authorities responded to marital crises by supporting individual marriage rights and female custody of children, neither of which made much sense in local African terms. The intention was to protect women, but the result was to leave women exposed and to weaken the pre-colonial systems that protected them. In early twentieth-century Southern Rhodesia, magistrates hoped to support women by offering them marital choice and independence. When confronted with women who had been unfaithful to their husbands, magistrates tended to 'release' them by handing out divorces, when what the husbands had come to court for was adultery compensation. Again, women were left

[17] Diana Jeater, *Marriage, Perversion and Power: The Construction of Moral Discourse in Southern Rhodesia 1894–1930* (Oxford, 1993); Musisi, ' "Bad Women" '.

[18] Jeater, *Marriage, Perversion and Power*; Elizabeth Schmidt, *Peasants, Traders, and Wives: Shona Women in the History of Zimbabwe* (London, 1992).

vulnerable and without protection, and the policy seriously exacerbated tensions between men and women.[19]

Conversely, in south-western Nigeria during the 1900s, women actively seeking divorce found it fairly easy to get support from British officials. As in British law, divorced women were not returned to dependent status, creating a phenomenon of legally independent women. The British administration formalized Yoruba divorce law by statute in 1907, and the following year at least one women won a divorce simply by stating, 'I am tired of staying with him, I would like to get another husband.'[20] Unlike in southern Africa, independent women in Yorubaland did not threaten the colony's economic base, because they continued to operate as independent producers. However, their enhanced access to divorce had fairly devastating effects on the economic position of men, who had often put themselves in vulnerable positions as indebted pawns in order to pay bridewealth. This situation continued until the 1920s, when economic downturn forced a change in policy towards agricultural production, and made the administration take note of the problems faced by abandoned husbands.[21]

In none of these cases, however, does it seem that imperal agents had planned these outcomes, or predicted the consequences of their intervention. Family breakdown and colonial responses all took place in the context of social upheaval, linked to political and economic changes. Both women and men had taken advantage of opportunities opened up by these changes to seek more autonomy. For women, that usually meant autonomy from fathers or husbands. Colonial policy on bridewealth and divorce was a complicating factor; it was not the main reason why changes in gender relationships were taking place.

Colonial officials were also forced to take an interest in adultery by African men. Indigenous mechanisms for coping with adultery had weakened steadily during the early twentieth century. Wage labour opportunities and new transport infrastructures posed problems for African marriages. On the one hand, wives often deserted their labour-migrant husbands because of the

[19] Sandra Burman, 'Fighting a Two-Pronged Attack: The Changing Legal Status of Women in Cape-ruled Basutoland', in Walker, ed., *Women and Gender*, pp. 48–75; Jeater, *Marriage, Perversion and Power.*

[20] Judith Byfield, 'Women, Marriage, Divorce and the Emerging Colonial State in Abeokuta (Nigeria) 1892–1904', in Hodgson and McCurdy, eds, '*Wicked' Women*, pp. 27–46.

[21] Andrea Cornwall, 'Wayward Women and Useless Men: Contest and Change in Gender Relations in Ado-Odo, S.W. Nigeria', in Hodgson and McCrudy, eds., '*Wicked Women*', pp. 67–84.

dramatic increase in their workloads. On the other hand, men could easily move out of the district in which they had seduced another man's wife, and so evade paying compensation to the wronged husband's family. African elders put pressure on the white administrations to provide them with some redress and colonial administrators yielded to their complaints. As a result, bridewealth was, in these contexts, treated as purchase, adultery became a form of theft that justified being treated as a criminal matter, and women were treated as property. As one colonial administrator explained it, 'A Native has paid lobolo for his wife and she is his property. Adultery therefore with a Native woman is a serious breach of the rights of property only comparable with the more serious kinds of theft . . . The Court should be authorized to assess damage at the same time, as in Stock Theft.'[22] The criminalization of adultery did not work as it was founded on a metropolitan, rather than a local, understanding of what 'adultery' was. African elders had wanted men to be criminally charged to ensure payment of compensation. The state, however, criminalized men and women for their moral transgressions.

Rather than accommodating existing African systems, colonial administrators altered gender relationships and the meaning of adultery. As with the marriage ordinances, the legislation was largely unenforceable, and African men found other ways to deal with the upheavals in marital relationships. Far from there being a 'patriarchal alliance' of white administrators and African elders conspiring to restrict African women, there was simply a mess of misunderstandings and colliding ideas about women and marriage throughout the African colonies during the early decades of the British Empire.[23]

The revival of Victorianism and the Morality of African Women

The robust imperial self-confidence in British society was shaken, both at home and in the Empire, by the experiences of the Great War. In Africa, local people had long resisted attempts to transform their gender relationships to mirror those in Britain. During the war years, many colonial authorities had to focus on protecting and stabilizing their territories and not alienating

[22] Native Commissioner, Ndanga to Superintendent of Natives, Victoria, 18 May 1914. National Archives of Zimbabwe, A3.21/50.2.

[23] Jeater, *Marriage, Perversion and Power.*

local populations. They had to pay more attention to local discontent, and they responded to complaints from senior men about the weakening of their controls over women and junior men. The adultery debates of this period contributed to the idea that control of African women was a moral issue, and that their sexual activities could legitimately be restricted by the state. This principle served a very useful purpose for colonial officials across the Empire in the coming decades.

The British Empire had moved away from overt projects of social transformation and 'civilizing' Africans by the 1920s. Instead, Indirect Rule, which had been a pragmatic solution to government for many years, became a conscious policy. Indigenous male authorities undertook to maintain administration and justice, in exchange for imperial protection of their sources of power. In many cases, this strategy was reduced to colonial officials conspiring with older African men to exert control over women and junior men. Rather than westernising social relations, Indirect Rule entrenched the conservative patriarchy of many African institutions at the same time as it created neo-traditions of female subordination.

Indirect Rule required a genuine 'patriarchal alliance' against female independence. However, several decades of social change and state support for female autonomy, in much of British Africa, had created significant numbers of independent women, who now needed to be brought back under 'tribal' control. Restraining women was easier said than done, not least because the 'tribal' structures that were presumed to support these women had been fractured, and class differentiation had created rural communities unwilling to accommodate 'surplus' women who could be earning cash in towns. Much frustration was experienced at the difficulties in restricting women's movements and economic independence. Failures to subordinate women exposed the weaknesses and limits of imperial power. Rather than acknowledging a problem with the policy, colonial officials found it easier to blame the inherent nature of African women. Their insubordination was attributed to their fundamentally immoral nature, in the same way that: 'Labeling the African worker as lazy was a way of acknowledging the limits of dominance, while attributing these limits to the basic nature of the dominated.'[24]

[24] Frederick Cooper, *On the African Waterfront: Urban Disorder and the Transformation of Work in Colonial Mombasa* (New Haven, Conn., 1987), p. 1.

So, by the 1920s, African women's sexuality had come to represent a range of threats to the Empire. What is more commonly understood as a 'Victorian' gender ideology came into its own in Africa just as women in the metropolis were finally emerging from its shadow. It was a reaction against women who had taken advantage of early opportunities opened up by colonial rule. Female sexuality *per se* was no longer an issue for white men, but it now resonated with other concerns, notably hygiene, town-planning, and prostitution. These issues had come to serve as metaphors for social disorder and difficulties in consolidating white rule. In 1920s Southern Rhodesia, frustration at the difficulties in controlling women's movements into urban spaces was expressed as a problem of sexual morality. In 1920s Kenya, urban segregation and restrictions on women's access to living space was justified in terms of their sexual promiscuity, and the hygiene threat posed by prostitution; in Namibia, medical tests for venereal disease bore little relationship to genuine medical practice, but allowed intimate intrusions into urban women's lives. In 1921, food shortages in Buganda were blamed on female sexual freedom.[25]

The link between female sexuality, prostitution, and degeneracy had been imported from Victorian England, but the policy outcomes in 1920s Africa were not a simple reflection of the original model. For example, in Victorian England, the powerful ideology linking prostitution and disease produced measures to force working-class women into dependence on men. In Kenya in the 1920s a similar obsession with prostitution and disease produced general restrictions on Africans' freedom of movement, which affected all independent African traders and the unemployed and justified a policy of urban segregation.[26]

Colonial gender ideology had become genuinely 'Victorian' in its attempts to eradicate what was defined as female 'sexuality' but was actually female independence. Interventions in women's lives had moved well beyond the attempts to improve their status in marriage. The emphasis was now on improving the behaviour of women, rather than improving the behaviour of men. The impact on women affected their economic independence, but also

[25] Jeater, *Marriage, Perversion and Power*, p. 255.; White, *Comforts of Home*; Claire C. Robertson, 'Transitions in Kenyan Patriarchy: Attempts to Control Nairobi Area traders, 1920–1963', in Kathleen Sheldon, ed., *Courtyards, Markets, City Streets: Urban Women in Africa* (Oxford, 1996), pp. 47–72; Patricia Hayes *et al*, eds., *Namibia under South African Rule: Mobility and Containment, 1915–1946* (Athens, Oh., 1998); Musisi, ' "Bad Women" ', p. 177.

[26] White, *Comforts of Home*, p. 46.

their sexual autonomy. Many 'respectable' women welcomed the new policies, and not all of those who fell foul of new regulations were trying to resist or escape male control.

Women started to impinge on colonial consciousness far more than they had done in the past, and 'women's issues' became a broader field than it had been at the turn of the century. There were new, overt restrictions on women's autonomy, but there were also attempts to force them into 'appropriate' work, make them farm differently, and change their domestic lives. Not all of these initiatives were carried out by colonial officials themselves; the logic of Indirect Rule left much of this work in the hands of local rulers. Between 1929 and 1932 in rural Asante, chiefs periodically ordered the arrest of all spinsters and held them prisoner until they found someone to agree to marry them. Unlike the 'respectable' spinsters who were coming under suspicion in the British metropolis for being sexually frustrated and 'unbalanced', these spinsters were under suspicion for being sexually active and spreading venereal disease. However, as Jean Allman demonstrates, the real problem was not these women's sexuality, but their success as independent cocoa producers.[27]

Most assaults on women's autonomy were targeted at those in the towns. 'Urban women' suddenly became visible to colonial authorities, where they had been invisible before.[28] There were various reasons why urban women began to disturb colonial authorities in the inter-war period, most of which were framed in terms of a concern for sexual morality. In white settler societies, town-planning progressed increasingly along segregated lines, and any urban Africans posed difficulties for zoning. Moreover, faced with African elders' refusal to release women from agricultural work, most colonial societies had adjusted to a system of male migrant labour. As male migrant labour became an inherent part of colonial economic structures, increased pressure was put on rural areas to provide social welfare for children and the elderly, who were largely excluded from the waged labour markets and were not productive farmers. These rural economies became increasingly dependent upon a combination of wage remittances and sustained female labour, while a higher proportion of male labour was absorbed in the waged economies in towns, areas of large-scale commercial farming,

[27] Jean Allman, 'Rounding up Spinsters: Gender Chaos and Unmarried Women in Colonial Asante', *JAH*, XXXVII, 2 (1996), pp. 195–214.

[28] Diana Jeater, 'No Place for a Woman: Gwelo Town, Southern Rhodesia, 1894–1920', *JSAS*, XXVI, 1 (2000), pp. 29–43.

and industrial production. As its economic development became predicated on migrant African male labour, the Empire developed its own interest in keeping African women working in the rural areas, sustaining the rural economies from which male labour was drawn.

Measures were designed to get women out-of-town, or to stop them coming to town in the first place, or to ensure that only 'respectable' women were allowed to settle there. In the self-governing settler society of South Africa, pass laws were attempted; elsewhere, restrictions on women's access to markets and housing were tried. But women still kept coming into the towns, pushed by rural poverty and pulled by the possibilities of earning cash. A growing literature on female urbanization, particularly for eastern and southern Africa, where towns were largely colonial creations, reveals that colonial intervention by itself was not effective, and could even be self-contradictory. In Nairobi, for example, the administration see-sawed between the need to encourage small food traders, who were predominantly women, and the wish to support African men in their attempts to limit female autonomy.[29]

Only when state restrictions had significant support within African communities was there a real impact on local gender relations. While indigenous and colonial authorities shared a concern about urban women, they did not share the same motives, and not all African men even shared the concern. Colonial restrictions on urban women in the 1920s bowed to concerns from rural 'tribal elders' about losing control of women, but many rural families relied on cash remittances from daughters in town. In southern and eastern Africa, the colonial agenda of segregation and migrant labour made urban women a particular problem for whites. In these societies, dependent on male labour migration, urban men were generally happy to have access to women, who offered them, in Luise White's phrase, 'the comforts of home'.[30] Consequently, state controls on female urbanization, while making women's lives difficult, proved largely ineffective in the 1920s and 1930s.

By contrast, in West Africa, where towns had flourished long before white rule, and women dominated the market place, segregation was not an issue. Opposition to female economic autonomy was in African rather than colonial hands. Egba men in south-western Nigeria asserted new control over urban women in the 1920s by greatly restricting their ability to divorce their

[29] Robertson, 'Transitions in Kenyan Patriarchy'.
[30] White, *The Comforts of Home*.

husbands. Women now had to pay 8 shillings to file for divorce. Their 'seducers' were liable for court costs. The whole of the bridewealth also had to be restored at once. The issue of women getting easy divorces had been around since the turn of the century, but a crisis in the cloth industry and competition from female cloth-dyers brought matters to a head.[31] This episode suggests that, for African men, the issue was not urbanization *per se*, and not female sexuality, but the relative economic power between men and women. It also shows how African gender struggles were more significant than state policy in influencing women's access to town.

Ironically, the colonial shift away from the 'civilizing' mission and towards a more 'Victorian' obsession with female sexuality accelerated the emergence of new systems of class differentiation within African communities, including more European models of marriage. By the 1930s in Africa colonial policies regarding independent women had given middle-class, and indeed, working-class, African women a real incentive to express themselves as 'respectable'. European models of marriage appealed to upwardly mobile urban African women, as a mark of their difference from the morally suspect independent women who had become targets of colonial hostility.

The trends towards more European models of marriage were not new, and were not the creation of colonial policy. Elite Christian families in Lagos had been signalling their difference from other urban dwellers for decades, by forming monogamous unions that indicated their higher status as educated and 'civilized'. In Buganda, Christian élites had tried to consolidate their position by raising bridewealth and limiting married women to 'respectable' parts of town as far back as the turn of the century. By the 1930s, however, colonial attacks on independent urban women had given new urgency to the need to signal oneself as 'respectable'. Even where women were not permanently in town, they could lay claim to 'respectability' when they visited husbands or relatives.[32] These attitudes endured into the 1960s, when a nurse in the Zambian Copperbelt could comment that she avoided some clubs in town because 'they are always crowded with low class people who go there for chibuku [African beer] ... The best club for us is Chilimana. No chibuku is sold there and the pub is decent. You find well behaved people

[31] Byfield, 'Women, Marriage, Divorce', p. 88.

[32] Kristin Mann, *Marrying Well: Marriage, Status and Social Change among the Educated Elite in Colonial Lagos* (Cambridge, 1985); Musisi, ' "Bad Women" '; Teresa Barnes, *'We Women Worked So Hard': Gender, Urbanization, and Social Reproduction in Colonial Harare, Zimbabwe, 1930–1956* (Oxford, 1999); Allman and Tashjian, *'I Will Not Eat Stone'.*

there [ladies and gentlemen who are] educated and or doing high grade jobs.'[33]

By the 1930s a package of ideas entailing monogamy, sobriety, and marital fidelity, which Teresa Barnes labels 'righteousness', was the difference between 'good' women and 'prostitutes' across most of British Africa. The ideology was in some ways similar to the idea of 'companionate marriage' that was gaining ground in the metropolis during the same period, and was encouraged by similar influences from imperial, consumer-oriented businesses. The domestic home became a place for sharing consumer purchases and reflecting household status. At the same time, increasing consumerism also had the opposite effect in some cases—attracting many other women into embracing 'wickedness', selling sex or beer in exchange for opportunities to enjoy leisure pursuits, dancing to imported jazz music, and purchasing new consumer goods.[34]

The shifting definitions of a 'good woman' within African communities were powered by social and class differentiation. None the less, these new African ideas about a 'good woman' made much more sense to colonial authorities than local gender ideologies had done a generation before. We might therefore expect to see metropolitan, colonial, and African ideas about appropriate behaviour for women marching in step in the 1930s. They did not. The role of women as agricultural producers in Africa still marked them out as different in kind from their counterparts in Europe. During the interwar years, women's agricultural work intensified significantly.

African Women, Colonial Labour, and Domestic Work

One of the most significant consequences of British imperialism for African women was the steady intensification of their workloads. From the beginning of imperial trade, men had taken advantage of emerging markets for cash crops to raise household production, exploiting the labour of wives and children. Indirect Rule policies had helped men to maintain control over women and utilize their labour power. Along with the struggle for control over the labour of women by African men came a later struggle

[33] Cited in Jane Parpart, ' "Wicked Women" and "Respectable Ladies": Reconfiguring Gender on the Zambian Copperbelt, 1936–1964', in Hodgson and McCurdy, eds., '*Wicked' Women*, p. 284.

[34] Barnes, '*We Women Worked so Hard*'; Timothy Burke, *Lifebuoy Men, Lux Women: Commodification, Consumption and Cleanliness in Modern Zimbabwe* (Durham, NC, 1996).

for control over the product of women's labour by colonial states. Colonial efforts to control the terms under which women participated in cash–crop production, which began in the inter-war period, also occurred in the context both of changing colonial ideas about what work was appropriate for African women and of increasing efforts, especially on the part of missionaries, to change the nature of the domestic sphere in African societies.

In many parts of British Africa, women had thought of, and protected, their agricultural output as independent from men's. However, colonial officials conceived of farmers as male, and expected men to control agricultural output.[35] Administrations had tended to concentrate on exploiting the male labour force, and had shown less interest in harnessing women's labour. This situation changed in the inter-war years. Colonial states began to take a direct interest in exploiting women's agricultural labour for their own purposes.

The worldwide Depression forced a re-evaluation of the financial benefits of Empire to the British economy. Attention turned to agricultural productivity and the need for more, and higher-yielding, cash-crop production. These years saw the beginnings of systematic agricultural extension projects, designed to increase African productivity and introduce new land-management techniques. This policy was linked to inter-war concerns about environmental degradation, and the post-war Labour government strongly supported it. After the war the Colonial Office was directed to make the Empire economically viable, through effective planning and investment in modernization.

By the late 1940s a 'second colonial occupation'[36] was in full sway, flooding the continent with technocrats whose brief was to develop and modernize African society, at whatever cost to 'traditional' rule. Across the colonial territories, senior men struggled to maintain control over families in which cash-based divisions of labour were playing a growing part. In West Africa, cash crop production of exports such as cocoa, groundnuts and palm oil,

[35] Schmidt, *Peasants, Traders, and Wives*; Dorothy Hodgson, 'Pastoralism, Patriarchy and History: Changing Gender Relations among Maasai in Tanganyika, 1890–1940', *JAH*, XL, 1 (1999), pp. 41–66; Beverly Grier, 'Pawns, Porters and Petty Traders: Women in the Transition to Cash Crop Agriculture in Colonial Ghana', *Signs*, XVII (1992), pp. 304–28; Mackenzie, *Land, Ecology and Resistance.*

[36] D. A. Low and J. M. Lonsdale, 'Introduction: Towards the New Order 1949–63', in D. A. Low and Alison Smith eds., *History of East Africa*, Vol. III, (Oxford, 1976), pp. 12–16.

rose significantly, and rural women had to work even harder to increase agricultural outputs in order to sustain the imperial economy. In East Africa, colonial officials appropriated huge numbers of female labourers for the building of terraces, as part of soil conservation projects.

As the colonial officials responsible for increasing the profitability of the Empire developed a greater interest in women's work, local policies towards women revealed an apparent inconsistency. On the one hand, particularly in West Africa, the continuation of Indirect Rule encouraged support for older forms of patriarchal authority. On the other hand, simultaneously with the attempts to uphold 'tradition', the 'second colonial occupation' required new working methods from rural women that directly challenged kin-based control over women's labour. Unfortunately, for African women the resulting tensions most often meant that 'modernization' entailed even greater entrenchment of patriarchal authority, as their workloads increased even further and resources were concentrated in the hands of male farmers.[37]

In an urban area such as the Zambian Copperbelt, modernization policies encouraged the development of social welfare initiatives and support for training programmes that would bring wives into more Western styles of household management based on the nuclear family. In rural areas such as the Central Province in Kenya, extended households under entrepreneurial patriarchs contributed to the state's agricultural betterment programmes by 'traditional' exploitation of female labour.[38] Imperial agents once again seemed unclear about whether African women needed firmer management, or more freedom.

The 'second colonial occupation' not only brought agriculturalists and environmentalists into Africa, but also health experts, bearing with them the message from Britain that the state had an interest in improving the health of infants and the standards of mothering. By the 1930s colonial agents had already focused a significant part of their attention on health and mothering; indeed, at times it became something of a fixation. This attention was a new

[37] Jean Allman, 'Of "Spinsters", "Concubines" and "Wicked Women": Reflections on Gender and Social Change in Colonial Asante', *Gender and History*, III (1991), pp. 176–89; George Chauncey, Jr., 'The Locus of Reproduction: Women's Labour in the Zambian Copperbelt, 1927–1953', *JSAS*, VII (1981), pp. 135–64; Mackenzie, *Land, Ecology and Resistance*; Hodgson, 'Pastoralism, Patriarchy and History'; Allman and Tashjian, *'I Will Not Eat Stone'.*

[38] Jane Parpart, ' "Where is your mother?": Gender, Urban Marriage, and Colonial Discourse on the Zambian Copperbelt, 1924–1945', *International Journal of African Historical Studies* (hereafter *IJAHS*), XXVII (1994), pp. 241–71; Parpart, ' "Wicked Women" and "Respectable Ladies" '; Mackenzie, *Land, Ecology and Resistance.*

departure, but it was rooted in established policies, particularly the 'Victorian' concern with female sexual morality, prostitution, and venereal disease of the 1920s. Worries about 'morality,' combined with the shift towards 'betterment', shaped the new emphasis on domestic work and primary health care. This message reflected a similar emphasis in inter-war British social policy, in which training was designed not only to teach nursing or child healthcare to women, but to ensure that as 'good mothers' they were the guardians of the society's morals.[39]

During the inter-war period, mission societies developed a much closer alliance with colonial officials in the 'domestication' of African women. Missions and colonial states had not always agreed on policies towards African women earlier in the century, as missions had wanted far greater interference in marriage than would have been sensible—or even possible—under colonial rule. However, once the churches' initial assaults against the power of male elders subsided, mission stations had turned to other aspects of Christian marriage. Opposition to forced marriages remained, but greater emphasis was given to domesticity and female dependence on men. Training for girls was designed to suit them for work as domestics in British households, but also to prepare them for the 'proper' management of their own households, as wives to mission-educated men.[40] In West Africa, where Indirect Rule was particularly entrenched, missions formed alliances with chiefs, male elders, and colonial officials to move women into new roles as proper mothers and dutiful wives, and thereby to reassert and maintain male control over them as producers and reproducers.[41] The obsession with domesticity—the 'correct' way to ice a cake, knit a cardigan, or set a dinner table—reflected similar interests in the metropolis, where a new generation

[39] Summers, 'Intimate Colonialism'; Vaughan, *Curing Their Ills*; Jean Allman, 'Making Mothers: Missionaries, Medical Officers, and Women's Work in Colonial Asante, 1924–45', *History Workshop Journal*, XXXVIII (1994), pp. 23–47. Nancy Rose Hunt, 'Le Bebe en Brousse: European Women, African Birth Spacing and Colonial Intervention in Breast Feeding in the Belgian Congo', *IJAHS*, XXI, 3 (1988), pp. 401–32, identifies a similar process in the Belgian Congo.

[40] Sheila Meintjes, 'Family and Gender in the Christian Community at Edendale, Natal, in Colonial Times', in Walker, ed, *Women and Gender*, pp. 125–45; Gaitskell, 'Devout Domesticity?'; Schmidt, *Peasants, Traders, and Wives*; Karen Tranberg Hansen, ed., *African Encounters with Domesticity* (New Brunswick, NJ, 1992); Terence Ranger, *Are We Not also Men? The Samkange Family and African Politics in Zimbabwe, 1920–64* (London, 1995).

[41] Allman and Tashjian, '*I Will Not Eat Stone*.'

of women's magazines was beginning to appear, aimed at the emerging 'new woman' as consumer and home-maker.

Again, these initiatives to redefine the nature of women's work as well as the type of spaces in which it was to be performed were successful because Africans, and specifically African women, now had an interest in supporting them. For example, nursing, which was a form of work that colonial officials and missionaries thought appropriate for African women because they saw it as inherently maternal, became a highly sought-after profession for women, providing them with financial independence as well as respectability. In African cities, 'modern' ideas about marriage relationships gained ground, particularly among the educated middle classes whose men found employment supporting the work of the colonial technical advisers. In 1927 in Nigeria the British West African Educated Women's Club supported the establishment of the Queen's College, which explicitly offered girls an education as wives and mothers, and did not even claim any vocational agenda.[42] The same was true of the popular Inanda seminary in South Africa.[43]

Previous missionary attempts at 'domestication' had been less successful. By the inter-war years, however, many African women were themselves concerned about 'moral' breakdown, though this had a slightly different meaning for them than it had for the health educators and colonial officials. 'Morality' within African societies had less to do with sexual promiscuity, and more to do with honouring obligations to kin and other allies, and taking responsibility for the maintenance of support networks. In many areas, missionaries' policies regarding female choice in marriage had previously been blamed for the breakdown in these networks, and the perceived increases in female promiscuity. African women's Christian purity leagues in southern Africa had been established to combat the immorality that the missions themselves were blamed for creating.[44] By the 1920s and 1930s, the new emphasis on domestic life rather than marriage systems had removed this taint from the missions.

The missions' domestic agenda now also had an appeal for élite African women, who, unlike many earlier converts, were enhancing their status through Christianity, rather than escaping from oppressive situations. By

[42] Rina Okonkwo, *Protest Movements in Lagos, 1908–1930* (Lampeter, Wales, 1995).

[43] Meintjes, 'Family and Gender'.

[44] Porterfield, 'Early New England Missionaries', p. 74; Deborah Gaitskell, ' "Wailing for Purity": Prayer Unions, African Mothers and Adolescent Daughters 1912–1940', in Marks and Rathbone, eds., *Industrialization and Social Change*, pp. 338–57.

the 1930s rural differentiation and social dislocation had made kinship obligations increasingly onerous for women, on whom the bulk of responsibility fell. Women's clubs, often run by churchwomen, provided help and support, as well as vocational training and advice about home management and child-rearing. Moreover, the new ideas about a woman's domestic responsibilities provided a way to avoid oppressive kin obligations, by establishing monogamous marriages, albeit at the price of losing support in turn. These new definitions of a woman's domestic role coincided with the search for markers of 'respectability' in urban life. By the mid-twentieth century, mission-educated women in many parts of the Empire expected a church marriage based on mutual attraction, with an educated wage-earning spouse.[45]

The post-war period in British Africa saw the ideology of the male breadwinner take root in African gender relationships. Although this had became a dominant aspect of gender relationships in Britain, very few Africans had any familiarity with it up until this time. The inter-war domesticity projects had encouraged couples who were intent on 'founding comfortable and happy homes where the man earns the money and his wife keeps the home and really tries to bring up the children'.[46] However, up to 1945, with the exception of a few Christian élite circles, women had tried to defend their separate economic spheres, and even 'domesticated' wives had expected to maintain their own income sources. Colonial authorities, meanwhile, particularly in West Africa, had thought of the African work force in terms of 'tribal' labour, available for unskilled seasonal or casual work, but not as a skilled working class. Where the dominant economic model was male migrant labour, which was especially true of eastern and southern Africa, wives were expected to support their families in the rural areas. It was a key feature of labour negotiations, for both African men and colonial officials, to argue that African families were different from European families, and that male earners had different sorts of dependants.[47] Yet the shift towards 'modernization' forced a reassessment of these models in colonial circles,

[45] Allman and Tashjian, *'I Will Not Eat Stone'*; Barnes, *'We Women Worked So Hard'*; Mann, *Marrying Well*; Ranger, *Are We Not also Men?*

[46] Cited in Gaitskell, 'Wailing for Purity', p. 339.

[47] Frederick Cooper, *Decolonization and African Society: The Labor Question in French and British Africa* (Cambridge, 1996); Lisa A. Lindsay, 'Domesticity and Difference: Male Breadwinners, Working Women, and Colonial Citizenship in the 1945 Nigerian General Strike', *American Historical Review*, CIV, 3 (June 1999), pp. 783–812.

beginning in the 1930s, but gaining rapid ground following the 1945 Labour victory in Britain, with its new determination to make the Empire economically viable. In West Africa, the colonial officials began to think of 'detribalized' African men as a stabilized urban working class—a skilled workforce of male breadwinners.

These new models were not unwelcome to African trade unionists. In the Nigerian general strike of 1945, women's interests in economic reform were subsumed in a campaign that presented women only as 'supporters' of men seeking a family wage. In Southern Rhodesia, meanwhile, the settler-run government was independent of Colonial Office directives, and the dominant segregation policy was designed to perpetuate the migrant-worker system. Even so, relations between men and women were a crucial aspect of strike actions, and a major demand in industrial unrest was for wages that would make it possible for a man to keep his wife and family with him at his place of work.[48] These pressures seemed to be coming from women as much as from men. None the less, as Lisa Lindsay points out with reference to Nigerian railway workers, the metropolitan ideals of a male breadwinner and a dependent wife came to the fore in labour disputes, but they coexisted with other ways of positioning family income, within different configurations of obligation and resource-distribution.[49] A man could be a husband and breadwinner in his trade union, but a brother or son or in-law with wider obligations when he was at home. Similarly, his wife could think of herself as a dependent wife and as an independent trader, daughter, and farmer. The addition of metropolitan ideas about gender to existing family models did not mean that older models had been abandoned.

Visible and Invisible Changes

Policies on marriage law, colonial cities, agricultural labour, and domestic roles were never central to the official ideologies of the British Empire because African women were of limited interest to colonial officials throughout Africa as well as to imperial rulers in London. As a result of this lack of

[48] Teresa Barnes, ' "So that a labourer could live with his family": Overlooked Factors in Social and Economic Strife in Urban Colonial Zimbabwe, 1945–1952', *JSAS*, XXI, 1 (1995), pp. 95–113; Barnes, *"We Women Worked So Hard"*; Ian Phimister, *Wangi Kolia: Coal, Capital and Labour in Colonial Zimbabwe 1894–1954*, (Harare, 1994).

[49] Lisa A. Lindsay, ' "No Need . . . to Think of Home?" Masculinity and Domestic Life on the Nigerian railway, c.1940–61', *JAH*, XXXIX, 3 (1998), pp. 439–66.

attention, the outcomes of these policies were often far from those that had been intended. Perhaps the most significant influence that British imperial rule had on African women was the consistent failure of its agents to notice them at all, especially in contexts where African women traditionally wielded power. The myopia of colonial officials in perceiving the powerful roles that women played in politics, economics, and religious ritual had lasting impact.

Colonial officials generally noticed women only where their preconceptions led them to expect women to be visible. They were aware of women as downtrodden wives in the early part of the century, then as prostitutes, and then as wives, mothers, and agricultural workers. Colonial officials responded to these two-dimensional stereotypes of African women with legislation and policy. The resulting laws and administrative actions affected women, but only in limited ways. Where the British Empire ended up affecting the lives of African women most was not in terms of the ways it saw them, but in terms of the ways it did *not* see them. It was not the laws and policies that were designed to affect women that really changed their lives, but rather those that seemed to overlook their very existence.

A simple explanation accounts for this failure: colonial men, and the majority of early British ethnographers, were men. They expected to deal with other men. For colonial officials, the meetings that they attended, which were the meetings of the African men's councils, were taken as being, by definition, the public councils. Women's meetings and rituals, by contrast, were assumed to be private meetings with no public consequence. African gender protocols, meanwhile, did not allow men to deal with women's matters; women, therefore, did not usually seek the involvement of the male white officials. Colonial officials never envisaged that women might have a role in government, law, administration or land ownership.[50]

The British overlooked the significance of women's institutions from the start. In pre-colonial times, the Asante kingdom in West Africa had included some powerful roles for women. When the British attempted to graft their Indirect Rule on to what they believed to be the traditional political system, they excluded women entirely. When, in the 1920s, the colonial ethnographer R. S. Rattray asked some elderly informants how this had happened, he was told, 'The white man never asked us this. You have dealings with and recognize only the men; we supposed the European considered women of

[50] Hodgson, 'Pastoralism, Patriarchy and History'.

no account, we know you do not recognize them as we have always done.'[51] Similarly, women in the nineteenth-century Egba state in south-western Nigeria had had important formal authority as title-holders; but, when the British formed the Egba United Government in 1898, no women chiefs were selected. The Council was enlarged several times over the next fifteen years, yet still no women chiefs were ever invited to join it.[52]

During the period of indirect rule, this colonial myopia began to have wide-reaching and serious consequences for African women. As Jean Allman and Victoria Tashjian noted with reference to Asante, historical work 'has not even begun to measure the social and political costs of an indirect rule that pushed women to the margins, an indirect rule that, aiming at restoring moral order, remapped the terrain of patriarchal power'. Maasai women in 1920s Tanganyika had their rights to vital cattle resources stripped by an indirect rule system that recognized only male rights. Men acquired new status as 'taxpayers', 'property owners', 'buyers' and 'sellers', while women were reduced to the margins, excluded from economics and politics, and gradually redefined as stupid, childlike, and themselves the 'property' of men.[53]

In the 1950s Kikuyu women fiercely defended initiation rites. The move away from Indirect Rule had been consolidated in the post-war period, and 'traditional' practices were now opposed by the state, in favour of a modern development agenda. Clitoridectomy was an integral part of girls' initiation, and was overseen by senior women in the 'council of entering'. However, it was banned in 1956 by the men's council, the *Njuri Ncheke*, on prompting from the District Commissioner, despite being entirely outside their 'traditional' area of legitimate jurisdiction. Appalled by the prospect of being barred from full adult status, and inspired by each other to resist, girls developed a remarkably successful covert self-excision movement. The colonial authorities, deep in the Mau Mau insurgency, interpreted this movement as evidence of resistance to colonial rule rather than as an assertion of women's authority *vis-à-vis* men's. Still thinking of women's issues in terms of agriculture and domesticity, the colonial authorities assumed that the self-excision movement was led by young men, resisting the authority of the

[51] Cited in Jean Allman, ' "England Swings Like a Pendulum Do?": Africanist Reflections on Cannadine's Retro-Empire,' *Journal of Colonialism and Colonial History*, III, 1 (2002), par. 7.

[52] Byfield, 'Women, Marriage, Divorce', p. 40.

[53] Allman and Tashjian, '*I Will Not Eat Stone*', p. 223; see also Ifi Amadiume, *Re-inventing Africa: Matriarchy, Religion, and Culture* (London, 1997); Hodgson, 'Pastoralism, Patriarchy and History'.

older men in the *Njuri Ncheke*, and saw the young women simply as pawns in their nationalist game.[54]

The most negative effects of Empire on women were because of the colonial inability to understand that African women and men did not have the same types of relationships as British women and men had back in the metropole. Moreover, metropolitan ideas about appropriate roles for African women were not consistent; indeed, they were frequently contradictory. The result of this misreading of gender relationships in British Africa was that African women were almost never seen for who they really were and were even more rarely heard. As Misty Bastian points out regarding Igbo women in West Africa, 'Women . . . literally had no access to official buildings or to the minds of those who sat in them.'[55]

The British Empire clearly had a complex and profound impact on women's lives; many women were able to assert greater personal autonomy under imperial rule, but collectively they had been dispossessed. But not only was Empire significant in the lives of African women; African women were also significant to the life of the British Empire. Across the century of British rule over much of Africa, as Allman and Tashjian emphasize, there was a steady intensification of women's workloads. 'Whether Shona, Asante, Luo, Igbo or Zulu, despite the range of "colonialisms"—whether there was intensive labor migration or not, whether there were white settlers and plantations or peasant cash cropping, whether there was matrilineal or patrilineal descent—African women's status declined, work burdens increased, and safety nets *disappeared*, as women bore increasing responsibility, across the continent, for social reproduction.'[56] The real importance of African women to Empire makes it even more striking that they remained largely invisible to the imperial authorities. This is the most lasting legacy of the Empire. The new states of Africa lowered the British flag with women not only facing greater work burdens than ever before, but also erased from state hierarchies and confined to the edges of power.

[54] Lynn M. Thomas, ' "*Ngaitana* (I will circumcise myself)": The Gender and Generational Politics of the 1956 Ban on Clitoridectomy in Meru, Kenya', in Hunt, Liu and Quataert, eds, *General Colonialisms.* pp. 16–41; Thomas, 'Imperial Concerns and "Women's Affairs": State Efforts to Regulate Clitoridectomy and Eradicate Abortion in Meru. Kenya, *c.* 1910–1950', *JAH* XXXIX, 1 (1998), pp. 121–46.

[55] Misty L. Bastian, 'Dancing Women and Colonial Men: The *Nwaobiala* of 1925', in Hodgson and McCurdy, eds, '*Wicked*' *Women*, p. 125.

[56] Allman and Tashjian, '*I Will Not Eat Stone*', p. 223.

Select Bibliography

JEAN ALLMAN, SUSAN GEIGER, and NAKANYIKE MUSISI, eds., *Women in African Colonial Histories* (Bloomington, Ind., 2002).

JEAN ALLMAN and VICTORIA TASHJIAN, *'I Will Not Eat Stone': A Women's History of Colonial Asante* (Oxford, 2000).

TERESA BARNES, *'We Women Worked So Hard': Gender, Urbanization, and Social Reproduction in Colonial Harare, Zimbabwe, 1930–1956* (Oxford, 1999).

SARA BERRY, *Chiefs Know their Boundaries: Essays on Property, Power and the Past in Asante, 1896–1996* (Oxford, 2000).

BARBARA BUSH, *Imperialism, Race and Resistance,* (London, 1999).

MARTIN CHANOCK, *Law, Custom and Social Order* (Cambridge, 1985).

KAREN TRANBERG HANSEN, ed., *African Encounters with Domesticity* (New Brunswick, NJ, 1992).

DOROTHY L. HODGSON and SHERYL A. MCCURDY, eds., *'Wicked' Women and the Reconfiguration of Gender in Africa* (Oxford, 2001).

NANCY ROSE HUNT, TESSIE R. LIU, and JEAN QUATAERT, eds., *Gendered Colonialisms in African History* (Oxford, 1997).

DIANA JEATER, *Marriage, Perversion and Power: The Construction of Moral Discourse in Southern Rhodesia 1894–1930* (Oxford, 1993).

FIONA D. MACKENZIE, *Land, Ecology and Resistance in Kenya, 1880–1952* (Edinburgh, 1998).

KRISTIN MANN, *Marrying Well: Marriage, Status and Social Change among the Educated Elite in Colonial Lagos* (Cambridge, 1985).

ELIZABETH SCHMIDT, *Peasants, Traders, and Wives: Shona Women in the History of Zimbabwe* (London, 1992).

KATHLEEN SHELDON, ed., *Courtyards, Markets, City Streets: Urban Women in Africa* (Oxford, 1996).

CHERRYL WALKER, ed., *Women and Gender in Southern Africa to 1945* (London, 1990).

LUISE WHITE, *The Comforts of Home: Prostitution in Colonial Nairobi* (Chicago, 1990).

10

African Participation in the British Empire

TIMOTHY H. PARSONS

Without African participation, there would have been no British Empire in Africa. Africans built the Empire, did the work of the Empire, sometimes ruled in the Empire, and often redirected the goals and efforts of the Empire to their own advantage. Why would Africans participate in a system of alien rule that robbed them of their sovereignty, promoted racial discrimination, and subjected them to the unmitigated forces of foreign economic exploitation? The vast majority of people simply had no choice. The British colonial regime coerced them into becoming taxpayers, wage labourers, and agricultural commodity producers. Those who refused faced prosecution as tax defaulters, trespassers, vagrants, and squatters. More problematic, however, were the motives of the African intermediaries who constituted the interface between colonial rulers and the subject African majority. These men (and occasionally women) served as chiefs, clerks, interpreters, soldiers, policemen, prison warders, clergymen, teachers, labour overseers, artisans, and household domestic workers. Few were motivated by feelings of loyalty to the Empire, but they enabled a handful of British administrators, missionaries, and entrepreneurs to govern and develop their African colonies. The factors that induced African intermediaries to take part in the colonial enterprise expose not only the relatively fragile inner workings of colonialism in Africa but also lay bare the mean realities of life for the majority of Africans within the British Empire.

Britain had depended on a small group of Anglicized Africans to protect its interests on the pre-colonial West African coast since the nineteenth century. During this era of informal empire, many influential Britons considered African colonies an impractical and unnecessary expense. As a result, Britain used local Africans to staff its small coastal enclaves and trading stations. Many of these educated intermediaries came from centuries old Afro-European communities that sprang from relations between European traders and local peoples. British influence in these cosmopolitan coastal societies expanded in the early nineteenth century with the establishment of

Sierra Leone as a haven for liberated slaves. Under the unifying influence of Anglican Protestantism, this heterogeneous settlement grew into a vibrant community with its own church, language, and culture. The Sierra Leonean Krios, as they came to be known, served as clerks, doctors, and missionaries in Britain's West African coastal territories.[1]

The British Empire offered considerable opportunities for westernized Africans during this period. John Africanus Horton earned a medical degree in Great Britain and joined the medical service in West Africa in 1859. Samuel Ajayi Crowther, who became the first African Bishop of the Anglican Church in 1864, led the Church Missionary Society's all-African mission to Nigeria. In southern Africa, where Britain imposed a franchise based on property and literacy in the formerly Dutch Cape Colony, British rule nurtured a small but prosperous non-European Cape élite that adopted the manners of English upper class to establish their gentlemanly credentials.[2] The Krios and other West African coastal élites also adopted English names, Victorian dress, and sent their children to British mission schools. These 'Afro-Victorians' held senior positions in local civil services and played a willing role in the expansion of British influence because they assumed that they would be its primary beneficiaries.

The rise of pseudo-scientific racism and social Darwinism following the formal partition of Africa in the late nineteenth century proved that the Afro-Victorians were sorely mistaken about the opportunities that the British Empire would afford them. Concluding that westernized Africans were too far removed from their own cultures to be of value in administering Britain's new territories, colonial officials purged Africans from the upper ranks of the West African civil services.

Yet fiscal and administrative necessity still forced them to rely on African assistance in making Britain's African Empire politically and economically viable. The metropolitan Treasury was absolutely adamant that the colonies cover the costs of their own administration, and most territories lacked a rudimentary tax-base and a self-sustaining export economy. Moreover, infectious disease, unfamiliar climates, and alien local cultures made it unappealing for Britons to settle in most parts of Africa. These fiscal and

[1] Christopher Fyfe, *A History of Sierra Leone* (London, 1963) and Akintola J. G. Wyse, *The Krio of Sierra Leone: An Interpretive History* (Washington, 1991).

[2] Andre Odendaal, 'South Africa's Black Victorians: Sport and Society in South Africa in the Nineteenth Century', in J. A. Mangan, ed., *Pleasure, Profit, Proselytism: British Culture and Sport at Home and Abroad* (London, 1988).

logistical problems forced the Colonial Office to govern the African territories with only a small handful of field officers. In 1925 it ruled approximately 20 million Nigerians with just two hundred administrators, a ratio of one per one hundred thousand people. By the late 1930s Lord Hailey listed the ratio of administrative officers to the greater African population as approximately one per 188,000 in the Gold Coast, one per 28,000 in Tanganyika, and one per 1,000 in Swaziland.[3]

Colonial officials lacked the understanding of African societies and sufficient police forces to impose their will directly on their African subjects. The small 70,000 regular British Army could not afford to expend its relatively limited resources in Africa. Colonial governments therefore needed trained Africans to provide the administrative, coercive, cultural, and commercial assistance to keep the colonies running. As Governor of Nigeria, Frederick Lugard estimated that he needed at least 5,000 African clerks to administer the colony, a relatively small number in comparison to the overall population. In 1931 employment rolls for the Gold Coast showed that clerks amounted to just 4.9 per cent of the total number of 134,425 registered workers. Similarly, domestic servants accounted for 6.6 per cent of the work force, policemen 1.3 per cent, mechanics 1.2 per cent, teachers 1.1 per cent, and soldiers just 0.8 per cent.[4] In other words, British rule was possible in Africa because colonial officials needed to induce only a small handful of Africans to participate directly in the colonial system.

The motives of these African intermediaries have been the subject of considerable debate. During colonial times, academics and imperial partisans celebrated them as prescient 'modernizers' who recognized the value of Britain's 'civilizing' mission. Yet even Africans who appeared to demonstrate their 'loyalty' to the Empire by wearing colonial medals and enthusiastically singing 'God Save the King' usually invoked and appropriated these symbols to use the mechanisms of colonial power to pursue specific goals in a local context. Nevertheless, a new generation of nationally minded historians in Africa and the West in the post-colonial era questioned African participation in the Empire. They hailed those who opposed colonialism by force as heroes, and considered the colonial intermediaries to be collaborators and traitors to a larger nationalist or pan-Africanist cause.

[3] Michael Crowder, *West Africa Under Colonial Rule* (London, 1968), p. 198 and Lord [Malcolm] Hailey, *An African Survey: A Study of Problems Arising in Africa South of the Sahara* (London, 1938), pp. 108, 226.

[4] A. W. Cardinall, *The Gold Coast, 1931* (Accra, [c.1931]), pp. 170–72.

Many historians now see this collaborator/resister dichotomy as too simplistic. Frederick Cooper considers it is more important to study how Africans perceived and re-imagined their local communities and daily lives under British rule.[5] Most Africans took a practical approach to survival during the colonial era and adopted tactics that shifted between opposition and co-operation with British rule as the situation dictated.[6] Colonialism created new social divisions and centres of power in local communities, and so the targets of African resistance during this period were never clear. Nevertheless, popular perceptions of Africans who worked directly with British colonialists continue to suggest that they betrayed a greater 'Africanness' by unfairly taking advantage of their relative status and authority to enrich themselves.

To be sure, there were relatively substantial rewards for playing an intermediary role in the Empire. In the early colonial era, African leaders could retain a measure of their authority by aligning themselves with the new British rulers. In southern Africa, limited co-operation with Britain earned Swaziland, Bechuanaland, and Nyasaland protectorate status under the more benevolent rule of the Colonial Office rather than incorporation into South Africa. Similarly, the administrative policy of governing through 'traditional' leaders, known as Indirect Rule, empowered Africans who depicted themselves successfully as arbitrators of African custom. On a more personal level, the most viable strategies for capital accumulation and social advancement were through either employment in the colonial administrative, coercive, and cultural fields or by organizing labour and producing agricultural commodities for colonial markets. Although taxation and the pressures of wage labour in the countryside could be extremely oppressive, the colonial era also gave peasant farmers the means to export their produce, which in turn raised the value of African labour.

The rewards that came from participation in the colonial enterprise did not mean that African intermediaries engaged in traitorous 'collaboration' with the alien British regime. Most Africans had a localized view of the world during the colonial era. Few had a sense of national attachment to colonial boundaries. Pan-Africanism was largely an élite ideology, and most individuals drew their sense of identity from ethnicity, faith, and local

[5] Frederick Cooper, 'Conflict and Connection: Rethinking Colonial African History', *American Historical Review*, XCIX (1994), pp. 1532, 1534.

[6] See Edward Steinhart, *Conflict and Collaboration: Kingdoms of Uganda* (Princeton, 1977) and A. A. Boahen, *African Perspectives on Colonialism* (Baltimore, 1987).

allegiances. Pre-colonial political institutions that failed to stand up to the European invaders lost much of their legitimacy in the eyes of their subjects. Even polities such as the Kingdom of Buganda that survived the partition by winning recognition from the British as 'Native Authorities' were vastly different in scope and character from their pre-colonial predecessors.

On an individual level, all Africans took part in the Empire to one degree or another, yet at very different levels of participation. The reach of the under-manned and under-funded territorial governments of the early colonial period was relatively short. Even the more mature and extensive colonial bureaucracies that grew out of British attempts to administer the colonies more efficiently and profitably following the Second World War had a limited capacity to reorder the daily lives of Africans in the countryside. Most rural communities experienced British rule through taxation and forced labour. As colonial policy accelerated the incorporation of farming and pastoral peoples into a monetized economy, those who tried to cling to the autonomy of pre-colonial patterns of pastoralism and subsistence agriculture faced marginalization and prosecution for squatting, trespassing, and tax evasion. Africans living closer to urban areas, mines, plantations, and centres of European settlement found colonial economic and social policies even more invasive.

Many Africans therefore made no distinction between legitimate and criminal forms of participation in the Empire. Having little faith in the legitimacy of British rule, they shifted back and forth between legal and larcenous strategies of accumulation as the situation dictated. Even the most trusted African intermediaries might engage in this type of behaviour. 'Native Authorities' used their status to acquire land and additional wives. Clerks embezzled government and company funds, and policemen extorted tribute from local communities. African civil servants of all stripes were often receptive to bribery. Teachers made off with school funds and took money from parents anxious to secure enrolment for their children. Farmers encroached on government land, and businessmen ignored licensing codes and dabbled in smuggling. Thus, 'conmen' and bandits were not heroes and chiefs and clerks were not collaborators. Given that British rule in Africa seemed relatively permanent, Africans participated in the Empire on terms that offered the greatest opportunity for personal enrichment and social advancement.

Most individuals had little choice but to build their lives within the confines of colonial society. Few had any inclination that British rule would last less than a century, and those who wished to get an education, enter a profession, learn an industrial trade, or engage in formal commerce had to do so within the limits of the colonial system. African healers, storytellers, and Islamic experts were often able to retain a greater degree of autonomy. For most Africans, however, participation was an attempt by common people to make colonialism more bearable. They were not traitors because there were few larger surviving African polities or institutions for them to betray. In the novel *No Longer At Ease*, Chinua Achebe's Obi, a young government clerk, wins a place in the Nigerian civil service because the people in his home village of Umofia taxed themselves to pay for his university education in England on the expectation that his training and subsequent career would pay them 'heavy dividends'.[7] In other words, Obi's strongest obligations were to his village and his kinsmen, not to his Igbo ethnic group, the Nigerian nation, or a larger sense of Africanness, and certainly not to the British Empire.

Changing Opportunities for Participation

For most Africans the difference between prosperity and poverty during the colonial era was determined by the circumstances under which they had to participate in the British Empire. These circumstances changed over time as the style and substance of British colonial rule shifted from informal empire in the nineteenth century, to direct coercion from partition to the First World War, to bureaucratized Indirect Rule in the inter-war era, to a search for more effective African allies in the face of increasing nationalist resistance after the Second World War. The inability of colonial authorities to win popular African support for any of these administrative systems forced them to court local allies as an alternative to the expense of naked authoritarianism. This 'dominance without hegemony' created opportunities for African intermediaries to exploit the limitations of the colonial state.[8]

The most coercive phase of British rule in Africa lasted from 1880 to 1914 when British soldiers, adventurers, settlers, and chartered concessionaries resorted to brute force to exert their will over resistant African societies. Drawing their authority from pseudo-scientific studies of African 'primitiveness', colonial officials viewed the Afro-Victorians and other educated

[7] Chinua Achebe, *No Longer At Ease* (New York, 1988).

[8] Cooper, 'Conflict and Connection', p. 1531; Cooper *Decolonization and African Society: The Labor Question in French and British Africa* (Cambridge, 1996), pp. 11–12.

Africans as base caricatures of Western gentlemen. During this period, the main opportunities for African participation in the Empire were as soldiers, porters, interpreters, commercial agents, and political allies. Now that they had a greater capacity to take a more direct role in running their African territories, British administrators dismissed westernized Africans as too 'detribalized' to be of value as colonial intermediaries. In South Africa, Britain abandoned the Cape élites when it came to terms with the Afrikaners after the South African War. Approximately 5 per cent of the Cape Colony's non-Europeans retained the right to vote until the 1930s, but British officials allowed Afrikaner nationalists to set exclusionary racial qualifications for citizenship in the new Union of South Africa.

The formalization of Indirect Rule during the inter-war era fixed patterns of African participation in the Empire. Increased economic development and accelerated European settlement in eastern and southern Africa created a greater need for African artisans, teachers, domestic workers, and policemen. With educated Africans relegated to minor clerical roles, colonial officials sought men with 'traditional' authority to be their key intermediaries as chiefs and headmen. In many societies these Native Authorities were actually new men whose sole claim to legitimacy was their ability to serve British interests. Under what Mahmood Mamdani has termed 'decentralized despotism' the colonial regime used arbitrarily appointed 'Native Courts' to empower chiefs to coerce rural Africans into forced labour, military conscription, and compulsory cultivation under the legitimizing guise of 'tribal custom'.[9]

Colonial officials hoped to use the power of 'tradition' to limit the influence of politically unreliable 'detribalized' educated Africans. In West Africa they ensured that appointed chiefs outnumbered the small handful of elected representatives of the westernized coastal communities in the Nigerian and Gold Coast Legislative Councils. Africans did not gain direct representation in the Legislative Councils of the settler-dominated colonies of eastern and central Africa until after the Second World War. Kenyan colonial authorities limited African political participation to carefully chosen Local Native Councils where District Officers directed the legislative agenda and held veto power over all Council activities. There were even fewer opportunities for African political participation in South Africa aside from consultative 'Tribal Councils' in the rural reserves.

[9] Mahmood Mamdani, *Citizen and Subject: Contemporary Africa and the Legacy of Late Colonialism* (Princeton, NJ, 1996), p. 52.

Patterns of African participation shifted again after the Second World War when colonial officials had to rethink their reliance on 'traditional' authorities. Faced with mounting opposition from African nationalists, they sought alliances with the small African educated and professional classes. Some of these people were from the older Afro-Victorian communities; others were more recent products of government and mission schools. Hoping to weaken African nationalism, colonial officials tried to build support for new democratic institutions by giving educated Africans a greater say in local affairs. They expanded African opportunities for participation by opening the civil service and the professions. This process of 'Africanization' was easier in West Africa than in eastern and central Africa where institutional racism proved far more resilient. In South Africa the 1947 electoral victory of the National Party on a platform of white supremacy meant that Africanization was out of the question in the Union. The development of apartheid as a governing ideology in South Africa ended opportunities for African advancement under the increasingly independent segregationist regime.

Shifting colonial distinctions of race, class, and gender determined the nature of individual African participation in the Empire. Although the Colonial Office denied the existence of an official colour bar (racial discrimination) in Africa, European administrators and settlers had considerable autonomy in discriminating against Africans in the civil service, schools, church, and commerce. Despite official commitments to 'non-racialism', informal racial discrimination limited African opportunity and advancement in almost every African colony. West African clerks and doctors served in separate African branches of the civil service in spite of the fact that some held higher degrees than their European counterparts. British administrators did not want to socialize with them or pay them equal wages, and justified dismissing African doctors on the grounds that European patients would not see them. No African in the Tanganyikan civil service rose higher than simple clerk after 1938, and East African authorities preferred Indians and Goans for mid-level positions in the civil service and the police on the grounds that they were more 'civilized'. In southern Africa, where European manpower was even more plentiful, few Africans rose to responsible administrative positions. British officials relied on African intermediaries out of political and economic necessity, but the need to maintain a sharp social division between the colonizer and the colonized meant that African participation in the Empire was sharply restricted by race.

Yet in terms of class, the relatively generous remuneration, privileges, and status of civil service made administrative employment one of the surest avenues to social advancement during the colonial era. Government employment allowed educated Africans to lead relatively affluent lives and often provided the financial resources that enabled them to invest in land and private trading ventures. African civil servants therefore guarded their prerogatives jealousy. They formed organizations like the Gambia Native Defensive Union during the First World War and the Tanganyika African Association in 1929 to protect their status and lobby colonial officials to improve their conditions of service.

In the non-governmental sector, African opportunities for participation in the Empire were largely shaped by the contradictions of Britain's economic goals in Africa. With significant direct financial support from London out of the question before the Second World War, each territory had to attract foreign investment. Yet colonial policy barred them from developing local enterprises that might compete with metropolitan commercial interests. Local officials therefore promoted export-based economies that produced cash crops and minerals for global markets. These agricultural and mining ventures relied on inexpensive African labour to compensate for limited capital investment and high production and transportation costs. Colonial regimes therefore had an incentive to limit African opportunities for accumulation, to discourage competition with European enterprises, and ensure a constant supply of cheap labour. Yet they also needed to stimulate African commodity production and consumption to boost export revenues and develop local markets for British goods.[10]

These restrictions put the majority of Africans in a difficult position. If they were unable to exploit the limited economic opportunities provided by British rule they had to survive either through subsistence agriculture and pastoralism, unskilled wage labour, or employment in the informal sector of the economy. In the early colonial era, British administrators filled their labour requirements through open coercion or by transforming African institutions of reciprocal labour obligations into direct tribute to the Native Authorities. By the inter-war era, the need for a more stable labour force, coupled with humanitarian criticism of forced labour, led colonial officials to rely primarily on direct taxation to drive Africans into wage labour. Land

[10] Sara Berry, *No Condition is Permanent: The Social Dynamics of Agrarian Change in Sub-Saharan Africa* (Madison, Wisc., 1993).

alienation and the creation of native reserves in the settler-dominated societies of Kenya, the Rhodesias, and South Africa forced Africans into the labour market by restricting their ability to practise pastoralism and subsistence agriculture. The threat of starvation or being arrested as a tax defaulter also compelled Africans to shift to agricultural commodity production. Those with insufficient access to land or markets had to seek paid work with governmental and private employers. In cases where there were insufficient opportunities for local employment, they had to travel great distances as labour migrants to work on African-owned cocoa and palm oil enterprises in West Africa, settler farms and corporate sisal plantations in East Africa, or the gold, copper, and diamond mines in South Africa and the Rhodesias.

There were relatively few opportunities for real social advancement in this form of African participation. A few successful farmers and migrant labourers prospered by investing their wages in land, stock, and commercial enterprises, and were often more efficient than settler farmers in producing for local and international markets. Yet discriminatory licensing laws, commodity marketing boards, transportation problems, and land shortages meant that African small-scale farmers and unskilled labourers often faced economic and social marginalization. Work in the police, army, prisons, railways, and docks offered reasonably lucrative employment to some unskilled and semi-skilled men in West and East Africa, but fears of armed Africans and 'civilized' labour policies reserving skilled positions for Europeans closed off most of these opportunities in southern Africa.

Gender was the final factor in shaping the degree and nature of African participation in the Empire. Colonial officials allied with older African men in their attempt to harness the forces of indigenous 'tradition'. Believing that chiefly power stemmed from patriarchal institutions of authority, field officers co-operated with male elders in using customary laws governing marriage and inheritance to exert social control over younger men and women.[11] Most territorial governments tried to maintain the integrity of 'traditional' rural society by confining women to the countryside with gender-biased pass laws and restrictive urban residency permits. However, colonial officials encouraged some women to settle in army barracks and copper-mining compounds on the assumption that African men were easier to discipline when they were married. Military officers and mine-owners

[11] Jane Parpart, 'Sexuality and Power on the Zambian Copperbelt, 1926–1964', in S. B. Stichter and J. L. Parpart, eds., *Patriarchy and Class* (Boulder, Colo., 1988).

used the privilege of married status for soldiers and miners as a powerful recruiting inducement, and believed that formalized family relationships discouraged drinking, gambling, fighting, and prostitution.

In the first decades of the colonial era it was also not unusual for junior British administrative officers to form their own conjugal relationships with Africans. Senior officials tolerated this 'concubinage' until scandalous reports of field officers using their authority to coerce sex from African women drew public attention. In 1908 fears of miscegenation and potential political subversion by mixed-race children led the Colonial Office to issue a circular barring its employees from having sexual contact with Africans. Nevertheless, it was not unusual for African women to seek greater privileges and autonomy by maintaining covert relationships with young unmarried British District Officers.[12]

Apart from these special cases, there were very few opportunities for African women to play a formal role in the colonial system. Aside from a small number of female elementary school teachers and social welfare workers, the African sectors of colonial bureaucracies were almost entirely male institutions. As a result, African women were largely confined to the informal sectors of the colonial economy. They played a dominant role in urban petty trading in Nigeria and the Gold Coast. In eastern and southern Africa there were fewer opportunities for female participation. Women seeking to escape the confines of rural society in these territories had to survive by working as domestic servants for European employers or by catering to African labour migrants. In the latter case they often supported themselves through bootlegging, prostitution, or urban agriculture.[13]

Varieties of Participation

Formal African participation in the colonial system fell into four broad categories: administrative, coercive, cultural, and commercial. British officials depended on Africans for administrative and coercive assistance in governing and policing the colonies. They also needed African participation in schools in order to produce clerks and tradesmen, and in churches to establish the humanitarian and civilizing credentials that legitimized British

[12] Ronald Hyam, 'Concubinage and the Colonial Service: The Crewe Circular, 1909', *Journal of Imperial and Commonwealth History*, XIV (1986), pp. 170–86; and Terence Gavaghan, *Of Lions and Dung Beetles* (Ilfracombe, Devon, 1999).

[13] Luise White, *The Comforts of Home: Prostitution in Colonial Nairobi* (Chicago, 1990).

rule. Finally, difficulties in attracting foreign investment forced British officials to rely on African commercial assistance in developing their African Empire.

Native authorities were the cornerstone of the rural sector of colonial bureaucracies. Born out of European manpower shortages, economic necessity, and the aristocratic biases of British officials, Indirect Rule relied on politically influential Africans to assist in colonial governance as emirs, paramount chiefs, chiefs, and village headmen. It was more of a philosophy than a concrete set of administrative regulations, and its actual application in individual colonies varied considerably. Inspired in part by British experiences in India, Indirect Rule was first implemented in Africa by Theophilus Shepstone in early colonial Natal to co-opt influential local rulers into the rural administration as tax collectors and labour organizers. He appointed new chiefs if there were no viable or sufficiently co-operative candidates in a particular location.[14]

After the partition of the rest of Africa by Britain and other European powers in the last decades of the nineteenth century, Frederick Lugard further refined and expanded this model as Governor of Nigeria. Seeking to co-opt local institutions of authority, Lugard transformed the Hausa Emirs of northern Nigeria into British intermediaries by making them tax collectors and arbiters of customary law. He stripped them of their sovereignty and military prerogatives, and placed a European 'resident' in each court to ensure that they did not become too independent. [15] British officials followed similar administrative engineering policies in the Kingdom of Buganda. Under the guise of Indirect Rule they transformed the Bugandan Kabaka and his nobles into colonial clients. In the early days of British rule in Uganda colonial officials used this Gandan civil service to pacify and govern the rest of the Protectorate.

British administrators were even more inventive in African societies that lacked centralized pre-colonial institutions of authority. In what British authorities termed the 'pagan and primitive' communities of Nigeria, Lugard transformed local dignitaries who could demonstrate a measure of 'traditional' authority into chiefs. Most of the 'warrant chiefs' in eastern Nigerian stateless communities had no claim to pre-colonial legitimacy and

[14] John Lambert, 'Chiefship in Early Colonial Natal, 1843–1879', *Journal of Southern African Studies* (*JSAS*), XXI (1995), pp. 269–85.

[15] Frederick Lugard, *The Dual Mandate in Tropical Africa* (London, 1965).

earned their positions by co-operating with British officials. Colonial administrators were equally flexible in eastern Africa. In the Uganda Protectorate District Officers governed the Lango, who had largely egalitarian institutions of authority, by selecting helpful members of the local community as their chiefs.[16] Similarly British administrators in southern Nyasaland found their chiefs from the ranks of *capitaos* (agricultural overseers) and even promoted the Governor's former cook.[17]

Indirect Rule was built on compromise, and the customary authority from which the colonial political intermediaries drew their authority was often highly fictive. Many chiefs therefore had difficulty collecting fines and taxes, mobilizing labour, and maintaining law and order. Participation in the Empire placed them in a difficult position. Although they were officially traditional rulers, they drew their authority from their ability to execute colonial policy rather than the support of their supposed constituents. Territorial governments paid the chiefs with either direct salaries or a share of local tax revenues, but these relatively limited rewards were small compensation for the social alienation that came with service to the colonial state. Field administrators therefore often turned a blind eye when they engaged in personal accumulation by using their offices to acquire land, commercial licences, and additional wives.

Not surprisingly, these prerogatives sparked tension between educated Africans and traditional authorities. S. I. Kale, an African teacher at the Church Missionary Society grammar school in Lagos, complained that Indirect Rule gave Nigerian headmen power far out of proportion to their authority in pre-colonial times, and complained that their administrative tyranny forced progressive young men to flee the countryside.[18] Asante chiefs on the Gold Coast who exceeded pre-colonial limits on their authority were often destooled by their resistive subjects. Yet the chiefs were not always entirely at odds with the educated élites. Many West African traditional authorities valued Western education and were receptive to democratic institutions that did not substantially undermine their authority. In regions where British officials gave local people a say in choosing a chief or headmen

[16] Beverly Gartrell, 'British Administrators, Colonial Chiefs, and the Comfort of Tradition: An Example from Uganda', *African Studies Review*, XXVI (1983), pp. 1–24.

[17] Tony Woods, '*Capitaos* and Chiefs: Oral Tradition and Colonial Society in Malawi', *International Journal of African Historical Studies*, XXIII (1990), pp. 259–68.

[18] S. I. Kale, 'Must Education Lead to Detribalization?', *Oversea Education*, XII (1941), pp. 60–64.

the electors often selected educated men. Nevertheless, the overall status and influence of the chiefs declined dramatically after the Second World War as politically minded Africans increasingly came to see them as standing in the way of economic development and eventual independence.

In comparison with the shifting power of the chiefs the status and influence of Africans in the formal civil service remained largely intact throughout the colonial era. Once Africans were relegated to subordinate positions in the colonial bureaucracies after partition, a simple primary school education became the main qualification for a junior clerkship. Educated and semi-educated intermediaries ran the courts, accounting offices, post offices, railway ticket offices, government technical departments, and district field offices. They often had considerable autonomy due to lax supervision, and it is not surprising that many enriched themselves by abusing their prerogatives. Court clerks and interpreters in south-eastern Nigeria used the Native Court system to issue summons and arrest warrants on their own authority. They exploited their link between District Officers and appointed warrant chiefs to extort bribes by taking advantage of the largely illiterate general population.[19] Most of these civil servants rarely faced social pressure to behave more responsibly because they came from westernized coastal enclaves and had few ties to local communities.

Yet the lot of a colonial clerk was not easy. Although their terms of service and unofficial prerogatives provided substantial opportunities for personal enrichment, they were often mistrusted and abused by their British superiors. Joyce Cary's *Mister Johnson* illustrates the common prejudice among colonial officials that African clerks were at best caricatures of educated men and at worst inherently lazy and corrupt.[20] These biases were due in part to the vulnerability that European field officers experienced living in the countryside amongst a sea of Africans. African clerks were their bridge to the general population, and they never could be sure that their administrative partners were not twisting their orders to serve their own ends. In the years leading up to the First World War, there were several notorious incidents in the region where District Officers beat and racially abused clerks for failing to show proper deference. African civil servants in eastern and southern Africa were largely spared this mistreatment because they never achieved the status or autonomy of their better-educated West African counterparts.

[19] See Jonathan Derrick, 'The "Native Clerk" in Colonial West Africa', *African Affairs*, LXXXII (1983), pp. 61–74.

[20] Joyce Cary, *Mister Johnson* (New York, 1964).

The West African clerks acquired a reputation for insubordination; that is, for standing up for their rights. The racial bar on African advancement in the colonial bureaucracies led many into politics. Others left government employment entirely to become private businessmen. E. F. Small, a Sierra Leonean clerk who served in the Freetown Post Office and the Gambian Public Works Department, quit the civil service when his superiors rejected his repeated applications for promotion. He worked for a French commercial firm and the Wesleyan Mission in the Gambia before becoming an organizer for the local branch of the National Congress of British West Africa. Small also tried to follow in the footsteps of Marcus Garvey by founding an African co-operative movement in the Gambia.[21] Not all African clerks, however, had an adversarial relationship with their British superiors. Robert Cudjoe, a Fante carpenter turned senior interpreter, became a valued member of the Nigerian civil service. Writing in the introduction to Cudjoe's short autobiography, a British field officer described his African colleague as the 'best of companions' who was 'trusted by all'. Cudjoe generally reciprocated these feelings: 'I very highly appreciate the kindness shown towards me by the past and present Nigerian Administrative Officers... under whose tactful ability and sportsmanship... I had the pleasure of serving'.[22]

British officials recruited African soldiers and policemen from an entirely different segment of the colonial society than they did their administrative intermediaries. Where education was a prerequisite for employment in the civil service, the colonial army and police forces preferred to recruit illiterate men from remote rural areas. British officers did not expect their African soldiers and policemen to think independently or question policy. The primary mission of rank-and-file colonial soldiers and policemen was to discourage overt political challenges to British rule, support the traditional authorities, and, in eastern and southern Africa, ensure the safety of European settler communities.

Britain would not have been able to subdue its African colonies without African soldiers. In the decades after partition of Africa, colonial authorities initially formed political and military alliances with African communities to augment their relatively meager regular forces. These 'native auxiliaries'

[21] Langley Ayodele, 'The Gambia Section of the National Congress of British West Africa', *Africa*, XLIX (1969), pp. 382–95.

[22] Robert Cudjoe, 'Some Reminiscences of a Senior Interpreter', *The Nigerian Field*, XVIII (1953), pp. 148, 164.

participated in the conquest of British Africa because they viewed the British as useful allies against local enemies. In Kenya, Maasai *moran* (young fighters) needed the captured livestock that they earned for helping defeat their Kalenjin and Luhya rivals because their own herds had been wiped out by rinderpest (bovine pleuro-pneumonia). British officials dismissed their local military allies once their political control of the colonies was secure.[23]

By the First World War most colonies maintained small conventional armies consisting entirely of African soldiers led by tiny cadres of British officers. These forces underpinned civil authority by arresting tax resistors, enforcing cattle quarantines, suppressing millenarian movements, and breaking strikes by African labourers and miners. In wartime they served the Empire as frontline combat troops. During the First World War, British military authorities also conscripted approximately one million 'carriers' to transport supplies and munitions during the conquest of German East Africa. Similarly, the Union government raised the South African Native Labour Contingent to serve as enlisted military labourers in metropolitan British ports during the conflict.

In West and East Africa, Africans served in the Royal West African Frontier Force and the King's African Rifles. These units were regionally based infantry regiments linking territorial battalions raised in the individual colonies. There were far fewer opportunities for African military participation in settler-dominated societies in the south. The governments of Southern Rhodesia and the Union of South Africa never raised peacetime African military units because they worried about the political consequences of arming even a small segment of their disenfranchised African majorities. Southern Rhodesia grudgingly created the Rhodesia African Rifles for service in the Far East during the Second World War, but South Africa would only allow Africans to join the unarmed Native Military Corps during the conflict. The Union also used its political influence to ensure that Africans in the High Commission territories of Bechuanaland, Basutoland, and Swaziland only served in the labour-oriented African Auxiliary Pioneer Corps.[24]

On the surface, it seems inexplicable that African soldiers would serve the authoritarian colonial regime. Yet colonial military authorities were careful never to use soldiers against their local communities. The majority of

[23] Richard Waller, 'The Maasai and the British 1895–1905: The Origins of an Alliance', *Journal of African History* (hereafter *JAH*), XVII (1976), pp. 529–53.

[24] Ashley Jackson, *Botswana 1939–1945: An African Country at War* (Oxford, 1999).

Africans in the first colonial units in West Africa during the late nineteenth century were former slaves. Once colonial armies were more established most African soldiers were technically volunteers. Military service was one of the most lucrative and prestigious forms of employment open to unskilled Africans. Although military pay scales were low compared to salaries in the administrative sector, they were relatively generous in comparison to what could be earned by unskilled civilian labour. Colonial authorities only resorted to formal conscription in wartime. In theory, the Colonial Office would only allow the conscription of Africans for non-combatant labour units. In practice, there were many instances where traditional authorities and District Officers forced Africans to join the army. Colonial officials would often replace chiefs and headmen who failed to meet specific recruiting quotas. During the Second World War, the Commissioner of Kenya's Nyanza Province ordered a man who refused to volunteer for service to dress like a woman as a sign of his cowardice. In other cases, Africans joined the army to avoid more unpopular forms of civil labour conscription that required service on settler farms, plantations, and public work projects. These informal methods of impressment allowed colonial officials to claim that all African combat troops had enlisted willingly.[25]

Many Africans were indeed volunteers. British officers believed that the best African soldiers came from specific ethnic groups that they deemed 'martial races'. According to colonial stereotypes, some of these 'warrior tribes' included Muslim communities from the West African savanna (known collectively as Hausa in British military parlance), the Kamba, Acholi, and Nyamwezi in East Africa, and the Tonga and Ngoni in Central Africa. In reality, the willingness of individuals to accept military discipline was determined by their integration into the colonial economy. Men who had access to enough land to support themselves through subsistence agriculture or pastoralism had little interest in military service. Moreover, elementary school graduates and successful commodity producers found military service equally unappealing. There was little truth in colonial stereotypes characterizing specific 'tribes' as having inborn military talents. The colonial army attracted Africans from all communities who could not otherwise earn enough money to support themselves and pay their taxes.[26]

[25] Timothy Parsons, *The African Rank-and-File: Social Implications of Colonial Service in the King's African Rifles*, 1902–1964 (Portsmouth, NH, 1999).

[26] Timothy Parsons, ' "Wakamba Warriors are Soldiers of the Queen": The Evolution of the Kamba as a Martial Race, 1890–1970', *Ethnohistory*, XLVI (1999).

Strict military discipline made it relatively difficult for individual soldiers to follow the example of civilian clerks in exploiting their status as government servants. Yet Africans often played upon the sympathies of British officers, who were concerned with maintaining morale, to get colonial military authorities to intervene on their behalf in a host of domestic matters including land tenure, grazing rights, business licences, and bridewealth disputes. Moreover, relatively generous military wages and useful vocational training often gave African ex-servicemen considerable status and influence in their home communities. Military service was therefore most appealing to unskilled and uneducated men from rural areas. British officers followed strict ethnic recruiting quotas, but Africans from societies deemed 'non-martial' by the recruiters masqueraded as members of 'martial races' to gain access to the colonial army.

British military authorities maintained control over African military intermediaries by isolating them from the rest of colonial society. Rigorous training, comparatively high wages, and exemptions from forced labour and taxation encouraged colonial soldiers to consider themselves superior to African civilians. British officers tried to further isolate their soldiers by regulating their relations with women. Following the practices of mine-owners in the Rhodesias, they tried to 'stabilize' the African soldiery by encouraging them to keep wives and children within the barracks in peacetime. Their attempt to regiment African military families created opportunities for women to participate in the coercive arm of the colonial system. In the Royal West African Frontier Force, soldiers 'wives' supplied domestic labour in the barracks and were overseen by a *magagjia*, or head woman, who wore a sergeant's sash and stripes. These women gained access to the prestige and resources of colonial military service by forming conjugal relationships with African soldiers. Yet barracks life also subjected military women to army discipline, and the spouse of the most senior African sergeant often beat disruptive women.[27]

African service in the colonial police forces required a different type of coercive participation. Colonial soldiers provided the threat of lethal force to stifle overt African political opposition to British rule. African policemen, on the other hand, played a much more direct role in ensuring compliance with colonial policy. The prevention and detection of crime were generally sec-

[27] Anthony Clayton and Killingray David, *Khaki and Blue: Military and Police in British Colonial Africa* (Athens, Oh., 1989).

ondary concerns for colonial police forces unless Europeans were the potential victims. Most colonies created separate branches of the police to deal with urban and rural areas. The Nigerian Police Force had jurisdiction over towns and villages, while the Native Authority Police maintained order in the countryside. Lacking the consent of the governed, British officials created a host of auxiliary and irregular police units to ensure that the restive African majority respected colonial laws and regulations. These included mine police to maintain discipline in the compounds, forest guards to keep squatters out of forest reserves, game wardens to prevent poaching, railway police to protect transportation routes, and, in the Gold Coast, escort police to guard shipments of bullion from the mines.[28]

The evolution of formal African police forces largely mirrored the development of colonial administrative policy. Before the First World War service in the colonial police was not very different from service in the colonial army. The original police units were paramilitary constabularies that played a direct role in stamping out African resistance. As in the early armies, colonial officials relied primarily on African allies and auxiliaries during this period. The Southern Rhodesian Matabeleland Native Police was made up almost entirely of men supplied by Lobengula, the last king of the Ndebele. In the inter-war era, colonial authorities raised village and 'tribal' police forces to enforce the authority of chiefs and the Native Courts. Native Authorities in Northern Rhodesia were responsible for order in the countryside, and exercised power through village special constables known as *kapasus*. Rank-and-file civil policemen had few responsibilities and served mostly as guards and patrolmen. Many colonies, especially those with large settler populations, also raised special paramilitary units to deal with mounting anti-colonial agitation following the Second World War. Police mobile forces in Kenya, Uganda, Northern Rhodesia, and Nyasaland trained for riot control, but were also equipped with armoured cars and automatic weapons. Most police forces during this period also included surveillance and intelligence branches to monitor and infiltrate African nationalist movements.[29]

[28] David Killingray, 'Guarding the Extending Frontier: Policing the Gold Coast, 1865–1913', in David Anderson and David Killingray, eds., *Policing the Empire: Government, Authority and Control, 1830–1940* (Manchester, 1991); E. I. Steinhart, 'Hunters, Poachers and Gamekeepers: Towards a Social History of Hunting in Colonial Kenya', *JAH*, XXX (1989), pp. 247–64.

[29] Robert Foran, *The Kenya Police, 1887–1960* (London, 1962); John McCracken, 'Coercion and Control in Nyasaland: Aspects of the History of a Colonial Police Force', *JAH*, XXVII (1986), pp. 127–47.

Rank-and-file policemen usually came from the same impoverished rural communities that supplied manpower to the armed forces. In the late nineteenth century the first members of the Gold Coast Armed Police, also known as the Hausa Police, were former slaves, some of whom had been purchased by an enterprising British commander specifically for this purpose. Africans were more willing to enlist in the colonial police after the First World War. They were drawn by relatively generous pay for unskilled labour, tax exemptions, service gratuities, and immunity from manual labour. In mining compounds in the Rhodesias, mine police received better pay, special uniforms, and superior housing. Many of these men were ex-servicemen who had already demonstrated a willingness to obey orders.

There were much greater opportunities for skilled and educated Africans to advance in the colonial police than there were in the colonial army. European manpower shortages created a need for capable Africans to interpret the criminal code, keep records, and investigate crimes. In West Africa elementary school graduates could reach intermediate ranks in the regular police forces. This was in sharp contrast to the situation in the army where the officer corps remained entirely European until the end of the Second World War when political considerations led colonial governments to commission a few Africans in the Royal West African Frontier Force. There were fewer opportunities for Africans in Britain's eastern and southern African colonies where inferior schools and settler biases meant that Europeans and Indians filled most of the skilled positions and intermediate ranks in the colonial police.

African policemen faced considerably more social stress than their military counterparts. Although they usually served away from their homes, their enforcement of repressive colonial laws and regulations made them unpopular in the larger African community. Most of the early police units experienced disciplinary problems and high desertion levels. African policemen also abused their authority by demanding bribes and social deference from civilians. These attempts at personal enrichment undercut the legitimacy and effectiveness of colonial police forces. Police 'corruption' became such a problem in Nigeria after the Second World War that one police Commissioner ordered his men to sew up the pockets of their uniforms. Although this behaviour was certainly larcenous, rank-and-file policemen had little reason to identify with the alien communities they policed or to uphold their oath of service to the colonial state. Even trusted intermediaries kept a close watch on their own interests. Senior Northern Rhodesian police officials found that African informers for the Special Branch often had their own ties to suspect political organizations. Thus, African policemen operated on both sides of the law as their interests dictated.

There were other, more informal, forms of African participation in the Empire. Colonial officials needed cultural intermediaries to transmit British values to the African majority through the media of the church and school. Most of these clergymen and teachers worked for the missions rather than the colonial state, but they built tacit consent for the colonial enterprise and provided a humanitarian justification for British rule. Although their semi-official role in the Empire seems relatively minor, they were potentially far more threatening to the stability of the colonial regime than insubordinate African soldiers or policemen. Their familiarity with the legitimizing ideologies of British rule gave them the ability to mobilize African resistance by adapting and reinterpreting Western cultural values to raise doubts about the morality of colonialism.

In most colonies British administrators compensated for fiscal and manpower shortages by sub-contracting responsibility for African social services to Christian missionaries. The missions' primary goal was to win converts, but most viewed schooling and health care as part of the evangelical process. Although individual missionaries criticized forced labour, land alienation, and overt racial discrimination, the missions played an integral role in bringing African daily life under the influence of the colonial state. Evangelism required intimate contact with Africans from all walks of life, and the missions relied on African religious instructors, known as catechists, to reach rural communities. In the 1910s the Church of Scotland Mission sent twenty-four African teacher-evangelists from the Livingstonia mission in Nyasaland to extend its sphere of influence into the neighbouring districts of Northern Rhodesia. David Kaunda and Helen Nyirenda, the parents of Zambia's first president, were the sole founders of an outstation at Lubwa that would grow into one of the premier African educational institutions in Northern Rhodesia.[30] It was much easier for Africans to advance within the Christian missionary community than in the colonial civil service, and many African clergymen acquired considerable prestige as interpreters of European culture for local communities. Although European mission leaders tried to maintain close supervision over their catechists and converts, the very nature of rural evangelism gave African clergymen a great deal of autonomy.

[30] At Ipenburg, *'All Good Men': The Development of Lubwa Mission, Chinsali, Zambia, 1905–1967* (Frankfurt, 1992).

The colonial education system was equally dependent on African cultural intermediaries. Literacy and fluency in English were keys to white collar employment, and Africans embraced Western education as the most viable means of social advancement during the colonial era. Many British administrators worried that a literary education in English would have a disruptive influence on 'traditional' African society, and Lugard tried to protect the authority of the Nigerian Emirs by banning Christian mission schools from the north. Colonial officials tried to further minimize the destabilizing influence of Western-style schooling by promoting a vocational curriculum in African vernacular languages to produce useful village handymen rather than ambitious clerks. In West Africa these efforts were undercut by well-established mission secondary schools that had been producing English-speaking clerks, clergymen, and doctors since the nineteenth century. Conversely, settlers in eastern and southern Africa used their influence to promote vernacular vocational schooling modelled on the industrial African-American education system of the segregated South.[31]

Humanitarian idealism and practical necessity obliged colonial governments to offer a literary education to their African subjects. Colonial schooling appeared to validate Britain's 'civilizing' mission in Africa. It also produced skilled artisans to serve British commercial interests and clerks for the lower levels of the civil service. Colonial officials hoped elementary civics courses would mitigate the destabilizing effects of Western education by teaching respect for Native Authorities and loyalty to the Empire. Most missionaries shared these goals and sought to attract converts with the promise of a commercially useful education. Thus, the territorial governments and the missions were willing partners in African education. Most colonies only supported one or two state-run schools, and delegated responsibility for the bulk of African education to the missions.

The quality of these schools was often quite low. Lacking the financial resources to hire Europeans with established teaching credentials, colonial educators relied on African teachers, many of whom had completed only a few years of elementary education. These teachers staffed the village, bush, and kraal schools that gave most Africans their first taste of Western-style education. Their simple curriculum focused on basic literacy in vernacular

[31] Kenneth King, *Pan-Africanism and Education: A Study of Race, Philanthropy and Education in the Southern United States and East Africa* (Oxford, 1971); R. Hunt Davis, 'Charles T Loram and the American Model for African Education in South Africa', in Peter Kallaway, ed., *Apartheid and Education: The Education of Black South Africa* (Johannesburg, 1984).

languages and had a strong religious bent.[32] Africans teachers at these small schools were extremely influential in rural communities because the missions lacked the ability to supervise them directly.

Colonial officials worried about the political dangers of unsupervised schools and tried to prevent African teachers from teaching subversive ideas. Most governments introduced mandatory registration for African schools and teachers during the inter-war era. Responding to the perception that Kikuyu schools taught anti-British propaganda during the Mau Mau Emergency in the 1950s, Kenyan authorities required all African educators to join a government sponsored union and hold a special teaching licence. Similarly, South Africa's 1953 Bantu Education Act took over all African schools from the missions, transformed African teachers into government servants, and created an official curriculum that reinforced the values of the Nationalist Party's apartheid system.[33]

These supervisory measures did little to blunt the social and political influence of African educators. Although teachers in African schools were often badly paid and overworked with extra-curricular obligations, teaching was still a relatively lucrative white-collar profession. African teachers were widely respected for their literacy and understanding of Western culture. They served on local government councils, church committees, and the managing boards of co-operative societies. Colonial teaching could also lead to a career in politics. Future African Presidents like Julius Nyerere of Tanzania and Kenneth Kaunda of Zambia were former teachers. South African schools were one of the few sources of employment for educated Africans, but low wages and racial discrimination radicalized young teachers in the 1940s. Many joined the African National Congress Youth League and recruited promising students for the anti-apartheid struggle.

Colonial officials tried to limit the potentially disruptive side effects of Western education by giving Christianity a strong place in the African curriculum. Yet their reliance on African participation in colonial schools and churches created opportunities for their cultural intermediaries. Although teachers and clergymen could not emulate African clerks and policemen in using their status to exploit the weaknesses of the colonial system

[32] J. W. C Dougall, *The Village Teacher's Guide: A Book of Guidance for African Teachers* (London, 1931); Southern Rhodesia, Department of Native Development, *Junior School Syllabus* (Salisbury, 1932).

[33] J. F. A Callander, *Handbook for Teachers* (Nairobi, 1961); Kallaway, ed., *Apartheid and Education.*

directly, they had access to the ideological underpinnings of British rule. Christianity and a Western education were keys to social advancement within the Empire. Eager to exploit the most viable means of personal enrichment within the narrow confines of the colonial system, educated Africans became frustrated by hypocritical racial and cultural discrimination within the schools and missions. They recognized that an 'adapted' industrial curriculum would not give them the skills or credentials for a professional or civil service career. As student protests and strikes became more common during the 1920s and 1930s, many Africans concluded that they needed direct access to the fruits of Western education and material culture.

African clergymen and teachers throughout the continent therefore joined with community leaders to establish their own independent churches and schools. In the 1920s, Reuben Spartas, a Gandan clerk and ex-serviceman, founded an independent African branch of the Greek Orthodox Church to circumvent the dominance of the Anglican and Roman Catholic missions in Uganda. Within ten years, Spartas' African Orthodox Church claimed over 5,000 members and supported thirty church centres, twenty-three schools, a monastery, and a convent. Similarly, the African-run American School Movement in South Africa established its own schools to circumvent government limitations on African education.[34] The heyday of Christian independence came in the inter-war years, but many African educational experiments eventually failed due to fiscal insolvency and government harassment. Aside from a greater emphasis on politics and English language instruction, most independent schools followed a curriculum that differed little from the mission programme of instruction. Thus, religious and educational independence was another form of participation in the Empire. Although the independent churches and schools rejected colonial political values, their primary goal was to gain access to the legitimizing ideologies of British rule and credentials for a white-collar career.

Given the limitations of employment in the administrative, coercive, and cultural sectors, many Africans sought greater mobility and autonomy in the commercial sphere. Lacking the ability and inclination to develop Africa along Western lines, British officials, businessmen, and investors sought African assistance in making the colonies economically viable. In addition

[34] F. B. Welbourn, *East African Rebels: A Study of Some Independent Churches* (London, 1961); Robert Edgar, 'African Educational Protest in South Africa: The American School Movement in the Transkei in the 1920s', in Kallaway, ed., *Apartheid and Education.*

to requiring large amounts of unskilled labour, they needed bookkeepers, mining and agricultural overseers, skilled artisans, and domestic labourers. They also depended on Africans to mobilize labour, organize local and regional trade, and consume Western imports. To some extent colonial officials relied on Syrians in West Africa and Indians in eastern and southern Africa to fill these roles, but these intermediaries were more expensive, politically unreliable, and tended to touch off popular resentment because many Africans believed that these non-Western middlemen were profiting at their expense.

The strength of the colonial economy ultimately depended on African commercial participation. As was the case in the administrative sphere, Western businesses could not function without African clerical assistance. Commercial clerks typed correspondence, managed accounts, and conducted sales. Skilled African labour was equally important. Before becoming a government interpreter in Nigeria, Robert Cudjoe worked as a carpenter building military barracks, administrative housing, and ferries. A small élite of African tradesmen also kept the colonial railways running. East African Railways and Harbours, a corporation run by the East Africa High Commission, rewarded and stabilized its skilled African labour force with generous pay, housing, and educational benefits. These jobs were so lucrative and prestigious that most of these tradesmen spent their entire working lives with the railway.[35]

Skilled Africans also played key intermediary roles in large European commercial enterprises. Although discriminatory legislation in South Africa and the Rhodesias reserved the best paying positions for Europeans, mine-owners still needed trained African overseers and drill sharpeners, carpenters, mechanics, and clerks. As in the East African railways, key African workers received substantially better pay and benefits than the average unskilled miner. These essential commercial intermediaries also traded on their economic importance to win concessions from their employers. Skilled miners were some of the most politically active segments of the African labour force and played leading roles in strikes and labour protests in mines in the Gold Coast and southern Africa.

There were also more informal commercial opportunities for Africans within the Empire. Just as crime and corruption were unsanctioned forms of

[35] R. D. Grillo, *African Railwaymen: Solidarity and Opposition in an East African Labour Force* (Cambridge, 1973).

African participation in the colonial administrative and coercive systems, ambitious Africans engaged in independent entrepreneurial activities that put them in direct competition with British business interests. Colonial rule helped commercialize African agriculture by opening new markets and expanding cash flows into rural economies. African farmers with sufficient access to land and labour responded to these opportunities by producing for the market. Other enterprising Africans tried to capitalize on this new wealth by becoming commodity speculators, transporters, and petty traders. Politically influential metropolitan capitalist interests, mine-owners, and settler farmers often managed to stifle African competition by claiming that these activities increased overall labour prices and produced adulterated products. Yet the forced economy of colonial rule meant that financially strapped territorial governments had at least to tolerate, if not encourage, indigenous African economic development.

African commodity production was most viable in West Africa where well-organized growers continued to produce cocoa, palm oil, and groundnuts for the lucrative export market. Prosperous Nigerian coastal cocoa farmers pooled their resources through the Agege Planters Union to lend money to small farmers, enforce crop quality standards, and encourage the spread of cocoa farming into the interior.[36] African commodity production was so efficient that export tariffs rather than taxes became the primary source of government revenue in British West Africa. Large expatriate growers had difficulty competing and British officials in Nigeria turned down Sir William Lever's request for a palm oil concession in the colony. Although European merchants effectively denied Africans direct access to export markets through discriminatory shipping monopolies, African growers stopped them from fixing low commodity prices by withholding their crops from market.

African commercial opportunities were far more limited in eastern and southern Africa. Nevertheless, the export of African cotton became a cornerstone of the Ugandan economy. In Kenya, where African agriculture was largely limited to the 'native reserves', lower capital costs and familiarity with local conditions made African farmers more effective in mobilizing labour and developing markets than settlers or plantation owners. Many less

[36] A. G. Hopkins, 'Innovation in a Colonial Context: African Origins of the Nigerian Cocoa-Farming Industry, 1880–1920', in Clive Dewey and A. G. Hopkins, eds., *The Imperial Impact: Studies in the Economic History of Africa and India* (London, 1978).

experienced European farmers needed government intervention to procure cheap labour and stifle African economic competition. Similarly, African cotton growers in southern Nyasaland outbid their European counterparts for African labour, and used secret societies to mobilize extra workers from local communities.[37] Conversely, entrenched settler interests in South African and Southern Rhodesia produced more discriminatory land and labour policies that made it far more difficult for Africans to compete directly with European farmers.

Given the degree of institutional discrimination that Africans experienced in government service, the missions, education, and commerce it is not surprising that many turned to more larcenous forms of participation in the Empire. The colonial regime was an alien autocratic institution that had little legitimacy or popular support. Few Africans felt a moral obligation to respect the sanctity of colonial laws. In this environment, activities that British officials termed 'corrupt' or 'criminal' became valid strategies for accumulation and personal advancement as Africans became proficient at exploiting the weaknesses of colonial institutions. In urban areas, burglary rings targeted government offices, churches, shops, and the homes of European settlers. East African 'confidence' men raised fraud and impersonation to an art-form by taking advantage of colonial administrators' relative ignorance of African society. During the Second World War they convinced civil and military officials to hand over tens of thousands of shillings by forging pay and discharge certificates and by posing as ex-servicemen. Africans coped with the colour bar in settler societies by creating fake registration documents and passes giving themselves access to 'white' areas. In South Africa, Sam Pholotho wrote his own work permit granting himself permission to hold a job as a railwayman in Johannesburg.[38] Some of these incidents were certainly the work of simple criminals, but for other Africans fraud and theft offered a viable means of participation in the colonial enterprise.

Conclusion

Africans did not limit themselves to one particular type of participation in the British Empire. Ambitious individuals valued the autonomy and growth

[37] Elias Mandala, *Work and Control in a Peasant Economy: A History of the Lower Tchiri Valley in Malawi, 1859–1960* (Madison, 1990).

[38] Kenya National Archives, MAA 2/3/16, MD 4/5/141, DC KAPT 1/12/61; Margaret Kiloh and Archie Sibeko, *A Fighting Union* (Randburg, South Africa, 2000).

potential of the commercial sector and many chiefs, clerks, senior soldiers and policemen, clergymen, and teachers used their earnings and status to acquire land or set up petty trading ventures. Erica Fiah was a Gandan mission teacher who served as an interpreter and medical assistant with British forces during the First World War. After his discharge he held a variety of jobs with government departments and private companies in Dar es Salaam. Angered by racial discrimination in pay and promotion, Fiah quit to become a prosperous merchant, moneylender, and landlord.[39] Haya Peters Mlelemba, an educated Yao from southern Nyasaland, left a series of jobs with private employers for similar reasons. He became a highly successful commercial farmer and business owner who grew as wealthy as most of the local European planters in pre-1914 Nyasaland.[40] It was also possible for Africans to shift from the commercial sphere to administration. By the inter-war era, Christian communities in West Africa often convinced colonial officials to appoint successful businessmen and mission graduates as their chiefs and headmen.

The need for African assistance in running the Empire in Africa exposed some of the most fundamental contradictions of the colonial system. The colonial regime needed help governing the African majority, but the Native Authorities proved unreliable partners. Lacking a legitimate basis for their authority, they had difficulty executing unpopular colonial policies and were unable to blunt African political opposition. British administrators distrusted the African clerical class, which would have been far more useful as a political ally, because they exposed the vulnerability of European field officers through their greater knowledge of African society. Colonial authorities needed African coercive assistance to impose their will on the subject majority but worried that African soldiers and policemen might turn on them. Building political legitimacy and loyalty to the Empire by making Western cultural values more widely accessible might have reduced the need to rule by threat of force, but British officials worried that Christianity and a Western secular education fostered African nationalism and disrupted the 'traditional' basis of Indirect Rule. Finally, Britain needed to develop its African colonies but was unwilling to tolerate commercial competition from Africans. Moreover, colonial officials worried that social stratification

[39] N. J. Westcott, 'An East African Radical: The Life of Erica Fiah', *JAH*, XXII (1981), pp. 85–101.

[40] Joey Power, ' "Individualism is the Antithesis of Indirect Rule": Cooperative Development and Indirect Rule in Colonial Malawi,' *JSAS*, XVIII (1992), pp. 317–347.

in rural African societies would further disrupt indirect rule. Given these inherent contradictions, the question is not why British colonial rule ended far sooner than expected in the late 1950s and early 1960s, but why it lasted so long.

Select Bibliography

DAVID ANDERSON and DAVID KILLINGRAY, eds., *Policing the Empire* (New York, 1991).

SARA BERRY, *No Condition is Permanent: The Social Dynamics of Agrarian Change in Sub-Saharan Africa* (Madison, Wisc. 1993).

A. A. BOAHEN, *African Perspectives on Colonialism* (Baltimore, 1987).

PHILIP BONNER, PETER DELIUS and DEBORAH POSEL, eds., *Apartheid's Genesis, 1935–1962* (Johannesburg, 1993).

MARSHALL CLOUGH, *Fighting Two Sides: Kenyan Chiefs and Politicians, 1918–1940* (Niwot, Colo., 1990).

FREDERICK COOPER, *Decolonization and African Society: The Labor Question in French and British Africa* (Cambridge, 1996).

JEFF CRISP, *The Story of an African Working Class: Ghanaian Miners' Struggles, 1870–1980* (London, 1984).

R. D. GRILLO, *African Railwaymen: Solidarity and Opposition in an East African Labour Force* (Cambridge, 1973).

KAREN TRANBERG HANSEN, ed., *African Encounters with Domesticity* (New Brunswick NJ, 1992).

ASHLEY JACKSON, *Botswana 1939–1945: An African Country at War* (Oxford, 1999).

DAVID KILLINGRAY and ANTHONY CLAYTON, *Khaki and Blue: Military and Police in British Colonial Africa* (Athens, Oh., 1989).

JOHN LONSDALE and BRUCE BERMAN, *Unhappy Valley: Conflict in Kenya & Africa*, 2 vols. (London, 1992).

MAHMOOD MAMDANI, *Citizen and Subject: Contemporary Africa and the Legacy of Late Colonialism* (Princeton, NJ, 1996).

JANE PARPART, *Labor and Capital on the African Copperbelt* (Philadelphia, 1983).

11

African Workers and Imperial Designs

FREDERICK COOPER

The decision of Parliament in 1833 to abolish slavery in its colonies marked the British Empire as the Empire of free labour. Such a formulation would, for over a century, remain central to how decision-makers thought of their own role; how they justified further colonization to the British public; and how Great Britain defined itself *vis-à-vis* other colonizing powers and pressured them into co-operating in suppressing slavery throughout the world. Free labour principles were also vital to the critics of British policy, and no charge rang louder than that which at times came from missionary or humanitarian circles, that the government was tolerating slavery 'under the British flag'.[1]

The relationship of Empire and coerced labour would, however, persist until nearly the final phase of the colonial system. In 1840 the Secretary of State for the Colonies, Lord [John] Russell, wrote of a 'new system of slavery'—indentured labour—that he feared was leading to death and misery across the British Empire.[2] In the 1940s forced labour was revived in several colonies of British Africa, most intensely in Kenya, Northern Rhodesia, and Nyasaland, as wartime demand for African exports mounted while the commodities that might have induced Africans into wage labour were in ever scarcer supply.[3] In the intervening years came a reality that not all defenders of free labour were willing to acknowledge: in the complex spatial system of an Empire, potential workers would not necessarily be living near the sites where they were required, and elsewhere, workers

[1] For examples of this, see Frederick Lugard, 'Slavery under the British Flag', *Nineteenth Century* (February) 1896, pp. 335–55; Joseph Pease, *How We Countenance Slavery* (London [British and Foreign Anti-Slavery Society], 1895); and the *Anti-Slavery Reporter* (London) throughout the 1890s and 1900s.

[2] Hugh Tinker, *A New System of Slavery: The Export of Indian Labour Overseas 1830–1920*, (London, 1974), frontispiece.

[3] Frederick Cooper, *Decolonization and African Society: The Labor Question in French and British Africa* (Cambridge, 1996), p. 125.

might have alternatives to the wages that employers would be willing to offer. Beyond this lies another elusive aspect of this long history: the abolition of slavery did not break the association between race and labour, but in some ways deepened the racialization of the labour question in the British Empire.

Before emancipation it was an open question as to whether blacks were capable of responding to market incentives and working like other people. The myth of the lazy black, and the idea that a special regime of regulation and control of black labour was needed, would be operative until the final decade of British rule in Africa. However, the eventual recognition that African workers could be thought of in the same way as other workers entailed an even firmer view of the dangerous and primitive nature of those Africans who did not make the transition to such a 'modern' framework.

Even more important, the free labour idea itself was quite inadequate to accommodate the mixtures of incentives and constraints that motivated people, in the diverse situations in which they lived. It could not explain why people would agree to work for wages, and even less so for how long, with what degree of assiduity, or with what forms of individual and collective efforts to alter or subvert the work regime. In much of the century of 'free' labour, British humanitarians arguing for the elimination of all forms of labour coercion shared with apologists for administrative or judicial sanctions against 'lazy' workers an unwillingness to ask what labour in an African or West Indian context actually meant. They did not want to think that work might be considered a social act, part of the solidarity and tensions within a family or within a village, and not just an individual response to wage incentives. They did not want to acknowledge the social and political embeddedness of labour in a capitalist society either. Both opponents of and apologists for administrative intervention in labour recruitment could easily become enmeshed in a moralistic dialogue, one assuming that an African who refused to become a regular, disciplined wage labourer did so because of his moral failings, the other that a state which forced people to work was immoral. Only near the end of the British Empire did debates over labour policy enter tentatively at least the realm of the social, and focus on the conditions that determined when and why someone might seek wage labour and how the conditions in the workplace shaped the way people worked and patterns of conflict over labour.

The story of Africans and labour in the British Empire, throughout the entire period from the 1830s to the 1950s, is one that connects to, but diverges from, the story of labour in the British Isles, for the particularity of the

African labourer in British discourse stood alongside the general concern with the significance of wage labour. And the history unfolds in space as much as in time: the question of physical displacement of workers in regional and imperial terms remained central to British thinking about African labour.

The British Empire was never a homogeneous national space, defined by its Englishness, that then exercised power over a clearly defined 'outside'. It was from the start a differentiated political unit: political power was defined in relation to Scotland, Wales, Ireland, Jamaica, North America, and even different parts of 'England'. The development of sugar plantations in the West Indies, owned and managed by British entrepreneurs and supplying Europe, took place within a framework of imperial power and regulated commerce within an imperial system, but depended on links beyond the territory that Britain actually controlled, notably to the sources of slaves in Africa and to sugar markets beyond the Empire. The campaign against the slave trade marked the fact that the colonies were not merely a space where a British élite could continuously exploit the labour of 'the other' but was a moral space as well, in which an argument, ultimately a convincing one, could be made that a certain form of labour recruitment and exploitation was a stain on the British Empire.

From the inception of the anti-slavery movement, British capitalists faced the difficult tasks of justifying wage labour within a developing capitalist economy and of explaining why some workers should be left to the mercies of the labour market when others within the same Empire were being held as slaves. The Empire was not a mere space for exercising national will, but was a highly differentiated polity containing actors with unequal voices, yet with the possibility of political relations *across* the lines of difference. Some, West Indian planters, say, might at one time have access to the centres of power in London, but rebellious slaves and humanitarian lobbies eventually changed the terms of debate over slavery and labour within the Empire.

Race, Labour, and Migration in a Post-Emancipation Empire

The story of people of African descent in the British West Indies in the age of emancipation is told elsewhere in this volume. Here, the question is the consequence of that experience on later imperial designs, policies, and ultimately, actions in Africa. In this connection, the work of Thomas Holt has been extremely revealing. He showed that in the debates in the early 1830s leading up to the Emancipation Act, of 1834 MPs and leading colonial officials had a certain openness of mind in regard to the relationship of race and labour. The most optimistic thought that once freed from the degradation of slavery, Africans would behave like any other rational economic actor, and, in the absence of land of their own, would seek employment. The more pessimistic feared an exception, whether born of racial difference or the experience of slavery itself, to the rules of political economy, hence the dangers of idleness, economic decline, and perhaps violence from the freed labour force. A firm colonial administration would keep an eye on ex-slaves, trying to prevent them from moving to remote parts of the islands, keeping them close to the 'civilizing' influence of government and the plantations where their labour was needed. Holt also shows that the entire framework in which officials considered the labour question—the dichotomy of virtuous work and 'savage sloth',—corresponded little to the way ex-slaves saw their options. Families sought to combine periods of wage labour with maintaining provision gardens, and agriculture with small-scale marketing. Ex-slaves would work, but not necessarily when and as long as planters wanted. For officials, however, the key test was sugar production, and this fell by half between 1839 and 1848 in the crucial case of Jamaica.[4]

From this pattern stemmed two tendencies in imperial thinking. The first was an increasing racialization of economic thought. The openness of the early 1830s diminished in the 1840s: blacks were showing themselves to be resistant and unwilling workers; their alternative vision of economic life counted for little in official circles. This kind of thinking would have its echoes in regard to Africa from the 1860s onward: official scepticism that Africans could be integrated into fruitful economic relations with Europe by market relations alone, and acceptance by missionaries that 'civilization' and Christianity, as much as commerce, required benevolent imperal intervention.

In Cape Colony in British South Africa, missionaries, white settlers, and government officials in the era of emancipation had begun a long debate over the forms of intervention in a region where African pastoralists and farmers existed alongside white settlers. At one pole were those those who wanted to treat Africans as potential trading partners, potential Christians,

[4] Thomas C. Holt, *The Problem of Freedom: Race, Labor, and Politics in Jamaica and Britain, 1832–1938* (Baltimore, 1992), p. 119.

and possibly potential citizens, while at the other were those who wanted to use whatever means necessary to press them into wage labour. The harsher view would prevail in South Africa as demands for labour escalated after the 1860s, while elsewhere the racialized view of African incapacity as economic actors was reinforced by claims that Africans needed to be saved from the tyranny and enslavement practiced by their own rulers. Such an argument became a key rationale for further assertions of control from the 1860s to the 1890s.

The second tendency in British thinking about labour in an imperial context concerned migration, both indentured labour primarily in the West Indies and migratory contract labour, as later practised in colonial Africa. The purists of the free labour market never liked long-term labour contracts. For them, free labour discipline meant the 'sanction of the sack': the worker should at any moment be free to work or not to work, but with the knowledge that not working could mean starvation. An indenture, a contract of several months or several years, resembled temporary slavery, for the indentured servant would have no incentive to show himself a good worker for the duration of the contract and discipline would depend on punishment rather than incentives and fear of losing the job.[5] The displacement of the contract worker from the place of residence to the place of work also echoed one of slavery's key elements, the deracination of the slave, his or her removal from networks of social support to a place where the employer was the sole figure of authority. All forms of contract labour would remain suspect in humanitarian circles throughout the colonial era.

Britain, like France and other imperial powers, saw contract labour as an unpleasant necessity in the nineteenth-century context for getting people from where they were plentiful to where they were needed. One response to the unease about indentured labour was to emphasize the point at which the 'free' nature of the engagement was most clear, the acceptance of a contract. The fetish of the contract, occluding the mixture of impoverishment, administrative pressure, false promises, and real hopes that affected labourers' decisions, was the homage the vice of indenture paid to the virtue of free labour.

[5] See Charles van Onselen, *Chibaro: African Mine Labour in Southern Rhodesia 1900–1933* (London, 1976). It is a stark illustration of both the types of abuses inherent in migratory contract labour in British Africa and the terms in which African workers perceived such contracts.

The networks and systems of labour recruitment, shipping, discipline, and (if workers lived long enough and did not desire to settle) return were solidly established in the 1840s, with the number of indentured workers peaking in the 1850s, and continued until around 1920. Around 1.4 million people went to destinations in the British Empire (out of 2 million indentured labourers worldwide). About 82 per cent of these were Indians; a small number were Africans now 'freely' choosing to go to areas where their ancestors had gone as slaves. Most went to sugar plantations, notably in the British West Indies and Mauritius. The scale was large, and hence it gave rise to an infrastructure, within and beyond the British Empire—the ability of which to supply labour in this manner raised the opportunity costs of any other way of getting workers. Despite the vigilance of metropolitan humanitarian groups the reality of the situation was that plantations were relatively isolated entities and disinterested supervision largely an illusion. What is most remarkable of all is that indentured labour was practised in parts of the British Empire until 1922.[6] It was ended above all because of the rising influence of nationalist parties in India. Workers on contracts of several months or longer, serving in places away from their homes and families, remained important in Africa long after that.

Colonial Conquest and the Failure of Imperial Policies

The idea of Africa as a slave-ridden continent, oppressed by its own tyrants and so kept off the path to civilization, Christianity, and commerce, was crucial to missionary propaganda and a common argument in explorers' accounts available to the reading public in Britain and a means of gathering metropolitan support for imperial intervention overseas.[7] As African troops under British command conquered more of the continent and installed colonial governments, policy-makers in London did, at least in some instances, think of themselves as affecting a transformation in the way labour was utilized. In coastal East Africa and inland West Africa (notably Northern

[6] David Northrup, *Indentured Labor in the Age of Imperialism, 1834–1922* (Cambridge, 1995), pp. 144–45, 156–60.

[7] Two of the most famous examples of this are David Livingstone, *Narrative of an Expedition on the Zambezi and Its Tributaries; and of the Discovery of the Lakes Shirwa and Nyassa, 1858–1864* (London, 1865), and John Hanning Speke, *Journal of the Discovery of the Source of the Nile* (Edinburgh, 1863). On the relationship between the anti-slavery movement and imperialism, see Suzanne Miers, *Britain and the Ending of the Slave Trade* (New York, 1975).

Nigeria), for example, the administration hoped both to maintain large units of production in the hands of indigenous landlords and transform slave labour into wage labour.[8] However, the practical task of ruling Africa meant colonial regimes had to come to grips with the complexities of slavery in Africa itself and with the difficulties of getting people already engaged within a wide range of systems of production to sell their labour. Colonial governments would soon face the limits of their own tools for understanding and intervening in African society.

Colonial revenues depended on the exports of crops grown by slaves and peasants. Imperial political hold in most colonies was very fragile, sometimes resting on alliances with African leaders who had an interest in slavery. British colonies moved promptly against the slave trade in its most virulent forms but wavered about slavery in its agricultural and domestic forms. They were not allowed to temporize in peace as the anti-slavery lobbies made tolerance of slavery in Africa their prime target. More important, the conquest disrupted the mechanisms of control and reproduction of African slave-owners, and slaves in many parts of British Africa quickly began to take matters under their own control.[9]

In East Africa the British government officially declared slavery illegal in 1897 in Zanzibar and 1907 in coastal Kenya.[10] But in both cases, Swahili-speaking, Muslim slaveowning families, some long resident in the area, others nineteenth-century immigrants from Arabia, kept the title to land and productive trees under Islamic law. The British recognized the title to land even as they rejected ownership of slaves. They hoped that these landowners would become indigenous capitalists, hiring wage labour, and that ex-slaves, with no access to land, would provide the labour force. Or else, they hoped, the old landlords would sell land, presumably to white settlers. The state denied ex-slaves land rights in the coastal zone, and used the coercive atmosphere of courts, in which slaves received freedom papers, to try to get them to agree to labour contracts with former masters. Instead, ex-masters and ex-slaves worked out other sorts of arrangements than wage

[8] See Frederick Cooper, *From Slaves to Squatters: Plantation Labor and Agriculture in Zanzibar and Coastal Kenya*, 1890–1925 (New Haven, Conn., 1980); Paul E. Lovejoy and Jan S. Hogendorn, *Slow Death for Slavery: The Course of Abolition in Northern Nigeria, 1897–1936* (Cambridge, 1993).

[9] This is a schematic summary of a complex process, whose variations can most readily be charted by the studies in Suzanne Miers and Richard Roberts, eds., *The End of Slavery in Africa* (Madison, Wisc., 1988).

[10] The following account of abolition in Zanzibar and coastal Kenya comes from Cooper, *From Slaves to Squatters*.

labour *per se*, involving long-term personal relations rather than contractual ones. Ex-slaves became, for the most part, squatters on the planters' land, combining a degree of cultivation with periodic forays into wage labour but rarely as permanent, year-round labourers. The owners benefited from people on the land whose presence demarcated ownership, and they obtained some labour from ex-slaves, but not the kind of steady, committed labour that British officials sought.

In Zanzibar, where a potentially lucrative clove crop needed to be harvested each year, further arrangements with people who had been outside the plantation economy were worked out by indigenous people rather than by the colonial regime. These reflected the social and spatial differentiation of the region. People from nearby villages on Zanzibar Island would pick cloves for several weeks each year, living off their own land or fishing the rest of the time. Immigrants from further away, especially the German-held (until 1919) mainland of Tanganyika would come on longer term contracts to tend the plantations in the non-harvest season. Such a system maintained Zanzibar, where the clove economy had been a major innovation of the mid-nineteenth century, as a significant export producer, but it depended on several socially distinct groups playing their individual roles in the productive process without trying to better their situation too much.

In coastal Kenya, the class compromise was similar in structure but less effective in practice. The coast, once the economic strong-point of the region, fell behind interior zones where either white settler or African peasant agriculture adapted itself to the possibilities and constraints of the colonial economy. Further afield in Africa, one finds other examples of failed transitions of a similar sort: a British effort to sustain a landed upper class while weaning it from slave labour. Such efforts were undermined from above as well as below, as élites saw more promise in maintaining social dominance or extracting an agricultural surplus from forms of social relations other than that of employer to employee.

Imperial conquest did bring an end to large-scale, long-distance versions of the slave trade and limited even the more localized forms of slave trading. Colonial rule made it possible for slaves to flee a harsh master, to transfer their dependence to other groups or individuals, to redefine relations of dependence, or to take their chances finding jobs in colonial cities, colonial armies, colonial railways, colonial schools, and mission stations. However, neither colonial conquest nor colonial rule could affect the type of transformation that imperial ideologies promised and metropolitan policies called for, a transformation that would replace labour coercion with market incentives. Instead, colonial rulers tried to pretend early on that the problems surrounding emancipation had been solved by defining slavery narrowly and legalistically, and by insisting that courts no longer recognized such a status. Slavery was generally considered a male issue; the ambiguities of the dependence of women, unless their mode of acquisition was too blatantly violent, were assimilated into the category of marriage where the courts were concerned.[11] Other relations of subordination were assimilated into tenancy or debt. These same rulers later blamed their failure to establish the conditions and discipline of European capitalism in Africa on Africans and their alleged cultural aversion to steady labour.

The sequence within British thinking in Africa in the early decades of the twentieth century is important, and it contains echoes of their thinking about the West Indies in the 1830s: an interventionist episode, followed by a confrontation with the complexity of the local situation and a realization that change could not be directed as desired, followed by an argument that the peculiarity of the ex-slave (and in this case of the ex-master as well) frustrated the application of universal principles of social and economic progress.

The post-1860s argument, popularized by David Livingstone and other missionaries, that Africa was a slave-ridden continent in need of Christian redemption did not narrowly apply to those parts of Africa affected by slavery. It applied to the peasants of British South Africa as well, and later to newly incorporated African colonies, such as Southern Rhodesia, where slavery was not an historic factor of large dimensions. Like slaves, peasants were not fully disciplined by a market economy; they could escape into self-subsistence. Like the brutalized slave, they were exceptions to the rule of economic rationality, and therefore in need of some kind of tutelage. Such conceptions of the backward cultivator ignored the considerable increase, especially in West Africa, of production for the expanding raw materials markets of industrializing Europe. Palm products from coastal West Africa and ground nuts from the Senegambia were among the growing exports of West Africa, and if slave labour was sometimes important in the growing or marketing of agricultural produce, so too was small-scale production organized by family units or sometimes by religious leaders whose disciples were building up new kinds of socio-economic organization.

[11] Lovejoy and Hogendorn, *Slow Death*, p. 111; Martin Chanock, *Law, Custom and Social Order: The Colonial Experience in Malawi and Zambia* (Cambridge, 1985), p. 169.

These dynamics were not well understood by even the more sympathetic of Europeans in Africa in the last half of the nineteenth century. Some missionaries in British South Africa looked to the emergence of more individualistic farming communities centred around mission stations. They were ambivalent about the fact that, from the 1860s, the new diamond mines were demanding more labour, sugar plantations needed migrants from the region and from India, and white farmers were demanding more wage labour as their markets grew. The discovery of gold in the 1880s rapidly compounded the pressures on the labour market. That African peasants in certain regions were, as a number of South African liberals claimed at the time and as scholars have since demonstrated, contributing to grain and cattle markets was ignored as the labour-seeking lobby grew in importance and influence. Although controls over the movement of Africans had been in place since at least the 1820s, they were used increasingly to channel Africans to their niches in the labour market, to weaken Africans' access to land, and to prevent intermediary forms of tenancy and squatting between landlord and cultivator from emerging. In actuality, Africans struggled for decades to maintain just such arrangements, often moving from place to place to try to find a co-operative white landowner who would let them combine labour, cultivation, marketing, and cattle raising. But the direction of change, in the 1890s and 1900s, turned against them. The British government, after victory in the Boer War, sustained the position of the big landowner and the big employer.

The transformation of semi-autonomous South African peasants into dependent labourers was, however, incomplete. It is not clear that government had the power to affect a complete transformation as blacks fought tenaciously to defend some access to land and cattle despite the intensity of settler land-grabbing in the region. Labour was for sale in small units of time, as African families tried to maintain multiple forms of access to resources. As Keletso Atkins has shown in regard to nineteenth-century Natal, the terms under which Africans sought work were not entirely dictated by the employers; day labour in her case study, other forms of short-term labour in other cases, reflected the working out of a *modus vivendi* between desires, habits, and attitudes towards work that were, it might seem, incompatible with one another.[12]

[12] Keletso Atkins, *The Moon is Dead! Give Us Our Money!: Cultural Origins of an African Work Ethic, Natal, South Africa, 1843–1900* (Portsmouth, NH, 1993).

The mixture did not reflect equal power of employees and employers, and in South Africa, it was particularly unequal.

Elsewhere in British Africa, officials retreated by the time of the First World War from their more reformist vision of remaking African work habits and African land tenure. They came to accept a wide range of arrangements. British Africa remained dotted with islands of wage labour—the settler farms of southern Rhodesia or central Kenya, the mines of northern Rhodesia, commercial hubs and ports in all colonies—surrounded by vast expanses where economic systems were poorly understood and largely left alone.

By the time of the First World War, the unreformed nature of African society was being proclaimed as a virtue of British colonial rule. In West Africa, this became the doctrine of 'Indirect Rule': the wise colonial ruler would only slowly attempt to induce change in African societies, and then within the framework of 'traditional' beliefs and 'traditional' authority. The representation of the African as traditional could serve not only in West Africa, where the export economy depended on small-scale cultivation by African families and extended kinship groups, supplemented at times by additional labour, but also in South Africa, where the mineral and agricultural economy depended on the exploitation of the labour of Africans whose access to productive resources had been systematically undermined. Here the 'reserves' were slowly becoming dumping grounds for people not in wage labour rather than forming sites of alternative economic possibilities. In both cases, official thinking recognized that Africans could work, but not that they could be workers. They were confined, in ideology more than in practice, to an essentialized domain of tradition, from which they were called forth, frequently or occasionally, to perform needed labour before being sent back again.

The Labour Question in Colonial Africa

One of the most revealing comments about British labour policy in the interwar years is to be found in a report from an assistant District Commissioner in coastal Kenya in 1918. He remarked that success in getting labour for white settlers from an African chief 'depended on how far he could be induced to exceed his instructions'.[13] Back in London the Colonial Secretary, Lord Milner, claimed, in regard to settler areas, that he wished to steer 'a middle

[13] Assistant District Commissioner, Kilifi, to Provincial Commissioner, 18 Oct. 1918, Kenya National Archives, CP 38/582.

course between allowing the natives to live in idleness and vice and using improper means to get them to work'.[14] Awareness of the limits of colonial power as much as concern that the anti-slavery lobby in England would create a fuss constrained officials to combine a dose of compulsion (more through the supposed authority of chiefs over 'their people' than through labour round-ups), a measure of incentives (more consumer goods), indirect coercion (taxes payable in cash), and a politics of depriving some regions of resources for cash cropping while endowing others with them. The patchwork of zones of peasant cultivation, labour reservoirs, and areas of white settlement covered much of southern and central Africa, as well as parts of East Africa but not West Africa, where there were no settlers, indigenous agricultural production was predominant, and cities with relatively flexible labour markets were better established.

When the copper mines of Northern Rhodesia came on stream in the late 1920s with their 16,000 workers, many officials and managers accepted the doctrine that a rapidly circulating labour force reduced the burden of social costs on capital, maintained tribal authority, and forestalled the social risks of proletarianization. Some mining companies, however, mildly questioned the wisdom of high turnover and male-only urban residence which followed from such an approach. They envisioned urban family life for a segment of the work force for a portion of their lives. In practice, women were not the passive, homemaking creatures the mine managers expected them to be. For some, being in a mining town created opportunities for an autonomy consistent with neither African nor British notions of patriarchy. Whether mining companies wanted it or not, a significant portion of miners—31 per cent according to one estimate from 1931—lived with their wives in the mining towns. Circular migration was never as strong on the ground as in official minds. Meanwhile, officials and African chiefs tried to reassert patriarchy in this changing and contested terrain, prosecuting women for alleged sexual misconduct in courts under indigenous authorities.[15] In the early 1930s, going further than this was dismissed as going against the nature of the African mind. As one Governor Sir Shenton Thomas of Nyasaland, said:

[14] *House of Lords Debates* 41 (14 July 1920), col. 155.

[15] George Chauncey, Jr., 'The Locus of Reproduction: Women's Labour in the Zambian Copperbelt, 1927–1953', *Journal of Southern African Studies*, (hereafter *JSAS*), VII (1981), pp. 135–64; Jane L. Parpart, 'Sexuality and Power on the Zambian Copperbelt: 1926–1964', in Sharon Stichter and Jane L. Parpart eds., *Patriarchy and Class: African Women in the Home and in the Workforce* (Boulder, Colo., 1988), pp. 115–38.

I wish to place on record that it would be absolutely incredible to any native in any country in which I have served that the Government should wish him to uproot himself, his wives, and his children from the place consecrated in his eyes by age-long associations, to abandon his relations to whom by native custom he is so closely tied, his plot of land, his flocks and his herds, and to betake himself to a new country.[16]

As with wage labour production, the successes of the rival economic model—cash cropping—were concentrated in exceptional areas of productivity within British Africa. The most important of these islands of relative prosperity came about without imperial planning or prodding. Palm oil production in coastal West Africa was part of the precolonial economy; the cocoa farmers of the Gold Coast and Western Nigeria obtained shoots from missionaries and developed cocoa production themselves at the end of the nineteenth century; and the farmers of Northern Nigeria grew peanuts when officials were trying to get them to grow cotton in the early decades of the twentieth century. Such farming systems were neither 'African', which in imperial ideology meant static and traditional, nor, capitalist in the sense that Marx envisaged. The cocoa labourer expected not only wages, but access to land to feed himself, a share of the crop, and in many cases long-term relations with the landowner, who might one day help him to acquire land and plant trees himself. In the Gold Coast—the first of the cocoa systems—this was changing in the 1930s, as good cocoa land was used up.[17]

Large public works projects, notably early railroad construction in West Africa, also required coercive official recruitment, while in East Africa, building the railway required massive imports of indentured Indian labourers.[18] But overall, labour for ports, railways, and commercial operations became part of increasingly differentiated patterns of migration and urban settlement. Urban labour markets grew; migratory patterns took in urban jobs as well as cocoa fields; mission-educated men filled clerical and teaching positions and were beginning to found mutual aid societies and trade unions in the 1920s.

[16] Governor, Nyasaland, to Passfield, 7 May 1931, Public Record Office [PRO], CO 795/43/36043.

[17] Gareth Austin, Labour, Land, and Capital in Ghana: From Slavery to Free Labour in Asante, 1807–1956 (Rochester, NY, 2005).

[18] Roger Thomas, 'Forced Labour in British West Africa: The Case of the Northern Territories of the Gold Coast, 1906–27', *Journal of African History* (hereafter *JAH*), XIV (1973), pp. 79–103; van Onselen, *Chibaro*; Michael Mason, 'Working in the Railway: Forced Labor in Northern Nigeria, 1907–1912', in Robin Cohen, Jean Copans, and Peter C. W. Gutkind, eds., *African Labor History* (Beverly Hills, Calif., 1978), pp. 56–79; R. D. Grillo, *African Railwaymen: Solidarity and Opposition in an East African Labour Force* (Cambridge, 1973).

With imperial policy, reinforced by the best anthropology of the day, focused on maintaining order through ethnic structures, a central tenet of the policy of Indirect Rule, the label 'detribalized' was attached to people who might otherwise have been called workers or town-dwellers. When the Depression struck British Africa, the possibility of sending wage labourers back to the security and invisibility of their villages and the continuing supplies of modest quantities of export crops even at low prices made Indirect Rule and circular migrancy appear to have been an especially wise approach. Several colonies which had labour departments in the 1920s closed them during the Depression, transferring their functions to the provincial administration, assisted by medical departments, so reaffirming the bureaucratic domination of the apparatus of Indirect Rule and the ideological power of 'tribe'.

In this context, free labour ideology was formalistic. Britain continued to see itself in the vanguard of progressive colonialism, marked above all by rejection of the brutality and coercion of past colonial regimes. Britain had been active in international congresses in 1884–85 and 1889–90 that set out the rules for modern colonization, notably that a colonizing power would suppress the slave trade in its territories and refrain from analogous practices itself. British representatives supported the anti-slavery resolution of the League of Nations in 1926 and the declaration against forced labour of the International Labour Organization of 1930. British citizens, humanitarian organizations, and at times the British government criticized King Leopold of Belgium, the Portuguese government in Angola, and the Liberian government for coercive labour practices in the early twentieth century.

Outside official circles came the beginnings of a critique of the labour system that went beyond the free labour ideology. In a book published in 1933 under the auspices of the International Missionary Council, it was argued that industrial labour and migrancy were 'shaking the foundations of Bantu life', leaving workers vulnerable to disease and antisocial behaviour in cities and leaving their communities economically vulnerable by their absence. Migration disrupted the one strong asset Africans had—the 'integrated solidarity and mutual dependence' of African communities—while back and forth movements made the efforts of missionaries to educate them all the harder. 'It is a striking inconsistency to encourage tribal integrity on the one hand under the system of indirect rule . . . and on the other hand to encourage its disruption by the present chaotic economic system.' The book's editor called for 'stabilization' at two levels, ensuring the conditions for sustained life in the village and turning mine labour into a long term proposition.[19]

This was precisely the point British official thinking avoided in the mid-1930s. That Africans routinely suffered from ill health, poor food, and other bad working conditions was most often seen in the official milieu not as a problem of Empire but as a consequence of their being primitive.

Labour and the Development Framework

Despite attempts to evade the labour question, it returned as a problem of Empire just before the centenary of the abolition of slavery in the Caribbean. Disturbances in St Kitts, Trinidad, and British Guiana in 1935, in Trinidad and Barbados in 1937, and in British Guiana and Jamaica in 1938 had begun as strikes, which spread in both rural and urban areas and sometimes took a violent direction. These movements touched a population where the boundaries of work and unemployment, of regular jobs and insecurity, were porous.[20] The climax came in 1938, exactly a century after the British had abolished the apprenticeship programme and proclaimed the former slaves of their colonies fully free. British officials had, for most of this century, been happy to take credit for emancipation, but in 1938 the West Indian governments decided to cancel centenary celebrations: the riots and strikes focused attention on the fact that poverty and anger were among the fruits of a century of British emancipation.

The first of a series of major strikes in British Africa began in 1935 as well. The Northern Rhodesian mineworkers strike of 1935 was organized without benefit of trade unions, and it spread from mine to mine, from mining town to mining town, by personal networks, dance societies, religious organizations, and eventually mass meetings. The movement embraced non-miners in the towns, and women as well as men.[21] Other general strikes occurred in

[19] J. Merle Davis, ed., *Modern Industry and the African: An Enquiry into the Effect of the Copper Mines of Central Africa upon Native Society and the Work of Christian Missions Made under the Auspices of the Department of Social and Industrial Research of the International Missionary Council* (London, 1933), pp. vii, 1–2.

[20] The most detailed study is Ken Post, *Arise Ye Starvelings: The Jamaican Labour Rebellion of 1938 and its Aftermath* (The Hague, 1978).

[21] Ian Henderson, 'Early African Leadership: The Copperbelt Disturbances of 1935 and 1940', *JSAS*, II (1975), pp. 83–97; Charles Perrings, *Black Mineworkers in Central Africa: Industrial Strategies and the Evolution of an African Proletariat in the Copperbelt 1911–41* (New York, 1979); Jane Parpart, *Labor and Capital on the African Copperbelt* (Philadelphia, 1983).

Dar es Salaam in 1939 and in Mombasa in 1934 and 1939. British officials first reacted to African workers' actions by reaffirming tribal authority.

Taken together, the events in the quite distinct social environments of the old plantation colonies of the West Indies and the migrant-labour dominated colonies of central Africa raised questions that did not fit in the old categories. London was shaken seriously, all the more because the strikes occurred as the Depression was easing and production increasing, as the dangers of war with Germany were looming, and as political movements in different colonies were making an ever-wider range of claims on imperial authority. Some have argued that the British Colonial Office was looking to fostering economic and social progress in the Empire, and seized on the riots as a means of persuading sceptics, but the archival evidence suggests that officials were knocked off balance by the pan-Empire protests and suffered a serious crisis of self-confidence.[22]

The reaction of officials in the Colonial Office was not to question Empire but to reform it from within. This entailed, first, urging colonies to create labour departments (or recreate them in the case of those African territories that had pushed labour issues into 'native administration'), so that specific attention would go to labour. The Colonial Office appointed its own Labour Adviser, Major G. St. J. Orde Browne, in 1938. Second, the Colonial Office, under Malcolm Macdonald, tried to deflect the labour question into a question of 'development'. It devised an argument for the use of metropolitan funds for the specific purpose of improving living conditions in the colonies, particularly the living conditions in urban areas and plantation areas. The implicit theory of economic and social processes behind the proposals was simple (and not something social scientists would care to sustain in such a simple form): bad conditions breed disorder. Faced with scepticism from fiscal conservatives, who argued plausibly enough that colonies were supposed to enrich the metropole rather than the other way around, the Colonial Office developed a double argument: investments that in the short run did not pay were necessary in extremely poor territories to create the conditions that would eventually enhance production. A better-educated, better-housed, better-fed labour force would imply more productive workers. Second, a more prosperous working class would be

[22] Stephen Constantine, *The Making of British Colonial Development Policy 1914–1940* (London, 1984), 233–57; J. M. Lee, *Colonial Development and Good Government* (Oxford, 1967); D. J. Morgan, *The Official History of Colonial Development* (London, 1980), 5 vols.

orderly and predictable and would save the Empire from embarrassment and danger. This rationale eventually resulted in the Colonial Development and Welfare (CD&W) Act of 1940, although wartime constraints prevented it from going into full effect (with added funding) until 1945.

The Act was a landmark in the history of the British Empire, and not only because it authorized the spending of the British taxpayer's money on projects that were not seen as profitable investments but as politically necessary expenditure on improvements in the standard of living of colonial people, and especially of colonial workers. The Act was conceptually important because it put Africans and West Indians into the same category. Both had a *social* existence. They could either work well or badly, preserve order or threaten the state, depending on their conditions of life.

The CD&W Act would focus on housing, water, hospitals, roads, and schools, alongside investments intended to produce more immediate returns. It was an important departure in imperial thinking, not least because it implied that the success of imperial policy could be measured not by such vague, and inherently self-referential, criteria as the claim to represent a superior 'civilization', but on more specific criteria of social progress: per capita income, literacy, life expectancy. The words of the Secretary of State for the Colonies, Oliver Stanley, in 1944 suggest how much the development framework, first articulated in 1939, was setting the terms of debate on future policy:

> the Colonial Empire means so much to us that we should be prepared to assume some burden for its future. If we are unable or unwilling to do so, are we justified in retaining, or should we be able to retain a Colonial Empire? . . . If these sums are wisely spent, and the plans devoted to increasing the real productive power of the Colonies, there will in the long run accrue considerable benefit to us . . . But I am not basing my argument on material gains to ourselves, important as I think these may be. My feeling is that in these years to come without the Commonwealth and Empire, this country will play a small role in world affairs, and that here we have an opportunity which may never recur, at a cost which is not extravagant, of setting the Colonial Empire on lines of development which will keep it in close and loyal contact with us.[23]

The Empire was indeed in question. Just as the initiative for the 1940 Act stemmed from expressions of popular anger in the West Indies and central

[23] Secretary of State Stanley to meeting of Colonial Economic Advisory Committee, 19 December 1944, PRO, CEAC (44)46, CO 852/588/2. These and related issues are discussed in detail in Cooper, *Decolonization and African Society*, pp. 111–24.

Africa, the success of the new initiative not least in the eyes of the Colonial Office would lie in the question of whether 'development' would in fact prevent 'disorder'.

From the Particular to the Universal

But the labour question in Africa could not, in fact, be shoehorned into the development framework, as became increasingly clear during the Second World War, when spending under the CD&W Act could not begin in earnest, and it was equally true in the decade or so after the war, when spending was rapidly increasing.

During the war, Northern Rhodesia, Kenya, Nigeria, and the Gold Coast experienced large-scale strikes.[24] Whatever the economic planners in London thought about managing development in a time of constraints, the political managers had to face the immediate reality: only significant concessions in wages would prevent the paralysis of transport and mining in export-oriented colonies. The 1940 miners' strike in Northern Rhodesia, like the 1935 one, spread from mine to mine and involved urban protest as much as industrial action. It was repressed with loss of life. The Kenyan port of Mombasa was on the edge of paralysing strikes in 1942 and again in 1945. Most government and railway workers in Nigeria struck in 1945. Mines and railways in the Gold Coast were on edge of major strikes at several points during the war.[25] All this occurred at a time when the services of workers was urgently needed, so officials were in a poor position to use coercion, and the neo-traditional legitimacy (the supposed loyalty of the African man to his chief) was of little relevance in workplaces and cities.

The common thread connecting these confrontations was the experience of African workers in cities, mines, and communications centres of growing wage labour without the social conditions necessary to sustain a working population. In the aftermath of the Depression, economic expansion throughout British Africa sent growing numbers of workers to cities where governments were unwilling to invest in housing, schools, and other facilities and where employers and officials held wages down even as prices rose. Such

[24] The following paragraphs summarize a much more detailed discussion of these events in Cooper, *Decolonization and African Society*, pp. 124–41.

[25] Henderson, 'Early African Leadership'; Frederick Cooper, *On the African Waterfront: Urban Disorder and Transformation of Work in Colonial Mombasa* (New Haven, Conn., 1987); Richard Jeffries, *Class, Power and Ideology in Ghana: The Railwaymen of Sekondi* (Cambridge, 1987).

rigidity was enhanced by officials' belief that Africans were by nature peasants and if they worked for wages it was only a temporary affair and a masculine affair at that. The city was not really a place in which African workers lived. The reality was more complex. The well-established West African port cities had substantial African populations including skilled workers as well as teachers and other professionals and the new influx brought both strains and political possibility to cities where African newspapers and organizations were already making political claims. In central and eastern Africa, British officials tried to control influx into most cities, but men did not necessarily leave when they were not working for wages and women often came to accompany a man or seek their fortunes independently even when they were supposed to be bringing up families in rural villages. Urban Africa was subject to tensions among incoming Africans and established residents, between Africans and Europeans, between men and women.

These were dynamic cities, with the potential for new social and political connections, and the combination of increasing numbers of immigrants and rising inflation from the late 1930s to the post-war period produced a volatile situation. In some cases, the Gold Coast and Nigeria for instance, trade unions led a number of effective strikes, but in others, like Mombasa, general strikes took place without trade union leadership. Urban movements were as much consumer revolts as strikes, for the self-employed market women as well as labouring men experienced similar strains on their livelihood. The difficulties of keeping a family alive, when wages were minimal even for the single man, were central to the popular, cross-occupational nature of protest in this era. For all the social differentiation within cities, communications within crowded neighbourhoods made mass mobilization possible in the intense conjuncture of the war years and post-war years.

The British Empire was discovering that the worker was not just a unit of labour power, but a human being living in specific conditions. Those living conditions might foster orderly compliance with a work regime, incipient anger, or collective action. They might foster high turnover or long-term service. Workers might learn on the job and become more productive or they could be caught in a vicious circle of low productivity justifying low wages and low expectations. Most important, the tendency of colonial labour systems to treat all African workers as something less than a real worker, as a unit of labour power temporarily extracted from a 'traditional' setting, produced a mass work force rather than a differentiated one. A Rhodesian official, for example, agonized over the effects of 'casual and precarious' urban living conditions, of the absence of family life, of the 'abnormal social structure' with a preponderance of young men, and hence of the dangers coming from 'the fluid mass of the irresponsible 18–35 age group'.[26] Hence, the great danger in an inflationary conjuncture was that strikes would not remain industrial disputes confined to particular businesses or industries but would spread. And indeed they did: the years 1939–1948 were the years of the general strike, city-wide as in Mombasa or Dar es Salaam in 1947 or country wide as in Nigeria in 1945. As with the 1930s strikes, they raised the spectre of imperial disorder, not just that of labour dispute.

The reports of colonial administrator in Africa in the colonies and Colonial Office staff in London consistently record this fear of labour action becoming mass disorder. 'If a strike develops we may not be able to confine it to the dimension of a mere trade union dispute' sums up the concern in the Copperbelt, while in Nigeria the Acting Governor noted 'the solidarity of all classes of Government servants in the demand for an improvement in their living conditions generally'. Governors confessed their impotence: 'there is very little more I can do in the way of positive action to end the strike'.[27] In London, Frederick Pedler, an example of a more perspicacious type of colonial official of this period, admitted that 'Before very long East Africa will have to change over, probably very suddenly, from low grade labour and very low wages to something much nearer the standard of European manual labour and the European labourer's wage.'[28]

If the political administration was acting in response to immediate threats, other voices within the administration were trying to find other ways to grapple with the new parameters of the labour question. The main forum for developing a new discourse on labour was a series of commissions that investigated labour conditions after each of the major strikes. One in Kenya in 1945 dramatically posed the problem as the coming into being of an 'urbanized working class'.[29] This and other commission reports

[26] Southern Rhodesia, 'Report of the Committee to Investigate the Economic, Social and Health Conditions of Africans Employed in Urban Areas', Jan. 1944.

[27] Minute, Arthur Dawe, 15 May 1941, PRO, CO 795/122/45109/7; Acting Governor, Nigeria, to Secretary of State, 21 May 1942, 28 May 1942 (telegram), 9 June 1942, PRO, CO 554/129/33669; Acting Governor, Nigeria, to Governor to Secretary of State, 13 July 1945, PRO, CO 583/275/30647/1.

[28] F. J. Pedler, Minute, 18 August 1939, PRO, CO 533/513/38397/2.

[29] *Report of Committee of Inquiry into Labour Unrest at Mombasa* [Phillips Report] (Nairobi, 1945).

recognized the fact that whatever officials thought of the desirability of Africans coming to live as well as to work near places of wage employment, the reality of their doing so had to be confronted. As a percentage of population, the numbers were small, but the very rotation of people into and out of work meant that a larger percentage of male Africans had experienced wage labour. In fact, in the Copperbelt and elsewhere more and more men were bringing their wives and children with them, and a variety of family forms, whether legal or not, were developing in cities. Efforts to repatriate workers after their stints in the mines or docks were done were proving impossible, and the increasing complexity of urban centres made it easier for Africans to establish themselves.

When officials in the Copperbelt began to talk of 'stabilization' in the 1940s, what they thought of as a desirable policy was already a pattern with which Africans had confronted them. The problem was to manage it.[30] The investigatory studies began to develop a language of social scientific control aimed at establishing at least a sense of order.[31] At the core of the new discourse was a set of old ideas, and the newness lay in their application to Africans. Officials had a model of an ideal working class before them, based on a simplified version of the past century of Western European history: workers as a stable category of people, reproducing new generations of workers socialized to industrial situations and urban living, internally differentiated by occupation, income, skill, and other fundamentally 'industrial' categories, incorporated into a set of stable institutions which, while potentially expressing class interest, were familiar and predictable enough to permit orderly negotiating. Social engineering in the post-war decade created the British welfare state, which was intended to promote orderly economic growth by keeping class conflict within certain bounds. Belief in rational planning and objective measurement and evaluation existed alongside acceptance of the fact that trade unions had a legitimate place in the order, that conflict would occur, and that conflict too could be handled effectively.

[30] Further discussion of stabilization in Northern Rhodesia, often considered a laboratory for the policy in British Africa, see Cooper, *Decolonization and African Society*, pp. 336–38, 346–47.

[31] For example, see Godfrey Wilson, *An Essay on the Economics of Detribalization in Northern Rhodesia*, Rhodes–Linvingstone Papers, 5 (Livingstone, Northern Rhodesia, 1941). See also James Ferguson, *Expectations of Modernity: Myths and Meanings of Urban Life in the Zambian Copperbelt* (Berkeley, 1999).

Applied to Africa, this vision required that colonial officials think of the African worker as the universal worker, as not very African. This was more pious wish than reality observed in any factory or dockyard. When, in the early and mid-1950s, social scientists began serious field research in mining towns, urban areas, and other centres of wage labour, they would soon reveal a more complex reality, one not dichotomized into a modern industrial sector and a backward traditional one.

Labour officers and other officials concerned with observing and managing the world of work in the post-war decade were none the less engaged in an important enterprise of imagination. The old Africa of pre-war officialdom was by and large a world of tribes, from which Africans exited for finite stints as workers and risked 'detribalization' whenever such a foray extended too long. The imaginative break between the wartime and post-war years enabled British officials to accept what was already a reality: the African presence in cities, railway lines, ports, and mines. It enabled them to think of this reality as normal and manageable, by techniques developed in managing conflict in Europe, and it enabled officials to work with institutions that had up to then been left unrecognized: trade unions, political parties, and the opinion of educated sectors of the African population. It entailed costs: if it were necessary for a new generation of African workers to be brought up in the social environment of a modern workplace or modern city, then wages high enough to support entire families would have to be paid. Schools and hospitals would have to be built. In this sense, the economic orientation of the development project and the social orientation of the new labor policy reinforced each other.

If the old thinking was premised on a dichotomy between a civilized West and a primitive Africa, the new one had its own dualities, only they did not line up so neatly in racial terms. Africans *could* become 'modern'. But those who did not, who stuck to old ways, might be accused of being willfully obstructive, hostile to a project that officials believed to be in their interest. Most important was the meaning attached to the name by which post-war labour policy was called: stabilization. This word did not imply that labour policy was directed at moving all of Africa toward wage labour, but rather that the working class that existed should become self-reproducing, that workers should remain on their jobs throughout their working lives and produce a new generation of workers within the urban or industrial milieu. The Kenyan Committee on African Wages, en route to recommending family instead of bachelor wages, assigned itself the task of providing 'such conditions, both social and economic, as will induce the African to sever his ties with tribal life and virtually start afresh in a new environment... We cannot hope to produce an effective African labour force until we have first removed the African from the enervating and retarding influence of his economic and cultural background.'[32] In short, it implied a separation of the working class from all that was African.

The Challenge of Labour Stabilization and the End of Empire

Officials hoped, of course, to stabilize not only labour but Empire. They accomplished neither, and the *dénouement* of colonial rule in Africa turned out to be remarkably rapid. It would be a mistake to see labour as the vanguard of independence movements in Africa, but it would be equally misleading to infer, from wage workers' minority status and unions' varied organizational capabilities, that the influence of labour was minor. Most important is to recognize the double importance of the labour question in the rapidly shifting politics of the end of Empire. First, labour was a serious question in itself, the focus of aspirations for better material conditions on the part of workers and a concern to imperial officials precisely because the narrowness of colonial economies gave power to relatively small numbers of workers in key nodes of the colonial spatial system. Second, the labour question was emblematic of a deeper crisis in imperialism, of the tension between the particular situation of Africans, described in colonial discourse as 'tradition', and the universal processes of history, or 'modernity' as these were understood in the language of development discourse.

From the point of view of imperial rulers, the long emphasis on the peculiarity of the African which had served to justify a certain kind of emancipation and a certain kind of colonization, was no longer a guide to understanding the current challenges facing British rule, particularly the general strikes and urban disturbances that had repeatedly occurred in Africa. Nor was the ideological coherence of the rule of 'difference' as useful as it once was: Hitler had given racial ideologies a bad name. Britain, like France, was now justifying its presence in Africa not on the basis of its inherent right of whites to rule blacks, but on its ability to foster 'development', to promote the potential equality among all human beings. Such a rationale had two big drawbacks: it was measurable, via economic indicators

[32] *Report of the Committee on African Wages* (Nairobi, 1954).

and potentially contradicted, as in the 1940s, by visible evidence of anger. Its obvious remedies—public services, investment, and higher wages—cost money.

Once the idea of difference ceased to be an unquestioned premise of colonial policy, the limit of how far development should go was not obvious, and could be taken to mean the standard of living of the most advanced parts of the British Empire, notably Britain itself. The era of Empire on the cheap was no long defensible, and the question facing Great Britain was whether it was willing to pay for an Empire based on the notions of equality and welfare. The Imperial government had, from the very start of the development debate, insisted that equal services and wages were not the implicit promise of imperial development. There were, however, other voices.

From the late 1940s through to the late 1950s, British imperial designs were caught between fear of the escalating costs of modernized imperialism and fear of the political and social consequences of not modernizing imperialism decisively enough. Policy-makers did not have the luxury of contemplating the two alternatives in the abstract, but faced active, claim-making movements. These were by no means limited to labour. By far the best studied are political parties, and especially the way in which a relatively well-educated, élite leadership sought mass support in the post-war years by the direct appeal of militant collective action and by the development of networks through a wide range of associations, in rural as well as urban areas. Labour unions are sometimes incorporated into the narrative of nationalist mobilization, and indeed social and political organizations reinforced each other's sense of militancy and the possibility of expanding claims in a charged atmosphere, but there were frequent tension between their claims.

The Gold Coast was the paradigmatic case. Its labour movement, notably in the railroads and mines, was well organized and waged important strikes during and after the war. In 1948, just as Kwame Nkrumah was invigorating the nationalist party, a consumer revolt broke out in Accra, reflecting the porous boundaries between workers and nonworkers in an urban setting and the common post-war problems of inflation, poor infrastructure, and poor living conditions.[33] When a march of ex-servicemen, seeking jobs and reintegration into post-war society, was fired on by police, a multiple-layered social situation turned into a tinderbox, with rioting, looting, and other

[33] For further details, see *Report of the Commission of Enquiry into Disturbances in the Gold Coast, 1948* (London, 1948); Dennis Austin, *Politics in Ghana 1946–1960* (London, 1964), pp. 66–72.

expressions of anger spreading throughout Accra and to other cities. The riots badly shook the government, which realized that armed forces could contain the revolt but not assure that workers would work or that urban order would be maintained. Officials simultaneously sought to co-opt a 'respectable' élite and isolate demagogic leaders from the volatile mass, only to find that it could not define who was the demagogue and who the respectable leader.

By 1949 colonial officials thought Nkrumah was engaged in an 'intensive drive to forge organised labour into the spear-head of his attack on ordered government'. London feared the Gold Coast was 'on the edge of revolution'.[34] Nkrumah indeed worked with labour unions to push a 'positive action' campaign, centred around a general strike, that would enlist labour in the cause of self-government and independence. But the British policy that sought to build labour stability around higher wages and a measure of collective bargaining was in fact paying off: organized labour was divided over Nkrumah's tactics, with some unions trying to make the most of what they could in wage gains within the framework of collective bargaining.

It was fear of disorder at the uncertain boundary between a working-class and young men shorn of their 'traditional' roots without having sunk urban ones that concerned the British government above all and which drove them to seek allies among 'respectable' colonial subjects in the Gold Coast. Predictably enough, these subjects saw in increasingly powerful territorial Assemblies and in increasingly open elections the best possibility for advancing their own, and their territory's interests, and the British government had little choice but to open the door to electoral democracy inch by inch. That the 1951 election under the new constitutional arrangements brought to power Nkrumah, who had been jailed for his role in positive action, revealed how little the colonial state could control political pressures that were leading to the dissolution of Empire in the Gold Coast. Whatever labour's role in the actual electoral process, the state's fear of the uncertain boundary of organized labour and disorganized society was crucial to creating the situation in which electoral decolonization was possible.

Nkrumah's party won the election and he became leader of a majority government with considerable power under continued British sovereignty.

[34] Acting Governor (Mangin) to Secretary of State, 3 June 1949, PRO, CO 96/797/31312/4/1949. The Secretary of State's fears are made clear in Richard Rathbone, ed., 'Introduction,' *British Documents on the End of Empire, Series B, Vol. 1: Ghana, Part I, 1941–1952* (London, 1992), p. xlviii.

In power, he feared the autonomy of trade unions and sought, much to the relief of the British, to co-opt them into his party-regime or to suppress them. By 1957, when the colony of the Gold Coast became the independent country of Ghana, labour had been marginalized as a political force, and its ability to make wage claims had considerably diminished. Nkrumah's radicalism was very much centred on separating the African nation from European imperialism, and the claims of organized labour to pay and benefits received short shrift in independent Ghana.[35]

Although Ghana forged the way for other independence movements, the variations of this pattern were important. In Kenya, the most important strike of the post-war era, a general strike in the port of Mombasa in 1947, was organized without benefit of trade union leadership but forced the government to respond with immediate wage increases and with a longer range programme of 'decasualizing' dockwork, turning day labourers into a regular, relatively well-paid work force, and seeking, with less success, to stabilize other forms of urban employment, so that a new generation of workers would emerge within the industrial, urban setting. The Kenyan government paid lip-service to the pro-trade union policy of the Colonial Office, but kept deciding that the actual unions that arose were not suitable for its purposes.[36]

Meanwhile, Kenyan families who had once had a measure of access to land resources while performing labour for white settlers in the Rift Valley were increasingly expelled and replaced by wage labourers, giving the owner greater flexibility in the use of land, labour, and, increasingly, machinery in the years of high prices for agricultural exports during the post-war era. To the extent that stabilization policies in the capital city of Nairobi, near the area of white-owned farms, were successful, they opened a gulf between the holder of a job and someone without one, which meant that expelled squatters had little chance of entering the regularized job sector. Better-off Africans who were finding a place as agricultural producers, increasingly possible around 1950, were rarely eager to welcome back expelled squatters to ancestral villages. The overlapping tensions between rural and urban areas eventually spawned

[35] For further information on Nkrumah's relationship with both 'modern' (labour) and 'traditional' (chiefs) organizations, see Jeffries, *Class, Power and Ideology*; Jeff Crisp, *The Story of an African Working Class: Ghanaian Miners' Struggles, 1870–1980* (London, 1984); Jean Marie Allman, *The Quills of the Porcupine: Asante Nationalism in an Emergent Ghana* (Madison, Wisc., 1993); Richard Rathbone, *Nkrumah and the Chiefs: The Politics of Chieftaincy in Ghana, 1951–1960* (Oxford, 2000).

[36] For a full description of this strike, see Cooper, *On the African Waterfront*, pp. 78–113.

an armed insurrection, some of whose leaders were former trade unionists from Nairobi who had been marginalized by the state's repression of trade union radicalism. The insurrection became known as Mau Mau, and after the declaration of an Emergency in 1952, it was brutally suppressed.[37]

While the British public was treated to propaganda about the alleged brutality of primitive rebels, the union movement finally was allowed to take root in Kenya, under the aegis of Tom Mboya. He skillfully portrayed effective unions as an alternative to mass disorder and won concrete gains for union members. Mboya rode the trade union federation to a position of influence in the nationalist movement for independence, whose earlier leaders, including Jomo Kenyatta, had been jailed. He was a key figure in the negotiations that led to independence in 1963. Mboya, and the Kenyan labour movement generally, was thus emblematic of a wider process of political positioning, making possible a kind of decolonization that Africanized political leadership without sharply breaking with the development-oriented social policies and export-oriented economic policies of late colonialism.[38]

Conclusion

In the 1830s British policy-makers briefly opened a window to thinking of the worker of African descent as potentially just like any other worker, capable of responding to the incentives of a free market in labour. Soon, however, the ex-slave of the British West Indian colonies was reclassified as a racial exception to a universal economic rule. It was only in the 1940s that the African (and West Indian) worker began to emerge from this vision of immutable distinctiveness, and this time he, and it was indeed a male figure that occupied the scene, appeared not so much as economic man but as social man. He was like any other worker, part of a collectivity of people who sold their labour and who had certain needs as a result of that fact. He needed not just to survive, but to be socialized into a milieu where the key

[37] Frederick Cooper, 'Mau Mau and the Discourses of Decolonization'. *JAH*, XXIX (1988), pp. 313–20. See also David Throup, *The Economic and Social Origins of Mau Mau, 1945–53* (London, 1987); Tabitha Kanogo, *Squatters and the Roots of Mau Mau, 1905–63* (London, 1987); On repression, see David Anderson, *Histories of the Hanged: Britain's Dirty War and the End of Empire* (New York, 2005).

[38] Cooper, *On the African Waterfront*, pp. 203–19; and David Goldsworthy, *Tom Mboya: The Man Kenya Wanted to Forget* (London, 1982).

distinctions were those of income and occupation, a differentiated social structure. To produce such a working class, a class separated not just from the property-owners for whom they worked but from those engaged in traditional forms of economic activity, required more than one generation, and therefore the worker's wife, who would raise the children, was a key figure in the new social vision. She should not be left behind in a village, where her traditionalist outlook and ignorance of modern health care, childrearing, and education would hold back her children. Family wages and family housing were thus crucial components of the new imperial design. Trade unions would be part of the picture too, for they embraced the worker in a predictable set of structures, far better than leaving him to mingle with other elements of the urban masses or be subject to politicians perceived to be populist demagogues.

On the surface, the reformulation of labour policy during and after the war took consideration of labour out of the racialized framework in which it had been stuck for the previous century. The potential of an African wage-worker to become a worker in the fullest sense of the term was acknowledged and supported, but race kept creeping into the world of work—in officials' promoting trade unionism in theory but not finding an African trade unionist who was quite suitable. Even more important was the way distinctions were made between a world of work, whose norms were seen as acultural and universal even if they derived from the social history of Europe, and an African world outside which was still defined by its cultural particularity. The very possibility opened to the African to become 'modern' cast in an even harsher light on the African who chose not to do so. That the new labour policy was called stabilization underscored that the task in Africa was not to make wage labour the basic form of production, as in ideal-typical capitalism, but to separate a domain of wage labour from a domain of traditional production and above all to insure that the reproduction of the wage earning class would take place uncontaminated by the primitiveness that lay outside it.

The dualistic vision so evident in the reports of labour officers and the various Commissions that studied different aspects of the labour question in the 1950s was unrealizable; in many ways it was a fantasy. African workers did not cease to be African; they did not cut themselves off from a wide range of social and cultural relationships. They might choose to live in a family arrangement other than that of the monogamous male breadwinner with his dependent wife and children. They might use their earnings to escape from rather than advance within wage labour, to improve a farm, to start a small business as an artisan. Their politics might not be about fostering their self-interest as workers, but in participating in the revitalization of village life or in a kind of populist nationalism.

Even in the mid-1950s, the best sociological studies were documenting a precarious world in African cities with a large area of overlap between wage and non-wage activities. Eventually this would be known as the informal sector, but from the start it represented the limits of the stabilization project of post-war British colonialism. If formal work remained largely a male bastion, the unregulated, unstabilized employment included a substantial female component, particularly in urban marketing. Still, the possibility of lifetime wage earnings sufficient to support a family and eventually a pension became, for many miners, railway workers, dockers, factory workers, and others with stable jobs a real possibility.

This did not imply that the acultural, modern worker of the bureaucrat's imagination had come into being. Lisa Lindsay's detailed study of Nigerian railworkers in the post-war era reveals that the most stable, best paid men were likely to retain close ties with communities of origin, using their wages to enhance their social and political position, that they were likely to live in extended families rather than the nuclear ones that social scientists associated with modern life, and that their earnings contributed capital to their wives' trading efforts and to other family enterprises. In Nigeria the Yoruba railwayman's aspirations were shaped not just by the possibilities of individual upward mobility opened up by unionized, stable labour, but by the idea of the 'big man', a figure of importance within a Yoruba community as well as in the world of skilled workers.[39]

That, in the independence era, such aspirations became increasingly unrealizable, as employment failed to grow, as inflation eroded pensions, and as African governments weakened unions and kept wages low, represented for many Africans the dashing of profound hope. Former railwaymen in Nigeria and ex-mine workers in Zambia suffered considerable deprivation and were saved from even worse not by the safety nets of modern industrial societies or even by trade union organization, but by the diverse social ties which they retained in both urban and rural communities.

[39] Lisa Lindsay, *Working with Gender: Wage, Labor and Social Change in Southwestern Nigeria* (Portmouth, NH, 2003); Ferguson, *Expectations of Modernity.*

For British officials, the exercise of imagining the African as a worker was an important one, for all its belittling and self-contradictory aspects. Labour was one dimension of imagining the possibility of an Africa that would reflect British influence, continue to trade, and to interact with Great Britain, and which could, however implausibly, be thought of as another offshoot of Britain after moving from the status of colony to that of Commonwealth member. Officials could imagine more plausibly, as the experience of Nkrumah first demonstrated, that African leaders could take over the painful task of disciplining labour movements, but that production would continue to take place in the forms which colonization had introduced. Thinking about workers and work, in short, helped make decolonization imaginable.

Once the bureaucracy of Empire took upon itself the task of superintending the details of labour organization and conflict in its African colonies from the mid-1930s, it learned lessons that colonialism on the cheap had not had to confront. The vision of the universal worker may have been for officials a way of asserting control, but for labour organizations it was a language in which to make claims: if you-want us to produce like a modern worker, then pay us like one. In the 1950s, the era of the general strike, like that of Mombasa in 1947, or the urban disturbance, like that in Accra in 1948, faded, but a more organized labour movement became adept at posing concrete demands, with the threat of amorphous violence lurking in the background.

As the costs of the policies necessary to reform imperialism grew, the possibility of a continued connection in a new guise between Britain and Africa seemed more attractive. Most important, perhaps, was the fact that colonial ideologies were making less and less sense in the 1950s, not just in an international arena heavily influenced by the self-determination doctrine but in social policy as well. If the African could be understood through the same social categories used for understanding workers in the metropole, maintaining the fiction of immutable difference between colonizer and colonized no longer served a purpose. Preserving an apparatus built to control and perpetuate such distinction appeared less useful than applying general mechanisms of social engineering to Africans.

By the late 1950s the British government knew that it was not going to get the disciplined, orderly work force it had hoped for, nor was the economic development programme producing the breakthroughs in productivity that were sought. The theory that incremental improvements in welfare would diffuse conflict was proving wrong as the contradictory effects of social change themselves provoked disputes and claim-making. By the end of the decade, Great Britain was ready to pass the messy realities of the labour question to the successor governments of its former colonies.

Select Bibliography

KELETSO ATKINS, *The Moon is Dead! Give Us Our Money!: Cultural Origins of an African Work Ethic, Natal, South Africa, 1843–1900* (Portsmouth, NH, 1993).

SARA BERRY, *No Condition is Permanent: The Social Dynamics of Agrarian Change in Sub-Saharan Africa* (Madison, 1993).

CAROLYN BROWN, '*We Were All Slaves*': *African Mines, Culture and Resistance at the Enugu Government Colliery* (Portsmouth, NH, 2003).

COLIN BUNDY, *The Rise and Fall of a South African Peasantry* (London, 1979).

FREDERICK COOPER, THOMAS C. HOLT, and REBECCA J. SCOTT, *Beyond Slavery: Explorations of Race, Labor, and Citizenship in Postemancipation Societies* (Chapel Hill, NC, 2000).

FREDERICK COOPER, *Decolonization and African Society: The Labor Question in French and British Africa.* (Cambridge, 1996).

JAMES FERGUSON, *Expectations of Modernity: Myths and Meanings of Urban Life on the Zambian Copperbelt* (Berkeley, 1999).

PATRICK HARRIES, *Work, Culture, and Identity: Migrant Laborers in Mozambique and South Africa, c. 1860–1910* (Portsmouth, NH, 1994).

RICHARD JEFFRIES, *Class, Power, and Ideology in Ghana: The Railwaymen of Sekondi* (Cambridge, 1978).

PAUL E. LOVEJOY and JAN HOGENDORN, *Slow Death for Slavery: The Course of Abolition in Northern Nigeria, 1897–1936* (Cambridge, 1993).

ELIAS MANDALA, *Work and Control in a Peasant Economy: A History of the Lower Tchiri Valley in Malawi, 1859–1960* (Madison,Wisc., 1990).

T. DUNBAR MOODIE, *Going for Gold: Men, Mines, and Migration* (Berkeley, 1994).

DAVID NORTHRUP, *Indentured Labor in the Age of Imperialism, 1834–1922* (Cambridge, 1995).

CLAIRE ROBERTSON, *Sharing the Same Bowl?: A Socioeconomic History of Women and Class in Accra, Ghana* (Bloomington, Ind. 1984).

RICHARD SANDBROOK and ROBIN COHEN, eds., *The Development of an African Working Class* (London, 1975).

HUGH TINKER, *A New System of Slavery: The Export of Indian Labour Overseas 1830–1920* (London, 1974).

CHARLES VAN ONSELEN, *The Seed Is Mine: The Life of Kas Maine, A South African Sharecropper, 1894–1985* (New York, 1996).

WILLIAM WORGER, *South Africa's City of Diamonds: Mine Workers and Monopoly Capitalism in Kimberley, 1867–1895* (New Haven, Conn., 1987).

12

The Black Experience in the British Caribbean in the Twentieth Century

HOWARD JOHNSON

The twentieth-century black experience in the British Caribbean varied over time and space and, at the individual level, largely reflected the position of peoples of African descent in the race–class hierarchy of their respective societies. Although the term 'black' encompasses the experiences of non-whites, ranging from those who were 'preserved in all... [their] opaque purity' to those of mixed race (some of whom looked white), it most often described those at the base of the social structure.[1] Throughout the region, blacks and browns constituted an overwhelming majority in most colonies, more than 90 per cent of the population, during the period 1921–46. In Jamaica, for example, that group formed 95.6 per cent of the total population of 1,237,063 in 1943. The main exceptions to this general pattern were British Guiana and Trinidad and Tobago where East Indians were a substantial minority amounting, in 1946, to over two-fifths of British Guiana's population and over one-third of Trinidad's and Tobago's.[2]

At the turn of the twentieth century and well beyond, blacks occupied the middle and bottom strata of a tripartite social structure inherited, in its essential features, from the slavery era. It is a system in which race and class remain interconnected. Writing in 1899 about Jamaican society, W. P. Livingstone, the English editor of the *Daily Gleaner* noted that colour distinctions influenced decisively relations between the classes: 'Broadly speaking, the position of all these classes is governed by the caste of colour.'[3] At the apex of most Caribbean societies was a white minority that maintained its social and economic (if not its political) dominance into the 1960s.

[1] Robert T. Hill, *Cuba and Puerto Rico* (New York, 1903), p. 738.

[2] R. R. Kuczynski, *Demographic Survey of the British Colonial Empire*, 3 vols. (London, 1953), III, pp. 27–30.

[3] W. P. Livingstone, *Black Jamaica: A Study in Evolution* (London, 1899), p. 165.

These élite whites remained socially exclusive in most colonies until the 1950s. Although there was no institutionalized colour bar, on the American South model, Barbados and the Bahamas were notorious for their long-lasting informal systems of segregation. In Barbados, in the late 1940s, there was only one public restaurant where blacks and whites could socialize in Bridgetown. In Jamaica, by contrast, social separation by race was confined to the private rather than the public sphere. As Morris Cargill, the white Jamaican journalist remembered of the 1930s, ' "keeping the niggers out" was a task to which the vast majority of whites addressed themselves constantly and with considerable enthusiasm'.[4]

In most British Caribbean societies, the descendants of free people of colour formed the core of the middle class. They had long differentiated themselves from the mass of the non-white population by their mercantile activities, ownership of land, access to a formal education, and entry into the professions. This group, occupying the upper tier of the middle class, also benefited, in Jamaica, from the decline in the sugar industry, which provided them with opportunities for joining the planter class. Light-skinned members of this group in Jamaica often aspired to whiteness forming the 'census whites' who were white by self-identification in the census records but were widely known to be of mixed ancestry.[5] By the late nineteenth century, the middle class expanded with the efforts to diversify British Caribbean economies away from sugar. In Trinidad and Grenada, the development of the cocoa industry and in Jamaica the expansion of banana production for export provided opportunities for lower-class blacks to achieve middle-class status. In 1891, the *Agricultural Record* noted the contribution of cocoa and other cash crops to the creation of a rural black middle class in Trinidad: 'Many ignorant black men will be found in this "Hinterland" living simple lives, but who have sons in the different Colleges, and by means of planting cocoa, coffee, etc., having acquired an independent estate of from two to eight or ten thousand pounds in value, and all this by patient industry, and starting without capital.'[6] The foregoing comment ignored the contribution of women, whether independently or as partners, to agricultural production and ultimately to class formation. In Trinidad, for example,

[4] Morris Cargill, *Jamaica Farewell* (New York, 1978), p. 90.

[5] Zora Neale Hurston, *Tell My Horse: Voodoo and Life in Haiti and Jamaica* (Perennial Library edn., New York, 1990), p. 8.

[6] Quoted in Howard Johnson, 'Merchant Credit and the Dispossession of the Cocoa Peasantry in Trinidad in the late Nineteenth Century', *Peasant Studies*, XV (1987), p. 35.

black women involved themselves in the cocoa industry as peasants, planters, and produce dealers. In Jamaica, women had long established themselves as producers and retailers in the internal marketing system, with responsibility for contributing to the family income.

The principal mechanism of middle-class formation (from the late nineteenth century onwards) was education at the primary and secondary levels. Equipped with an elementary education, blacks found employment as elementary school teachers, clergymen, policemen, postmasters/mistresses, and estate personnel. Although they were employed in clerical positions in the commercial sector in British Guiana, those positions in Barbados and Jamaica remained mainly the preserve of the whites and browns into the 1960s. This lower middle class of school teachers and clergymen would provide an important source of black leadership in the twentieth century. A secondary school education (to which few blacks initially had access) provided the necessary qualifications for entry into the professions and the lower levels of the colonial bureaucracy. In the major colonies, scholarships based on the results of English-derived examinations provided limited opportunities for a university education.

Educational opportunities created a middle-class élite whose members were able to manipulate English culture and were separated from lower-class blacks by their cultural 'refinement'. In the early twentieth century, they would base their claims to supersede whites in senior administrative positions and political representation on their cultural assimilation. C. L. R. James, in 1933, advanced this élite's characteristic argument: 'Cut off from all contact with Africa for a century and a quarter, they present today the extraordinary spectacle of a people who, in language and social customs, religion, education and outlook are essentially Western and, indeed, far more advanced in Western culture than many a European community.'[7]

Although diverse in their origins and occupations, the middle class shared an obsession with colour distinctions. Considerations of skin colour and physical attributes (preferably European-type) influenced marriage decisions and casual social relationships. Individuals were generally reluctant to associate with those of darker skin and were especially intent on distancing themselves from the lower class.

Across the region, the lower class mainly consisted of a landless proletariat, cultivators partly dependent on wage labour, and peasants capable of

[7] C. L. R. James, 'The Case for West Indian Self-Government'. Reprinted in Anna Grimshaw, ed., *The C. L. R. James Reader* (Oxford, 1992), p. 48.

supporting themselves from the proceeds of their own plots. In Jamaica, for example, the peasant sector had expanded in the late nineteenth century with the cultivation of cash crops such as coffee, ginger, tobacco, and bananas. In the towns, there were regularly employed labourers (including artisans and those in domestic service) and a reservoir of casual labourers who struggled to eke out an existence with economic activities which were often illicit. At the base of the social structure, the black man, as Marcus Garvey observed in 1916, was 'trampled on by all the shades above' in Jamaica. Employers treated him 'like a mule' and 'so much brute force'. In the domestic setting, Jamaican housewives, who viewed their servants as little more than 'animated machine[s]', substituted the 'lash of the tongue' for the whip.[8]

Unlike the middle classes which aspired to 'Englishness', the black lower class retained a strong identification with Afro-creole culture. The cultural divisions were reflected in the cosmology of folk beliefs, the religious observances, and the leisure-time activities of the lower classes. In Jamaica, a belief in *obeah* (an African-derived practice of sorcery involving the use of charms, poisons, and a control of the spirits) persisted. A correspondent to the *Jamaica Times* in 1901 contended: 'In our country districts, one half of our people either believes in, or practice Obeahism; and their beliefs and practices are promoted or increased by some who assume a religious form, and more under the title of "Revivalists." '[9] The cultural divergence was also evident in religious allegiances. Middle-class Jamaicans remained loyal to the mainstream churches whereas the black lower classes often attached themselves to syncretic Afro-Christian religious cults such as Myal, Revival, and Pocomania (Pukimina). Members of the middle class were especially anxious to distance themselves from the lingering manifestations of the African cultural heritage. As 'Climaticus' commented in 1902:

> When I say that our people are naturally inclined to be religious, I did not mean that they are naturally inclined to christianity. The heritage of slavery, spiritual blindness, ignorance and superstition cannot be got rid of in sixty or seventy years. The fetischism of Africa, the natural religion of our forefathers that be gat us, was not a merely surface religion, but went deep down into their constitution even to the marrow of their bones.[10]

[8] Quoted in Robert A. Hill, ed., *The Marcus Garvey and Universal Negro Improvement Association Papers, 1826–August 1919* (Berkeley, 1983), I, p. 179; Livingstone, *Black Jamaica*, p. 168.

[9] Letter by R. E. F., *Jamaica Times*, 25 May 1901.

[10] 'Climaticus', 'The Visit of the Keswick Delegates', *Jamaica Times*, 6 Dec. 1902.

Throughout the British Caribbean, the middle classes in the early twentieth century devalued folk cultural forms in song, dance, and stories. In Trinidad, where Carnival and the Calypso were essentially confined to the creole masses, the 'respectable' called for greater control over Carnival, with its potential for the expression of class antagonisms, and for the censorship of Calypso with its bawdy lyrics and political commentary.

The structure of social inequality was reinforced by the dual system of education, reflecting class divisions, which had emerged by the end of the nineteenth century. Elementary education, with its emphasis on teaching basic skills in reading, writing, and arithmetic, was intended for the lower class. Secondary education was initially designed for the brown and white upper and upper-middle classes. There was little attempt to turn the elementary and secondary tracks of the educational system into sequential stages. In most colonies, secondary schools served a small minority of the eligible population into the 1960s. Blacks who received a secondary education often found their employment opportunities limited. Writing about his career prospects on entering the Combermere School in Barbados in 1944, Austin Clarke (the Barbadian novelist) noted: 'It would turn me into a civil servant, if I did well. If I didn't do well, it would turn me into a sanitary inspector. If I did worse than that, into a "book-keeper," on one of the many sugar plantations . . . .'[11] Employment opportunities for educated women were equally circumscribed. Their options included working as teachers, nurses, clerks, secretaries, and typists.

By the first decade of the twentieth century, the abandonment of sugar production in some colonies and the reorganization of the industry in others resulted in the growth of unemployment, underemployment, and depressed wage levels. In Trinidad and British Guiana where creole blacks had, with indentured Indian immigration, moved to the top of the plantation hierarchy, estate amalgamation and modernization reduced the demand for factory workers and skilled artisans such as carpenters, masons, and coopers. In British Guiana, this crisis in plantation employment forced creole blacks to seek a living beyond the littoral into the interior, prospecting for diamonds and gold either as wage labourers or increasingly on their own account as independent 'pork-knockers'. Retrenchment in the sugar industry adversely affected not only those for whom estates had previously provided full-time employment but also those who had supplemented their income by

[11] Austin Clarke, *Growing Up Stupid Under the Union Jack* (Havana, 1980), p. 8.

occasional wage labour. In Jamaica and Grenada, the impact of the sugar crisis had been modified by the expansion of small holdings and a shift to export crop production by the peasants. There were, however, indications that the supply of land available for peasant settlement in Jamaica was becoming exhausted. The expansion of the banana industry as a plantation crop provided aspiring peasants with formidable competitors in the market for cultivable lands, made available by the decline of the sugar industry.

In some colonies, agricultural labourers without jobs or steady employment migrated in increasing numbers to the capital towns where they hoped to find work and raise their living standards. In Trinidad this urban drift included cocoa-growing peasants dispossessed of their properties by merchant-creditors. In Barbados there was a steady movement of people from the rural parishes to suburban St Michael between 1871 and 1921. By 1921 St Michael, which constituted 10 per cent of the island's total area, held more than one quarter of the island's population. Between 1911 and 1943 the population of the city of Kingston grew faster than that of the island as a whole. In the urban centres, women found employment as petty traders or domestic servants. H. G. De Lisser noted in 1913 that young women in Kingston had the option of joining 'the ranks of the domestic servants, the washerwomen, the cake-sellers'.[12] Almost one in four women in Georgetown, British Guiana was a domestic servant in 1905. Men worked as skilled artisans and performed the menial tasks associated with the commercial economy. Despite migrant expectations, urban employment opportunities did not keep pace with the number of labourers displaced by the plantation economy. In opting for urban life, migrants often exchanged rural poverty for destitution and squalor in the overcrowded and insanitary urban slums which promoted the spread of diseases. The 'slum-suburbs' of Kingston had their counterparts in the barrack yards of Port of Spain and the tenement houses of Bridgetown and Georgetown.

For many, external migration offered a solution to the problem of persistent poverty. The employment opportunities to which labour responded were generated primarily by the expansion of American capital investment in Central America and the Caribbean. This outward movement disguised the gravity of the economic crisis, as many island communities became remittance societies. In the Bahamas, where the major agricultural export staples had declined by the 1900s, labourers escaped depressed conditions and the

[12] H. G. De Lisser, *In Jamaica and Cuba* (Kingston, Jamaica, 1910), p. 111.

credit and truck systems (mechanisms of labour control) to work in South Florida. Between 1901 and 1924, when restrictive legislation was enacted, 102,000 Caribbean migrants entered the United States, most of whom were British West Indians. From the late nineteenth century labourers from the Leeward and Windward Islands migrated to the Dominican Republic, on a seasonal basis, where they worked mainly on US-owned sugar plantations. The level of dependence on Dominican employment in these islands can be gauged from the fact that, in some years, up to 90 per cent of Anguilla's male population left for that country.

The principal destination for West Indian labour migrants in the early twentieth century was Panama where the United States began work on an isthmian canal in 1904. Between 1905 and 1913, the Isthmian Canal Commission (ICC) recruited approximately 20,000 contract labourers in Barbados. However, most labourers (male and female) went to Panama independently. An additional 40,000 Barbadians and from 80,000 to 90,000 Jamaicans journeyed to Panama in those years, as did labourers from other British Caribbean colonies. With the completion of the Canal in 1914, some migrants left for the banana plantations of Costa Rica and Spanish Honduras and the sugar plantations of eastern Cuba, seeking wages comparable to those of the Canal Zone. Between 1911 and 1921 the estimated net emigration to Cuba from Jamaica amounted to 22,000. In the Eastern Caribbean, the establishment of oil refineries (to process Venezuelan petroleum) on Curaçao in 1918 and on Aruba in 1929 attracted labourers from adjoining British colonies.

External migration had significant implications for the colonies' family structure. This outward movement was sex-selective in nature, for young able-bodied men ventured abroad leaving their wives to assume responsibility for maintaining the household. It is estimated that in Barbados, 70 per cent of the migrants in the period 1861–1921 were male. This temporary arrangement often became permanent if wives were deserted, husbands died overseas, or remittances otherwise ceased. The effect of these developments was to accelerate the trend towards female-headed households which was discernible from the period of slavery. As the West India Royal Commission noted: 'The argument that the man is the head of the household and is responsible for the financial upkeep of the family has less force in the West Indies where . . . the woman so often is the supporter of the home.'[13]

[13] *West India Royal Commission Report, 1938–39*, Cmd. 6607 (London, 1945), p. 220.

By the 1920s large-scale emigration ended as the economies of the host countries entered a downward phase. With deteriorating conditions, the governments of the receiving countries enacted discriminatory legislation in the 1920s and 1930s to restrict the entry of foreign labourers and protect native workers from competition. Faced with reduced employment opportunities, hostility to foreigners, and destitution, many migrants returned home where economic conditions had deteriorated during their absence. The repatriation of migrants, often penniless, ended the remittances which had supported family members and (especially in Barbados) modified the rigid social structure by financing land purchases. Moreover, returning immigrants increased 'the reserve army of labour' of the unemployed and underemployed. Many colonists, accustomed to freedom of movement, responded to immigration restrictions with frustration.

In the inter-war years, there were several additional sources of lower-class discontent. Across the region, the wartime inflation in the price of basic consumer items, which resulted in an upward spiral in living costs and an erosion of the purchasing power of wages, persisted into the early peacetime years. The colonies also experienced a prolonged slowdown as the prices for agricultural exports (on which their economies remained largely dependent) fell sharply as supplies exceeded effective demand in the metropolitan markets. The sugar industry, for example, which had revived during the First World War as warfare disrupted continental beet sugar production, competed not only with traditional producers but also a government-subsidized British beet sugar industry. Some agricultural staples suffered from the effects of plant disease and hurricane damage. Economic conditions worsened with the global economic Depression which further reduced the demand for agricultural exports in the 1930s.

Throughout the British Caribbean, the sustained economic downturn had devastating consequences for the working classes. In some industries, employers responded to the falling prices for their commodities by reducing already low wages. The region's sugar industry continued the earlier strategy of plantation rationalization. The resulting gains in productivity were generally accompanied by a reduced demand for labour. A parallel development was the process of corporatization by which privately owned estates were gradually replaced by extensive plantations owned (except in Barbados) by externally based multinational corporations. The emergence of these monopoly corporations had important implications for labour relations throughout the sugar industry. Impersonal relations between capital and labour superseded the personalized and often paternalistic relations of the small estates.

In Jamaica's banana industry, the spread of Panama disease resulted in large-scale labour displacement. On the large plantations, the abandonment of land affected by the disease led to the widespread unemployment of plantation labourers. Peasant cultivators often destroyed both the infected plants and the food crops with which they had been interplanted. These actions, which removed the sources of their livelihood and subsistence, frequently forced them into an overcrowded labour market.

Two additional developments led to increased numbers seeking waged employment in Jamaica. First, many small and medium-sized peasant holdings had become fragmented, by sale and inheritance, into units so small that their owners were compelled to rely mainly on wage labour for a living. Second, the rapid increase in the island's population (by 50 per cent between 1911 and 1943), without a proportionate availability of new areas for land settlement, resulted in the emergence of a substantial body of landless proletarians.

In Jamaica, and elsewhere in the British Caribbean, population growth exacerbated the problems of underemployment and unemployment. This population increase reflected the downward trend in mortality rates as public health facilities improved. The inability of the region's economy to provide this steadily growing labour force with productive employment became a major and pervasive problem in the interwar years. In Trinidad and British Guiana, the mineral-extractive industries of petroleum and bauxite respectively were capital rather than labour intensive. Although the petroleum industry accounted in 1938 for nearly 60 per cent of Trinidad's exports, it employed less than 15,000 operatives in a population of over 450,000. In British Guiana, the bauxite industry employed approximately 1,300 workers.

By the early 1900s deteriorating material conditions for the working classes and the static position of blacks at the base of the race-class hierarchy prompted a class and racial consciousness in areas of the British Caribbean. This heightened awareness was expressed not merely in spontaneous protest but in the formation of organizations to improve labour conditions and promote a sense of black pride and identity as an essential component of racial upliftment. Although the two forms of consciousness are discussed separately, there are inevitably areas of overlap. Economic and labour grievances generally had a racial dimension.

The growth of the movement to instill racial self-respect was associated with regional and international developments. The first of those was the emergence of a black middle class whose members resented their exclusion from political participation and their experience of racial discrimination. The second was the establishment of Pan-African organizations throughout the African diaspora, a response to the European expansion in Africa in the late nineteenth century. In 1901 the Pan-African Association was established in both Jamaica and Trinidad after the visit of Henry Sylvester Williams, a Trinidadian, who had co-founded the organization in London in 1897. The early enthusiasm for this organization was not sustained and in Jamaica the association was defunct by 1902. Pan-Africanism later found institutional expression in the Garveyite movement.

Throughout the British Caribbean, the ideas of Marcus Mosiah Garvey proved the most significant factor in the growth of racial consciousness in the early twentieth century. He formed the Universal Negro Improvement Association (UNIA) in his native Jamaica in 1914 but his influence became widespread only after he left for the United States in 1916. The source of Garvey's appeal to Caribbean peoples was his effort to 'promote the spirit of race pride and love' and his assertion of a black nationalism which emphasized 'the beauty and dignity of being black and the ancestral heritage of Africa'.[14] His views, which were widely disseminated by the organization's newspaper, the *Negro World* and the reprinting of its articles in regional newspapers such as Trinidad's the *People* and St Kitts' *Union Messenger*, were thought to have influenced participants in the 1919 labour disturbances in British Honduras and Trinidad. In 1919–20 the colonial authorities in British Honduras, British Guiana, St Vincent and Trinidad banned the circulation of the paper. In the inter-war years, Garveyites would actively participate in labour and political movements throughout the region and influence public opinion in the black press.

Race consciousness, which manifested itself in the establishment of organizations with middle-class leadership, was an inescapable element of working-class experience. Members of the working class were especially aware of the unequal distribution of economic resources along racial lines. In the early 1900s their frustrated hopes for economic betterment and social change were often expressed in Afro-creole religious forms such as Revival in

[14] Ken Post, *Arise Ye Starvelings: The Jamaican Labour Rebellion and Its Aftermath* (The Hague, 1978), p. 144.

Jamaica which (like its antecedent Myal) had a political dimension. Alexander Bedward, who attracted a colonial-wide following from the 1890s into the 1920s, was in the millennial Native Baptist tradition. His concerns were primarily religious but the statements ascribed to him indicate his awareness of race as a factor in the structure of Jamaican society. By the 1930s a religious and political movement known as 'Ethiopianism' (black nationalist in orientation, with Ethiopia as a symbol of an idealized Africa) attracted broad-based popular support. This movement culminated in the emergence of the Rastafarian religion in Jamaica in 1933–34, the central tenet of which was the divinity of Emperor Haile Selassie of Ethiopia. In October 1935 the Italian invasion of Ethiopia evoked anti-white feeling and an ethnic consciousness throughout the region.

A class consciousness (which paralleled the rise of race consciousness) became evident in the late nineteenth century. Class struggle in its many forms had been a feature of post-emancipation society but it was only in the late 1890s that workers organized themselves to improve wages and working conditions. Initially, the early labour organizations represented groups of skilled urban workers. The Trinidad Workingmen's Association (TWA), which was established in 1897, drew its early support from skilled artisans but eventually included unskilled railway and waterfront workers. This organization combined the functions of a trade union and a political pressure group, thus broadening its appeal beyond the working class. With the exception of an abortive waterfront workers' strike in 1902, the TWA concentrated on political reforms rather than on trade union activities. The earliest of the Jamaican labour organizations was the Carpenters, Bricklayers and Painters Union founded in 1898. In 1901 tailors and shoemakers established a union and in 1907 separate unions were formed by printers and cigar makers. None of the Jamaican unions survived beyond the first decade of the twentieth century.

In British Guiana no lasting labour organization emerged before 1918 despite evidence of working-class militancy. The steady deterioration in wage rates and working conditions in the plantation sector from the late 1880s resulted in strikes in 1903, 1904 and 1905. The strikes of November–December 1905 mainly involved rural and urban Afro-creoles who demanded an increase in wage rates. With the exception of the 1906 waterfront strike in Georgetown, strike action (mainly in the sugar belt in successive years from 1908 to 1913) was spontaneous and unorganized.

By the beginning of the First World War, trade unions in Jamaica and Trinidad ceased to function effectively and, in other territories, failed to emerge. However, wartime economic conditions resulted in working-class militancy and revitalised efforts to organize labour. Prices for necessities had risen sharply but wages remained unchanged despite improved prices for export commodities such as sugar and cocoa during the war. The strikes of 1917–18 in British Guiana, Trinidad, St Lucia, St Kitts, and Jamaica reflected worker dissatisfaction with wages and working conditions. These strikes, which resulted in wage increases, gave new impetus to the organization of trade unions. In Jamaica, the Jamaican Federation of Labour was formed in 1917 from newly-established trade unions. In 1919, the TWA was revived to focus on working-class issues and the British Guiana Labour Union was formed. In St Kitts a 1916 law frustrated an attempt to establish a trade union by making its formation illegal.

The St Kitts' experience demonstrated the ability of colonial legislatures (dominated by the planter class) to obstruct the development of trade unionism. In the inter-war years, capital and government, in the colonial context, connived to limit the effectiveness of the existing trade unions in defiance of successive Colonial Office directives. By the mid-1930s, forming a trade union or taking strike action remained a criminal offence except for colonies where legislation had been enacted. These included Jamaica in 1919, British Guiana in 1921, the Leeward Islands in 1931, Trinidad and Tobago in 1932 and Grenada and St Lucia in 1933. However, peaceful picketing was outlawed in all colonies and trade unions were liable for employees' claims for losses sustained as a result of breach of contract or strikes, except in British Guiana. Up to the late 1930s no provisions were made either for bringing legitimate grievances to the attention of the employer class or for resolving labour disputes. With the labouring population throughout the British Caribbean largely unorganized and their economic interests virtually unprotected, employers (especially in the agricultural sector) combined to dictate wage levels.

Although members of the middle class were involved in projects for racial upliftment and organizing labour, their main preoccupation was with constitutional reform. Middle-class agitation for constitutional reform was most marked in the inter-war years but it had originated as a response to the introduction of Crown Colony government by 1898 in most colonies (except for Barbados, the Bahamas, and British Guiana) that had previously enjoyed representative government. Crown Colony government was primarily intended to limit the growing political participation of coloured and black men and forestall any threat which their anticipated dominance might pose to metropolitan economic interests. Members of the middle class had several objections to Crown Colony government. First, it barred them from political participation for, until the early 1920s, the only Crown Colony with an elective element was Jamaica. Second, it effectively stalled the careers of middle-class professionals since senior appointments in the civil service were reserved for white expatriates. In Jamaica, for example, this development reversed the pre-1865 trend towards admitting men of colour to senior posts. Finally, the middle class realized that the Crown Colony system, theoretically a benevolent and impartial autocracy, had developed into an oligarchy, reflecting the interests of an economic élite that shaped government policy by unofficial representation on the colonial legislatures and through social contact.

In the early 1900s middle-class reform organizations, which lobbied for constitutional reform, racial parity in the civil service and, in some cases, a federation of the colonies, were established in the British Caribbean. An early example of this type of organization was the short-lived National Club which was founded in Jamaica in 1909 by S.A.G. Cox who had experienced racial discrimination as a civil servant. As early as 1910 the National Club was demanding self-government on the same terms as the settler colonies of Canada and Australia. It was assumed that self-government would result in senior positions being filled by natives. In the Eastern Caribbean, a group of middle-class men in Grenada formed a Representative Government Association in 1914 and petitioned the Colonial Office for the restoration of the colony's representative institutions. The Colonial Office's concession of a few elected members to Grenada's Legislative Council, at the end of the First World War, led to the establishment of similar organizations in other colonies and petitions for representative government. In Trinidad, for example, the news of the concession to Grenada revitalized the movement for constitutional reform which had been especially active in the years 1885–88 and 1892–95. These demands for constitutional reform prompted the Colonial Office to send E. F. L. Wood, Parliamentary Under-Secretary of State for the Colonies, to visit the colonies in 1921–22 to investigate.

Wood's recommendation that the Crown Colony system be retained, reflected current Colonial Office thinking on the unsuitability of representative institutions for non-white tropical dependencies. He regarded such a government as unsuited to the plural societies of the British Caribbean with their sharp divisions along ethnic and religious lines (as in Trinidad) and substantial sections of the 'backward and politically undeveloped'.[15] This assertion of the backwardness of the black majority was an index of the centrality of race (especially the idea of white Anglo-Saxon superiority) to the imperial project by the late nineteenth century. The need to protect the hegemony of white capital from the threat of a politically empowered black majority limited the scope of Wood's recommendations for constitutional reform. He recommended the introduction of the elective principle as a concession to the black and brown intelligentsia politicized by foreign travel and wartime experiences. His main proposal for constitutional reform was implemented in 1924 when unofficial members, elected on a restricted franchise, were added to the Legislative Councils of Trinidad and Tobago, the Windward Islands, and Dominica. In 1928 the Colonial Office imposed Crown Colony government in British Guiana when it became clear that the planter–merchant coalition would no longer exercise state power.

In the inter-war years, a significant number of politically oriented organizations emerged which extended political activism, beyond the narrow middle-class emphasis on constitutional reform, to include issues of class, race and (especially in Jamaica) nationalism. Women and members of the working class participated in these organizations although their leadership was predominantly male and middle class. Their membership also included First World War veterans, whose wartime experience of racial discrimination made them sensitive to racial and class injustice, and returning migrants who were impatient with the lack of change in their home societies. Anti-establishment in nature, these organizations criticized the form of colonial rule but did not question the Imperial connection. They provided their membership with leadership opportunities and experience in organizational skills.

In Jamaica, the leadership of the anti-establishment organizations came primarily from the black petty bourgeoisie especially teachers, clergymen, journalists, urban artisans and middle farmers, some of whom had served a political 'apprenticeship' in the Jamaica Union of Teachers and the Jamaica Agricultural Society. These groups (largely Kingston-based) articulated a growing sense of a Jamaican identity and stressed the need for democratic change leading to self-government. They included the Jamaica League

[15] Quoted in Ann Spackman, ed., *Constitutional Development of the West Indies, 1922–1968: A Selection from the Major Documents* (Bridgetown, Barbados, 1975), pp. 76–78.

(1913–22) and the Jamaica Reform Club (1923–33), which adopted the motto 'Jamaica for Jamaicans' and advocated universal adult suffrage. The most widely influential organization was the Universal Negro Improvement Association (UNIA) under the leadership of Garvey, who resided in the colony between 1928 and 1935. He contributed to the growth of a national consciousness by rejecting the existing system of racial values, thus countering the 'carefully nurtured sense of inferiority' which was a feature of the colonial experience.[16] In the late 1930s, two organizations with nationalist agendas were launched: the Jamaica Progressive League and the National Reform Association. Progressive political ideas and the new nationalism were widely discussed in the *Public Opinion*, a weekly journal which began publication in 1936. The political awakening of this period was reflected in the formation of citizens' associations, study groups, and literary associations in both rural and urban contexts. These were not overtly political organizations but their meetings became a forum for the discussion of social and political issues.

In Trinidad and Tobago, political activism in the years before 1937 was closely associated with the Trinidad Workingmen's Association (TWA) and Captain A. A. Cipriani, a white Creole who assumed the presidency of the organization in 1923 on the invitation of its black leadership. Under his leadership, the TWA attracted both black and Indian adherents. In 1936 the organization (by then renamed the Trinidad Labour Party) had an estimated membership of 125,000. The name change reflected a shift in focus from working-class concerns to the achievement of political reform. Members of the TWA disillusioned by this reformist approach sometimes joined the Negro Welfare Cultural and Social Association (an organization which combined a Marxist-Leninist influence with a black nationalist orientation) which was established in 1934.

In Trinidad and Tobago and Jamaica middle-class women became active participants in the social and political movements of the inter-war years. In 1921 Audrey Jeffers formed the Coterie of Social Workers in Port of Spain. This organization focused its attention on providing social services for the colony's women and children and eventually demanded a greater political role for women. In 1936 Jeffers became the first woman to hold elective political office in the colony. A Jamaican counterpart to the Coterie appeared in 1936 when a group of middle-class black women formed the Women's

[16] Richard Hart, *From Occupation to Independence: A Short History of the Peoples of the English-Speaking Caribbean Region* (London, 1998), p. 94.

Liberal Club. The organization's objectives included advancing the status of Jamaican women, encouraging them to develop a civic consciousness, an involvement in politics, and the fostering of a national spirit. This militancy was a response to gender discrimination in societies where women, up to the 1930s, had few opportunities for political participation. In those colonies where women were eligible for the vote or to stand for election, the property and income qualifications guaranteed that few satisfied them.

In Barbados the working and middle classes, which had hitherto remained silent on social and economic issues, began to organize to effect change in the inter-war years. The dominance of an agro-commercial bourgeoisie in the economy and in politics undoubtedly muted the criticism of a small black middle class, largely dependent on its patronage. The major figure in the evolving critique of conditions under the white oligarchy was Dr C. D. O'Neale who founded the Democratic League—the colony's first political party—in 1924. This organization attracted support from middle-class professionals and sections of the working class, especially the members of the UNIA. In 1926 O'Neale also launched the Workingmen's Association which failed to mobilize workers for trade union activity on a long-term basis. Although the Democratic League disintegrated after O'Neale's death in 1936, friendly societies and lodges continued to foster skills of political organization and mobilization among their working-class membership

By the late 1930s, organizations whose leadership, memberships, and concerns were primarily working-class were established in Jamaica and Trinidad. In Trinidad, T. U. Butler formed the British Empire Workers and Citizens Home Rule Party, in 1936, which addressed working-class grievances. In rural Jamaica, new groups expressed the class grievances of peasants and agro-proletarians and presented their concerns to the colonial authorities and the wider public. The emergence of these organizations reflected the growing economic pressure experienced by peasants who were unable to pay the annual land tax and often cultivated land rented from large proprietors on an insecure tenure. In 1938, for example, a peasant organization, the Poor Man's Improvement Land Settlement and Labour Association (PMILSA) was formed, in the parish of Clarendon, by Robert E. Rumble.

In Trinidad, working-class discontent with existing conditions was expressed not only in organized action but through the medium of the Calypso. During the 1930s calypsoes documented a wide spectrum of social and economic experiences and became 'the major forum for the expression of working-class dissent'. In 1934, for example, 'Workers' Appeal' by the calypsonian the Growling Tiger dealt with the chronic problems of unemployment, hunger and starvation:

> Anywhere you go you must meet people sad
> They search for employment: none can be had
> They start to drop down dead in the street
> Nothing to eat and nowhere to sleep
> All kind-hearted employers I appeal now to you
> Give us some work to do.

In that same year, the colonial government censored the performance of Calypso and two years later, calypso records.[17]

Evidence of deteriorating social and economic conditions and working-class efforts to publicize their plight did not prompt effective ameliorative action by the colonial or metropolitan governments. This official complacency is partly explained by the fact that the black majority remained largely unrepresented in most colonies where legislatures were controlled by nominated members, representing the propertied interests, and unofficials elected on a restricted franchise. Equally important was the lingering influence of laissez-faire ideas—the dominant social philosophy of the Victorian era—which viewed government's role in social and economic matters as one of non-interference. In the inter-war years, the nineteenth-century orthodoxy, that a colony should have only those services which it could afford to maintain from its own resources, dominated the thinking of the Treasury and the Colonial Office

Official attention to working-class demands came only with the series of labour rebellions which occurred with alarming regularity throughout the British Caribbean between 1934 and 1939. Strikes and riots were the familiar methods by which workers, who were virtually unrepresented in the political process, took political action. Those of the late 1930s were unprecedented in scope and scale, affecting most sectors of the colonial economies, and for that reason attracted greater public attention. In British Honduras, labour agitation which began in February 1934 developed into a riot in September. In that same year labour disturbances affected sections of the sugar belt in both Trinidad and British Guiana. In January 1935 a general strike of agricultural labourers in St Kitts was followed by a strike in Trinidad's oilfields and a hunger march to Port of Spain in March. In Jamaica labour protests broke

[17] Gordon Rohlehr, *Calypso and Society in Pre-Independence Trinidad* (Port of Spain, Trinidad, 1990), pp. 125, 186.

out in May among banana workers in the town of Oracabessa and dock-workers in Falmouth. In September and October, labourers rioted at several estates in British Guiana. Riots occurred in Kingstown and Camden Park on St Vincent in October. There were no labour disturbances in 1936 but in the following year they resumed on a larger scale than those of 1934–35. In Trinidad, the strikes and riots of 1937 began in the oilfields and eventually spread to the sugar belt and the towns. In Barbados the disorders affected both Bridgetown and the rural areas. In 1938 there were island-wide disturbances in Jamaica during the months of May and June. In February 1939 a major strike broke out at the Plantation Leonora in British Guiana.

The Colonial Office responded to the series of labour rebellions of 1937–38 with coercion, commissions of inquiry, conciliation, and eventually reform. In Trinidad and Barbados, martial law was declared, British forces were despatched to restore public order, and commissions of inquiry established to investigate the causes of these outbreaks. With the outbreak of the Jamaican disturbances in May 1938, Colonial Office officials abandoned the policy of colonial self-sufficiency by which individual colonies would finance the slow introduction of reforms from their own resources and accepted the principle that the British government should finance schemes for economic development and social welfare which the colonies could not afford. A West India Royal Commission, chaired by Lord Moyne, was directed to investigate social and economic conditions in the British Caribbean and make recommendations. The terms of reference reflected the new importance that working-class demands assumed in the making of colonial policy after their 'extra-constitutional' direct action of the late 1930s.

The Commissioners, who reported in December 1939, recognized that colonial discontent was no longer 'a mere blind protest against a worsening of conditions, but a positive demand for the creation of new conditions that will render a better and less restricted life'.[18] Comprehensive in their analysis of the underlying economic problems at the colonies, the Commissioners offered no general strategy for the economic transformation of the region. They noted, for example, that the colonies would need a substantial and sustained expansion of economic activity (with a reduced dependence on export production) to cope with the chronic problems of underemployment and unemployment. The Commissioners expressed concern over rapid population growth in the British Caribbean (at a rate of between 1.5 and

[18] *West India Royal Commission Report*, p. 8.

2 per cent annually), which increased intermittent employment and underemployment, and urged a reduction in the birth rate, warning that the colonies would soon face the formidable task of providing gainful employment for individuals of working age. The Commissioners acknowledged the importance of a programme of land settlement for promoting the development of a class of smallholders and reducing underemployment, but rejected it as too expensive. They did not regard industrial development as a panacea for the region's economic problems, anticipating that the manufacturing sector would remain small-scale and thus unable to reduce unemployment levels significantly.

The Commission's main recommendation was that the British government should assume financial responsibility for essential social services which the colonies could not afford. To implement such schemes, the Commissioners proposed the establishment of a West Indian Welfare Fund, to be financed by an annual grant of £1 m from the British government over a twenty-year period. It also recommended the appointment of a Comptroller (directly responsible to the Secretary of State for the Colonies) and a staff of advisers whose expertise would be available to colonial administrations. In 1940, the Commission's proposal for the British Caribbean was superseded by an ambitious Empire-wide programme. The Colonial Development and Welfare Act of that year allocated £5 m yearly to colonial development and welfare for a ten-year period and £500,000 for colonial research annually for an indefinite term.

In the first fifteen years of its existence, the programme of colonial development and welfare (originally conceived to ameliorate West Indian conditions) failed to produce the anticipated results. The implementation of major development and welfare projects was delayed by wartime mobilization and the competition for scarce material resources. As early as 1941, some colonies were remitting funds to Britain in support of the war effort instead of receiving the promised financial assistance. In fact colonial resources in the main financed the development projects undertaken. Progress on planned projects was, moreover, slowed by the method of implementation and the resilience of ideas on colonial self-efficiency. Final decisions on projects and on funding were made by Colonial Office officials who were reluctant to initiate welfare projects where individual colonies would be unable to finance the recurrent costs from their own resources. By the early 1950s the inadequacies of the programme of colonial development and welfare were evident. Colonial Office officials clearly regarded the metropolitan commitment as a short-term one and expected that individual colonies would increasingly assume financial responsibility for development and welfare projects. They had, moreover, begun to despair of achieving viable economies and self-sufficiency in the smaller colonies, despite years of funding development projects.

The gradual introduction of representative government in the British Caribbean after 1940 was tacit acknowledgement that the system of élite control was no longer tenable. It was an incremental process which involved at different stages, the extension of the franchise, universal adult suffrage, increases in unofficial representation, and the eventual concession of elected majorities in the legislatures. This slow pace indicated the Colonial Office's lingering doubts about the suitability of representative institutions in societies with black majorities. The Moyne Commission had not proposed the immediate introduction of universal adult suffrage but recommended that 'universal suffrage should be the ultimate goal'.[19] In 1944 Jamaica was granted a new constitution with universal adult suffrage primarily as a result of United States pressures. Adult suffrage was subsequently introduced in Trinidad and Tobago in 1945, in Barbados in 1950, the Leeward and Windward Islands in 1951, British Guiana in 1953 and in British Honduras in 1954. Elected majorities were granted to Trinidad and Tobago in 1950, to Grenada, St Vincent, St Lucia, Dominica, Antigua, St Kitts-Nevis, Montserrat, and the Leeward Islands Federation in 1954, and to British Honduras and the British Virgin Islands in 1954. By the late 1950s Barbados and Jamaica had already been granted the ministerial system and advanced, in 1958 and 1959 respectively, to full internal self-government, with responsibility for internal affairs. The pace of constitutional development mainly reflected the British government's assessment of each colony's readiness to move to the next stage but reforms were generally introduced after political agitation in the colonies.

Throughout the British Caribbean, the transition to representative government coincided with the emergence of viable trade unions and political parties which pressed for constitutional change. In most colonies the labour disturbances began and spread without leadership or support from a formal trade-union organization. However, middle-class leaders quickly emerged who took advantage of the spontaneous working-class protest as the vehicle for their own political advancement. In the aftermath of the disturbances, these leaders recognized the opportunities for organizing the working

[19] *West India Royal Commission Report*, p. 380.

classes. It was a process facilitated by the colonial and metropolitan governments' interest in fostering 'legitimate' labour movements. In Trinidad, Adrian Cola Rienzi, an Indo-Trinidadian lawyer, formed the Oilfield Workers' Trade Union, which was predominantly Afro-Trinidadian in composition, and the All Trinidad Sugar Estates and Factories Workers' Trade Union which was overwhelmingly Indian. In Barbados and St Kitts, middle-class political organizations formed links with the working classes after the disturbances. In 1941 the Barbados Workers Union was organized as the offshoot of the Progressive League, with Grantley Adams, an Oxford-educated lawyer as President. In St Kitts, the St Kitts Trades and Labour Union was established in 1940 under the middle-class leadership of members of the Workers' League. In Jamaica the 1938 disturbances led to the formation of the Bustamante Industrial Trade Union by W. A. Bustamante, a businessman.

In most colonies, the colonial and British governments attempted to shape the development of the trade unions, usually with the collaboration of middle-class trade unionists. After the disturbances, the Colonial Office was especially concerned that 'responsible' trade unionism, compatible with the interests of colonial business, should be established. Legislation guaranteed trade unions the right of peaceful picketing and protection from legal action but colonial governments retained control over the development of trade unions by the establishment of labour departments. These departments, which worked closely with the British Trades Union Congress, were expected to provide guidance and supervision to trade unions, in part, by emphasizing the distinction between industrial disputes and political militancy. In the cold war context, US trade unions also influenced the direction in which British Caribbean trade unionism developed. In Jamaica, for example, the United Steelworkers of America worked closely with the National Workers' Union to exercise control over the bauxite-alumina workers and ensure a stable business environment for the exploitation of the island's bauxite reserves. By the early 1950s, Jamaica supplied the United States with more than 50 per cent of its imports of alumina, a strategic raw material.

In some colonies, the years following the disturbances were marked by the emergence of political parties which relied on allied trade unions for their mass voting support. Among them was the Progressive League in Barbados which became the Barbados Labour Party in 1944. In Jamaica W. A. Bustamante led both the Bustamante Industrial Trade Union (BITU) and the Jamaica Labour Party by 1943. In 1946 Robert Bradshaw founded the

St Kitts Labour Party for which the St Kitts Trade and Labour Union provided the mass base. In both Antigua and Grenada, trade unions formed the core of support for political parties which were later established. The Antigua Labour Party developed from the Antigua Trades and Labour Union which was founded in 1939. By the late 1940s Vere Bird led both organizations. The Grenada Manual and Mental Workers' Union, established by Eric Gairy in 1950, formed the basis of his Grenada People's Party launched in the following year. The institutionalization of the labour movement was often accompanied by the rise of 'charismatic authoritarian leaders' such as Bustamante, Bradshaw, Bird, and Gairy. They regarded the labour organizations as their 'personal vehicle rather than the organised expression of working-class aspirations'.[20]

Although the Colonial Office opposed the development of links between political parties and trade unions (arguing that trade unions should limit their activities to industrial action) the trend persisted throughout the region. Political parties with a trade-union base integrated the working classes into colonial politics and eventually mobilized their support for political demands such as universal adult suffrage and self-government. Political parties such as the People's National Party of Jamaica and the Barbados Labour Party (despite its trade-union base) reflected their middle-class leadership by focusing on the struggle for self-government rather than on social and economic change.

By the 1940s a nationalist consciousness among the middle classes manifested itself not only in political activities but in a sense of cultural identity. The cultural divide between the middle and working classes narrowed as members of the intelligentsia celebrated Afro-creole culture as authentic and non-European. In Jamaica the urban brown middle class emphasized the existence of a collective cultural identity based on a shared creole folk culture. In Trinidad, the Calypso and Carnival, hitherto primarily the cultural expression of the working class, came eventually to define the national culture. Across the region, working-class life provided the source material for literary production. In the inter-war years Trinidad writers attempted to produce a distinctly West Indian body of literature which was published locally in two magazines, *Trinidad* (1929–30) and the *Beacon* (1931–33, 1939). In their short fiction, middle-class writers including the Afro-Trinidadians

[20] O. Nigel Bolland, *The Politics of Labour in the British Caribbean: The Social Origins of Authoritarianism and Democracy in the Labour Movement* (Kingston, Jamaica, 2001), pp. 515, 582.

C. L. R. James and C. A. Thomasos used 'West Indian settings, speech, characters and conflicts', focusing on urban working-class life in the barrack yard. In 1942 *Bim* was launched in Barbados by Frank Collymore, and in British Guiana in 1945 A. J. Seymour, in the first issue of *Kyk-over-al*, expressed the hope that it would be 'an instrument to forge a Guianese people'.[21] In Jamaica in 1943 the sculptor Edna Manley founded the literary journal *Focus*. She had earlier gathered around her a group of artists who together developed a distinctively Jamaican iconography. Two Jamaican novelists reflected in their work a national consciousness and the new interest in the 'folk.' V. S. Reid's *New Day* (1949) celebrated, in a fictional account, Jamaica's new constitution with universal suffrage in 1944, using as his narrator a representative of the rural peasantry. In his novels, *The Hills Were Joyful Together* (1953) and *Brother Man* (1954), Roger Mais described the poverty and squalor experienced by the urban working class and gave a sympathetic portrayal of the Rastafarian.

Although a nationalist consciousness had developed in the British Caribbean by the late 1940s, the intense nationalism and anti-colonialism which marked the African and Asian colonies was not evident. As Raymond T. Smith has observed: 'Caribbean nationalism has always lacked the coherent form that might have been supplied by a traditional culture.'[22] In most colonies, nationalist sentiment was still largely confined to the middle class. The main focus of working-class loyalty remained the British monarchy which was first associated with slave emancipation. This loyalty had been further encouraged by the educational system and the Empire-day celebrations of the twentieth century. The British government regarded nationalism as non-threatening and compatible with metropolitan interests. Colonial nationalists did not demand changes in the existing social and economic structure, choosing instead to concentrate on the eventual attainment of self-government within the British Commonwealth. The gradual modification of the Crown Colony system had not conflicted with the protection of Britain's economic interests in the region.

[21] Reinhard W. Sander, *The Trinidad Awakening: West Indian Literature of the Nineteen-Thirties* (New York, 1988), p. 9; Kenneth Ramchand, *The West Indian Novel and its Background* (London, 1970), pp. 71–72.

[22] Raymond T. Smith, 'Social Stratification, Cultural Pluralism and Integration in West Indian Societies', in S. Lewis and T. G. Mathews, eds., *Caribbean Integration: Papers on Social, Political and Economic Integration* (Rio Piedras, Puerto Rico, 1967), p. 242.

An exception to this trend was British Guiana, where the British government suspended the constitution on 9 October 1953, after landing troops in Georgetown, overthrowing the democratically elected government of the People's Progressive Party led by Dr Cheddi Jagan. This suspension came 133 days after the Party, in the first election under adult suffrage, received the support of the African and East Indian communities, winning eighteen of the twenty-four seats in the Legislative Council. The British government justified its action by claiming that it was necessary to prevent the establishment of a Communist state within the British Commonwealth. At the height of the cold war, the Colonial Office, the British Cabinet (and the US government) believed that British Guiana and its ruling party were threatened with subversion from the Soviet Union, which was strongly opposed to the continued existence of the British Empire. More important, however, was the economic threat from a colonial government whose members were intent on initiating, with popular support, radical political and economic reforms which would adversely affect foreign-owned sugar and bauxite companies.

The long-term effect of the British intervention was to polarize the Guianese population along ethnic lines. The British government worked to destroy the People's Progressive Party as a broadly based national movement by dividing the anti-colonial forces. It swung its support to Forbes Burnham, a black lawyer who was regarded by the colonial administration as a viable alternative to the left-wing Jagan. Burnham split the party into two factions in 1955 and in 1957 established the People's National Congress. By 1957 the pattern of racial polarization (which has remained a feature of Guianese politics) was clear as African and Indian politicians of separate parties increasingly appealed to ethnic fears to obtain votes. There were similar developments in post-war Trinidad where, with the introduction of adult suffrage, political parties organized along ethnic lines exploited the tensions between blacks and Indians.

The political and economic reforms of the post-war years modified but did not reorder the existing social and economic structure of the British Caribbean. In most colonies, the control of the state apparatus passed gradually to the members of the black and brown middle classes with the introduction of adult suffrage. Members of the white élite largely retreated from participation in the electoral process but continued to exercise effective power as they survived and adapted to the black democracies. This power derived from the white minorities' control of the colonial economy which remained unchallenged. In Barbados, for example, the diversification of the economy to include light manufacturing and tourism by the 1950s provided the white corporate bourgeoisie with additional opportunities for expanding their operations. In Trinidad, the white élite extended its economic interests beyond plantation agriculture and commerce to include manufacturing, real estate development, and finance.

Among the major beneficiaries of the social and economic developments of this period were the members of the middle class. In many colonies, the opportunities for government-related employment increased with the changing and expanding role of the colonial state. Members of the educated middle class found jobs as teachers, civil servants, and professionals. In some colonies such as Jamaica and Trinidad, the operations of the mineral-extractive industries resulted in the emergence of enclaves of well-paid, mid-level employees (often segregated residentially from the white expatriate management) in a wider setting of poverty and discontent. The widening gap between the middle and lower classes was readily apparent. Writing of Jamaica in the 1950s, Rex Nettleford has observed: 'Successive salary revisions, new houses, motor cars were the barometers of the new benefits which flowed in directions away from the black lower classes.'[23]

In the post-war wars, the problems of unemployment and underemployment persisted as a burgeoning population continued to outpace employment opportunities. In most colonies, the plantation monopoly of arable land continued. In Jamaica and Trinidad, moreover, the bauxite and oil companies respectively acquired prime agricultural land with proven or probable mineral reserves, thus limiting the supply of land available for peasant production. Across the British Caribbean emigration once again assumed importance as a survival strategy. As politicians failed in their efforts to provide job opportunities for an expanding labour force, they increasingly adopted mass migration as a central feature of their economic policy. Although some individuals (especially in the Bahamas and Jamaica) went to the United States as short-term contract labourers on government-sponsored programmes, most left spontaneously for destinations within the Caribbean and for Britain. Immigrants from the Leeward and Windward Islands went to Trinidad, Aruba, and Curaçao where they found employment in the oil industry. The development of the tourist industry (with its

[23] Rex M. Nettleford, *Mirror Mirror: Identity, Race and Protest in Jamaica* (Kingston, Jamaica, 1970), p. 48.

demand for labourers in construction and the service occupations) in the US Virgin Islands also attracted migrants from the Eastern Caribbean. The major destination was, however, Britain where the demand for labour for post-war reconstruction resulted in massive migration from the British Caribbean. It has been estimated that between 230,000 and 280,000 West Indians entered Britain from 1951 to 1961.

External migration coincided with the efforts of colonial governments in Jamaica, Trinidad, and Barbados to diversify their economies and create jobs. In Jamaica, the post-war economic boom was partly based on the growth of tourism and on traditional agricultural exports such as sugar and bananas. The main boost to the Jamaican economy came, however, from bauxite--aluminum production and secondary industries. By 1957 the Jamaican government had renegotiated the terms of its agreement with the bauxite companies and increased the level of income from that source. The Jamaican government also adopted a strategy of industrialization which was based on attracting foreign investors to produce primarily for the domestic market. In Barbados, the diversification programme centred on tourism and light manufacturing. Although Trinidad also pursued a strategy of 'industrialisation by invitation', along lines suggested by the West-Indian economist W. Arthur Lewis, its prosperity remained dependent on its oil industry. Manufacturing, tourism, and the extractive industries were capital-intensive and failed to create adequate employment for the region's steadily increasing labour force. Manufacturing and tourism, moreover, relied on high levels of imports and thus had few linkages with other sectors of the host economy. Although the conventional gauges of economic growth, such as per capita income, recorded a favourable trend in these colonies, they concealed the persistent problems of unemployment and underemployment which the development of new sectors of economic activity had done little to abate.

By the late 1950s, the British government was more concerned about the failure of the smaller British Caribbean colonies to become economically viable than the inability of the larger colonies to provide productive employment for their labour force. Treasury officials increasingly feared that these colonies could become a permanent drain on British resources in a period of economic decline. An index of the British government's anxiety about the costs of Empire was Prime Minister Harold Macmillan's request in 1957 for a cost–benefit analysis of the colonies, which confirmed the declining economic and military value of the Empire. In the British Caribbean, the

Colonial Office had hoped that that a West Indian Federation, which was finally established in 1958, would create a viable political and economic unit that would become financially self-sufficient and thus qualified for self-government. By the end of the decade, however, it was already clear that the Federation would not provide the mechanism by which the more prosperous colonies (especially Jamaica and Trinidad) would assume financial responsibility for their impoverished regional partners. Britain's application for membership in the European Economic Community in 1961 signalled an intention to place its relationship with the colonial Empire on a new footing. In 1959 Iain Macleod had been appointed Colonial Secretary with instructions to hasten the process of decolonization.

The way was cleared for the decolonization of the British Caribbean in January 1960 when Macleod assured the Jamaican government that he regarded the colony as qualified for independence on its own. Up to that point, the Colonial Office had envisaged that the colonies would achieve nationhood not individually but as part of a West Indian Federation. It was not, however, until 19 September 1961, after the Jamaicans voted to withdraw from the Federation, that Jamaica left the union. The years of the Federation's existence were marked by intercolonial disputes on a range of issues, including the freedom of movement of people throughout the region, the financing of the Federal government, the co-ordination of fiscal, customs, and tariff policy, and the representation of individual units in the federal legislature. The main tensions were generated, however, by the attempts of nine of the constituent units to accommodate the demands of a Jamaican government which was increasingly intent on pursuing an independent line on plans for economic development. Jamaica, under the leadership of Norman Manley, viewed a stronger federal structure as incompatible with its development programme. In Trinidad, Dr Eric Williams of the ruling People's National Movement, which had come to power in 1956, supported the strengthening of a Federation that would advance to Dominion status.

For Eric Williams, the political implications of Jamaica's withdrawal from the Federation were clear. He feared that Trinidad would have to assume financial responsibility for the eight less developed territories. Four months later, Trinidad declined to participate in an Eastern Caribbean Federation. The West Indian Federation came to an end on 31 May 1962, thus preparing the way for independence by each territory.

By 1962 the earlier British criteria for granting independence—size and economic viability—were no longer strictly applied. The willingness to grant independence to the British Caribbean colonies was influenced not only by metropolitan economic considerations but also by earlier grants of independence to colonies which were often smaller and poorer. Between 1962 and 1966 the four main colonies—Jamaica, Trinidad and Tobago, Barbados, and British Guiana (which had chosen not to join the Federation)—became independent. By the early 1980s, the British government had disengaged from its colonial entanglements, except for a few dependent territories such as the Cayman Islands and the Turks and Caicos Islands, which have chosen to remain colonies.

At the time of decolonization, the problems of unemployment and chronic underemployment (and the associated social ills) evident from the opening years of the twentieth century, remained unsolved. In the aftermath of the 1930s labour rebellions, these problems had been identified, analysed, and addressed by both the metropolitan and colonial governments. In the major colonies, successive administrations attempted to diversify their economies, hitherto reliant on agricultural export staples. However, the capital-intensive tourist, manufacturing, and mineral-extractive industries could not absorb the rapidly expanding labour force. Once again, many saw emigration as the only means of coping. Even in the most prosperous colonies (where the middle and upper classes were the main beneficiaries of economic growth), the disparities in income between rich and poor widened, thus bringing class and colour differences more sharply into focus. By the 1950s, there were signs of deeply rooted grievances and tensions among the black lower classes in some societies. In Jamaica, for example, increased support for the Rastafarian movement brought to public attention the failure of governments since 1944 to improve the material conditions of the black majority. At independence, the position of the black majority in Jamaican society was, perhaps unintentionally, acknowledged in the selection of the colour black, to symbolize hardship, for Jamaica's national flag. Across the British Caribbean, colonies advanced to independence without a disruption of the long-entrenched social structure, with its colour/class correlation.

Select Bibliography

O. NIGEL BOLLAND, *The Politics of Labour in the British Caribbean: The Social Origins of Authoritarianism and Democracy in the Labour Movement* (Kingston, Jamaica, 2001).

GREAT BRITAIN, *The West Indian Royal Commission Report, 1938–39*, Cmd. 6607 (London, 1945).

JEFFREY HARROD, *Trade Union Foreign Policy: A Study of British and American Trade Union Activities in Jamaica* (London, 1972).

RICHARD HART, 'Origin and Development of the Working Class in the English-Speaking Caribbean Area: 1897–1937', in Malcolm Cross and Gad Heuman, eds., *Labour in the Caribbean* (London, 1988).

HOWARD JOHNSON, 'The British Caribbean from Demobilization to Constitutional Decolonization', *Oxford History of the British Empire*, 5 vols. (Oxford, 1998, 1999), IV, Judith M. Brown and Wm. Roger Louis, eds., *The Twentieth Century* (1999), pp. 597–622.

—— 'The West Indies and the Conversion of the British Official Classes to the Development Idea,' *Journal of Commonwealth and Comparative Politics*, XV (1977), pp. 58–83.

CECILIA A. KARCH, 'The Growth of the Corporate Economy in Barbados: Class/Race Factors, 1890–1977', in Susan Craig, ed., *Contemporary Caribbean: A Sociological Reader*, 2 vols. (Maracas, Trinidad, 1981), I, pp. 213–24.

GORDON K. LEWIS, *The Growth of the Modern West Indies* (London, 1968).

W. P. LIVINGSTONE, *Black Jamaica: A Study in Evolution* (London, 1899).

JAY R. MANDLE, 'British Caribbean Economic History', in Franklin W. Knight and Colin A. Palmer, eds., *The Modern Caribbean* (Chapel Hill, NC, 1989), pp. 229–58.

ROBERTO MÁRQUEZ, 'Nationalism, Nation, and Ideology: Trends in the Emergence of a Caribbean Literature', in Franklin W. Knight and Colin A. Palmer, *The Modern Caribbean*, pp. 293–340.

JOYCELIN MASSIAH, *Women as Heads of Households in the Caribbean: Family Structure and Feminine Status* (Paris, 1983).

TREVOR MUNROE, *The Politics of Constitutional Decolonization: Jamaica, 1944–62* (Mona, Jamaica, 1972).

REX M. NETTLEFORD, *Mirror Mirror: Identity, Race and Protest in Jamaica* (Kingston, Jamaica, 1970).

KEN POST, *Arise Ye Starvelings: The Jamaican Labour Rebellion and Its Aftermath* (The Hague, 1978).

—— *Strike the Iron: A Colony at War, 1939–1945*, 2 vols. (Atlantic Highlands, NJ, 1981).

BONHAM C. RICHARDSON, 'Caribbean Migrations, 1838–1985' in Knight and Palmer, eds., *The Modern Caribbean*, pp. 203–28.

SELWYN D. RYAN, *Race and Nationalism in Trinidad and Tobago: A Study of Decolonization in a Multiracial Society* (Toronto, 1972).

OLIVE SENIOR, *Working Miracles: Women's Lives in the English-Speaking Caribbean* (Cave Hill, Barbados, 1991).

RAYMOND T. SMITH, 'Race and Class in the Post-Emancipation Caribbean', in Robert Ross, ed., *Racism and Colonialism* (The Hague, 1982).

13

The Black Experience in Twentieth-Century Britain

WINSTON JAMES

The black presence in Britain can be traced as far back as Roman times, but only in the second half of the twentieth century did it become conspicuous and assume definite form. The small and beleaguered black communities in London, Liverpool, and Cardiff notwithstanding, as late as the 1930s, Britain served more as a crossroads for black people in the Empire and elsewhere than as a site of permanent settlement. Students, entertainers, seamen, lawyers, writers, businessmen, petitioners, and black colonial civil servants sojourned in the imperial metropolis, but few made it their home. A wave of migration from the Caribbean following in the tumultuous wake of the Second World War was a major instrument of change, creating a substantial, settled black community sprinkled across the urban centres of England and Wales. From no more than a few thousand in 1900, Britain's population of African and Afro-Caribbean descent reached a million at the end of the century. Though amounting to no more than 2 per cent of the general population in 2000, black Britons have been and remain highly concentrated in English cities such as Birmingham, Liverpool, and Manchester. But London, home to more than half of black Britons, has always been the pre-eminent site of black settlement. In the London boroughs of Lambeth and Hackney one in every six residents is of Afro-Caribbean descent. Though few in absolute and relative terms, black Britons have exerted and continue to exert a profound influence upon the nation's culture, especially its popular culture.

The history of black Britain has been a history of struggle and no less so in the twentieth century than before. The specific grievances have changed over time, but the fundamental objectives of their exertions remain the same.

I would like to thank Philip Morgan and Sean Hawkins for their comments on earlier drafts of this chapter, and also for their forbearance.

Respect, equality of opportunity, and justice have been their yearning, the core of their entreaties and demands over the centuries and generations. The lives of black Britons have been persistently blighted by racial prejudice and discrimination. Though no longer viewed with contempt and pity as they generally were at the beginning of the century, black people still suffer gross discrimination in almost every area of British life and have not been fully accepted as full members of the British nation. Progress has undoubtedly been made, but it has come slowly, unevenly and at a heavy price.

The story of the black experience in twentieth-century Britain is forbiddingly complex, far more so than is generally appreciated. It is one of nationalities formed within the British Empire—of Jamaicans, Barbadians, and other Caribbeans along with Ghanaians, Nigerians, and other continental Africans—meeting one another generally for the first time and doing so on British soil. It is the story of tensions as well as new self-identifications and solidarities forged among these groups in the crucible of Britain; of Guyanese and Kenyans not only becoming Caribbeans and Africans, respectively, but also their embracing more expansive and inclusive identifications as 'Negro' and 'black'.[1] London, especially, was not only a site of residence for continental Africans and Africans from the Americas; it was also, prior to the Second World War, the planet's primary crossroads at which black people came to a greater sense of group consciousness. Paul Robeson 'discovered' Africa in London, where, as he wrote, 'I came to consider that I was an African.' He was not the first or the last to undergo such a metamorphosis in Britain. Many others underwent a similar transformation through the contact with continental Africans that London and Britain more generally afforded.[2]

The black presence in twentieth-century Britain was never homogeneous or static. The black population was skewed in its largely working-class composition, but also consisted of students, lawyers, and doctors as well as seamen, nurses, soldiers, bus conductors, and clerks. This chapter will focus on the large group of workers while not neglecting the small intelligentsia.

[1] I have used the terms 'self-identification' and 'identification' instead of 'identity' quite deliberately in order to avoid some of the confusion so ably identified and exposed by Rogers Brubaker and Frederick Cooper in 'Beyond "Identity" ', *Theory and Society*, XXIX (2000), pp. 1–47.

[2] Paul Robeson, 'How I Discovered Africa', *Freedom*, June 1953, reprinted in Philip S. Foner, ed., *Paul Robeson Speaks: Writings, Speeches, Interviews, 1918–1974* (New York, 1978), pp. 351–53; and Robeson, *Here I Stand*, ([1958]Boston, 1988), p. 33.

The black story was punctuated by the rhythm and exigencies of war, the boom and bust of capitalist economic cycles at the periphery (whether colony or neo-colony) and in Britain itself. Similarly, it was shaped by the shifts and turns in British immigration policies as well as by racist attacks and black resistance. It witnessed black–white alliance and black–white conflict, the struggle for housing and the struggle for work. It saw progress and retrogression. What follows, then, does not pretend to be more than an overview of the broad contours of this history organized, chronologically, around the struggles and achievements of two distinct but interconnected groups of black people in twentieth-century Britain: workers and intellectuals. It should be pointed out at the outset that it is preferable to use the terms 'migrants', 'settlers', and 'black Britons', as opposed to 'immigrants', when describing black people in Britain, because that is precisely what the vast majority were. Strictly speaking, there have been relatively few black *immigrants* to Britain. Most of those who entered Britain in the twentieth century, including the post-war years, were simply moving from one part of the British empire to another *as British citizens*. The movement was therefore more akin to internal migration than immigration as such. Unless one is prepared to call Yorkshiremen in London immigrants, then one should not call Barbadians entering London on British passports immigrants. The immigrant label attached to such persons largely developed in the 1960s precisely to deprive black Britons of their citizenship rights.

Black Britain before the First World War

Given Britain's imperial network of maritime commerce with its African and Caribbean colonies, the primary sites of residence of Africans and Caribbeans in early twentieth-century Britain were the port cities—Liverpool, London, Bristol, and Cardiff. True, students and intellectuals gravitated to Edinburgh, Glasgow, Oxford and Cambridge, in addition to London, but the majority of the black population consisted of proletarians connected to Britain's seafaring activity. As late as the mid-1950s, Michael Banton found that 'in Stepney and many other parts of the country the general public have tended to think of the coloured men as being seamen by trade and by nature, who, though they may take work ashore, are never permanent residents'. The 1911 census gives a figure of just under 14,000 Caribbean- and African-born people living in Britain, but this number excludes people of African descent born in Britain and includes whites born in the Caribbean and

Africa.[3] Still, set against a UK population of approximately 46 million, the black presence was tiny.

Its size, however, did nothing to mitigate the general hostility with which the black population was treated or the precariousness of black people's lives. Thinking it would be relatively easy to get work on British ships and docks, many West African and Caribbean seamen disembarked in British ports only to find their small savings slipping through their fingers with little prospect of work. The seamen's unions exerted themselves to block the employment of black people; some white British sailors refused to sail with non-European men. Instead of devising means to combat discrimination against black British subjects, a 1910 parliamentary Committee of Inquiry into Distressed Colonial and Indian Subjects recommended 'repatriation', even though it identified 'a prejudice in the labour market against the coloured British subject' as the major reason for their distress.[4]

The use of the term 'repatriation' in such a context is highly significant. After all, by law, 'coloured' British subjects had the same right of abode in Britain as non-coloured, white, British subjects. The term 'repatriation' is therefore inappropriate, a euphemism for what was really deportation and exile. (How can one be repatriated *from* one's own country?) The general attitude of the Committee would remain characteristic of the British ruling class for the duration of the twentieth century. British subjects who happened to be black, were discriminated against, they were physically attacked and even killed. What was to be done? Deport the victims, pass laws to prevent other black people from entering the country, i.e., deprive them of their rights as British subjects. The problem was the victim, not the aggression and the aggressors.

Although seamen were by far the largest contingent of Britain's black working class before the First World War, black workers included many butlers and domestics. Often invisible, isolated, and scattered across the British Isles, they emerge into view through court cases (often involving cruelty on the part of employers) and plaintive entreaties to charitable

[3] Michael Banton, *The Coloured Quarter: Negro Immigrants in an English City* (London, 1955), pp. 127, 67.

[4] Banton, *Coloured Quarter*, p. 34; Laura Tabili, *'We Ask for British Justice': Workers and Racial Difference in Late Imperial Britain* (Ithaca, NY, 1994), chaps. 2–7; Peter Fryer, *Staying Power: The History of Black People in Britain* (London, 1984), p. 295; Report of the Committee on Distressed Colonial and Indian Subject, Cmnd. 5133 (April 1910), p. 20, quoted in Carlton Wilson, 'A Hidden History: The Black Experience in Liverpool, England, 1919–1945', Ph.D. dissertation, University of North Carolina, Chapel Hill, 1992, p. 130.

organizations and the Colonial Office. Most were brought to Britain by their British employers returning from Africa and the Caribbean. Still others accompanied their American employers to Britain.[5]

The most visible and vocal group comprised students and professionals, based largely, but not exclusively, in the capital. London was not only the capital of the largest Empire the world had ever known, but also, by that very token, the magnet that drew anti-colonial petitioners and fighters to the British Isles. As in the eighteenth and nineteenth centuries, London was the primary British site of organized black resistance to British colonialism and racism. In 1897 the capital saw the formation of the African Association, which aimed 'to facilitate friendly intercourse among Africans in general [and] to promote and protect the interests of all subjects claiming African descent, wholly or in part, in British Colonies and other places, especially in Africa'.[6] Its driving force was a young Trinidadian law student, Henry Sylvester Williams. The organizers of the 1900 Pan-African Conference, who were members of the Association, had lived in Britain's colonies as well as the imperial capital and had experienced and witnessed the bitter fruits of the empire's excesses and racist practices. In their 'Address to the Nations of the World', the conferees confidently and sombrely announced that 'the problem of the twentieth century is the problem of the colour-line.'[7]

In 1912 a remarkable and enigmatic Sudanese-Egyptian intellectual, Dusé Mohamed (later Dusé Mohamed Ali), founded the *African Times and Orient Review* (*ATOR*). A political, commercial and cultural journal with a decidedly 'Pan-Oriental' and 'Pan-African' stance, the *ATOR*, as Mohamed explained in its first issue, was located 'at the seat of the British Empire' and intended to 'lay the aims, desires, and intentions of the Black, Brown, and Yellow Races—within and without the Empire—at the throne of Caesar'. For 'the voices of millions of Britain's enlightened dark races are never heard; their capacity underrated'. This lack of understanding of both African and Oriental had produced non-appreciation, and non-appreciation had, Mohamed Ali

[5] Jeffrey Green, *Black Edwardians: Black People in Britain, 1901–1914* (London, 1998), chap. 3.

[6] Quoted in Owen Mathurin, *Henry Sylvester Williams and the Origins of the Pan-African Movement, 1869–1911* (Westport, Conn., 1976), p. 41.

[7] Pan-African Conference, 'Address to the Nations of the World', reprinted in J. Ayo Langley, ed., *Ideologies of Liberation in Black Africa, 1856–1970: Documents on Modern African Political Thought from Colonial Times to the Present* (London, 1979), pp. 738–39; J. Ayodele Langley, *Pan-Africanism and Nationalism in West Africa, 1900–1945* (London, 1973), p. 189.

wrote, 'unleashed the hydr[a]-headed monster of derision, contempt, and repression'. Whether out of political tactics or genuine belief he also declared: 'We, as natives and loyal subjects of the British Empire, hold too high an opinion of Anglo-Saxon chivalry to believe other than that African and Oriental wrongs have but to be made manifest in order that they may be righted.' This very position was undermined by the colonial wrongs exposed by the magazine that went unheeded by the British authorities.[8]

Racism was a fact of black life in Britain, but racism's manifestation and intensity varied significantly over time and space. It also varied across sectors of the economy and labour force. For example, John Archer, who was born in the dock area of Liverpool in 1863, the son of a Barbadian ship's steward, Richard Archer, and Mary Burns Archer, an illiterate Irish Catholic, was elected the fourteenth Mayor of Battersea in 1913. 'You have made history to-night,' Archer told the council. 'Battersea has done many things in the past, but the greatest thing it has done is to show that it has no racial prejudice, and that it recognises a man for the work he has done.' Archer's case in Battersea suggests that the political culture of a community cannot be overlooked in understanding the local black experience.[9]

Some of the most virulent forms of racism manifested themselves in areas of the labour force where direct competition between black and white workers was greatest; or to be more precise, where white workers perceived the competition in racial terms. Thus relations between black and white seamen and dock workers in Liverpool, Cardiff, and the East End of London were among the most combustible and it was primarily in those cities that racist explosions occurred in 1919. But even in those areas, despite the suspicion and tension that were more or less always present, outright conflict took place only during hard times and retrenchment in jobs. When work was plentiful, conflict was minimal or nonexistent.[10]

A more virulent racism lurked among the intelligentsia and the British middle classes more generally. For, very much abroad in Britain, especially since the second half of the nineteenth century, were notions of European (especially English) genetic superiority and the inferiority of non-European peoples (especially those of African descent). Moreover, supposedly backed by science, the idea of a racial hierarchy gained in respectability

[8] 'Foreword', *African Times and Orient Review*, I, 1 (July 1912), p. i.

[9] Barry Kosmin, 'J. R. Archer (1863–1932): A Pan-Africanist in the Battersea Labour Movement', *New Community*, vii, (1978–79), pp. 430, 436; quotation in Fryer, *Staying Power*, p. 291.

[10] Kenneth Lunn, ed., *Race and Labour in Twentieth-Century Britain* (London, 1985).

over time.[11] While it is commonplace to view the white British working class as infected carriers of the virus of racism, the evidence suggests that the primary culprits were members of the middle class and British officialdom, not least because the latter were far more literate and therefore more exposed to racist ideas.

The racist ambience of Britain was such that it had a profound effect upon non-Europeans and especially those of African descent who entered it. When Kobina Sekyi, a scion of an aristocratic Fante family in Ghana, came to Britain in 1910 to study at the University of London, he was, he admitted, an extreme Anglophile, an Anglomaniac, he said. But because of the racism he experienced, Sekyi became extremely disillusioned with Britain, learned to hate things British and, by extension, things European. By the time he returned to the Gold Coast in 1913 after gaining his degree in philosophy from University College, Sekyi was a changed man. As if the experience of his first sojourn was not bad enough, fate would have it that on his way back to Britain in 1915 to read for a law degree, his ship was sunk by a German U-Boat in the Irish Sea. Some of the passengers were killed. Sekyi managed to clamber aboard a lifeboat. One Englishman, on seeing Sekyi in the lifeboat, shouted at him, telling Sekyi that he, as a black man, had no right to be alive when whites were drowning. This traumatic event led Sekyi to conclude that African interests and values were incompatible with those of the British. Sekyi became a fervent African traditionalist and nationalist, rejecting European clothes along with what he perceived as European values. He articulated these ideas in various articles and most notably in his 1915 play, *The Blinkards* and his moving, autobiographical short story, 'The Anglo-Fanti', published in 1918.[12]

Traumatic experiences, such as Sekyi's, European overlordship in Africa, and the ready acceptance of 'scientific' racist ideas in influential circles gave momentum to the stream of black vindicationist literature that emerged in

[11] Philip Curtin, *The Image of Africa: British Ideas and Action, 1780–1850* (Madison, Wisc., 1964); Douglas Lorimer, *Colour, Class and the Victorians: English Attitudes to the Negro in the Mid-nineteenth Century* (Leicester, 1978); Nancy Stepan, *The Idea of Race in Science: Great Britain, 1800–1960* (London, 1982); Paul Rich, *Race and Empire in British Politics*, 2nd edn. (Cambridge, 1990).

[12] *The Blinkards: A Comedy* and *The Anglo-Fanti—A Short Story* (Accra, 1997). His core ideas were articulated in 'The Future of Subject Peoples', *African Times and Orient Review* (Oct.–Dec. 1917). See also J. Ayo Langley, 'Modernization and its Malcontents: Kobena Sekyi of Ghana and the Re-statement of African Political Theory (1892–1956)', *Research Review* (Ghana), VI, 3 (Trinity Term 1970), pp. 1–61, and his *Pan-Africanism and Nationalism.*

the second half of the nineteenth century and continued into the twentieth. This urgent counter-discourse was aimed, as one of its distinguished and early practitioners, William Rainy, put it, at 'the wide-spread conspiracy' to 'lower the Negro in the scale of creation'.[13]

Black Struggle and Survival from the First to the Second World War

Bad though it was in many ways, the period prior to the First World War seems in retrospect almost benign for black people in Britain. The war itself brought prosperity to many of the black seamen beached on Britain's ports but great suffering and heartache to those who served directly in the war. The anguish and disillusionment that black men experienced in the British Army stemmed largely from the fact that the British military authorities did not want them in the armed forces in the first place—and said so openly. The attitude of the rank and file was no different. When members of the British West Indies Regiment (BWIR) arrived in Alexandria, Egypt, in August 1916 after an appalling thirty-five-day journey across the Atlantic from British Honduras, they marched tired and hungry to a hut reserved for British soldiers. On the way they sang 'Rule Britannia'. 'Who gave you niggers authority to sing that?' the white soldiers scornfully demanded. 'Clear out of this building—only British troops admitted here.'[14] For the duration of the war, the men of the BWIR experienced inferior food, poor transportation, menial work, and substandard medical care. And they received a barrage of racist verbal abuse. Individual black resistance was commonplace, and in Taranto, Italy, in December 1918 black soldiers finally revolted. Many of the men from the BWIR were temporarily stationed in Britain after the armistice until transportation could be secured to take them back to the Caribbean. Some settled in the UK. Many of those who made it back

[13] Quoted in Nemata Blyden, *West Indians in West Africa, 1808–1880* (Rochester, NY, 2000), p. 151. William Rainy was the author of *The Censor Censured, or the Calumnies of Captain Burton Against the Africans of Sierra Leone* (London, 1865), one of the earliest and most sustained anti-racist polemics written by a black colonial. Africanus Horton, Edward Blyden, Theophilus Scholes, John Mensah Sarbah, Sol Plaatje and J. E. Casely Hayford were among the most distinguished and influential who followed in Rainy's wake.

[14] Winston James, *Holding Aloft the Banner of Ethiopia: Caribbean Radicalism in Early Twentieth-Century America* (London, 1998), p. 52–64, quotation at p. 56; C. L. Joseph, 'The British West Indies Regiment, 1914–1918', *Journal of Caribbean History*, II (May 1971), pp. 94–124; Glenford Howe, *Race, War and Nationalism: A Social History of West Indians in the First World War* (Kingston, Jamaica, 2002).

to the Caribbean alive served in the vanguard of the 1919 uprisings in the British Caribbean.[15]

In the end over 15,000 men, with two-thirds from Jamaica alone, went overseas with the BWIR in defence of the Empire. Almost 10 per cent never made it back home, with almost 1,100 of these dying from diseases contracted under the most appalling conditions. Another 700 were maimed during the war. At war's end, Africa, the prize of much of the fighting, had lost as many as 250,000 of the 2 million of its people mobilized by the European combatants. The sacrifice—voluntarily and involuntarily—was not only in the form of blood but treasure. In the British Caribbean, individual citizens and the local colonial authorities offered approximately £2 m to the war effort—a major tribute for a small and impoverished region.[16] The contribution of colonial subjects did not end there. Some, probably numbering in the hundreds from the British Caribbean alone, made their way to Britain under their own steam to join Kitchener's army. Others, who were resident in Britain, also joined up. Many were refused admission into the army on the grounds of colour, but others, mainly because the recruitment was haphazard and the protocols of colour varied from place to place, successfully entered Britain's armed forces.[17]

In British ports, previously scorned black hands were put to essential work. With many of their white British counterparts conscripted or drawn into the armed forces, black workers found jobs more plentiful. Opportunity and the exigencies of war combined to increase the black presence with immigration. Black labourers were welcomed in the munitions industries;

[15] W. F. Elkins, 'A Source of Black Nationalism in the Caribbean: The Revolt of the British West Indies Regiment at Taranto, Italy', *Science and Society*, XXXIV, 1 (Spring 1970), and 'Black Power in the British West Indies: The Trinidad Longshoremen's Strike of 1919', *Science and Society*, XXXIII, 1 (Winter 1969); Tony Martin, *The Pan-African Connection: From Slavery to Garvey and Beyond* (Cambridge, Mass., 1983), pp. 47–58; James, *Holding Aloft the Banner of Ethiopia*, pp. 64–66.

[16] Melvin E. Page, 'Introduction: Black Men in a White Man's War', in Melvin E. Page, ed., *Africa and the First World War* (Basingstoke, 1987), p. 14; Joseph, 'The British West Indies Regiment, 1914–1918', pp. 101–24; Howe, *Race, War and Nationalism*, p. 4.

[17] David Killingray, 'All the King's Men? Blacks in the British Army in the First World War, 1914–1918', in Rainer Lotz and Ian Pegg, eds., *Under the Imperial Carpet: Essays in Black History, 1780–1950* (Crawley, England, 1986), pp. 164–81; and 'Race and Rank in the British Army in the Twentieth Century', *Ethnic and Racial Studies*, X, 3 (July 1987), pp. 276–90; Philip Sherlock, *Norman Manley: A Biography* (London, 1980), pp. 58–60. Laura Tabili reports the existence of 'at least one "Coloured" unit' formed by men living in Britain, '*We Ask for British Justice*', p. 16, but the evidence of such a unit or units is questionable.

the British authorities even brought some into the country to work for the war effort.[18] In the aftermath of the war, however, there was a rapid deterioration in the conditions and prospects of black people in Britain and a new spurt of anti-racist agitation. The relative prosperity that came with the outbreak of war vanished as quickly with the end of hostilities in the fall of 1918. The maritime trades were hit especially hard. Unemployment and wage cuts became the order of the day. The most vulnerable were black seamen. Competition for work became fierce and the racial cleavage among the working class, especially in the port cities, widened catastrophically. Unemployment, especially among the demobilized servicemen, was rife. Black men, especially black seamen, became easy scapegoats. From January to August 1919 a series of riots broke out. Black and other non-European men and women were viciously attacked in Britain's port cities. Black men were stabbed and beaten by angry mobs, their homes, furniture, and hostels ransacked and burnt. In 1920 another full-scale riot occurred in Hull and a smaller one in Limehouse, in London's East End. The system of justice failed black Britons in the aftermath of the riots: black men were disproportionately charged with offences and given harsher sentences than the true aggressors.[19]

Instead of dealing with the problem of racism, the British authorities punished the victims further through 'repatriation'. White colonial munitions workers who had come over during the war were also encouraged to

[18] Kenneth Little, *Negroes in Britain: A Study of Racial Relations in English Society*, rev. edn. (London, 1972), pp. 78–79; Banton, *Coloured Quarter*, p. 33; Dick Lawless, 'The Role of Seamen's Agents in the Migration for Employment of Arab Seafarers in the Early Twentieth Century', and Diane Frost, 'Racism, Work and Unemployment: West African Seamen in Liverpool, 1880s–1960s', both in Diane Frost, ed., *Ethnic Labour and British Imperial Trade: A History of Ethnic Seafarers in the UK* (London, 1995); P. C. Lewis and G. W. Gordon, 'We Were in Cardiff', *Keys*, III, 1 (July–Sept. 1935), p. 4.

[19] Roy May and Robin Cohen, 'The Interaction between Race and Colonialism: A Case Study of the Liverpool Riots of 1919', *Race and Class*, XVI, 2 (1974); Neil Evans, 'The South Wales Race Riots of 1919', *Llafur: Journal of Welsh Labour History*, 3, 1 (1980); and, 'Across the Universe: Racial Violence and the Post-War Crisis in Imperial Britain, 1919–25', in Frost, ed., *Ethnic Labour and British Imperial Trade*; Andrea Murphy, *From the Empire to the Rialto: Racism and Reaction in Liverpool, 1918–1948* (Birkenhead, 1995), chap. 1; Jacqueline Jenkinson, 'The 1919 Race Riots in Britain: A Survey', in Lotz and Pegg, eds., *Under the Imperial Carpet*. The most comprehensive analysis is Jacqueline Jenkinson's fine study, 'The 1919 Race Riots in Britain: Their Backgrounds and Consequences', Ph.D. dissertation, University of Edinburgh, 1987. For a rare account of the riots from a black eye-witness and victim, see Ernest Marke, *Old Man Trouble: The Memoirs of a Stowaway, Mutineer, Bootlegger, Crocuser and Soho Club Owner* (London, 1975), pp. 25–32.

return to their native land, but the treatment they received was worlds apart from that inflicted upon black colonials. From the outset, white colonials were offered a £5 resettlement allowance, while black colonials were not. Only after the 1919 riots, coupled with the reluctance of black colonials to be repatriated, were the financial inducements which had long been offered to white colonials now offered to black Britons.[20] To 'get rid of the coloured population', an inter-departmental committee (comprising representatives of the Colonial Office, the Board of Trade, Home Office, Local Government Board, India Office, Ministry of Labour, and the Ministry of Shipping), devised the establishment of Repatriation Committees in the primary areas of black settlement and disturbance. Conspicuously absent was any representation from the black seamen or the non-European community more generally. The Repatriation Committees succeeded in removing probably as many as 3,000 black people from the British Isles between June 1919 and 1921—almost 15 per cent of the estimated 20,000 black people who resided in Britain in 1920.[21] On the supreme logic that the cessation of rioting in 1920 was an unquestionable mark of the success of their scheme, the Repatriation Committees congratulated themselves and disbanded soon thereafter.

White trade unionists and veterans were not just advocates of repatriation, but key participants in the attacks on black Britons, including black veterans. The National Sailor's and Firemen's Union advocated the firing of black people to make room for 'British' workers. To drive the demand home, many of them refused to serve on ships with black members. The employers were generally happy to oblige. The socialist organizations and their press refused to condemn the racist violence. There was one exception to this silence on the left: Sylvia Pankhurst's Workers' Socialist Federation and its newspaper,

[20] Jenkinson, 'The 1919 Race Riots in Britain: Their Backgrounds and Consequences', pp. 185–87; Murphy, *From the Empire to the Rialto*, pp. 22–23. On compulsory repatriation see copy of letter from Chief Constable's Office, Chelsea, 21 Nov. 1919, PRO, MEPO [*Metropolitan Police Records*] 2/1779.

[21] Jenkinson, 'The 1919 Race Riots in Britain: Their Backgrounds and Consequences', p. 190, estimates that about 2,000 were removed from the country, but she apparently failed to take into account the figures provided by the police of people on board ships they examined prior to sailing. Hundreds of passengers were involved in the London metropolitan area alone. For the directive and some subsequent reports see Under Secretary of State, Home Office to Commissioner of Police of the Metropolis, 20 Jan. 1920; Assistant Commissioner, [Metropolitan Police] to Under Secretary of State, 24 Jan. 1920, 2 Feb. 1920; and M. Mosey, Chief Superintendent, Mercantile Marine Office to Superintendent Hopkins, Marylebone Police Station, 9 Jan. 1920, PRO, MEPO 2/1780.

the *Workers' Dreadnought.* In 'Stabbing Negroes in the London Dock Area' Pankhurst submitted 'a few questions for the consideration of those who have been negro hunting':

Do you wish to exclude all blacks from England?

If so, do you not think that blacks might justly ask that the British should at the same time keep out of the black peoples' countries?

Do you not know that capitalists, and especially British capitalists, have seized, by force of arms, the countries inhabited by black people and are ruling those countries and the black inhabitants for their own profit?[22]

Uncommonly courageous and decent, Pankhurst sought to lead, not follow; to break the prejudices among some of her own constituents in London's East End rather than pander to them or remain silent.

The black population rallied in defence of its members by creating ad-hoc and more formal organizations. In Liverpool, the National African Sailor's and Fireman's Union was established, but was short-lived. More enduring was the African Progress Union (APU), which derived its driving force from London-based black professionals and students. It aimed to promote the 'general welfare of Africans and Afro-Peoples'; to establish in London a 'Home from Home', where members of the Association 'may meet for social recreation and intellectual improvement'; to spread 'knowledge of the history and achievements of Africans and Afro-Peoples past and present'; and to 'create and maintain a public sentiment in favour of brotherhood in its broadest sense'.[23]

Emerging at the same time as the APU was the Society of Peoples of African Origin (SPAO). Its objectives were, as one of its members admitted, 'identical' to those of the APU and so the two eventually amalgamated to form the Society of African Peoples, which was formally launched in Holborn in July 1919. But the merger was apparently more formal than real, with both organizations functioning much as they had done before.[24] The major

[22] *Workers' Dreadnought,* June 7, 1919.

[23] Jenkinson, 'The 1919 Race Riots in Britain', pp. 196–97; 'African Progress Union', *African Telegraph,* Dec. 1918, pp. 89–90, quotation on p. 89; 'Reception by Committee for the Welfare of Africans in Europe', *African Telegraph,* May–June 1919, pp. 211–12; Jeffrey Green, 'Edward T. Nelson', *New Community,* XII, 1 (Winter 1984–85), pp. 149–54; Murphy, *From the Empire to the Rialto,* pp. 32–38.

[24] 'Inauguration Dinner of the Society of African Peoples', *African Telegraph,* July-Aug. 1919, pp. 269–71; W. F. Elkins, 'Hercules and the Society of Peoples of African Origin', *Caribbean*

distinction between the SPAO and the APU was that the former had a mouthpiece, the *African Telegraph*, and the latter did not. Founded in 1914, the *African Telegraph* was owned and edited by a Sierra Leonean and London-based businessman, John Eldred Taylor. He approached Felix Hercules in late 1918 and offered him the editorship of the *African Telegraph*. Hercules transformed the *Telegraph* and made it into a more forthright anti-colonial and Pan-Africanist voice, intervening strongly in discussions of the war, the riots, and the place of black people in the post-war world.

Felix Eugene Michael Hercules was born in Venezuela in 1888 of Trinidadian parents. He grew up in Trinidad, where his father was a civil servant. After teaching for some years in the island, he decided to travel to Britain during the war, where he received a B.A. degree from the University of London. Hercules underwent the radical transformation born of disillusionment associated with the black migrant experience in Britain.[25] Hercules served not only as editor of the *African Telegraph* but also the general secretary of the Society of Peoples of African Origin and associate secretary of the African Progress Union, simultaneously. In these capacities, but especially as editor, he intervened in the crisis of 1919. In the December 1918 issue of the magazine, Hercules carried a damning report of 'The Belmont Hospital Affair', detailing the gruesome and violent attack upon fifty, mainly limbless, black soldiers who were patients in this Liverpool hospital, by some 500 to 600 white, racist soldiers. Hercules was appalled at the way in which the white press vilified the black soldiers. He called upon the local and central government authorities to address the black veterans' needs, reminding readers of the extraordinary sacrifices these men had made for the country during the war. He noted with indignation the British authorities' exclusion of all black British soldiers from the Victory March, despite their having fought 'as stubbornly and as valiantly as their white comrades'.[26]

The greatest casualty of the events of 1919 was the image of Britain as the Motherland in the eyes of black Britons. As late as December 1918, Hercules

Studies, XI, 4 (Jan. 1972), p. 45; Jeffrey Green, 'The African Progress Union of London, 1918–1925: A Black Pressure Group', paper presented at the Institute of Commonwealth Studies, University of London, 5 Feb. 1991.

[25] F. E. M. Hercules, 'The African and Nationalism', *African Telegraph*, Dec. 1918, p. 84.

[26] Elkins, 'Hercules and the Society of Peoples of African Origin', p. 48; F. E. M. Hercules, 'The African and Nationalism' and 'The Belmont Hospital Affair', *African Telegraph*, Dec. 1918, pp. 84 and 94–95; 'The African Progress Union', *African Telegraph*, Jan.–Feb. 1919, p. 111; and 'The Victory March', *African Telegraph*, July–Aug. 1919, quotation on p. 242.

had penned a cloying seven-stanza poem, 'To Britain!', declaring his love for his mother country: 'We love thee, Britain!' ran the refrain. He begged Britain to 'treat us well', but the love expressed in the poem was unconditional. And it was an unrequited love. Less than a year after writing the poem, Hercules drew up a balance sheet of the black man's position after the war. During the war, he wrote, the black man fought 'shoulder to shoulder' with fellow Britons and the allies in every theatre of the war, and 'fought splendidly for democracy, for liberty, justice and freedom'. After 'specious promises' made to black soldiers, and loyalty to Britain that was 'a lesson to others', 'Black men all the world over are asking to-day: What have we got? What are we going to get out of it all? The answer, in effect, comes clear, convincing, and conclusive: *"Go back to your kennel, you damned dog of a nigger!"* ' After a tour of the Caribbean where he had been harried by the colonial authorities, Hercules ended up in New York, where he soon disappeared from the historical record. Towards the end of 1919 the *African Telegraph* was driven into bankruptcy by a cynical, government-sponsored libel case for an article which it published the previous year condemning the stripping and public flogging of women in Nigeria by agents of the colonial state. The emigration of Hercules and the death of the *African Telegraph* was a double blow to black Britain.[27]

Hercules's articulation of the betrayal of black Britons foreshadowed the British state's clampdown on the black population. The most brutal, cynical, and notorious measure was the Special Restriction (Coloured Alien Seamen) Order of 1925. It was the first in a long line of explicitly racist immigration legislation in twentieth-century Britain, and was the first to attract widespread notice and black opposition. The order, issued by the Aliens Department of the Home Office, stipulated that undocumented non-white seamen in Britain should register as aliens. As a result, clearly foreseen by the authorities, a large number of *bona fide* black British subjects were registered as aliens, which, in turn, diminished their ability to work. Many legitimate black residents were threatened with deportation and some were indeed deported under the provision of the order.[28]

[27] F. E. M. Hercules, 'To Britain!' *African Telegraph*, Dec. 1918, p. 78; 'Discrimination and Disintegration', July–Aug. 1919, p. 253, emphasis in the original; Elkins, 'Hercules and the Society of Peoples of African Origin', pp. 53–59; Ian Duffield, 'John Eldred Taylor and West African Opposition to Indirect Rule in Nigeria', *African Affairs*, LXX, 280 (1971), esp. pp. 262–68.

[28] Laura Tabili, 'The Construction of Racial Difference in Twentieth-century Britain: The Special Restricted (Coloured Seamen) Order, 1925, *Journal of British Studies*, XXXIII (1994), p. 81 and n.86.

The racist dimension of the 1925 Order was undergirded by its application only to black people. The most scandalous and cynical dimension of the order was the way in which it was administered. The police frequently confiscated the passports of black seamen and then registered them as aliens! The League of Coloured Peoples (LCP), which was founded in 1931 by a Jamaican doctor, Harold Moody, to oppose the colour bar, brought to public attention some peculiarities in the administering of the order and their consequences for the victims. From a detailed 1935 investigation of the situation in Cardiff, the LCP noted that, 'Threats of arrest and imprisonment were not uncommon if a seaman refused his passport when demanded'. Although not revealed at the time, the Home Office had given the police instructions to do so.[29]

Black seamen raised their voice in protest. As soon as the order came into effect in April 1925, a group of twenty-six Caribbean and West African seaman based at the Missions to Seamen in Barry Dock in the Bristol Channel wrote to the Colonial Office: 'If we are classed as aliens our brothers who have made the supreme sacrifice on various battle fields of the Great War for the preservation, flag, prestige, honour and future welfare of the British Empire can be termed mercenaries. We know, feel, and believe that every breast was bared in freedom's cause, every eye, heart, soul wish and imagination pointed to the same goal as the truest Englishman that ever lived.' 'We sincerely believe,' they concluded, 'that our government will rectify what we believe to be a mistake.' 'Their' government did not.

The Colonial Office expressed opposition to the policy of the Home Office, not on the grounds of the justice of the men's claim, but by the algebra of colonial rule. Even the Foreign Office, which normally kept its distance from matters colonial, felt impelled to intervene. No less a figure than the Foreign Secretary, Austen Chamberlain, demanded a resolution of the crisis, lest adverse publicity in the colonies 'serve as a peg on which to hang anti-British propaganda'. Remarkably, despite the protests, the Home Office stuck to its guns, an index of the level of general support in government for the policy.[30]

[29] Little, *Negroes in Britain*, pp. 86–87; Tabili, 'The Construction of Racial Difference', pp. 54–98, esp. 76–77 and 84–85; quotation from George W. Brown, 'Investigation of Coloured Colonial Seamen in Cardiff. April 13th–20th, 1935, *Keys*, Oct.–Dec. 1935, p. 19; David Vaughan, *Negro Victory: The Life Story of Dr. Harold Moody* (London, 1950); Roderick Macdonald, 'Dr. Harold Arundel Moody and the League of Coloured Peoples, 1931–1947: A Retrospective View', *Race*, XIV, 3 (Jan. 1973), pp. 291–310.

[30] Tabili, *'We Ask for British Justice'*, pp. 113, 123, 125–28; quotations at pp. 113, 125 and 128.

Britain's black workers were not the only ones who led blighted lives; the black middle class suffered, too. Taunted on the streets, they had trouble finding lodgings. In the 1930s and early 1940s, a study of 701 lodging providers (catering mainly to students) found only a dozen willing to take 'coloured persons'. Like their working class counterparts, the black middle class were frequently refused service. As students—especially in the field of medicine—black people frequently suffered ostracism and verbal abuse not only from white peers, but also sometimes from the teaching staff.[31] White doctors and lawyers gave their black colleagues similar advice: go back 'home' and practice in 'your own country'. But that was more easily said than done. Under colonialism, their 'own country' was no longer their own, but Britain's; and Britain, according to imperial propaganda, was their mother country. The difficulty for black doctors was compounded by the fact that the West African Medical Staff (WAMS), an arm of the colonial civil service and the chief employer of doctors in British West Africa, had banned doctors of 'non-European parentage' from its employ as early as 1906. Black doctors who wished to practice in the region hardly had a chance to do so. However, those Caribbean and African doctors able to establish successful practices in Britain, especially in white working-class areas, won the respect of their patients.[32]

The 1930s was one of the most crucial decades in the history of black Britain. The consequence of what we may call the alienization of black British subjects became even more dire during the Depression, and for black seamen it became especially bleak after 1935. For in that year the government, under pressure from the battered shipping industry, provided the latter with a subsidy, one of the key conditions of which was the exclusion of alien seamen from employment on British ships. Black Britons who, through legislative

[31] Little, *Negroes in Britain*, pp. 293–303; Una Marson, 'Nigger', *Keys*, July 1933, pp. 8–9; Elkins, 'Hercules and the Society of Peoples of African Origin', p. 53; Winston James, 'A Race Outcast from an Outcast Class: Claude McKay's Experience and Analysis of Britain', in Bill Schwarz, ed., *West Indian Intellectuals in Britain* (Manchester, 2003), pp. 74–75; Theophilus E. Samuel Scholes, *Glimpses of the Ages, or the 'Superior' and 'Inferior' Races, So-Called, Discussed in the Light of Science and History*, 2 vols. (London, 1908), II, pp. 176–79.

[32] 'Barred by Colour', *African Times and Orient Review*, May 1913, p. 334; Adell Patton, Jr., *Physicians, Colonial Racism, and Diaspora in West Africa* (Gainesville, Fla., 1996), pp. 125–32; Scholes, *Glimpses of the Ages*, II, pp. 165–67; Jeffrey Green, 'West Indian Doctors in London: John Alcindor (1873–1924); James Jackson Brown (1882–1953)', *Journal of Caribbean History*, XX, 1 (1985–86), pp. 49–77; and 'John Alcindor (1873–1924): A Migrant's Biography', *Immigrants and Minorities*, VI, 2, July 1987, pp. 174–89.

and administrative subterfuge, had been earlier deprived of their citizenship were now prevented from holding on to an economic lifeline in a desperate time.[33] The decade also witnessed the birth and emergence of a number of new black organizations and a level of black activism that was unprecedented. The focus of attention was both domestic and international, and the level of engagement in matters political by the black middle class reached a new height. These features of the new decade were partly due to the increase in the black population, but mainly to new challenges that could not be easily ignored.

Though estimates of the size of Britain's black population are notoriously unreliable, all the evidence suggests that the black population declined in the 1920s (no doubt partly because of the terror, deportations, and state repression in 1919 and after) and increased in the 1930s. A number of developments account for the growth: the beaching of black seamen on British shores who found it virtually impossible to find work; an understandable reluctance of black men to return to Africa and the Caribbean, places that were even more ravaged by the depression than Britain itself; natural increase, or to be more precise the growth in the number of offspring that came from the union of black men and white women—the so-called 'half-castes'—especially in the port cities; and an increase in the number of students from the Caribbean and Africa in the British Isles.[34]

In addition to this growth in the black population was the fortuitous arrival, almost simultaneously, of a cohort of experienced and talented black activists complementing those already domiciled in Britain. George Padmore, C. L. R. James, Thomas Griffith (who later adopted the name T. Ras Makonnen), Amy Ashwood Garvey, Jomo Kenyatta, Paul Robeson, and Marcus Garvey were all living in London by the mid-1930s. I. T. A. Wallace-Johnson, the distinguished Sierra Leonean and West African trade unionist and journalist arrived in 1937 and worked closely with Padmore.

Outside of the local black organizations in Cardiff and Liverpool there were several noteworthy groups extant and active before the crisis of the

[33] Brown, 'Investigation of the Coloured Colonial Seamen in Cardiff', p. 20; Tabili, 'The Construction of Racial Difference', p. 85; P. Cecil Lewis, 'Cardiff Report—General Survey', *Keys*, Oct.-Dec. 1935, p. 16.

[34] Little, *Negroes in Britain*, pp. 107–08; Banton, *Coloured Quarter*, p. 67; Wilson, 'A Hidden History', pp. 201–05; Hakim Adi, 'West African Students in Britain, 1900–1960: The Politics of Exile', in David Killingray, ed., *Africans in Britain* (London, 1994), pp. 107–08; Brown, 'Investigation of Coloured Colonial Seamen in Cardiff', p. 20.

mid-1930s, but they were largely usurped as black politics became decidedly more radical and anti-colonial. One of these, the West African Student Union (WASU), was founded in 1925 at the urging of the distinguished Sierra Leonean Dr Herbert Bankole-Bright, a former medical student at Edinburgh University, member of the Legislative Council in Sierra Leone and the National Congress of British West Africa. Disproportionately comprising the scions of the West African coastal merchant elite and aristocracy, WASU paid scant attention to the plight of West African workers in Britain. The organization was more concerned with Britain's insulting colour bar on its members. Its other aims were very similar to those of the earlier APU. For the first decade of its existence much of WASU's energy was focused on the establishment of an African student hostel in London, but by the mid-1930s, it took on a more explicitly anti-colonial position, some of its members joining the Communist Party (CP), making alliance with organizations led by the CP, such as the League Against Imperialism (LAI), and the more radical Pan-Africanist organisations established under the leadership of George Padmore.[35]

The most explicitly radical and Pan-African group to emerge during this period was that which formed around Padmore. One of the most distinguished Pan-Africanists of the twentieth century, Padmore was born in Arouca, Trinidad, also the birthplace of Sylvester Williams. Soon after arriving in London in 1934, he launched or helped to launch, successively, the International African Friends of Abyssinia, the International African Service Bureau (IASB), and the Pan-African Federation (PAF) with like-minded Caribbeans and Africans, most notably Ras Makonnen, Wallace-Johnson, Amy Ashwood Garvey, Kenyatta, and James, another fellow Trinidadian and childhood friend. Padmore's office and small flat in central London became the workshop of the African anti-colonial struggle. Kwame Nkrumah and Kenyatta were two of the more distinguished African nationalists to pass through their apprenticeship under Padmore's guidance. Padmore later served as Nkrumah's advisor on African affairs in the newly independent Ghana.[36]

[35] Hakim Adi, *West Africans in Britain, 1900–1960* (London, 1998), pp. 32–34.

[36] J. R. Hooker's *Black Revolutionary: George Padmore's Path From Communism to Pan-Africanism* (New York, 1967) is the only biography of Padmore. But see also: Imanuel Geiss, *The Pan-African Movement*, trans. Ann Keep (London, 1974), chaps. 16–20; Penny von Eschen, *Race Against Empire: Black Americans and Anticolonialism, 1937–1957* (Ithaca, NY, 1997); Philippe Dewitte, *Les Mouvements Nègres en France, 1919–1939* (Paris, 1985); and the memoirs of some his

Two major international developments contributed to an unprecedented level of black activism and Pan-Africanist upsurge in the 1930s. The first began in British Honduras (Belize) but quickly ripped through the Caribbean archipelago like a hurricane, and its powerful ripples were soon mirrored in British colonies in Africa. Almost every Caribbean territory, including some non-British ones, was hit by worker revolt. Exploitative, capitalist colonial rule combined with the devastation of the Great Depression was too much for the Caribbean working class to bear. In the British Caribbean, the uprisings continued for almost four years, culminating in the Jamaica labour rebellion of 1938. Scores of people were killed, hundreds injured, millions of pounds of property destroyed. The black organizations, especially Padmore's IASB, analysed the events and argued the case for self-government. The LCP, under the leadership of Moody, pressed the Colonial Office for an inquiry and even managed to help formulate the terms of reference of the Royal Commission, chaired by Lord Moyne, which was sent out to investigate and make recommendations. In hindsight the labour revolts of the 1930s marked a crucial phase in the anti-colonial struggle in the British colonies of the Caribbean and Africa. Through the Moyne Commission, the demands for trade union rights, universal adult suffrage, and self-government were relayed to the British ruling class; which responded with the Colonial Development and Welfare Act of 1940. And many of these demands were conceded, beginning in Jamaica, before the end of the Second World War.[37]

The second event, Mussolini's invasion of Ethiopia and his savage suppression of its people, was the most important in generating solidarity and Pan-African agitation in Britain. No event had so outraged the black world, and none had elicited such outpouring of solidarity and support among black people on the African continent, the Americas, and Europe. The inactivity and de facto complicity of the Great Powers, including Britain,

associates and comrades: Ras Makonnen, *Pan-Africanism From Within* (Nairobi, 1973); C.L.R. James, 'George Padmore: Black Marxist Revolutionary—A Memoir', in his *At the Rendezvous of Victory: Selected Writings* (London, 1984); Dudley Thompson, *From Kingston to Kenya: The Making of a Pan-Africanist Lawyer* (Dover, Mass., 1993); and Peter Abrahams, *The Black Experience in the Twentieth Century: An Autobiography* (Bloomington, Ind., 2000).

[37] See W. Arthur Lewis, *Labour in the West Indies: The Birth of a Workers' Movement* (London, 1939); Ken Post, *Arise Ye Starvelings: The Jamaican Labour Rebellion of 1938 and Its Aftermath* (The Hague, 1978); Roy Thomas, ed., *The Trinidadian Labour Riots of 1937: Perspectives 50 Years Later* (St Augustine, 1987); O. Nigel Bolland, *On the March: Labour Rebellions in the British Caribbean* (Kingston, Jamaica, 1995).

in the conquest of Ethiopia astonished and appalled black Britons and those in the Empire. The articles of the League of Nations had stipulated that an attack upon one member was an attack on all and demanded collective action to repulse aggression. All this was a dead letter when it came to Ethiopia. Like many others, C. L. R. James, who co-founded the International Friends of Abyssinia in 1934, publicly offered to enlist in the Ethiopian army. Padmore was deeply affected by the whole episode and transmuted his rage into frenetic activity in the cause of African independence and anti-colonialism that never abated until he died.[38]

Black Subjects and British Nationality after the Second World War

The Second World War constitutes the most important watershed in the history of twentieth-century black Britain. It induced exponential growth in the black population in the post-war years, an increase that began during the war. For black Britons who had endured the long hardship of the Great Depression, the preparation for and the outbreak of war brought a welcome respite from terrible economic privations. War brought its own peculiar dangers and hardships, but they were different to those encountered and experienced during the decade-long depression. Advertised as a war against fascism and racism, the Second World War provided additional ideological and political leverage to the anti-racist struggle in Britain and the anti-imperialist ones in the colonies from which the new black migrants came.

The black population in Britain was substantially augmented by Caribbeans, Africans, and African-Americans who entered the country to assist in the war effort. The precise number of local black people and those from the colonies who served in the army is unkown, but it was in the thousands. In addition, some 10,000 Caribbeans served in the Royal Air Force (RAF), primarily as ground staff but also as pilots and gunners. Thousands more were also brought in to work in Britain's munitions industry, especially as technicians. Over a thousand British Hondurans (Belizeans) were brought in as forestry workers in Scotland. Some 600 Caribbean women

[38] S. K. B. Asante, *Pan-African Protest: West Africa and the Italo-Ethiopian Crisis, 1934–1941* (London, 1977); and 'The Impact of the Italo-Ethiopian Crisis of 1935–36 on the Pan-African Movement in Britain', *Transactions of the Historical Society of Ghana*, XIII, 2, pp. 217–27; Makonnen, *Pan-Africanism From Within*, chap. 8; Kent Worcester, *C. L. R. James: A Political Biography* (Albany, NY, 1996), p. 32; Kwame Nkrumah, *The Autobiography of Kwame Nkrumah* ([1957] London, 1973), pp. 22–23.

were recruited into the Auxiliary Territorial Service, the only women's unit to seek recruits in the islands, 100 of whom served in Britain. An indeterminate number of black women served in the Women's Auxillary Air Force and other units. By 1945, seventy men of non-European descent from the colonial territories had gained commissions after much resistance from the authorities. Over 130,000 black American GIs served in Britain.[39]

Black British veterans of the Second World War, according to their testimonies, encountered relatively little racism from ordinary British people, but this could not always be said of their immediate officers and the War Office. The most vulgar and violent forms of racism experienced by black servicemen and civilians during the war came from white American servicemen stationed in Britain. They particularly resented the relative insouciance with which black men and white British women interacted. The dance hall floor became one of the primary sites of racist attacks initiated by white Americans. One victim, a member of the Royal Air Force (RAF), asked whether it was fair or just 'to ask me to risk my life nightly over enemy territory' when acts of virulent racism could occur on British soil and not just from the Americans. For the most part, the authorities sought to appease rather than challenge American Jim Crow norms in Britain.[40]

Partly in response to such acts of racism, Padmore, Makonnen and their colleagues busily prepared for the anti-colonial showdown in the post-war years. Between 15 and 19 October, 1945, the Fifth Pan-African Congress met in Manchester. With more than 100 delegates representing twenty-one countries and nineteen British-based organizations, the Congress called without equivocation for self-determination for all colonized peoples, the expansion and protection of the rights of workers, and an end to the colour bar in Britain. Thoroughly internationalist in outlook, it extended solidarity to all

[39] Marika Sherwood, *Many Struggles: West Indian Workers and Service Personnel in Britain (1939–1945)* (London, 1985); Thompson, *From Kingston to Kenya*; E. Martin Noble, *Jamaica Airman: A Black Airman in Britain, 1943 and After* (London, 1984); Amos Ford, *Telling the Truth: The Life and Times of the British Honduras Forestry Unit in Scotland (1941–44)* (London, 1985); Killingray, 'Race and Rank in the British Army', pp. 280–82; Graham Smith, *When Jim Crow Met John Bull: Black American Soldiers in World War II Britain* (London, 1987); Wilson, 'A Hidden History', chap. 8; Ben Bousquet and Colin Douglas, *West Indian Women at War: British Racism in World War II* (London, 1991).

[40] Thompson, *From Kingston to Kenya*; Noble, *Jamaica Airman*; Ford, *Telling the Truth*; Bousquet and Douglas, *West Indian Women at War*; Sherwood, *Many Struggles*; and Smith, *When Jim Crow Met John Bull*, esp. chap. 3; *Sunday Pictorial*, 19 August 1943; and Wilson, 'A Hidden History', pp. 529–33.

oppressed groups around the world regardless of colour. Hastings Banda, W. E. B. Du Bois, and, Ken Hill, as well as Amy Ashwood Garvey, Kenyatta, Wallace-Johnson, and Nkrumah were among some of the more distinguished delegates. Of these, Nkrumah would become the leader of Ghana, the first independent black state in sub-Saharan Africa, followed by Kenyatta in Kenya, and Banda in Malawi. The Congress's impact was more far-reaching internationally than domestically, but it had joined the struggles of black people and those in the colonies far more concretely than had been previously achieved. It was a rallying cry and a harbinger of the demise of the British Empire.[41]

After the election of Clement Attlee's Labour government, Padmore sent an 'Open Letter to the Prime Minister' on behalf of the PAF welcoming Labour's 'great victory', for which they, as colonials, 'have hoped and worked alongside Britain's workers'. This victory, the letter continued, 'makes possible the inauguration of the century of the common man.... The dark-skinned workers, no less than the pale-skinned, want freedom from war, want and fear'. To condemn German, Japanese, and Italian imperialism while condoning that of Britain would be 'more than dishonest, it would be a betrayal of the sacrifice and sufferings and the toil and sweat of the common people of this country. All imperialism is evil.' As an expression of 'Socialist goodwill', the Labour government should, the letter suggested, implement several immediate reforms. Among these, discrimination based on 'race, colour or creed' in Britain should be made a 'punishable offence'.[42] Attlee did not reply to the letter. Instead of moving in the direction the PAF suggested, the government exerted itself in holding on to the Empire; Attlee did not want Labour to be blamed for 'losing' the Empire.

Furthermore, instead of tackling the colour bar, the Labour government exerted itself in trying to prevent the migration of black people to Britain, whether or not they were British subjects. Some of the black ex-soldiers and former workers brought in during the war decided to remain in Britain, although the vast majority returned to the colonies. But on discovering the

[41] George Padmore, ed., *Colonial and Coloured Unity: A Programme of Action—History of the Pan-African Congress* (Manchester, 1947); Hakim Adi and Marika Sherwood, *The 1945 Manchester Pan-African Congress Revisted* (London, 1995), esp. chap 1; Hooker, *Black Revolutionary*, chap. 6; Geiss, *Pan-African Movement*, chaps. 19 and 20; Langley, *Pan-Africanism and Nationalism in West Africa, 1900–1945*, esp. chap. 9.

[42] Quoted in Adi and Sherwood, *The 1945 Manchester Pan-African Congress Revisted*, pp. 23–24.

depressed state of the economies there, a significant number decided to go back to Britain where post-war reconstruction enhanced the prospect of finding employment. As the Colonial Secretary, Arthur Creech-Jones, pointed out in 1947, it was well-known in the Caribbean that Britain was experiencing a 'labour shortage' and that a massive government campaign was underway to recruit displaced persons from Europe, under the European Voluntary Workers (EVW) scheme among others. Governor Huggins of Jamaica and other Caribbean Governors urged the British government to extend the scheme to Caribbean workers. But the government refused.[43]

To discourage black migration, the Welfare Officer of the Colonial Office toured the Caribbean in early 1947 to dispel the idea that there were jobs to be had in England. He informed incredulous governors and the local press that jobs seen advertised in the British newspapers were 'paper vacancies', not real jobs. The ruse did not work and the workers came, despite efforts to slow down the issuing of passports. When in 1947 the SS *Ormonde* arrived in London with 110 Jamaican migrants on board, government departments were anxious that it not become the beginning of a trend of black migration. A year later, the SS *Empire Windrush*'s arrival with 492 Jamaican migrants created panic and mutual recrimination, with the Colonial Office blamed for the catastrophe of the 'argosy' or 'invasion' of Britain by blackamoors. Since as British subjects the Jamaicans could not very well be prevented from landing, the aim became to spread them out across the country, some being placed in jobs as far away as Scotland, others in Gloucester, the Midlands and South Wales.[44]

Within two days of the docking of the *Empire Windrush*, a group of eleven Labour MPs wrote Attlee urging him to place controls on black 'immigration' to Britain. The Prime Minister took several months to respond and crafted a careful reply. Outlining the legal position, he stated that it was 'traditional that British subjects, whether of dominion or Colonial origin (and of whatever race or colour), should be freely admissible to the United Kingdom. This tradition is not, in my view, to be lightly discarded, particularly at a time when we are importing foreign labour in large numbers.' He was careful, however, not to rule out immigration controls in

[43] Clive Harris, 'Post-War Migration and the Industrial Reserve Army', in Winston James and Clive Harris, eds., *Inside Babylon: The Caribbean Diaspora in Britain* (London, 1993), pp. 9–54.

[44] Ibid., pp. 22–24.

the future: 'If our policy were to result in a great influx of undesirables, we might, however unwillingly, have to reconsider modifying it.'[45]

Behind closed doors, however, Attlee's position was quite different. In Cabinet, Creech-Jones was dragged over the coals for not 'having kept the lid on things' sufficiently in the colonies to prevent the 'invasion' of Jamaicans and was urged to 'ensure that further similar movements either from Jamaica or elsewhere in the colonial empire are detected and checked before they can reach such an embarrassing stage'. Attlee asked whether the *Windrush* migrants might be diverted to groundnut projects in East Africa. Government officials explored the possibility of settling others from the densely-populated islands to British Honduras and British Guiana where land, they said, was more plentiful. In addition, a whole series of devious administrative devices, such as deliberate delay in issuing passports, were deployed to impede the migration of black people and other non-Europeans to Britain. The British authorities even got the French in West Africa to collude in some of these measures to hinder the migration of West African British subjects to the UK.[46]

The Conservative government of Winston Churchill, which came to power in October 1951, pursued the idea of restricting 'coloured' immigration with even greater vigour than did its Labour predecessor. Even more than Labour, the Tories abhorred the idea of black people migrating and settling in Britain. They feared the contamination of the British 'stock', or as the Marquis of Salisbury, a member of Churchill's Cabinet, put it, 'the racial character of the English people'.[47] Anticipating the racist language of Peter Griffiths, Enoch Powell, and Margaret Thatcher, Churchill himself had told Sir Hugh Foot, Governor of Jamaica, that he opposed Jamaican migration to Britain because he hated the idea of a 'magpie society'. 'That would never do', he declared.[48] Harold Macmillan recalled that in 1955 Churchill suggested

[45] Clive Harris, 'Post-War Migration and the Industrial Reserve Army', p. 24; Bob Carter, Clive Harris and Shirley Joshi, 'The 1951–55 Conservative Government and the Racialization of Black Immigration', in James and Harris, *Inside Babylon*, p. 56; C. Atlee to J. D. Murray, 5 September 1948, [CO 876/88, f.11030/26] quoted in Clive Harris, 'British Capitalism, Migration and Relative Surplus-Population', *Migration*, I (1987), p. 87 n. 31.

[46] Harris, 'British Capitalism, Migration and Relative Surplus-Population', pp. 63–64, quotation at p. 63; and Carter and others, 'The 1951–55 Conservative Government', p. 57; Kathleen Paul, *Whitewashing Britain: Race and Citizenship in the Postwar Era* (Ithaca, NY, 1997), pp. 151–53.

[47] Quoted in Carter and others, 'The 1951–55 Conservative Government', p. 65.

[48] Quoted in Zig Layton-Henry, *The Politics of Race in Britain* (London, 1984), p. 32.

that ' "Keep Britain White" might be a good slogan for the forthcoming election.'[49]

Churchill complained to one of his junior colleagues, Sir Ian Gilmour, in 1954 that 'Immigration is the most important subject facing this country but I cannot get any of my ministers to take any notice.'[50] The archival evidence tells a different story. There was striking ministerial unanimity around the idea of blocking black migration to Britain. The problems for Churchill lay elsewhere: how to make a 'strong case' for such drastic action, entailing the *de facto* abrogation of the 1948 Nationality Act, and how to craft legislation aimed solely at keeping out black British subjects without appearing to do so. Building a 'strong case' involved the gathering and analysing of data to show that black settlers constituted a 'problem' which called for targeted immigration controls. Successive working parties could never find enough negative information to make a case sufficiently persuasive to win parliamentary and public approval. Both the Labour and Conservative governments up to 1961 did not believe that parliamentary and public opinion had 'crystallized' enough against black migration to facilitate the legislation they had in mind. In light of this, the Conservative governments in particular, exerted enormous effort in shaping, or, as one civil servant irreverently put it, 'cook[ing]', public opinion against black people.[51] The other problem with a bill aimed only at 'coloured' colonials was the anticipated negative reaction from the colonies and wider international opinion. Would it not add force to the nationalist and anti-colonial 'wind of change' then blowing in Britain's colonies in Africa and the Caribbean? And what of the boast of a multi-racial and harmonious British Commonwealth of Nations? As Churchill's private secretary, Sir David Hunt, put it: 'The minute we said we've got to keep these black chaps out, the whole Commonwealth lark would have blown up.'[52]

[49] Harold Macmillan, *At the End of the Day, 1961–1936* (New York, 1973), pp. 73–74. The remark is corroborated by *The Macmillan Diaries: The Cabinet Years, 1950–1957*, Peter Catterall, ed. (London, 2003), with a slight variation. The entry for 20 Jan. 1955 reads: 'More Discussion about West Indian immigrants. A Bill is being drafted—but it's not an easy problem. P. M. [Churchill] thinks "Keep England White" a good slogan!' p. 382.

[50] Quoted in Layton-Henry, *Politics of Race in Britain*, p. 32.

[51] Carter and others, 'The 1951–55 Conservative Government', pp. 66–67; for Macmillan's agonizing over the problem of interfering with 'the traditional freedom of movement between the countries of the Commonwealth and the Motherland,' see his *At the End of the Day*, pp. 73–83.

[52] Quoted in Paul, *Whitewashing Britain*, p. 142; also see chaps. 5 and 6, and Bob Carter and Shirley Joshi, 'The Role of Labour in Creating a Racist Britain', *Race and Class*, 25, 3 (Winter 1984), pp. 53–70

Such considerations became moot, at best secondary, by October 1961 when the Conservatives tabled the Commonwealth Immigrants Bill. Condemned as racist by Hugh Gaitskell, leader of the Labour Party, it nevertheless passed into law the following year. Harold Wilson's Labour government, which came to power in 1964, did not repeal the Act, despite the Labour Party's earlier official opposition to it. On taking office, Wilson in fact promised to maintain and strengthen the Act, and indeed did so. Moreover, Labour passed a second Commonwealth Immigrants Act in 1968, which successfully deprived Asians of British nationality from entering Britain during the political crises of the late 1960s in East Africa. In 1971, by which time British public opinion against 'coloured' immigration had finally crystallized, the Conservatives passed another Immigration Act that was even more draconian and more blatantly racist in its language and more explicit in intent. It effectively brought to a close primary migration of black people to Britain. Dependents, mainly children, could enter but virtually no other black person.[53]

One of the arguments repeatedly used by the apologists of racist immigration controls was that Britain was an 'overcrowded' island. But this argument was never used in relation to the hundreds of thousands of continental Europeans who were encouraged to migrate to Britain in the post-war years. Most remarkably, it was never used in official circles against Irish immigration to Britain. Irish immigrants entered Britain unimpeded at the rate of 50,000 to 60,000 per year. Yet the Afro-Caribbeans who were entering at a rate of 1,000 to 2,000 per year at the time drew official attention and opprobrium. By 1951 there were an estimated 15,000 Caribbean migrants in Britain compared to nearly 750,000 Irish immigrants.[54] From reading the official documents one could be forgiven for thinking that the figures were reversed. The inconsistency did not go unnoticed. In 1955 when a draft immigration bill was being considered by a parliamentary committee, some members asked: 'Why should mainly loyal and hard-working Jamaicans be discriminated against when ten times that quantity of disloyal

[53] Ian Macdonald and Nicholas Blake, *Immigration Law and Practice in the United Kingdom*, 4th edn. (London, 1995), esp. chap. 1; Layton-Henry, *Politics of Race in Britain*, chap. 3.

[54] Figures from E. J. B. Rose and others *Colour and Citizenship: A Report on British Race Relations* (London, 1969), p. 97; and Paul, *Whitewashing Britain*, p. 93. Between 1951 and 1971 when the issue of immigration was most hotly debated, there were 55,000 more people leaving than entering Britain. See Ceri Peach, Vaughan Robinson, Julia Maxted and Judith Chance, 'Immigration and Ethnicity', in A. H. Halsey, ed., *British Social Trends Since 1900: A Guide to the Changing Social Structure of Britain* (Basingstoke, England, 1988), p. 562, Table 14.1.

Southern Irish (some of them Sinn Feiners) come and go as they please?' Churchill's working party answered that objection in its report: the Irish 'are not—whether they like it or not—a different race from the ordinary inhabitants of Great Britain'.[55]

Loyalty, Racism, and Disillusionment

Despite the obstacles placed in their way, large numbers of black people still managed to get into Britain. Many of them slipped in before the 1962 immigration act came into effect. From under 21,000 in 1951, the Caribbean- and West African-born black population in England and Wales grew to over 360,000 by 1966. More than half came from Jamaica alone, and just over 43,000, about 12 per cent, migrated from West Africa. Ambitious, energetic and in the prime of life, they came disproportionately from the skilled proletariat, the black artisanry—carpenters, electricians, masons, mechanics, dressmakers—many of whom had served a long and arduous apprenticeship in their country of origin. Caribbean governments repeatedly bemoaned the loss of their best workers, and studies by economists undergirded these pronouncements, adding dire calculations of the implications for economic development. Professionals, students, and white-collar workers also migrated in significant numbers, particularly from West Africa.

The post-war black migration differed from that before the war. Black women, who were few in number in the early years, comprised a large part of the post-war cohort of migrants. So much so that between 1961 and 1966 more black women than men migrated to Britain. Indeed, the pattern was such that there were more Jamaican women than Jamaican men in London by 1966. Different too, was the destination of the migrants. The seaport cities of Cardiff and Liverpool no longer had the magnetic pull that they had in the pre-war years. London became more important than ever, with the overwhelming majority settling there, with the next largest group of migrants settling in the Midlands, especially Birmingham, followed by Manchester. Black migrants were thus far more urbanized than the rest of the British population.[56]

[55] Quotations from Carter and others, 'The 1951–55 Conservative Government', pp. 67 and 69. See Paul, *Whitewashing Britain*, chap. 4, for the Government's handling of the Irish immigration question.

[56] Rose and others, *Colour and Citizenship* provide the most detailed profile of the post-war migrants. See also Ceri Peach, *West Indian Migration to Britain: A Social Geography* (London, 1968).

Because of the pervasive racism they encountered in the labour market, post-war black migrants secured openings primarily in the most vulnerable and undesirable sectors of the British economy. The post-war boom provided unparalleled opportunity for members of the white working class to move from low-paid and generally undesirable jobs to better ones. Although there was room at the top and in the middle of the labour force, black workers were disproportionately placed at the bottom. Indeed, many employers turned to black labour primarily because white workers refused to work for them. Thus skilled black workers were downgraded to semi-skilled and unskilled labourers in Britain. Moreover, from the 1950s onwards, in both the private and public sectors, employers (partly due to union pressure) were unwilling to allow black workers to take up apprenticeships and join training programmes. Black professional and white collar workers had even greater difficulty in finding work commensurate with their skills.[57] A Trinidadian accountant might become a London bus conductor; a Jamaican seamstress might find herself in a fruit-canning factory in Manchester.

In the search for shelter, the modes and pattern of discrimination were even more explicit and painful than those encountered in the search for work. Rooms for rent disappeared once a black would-be tenant knocked on the door. When accommodation was finally secured, it was almost invariably at a higher rent than a white person would have been charged. The practice of overcharging was so commonplace that the sociologists dubbed it the 'colour tax', the surcharge for having a black face. Moreover, these openings in the housing market were generally located in the most run-down and blighted areas of Britain's urban centres. High rents and the artificial scarcity of accommodation led to overcrowding, as black compatriots sublet to one another, and slumlords, such as the notorious Peter Rachman in Notting Hill, cashed in by overcharging and over-stuffing their buildings with black tenants who had little if any choice.[58]

The black settlers were as likely to be unwelcome in pubs as in churches. Because of this hostility, black people would stay at home, inviting their

[57] Harris, 'Post-War Migration', esp. pp. 29–31; also see Ralph Fevre, *Cheap Labour and Racial Discrimination* (London, 1984); and Dennis Brooks, *Race and Labour in London Transport* (London, 1975).

[58] The sociological literature on the subject is vast, but see in particular J. Rex and R. Moore, *Race, Community and Conflict* (London, 1967); Shirley Green, *Rachman* (London, 1979); and Edward Pilkington, *Beyond the Mother Country: West Indians and the Notting Hill White Riots* (London, 1988).

friends, fellow black pariahs, for a drink, a game of dominoes, or to listen to some music. Soon, enterprising members of the black community opened black clubs and other places of entertainment. Similarly, the religious-minded formed their own places of worship, avoiding the scorn of white Christians as they worshipped their God.

In many parts of Britain it was often unsafe and generally unpleasant for a black person to walk the streets, especially at night. Hostile stares and racist epithets would often follow black pedestrians. Less frequently, a black person suffered an unprovoked physical attack, especially by young white hoodlums who called themselves Teddy Boys, many of whom were indistinguishable from Oswald Moseley's band of fascist followers. In the late 1950s many of them engaged in what they called 'nigger hunting', the sudden attack on an unsuspecting black person or persons in superior numbers.[59]

Soon after their children started entering British schools, black parents discovered that they were disproportionately placed in the low streams. Many normal black children, as studies later revealed, were even placed in classes and schools designated for the educationally subnormal. Studies also revealed that white teachers were far more ready to suspend and expel black students (especially boys) than they were their white counterparts. The problem of the education of black children in Britain was to fuel black political activity in the 1960s and 1970s especially. Black parents, their children, and progressive white educationalists protested and set up supplementary schools, which generally met all day on Saturdays. These schools, which could be found in black communities all over the country, provided the general curricular offerings (such as basic English and mathematics) along with the teaching of black historical and cultural studies. Many black undergraduate and post-graduate students in university towns such as London, Birmingham, Manchester, and Leeds devoted their Saturdays to teaching in these schools alongside the children's parents.[60]

The general hostility traumatized many black migrants. Some, despite the economic hardships back home, were so horrified by the experience that they decided to return to the Caribbean as soon as they had put together the fare.

[59] Pilkington, *Beyond the Mother Country*, esp. chap. 7.

[60] Bernard Coard, *How the West Indian Child is Made Educationally Sub-normal in the British Educational System* (London, 1971); Maureen Stone, *The Education of the Black Child in Britain: The Myth of Multi-racial Education* (London, 1981); Sally Tomlinson, *Educational Sub-normality: A Study in Decision-Making* (London, 1981); Beverley Bryan and others, *The Heart of the Race: Black Women's Lives in Britain* (London, 1985), chap. 2.

Still others suffered severe psychological distress from which they found it difficult to recover. Many resolved to fight the system of racism and organize politically, joining reformist organizations such as the Campaign Against Racial Discrimination (CARD), very much in the tradition of Harold Moody's LCP. Others joined organizations such as the British Communist Party; still others formed organizations of their own with names such as the Black Unity and Freedom Party, the Black Liberation Front, the Race Today Collective. Britain also had its own Black Panther Party. In the 1970s and 1980s a significant number of young black radicals, mainly students and former students, joined revolutionary socialist (mainly Trotskyist) organizations such as the Socialist Workers' Party (SWP), and the International Marxist Group. Black people also joined and were actively engaged in the Anti-Nazi League, which was formed and led by the SWP, to fight against the resurgence of fascist groups such as the National Front and the British National Party. Black women were actively engaged in all of these efforts, quite often taking on a leadership role. But in the 1970s and 1980s, in order to more effectively combat the dual oppression of race and sex, they established a number of autonomous black women's organizations such as the Brixton Black Women's Group and later, in 1978, the Organization of Women of Asian and African Descent (OWAAD). It was also at this moment that the problem of homophobia within the black community was exposed, debated, and challenged. Black women, especially an increasingly visible black lesbian community, led the struggle for greater tolerance and acceptance of gay people.[61]

The plight of black migrants, especially in the 1950s and 1960s, would undoubtedly have been less harrowing and prolonged had the British authorities taken measures to condemn and proscribe racist practices in the country. The Pan-African Federation and the Pan-African Congress had called for such measures as early as 1945. Both Labour and Conservative governments refused to act. Indeed, the Conservatives, from Churchill to Thatcher, were far more interested in inflaming public opinion against black people than combating racism. Only after the 1958 riots did the Labour Party condescend to give serious consideration to anti-discrimination legislation, which yielded the virtually toothless Race Relations Act of 1965.

[61] A. Sivanandan, *A Different Hunger: Writings on Black Resistance* (London, 1982), pp. 3–54; see special issue of *Feminist Review*, 17 (July 1984); Bryan and others, *Heart of the Race*, esp. chap. 4; Centre for Contemporary Cultural Studies, *The Empire Strikes Back: Race and Racism in 70s Britain* (London, 1982), chap. 6.

The Race Relations Board that was established to administer the Act, found that its remit was so narrowly defined that 73 per cent of complaints of racism lodged in its first year of operation was outside its scope; in the following year the proportion rose to 83 per cent of its 690 complaints. The Act was strengthened in 1976, but it was still too weak and far too late, given the urgency and seriousness of black people's suffering.[62]

While the Labour Party was scratching its head over what to do about racism in Britain, Peter Griffiths, a Conservative candidate won a Midlands parliamentary seat in the 1964 general elections with the slogan: 'If You Want A Nigger for Your Neighbour Vote Labour'. Four years later, Enoch Powell, a senior Conservative MP, gave his infamous 'Rivers of Blood' speech, which called for the 'repatriation' of black people from Britain. Edward Heath, the leader of the Conservative opposition in Parliament sacked him from the shadow cabinet, but East End dockers left work and marched in the centre of London in defence of 'our Enoch'. Neither Griffiths nor Powell was expelled from the Conservative Party. The Labour Party, instead of vigorously tackling these racist rantings, determined that the problem was indeed the black presence. But since it would not or could not stoop to forcibly 'repatriate' black Britons, decided instead to prevent others of dark hue from entering the country.[63]

Such incidents and behaviour combined with the reluctance of the British government to deal with the racism that black people faced in their everyday lives contributed to a profound sense of disillusionment. The root cause of the disillusionment and growing bitterness among black Britons was the clash of two logics within British imperialism—that of the Empire and that of the metropole. At home, especially in the Caribbean, which had endured 300 years of British colonialism, black people had been taught that they were British and came to think of themselves as such. They imbibed even such obscenely jingoistic tunes as 'Rule Britannia', which they sang, not only without objection but also with genuine pride. The same pride accompanied the annual celebration of Empire Day. British officialdom in the colonies deliberately and assiduously cultivated such ideas and practices in order to extend their hegemony among the people. 'Missis Queen' or 'Victoria the Good', loved them. When the local ruling class tormented them to excess, they sent petitions to the Mother Country via the Colonial Office to get relief.

[62] Layton-Henry, *Politics of Race in Britain*, chap. 9.

[63] Paul Foot, *The Rise of Enoch Powell* (London, 1969).

Their movement to Britain was never perceived as immigration as such.[64] They saw it more as internal migration, as if a man was moving from the parish of Hanover in the west of Jamaica to Portland in the east; like an Englishman going from Manchester to London. In strictly juridical terms they were perfectly correct, a point upon which John Stuart Mill might have insisted.[65] The *logic of the Empire* mandated that Barbados was not just 'Little England', but England overseas, separated from the 'mainland', the Mother Land, by the accident of an ocean. The *Evening Standard*, at least momentarily, subscribed to the logic when it greeted the passengers of the *Empire Windrush* with the headline, 'WELCOME HOME'.[66]

The other logic of British imperialism, the *logic of the metropole*, was more powerful and overrode the *logic of the Empire*. The British ruling class saw black people as colonials, and as such inferiors, Kipling's 'lesser breeds', perfectly suited by Nature to be hewers of wood and drawers of water, cutters of sugar cane, providers of valuable raw material and tropical products, and captive markets of British manufactures. In the colony, they could be British, but not in Britain, the white man's country, the home of superior beings, whom God had specially endowed with the gift of rulership. In short, the Nigerians and Antiguans belonged *to* the Mother Country but not *in* the Mother Country.

These two logics were to be kept separate: the Natives would be fed the lie of their Britishness while in the colonies, and were only to discover otherwise when they tried to enter Britain. The need to separate these conflicting and incommensurate logics lay behind a Colonial Office letter sent to the 'West Indies Governors' in 1958. The letter informed the Governors that the pressure for a ban on coloured immigration to Britain had nothing to do with the British Government at all, but emanated 'from individuals, often belonging to the lunatic fringe'.[67] As the Colonial Office knew full well at the time, the government had fully subscribed to the sustained post-war British state policy of keeping black people out and keeping Britain white.

[64] Richard Hart, 'Jamaica and Self-Determination, 1660–1970', *Race*, XIII, 3, Jan. 1972, pp. 271–97; Gordon Lewis, *Main Currents in Caribbean Thought: The Historical Evolution of Caribbean Society in Its Ideological Aspects, 1492–1900* (Baltimore, 1983), pp. 307–10; Winston James, *A Fierce Hatred of Injustice: Claude McKay's Jamaica and His Poetry of Rebellion* (London, 2000), pp. 91–97.

[65] John Stuart Mill, *Principles of Political Economy* (London, 1900), p. 454; George Lamming, 'Sea of Stories', *Guardian*, 24 Oct. 2002.

[66] *Evening Standard*, 21 June 1948; quoted in Fryer, *Staying Power*, p. 372.

[67] Quoted in Paul, *Whitewashing Britain*, p. 153.

The collision of these two logics generated terrible disillusionment among black migrants. They left British Guiana and British Honduras as proud black Britons and arrived in Britain as niggers. The shocking discovery of their inferior status profoundly affected the self-conception and political consciousness of the black settlers. Jamaicans in Britain became more than Jamaican; they became 'West Indian', 'Afro-Caribbean', 'black'. Some even identified themselves as 'African'. 'Most West Indians of my generation were born in England', noted the distinguished Caribbean intellectual, George Lamming, who had himself migrated to London in 1950.[68] What he meant is, prior to migration, Jamaicans and Barbadians identified themselves in insular terms within the Caribbean, but in Britain assumed a pan-Caribbean self-identification, transformed into 'West Indians.' The process was equally true of continental Africans. Ghanaians became more than Ghanaians. They became 'African' and 'black'. 'Pan-Africanism', after all, was not born on the continent, but emerged from the merciless crucible of exile in a racist world. The petty antagonisms between different island groups and between different African nationalities would be eroded over time in Britain, thanks to the centripetal power of the racism each black person experienced. The racism was even powerful enough to bring together to a remarkable degree Afro- and Indo-Caribbeans, two groups that had a long history of antagonism and tension in Guyana and Trinidad. The 'light-skinned' Caribbean person, who had such misplaced airs and contempt for darker islanders at home, in Britain was called a 'nig-nog', 'sambo' and other choice names by racists. The transformation this elicited—the overthrowing of old prejudices and the birth of a new, black self-identification—led one such person to declare that: 'England has at last done [her] a favour.'[69]

Life for black Britons was not unrelievedly grim. Had it been so, far many more would have made their way back to the Caribbean and West Africa. Despite the pervasiveness of racism in Britain, the migrants came into contact with many decent white people. Friendships and alliances developed across racial lines in the workplace. One notable feature of the early years that has continued to the present was the large number of black migrants who

[68] George Lamming, *The Pleasures of Exile* (1960; London, 1984), p. 214.

[69] Donald Hinds, *Journey to an Illusion: The West Indian in Britain* (London, 1966), pp. 16–17; Patricia Madoo, 'The Transition from "Light Skinned" to "Coloured" ', in H. Tajfel and J. Dawson, eds., *Disappointed Guests* (London, 1965), p. 62, for quotation; and Winston James, 'Migration, Racism and Identity Formation: The Caribbean Experience in Britain', in James and Harris, *Inside Babylon*, pp. 231–87.

joined and became active in the trade unions. Indeed, trade union membership among them has always been higher than that among their white counterparts, which gives the lie to the fear and calumny that black workers would not join unions and would undermine the labour movement. Materially, black migrants were generally better off in Britain, some significantly so, than they had been in the Caribbean and Africa. The low-paid jobs in Britain generally provided a higher income than even many of the more high-status jobs in the Caribbean Africa that some migrants had before emigration. And as the economic crisis deepened in the Caribbean in the 1960s and 1970s, only the most determined chose to leave Britain and the security provided by the post-war welfare state.

Mainly young people in their twenties and early thirties, the black migrants soon became more enterprising in their search for entertainment. The men, especially, risked the dangers of the night streets to dance at the black nightclubs and the more open-minded white-owned ones. Aldwyn Roberts, better known as the calypsonian 'Lord Kitchener', was among the few Trinidadians who arrived on the *Empire Windrush* in 1948. He first lived and worked in London and then settled in Manchester, but travelled the country with his calypso band. He, more than anyone, helped to popularize this Caribbean musical form in Britain. The Jamaicans brought ska and rock steady, precursors of reggae music, which won a massive following not only among the black settlers but also among British youth, including the more progressive wing of the Teddy Boys in the 1950s and 1960s. Some of the migrants also played in jazz bands. Records were brought and imported in increasing numbers from the Caribbean and the United States, and London, Birmingham, Manchester, and other British cities were the venues of calypsonians and Jamaican musicians touring the country. The British public had never had such a wide and sustained exposure to Caribbean musical forms. There was home-grown black talent, too, emerging from an earlier phase of black migration. Cleo Laine, a woman of mixed descent, (Jamaican father, white English mother), emerged in the 1950s as Britain's pre-eminent female jazz vocalist. Out of 'Tiger Bay', Cardiff's black community, came Shirley Bassey, the daughter of a Nigerian seaman and his Welsh wife, a singer of extraordinary range and talent. Such was their popularity that Laine and Bassey were among the very few black women who could be seen on British television in the 1960s. Black Britons also took pride in the achievement of the highly talented Rudolph Dunbar, a classical musician and conductor, who had migrated as a young man from Guyana (via New York's Julliard

School of Music) to Britain in 1928. As early as the 1940s and 1950s, he conducted the Berlin Philharmonic Orchestra, the London Philharmonic Orchestra and the orchestras of the Paris Conservatoire, and the National Symphony of Paris. All of these occasions were, however, rather episodic and ad hoc, for Dunbar was never given the opportunity his widely-recognised talent deserved. In the 1950s and 1960s, London served as the incubator of the post-war, Anglophone-Caribbean novel. It was then and there that Wilson Harris, John Hearne, George Lamming, Roger Mais, Edgar Mittelholzer, V. S. Naipaul, Orlando Patterson, Andrew Salkey, Sam Selvon, and Sylvia Wynter, among others, honed their skill as fiction writers. Moreover, it was London publishers who brought out their books, and the BBC's 'Caribbean Voices' programme provided them with much needed, if modest, bread. The fiction produced—remarkable in both quantity and quality—in those two decades, served as a mirror not only to the Caribbean but also Britain, including reflections on the black experience in the metropole itself.[70]

In the late 1950, the black community in Notting Hill, under the leadership of Claudia Jones, started what became known as the Notting Hill Carnival. Jones, a Trinidadian, had migrated as a child with her parents to New York. She joined the Communist Party while still at school and was deported to Britain during the anti-Communist witch-hunts of the 1950s in the US. She remained politically active in Britain and started the first black newspaper, the bold *West Indian Gazette*, in 1958. But she recognized the need for black enjoyment as well as struggle and, with her close associates, started the Notting Hill Carnival in 1959.[71] By the 1980s, the Carnival was the largest street festival in all of Europe drawing revellers every August Bank Holiday from the continent, the United States, the Caribbean, and even from Brazil.

Perhaps the source of the greatest pride for the black settlers was the West Indies cricket team and its remarkable achievements and pre-eminence in the 1950s and 1960s. The 'Windies', as the team was popularly known, boasted the world's best batsmen and bowlers, including Garfield Sobers. They provided excellent entertainment for their discerning and knowledgeable black fans. Moreover, these black men almost invariably beat the English at

[70] Susan Okokon, *Black Londoners, 1880–1990* (Stroud, Glos., 1998), pp. 9–10, 24–25; Kenneth Ramchand, *The West Indian Novel and its Background* (London, 1970); Glyne Griffith, 'Deconstructing Nationalisms: Henry Swanzy, *Caribbean Voices* and the Development of West Indian Literature,' *Small Axe*, 10, (September 2001), pp. 1–20.

[71] Marika Sherwood and others, *Claudia Jones: A Life in Exile* (London, 1999), esp. pp. 150–62.

'their own game'. When the team toured Britain during the test season, it was assured of a loyal and boisterous band of black supporters, men and women, in the stands.

Conclusion

The period stretching from the late 1970s to the end of the 1980s, dominated as it was by economic and political Thatcherism, was the worst for black settlers and their children in Britain since the dark days of the early 1950s. It is not surprising that it was during this moment of disillusionment and anger that radical dub-poet, Linton Kwesi Johnson, who went to England when he was 10 years old, wrote his most resonant poem. Written in his native Jamaican Creole it declared: 'Inglan is a bitch/ dere's no escapin' it/ Inglan is a bitch/ dere's no runnin' whey fram it.'[72]

Margaret Thatcher's hostility toward the black presence in Britain was well-known even before she came to power. In a television interview the year before she came to power, Thatcher, 'a sincere racist', as Sivanandan noted, stated that people were understandably fearful of being 'swamped' by non-white 'immigrants'.[73] 'We are a *British* nation with *British* characteristics', she insisted. 'Every nation can take some minorities, and in many ways they add to the richness and variety of this country. But the moment a minority threatens to become a big one, people get frightened.'[74] To Thatcher and so many before and after her, one could not be black and British. True to her pronouncement, the Conservative government tightened even further the already draconian immigration rules as they applied to would-be non-white 'immigrants'. In 1981 her government passed the British Nationality Act, the most radical and unapologetically racist of all, that, most notably, deprived non-white overseas British nationals of the right of abode in Britain. Perhaps the most radical and astonishing of all its provisions was the denial of automatic citizenship to those born in Britain; if the parents had entered the country illegally, or if they were neither 'settled' residents nor citizens then

[72] Linton Kwesi Johnson, 'Inglan is a Bitch', in his *Tings an Times: Selected Poems* (Newcastle upon Tyne, 1991), pp. 13–14.

[73] A. Sivanandan, 'Challenging Racism: Strategies for the 80s', *Race and Class*, XXV, 2 (1983), p. 6.

[74] Thatcher quoted in John Solomos, *Race and Racism in Contemporary Britain* (London, 1989), p. 130, emphasis added in keeping with the tone of her televised comments which I saw at the time.

the British-born child was deprived of automatic British citizenship. Since primary black immigration had effectively been stopped already, the Act's practical impact was limited as far as black people were concerned. What the act *did* was to reaffirm in black people's minds that the government did not welcome their presence. Unsurprisingly, during the 1980s many of the early black migrants chose to return to the Caribbean. Some were now reaching retirement age, others were made redundant thanks to the collapse of British industry, but all shared a new disillusionment with Britain, akin to the shock of the early years.[75]

The greatest impact on black Britons of the crisis of the 1970s and 1980s was economic. Migrants had gravitated to the most vulnerable areas of the British economy: manufacturing and the public sector, especially the National Health Service. Thanks largely to the monetary and fiscal policies of the Thatcher governments, these parts of the economy went into terminal decline. British manufacturing, battered by international competition and choked by high interests rates, staggered and fell. The industries that collapsed most catastrophically were precisely the ones in which a disproportionate number of black people worked. Black unemployment thus rose far more rapidly than that of white workers. Similarly, government cuts in the public sector severely affected black workers. School leavers, especially black working-class ones, found it more difficult than ever to find work. Black youth unemployment became scandalously high and black youngsters were discriminated against on the youth training schemes that had been instituted. Police powers were expanded and police harassment of young black people occurred on an unprecedented scale. The 'sus' law, as it was commonly called, a provision that gave the police wide powers of arrest on the merest suspicion, was also widely abused when it came to black people. Beatings of black men while in police custody were common and there were more than a few suspicious deaths of black people in police stations. Physical attacks and murders of non-whites, especially Asians, by fascists such as members of the National Front, were becoming all too common. Counter-demonstrators against marching fascists were frequently violently suppressed by the police. These forces came together to trigger a series of unprecedented urban revolts in 1980 and 1981, most notably in Bristol,

[75] Macdonald and Blake, *Immigration Law and Practice in the United Kingdom*, pp. 130–47; Layton-Henry, *Politics of Race in Britain*, pp. 147–60; T. Kellman, 'Black Moods in Britain', *Caribbean Contact*, May 1984; James, 'Migration, Racism and Identity Formation', pp. 245–50.

Brixton (London), and Toxteth in Liverpool. One of their most remarkable features was the combination of black and white youths in attacks upon the police and property.[76]

Despite Thatcherism, the general British public gradually reconciled itself to a black presence. In the 1980s Bill Morris, a Jamaican migrant, became the deputy general secretary and in 1991 the general secretary of Britain's largest trade union, the Transport and General Workers Union. In 1987 three black people were elected to the House of Commons for the first time in British history. (In 2002, the first black member of a British Cabinet was appointed.) The black presence in the media, especially the electronic media, became more conspicuous, and the depiction of black people more positive. Since the 1980s major strides have been made in entertainment, with black athletes and footballers in particular making major inroads in their sports. During the 1980s the England cricket selectors even included a Barbadian-born player in the test team.

Black Britons registered their greatest impact in the field of music. In the 1970s and 1980s reggae became extremely popular in Britain, thanks largely to wide appeal of groups such as Bob Marley and the Wailers. Multiracial bands, such as UB40, came to prominence singing about the plight of the unemployed and developed a wide following among black and white youth. Soul II Soul, founded by the son of Antiguan migrants, became one of Britain's most popular music groups. Both black and white youth enjoyed and participated in sound-system and dub music, leading some to speak in an overly optimistic manner about a 'two-tone' Britain. A fusion of Asian and reggae music also became popular.[77] Ever since the 1980s, far more white than black people revel in the Notting Hill Carnival. In the 1990s the leader of the Conservative Party attended the event.

Thanks in large measure to central and local government policy of black dispersal in the 1960s, Britain's black and white working-class children have grown up together, getting to know each other in ways almost unimaginable in the United States. This educational and social mixing has helped to

[76] Stuart Hall and others, *Policing the Crisis: Mugging, the State, and Law and Order* (London, 1978); Institute of Race Relations, *Police Against Black People* (London, 1979); Sivanandan, *A Different Hunger*; M. Kettle and L. Hodges, *Uprising!* (London, 1982).

[77] Paul Gilroy, *There Ain't No Black in the Union Jack: The Cultural Politics of Race and Nation* (London, 1987); Paul Gilroy and Errol Lawrence, 'Two-Tone Britain: White and Black Youth and the Politics of Anti-Racism', in Philip Cohen and Harwant Bains, eds., *Multi-Racist Britain* (London, 1988), pp. 121–51; Kwesi-Owusu, ed., *Storms of the Heart: An Anthology of Black Arts and Culture* (London, 1988); and James, 'Migration, Racism and Identity Formation', pp. 264–65.

generate a remarkable level of intermingling, especially among young people, across racial lines.[78] But the insouciance of social interaction is still not reflected in the workplace. Black people have experienced significant social mobility over the years, but significantly less than whites, and some groups of Asians. Their children are also still to be found in disproportionate numbers in inferior schools. Racism persists in various ways, if less crudely than previously.[79] Although all was far from well for black people in Britain at the end of the twentieth century, there has been remarkable progress. It is noteworthy, too, that at century's end, Britain revelled in the inter-racial *charivari* created by Zadie Smith in her best-selling novel, *White Teeth*, which was later dramatized on British television. But less than a year before Smith's celebration of multi-racial London appeared, a more disturbing item entered the public domain in the non-fiction genre. Widely commented upon in the press but seldom read, the Macpherson Report, as it became known, opened the window on an uglier side of Britain, providing gruesome detail of the slaughter of an eighteen-year-old, black British student, Stephen Lawrence, and the extraordinary racism and negligence of the police in pursuing his murderers. Stephen's parents suffered a double blow—the brutal murder of their son, and their son's murderers escaping punishment—thanks to police bungling of the case. The Smith and Macpherson publications complement each other and are best read as a diptych of filtered sunlight (*White Teeth* after all is a work of fiction) and shadows. For despite the positive developments, the struggle most certainly continues for black people in Britain in the twenty-first century.[80]

[78] James 'Migration, Racism and Identity Formation', pp. 258–62; Suzanne Model and Gene Fisher, 'Unions Between Blacks and Whites: England and the US Compared', *Ethnic and Racial Studies*, XXV, 5 (Sept 2002), pp. 728–54.

[79] Tariq Modood and others, *Ethnic Minorities in Britain: Diversity and Disadvantage* (London, 1997) and Runnymede Trust Commission on the Future of Multi-Ethnic Britain, *The Future of Multi-Ethnic Britain* (London, 2000).

[80] Zadie Smith, *White Teeth* (London, 2000); Sir William Macpherson of Cluny, *The Stephen Lawrence Inquiry* (London, 1999)

Select Bibliography

Hakim Adi, *West Africans in Britain, 1900–1960* (London, 1998).

Michael Banton, *The Coloured Quarter: Negro Immigrants in an English City* (London, 1955).

BEN BOUSQUET and COLIN DOUGLAS, *West Indian Women at War: British Racism in World War II* (London, 1991).

BEVERLEY BRYAN and others, *The Heart of the Race: Black Women's Lives in Britain* (London, 1985).

Centre for Contemporary Cultural Studies, *The Empire Strikes Back: Race and Racism in 70s Britain* (London, 1982).

PETER FRYER, *Staying Power: The History of Black People in Britain* (London, 1984).

IMANUEL GEISS, *The Pan-African Movement*, trans. Ann Keep (London, 1974).

STUART HALL and others *Policing the Crisis: Mugging, the State, and Law and Order* (London, 1978).

DONALD HINDS, *Journey to an Illusion: The West Indian in Britain* (London, 1966).

WINSTON JAMES and CLIVE HARRIS, eds., *Inside Babylon: The Caribbean Diaspora in Britain* (London, 1993).

DAVID KILLINGRAY, ed., *Africans in Britain* (London, 1994).

KENNETH LITTLE, *Negroes in Britain: A Study of Racial Relations in English Society*, rev. edn., (London, 1972).

KENNETH LUNN, ed., *Race and Labour in Twentieth-Century Britain* (London, 1985).

ROBERT MILES, *Racism and Migrant Labour* (London, 1982).

TARIQ MODOOD and others, *Ethnic Minorities in Britain: Diversity and Disadvantage* (London, 1997).

KATHLEEN Paul, *Whitewashing Britain: Race and Citizenship in the Postwar Era* (Ithaca, NY, 1997).

CERI PEACH, *West Indian Migration to Britain: A Social Geography* (London, 1968).

EDWARD PILKINGTON, *Beyond the Mother Country: West Indians and the Notting Hill White Riots* (London, 1988).

E. J. B. ROSE and others, *Colour and Citizenship: A Report on British Race Relations* (London, 1969).

BILL SCHWARZ, ed., *West Indian Intellectuals in Britain* (Manchester, 2003).

A. SIVANANDAN, *A Different Hunger: Writings on Black Resistance* (London, 1982).

GRAHAM SMITH, *When Jim Crow Met John Bull: Black American Soldiers in World War II Britain* (London, 1987).

LAURA TABILI, *'We Ask for British Justice': Workers and Racial Difference in Late Imperial Britain* (Ithaca, NY, 1994).

14

Language, Race, and the Legacies of the British Empire

KWAME ANTHONY APPIAH

My father's world was the world of law courts where he went to work, dressed in his dark European suits, carrying the white wig of the British barrister (which he wore after independence as in the colonial period), a rose from the garden (my mother's garden) always in his buttonhole, and the world of Parliament, where he went in the first years I can remember, an opponent now of his old friend Kwame Nkrumah. These worlds we, his children, knew only because our parents spoke of them. The world of the little church, Saint George's, where we went to Sunday school with Baptists and Copts and Catholics and Methodists and Anglicans, from other parts of the country, other parts of the continent, other parts of the world, we knew inside out, knew because it was central to our friendships, our learning, our beliefs.

The world of my childhood was a product of a complicated negotiation of cultures, British and Asante, that had been underway for several generations before this part of Africa became part of the British Empire; a process that continued after the formal end of Empire. As a child, these were not bifurcated or antagonistic worlds, but simply the worlds of my parents that had met and been resolved in their marriage. When I was about eight, I fell very ill. Towards the end of my couple of months in bed in the local hospital, the English Queen paid her first post-independence visit to Ghana. She and

The material in this essay was previously published in Kwame Anthony Appiah, *In My Father's House: Africa in the Philosophy of Culture* (New York, 1992). The present chapter is a reworking of that material into a new argument dealing exclusively with the legacies of the British Empire. Readers should consult the original work, which has had, along with the work of V. Y. Mudimbe, a profound influence on debates and discourses relating to African culture. See also the following works, which explore questions of black culture in the context of the British imperial legacy: Paul Gilroy, *The Black Atlantic: Modernity and Its Double Consciousness* (Cambridge, Mass., 1993); Simon Gikandi, *Maps of Englishness: Writing Identity in the Culture of Colonialism* (New York, 1996); Gaurav Desai, *Subject to Colonialism: African Self-Fashioning and the Colonial Library* (Durham, NC, 2001).

her husband and the President of Ghana, Osagyefo Dr Kwame Nkrumah, duly arrived in Kumasi and made their way through the hospital, passing, as they did so, by my bed. The Queen, whose mastery of small talk is proverbial, asked me how I was, and I, in a literal fever of excitement at meeting my mother's Queen and my father's President, mumbled . . . that I was quite well. That these two worlds could be brought together in this moment of childlike, post-imperial excitement is a testament to my parents and, in particular, to the lessons of my father's life.

In 1945 my father was with Nkrumah and Du Bois at the Pan-African Congress in Manchester, England; in 1974 he was one of the very few from the 1945 Congress (he himself met no other) who attended the Congress, hosted by Julius Nyerere, in Dar es Salaam. By then Du Bois and Nkrumah were gone. In 1972 my father had gone to Guinée to negotiate the return of Nkrumah's body for a Ghanaian state funeral; his office, in those days, in Christiansborg Castle in Accra, was a few short steps from Du Bois' grave. My father was, I think, as complete a Pan-Africanist as either of them; yet he also taught us, his children, to be as completely untempted by racism as he was. The power and relevance of that lesson, as with the example of my father's life, is appreciable only through an understanding of the relationship between language, race, and identity as experienced by people whose lives were altered by colonialism, in this case by their experience of the British Empire.[1]

Throughout the former colonies of the British Empire in Africa, as well as the Caribbean and the United States, the English language is a marker of a cultural legacy that many Africans and people of African descent have inherited, but also a legacy to which they have made an abiding contribution. It is of course a legacy that connects all people of the English-speaking Commonwealth, but in Africa in particular the legacy is more complicated and more contested than in most other parts of this world. In Africa, English competes with very strong and vibrant indigenous vernaculars, and although inflected with elements from the cultures that produced these languages, English remains largely a lingua franca, not a primary mode of communication. Yet its role as a lingua franca should not be underestimated; English has been, along with other former colonial languages, not merely imposed or imitated but later frequently appropriated and reworked, an important medium in the construction of African identity—whether that identity is seen as continental or as Pan-African, that is, as belonging to all people of African descent.

[1] See Joe Appiah, *Joe Appiah: The Autobiography of an African Patriot* (New York, 1990).

On 26 July 1860, Alexander Crummell, African-American by birth, Liberian by adoption, an Episcopalian priest with a University of Cambridge education, addressed the citizens of Maryland County, at Cape Palmas. Although Liberia was not to be recognized by the United States for another two years, the occasion was, by Crummell's reckoning, the thirteenth anniversary of her independence. So it is particularly striking that his title was 'The English Language in Liberia' and his theme that the Africans 'exiled' in slavery to the New World had been given by divine providence 'at least this one item of compensation, namely, the possession of the Anglo-Saxon tongue'. Crummell, who is widely regarded as one of the fathers of African nationalism, had not the slightest doubt that English was a language superior to the 'various tongues and dialects' of the indigenous African populations; superior in its euphony, its conceptual resources, and its capacity to express the 'supernal truths' of Christianity.[2] Now, over a century later, more than half of the population of black Africa lives in countries where English is an official language.

Perhaps the Reverend Crummell would have been pleased with this news, but he would have little cause to be sanguine. For English as the language of government is the first language of a very few and is securely possessed by only a small proportion of the population; in most of the Anglophone states even the educated élite learned at least one of the hundreds of indigenous languages as well—and almost always before—English. Anglophone élites not only use the colonial languages as the medium of government but know and often admire the literature of their ex-colonizers, and have chosen to make a modern African literature in English.

This is not to deny that there are strong living traditions of oral culture—religious, mythological, poetic, and narrative—in most of the 'traditional' languages of sub-Saharan Africa, or to ignore the importance of a few written traditional languages. But to find their way out of their community, and acquire national, let alone international, recognition, most traditional languages—the obvious exception being Swahili—have to be translated. Few black African states have the privilege of corresponding to a single traditional linguistic community. And for this reason alone, most of the writers who have sought to create a national tradition, transcending the ethnic divisions of Africa's new states, have had to write in European languages or risk being

[2] Alexander Crummell, 'The English Language in Liberia', in *The Future of Africa: Being Addresses Sermons Etc., Etc., Delivered in the Republic of Liberia* (1892; Detroit, 1969).

seen as particularistic, identifying with old rather than new loyalties. For example, the decision of the Kenyan writer Ngugi wa Thiong'o to write in his mother tongue, Gikuyu, led many even within his nation to see him—wrongly, in my view—as a sort of Gikuyu imperialist (and this is no trivial issue in the context of inter-ethnic relations in Kenya).[3]

It should be said that there are other more or less honourable reasons for the extraordinary persistence of the colonial languages. We cannot ignore, for example, on the honourable side, the practical difficulties of developing a modern educational system in a language in which none of the manuals and textbooks have been written; nor should we forget, in the debit column, the less noble possibility that these foreign languages, whose possession had marked the colonial élite, became too precious as marks of status to be given up by the class that inherited the colonial state. Together such disparate forces have conspired to ensure that the most important body of writing in sub-Saharan Africa even after independence continues to be in English, French, and Portuguese. For many of its most important cultural purposes, most African intellectuals, south of the Sahara, are what we can call 'Europhone', and the majority of these are Anglophone.

A concern with the relations of 'traditional' and 'modern' conceptual worlds, with the integration of inherited modes of understanding and newly acquired theories, concepts, and beliefs, is bound to be of especial importance in the lives of those of us who think and write about the future of Africa in terms that are largely borrowed from elsewhere. We may acknowledge that the truth is the property of no culture, that we should take the truths we need wherever we find them. But for truths to become the basis of national policy and, more widely, of national life, they must be believed, and whether or not whatever new truths we take from the West *will* be believed depends, in large measure, on how we are able to manage relations between our conceptual heritage and the ideas that rush at us from worlds elsewhere.

Crummell's peroration is most easily available to us in a collection of his writings first published in 1862 and entitled *The Future of Africa*. It is a mark of the success of a picture of the world that he shared, that few of the readers of this book in the last hundred years—few, that is, of the Europeans, Americans, and Africans equipped with English to read it—will have found anything odd in this title, its author's particular interest in Africa's

[3] Ngugi wa Thiong'o, *Decolonising the Mind: The Politics of Language in African Literature* (London, 1986).

future, or of his claim to speak for a continent. It is a picture that Crummell learned in America and confirmed in England; though it would have astonished most of the 'native' population of Liberia, this picture has become in our century the common property of much of humankind. And at its root is an understanding of the world that we will do well to examine, to question perhaps, in the end, to reject.

At the core of Crummell's vision is a single guiding concept: race. Crummell's 'Africa' is the motherland of the Negro race, and his right to act in it, to speak for it, to plot its future, derived—in his conception—from the fact that he too was a Negro. More than this, Crummell held that there was a common destiny for the people of Africa—by which we are always to understand the black people—not because they shared a common ecology, nor because they had a common historical experience or faced a common threat from imperial Europe, but because they belonged to this one race. What made Africa one for him was that it was the home of the Negro, as England was the home of the Anglo-Saxon, or Germany the home of the Teuton. Crummell was one of the first people to speak *as* a Negro in Africa, and his writings effectively inaugurated the discourse of Pan-Africanism.

The centrality of race in the history of African nationalism is both widely assumed and often ignored. There were many colonial students from British Africa gathered in London in the years after the Second World War—a war in which many Africans died in the name of liberty—and their common search for political independence from a single metropolitan state naturally brought them together. They were brought together too by the fact that the British—those who helped as well as those who hindered—saw them all as Africans, first of all. But they were able to articulate a common vision of post-colonial Africa through a discourse inherited from pre-war Pan-Africanism, and that discourse was the product, largely, of black citizens of the New World.

Since what bound those African-American and Afro-Caribbean Pan-Africanists together was the partially African heritage they shared, and since that ancestry mattered in the New World through its various folk theories of race, a racial understanding of their solidarity was, perhaps, an inevitable development. This was reinforced by the fact that a few crucial figures—Nkrumah among them—had travelled in the opposite direction from Crummell, seeking education in the black colleges of the United States.

What race meant to the new African affectively, however, was not, on the whole, what it meant to educated blacks in the New World. For many

African-Americans, raised in segregated American society and exposed to the crudest forms of discrimination, social intercourse with white people was painful and uneasy. Many of the Africans, on the other hand (my father among them) took back to their homes European wives and warm memories of European friends; few of them, even from the 'settler' cultures of East and southern Africa, seem to have been committed to ideas of racial separation or to doctrines of racial hatred. Since they came from cultures where black people were in the majority and where lives continued to be largely controlled by indigenous moral and cognitive conceptions, they had no reason to believe that they were inferior to white people and they had, correspondingly, less reason to resent them.

This fact is of crucial importance in understanding the psychology of post-colonial Africa. For though this claim, will, I think, be easily accepted by most of those who experienced, as I did, an African upbringing in British Africa in the later twentieth century, it will seem unobvious to outside observers, largely, I believe, on the basis of one important source of misunderstanding.

It will seem to most European and American outsiders that nothing could be a more obvious basis for resentment than the experience of a colonized people forced to accept the swaggering presence of the colonizer. It will seem obvious, because a comparison will be assumed with the situation of New World blacks.

My own sense of that situation came first, I think, from reading the copy of Fernando Henriquez's *Family and Color in Jamaica* that George Padmore, the West Indian Pan-Africanist, gave my parents as a wedding present. And one cannot read Eldridge Cleaver's *Soul on Ice*, for example, without gathering a powerful sense of what it must be to belong to a stigmatized subculture, to live in a world in which everything from your body to your language is defined by the 'mainstream' as inferior. But to read the situation of those colonial subjects who grew to adulthood before the 1950s in this way is to make an assumption that Wole Soyinka has identified as the assumption of the 'potential equality *in every given situation* of the alien culture and the indigenous, on the actual soil of the latter'.[4] And what undercuts this assumption is the fact that the experience of the vast majority of these citizens for Europe's African colonies was one of an essentially shallow cultural penetration by the colonizer.

[4] Wole Soyinka, *Death and the King's Horseman* (London, 1975), author's note.

If we read Soyinka's own *Aké*, a childhood autobiography of an upbringing in pre-war colonial Nigeria—or the more explicitly fictionalized narratives of his countryman, Chinua Achebe—we shall be powerfully informed of the ways in which even these children who were extracted from the traditional culture of their parents and grandparents and thrust into the colonial school were nevertheless fully enmeshed in a primary experience of their own traditions.

Most of us who were raised during and for some time after the colonial era are sharply aware of the ways in which the colonizers were never as fully in control as our elders allowed them to appear. We all experienced the persistent power of our own cognitive and moral traditions: in religion, in such social occasions as the funeral, in our experience of music, in our practice of the dance, and, of course, in the intimacy of family life. Colonial authority sought to stigmatize our traditional religious beliefs, and we conspired in this fiction by concealing our disregard for much that was European in Christianity in 'syncretisms'.

What the post-war generation of British Africans took from their time in Europe, therefore, was not a resentment of 'white' culture. What they took, instead, from their shared experience was a sense that they, as Africans, had a great deal in common: they took it for granted, along with everybody else, that this common feeling was connected with their shared 'African-ness', and they largely accepted the European view that this meant their shared race.

Crummell believed that each race has a different moral status, quite independent of the moral characteristics entailed by its racial essence. So, for example, when he is discussing 'The Relations and Duties of Free Colored Men in America to Africa', he speaks of the demands that Africa makes on black people everywhere as 'a natural call', as a 'grand and noble work laid out in the Divine Providence', as if the different moral status of the various races derives not from their different moral characters but from their being assigned different tasks by God.[5] On this view, there could be an allocation of morally different tasks without any special difference in moral or cognitive capacity.

Crummell's model here, like that of most nineteenth-century black nationalists, was, of course, the biblical history of the Jews: Jehovah chose the children of Israel and made a covenant with them as his people and that was

[5] Alexander Crummell, 'The Relations and Duties of Free Colored Men in America to Africa', in H. Brotz, ed., *Negro Social and Political Thought* (New York, 1966), pp. 185, 175.

what gave them a special moral role in history. But he did not give them any special biological or intellectual equipment for their special task.

Pan-Africanism inherited Crummell's commitment to the idea that race is intrinsically morally significant. We cannot say it inherited the idea *from* Crummell, since in his day it was the common intellectual property of the West. We can see Crummell as emblematic of the influence of this racism on black intellectuals, an influence that is profoundly etched in the rhetoric of post-war African nationalism. It is striking how much of Crummell we can hear, for example, in Ghana's first Prime Minister, Nkrumah, as he reports, in the *Autobiography of Kwame Nkrumah*, a speech made in Liberia in 1952, nearly a century after the speech of Crummell's with which I began:

> I pointed out that it was providence that had preserved the Negroes during their years of trial in exile in the United States of America and the West Indies; that is was the same providence which took care of Moses and Israelites in Egypt centuries before. 'A greater exodus is coming in Africa today', I declared, 'and that exodus will be established when there is a united, free and independent West Africa.'
>
> 'Africa for the Africans!' I cried . . . 'A free and independent state in Africa. We want to be able to govern ourselves in this country of ours without outside interference.'[6]

There is no difficulty in inserting this last paragraph from Nkrumah into a discussion of Alexander Crummell. For Nkrumah, as for Crummell, African-Americans who came to Africa (as Du Bois came to Ghana at Nkrumah's invitation) were going back—providentially—to their natural, racial, home.

The politics of race that I have described—one that derived from commonplaces of European nationalism—was central to Crummell's ideology. But his nationalism differed from that of his European predecessors and contemporaries in important ways, which emerge if we explore the politics of language with which I began. Crummell's engagement with the issue of the transfer of English to the African Negro runs counter to a strong tradition of European nationalist thought, which saw language as the expression of the nation's spirit. There is no evidence, however, that Crummell ever agonized over his rejection of Africa's many 'tongues and dialects', and for this there is,

6 Kwame Nkrumah, *Autobiography of Kwame Nkrumah* (1957; London, 1973), pp. 152–53.

I think, a simple explanation. For Crummell, as 'The English Language in Liberia' makes clear, it is not English as the *Sprachgeist*[7] of the Anglo-Saxons that matters; it is English as the vehicle of Christianity and—what he would have seen as much the same thing—civilization and progress. Crummell inherited not only the received European conception of race but also the received understanding both of the nature of civilization and of the African's lack of it. Crummell shared with his European and American contemporaries (those of them, at least, who had any view of the matter at all) an essentially negative sense of traditional culture in Africa as anarchic, unprincipled, ignorant, defined by the absence of all the positive traits of civilization as 'savage'.

Crummell's thinking anticipated that of many political leaders among the immigrants who came to the United Kingdom after the Second World War from throughout the British Empire. Their alliance turned all nonwhite people into Blacks, whether from Africa, the Caribbean, or South Asia.

Martin Farquhar Tupper, an Englishman who lived through most of the nineteenth century, was an extremely prolific and successful writer who today is known only to those with a historical interest in popular writers of the nineteenth century or an antiquarian interest in bad verse. But in 1850, at the height of his popularity, he published these soon-to-be-famous words in a new journal called the *Anglo-Saxon*:

> Stretch forth! stretch forth! from the south to the north,
> From the east to the west,—stretch forth! stretch forth!
> Strengthen thy stakes and lengthen thy cords,—
> The world is a tent for the world's true lords!
> Break forth and spread over every place
> The world is a world for the Saxon race!

The poem's tone is emblematic of an important development in the way educated Englishmen and women thought of themselves and of what it was that made them English—a development that was itself part of a wider movement of ideas in Europe and North America. Tupper's assumptions, which amounted to a new theory of race, colour our modern understanding of literature—indeed of most symbolic culture—in fundamental ways, and

[7] This term comes from the work of J. G. Herder (1744–1803), a prophet of German nationalism and founding philosopher of the modern ideology of nationhood. For Herder, the spirit of the nation was expressed above all in its language, its *Sprachgeist*.

this despite the fact that many of these assumptions have been officially discarded.

Race, nation, literature: these terms are bound together in the recent intellectual history of the West. While the ideas of racialism (i.e., the view that there are heritable characteristics, possessed by members of our species, which allow us to divide them into small sets of races, in such a way that members of these races share certain traits and tendencies with each other (that they do not share with members of any other race) are familiar and no one needs to be reminded of the connection between racialism and the sort of imperialism that Tupper celebrated, it is perhaps a less familiar thought that many of those works that are central to the recent history of our understanding of what *literature* is are also thematically preoccupied with racial issues. But the reason for this is not far to seek: it lies in the dual connection made in eighteenth- and nineteenth-century Euro-American thought between, on the one hand, race and nationality, and, on the other, nationality and literature. In short, the nation is the key middle term in understanding the relations between the concept of *race* and idea of literature.

I began with the tradition that leads through Tupper to the present day not merely because it informs recent African criticism, but also because I want to insist on the extent to which the issues of language and nation are so central not only to the situation of Anglophone writers in sub-Saharan Africa, but also to the problems of European and American criticism. This is not—as it is often presented as being—a voyage into the exotic, a flirtation with a distant Other. Voltaire or one of his *philosophe* comrades in a European culture before the heyday of the world empires once said that when we travel, what we discover is always ourselves. It seems to me that this thought has, so to speak, become true. In the world after those world empires, a world where centre and periphery are mutually constitutive, political life may be conceived of (however misleadingly) in national terms, but what Voltaire might have called the life of the mind cannot. If I seek to locate my discussion of the African situation with a few elements of context, then, it is in part so that others can recognize how much of that situation is familiar territory.

That the territory *is* so familiar is a consequence of the way in which Anglophone intellectuals from what I will call, with reservations, the Black World, are a historical product of an encounter with the West in what Paul Gilroy has called the Black Atlantic. Most African writers have received a Western-style education; their ambiguous relations to the world of their foremothers and forefathers and to the world of the industrialized countries are part of their distinctive cultural (dis)location, a condition that Abiola Irele has eloquently described in 'In Praise of Alienation':

> We are wedged uncomfortably between the values of our traditional culture and those of the West. The process of change which we are going through has created a dualism of life which we experience at the moment less as a mode of challenging complexity that as one of confused disparateness.[8]

Of course, there are influences—some of them important—that run from the precolonial intellectual culture to those who have received colonial or postcolonial educations in the Western manner. Nevertheless, in sub-Saharan Africa, most literate people are literate in the colonial languages and the only writing with a genuinely subcontinental audience and address is in English or French.

Language is, of course, a synecdoche. When the colonialist attempted to tame the threatening cultural alterity of the African (whether through what the French call *assimilation* or through the agency of missionary 'conversion', which was the main source of access to English culture in British Africa), the instrument of pedagogy was their most formidable weapon. So that the problem is not only, or not so much, the English or the French or the Portuguese languages as the cultural imposition that they each represent. Colonial education, in short, produced a generation immersed in the literature of the colonizers, a literature that often reflected and transmitted the imperialist vision.

This is, surely, no new thing: literary pedagogy played a similar role in Roman education in the provinces of that empire, an empire that still provides perhaps our most powerful paradigm of imperialism. The weapon of pedagogy changes hands simply because we turn from reading Buchan and Conrad and Graham Greene to reading Abrahams, Achebe, Armah—to begin an alphabet of writers in the Heinemann African Writers Series, which constitutes in the most concrete sense the pedagogical cannon of Anglophone African writing.[9] The decolonized subject people write themselves,

[8] Abiola Irele, 'In Praise of Alienation', in V. Y. Mudimbe, ed., *The Surreptitious Speech: Présence Africaine and the Politics of Otherness 1947–1987* (Chicago, 1992), pp. 212–13.

[9] Peter Abrahams, Chinua Achebe, and Ayi Kwei Armah, who were born, respectively, in 1919, 1930, and 1939, were at one time the first three authors on the alphabetic list of authors in the African Writers Series, which has been published by Heinemann since 1962.

now, as the subject of a literature of their own. The simple gesture of writing for and about oneself has a profound political significance.

Writing for and about ourselves, then, helps constitute the modern community of the nation, but we do it largely in languages imposed by 'the might of the legions'. Now that the objects of British imperialism have at last become the subjects of a discourse addressed both to each other and to the West, the English language and its intellectual disciplines have been 'turned', like double agents, from the projects of the metropole to the intellectual work of post colonial cultural life.

But though officially in the service of new masters, these tools remain, like all double agents, perpetually under suspicion. Even when the colonizer's language is creolized, even when the imperialist's vision is playfully subverted in the lyrics of popular songs, there remains the suspicion that a hostile *Sprachgeist* is at work. Both the complaints against defilement by alien traditions in an alien tongue and the defences of them as a practical necessity seem often to reduce to a dispute between a sentimental Herderian conception of Africa's languages and traditions as expressive of the collective essence of a pristine traditional community, on the one hand, and, on the other, a positivistic conception of English, as both a language and a culture inscribed within a language, a mere tool; a tool that can be cleansed of the accompanying imperialist—and, more specifically, racist—modes of thought.

The former view is often at the heart of what we can call 'nativism': the claim that true African independence requires a literature of one's own. Echoing the debate in nineteenth-century Russia between 'Westerners' and 'Slavophiles', the debate in Africa presents itself as an opposition between 'universalism' and 'particularism', the latter defining itself, above all else, by its opposition to the former. Operating with a typology of inside and outside—indigene and alien, Western and traditional—the apostles of nativism are able in contemporary Africa to mobilize the undoubted power of a nationalist rhetoric, one in which the literature of one's own is that of one's own nation. The problem with nativism is not its nationalism, but the typology of nation it constructs. For example, in the now-classic manifesto of African cultural nationalism, *Toward the Decolonization of African Literature*—written by three Nigerians (Chinweizu, Onwuchekwa Jemie, and Ihechukwu Madubuike) all of them encumbered with extensive Western university educations—the authors wrestle the critical ethnocentrism of their Eurocentric opponents to the ground in the name of an Afrocentric particularism. They assert that 'most of the objections to thematic and ideological matters in the African novel sound like admonitions from imperialist motherhens to their wayward or outright rebellious captive chickens. They cluck: "Be Universal! Be Universal!" '[10] And they condemn

> the modernist retreat of our poets into privatist universalism [which] makes it quite easy of them to shed whatever African nationalist consciousness they have before they cross the threshold into the sanctum of 'poetry in the clouds'. And that suits the English literary establishment just fine, since they would much prefer it if an African nationalist consciousness, inevitably anti-British, was not promoted or cultivated, through literature, in the young African elite.[11]

Their central insistence is that 'African literature *is* an autonomous entity separate and apart from all other literature. It has its own traditions, model, and norms.'[12]

Railing against the cultural hegemony of the West, the nativists are of its party without knowing it. Their sense of defiance is determined less by 'indigenous' notions of resistance than by the dictates of the West's own Herderian legacy—its highly elaborate ideologies of national autonomy, of language, and literature as their cultural substrates. Nativist nostalgia, in short, is largely fueleed by that Western sentimentalism so familiar after Rousseau; few things, then, are less native than nativism in its current forms.

I think that once we see the larger context more clearly, we will be less prone to the anxieties of nativism, less likely to be seduced by the rhetoric of ancestral purity. More than a quarter of a century ago, Frantz Fanon exposed the artificiality of nativist intellectuals, whose ersatz populism only estranges them from the *Volk* they venerate. The intellectual 'sets a high value on the customs, traditions, and the appearances of his people, but his inevitable, painful experience only seems to be a banal search for exoticism. The sari becomes sacred, the shoes that come from Paris or Italy are left off in favor of pampooties, which suddenly the language of the ruling power is felt to burn your lips.'[13] Inevitably, though, the 'culture that the intellectual leans toward is often no more than a stock of particularisms. He wishes to attach himself to the people, but instead he only catches hold of their outer garments.'[14] Fanon does not dismiss the products of the modern cultural worker in the

[10] Chinweizu, Onwuchekwa Jemie, and Ihechukwu Madubuike, *Toward the Decolonization of African Literature* (Durham, NC, 1980), p. 89.

[11] Ibid., p. 151.

[12] Ibid., p. 4.

[13] Frantz Fanon, *The Wretched of the Earth* (New York, 1968), p. 221.

[14] Ibid., pp. 223–24.

colonial and postcolonial era, but he urges that the native poet who has taken his people as subject 'cannot go forward resolutely unless he realizes the extent of his estrangement from them'.[15] Intellectuals betray this estrangement by a fetishistic attitude toward the customs, folklore, and vernacular traditions of their people, an attitude that, Fanon argues, must, in the end, set them against the people in their time of struggle.

One focus of this estrangement that has not, perhaps, been sufficiently appreciated is the very conception of an African identity. Although most discourse about African literature has moved beyond the monolithic notions of negritude or the 'African personality', the constructed nature of modern African identity (like all identities) is not widely enough understood. Terence Ranger has written of how the British nationalist's 'own respect for "tradition" disposed them to look with favour upon what they took to be traditional in Africa.'[16] British colonial officers, travelling in the footsteps of Lord Lugard (and with the support of that curious creature, the government anthropologist) collected, organized, and enforced these 'traditions', and such works as Rattray's *Ashanti Law and Constitution* had the effect of monumentalizing the flexible operations of pre-colonial systems of social control as what came to be called 'customary law'. Ironically, for many contemporary African intellectuals, these invented traditions have now acquired the status of national mythology and the invented past of Africa has come to play a role in the political dynamics of the modern state: 'The invented traditions imported from Europe not only provided whites with models of command but also offered many Africans models of "modern" behaviour. The invented traditions of African societies—whether invented by the Europeans or by Africans themselves in response—distorted the past but became in themselves realities through which a good deal of colonial encounter was expressed.'[17]

So it is, Ranger observes, that those like Ngugi wa Thiong' o, the Kenyan writer who chose to write in Gikuyu rather than English, 'who repudiate bourgeois elite culture face the ironic danger of embracing another set of colonial inventions instead'.[18] The English, who knew all about nations, could extend a similar comprehension to its stand-in, the 'tribe', and that

[15] Frantz Fanon, *The Wretched of the Earth* (New York, 1968), p. 226.

[16] Terence Ranger, 'The Invention of Tradition in Colonial Africa,' in Eric Hobsbawm and Terence Ranger, eds., *The Invention of Tradition* (Cambridge, 1983), p. 212.

[17] Ibid.

[18] Ibid., p. 262.

could mean inventing tribes where none quite existed before. The very invention of Africa (as something more than a geographical entity) must be understood, ultimately, as an outgrowth of European racialism; the notion of Pan-Africanism was founded on the notion of the African, which was, in turn, founded not on any genuine cultural commonality but on the very European concept of the Negro. 'The Negro', Fanon writes, is 'never so much a Negro as since he has been dominated by whites'.[19] But the reality is that the very category of the Negro is at root a European product: for the 'whites' invented the Negroes in order to dominate them. Simply put, the course of cultural nationalism in Africa has been to make real the imaginary identities to which Europe has subjected us.

The nativist's injunction to read literature by means of a theory drawn from the text's own cultural or intellectual inheritance is highly problematic precisely because it ignores the multiplicity of the heritage of the modern African writer. To insist on nativism on these grounds would be to ignore plain facts: to ignore the undeniable datum that Soyinka's references to Euripides are as real as his appeal to Ogun (and also to Brazilian syncretisms of Yoruba and Christian religions); or Achebe's report apropos of his reading as a child, that 'the main things were the Bible and the Book of Common Prayer and the [English] Hymn Book'.[20] The nativist practice of denying foreign legacies and the hybridity of African cultures obscures the history of contact and 'contamination' as a fundamental experience of the British Empire for both African cultures and African intellectuals.[21]

For all our gestures of piety toward the household gods cannot disguise that fact that the 'intellectual' is the product of a particular social formation—that, as Gayatri Spivak has observed, there is a sense in which the 'third-world intellectual' is a contradiction in terms precisely because intellectuals from the Third World are the product of the historical encounter with the West.[22]

[19] Fanon, *Wretched of the Earth*, p. 212. [20] Chinua Achebe, Interview, 26 Feb. 1982.

[21] This sort of 'contamination' plays a much larger role in the history of most cultures than is usually acknowledged. Rather than thinking of the history of the world as the development of a series of isolated cultures it would be truer (though no doubt slightly exaggerated) to say that hybridity is the norm. I would offer three extremely diverse cases in evidence: Hellenistic style in Gandhara sculpture; the role of Buddhism (which originates in South Asia) in East Asian civilizations; North African musical styles in Spanish music.

[22] Gayatri C. Spivak, *In Other Worlds: Essays in Cultural Politics* (New York, 1988).

African writing raises a set of difficulties that stem from one of the characteristics of the cultural situation of African writers in the colonial languages: namely, the fact that they normally conceive of themselves as addressing a readership that encompasses communities wider than any 'traditional' culture. When authors write in English or French about lives in their own countries in all their specificity, they necessarily find themselves accounting for features of those lives that derive from that specificity. This entails the use of particular concepts of, for example, kinship and family, marriage and status. The presentation of such details has often been read, especially by people outside Africa, as anthropologizing. We are told that Achebe's *Arrow of God*, for example, fails, in part, because it cannot take its setting for granted; that Achebe is always telling us what we need to know, acknowledging the reader's distance from Igbo traditions, and thus, allegedly, identifying the intended reader as a foreigner. I have heard the same point made about Soyinka's dramas, and I confess to finding it difficult to accept. For there are reasons, reasons highly specific to the situation of black African writing in metropolitan languages, why this is a mistake.

There is one trivial reason. Achebe and Soyinka are very consciously writing for Nigerian—and not just Igbo or Yoruba—audiences. The fact that a certain amount of detail is introduced in order to specify a thick description of the cultural milieu simply does not imply a foreign—if that means a non-African—reader. That is the first point. But it *is*, essentially, trivial because of a second point. To make that point I should begin with a not-to-be-neglected fact: Achebe and Soyinka are popular writers at home. If the presence of these accumulations of allegedly ethnographic detail were indeed a way of identifying an alien reader, why do Nigerian (and more specifically Yoruba and Igbo) readers not find them alienating? The fact is that the accumulation of detail is a device not of alienation but of incorporation.

Part of what is meant by calling, say, Achebe's *Things Fall Apart* 'anthropologizing' is that the narrator tells us so much about the culture that could, in this way, have been shown. I have already suggested that 'the gesture of writing for and about oneself' is not simply a matter of creating texts addressed to a European Other. For those of us raised largely with texts that barely acknowledged the specificity of our existence, each work that simply places before us the world we already know—and this is a point that has been made eloquently by feminism—can provide a moment of self-validation. At the same time, the reason that Africa cannot take an African cultural or political or intellectual life for granted is that there is no such thing: there are only so many traditions with the complex relationships—and, as often, their lack of any relationship—to each other.

Soyinka, on the other hand, has a much different project in mind. (Like Achebe, he writes in English; but this, like many obvious facts, is one whose obviousness may lead us to underrate its importance and its obscurities. For if it is obvious that Soyinka's language is English, it is hard to question whose English he writes.) He wishes to show how an African writer can take Africa for granted in his work, drawing on the 'world-view and social structure of his own [African] people',[23] and because he wishes to represent what is African about his and other African writing as arising endogenously out of Africa's shared metaphysical resources.

However, where there is commonality between cultures is not through an 'African' connection, but through a 'black', that is, colonial, connection. In *Myth, Literature and the African World*, Soyinka recognizes that, despite the differences between the histories of British, French, and Portuguese ex-colonies, there is a deep and deeply self-conscious continuity between the problems and projects of decolonized Africans. Yet he also wants to give an account of that continuity that is both metaphysical and endogenous. The desire to give an account that is endogenous is, I think, primary. There is something disconcerting for a Pan-Africanist in the thesis (which I here state at its most extreme) that what Africans have in common is fundamentally that European racism failed to take them seriously, that European imperialism exploited them. Soyinka will not admit the presupposition of Achebe's question: 'When you see an African what does it mean to a white man?'[24]—the presupposition that the African identity is, in part, the product of a European gaze.

I had better insist that I do not think that this *is* all that Africans have culturally in common. But even if the other similarities that Africans share were to be found only in Africa—and they aren't—they would not, even with the similarities of colonial history, justify the assumption of metaphysical or mythic unity, except on the most horrifyingly determinist assumptions. In denying a metaphysical and mythic unity to African conceptions, then, I have *not* denied that 'African literature' is a useful category. I have insisted that the

[23] Wole Soyinka, *Myth, Literature and the African World* (Cambridge, 1976), p. xii.

[24] Chinua Achebe, 'An Interview with Chinua Achebe', *Times Literary Supplement*, 26 Feb. 1982. Some of the material cited in this chap. comes from unpublished portions of this interview with Anthony Appiah, D. A. N. Jones, and John Ryle in the summer of 1981.

social-historical situation of African writers generates a common set of problems. But notice that it is precisely not a metaphysical consensus that creates this shared situation. It is, *inter alia*, the transition from 'traditional' to 'modern' loyalties; the experience of colonialism; the racial theories and prejudices of Europe, which provide both the language and the text of literary experience; the growth of both literacy and the modern economy. And it is because these are changes that were to a large extent thrust upon African peoples by European imperialism, precisely because they are exogenous, that Soyinka, in my view, revolts against seeing them as the major determinants of the situation of the African writer.

Once he is committed to an endogenous account of this situation, what is left by unity in metaphysics? Shaka and Osei Tutu—founders, respectively, of the Zulu and Asante nations—do not belong in the same narrative, spoke different languages, and had conceptions of kinship (to bow to the ethnographer's idol) that were centrally patrilineal and matrilineal, respectively. Because he creates an endogenous account, Soyinka is enmeshed in Europe's myth of Africa—an essential, authentic, and different place. Because he cannot see either Christianity or Islam as endogenous (even in their more syncretic forms), he is left to reflect on African traditional religions, and these have always seemed from Europe's point of view to be much of a muchness.

Postcoloniality is the condition of what we might ungenerously call a comprador intelligentsia: of a relatively small, Western-style, Western-trained, group of writers and thinkers who mediate the trade in cultural commodities of world capitalism at the periphery. In the West they are known through the Africa they offer; their compatriots know them both through the West they present to Africa and through an Africa they have invented for the world, for each other, and for Africa.

All aspects of contemporary African cultural life—including music and some sculpture and painting, even some writings with which the West is largely not familiar—have been influenced, often powerfully, by the transition of African societies *through* colonialism, but they are not all in the relevant sense *post*-colonial. For the *post* in postcolonial, like the *post* in post-modern is the *post* of the space clearing gesture, whereby the exponents of post-colonialism try to construct a new space that stands in marked contrast to the space of the colonial past. They do so in order to sell art and ideas that have become increasingly commodified, and so need to mark with difference in order to distinguish them from those of other producers. Many areas of contemporary African cultural life—what has come to be theorized as popular culture, in particular—are not in this way concerned with transcending, with going beyond, coloniality. Indeed, it might be said to be a mark of popular culture that its borrowings from the international cultural forms are remarkably insensitive to—not so much dismissive of as blind to—the issues of neo-colonialism or 'cultural imperialism'.

However, what is called 'syncretism', often taken as a sign of post-colonial culture, is made possible by the international exchange of commodities, of which imperialism was an important, but not unique, episode; it is not a consequence of a space-clearing gesture. If there is a lesson in the broad shape of the circulation of cultures, it is surely that we are all already contaminated by each other, that there is no longer a fully autochthonous *echt*-African culture awaiting salvage by our artists (just as there is, of course, no American culture without African roots). And there is a clear sense in some post-colonial writing that the postulation of a unitary Africa over against a monolithic West—the binarism of the Self and the Other—is the last of the shibboleths of the imperialism that we must learn to live without.

Achebe writes powerfully: 'It is of course true that the African identity is still in the making. There isn't a final identity that is African. But, at the same time, there is an identity coming into existence. And it has a certain context and a certain meaning. Because if somebody meets you, say, in a shop in Cambridge, he says, "Are you from Africa?" Which means that Africa means something to some people. Each of these tags has a meaning, and a penalty and a responsibility.' He continues, 'All these tags, unfortunately for the black man, are tags of disability.'[25] And they are tags of disability because they are disabling; which is, in essence, my complaint against Africa as a racial mythology—the Africa of Crummell and of the nativist critics (from the Old); against Africa as a shared metaphysics—the Africa of Soyinka; against Africa as a fancied past of shared glories—the Africa of Diop and the 'Egyptianists'.

The cultural life of most of black Africa remained largely unaffected by European ideas until the last years of the nineteenth century, and most cultures began the twentieth century with ways of life formed very little by direct contact with Europe. The major cultural impact of Europe is largely a

[25] Chinua Achebe, 'An Interview with Chinua Achebe'.

product of the period since the First World War. To understand the variety of Africa's contemporary cultures, therefore, we need first to recall the variety of the precolonial cultures. Differences in colonial experience have also played their part in shaping the continent's diversities, but even identical colonial policies identically implemented working on the very different cultural materials would surely have produced widely varying results. To speak of an African identity in the nineteenth century—if an identity is a coalescence of mutually responsive (if sometimes conflicting) modes of conduct, habits of thought, and patterns of evaluation; in short, a coherent kind of human social psychology—would have been 'to give to aery nothing a local habitation and a name'.[26] To speak of a fixed African identity even in the twentieth century is still premature. Yet there is no doubt that now an African identity is coming into being. It is a new thing, it is the product of history. Yet the bases through which so far it has largely been theorized—race, a common historical experience, a shared metaphysics—presuppose falsehoods too serious for us to ignore.

[26] William Shakespeare, *A Midsummer Night's Dream.* Act v. Sc. 1.

Select Bibliography

CHINUA ACHEBE, *Things Fall Apart* (London, 1958).

—— *Arrow of God* (London, 1964).

KWAME ANTHONY APPIAH, *In My Father's House: Africa in the Philosophy of Culture* (New York, 1992).

JOE APPIAH, *Joe Appiah: The Autobiography of an African Patriot* (New York, 1990).

CHINWEIZU, ONWUCHEKWA JEMIE, AND IHECHUKWU MADUBUIKE, *Toward the Decolonization of African Literature* (Durham, NC, 1980).

ELDRIDGE CLEAVER, *Soul on Ice* (New York, 1967).

ALEXANDER CRUMMELL, *The Future of Africa: Being Addresses Sermons Etc., Etc., Delivered in the Republic of Liberia* (1862; Detroit, 1969).

FRANTZ FANON, *The Wretched of the Earth* (New York, 1968).

FERNANDO HENRIQUEZ, *Family and Colour in Jamaica* (London, 1953).

ABIOLA IRELE, 'In Praise of Alienation', in V. Y. Mudimbe ed., *The Surreptitious Speech: Présence Africaine and the Politics of Otherness 1947–1987* (Chicago, 1992).

V. Y. MUDIMBE, *The Invention of Africa* (Bloomington, Ind., 1988).

KWAME NKRUMAH, *Autobiography of Kwame Nkrumah* (London [1957], 1973)

NGUGI WA THIONG'O, *Decolonising the Mind: The Politics of Language in African Literature* (London, 1986).

TERENCE RANGER, 'The Invention of Tradition in Colonial Africa', in Eric Hobsbawm and Terence Ranger, eds., *The Invention of Tradition* (Cambridge, 1983).

R. S. RATTRAY, *Ashanti Law and Constitution* (Oxford, 1929).

WOLE SOYINKA, *Death and the King's Horseman* (London, 1975).

—— *Myth, Literature and the African World* (Cambridge, 1976)

—— *Aké: The Years of Childhood* (London, 1981).

INDEX